LIFE HISTORIES
OF NORTH AMERICAN
MARSH BIRDS

by Arthur Cleveland Bent

Dover Publications, Inc., New York

Published in Canada by General Publishing Company, Ltd., 30 Lesmill Road, Don Mills, Toronto, Ontario.

Published in the United Kingdom by Constable and Company, Ltd., 10 Orange Street, London W. C. 2.

This Dover edition, first published in 1963, is an unabridged and unaltered republication of the work first published by the United States Government Printing Office in 1926 as Smithsonian Institution United States National Museum *Bulletin 135.*

Standard Book Number: 486-21082-0
Library of Congress Catalog Card Number: 63-17922

Manufactured in the United States of America
Dover Publications, Inc.
180 Varick Street
New York, N.Y. 10014

ADVERTISEMENT

The scientific publications of the National Museum include two series, known, respectively, as *Proceedings* and *Bulletin*.

The *Proceedings*, begun in 1878, is intended primarily as a medium for the publication of original papers, based on the collections of the National Museum, that set forth newly acquired facts in biology, anthropology, and geology, with descriptions of new forms and revisions of limited groups. Copies of each paper, in pamphlet form, are distributed as published to libraries and scientifiic organizations and to specialists and others interested in the different subjects. The dates at which these separate papers are published are recorded in the table of contents of each of the volumes.

The *Bulletin*, the first of which was issued in 1875, consists of a series of separate publications comprising monographs of large zoological groups and other general systematic treatises (occasionally in several volumes), faunal works, reports of expeditions, catalogues of type-specimens, special collections, and other material of similar nature. The majority of the volumes are octavo in size, but a quarto size has been adopted in a few instances in which large plates were regarded as indispensable. In the *Bulletin* series appear volumes under the heading *Contributions from the United States National Herbarium*, in octavo form, published by the National Museum since 1902, which contain papers relating to the botanical collections of the Museum.

The present work forms No. 135 of the *Bulletin* series.

ALEXANDER WETMORE,
Assistant Secretary, Smithsonian Instituition.

WASHINGTON, D. C., *December 16, 1926.*

INTRODUCTION

This is the sixth in a series of bulletins of the United States National Museum on the life histories of North American birds. Previous numbers have been issued as follows:

107. Life Histories of North American Diving Birds, 1919.
113. Life Histories of North American Gulls and Terns, 1921.
121. Life Histories of North American Petrels, Pelicans, and their Allies, 1922.
126. Life Histories of North American Wildfowl, 1923.
130. Life Histories of North American Wildfowl, 1925.

The same general plan has been followed, as fully explained in Bulletin 107, and the same sources of information have been utilized.

The classification and nomenclature adopted by the American Ornithologists' Union, in its latest check list and its supplements, have been followed, mainly, with such few changes as, in the author's opinion, will be, or should be, made to bring the work up to date and in line with recent advances in the science.

The main ranges are as accurately outlined as limited space will permit; the normal migrations are given in sufficient detail to indicate the usual movements of the species; no attempt has been made to give all records, for economy in space, and no pretence at complete perfection is claimed. Many published records, often repeated, have been investigated and discarded; many apparently doubtful records have been verified; some published records, impossible to either verify or disprove, have been accepted if the evidence seemed to warrant it.

The egg dates are the condensed results of a mass of records taken from the data in a large number of the best egg collections in the country, as well as from contributed field notes and from a few published sources. They indicate the dates on which eggs have been actually found in various parts of the country, showing the earliest and latest dates and the limits between which half the dates fall, the height of the season.

The plumages are described only in enough detail to enable the reader to trace the sequence of molts and plumages from birth to maturity and to recognize the birds in the different stages and at the

different seasons.   No attempt has been made to fully describe adult
plumages; this has been already well done in the many manuals.
The names of colors, when in quotation marks, are taken from Ridgway's Color Standards and Nomenclature (1912) and the terms used
to describe the shapes of eggs are taken from his Nomenclature of
Colors (1886 edition).   The heavy-faced type in the measurements
of eggs indicate the four extremes of measurements.

Many of those who contributed material for former volumes have
rendered a similiar service in this case.   In addition to those whose
contributions have been acknowledged previously, our thanks are
due to the following new contributors: Photographs, notes, or data
have been contributed by Griffing Bancroft, C. T. Barnes, O. E.
Baynard, R. H. Beck, Hiram Bingham, C. L. Broley, A. R. Cahn, B. R.
Chamberlain, B. H. Christy, J. H. Connery, A. H. Cordier, William
Dodd, Eastman Kodak Company, J. M. Edson, W. G. Fargo, W. H.
Fisher, I. N. Gabrielson, D. S. Gage, E. W. Hadeler, R. B. Harding, Paul
Harrington, C. G. Harrold, R. W. Hendee, H. M. Holland, E. G. Holt,
J. S. Huxley, E. R. P. Janvrin, Antonin Jay, G. A. Langelier, J. E.
Law, A. G. Lawerence, A. A. V. P. Lechner, R. J. Longstreet, J. B.
May, Dan McCowan, H. T. Middleton, N. D. Moser, J. E. Patterson
R. B. Ramp, T. E. Randall, F. W. Rapp, Russell Reid, C. C. Sanborn,
E. T. Seton, G. F. Simmons, Alexander Sprunt, F. A. E. Starr, O. A.
Stevens, H. S. Swarth, L. W. Turrell, and R. L. Walp.

Receipt of material from over 200 contributors has been acknowledged in previous volumes.

Through the courtesy of the Biological Survey, the services of
Frederick C. Lincoln were secured to compile the distribution para-
graphs.   With the matchless reference files of the Biological Survey
at his disposal and with some advice and help from Dr. Harry C.
Oberholser, his many hours of careful and thorough work have produced results far more satisfactory than could have been attained by
the author, who claims no credit and assumes no responsibility for
this part of the work.   The few minor changes made in the system
do not materially alter the general plan.

F. Seymour Hersey has handled the egg measurements and the egg
dates very satisfactorily; both of these involved collecting and working over a great mass of details, involving long hours of tedious
work which he volunteered to do.

Dr. Charles W. Townsend has written the life histories of five
species.   Rev. P. B. Peabody furnished a generous supply of notes
and photographs regarding the yellow rail.   A notable contribution
has been made by Thomas E. Penard, who compiled and wrote the

entire life history of the scarlet ibis, and furnished much of the material for that of the jabiru; all this involved a large amount of research in publications which are unknown to most of us. Credit should have been given, in the previous volume, to W. E. Clyde Todd for permission to use certain notes made by O. J. Murie in the Hudson Bay region.

The manuscript for this volume was completed in December, 1925. Contributions received since will be acknowledged later. Only information of great importance could be added. Contributions for the shore-bird volume should be sent, at once, to—

THE AUTHOR

TABLE OF CONTENTS

	Page.
Order Odontoglossae	1
Family Phoenicopteridae	1
Phoenicopterus ruber	1
American flamingo	1
Habits	1
Distribution	12
Order Herodiones	13
Family Plataleidae	13
Ajaia ajaia	13
Roseate spoonbill	13
Habits	13
Distribution	22
Family Threskionithidae	23
Guara alba	23
White ibis	23
Habits	23
Distribution	33
Guara rubra	33
Scarlet ibis	33
Habits	33
Distribution	45
Plegadis falcinellus	45
Glossy ibis	45
Habits	45
Distribution	51
Plegadis guarauna	52
White-faced glossy ibis	52
Habits	52
Distribution	56
Family Ciconiidae	57
Mycteria americana	57
Wood ibis	57
Habits	57
Distribution	65
Jabiru mycteria	66
Jabiru	66
Habits	66
Distribution	72
Family Ardeidae	72
Botaurus lentiginosus	72
American bittern	72
Habits	72
Distribution	82
Ixobrychus exilis exilis	84
Least bittern	84
Habits	84
Distribution	91
Ardea occidentalis	93
Great white heron	93
Habits	93
Distribution	100
Ardea herodias herodias	101
Great blue heron	101
Habits	101
Distribution	113
Ardea herodias fannini	114
Northwest coast heron	114
Habits	114
Distribution	117

Order Herodiones—Continued.
  Family Ardeidae—Continued.   Page

	Page
Ardea herodias wardi	118
Ward heron	118
Habits	118
Distribution	122
Ardea herodias treganzai	123
Treganza heron	123
Habits	123
Distribution	126
Ardea herodias hyperonca	127
California heron	127
Habits	127
Distribution	130
Ardea herodias sanctilucae	130
Espiritu Santo heron	130
Habits	130
Distribution	130
Ardea cinerea cinerea	131
European heron	131
Habits	131
Distribution	133
Casmerodius egretta	133
American egret	133
Habits	133
Distribution	144
Egretta candidissima candidissima	146
Snowy egret	146
Habits	146
Distribution	154
Egretta candidissima brewsteri	156
Brewster egret	156
Habits	156
Distribution	157
Dichromanassa rufescens	157
Reddish egret	157
Habits	157
Distribution	166
Hydranassa tricolor ruficollis	167
Louisiana heron	167
Habits	167
Distribution	176
Florida caerulea	177
Little blue heron	177
Habits	177
Distribution	184
Butorides virescens virescens	185
Green heron	185
Habits	185
Distribution	192
Butorides virescens frazari	194
Frazar green heron	194
Habits	194
Distribution	194
Butorides virescens anthonyi	195
Anthony green heron	195
Habits	195
Distribution	196
Nycticorax nycticorax naevius	197
Black-crowned night heron	197
Habits	197
Distribution	210
Nyctanassa violacea	213
Yellow-crowned night heron	213
Habits	213
Distribution	218

Page

Order Paludicolae_____ 219
  Family Megalornithidae_____ 219
    Megalornis americanus_____ 219
      Whooping crane_____ 219
        Habits_____ 219
        Distribution_____ 230
    Megalornis canadensis_____ 231
      Little brown crane_____ 231
        Habits_____ 231
        Distribution_____ 239
    Megalornis mexicanus_____ 241
      Sandhill crane_____ 241
        Habits_____ 241
        Distribution_____ 250
    Megalornis canadensis mexicanus_____ 250
    Megalornis canadensis pratensis_____ 253
  Family Aramidae_____ 254
    Aramus vociferus vociferus_____ 254
      Limpkin_____ 254
        Habits_____ 254
        Distribution_____ 259
  Family Rallidae_____ 260
    Rallus elegans_____ 260
      King rail_____ 260
        Habits_____ 260
        Distribution_____ 264
    Rallus beldingi_____ 266
      Belding rail_____ 266
        Habits_____ 266
        Distribution_____ 267
    Rallus obsoletus_____ 267
      California clapper rail_____ 267
        Habits_____ 267
        Distribution_____ 272
    Rallus levipes_____ 272
      Light-footed rail_____ 272
        Habits_____ 272
        Distribution_____ 275
    Rallus yumanensis_____ 275
      Yuma clapper rail_____ 275
        Habits_____ 275
        Distribution_____ 277
    Rallus longirostris crepitans_____ 277
      Clapper rail_____ 277
        Habits_____ 277
        Distribution_____ 282
    Rallus longirostris saturatus_____ 283
      Louisiana clapper rail_____ 283
        Habits_____ 283
        Distribution_____ 287
    Rallus longirostris scotti_____ 287
      Florida clapper rail_____ 287
        Habits_____ 287
        Distribution_____ 290
    Rallus longirostris waynei_____ 290
      Wayne clapper rail_____ 290
        Habits_____ 290
        Distribution_____ 292
    Rallus virginianus_____ 292
      Virginia rail_____ 292
        Habits_____ 292
        Distribution_____ 298
    Porzana porzana_____ 301
      Spotted crake_____ 301
        Habits_____ 301
        Distribution_____ 302

Order Paludicolae—Continued.
    Family Rallidae—Continued.   **Page**
      Porzana carolina _____ 303
      Sora rail _____ 303
        Habits _____ 303
        Distribution _____ 313
      Coturnicops noveboracensis _____ 316
      Yellow rail _____ 316
        Habits _____ 316
        Distribution _____ 324
      Creciscus jamaicensis _____ 326
      Black rail _____ 326
        Habits _____ 326
        Distribution _____ 331
      Creciscus coturniculus _____ 332
      Farallon rail _____ 332
        Habits _____ 332
        Distribution _____ 336
      Crex crex _____ 337
      Corn crake _____ 337
        Habits _____ 337
        Distribution _____ 338
      Ionornis martinicus _____ 339
      Purple gallinule _____ 339
        Habits _____ 339
        Distribution _____ 344
      Gallinula chloropus cachinnans _____ 346
      Florida gallinule _____ 346
        Habits _____ 346
        Distribution _____ 353
      Fulica atra _____ 356
      European coot _____ 356
        Habits _____ 356
        Distribution _____ 358
      Fulica americana _____ 358
      American coot _____ 358
        Habits _____ 358
        Distribution _____ 367
References to bibliography _____ 373
Index _____ 387

LIFE HISTORIES OF NORTH AMERICAN MARSH BIRDS
ORDERS ODONTOGLOSSAE, HERODIONES, AND PALUDICOLAE

By Arthur Cleveland Bent,

of Taunton, Massachusetts

Order ODONTOGLOSSAE. Lamellirostral Grallatores
Family PHOENICOPTERIDAE, Flamingoes

PHOENICOPTERUS RUBER Linnaeus

AMERICAN FLAMINGO

HABITS

I have never been privileged to see this gorgeous bird in its natural surroundings. But, having visited some of its former haunts in southern Florida, it is not difficult to picture in imagination the thrill of pleasure which others have enjoyed in their first sight of even a distant flock of these magnificent birds, perhaps a mile or more away across a broad, flat, shimmering waste of whitish marl, a glowing band of brilliant pink against a background of dark-green mangroves. It has always been a shy species, as even the earliest writers refer to the difficulty of approaching it in the open situations where it loves to congregate, to feed in the shallow muddy waters, and where its sentinels are always on the alert. Its favorite haunts are far from civilization, for it shuns human society and is soon driven away from much-frequented places to live its even, quiet life in the remote wilderness of the broad, shallow, muddy bays or estuaries of our tropical coasts. Dr. Frank M. Chapman (1908) describes it very well when he says:

There are larger birds than the flamingo, and birds with more brilliant plumage but no other large bird is so brightly colored and no other brightly colored bird is so large. In brief, size and beauty of plume united, reach their maximum of development in this remarkable bird, while the open nature of its haunts and its gregariousness seem specially designed to display its marked characteristics of form and color to the most striking advantage.

1

The flamingo is no longer to be found, except possibly as a rare straggler, on the North American Continent, but in Audubon's time it was fairly abundant in extreme southern Florida. Even in those days it was relentlessly pursued and was becoming quite shy. Gustavus Wurdemann (1861), in a letter written to the Smithsonian Institution in 1857, wrote:

The flamingo is known to but a very few inhabitants of this state, because it is confined to the immediate neighborhood of the most southern portion of the peninsula, Cape Sable, and the keys in its vicinity. It was seen by the first settlers at Indian River, but abandoned these regions immediately, and never returned thither after having been fired upon.

In the same letter he refers to a flock of 500 flamingos seen near Indian Key, in the Bay of Florida, and graphically describes his experiences in chasing and capturing, with a native hunter, some hundred or so of these beautiful birds, which were molting and unable to fly.

Evidently this flock of flamingos, or its descendants, was able to survive in this remote and inaccessible portion of Florida long after the species had disappeared from other sections. It was supposed to breed somewhere in that vicinity, but the breeding grounds were never found. W. E. D. Scott (1887) reported that the last birds were killed in Tampa Bay in 1885 and that they disappeared from Cape Romano and all points north of that at about that time. But in February, 1890, he found a large flock frequenting a bay 18 miles east of Cape Sable, about which he (1890) writes as follows:

It was some 9 or 10 miles from our anchorage to the mouth of the first of the three bays I have mentioned—a long way to go in a skiff. But both of our boats were soon manned and we began the details of the exploration. Rounding the point opening the first or more westerly of the bays, we found that it was about a mile and a half in width and some 3 miles deep into the land, with a decided bend to the west. No birds were to be seen till this bend was in turn opened, and there, still a mile or more away, was presented a truly wonderful sight. Stretched out for fully three-quarters of a mile, and about 300 yards from the mainland shore, was a band of rosy, firelike color. This band was unbroken, and seemed to be very even, though curving with the contour of the shore. Now and again a flame or series of flames seemed to shoot up above the level of the line. This proved when examined through the glass to be caused by one or more birds raising their heads to look about or to rest themselves, for when first noticed all were feeding, with their heads most of the time buried in the shallow water, searching the mud for the small shellfish which appear to be the favorite food at this point.

Presently some of the birds saw the boats, and the alarm was given. Slowly the line began to contract toward the center, and the birds were soon in a compact body, appearing now like a large field of red upon the water, and the resemblance to flames was much increased by the constant movements of the heads and necks of the different individuals. In a few moments they began to rise and soon they were all in full flight, passing out of the bay and over the point of land to the east in long lines and in V-shaped parties, recalling to mind the flight of wild geese. If the color on the water was novel, that of the flock while in the air was truly surprising, a cloud of flame-colored pink, like the hues of a brilliant sunset. As far as we could descry the birds, the color was the great conspicuous feature. Looked at through the glass, while in flight, the individuals composing the flock were seen to be mostly adults. I saw only a small division of the lighter colored immature birds. These seemed to have their own particular position in the flock, and on this and subsequent occasions, when seen, these younger individuals were always alone. As nearly as could be estimated there were at least 1,000 birds in this flock, and of these all but about 50 appeared to be adults.

Twelve years later, on March 26, 1902, Dr. Reginald Heber Howe, jr. (1902) "observed a flock of from 500 to 1,000 birds in a little bay to the east of Cape Sable," probably in the same locality. This was about the last of the flamingo in Florida, for in the following year, 1903, I spent parts of April and May in this vicinity, visiting Indian Key, where Audubon saw his first flock, and exploring the coast and islands from Cape Sable to a bay called Snake Bight, which I judge from their descriptions to be the place where Scott and Howe saw the two flocks referred to above. I made another visit to this same region in March and April in 1908, but saw no signs of flamingos on either trip. Perhaps they may still visit that region occasionally in winter, but the resident birds are gone.

In past years the flamingo probably visited the coasts of Louisiana and Texas, occasionally if not regularly, but no specimens have been taken there in recent years. W. L. McAtee (1911) reported seeing one at Cameron, Louisiana, on December 6, 1910. And R. D. Camp told me that he saw one at Bahia Grande, Cameron County, Texas, on October 15, 1912 and in September, 1915.

Nesting.—There was much controversy among the earlier writers as to the nesting habits of the flamingo; very little was known about it and there was an erroneous impression that the nest was a tall, truncated cone on which the bird sat astride, with its long legs reaching down to the ground on either side; it was so illustrated in drawings and in mounted groups. C. J. Maynard (1888) was the first to discover and describe a colony of American flamingos, establishing the fact that the flamingo sits on its nest with its legs folded under it, just as any other bird does. He gives a graphic account of his experiences in finding a large colony on Andros Island, in the Bahamas, on May 14, 1884, in which he describes the nesting rookery, as follows:

The rookery occupied about a half acre of land, or rather what was once land, for all, or nearly all, were surrounded by water, and were built on a kind of peninsula which had water on three sides of it. The nests were constructed wholly of marl piled layer upon layer, without waiting for any layer to dry, for in some cases the bottom was as soft as the top. In scooping up the marl the birds evidently use the lower mandible of the bill, while it is spread and flattened with the feet. The clay is not gathered at random about the nest, but from a pit on either side, or often from three pits, and it is the joining of these pits that causes the nests to be surrounded with water.   None of the nests are constructed quite to the margin of the peninsula, thus a dike nearly surrounds the rookery.   I say nearly, for this was broken through on the southern end, and the water from the creeks flowed in, thus the slight inland tide rose and fell among the nests.

The nests were, as a rule, not over 2 feet apart, measuring from their base, but they were generally constructed in groups of from three to seven or eight, each one being joined to one or two of the others at the base, oftentimes for a foot or more.   This rookery had evidently been used for at least one year previous to this, as we saw many nests, especially the higher ones, which had to all appearances been constructed on top of an old foundation.   New nests built throughout of soft marl were, on the average, only a foot high, and were built in a certain part of the rookery.   All of the nests in the older part of the rookery contained eggs, as a rule only one being deposited, and this was placed on the slightly cup-shaped top of the truncated pyramid.   Incubation had begun, and in nearly all the eggs the embryos were considerably advanced.   Thus we could judge that the birds had laid all the eggs that they would that season.   We estimated that there were in the neighborhood of 2,000 nests, and in all of these we found only some 50 sets of 2 eggs, and three in one case only.

For most of our information about the nesting habits of the flamingo we are indebted to Dr. Frank M. Chapman and I shall quote freely from his various papers on the subject, based on his explorations in the Bahama Islands.   As to the localities selected for nesting sites he (1902) says:

Exploration of the surrounding country showed that it was regularly frequented by flamingos in numbers during the nesting season.   Within a radius of a mile no less than eight groups of nests were discovered.   They showed successive stages of decay, from the old nests, which had almost disappeared before the action of the elements, to those which were in an excellent state of preservation and were doubtless occupied the preceding year.   Some were placed among young, others among fully grown mangroves, and one colony, probably inhabited in 1900, was situated on a sand bar 200 yards from the nearest vegetation.   All the colonies found contained at least several hundred nests, and the one on the sand bar, by actual count of a measured section, was composed of 2,000 mud dwellings.   What an amazing sight this settlement must have presented when occupied, with the stately males, as is their habit, standing on guard near their sitting mates.

In the above named localities the birds were not on their nests at the time of his visit, but on June 7, 1904, he again visited the same locality with marked success.   In describing his approach to the rookery he (1908) writes:

All day we had been following broad, shallow creeks, which, meeting other creeks widened at intervals into lagoons, while, on every side, the country spread away into the low, flat swash, neither land nor water and wholly worthless for everything—except flamingos.

At last his guide pointed across the swash to a thin pink line, distant at least a mile, but showing plainly against the green of the mangroves.

At a distance of about 300 yards, the wind being from us, toward the birds, we first heard their honking notes of alarm, which increased to a wave of deep sound. Soon the birds began to rise, standing on their nests, facing the wind and waving their black, vermilion-lined wings. As we came a little nearer, in stately fashion the birds began to move; uniformly, like a great body of troops, they stepped slowly forward, pinions waving and trumpets sounding, and then, when we were still 150 yards away, the leaders sprang into the air. File after file of the winged host followed. The very earth seemed to erupt birds, as flaming masses streamed heavenward. It was an appalling sight.

Referring to the nesting ground and nests in this colony, Doctor Chapman (1905) says:

The nesting ground selected by this colony of flamingos was an extension of that occupied by probably the same colony of birds in 1901. In that year the nests were placed among large red mangrove bushes where but few could be seen at one time. The area occupied in 1904 is more open in character, the only conspicuous vegetation being coarse grasses, buttonwood shoots, and one good-sized buttonwood bush. It is evident that in selecting a nesting site the birds are governed not by the nature of the vegetation, but by the height of the water. Since nesting material is not carried but is used where it is found, the birds must build where the ground is sufficiently muddy to be readily worked.

The main colony occupied an area of approximately 3,450 square yards, with an average of about 50 nests to each 100 square yards, or two square yards to a nest; but often the nests were built so close together that they touched each other.

As to the composition of the nests he (1905) says:

The material of which the nest is composed depends, as one might suppose, upon the nature of the spot in which it is built. The nests of 1902, placed on the marl bar, were composed wholly of marl; but under other conditions leaves, roots, and twigs may enter into the composition of the nest to a greater or less extent, and I saw several nests in which sticks played as prominent a part as mud. While I did not see flamingos actually building their nests, I saw them adding to nests in which the egg had already been laid. Standing with a foot on each side of the nest mud was dragged up the side of the nest with the bill and pressed into position with both bill and feet. Doubtless the method was similar to that employed in building a new nest.

The measurements of six nests, selected to show the range of variation in size, varied in height from 5 to 13 inches, in diameter at the base from 18 to 23 inches and in diameter at the top from 12 to 14 inches. The height of the nest is evidently varied to suit the water conditions and after frequent heavy rains the lower nests are often washed out.

Flamingos, when not too much disturbed, generally return to the same breeding grounds year after year. That they are much attached to and not easily frightened away from their nests is shown by the interesting group activities described by Doctor Chapman (1908) and by the ease with which he so successfully concealed himself in his blind in the very heart of the rookery, where he took such a wonderful series of photographs. When he first entered the rookery "the birds, after flying only a short distance to the windward, turned abruptly and with set wings sailed over him, a rushing, fiery cloud, to alight in a lagoon bordering the western side of the rookery." A short time later they rose again and "with harsh honkings bore down upon him. The birds in close array came toward him without a waver, and for a few moments one might well have believed they were about to attack; but with a mighty roar of wings and clanging of horns, they passed overhead, turned, and on set wings again shot back to the lagoon." The next day, when he was finally settled in his blind, they twice rose in a body and swept over the rookery to reconnoiter, and then:

Without further delay, the birds returned to their homes. They came on foot a great red cohort, marching steadily toward me. I felt like a spy in an enemy's camp. Might not at least one pair of the nearly 4,000 eyes detect something unnatural in the newly-grown bush almost within their city gates? No sign of alarm, however, was shown; without confusing, and as if trained to the evolution, the birds advanced with stately tread to their nests. There was a bowing of a forest of slender necks as each bird lightly touched its egg or nest with its bill; then, all talking loudly, they stood up on their nests; the black wings were waved for a moment, and bird after bird dropped forward on its egg. After a vigorous wriggling motion, designed evidently to bring the egg into close contact with the skin, the body was still, but the long neck and head were for a time in constant motion, preening, picking material at the base of the nest, dabbling in a near-by puddle, or perhaps drinking from it. Occasionally a bird sparred with one of the three or four neighbors which were within reach, when, bill grasping bill, there ensued a brief and harmless test of strength.

The American flamingo also breeds in the Galapagos Islands. Here according to Edward W. Gifford (1913), "the nests are always built near the water, either on some very low, flat, rocky islet or on a beach." Evidently the nests in this region "are not endangered to any great extent by the rise of the water," and are therefore built much lower. Most of the nests were from 4 to 8 inches high, none were higher than 12 inches and one "egg was laid on a level bit of lava rock," with mud an inch deep scraped around it.

Eggs.—The flamingo lays ordinarily only one egg or raises only a single young bird in a season; two or even three eggs have been found in a nest. The egg is from elliptical ovate to elongate ovate in shape. It is always somewhat rough and chalky, and sometimes very rough with a lumpy surface and with deep scratches. It is dull white, dirty white, or rarely pinkish white in color. The measurements of 41 eggs average 91.3 by 55.4 millimeters; the eggs showing the four extremes measure 99 by 54; 96.5 by 59.4; 85 by 55.5; and 96.1 by 51.9 millimeters.

Young.—The period of incubation does not seem to have been definitely determined for the American bird, but William Evans (1891) gives it as 30 to 32 days for a closely related foreign species. Incubation is performed by both sexes. Doctor Chapman (1905) says:

The birds changed places early in the morning and late in the afternoon. They left or returned to the rookery singly or in flocks containing as many as

50 birds. The individual, therefore, which incubated or cared for the young during the day fed at night, while the one which had been feeding during the day passed the night in the rookery. There was no relation between sex and the time of day occupied in parental duties, both sexes being represented during the day and hence, doubtless, during the night also.

As the egg pipped the parent bird was seen to stand over it and move it with the bill until the opening was uppermost, thus giving the hatching chick access to the air. When incubating, as well as when brooding, the bird sits upon the nest with the legs folded. In assuming this position, the bird first stands upon the nest with its toes on the rim, then drops forward, the toes remaining at about the same point, while the heel projects slightly beyond the tail, and the tarsus is visible for the entire length. In arising the bill is pressed into the side of the nest and for a moment thus forms a tripod with the legs.

The young flamingo when hatched is sufficiently developed to leave the nest before it is dry, under the stimulus of an apparently instinctive fear. At my approach young birds with their plumage still wet from the egg would crawl over the edge of the nest and fall to the ground or water below, when their strength seemed to fail them. A few hours later, when the plumage was dry, chicks could swim and run readily, and when they were a day old they invariably left the nest as I drew near. When not disturbed the young remain in the nest three or four days. During this time they are brooded by the parents.

Their food consists of a blackish liquid, doubtless the juices of partially digested *Ceritheum*, which they receive from the parent's bill, a drop at a time by regurgitation. The parent administers food while standing over the chick with lowered head and neck, or while brooding it, when the head of the young appears from beneath the parent's wing between the body and the humerus. Food was generally given in response to the young bird's open-mouthed appeal, and its administration was preceded by movements of the neck which evidently assisted the act of regurgitation.

While in the nest the young bird eats also the shell of the egg from which it was hatched. This soon becomes broken into small pieces which are readily picked up by the then straight-billed chick, doubtless with greater facility than its bent-billed parent could exhibit. This shell-eating habit appears to be invariable. Numerous chicks were seen exhibiting it, and eggshells were found in the stomachs of nearly 20 young examined. Possibly the development of this habit may be due to the limited nature of the parent's food, together with the fact that heavy rains may not only place the chick upon an islet but submerge available feeding areas. Consequently it is important that the food furnished by the parent be supplemented by a supply of bone-forming material which the chick finds in the nest. The young bird evidently continues under the care of the parent after leaving the nest and, for a time at least, is still fed by regurgitation. Young birds two days old, which jumped from their nests near my blind as I entered it, found their way home in response to the call of the parent and climbed back into the nest with the aid of bill, wings, and feet, without assistance from the parent. When not guided by the parent, chicks which had left the nest prematurely and were attempting to return to it, apparently recognized neither their nest nor parent. They endeavored to climb up the nearest nest on which an adult was sitting, but were not welcomed; threatening, sinuous gestures of the long neck being followed, should the chick persist, by a slight nip on the nape, when the lost young bird continued in its search for home.

Young birds which he took away from the rookery alive and attempted to raise in captivity lived long enough to throw some light on their habits and development. He (1904) writes:

It is an exceedingly interesting fact that the bill of the young flamingo is straight and wholly unlike the singular, bent bill of the adult. Signs of a Roman nose, so to speak, first appear when the chick is about two weeks old, and at this time he begins to feed after the manner of adults. That is, the upper mandible is held almost parallel with the ground, and even pressed into the muddy bottoms on which the bird feeds. It is then moved rapidly and sends a jet of water through the bill which washes away the sand or mud taken in with the food. Like the old bird, the young one now often treads water or dances when feeding, to float its food off the bottom so that it can be more readily secured.

The note of very young birds is a puppylike barking. This is soon followed by a kind of squealing whistle, and this, in turn, by a chirruping crow which persist until the bird is at least two months old. The whistling note was the characteristic one at the time of which I write, and, under proper conditions, the chorus of young birds could be plainly heard, day or night, at my tent a mile away.

Plumages.—When first hatched the young flamingo is thickly and uniformly covered, except on the lores and orbital region with pure white down, tinged more or less with bluish gray on the crown and back. When about a month old the first coat of white down is replaced by a second growth of down which is uniform ashy gray in color. The juvenal plumage appears first on the scapulars and sides of the breast, at an age of about five weeks. Doctor Chapman (1905) describes this plumage as follows:

The general color is grayish brown with a tinge of pink upon the underparts and wings. The feathers of the back have well-marked black shaft-streaks; the tail is pale pinkish white, externally edged with blackish; the primaries are black, the secondaries black internally margined with white except at the tips; the primary coverts are all pinkish, blackish at the tip and on the inner vane; the lesser, median, and greater coverts are generally pinkish basally, blackish at the tip; the axillars are pink; the abdomen is pinkish washed with brown.

Specimens taken in February, March, May, and July all show continuous molt from the juvenal into an older plumage which is unmistakably immature. This transition plumage might be called the first winter or the first nuptial plumage, for it covers both seasons, but it represents a constantly changing progress toward maturity. The head, neck, and mantle become gradually suffused with pale salmon pink, by the growth of new feathers, apparantly working from the head downward and beginning in December. The primary-coverts and the lesser wing-coverts are molted during the early spring and the median coverts a little later; but the juvenal greater wing-coverts and scapulars are apparently retained until July. Many of the new pink feathers in the coverts, particularly the larger feathers, have dusky shaft-streaks or dusky tips. The underparts gradually become pinker during spring By July the young bird is mostly pale pink except for the juvenal greater wing-coverts, the dusky shaft-streaks and the dusky tips on the scapulars.

During the summer, probably in July and August, a complete molt takes place, at which time the young bird assumes the adult plumage, or one closely resembling it, in which a few signs of immaturity may be retained in the way of dusky shaft-streaks or dusky tips in some of the wing coverts.

Doctor Chapman (1905) says of the molt of adults:

The molt begins while the birds are still nesting. Specimens taken June 13 have new feathers appearing in numbers on the crown and scapulars. At this time the old plumage is much worn and faded. The back, in some specimens, is nearly white, and the long scapulars are so abraded that little but the shaft remains on the terminal third. The upper and under wing coverts, and especially the axillars, show less change than other portions of the plumage. As far as I could learn from the usually inaccurate testimony of the negroes, the moult continues through July and part of August; the flight feathers being shed in the latter month.

Food.—Doctor Chapman (1905) says of the food of the flamingo:

The stomachs of all the adults examined contained only the remains of shells of the genus *Ceritheum*, which are evidently swallowed entire and ground up in the stomach, the walls of which are exceedingly thick and muscular. The birds sometimes fed in water which reached to their bodies, and the treading or dancing motion, which has been well described by former writers, was employed while the head was submerged.

He did not observe that the birds posted sentinels while feeding; but W. E. D. Scott (1890) describes the operation quite fully, as follows:

All the time the birds were feeding there were three small parties, varying from two to five individuals, that were apparently doing a sort of picket duty. At each end of the line and about 100 yards from it was posted one of these parties, offshore and at the center of the line and some hundred yards away the third party was stationed. About every half hour the individuals composing these picket squads would take wing, fly to the flock in line and alight, and presently, that is in less than a minute, another or part of the same picket squad would leave the flock and fly to the point left but a few minutes before. I am not sure that the entire squad was changed at such times, but the pickets taking the place that had been left only a few minutes before, were generally one or two more or less in number than the party they apparently relieved. I never saw more than five individuals in a party, and now and then there was only a single sentinel, but generally from three to five. The birds at these outposts did not appear to be feeding, but were apparently guarding against any attempt to surprise the main body.

C. J. Maynard (1896) obtained some evidence that the flamingo feeds at night; he writes:

At one time, late in January, we had penetrated into the interior of the island many miles, and had reached the borders of a large, shallow lake, near the shore of which was a mangrove island. During the daytime we had seen numbers of flamingos and I was assured by my guide that they fed near this island at night. Accordingly about sunset we concealed ourselves among the mangroves of the island and awaited the coming of the flamingos. As the sun disappeared numerous cormorants, pelicans, and herons began to settle on the low trees over our heads, and one large brown pelican alighted so near me that I could have touched it with my gun barrel. As soon as the short twilight gave place to darkness, we heard the honk of the flamingos and soon they began to arrive, each group alighting with a splash in the water near. Soon hundreds had gathered, and although we could hear them wallowing about, so dense was the darkness that neither my guide or myself could see a single bird.

Behavior.—J. L. Bonhote (1903) gives us an interesting picture of the behavior of a large flock of flamingos, writing as follows:

I had been watching at a distance an immense flock of 700 or a 1,000, feeding, preening, and wading about, and, desiring a closer inspection, had approached to within 20 yards of the nearest bird when I stumbled and thus gave them the alarm. As soon as they saw me they all bunched up together, their long necks stretched up as high as possible, and all I could see was a mass of living scarlet streaks. Although I remained absolutely quiet, the birds would not settle down again; at first four or five, then the layer about four deep nearest me, then the next layer, and so on and so on, slowly rose expanding their jet black wings and displaying, as they did so, the pink of their backs and the gorgeous scarlet of their under wing coverts. Thus they went slowly filing off in a long irregular column till not one was left, and, as they wended their way across the sky, one saw first the contrast of black and scarlet till it gave place to an intermittant line of red, gradually fading away in a pink haze on the eastern horizon. Such a blaze of moving color, set in the deep blue of a tropical sky in the light of the afternoon sun, forms a spectacle of natural beauty which cannot be surpassed.

Doctor Chapman (1908) writes:

Flamingos in flight resemble no other bird known to me. With legs and neck fully outstreched, and the comparatively small wings set halfway between bill and toes, they look as if they might fly backward or forward with equal ease. They progress more rapidly than a heron, and, when hurried, fly with a singular serpentine motion of the neck and body, as if they were crawling in the air.

As noon approached, the birds disposed themselves for sleep. The long necks were arranged in sundry coils and curves, the heads tucked snugly beneath the feathers of the back, and, for the first time, there was silence in the red city. Suddenly—one could never tell whence it came—the honking alarm note was given. Instantly, and with remarkable effect, the snakelike necks shot up all over the glowing bed of color before me, transforming it into a writhing mass of flaming serpents; then as the alarm note continued and was taken up by a thousand throats, the birds, like a vast congregation, with dignified precision of movement, gravely arose, pressing their bills into the nests to assist themselves. Under circumstances of this kind the birds rarely left their nests, and it was difficult to determine the cause of their alarm. Often, doubtless, it was baseless, but at times it was due to a circling turkey vulture, the gaunt ogre of flamingodom, which, in the absence of the parent birds, is said to eat not only eggs but nestlings. Possibly some slight sound from my tent, where, with ill-controlled excitement, I was making photograph after photograph, may have occasioned the deep-voiced warning *huh-huh-huh.*

Of the notes of the flamingo, he (1905) says:

The notes of the adults are varied in character. The commonest is the loud *huh-huh-huh*, already mentioned, the second syllable of which is strongly accented. This call was given in a low, deep tone and in a higher one of less volume, a difference which I considered sexual, the louder voice being, presumably, that of the male. This was the alarm call, and indeed was heard whenever there was any commotion in the colony. Other calls were a deep nasal, resonant *honk*,

honk, honk, honk, even more gooselike in tone than the first call mentioned, a henlike, drawled *cah-cah-cah-cah,* and a broken *cut-leek.*

That the flamingo can run well on its long legs, when wounded or when molting and unable to fly, is well illustrated by the following instance noted by Mr. Gifford (1913):

Where the ground is clear, and the bird's movements are unimpeded by rocks and bushes, the flamingo is a good runner, being able to cover ground very rapidly, and giving a person a lively chase. At James Bay, James Island, a young bird not quite able to fly got through the bushes from the lagoon to the ocean beach. I pursued it for nearly half a mile south along the beach late one afternoon. I was, however, unable to overtake it before it reached the rocks at the end of the beach. Perceiving that it would be caught if it remained on the beach, the bird stepped into the water and struck boldly out from shore, swimming over an eighth of a mile. As soon as I left the beach, it returned and commenced walking up and down again in the attempt to find its way back to the lagoon. The following morning it had disappeared.

At a lagoon 4 or 5 miles northwest of Sullivan Bay, James Island, on July 28, an adult bird was found without flight feathers. New ones were just appearing, which were very tender, bleeding profusely when bruised. This bird was a fast runner, racing up and down the smooth beach of the lagoon, until finally it was chased into a cul-de-sac. It tried to escape through the brush, but of course tripped and fell, bruising its wings, feet, and bill. It realized its inability to fly, for it did not make any attempt to use its wings until the very last.

D. P. Ingram (1894) relates the following incident, which shows that the flamingo is also a good swimmer:

A flock of American flamingos came flying down about parallel with the coast, and about 100 yards out over the water. When nearly opposite I selected my bird and gave him one barrel, which brought him down at once. I immediately selected my next bird and gave him the other barrel. The game was a long distance off at the first and had turned their course somewhat and were still further off at the second shot. I saw that my bird was hit but did not at once come down, but left the flock and turned his course at about right angles, directly out over the ocean, gradually lowering, and after flying about half a mile it struck the water. One of my men, who was a very expert sculler and who was on my large boat, which lay at anchor out about 200 yards distant, at once took his small boat and started for my prize, expecting to go and pick it up as it was down in the water. He soon saw that the bird was making about as good headway out in the ocean as he was, when he doubled his energy. When he had approached within about 50 yards of the bird it arose and flew, this time going about the same distance that it did the first time, before it was again compelled to take to the water. He then gave up the chase, being fully a mile and a half from shore, the bird having made almost two-thirds as good time as he could in sculling his boat. When the bird raised to fly he was somewhere in from 30 to 50 fathoms of water.

Enemies.—Aside from man flamingos have few enemies. There are very few predacious animals or birds, in the regions they inhabit, which are large enough to prey on the adults; and the adults, though gentle and practically defenseless, are generally wary enough to escape even from man. Young birds and eggs are often destroyed by turkey buzzards, and the presence of one of these vultures near a breeding rookery always causes considerable excitement. Much mortality among young birds and eggs is also caused by heavy rains, flooding the rookeries. But the worst enemies of these birds are the Bahama negroes who raid the rookeries before the young birds are able to fly and round them up in large numbers. The young birds are easily caught and form an important food supply for the natives; what birds they can not dispose of at once are salted down in brine for future use. The negroes are also very skillful in capturing the old birds by stealthy approach behind a screen of branches. A heavy toll has been thus levied for many years on the eggs, young birds, and adults until these beautiful birds seemed to be threatened with extermination. But fortunately, now that suitable laws have been enacted, the flamingos are receiving a reasonable degree of protection and there is hope that these interesting birds will long continue to give color to the Bahama landscape.

DISTRIBUTION

Range.—Tropical zones of the Americas, including the islands of the Caribbean Sea. East to southern Florida, (formerly Cape Sable); the Bahama Islands, (great Abaco, Andros, etc.); eastern Venezuela, (formerly the Delta of the Orinoco River); and French Guiana, (formerly, Cayenne). South to east central Brazil (Praia de cajutuba). West to the Galapagos Archipelago (Charles Island). North to Cuba (Isle of Pines) and Yucatan (formerly, Rio Lagartos). The flamingo apparently does not breed in the interior of South America and it has become extinct over much of the area where it once bred in large numbers.

Casual records.—Nonmigratory in the usual sense of the word, the flamingo is known outside of its breeding range only as a casual or accidental visitor. One was taken on De Bardien Island, South Carolina, September 17 or 18, 1876, and Audubon states that others had been taken in the vicinity of Charleston. One was seen at Bermuda in 1849; there are several records for both coasts of Florida and for many of the islands in the Carribbean Sea, where it is not known as a breeder. Nelson and Goldman collected specimens at San Felipe, Yucatan, April 23, 1901, and McAtee saw a single individual in Cameron Parish, western Louisiana, December 6, 1910. Most supposed records for this bird for the State of Texas have been found to refer to the roseate spoonbill, which bears the name "flamingo" among the natives of the Texan coast; but the author is inclined to accept a sight record made by R. D. Camp at Bahia Grande October 15, 1912, after a severe Gulf storm.

Egg dates.—Bahama Islands: 32 records, March 2 to July 14; 16 records, May 11 to 16. Galapagos Islands, February 26.

Order HERODIONES, Herons, Storks, Ibises, etc.

Family PLATALEIDAE. Spoonbills

AJAIA AJAJA (Linnaeus)

ROSEATE SPOONBILL

HABITS

This unique and beautiful species is one of the many which have paid the supreme penalty for their beauty and been sacrificed by the avaricious hand of man, who can never resist the temptation to destroy and appropriate to his own selfish use nature's most charming creatures. He never seems to realize that others might like to enjoy an occasional glimpse at a group of these gorgeous birds, clearly outlined in pink and white against a background of dark green mangroves; nor does he appreciate how much a Florida landscape is enhanced by the sight of a flock of "pink curlews" fading away over the tree tops, until the glow of rose-colored wings is lost in the distant blue of the sky. All his sordid mind can grasp is the thought of a pair of pretty wings and the money they will bring when made into ladies' fans! And so a splendid bird, once common in Florida and all along the Gulf coast to Texas, has been gradually driven from its former haunts and is making its last stand in a few remote and isolated localities. The roseate spoonbill never enjoyed a wide distribution, nor was it ever found commonly very far inland. Audubon (1840) implies that in his time it wandered as far north as North Carolina, though it was not common even in South Carolina; he also speaks of a specimen sent to Wilson from Natchez, Mississippi. Dr. Frank M. Chapman (1914) writes:

In 1858, when Dr. Henry Bryant visited Pelican Island, on Indian River, he found not only brown pelicans, but also roseate spoonbills nesting there. But even at that early date these beautiful and interesting birds were prey for the plumer, some of whom, Dr. Bryant writes, were killing as many as 60 spoonbills a day, and sending their wings to St. Augustine to be sold as fans. From that time almost to this, " Pink Curlews," as the Floridan calls them, have been a mark for every man with a gun. Only a remnant was left when the National Association of Audubon Societies protested against the further wanton destruction of bird life, and through its wardens and by the establishment of reservations, attempted to do for Florida what the State had not enough foresight to do for itself.

Writing at the time when the destruction of plume birds was flourishing, W. E. D. Scott (1889) says:

The record in regard to the species in question is even more shocking than that of the flamingo. The roseate spoonbill was 10 years ago an abundant bird on the Gulf Coast of Florida, as far north at least as the mouth of the Anclote River. The birds bred in enormous rookeries in the region about Cape Romano and to the south of that point. These rookeries have been described to me by men who helped to destroy them, as being frequently of many acres in extent and affording breeding grounds to thousands of roseate spoonbills. The birds bred in January and were in the best plumage late in November and in December. They do not seem to have bred north of Charlotte Harbor, so far as I am able to ascertain, but immediately after the breeding season was finished, and as soon as the young were able to shift for themselves, there was a great dispersal of the birds to the northward, particularly along the coast, though they were common at points in the interior. All this is changed. I have spent the past four winters and two summers in Florida. My old hunting grounds have all been carefully retraversed, some of them many times, and the roseate spoonbill is almost as great a stranger to me as to my fellow workers who live the year round in Massachusetts.

Nesting.—I have twice visited one of the few remaining breeding resorts of the roseate spoonbill in Florida, in 1903 and 1908. We had toiled all day, dragging our skiffs over miles of mud flats, poling them through several lakes and laboriously pushing and hauling them through the tortuous channels of sluggish streams, choked with roots and fallen tree trunks, in the almost impenetrable mangrove swamps of extreme southern Florida. The afternoon was well spent when we emerged on the open waters of Cuthbert Lake and saw ahead of us the object of our search, a mangrove island, about a mile distant, literally covered with birds. It was a beautiful sight as the afternoon sun shone full upon it; hundreds of white and blue herons, and a score or two of beautiful "pink curlews" could be plainly seen against the dark green of the mangroves, like feathered gems on a cushion of green velvet. As we drew nearer the picture became more animated, we could see the birds more clearly and we began to realize what a variety of birds and what a host of them the far famed Cuthbert rookery contained. The taller trees in the center of the island were dotted with the great white American egrets, perhaps 300 or 400 of them, watching us from points of vantage; on the mangroves below them, among the hundreds of white ibises, we could see about 75 or 100 of the rare roseate spoonbills; the outer edges of the mangroves, growing in the water, were black with Florida cormorants and anhingas; and everywhere were flocks and clouds of Louisiana and little blue herons. The egrets and the spoonbills were the first to leave; the former rose deliberately, long before we were within gunshot range, and flapped lazily away on their broad white wings; the latter were equally shy, flying around the island, circling to a considerable height and then flying straight away, with their necks outstreched and their feet extended, in long lines or in wedge-shaped flocks; we watched them longingly as they faded away in the distant sky with the blush of sunset glowing through their roseate wings. Then hundreds of white ibises were rising from the mangroves with a mighty roar of wings and scores of cormorants were dropping off the outer branches into the water. When fairly in their midst, the air seemed full of the smaller herons, flopping up ahead of us, drifting around the island and floating over us; and mingled with them were circling water turkeys, soaring turkey vultures, and hovering fish crows, ready to pounce on unprotected eggs.

We landed on the island and found it much like other islands of its class in southern Florida; it was not over two acres in total extent, with not over an acre of dry land in the center. The dry land was covered mainly with black mangroves, mixed with some white button-woods; it was surrounded by a wide belt of red mangroves growing in the mud and water, which was 3 feet deep at the outer edge.

The nesting sites of the roseate spoonbills were in the densest part of the red mangroves among the nests of the white ibises. On my first trip to this rookery, on May 1, 1903, we saw only 12 spoonbills in the colony and found only three nests, one containing a single heavily incubated egg, one a handsome set of three eggs and the other holding two downy young, not quite half grown. The nests were all on nearly horizontal branches of the red mangroves, near the edge of the water, and were from 12 to 15 feet above the mud or water. They were easily recognized as they were quite different from the other nests in the rookery; they were larger than the nests of the ibises or the small herons and were made of larger sticks; they were about the size of a water turkey's nest, but were more neatly made without the use of dead leaves, so characteristic of the latter species. The nests were deeply hollowed and were lined with strips of inner bark and water moss. At the time of my second visit, on March 29, 1908, the spoonbills had increased to 75 or more, but we were too early to find them well along with their nesting. A number of nests had been built or were in process of construction, but only four contained fresh eggs; there were one set of four, one set of three eggs and two nests with one egg each. All of the nests were grouped together, well inside the rookery, in the densest and most shady portion and placed on the lower branches of the red mangroves with more or less water or soft mud under them. The nest containing the set of four eggs was about 10 feet up on a horizontal branch; it was a large nest of course sticks, lined with finer twigs and with the dead and yellow leaves of the red mangrove; it measured 16 inches in outside diameter, 7 inches inside and was hollowed to a depth of about 2 inches. The other nests were similarly constructed.

One of the principal objects of my trip to Texas in 1923 was to find the breeding grounds of the roseate spoonbills; many observers had seen them in flocks at various points along the coast, but their nesting places had not been discovered. We were told that they nested on the islands in the bays, where the herons breed; and George Finlay Simmons said he had found nests and young birds on one of the islands late in the season. The nests were built on the ground among the sunflowers after the herons had finished breeding and gone; and Mr. Simmons said he found pink feathers in some of the nests. Such nesting habits, so different from the customary habits of the species, must have been very unusual or merely casual.

But I think we solved the mystery when we found large numbers of roseate spoonbills nesting in the midst of an immense rookery of white ibises away off in the wilds of Victoria County. It took us four days to locate this rookery, by watching the lines of flight of the birds to and from their feeding grounds, in an immense tract of swamps and heavily forested country in the lowlands along the Guadalupe River. This rookery is more fully described under the white ibis. The center of abundance of the spoonbills was a partially dry, but muddy, spot surrounded by water where a group of large trees, water oaks, and large elms, afforded some shade over a denser growth of small trees and bushes below. Here a great many nests were grouped closely together, from 6 to 15 feet above the ground, in the smaller trees and bushes. Spoonbill's nests were also scattered all over the rookery among the nests of the white ibises, but usually in the more shady places. The spoonbills' nests were easily recognized as they were larger, better made and more deeply hollowed; they were made of larger sticks and were lined with small twigs and with leaves, both green and dry. Most of the nests at that date, May 30, held three or four eggs, but many had small, pink, downy young; we did not find any large young.

Eggs.—The roseate spoonbill lays ordinarily three eggs, sometimes only two, often four eggs and very rarely five. The eggs are easily recognized. In shape they vary from ovate to elliptical ovate or even elongate ovate. The shell is thick and rather roughly granulated, with no gloss. The ground color is usually dull or dirty white and the egg is more or less evenly covered with spots and small blotches of various shades of brown, "chestnut," "auburn," "russet," or "tawny"; occasionally the markings are concentrated around the larger end. A particularly handsome set has a pinkish, creamy white ground color, more or less uniformly covered with dashes and spots of lavender, purple and drab, over which spots of various shades of brown are quite evenly distributed. The measurements of 40 eggs average 65 by 43.9 millimeters; the eggs showing the four extremes measured **71.5** by 42.5, 68.1 by **47, 60.2** by 44.4, and 66 by **41** millimeters.

Young.—The two young, referred to above, in the feeble, helpless stage, unable to stand as yet, were curious looking birds, flabby and fat, with enormous abdomens and soft ducklike bills; their color including bill, feet, legs, and entire skin, was a beautiful, deep, rich, salmon pink; they were scantily covered with short, white down, which was insufficient to conceal the color of the skin; the wing quills were well started, but still in sheaths. The bright pink color was very conspicuous at quite a distance and could be seen through the interstices of the nest, which was covered with whitish excrement, as were also the surrounding branches and the ground below; they are no neater than herons in this respect.

Dr. Frank M. Chapman (1914) says of the behavior of the young birds:

On April 17, 1910, I found a colony of about 200 pairs of roseate spoonbills on Pajaro Island, in Tamiahua Lagoon, on the Gulf coast of Mexico, south of Tampico. Most of the nests contained well-grown young at least a month old and probably older. Allowing a month for hatching, and it is evident that these birds begin to lay about the middle of February. In the Mexican colony, four was the usual number of young. They were well-behaved youngsters and, in the absence of their parents, rested peacefully in their homes, or occasionally ventured on thrilling excursions of a few feet to the adjoining limbs. But when their parents returned, they were all attention and on the alert for food. At such times they usually stood in a row on the edge of the nest facing the old birds, and in most comical manner swung the head and neck up and down. I have seen balanced mechanical toys which would make almost exactly the same motion. The toys, however, were silent, while the little spoonbills all joined in a chorus of tremulous, trilling whistles, which grew louder and more rapid as the parent approached. What their parents brought them I could not see, nor, for that matter, could they. But with a confidence born of experience, the bird that had the first opportunity pushed its bill and head far down its parent's bill to get what ever was there. This singular operation sometimes lasted as long as 10 seconds, and it was terminated only by the parent which, much against the will of its offspring, disengaged itself; then, after a short rest, a second youngster was fed, and thus in due time the whole family was satisfied. The young now sank contentedly back in the nest, and the old ones stood quietly by, or went back to the shores and marshes for further supplies.

Audubon (1840) says:

During the moult, which takes place in Florida late in May, the young of the preceding year conceal themselves among the close branches of the mangroves and other trees growing over narrow inlets, between secluded keys, or on bayous where they spend the whole day, and whence it is difficult to start them. Toward night they return to their feeding grounds, generally keeping apart from the old birds.

Plumages.—The downy, young, roseate spoonbill is a "pink curlew" and a real "spoonbill." The living young when seen in the nest is decidedly pink in appearance, bright, rich salmon pink, but this is due entirely to the color of the skin; the bill and feet are practically the same color. This color fades more or less in the dried skin to "orange pink" or "light salmon orange" and in some cases to dull yellow or buff; one specimen that I have had in my collection for over 20 years is still quite pink. The bill is broad and flat, like a duck's bill, and somewhat decurved. The young bird, when first hatched, is entirely covered with a sparse growth of short white down, through which the pink skin shows plainly. The down increases in length and density until the bird is entirely covered with thick wooly down. The wing quills appear at an early age and the first, or juvenal plumage is aquired before the young bird leaves the nest. This is mainly white, with a slight suffusion of pink under the wings and in the tail; the crown, cheeks, and throat are covered with white plumage, and not naked as in adults; in the juvenal wing the outer primaries are dusky-tipped, about half of the outer webs and less than half of the inner webs, the amount of dusky decreasing inwardly; the primary coverts and the greater wing coverts, are similarly marked.

The first winter plumage is a continuation of the juvenal with progressive changes toward maturity. The head and neck remain white, but the mantle and breast become gradually pinker. In some juvenal birds a little carmine appears in the lesser wing coverts and upper tail coverts during the winter and spring, but usually there is no trace of this color during the first year. The dusky-tipped wing coverts are molted before spring, but not the remiges. The tail is molted and replaced by one which is very pale buff. The feathered head and the juvenal primaries are retained until the first complete molt takes place in summer, from June to September.

At this molt, the first postnuptial, the young bird assumes a plumage which is much like that of the winter adult. The head, crown, cheeks, and throat, become wholly or partially naked; the wings, tail, and body are all pink, but with no carmine; and the neck and part of the breast are white. Sometimes this second winter plumage is worn without much change through the following spring; but usually at the second prenuptial molt, in late winter or early spring, a second nuptial plumage is assumed, including the buff tail, the carmine lesser wing coverts and more or less of the roseate and carmine colors in the body plumage. This plumage is much like the adult nuptial, but the highest perfection of plumage is not assumed until the following year, when the young bird is nearly three years old.

The adult apparently has a complete postnuptial molt in summer, mainly in July, August, and September, and an incomplete prenuptial molt in January, February, and March, which involves the tail, the lesser wing coverts and most of the contour plumage. In the highest perfection of the adult nuptial plumage there is much rich carmine in the lesser wing coverts and in the upper and lower tail coverts; a bunch of curly carmine feathers adorns the center of the breast, which is also suffused with pink and with "ochraceous buff"; sometimes the neck is mottled with a few carmine feathers; and the tail is a rich "ochraceous buff." I have seen birds in full nuptial plumage in November and December, but am inclined to think that these are exceptional. In most of the birds that I have called winter adults the carmine markings have been lacking or nearly so, the pink colors have been paler and more restricted and the tails have been pink instead of buff; however, these may be second winter birds and adults may show very little seasonal change; but material showing the postnuptial molt of adults is scarce.

Food.—Audubon (1840) has described the feeding habits of this species very well, as follows:

They are as nocturnal as the night heron, and, although they seek for food at times during the middle of the day, their principal feeding time is from near sunset until daylight. To all such feeding grounds as are exposed to the tides, they be · take themselves when it is low water, and search for food along the shallow margins until driven off by the returning tide. Few birds are better aware of the hours at which the waters are high or low, and when it is near ebb you see them wending their way to the shore. Whenever a feeding place seems to be productive, the spoonbills are wont to return to it until they have been much disturbed, and persons aware of this fact may waylay them with success, as at such times one may shoot them while passing overhead. To procure their food, the spoonbills first generally alight near the water, into which they then wade up to the tibia, and immerse their bills in the water or soft mud, sometimes with the head and even the whole neck beneath the surface. They frequently withdraw these parts, however, and look around to ascertain if danger is near. They move their partially opened mandibles laterally to and fro with a considerable degree of elegance, munching the fry, insects, or small shellfish, which they secure, before swallowing them. When there are many together, one usually acts as sentinel, unless a heron should be near; and in either case you may despair of approaching them. I have never seen one of these birds feeding in fresh water, although I have been told that this is sometimes the case. To all those keys in the Floridas, in which ponds have been dug for the making of salt, they usually repair in the evening for the purpose of feeding; but the shallow inlets in the great salt marshes of our southern coasts are their favorite places of resort.

N. B. Moore says in his notes that this species feeds in both salt and fresh water and that he has found in the stomachs fishes, prawns or shrimps, and coleopterous insects.

There are very little other data available as to the food of the roseate spoonbill, but G. B. Benners (1887) says:

I noticed one of these birds while feeding, and after it caught a fish it would beat it against the water before swallowing it. This was done apparently for the purpose of killing the fish.

Behavior.—In flight the spoonbills show their relationship to the ibises; when flying in flocks they usually form in diagonal lines or in wedge-shaped flocks, each bird a little behind and to one side of the bird ahead of it, so as to take advantage of the aerial waves caused by the advancing flock, after the manner of wild geese. The head and neck are fully outstretched, with the bill pointing straight forward, and the feet are extended backward under the tail and projecting beyond it. The wings, which are large for the size of the bird, beat the air steadily with rather slow, long strokes. I have occasionally seen spoonbills set their wings and scale like ibises, but this is not so customary with spoonbills as with pelicans, cormorants, and ibises.

Audubon's (1840) account of their behavior is well worth quoting; he writes:

The sight of a flock of 15 or 20 of these full-dressed birds is extremely pleasing to the student of nature, should he conceal himself from their view, for then he may observe their movements and manners to advantage. Now, they all stand with their wings widely extended to receive the sun's rays, or perhaps to court the cooling breeze, or they enjoy either seated on their tarsi. Again they all stalk about with graceful steps along the margin of the muddy pool, or wade in the shallows in search of food. After awhile they rise simultaneously on wing, and gradually ascend in a spiral manner to a great height, where you see them crossing each other in a thousand ways, like so many vultures or ibises. At length, tired of this pastime, or perhaps urged by hunger, they return to their feeding grounds in a zigzag course, and plunge through the air, as if displaying their powers of flight before you. These birds fly with their necks stretched forward to their full length, and their legs and feet extended behind, moving otherwise in the manner of herons, or with easy flappings, until about to alight, when they sail with expanded wings, passing once or twice over the spot, and then gently coming to the ground, on which they run a few steps. When traveling to a distant place they proceed in regular ranks, but on ordinary occasions they fly in a confused manner. When the sun is shining, and they are wheeling on wing previous to alighting, their roseate tints exhibit a richer glow, which is surpassed only by the brilliancy of the scarlet ibis and the American flamingo.

The vocal performances of the roseate spoonbill are not elaborate or conspicuous. The only note I heard from them on their breeding grounds was a grunting croak in a low key and so subdued as not to be audible at any great distance. Doctor Chapman (1914) refers to it as "a low, croaking call." Audubon does not mention it. Mr. Benners (1887) describes it as "a sort of cluck like a hen."

Fall.—After the breeding season is over, either early or late in the spring, these birds spread out over a wider territory, which they occupy more or less regularly during the summer, fall, and early winter. This spreading out includes what might be called a northward migration; it is between breeding seasons that the northward extension of range is made. The birds which breed on the east coast of Mexico, in the lagoons south of Tampico, migrate in the spring northward to the coast of Texas and perhaps beyond. On this subject Samuel N. Rhoads (1892) writes:

On the 28th of May, accompanied by Mr. Priour, I sailed down to the mouth of the Nueces River in search of these birds. At a distance of 2 miles a couple of large flocks could be described as a dull rosy streak along the water's edge. We approached near enough to make, with the aid of a glass, an excellent survey of the flocks in the act of feeding before they noticed our presence. When within about 200 yards of them, the whole company of four or five hundred individuals simultaneously raised their heads and faced about. On approaching some 50 yards nearer, the sudden righting about just mentioned was succeeded by a most interesting series of maneuvers, consisting of a contraction and filling in of all the gaps in the line; and just as this was completed, with a rush of wings and a glorious burst of color, they arose. Many other detachments joined them until the entire flock numbered about 600. Most of these alighted some 2 miles off, while a few returned to their former feeding ground. The spoonbills now leave the vicinity of Corpus Christi the latter part of February, and though a few stragglers sometimes remain all the year, none have been known to breed on the Texas coast of late years. This state of affairs is probably due to their persecution and to the destruction of the forests between Corpus Christi and Brownsville, which used to reach nearer the river mouths, affording this formerly abundant species suitable rookery sites. It is probable that most of the flock of birds seen on Nueces Bay were raised somewhere on the coast south of Brownsville. After raising their young in comparative safety, they return yearly to this spot to spend the summer and early winter months, arriving in considerable numbers, even so early as the latter part of April, and attaining their maximum numbers in the latter part of May. Their evident attachment to the vicinity of Nueces Bay must be due to the facilities it affords them in the great item of food supply, for the reception accorded these birds by Corpus Christi gunners is far from encouraging.

The spoonbills which breed in southern Florida wander far northward after the breeding season; Audubon (1840) took one 10 miles north of Charleston, South Carolina, and says:

The spoonbills are so sensible of cold, that those which spend the winter on the Keys, near Cape Sable in Florida, rarely leave those parts for the neighborhood of St. Augustine before the first days of March. But after this you may find them along most of the water courses running parallel to the coast, and distant about half a mile or a mile from it. I saw none on any part of the St. John's river; and from all the answers which I obtained to my various inquiries respecting this bird, I feel confident that it never breeds in the interior of the peninsula, nor is ever seen there in winter. The roseate spoonbill is found for the most part along the marshy and muddy borders of estuaries, the mouths of rivers, ponds, or sea islands or keys partially overgrown with bushes, and perhaps still more commonly along the shores of those singular salt-water bayous so abundant within a mile or so of the shores, where they can reside and breed in perfect security in the midst of an abundance of food. It is more or less gregarious at all seasons, and it is rare to meet with fewer than half a dozen together, unless they have been dispersed by a tempest, in which case one of them is now and then found in a situation where you would least expect it. At the approach of the breeding season, these small flocks collect to form great bodies, as is the manner of the ibises, and resort to their former places of residence, to which they regularly return, like herons.

Warden Kroegel, of Pelican Island, saw a flock of 60, in June, 1913, on the Mesquite Inlet Reservation, far north of the breeding range of this species.

Winter.—In southern Florida the roseate spoonbill is resident all the year round, but it frequents different localities in winter and wanders about more, feeding in large flocks in the shallows of the Bay of Florida, in the muddy inlets along the shore and in the shallow lakes and sloughs near the coast. One of their favorite feeding grounds is a large, so-called "slough" near Cape Sable, but very different in character from the typical western prairie slough. This is apparently a submerged forest, killed by inundations from the sea, the remains of which are still standing, tall, dead trees, many of them of large size, bare and bleached. During the fall and early winter the slough is full of water but at the time we were there, in April, it was partially dry in spots, but mostly soft and boggy, with sluggish streams and numerous shallow muddy pools scattered through it, forming fine feeding grounds for spoonbills, ibises, and other water birds. There is another favorite resort of the spoonbills on one of the keys which has a fair sized lake in the centre. Large flocks of "pink curlews," as they are called by the natives, had been seen almost daily flying to and from this lake. Owing to this fact we were led to suppose that we might find a breeding rookery here, but a day's search failed to reveal even a single bird. I am inclined to infer that they come here only to feed in the shallow muddy waters of the lake or to roost in the mangroves around it.

I have seen and several other observers have reported seeing flocks of roseate spoonbills, numbering from half a dozen to 50 or 60 birds, at various points on the coast of Texas during the spring. One large flock constantly frequented the chain of islands between Mesquite and San Antonio Bays on May 15 and 16; we spent some time chasing them from one island to another, but could not drive them away from that vicinity. Our guides felt confident that they would nest there in June, as it was here that Mr. Simmons had found the nests referred to above. The theory has also been advanced that these are birds which have bred on the coast of Mexico earlier in the season and wandered north after the breeding season. Most of these birds that I saw were in immature plumage, though some few seemed to be nearly adult, perhaps barren or unmated birds. I believe that they were all nonbreeders and were simply wandering around in flocks.

DISTRIBUTION

Range.—South and Central America, islands of the Carribbean Sea, and the Gulf and south Atlantic coasts of the United States. East to the Atlantic coast of Florida (Indian River), the Bahama Islands (Great Inagua), eastern Brazil, (Para). South to the central part of eastern Argentina (near Buenos Aires). West to the coast of Chile (Santiago), Peru (Lower Ucayali River), Costa Rica (La Palma), Nicaragua (San Juan del Sur), and Sinaloa (Mazatlan). North to Sinaloa (Mazatlan), Texas (Galveston Bay, Victoria County, and Beamont), and the coast of Louisiana (Cameron Parish and Lake Arthur). This range has been greatly restricted within the last few decades and the species is now probably extirpated from most of the Antillean Islands and from other regions where it was formerly a common breeder. In South America it is resident and of general distribution on both coasts and in the interior along the larger rivers

Casual Records.—Although the spoonbill is resident throughout its breeding range, small flocks and solitary birds have been recorded from long distances both to the north and to the south. A greatly emaciated specimen was collected near Kidney Cove and the remains of a second were found at Whalebone Bay, Falkland Islands, in July, 1860, while Sclater and Hudson record a specimen from the Straits of Magellan.

In the United States stragglers have been taken or noted in California (San Bernardino, June 20, 1903); Utah (Wendover, July 2, 1919); Colorado (Howardsville, June, 1888, and Pueblo, August, 1890); Kansas (Douglas, March 20, 1899); Wisconsin, (near Janesville, August, 1845); Indiana (Vincennes, spring of 1856, and Portland, July 14, 1889), and South Carolina (Charleston, June, 1879, and Yemassee, fall of 1885).

Egg dates.—Florida: 25 records, January 4 to June 6; 13 records, January 16 to May 1. Louisiana: 8 records, May 22 to June 2.

Family THRESKIONITHIDAE, Ibises.

GUARA ALBA (Linnaeus)

WHITE IBIS

HABITS

The sluggish upper waters of the St. Johns River in Florida are spread out into extensive marshes, broad lakes, and small ponds, choked with water hyacinths, "lettuce," and "bonnets," and dotted with floating boggy islets or more substantial islands overgrown with willow thickets. Here we found a paradise for water birds, many miles from the haunts of man, in which Florida ducks and various species of herons and gallinules were breeding in security. It was a joy to watch the graceful aerial evolutions of the stately wood ibises and to mark the morning and evening flights of the white ibises between their feeding ground and their rookeries in distant swampy thickets. Sometimes in large, loose flocks and sometimes in long, straggling lines, they were always recognizable by their snowy whiteness and their rapid wing beats. Wherever we went in southern Florida we frequently found them on inland lakes and streams, feeding in the shallow, muddy waters, or flying out ahead of us as we navigated the narrow creeks in the mangrove swamps. Once I suprised a large flock of them in a little sunlit, muddy pool in a big cypress swamp; they were feeding on the muddy shores, dozing on the fallen logs or preening their feathers as they sat on the stumps and the branches of the surrounding trees; what a cloud of dazzling whiteness and what a clatter of many black-tipped wings, as they all rose and went dodging off among the trees.

But, perhaps, my most interesting experience with the white ibis was in Texas, in 1923, where after much effort we succeeded in locating a big breeding rookery in Victoria County. Somewhere in the valley of the Guadalupe River, we had heard, was a colony of this species. With the help of what local talent we could find, we explored the swamp and bayou forests along the river, where the large cypress, tupelo, gum, water oak, and magnolia trees were draped in long festoons of Spanish moss; we skirted the borders of numerous lakes and open marshes; and we penetrated the dense marshy thickets of willows, button-bushes, huisache, and other brush, wading through miles of muddy water and fighting our way through thorny tangles. Frequently we saw the ibises flying over us, but always they went on beyond us to some distant point, tolling us on and on, deeper and deeper into the recesses of an immense tract of endless swamps, streams, and ponds. By taking observations from the tops of the highest trees we could find, we finally got their bearings from several directions and located their rookery about 3 miles away. Apparently their feeding grounds were scattered all over this big tract, in the more open marshes and meadows. Birds were constantly flying to and fro between their feeding grounds and their breeding rookery, but towards dark their movements were all in the direction of the latter. We eventually found the rookery, to which I shall refer later.

Courtship.—I have never seen the courtship of this species, nor can I find anything about it in print. As the breeding season approaches, the bill, face, gular pouch, and legs of the male, which at other seasons are dull flesh color, become deep, brilliant red in color and form a striking contrast with the white plumage. Evidently a decided distention of the gular pouch forms an important part of the nuptial display. Audubon (1840) says: "The males at this season have the gular pouch of a rich orange color, and somewhat resembling in shape that of the frigate pelican, although proportionally less." C. J. Pennock refers to this twice in his notes sent to me on the habits of this species in Florida. On April 1, 1917, the birds were apparently mating and were indulging in a series of outlandish noises; watching them at a distance of 40 or 50 feet, with a pair of good glasses, it appeared that the males distended the gular pouch to the size of "a good-sized lemon" and contracted it again as they uttered "their dulcet notes"; he describes the color of it as "rich deep vermilion or Turkey red." Again on May 29, 1917, he observed another bird, within 20 feet, make a similar display and estimated that the pouch extended about an inch and a half below the bill, "fiery red in color, the bill, face and legs being of the same color."

Nesting.—Audubon (1840) gives a description of an interesting colony which he found on an island 6 miles from Cape Sable, Florida. Besides the ibises there were—

Breeding there the brown pelican, the purple, the Louisiana, the white, and the green herons, two species of gallinule, the cardinal grosbeak, crows, and pigeons. The vegetation consists of a few tall mangroves, thousands of wild plum trees, several species of cactus, some of them nearly as thick as a man's body, and more than 20 feet high, different sorts of smilax, grape vines, cane, palmettoes, Spanish bayonets, and the rankest nettles I ever saw. As we entered that well-known place, we saw nests on every bush, cactus, or tree. Whether the number was one thousand or ten I can not say, but this I well know—I counted 47 on a single plum tree. These nests of the white ibis measure about 15 inches in their greatest diameter, and are formed of dry twigs intermixed with fibrous roots and green branches of the trees growing on the island, which this bird easily breaks with its bill; the interior, which is flat, being finished with leaves of the cane and some other plants.

On my two visits to Cape Sable in 1903 and 1908 we found no signs of this rookery and no island that answered his description. Most of the colonies of white ibises that I have seen have been in fresh-water lakes or marshes at some distance from the coast. My first experience with the nesting habits of this species was in the great Cuthbert rookery in Monroe County, Fla., to which I have made two visits, and which I have fully described under the preceding species. As we approached the little island the ibises arose in a great white cloud from the red mangroves and circled about over our heads, uttering their peculiar grunting notes of protest. We estimated that there were about 1,000 ibises in the colony. They soon settled down into the trees again when we landed and were constantly peering at us through the foliage while we were examining their nests. The ibises' nests occupied the intermediate belt, on the outer edge of the larger trees on the dry land and on the inner edge of the red mangroves over the mud and shallow water, the interior of the island being occupied by the herons and the outer edge of the mangroves by the cormorants. The nests were rather closely grouped, at heights varying from 8 to 15 feet on the horizontal branches of the mangroves, often on very slender branches; only a few were placed in the white "buttonwoods." They were very carelessly and loosely made of dry and green leaves of the mangroves, held together with a few small sticks and lined with fresh green leaves. The nests are probably added to as the eggs are laid or as incubation advances. The nests which contained only one egg were very small, flimsy structures, hardly large enough to hold the egg, often measuring only six inches across, while those with three eggs were larger, 10 inches or more across, and better made. They generally lay four eggs, and in such cases have large and well-built nests. At the time of our visit, May 1, 1903, the ibises in this rookery were only just beginning to lay, as most of the nests contained one or two eggs, none more than three, and all the eggs we collected were fresh. This was rather remarkable, considering that 15 days later, at Alligator Lake, where these ibises were breeding in immense numbers, they had young of all ages, many of them able to fly.

On the west coast of Florida, in Pinellas County, I found two breeding colonies, which I visited several times during the spring of 1925. A small colony of 60 or 75 pairs occupied a small island in Holmes Pond, about 3 miles north of Clearwater. This is a marshy pond overgrown with pickerel weed and arrowhead around the border, and with "bonnets" (*Nymphaea*) and white pond lilies in the deeper portions; there are a few boggy islands in it covered with small trees and bushes and some scattered patches of saw grass.

When Mr. Baynard first showed me this pond, on December 27, 1924, no ibises were seen or even mentioned; so I was surprised to find on my next visit, on April 7, a fine little colony established there and well along with its nesting. I waded out to the island in water more than waist deep and found an interesting little mixed colony of Ward, little blue, Louisiana, and black crowned night herons among which the ibises were nesting. It was a treacherous, boggy, half-floating island, thickly overgrown with large elders (the largest I have ever seen), willows, bays, wax myrtles, and a tangle of small bushes and vines. The nests of the ibises were placed at the lower levels, from 6 to 10 feet above the mud or water, and were similar in construction to those described above. Some of the nests were not yet finished, some held incomplete sets and some had three or four eggs. I visited this colony again on April 22, when some of the nests contained small young.

One of the largest and most prosperous colonies of Florida water birds that I have ever seen is on a large island known as Bird Key, in Boca Ceiga Bay, Pinellas County. It is now permanently established as a United States Bird Reservation, under the auspices of the Biological Survey, and is carefully guarded by an efficient warden, Harold Bennett. The whole island is heavily and thickly wooded with red and black mangroves, buttonwoods, willows, bays, and other trees and shrubs; the principal forest growth is made up of large black mangroves, many of which are 25 or 30 feet high and some higher. I made seven trips to this rookery during the winter and and spring of 1924 and 1925. When Mr. Bennett first took me to the island, on December 23, very few birds were in evidence, except that a number of Ward herons were already nesting in the tops of the tallest trees; they increased in numbers later. I did not visit the island again until March 11, when I found things in full swing; thousands of American egrets were well along with their nesting and apparently all had eggs; the Florida cormorants were still more abundant and were busy with their courtships and nest building in the tops of the tall black mangroves; the Ward heron's nests mostly contained young; and a small colony of yellow-crowned night herons, in another part of the island, were building their nests. Only a few white ibises were seen, feeding in the muddy pond holes or flying over, they had not yet begun nesting. It was not until April 7 that we found the ibises well started with their nesting; they were located in another portion of the island, where there were several muddy ponds surrounded by red mangroves of small or medium size and where the muddy soil was covered with a foot or so of water at high tide. Many nests were in process of construction and some held one or two eggs. The nests were typical of the species, placed at low elevations in the smaller red mangroves, closely grouped and poorly made of twigs and green leaves of the mangroves. Surrounding them and mixed with them to a certain extent were the nests of large numbers of Louisiana herons and a few snowy egrets. I twice saw two roseate spoonbills in their vicinity, but could find no nest. A few little blue, green, and black-crowned night herons were also seen on the island. Brown pelicans were first seen building their nests, on the flat tops of the low mangroves, on April 14, and on April 21 some of them had eggs. On the latter date some of the ibises had small young in the nests, peeping loudly like young chickens. I was unable to visit this most interesting rookery again, but hope it will continue to flourish.

The northernmost breeding colony of white ibises that I have ever heard of was discovered by that veteran ornithologist, Arthur T. Wayne (1922), on May 20, 1922, in Charleston County, South Carolina. It was "in a heavily wooded reservoir of cypress trees" in a large swamp known as Penny Dam Backwater. "Nests were placed in practically every cypress bush, one small bush containing five, each of which held from two to three eggs. All the nests were built in small cypress trees or bushes over water varying from 3 to 4 feet in depth." In describing the nests he says:

The foundation in many cases consisted of Spanish moss (*Dendropogon usneoides*) lined with this material in the gray (living) state together with cypress twigs in leaf, and with a base and support of dead cypress twigs arranged in a circular manner. A typical nest measures from out to out 2 feet, and is circular in outline.

Besides the ibises, there were breeding in the rookery water-turkeys, American egrets in large numbers, Louisiana herons, little blue herons, black-crowned night herons, and grackles. Although Mr. Wayne had hunted through this swamp practically every season for the past 30 years, he had never found the white ibises nesting here before.

Eggs.—The white ibis lays ordinarily four eggs, sometimes only three or even two and very rarely five. Average eggs vary in shape from ovate to elliptical ovate; extremes are blunt, short ovate or elongate ovate. The shell is smooth or finely granulated and without any gloss. The ground color is usually bluish or greenish white, varying in the brightest specimens from "pale olivine" to "pale glaucous-green"; in some eggs the ground color is pale buff, from "cream buff" to "pale olive buff." The eggs are usually handsomely marked with wide variation in patterns. They are irregularly spotted and blotched with various shades of brown; the commonest shades on the handsomest eggs are "bay," "chestnut," and "auburn"; the darkest markings vary from "light seal brown" to "cinnamon brown," and the lighter markings from "buckthorn brown" to "clay color." Sometimes the eggs are uniformly spotted all over the entire surface, with or without large blotches; sometimes the spots or blotches are concentrated at the larger end; and sometimes the eggs are very sparingly marked or even nearly immaculate. The measurements of 80 eggs average 57.6 by 38.3 millimeters; the eggs showing the four extremes measure 65.2 by 39.2, 53 by 42.3, 52 by 38 and 54.5 by 34 millimeters.

Young.—The period of incubation is said to be 21 days. Audubon (1840) says:

The young birds, which are at first covered with a thick down of a dark gray color, are fed by regurgitation. They take about five weeks to be able to fly, although they leave the nest at the end of three weeks, and stand on the branches, or on the ground, waiting the arrival of their parents with food, which consists principally of small fiddler crabs and crayfish. On some occasions, I have found them at this age miles away from the breeding places, and in this state they are easily caught. As soon as the young are able to provide for themselves, the old birds leave them, and the different individuals are then seen searching for food apart.

The breeding rookery I visited in Victoria County, Texas, on May 30, 1923, referred to above, gave me my best impression of the behavior of young white ibises, for we reached it at the time of their greatest activity. Having previously located the probable site of the rookery from a distance we found it quite a long trip into it, through a series of meadows, swamps, thickets, and groves of heavy forest growth. When we reached the thickest and wettest part of the big swamp where the willows, cypress, water oaks, and button bushes grew, and where the drier spots supported a heavy growth of live oaks, elms, tupelos, sweet gums, and black gums, festooned with long beards of Spanish moss, we began to see the birds flying from their nests. Way up in the tallest trees were the nests of the Ward herons and lower down those of the Mexican cormorants and water turkeys and in a clump of willows on the edge of an open space was a colony of American egrets. The air was full of white ibises, flying about in all directions, and often with them came a flash of pink and carmine, as a band of roseate spoonbills flew out into the open, circled and returned to alight on the bare tops of some tall dead trees, favorite perches, which were often filled with both of these species. We were now in the center of the rookery; wading in mud and water nearly to our armpits, where big alligators had left their tracks on the exposed mud banks, we soon came to the main nesting grounds of the white ibises, in a thick growth of small trees and button bushes. The place seemed alive with them; every tree and bush was as full of their nests as possible, at heights varying from 4 feet above the water to 14 feet or more. The nests were much smaller than the spoonbill's nests, were made of lighter sticks and were not so well made; they were lined with dry and green leaves. Some nests still contained three or four eggs, but by far the greater number contained, or had contained, young of various ages. Only the smaller young remained in the nests when we approached; all that were half grown or more began climbing out of the nests and traveling through the branches to get away from us; there were hundreds of them, scrambling through the trees and bushes in droves; it was a lively scene. Though awkward and ungainly in appearance, they were really expert climbers and made surprisingly good progress, using bills and wings as well as feet, in climbing and performing many acrobatic stunts. Short falls were frequent and often they fell into the water; where they went flopping off over the shallows or even swimming in the deep open water. If not too hard pressed, they preferred to huddle together in the tops of the trees. Many of them were already on the wing. How the parents ever find their young in such confusion is a mystery.

Plumages.—The downy, young, white ibis is far from white. The head is glossy black, the throat and neck brownish black, the back is "mouse gray" and the under parts "pale mouse gray." The down is short and thick on the head and short and scanty on the body. The bill is pale flesh color with a black tip.

The juvenal plumage is a striking combination of dark brown and white in marked contrast. The head and neck are mottled with dark brown and grayish white; the upper back, wings and outer half of the tail, are "clove brown" or "warm sepia"; the lower back, upper tail coverts and entire under parts are pure white. This plumage is worn through the first summer and fall, without much change except a gradual fading; by January the browns have faded to light, dingy shades. In December the first prenuptial molt begins, with the appearance of a few white feathers in the back. The molt then spreads during the late winter and early spring, involving the scapulars, wing coverts, and tail, in varying amounts; generally some of the juvenal rectrices are retained until the first postnuptial molt; and sometimes a few new white secondaries are acquired during the spring. In this first nuptial plumage young birds show a great variety of color patterns, but there is always more or less white, usually a preponderence of it, in the mantle and body plumage and the head and neck is always mottled with dusky and white.

At the first complete postnuptial molt, during the following summer, the young bird assumes a plumage which is nearly adult, including the white primaries with the bluish black tips; but some signs of immaturity remain all through the second winter and spring. Young birds breed in the second nuptial plumage, in which the head and neck is still more or less mottled with dusky and a few brown feathers are retained in the body plumage. At the second postnuptial molt, when over 2 years old, the young bird assumes the fully adult dress.

Adults apparently have a complete postnuptial molt and an incomplete prenuptial molt. The winter plumage of the adult, worn in the fall and early winter, differs from the nuptial only in having more or less dusky mottling in the crown and hind neck; the bill, face, and legs at this season are dull flesh color. The mottling on the head and neck disappears at the prenuptial molt and the naked parts become brilliant red, bright vermilion, or Turkey red; the gular pouch is distended in the nuptial display.

Food.—A large breeding colony of ibises must soon exhaust the food supply in the immediate vicinity of its rookery, although the proximity of a good food supply largely governs the selection of a nesting site. For this reason ibises often have to travel long distances to and from their feeding grounds. These flights occur mainly in the early morning and in the evening in the inland localities and at the proper stages of the tides on the seacoast. Their favorite feeding grounds are in the muddy, shallow waters of small lakes, ponds, and bayous, or on the fresh or salt water marshes or meadows, where crawfish and fiddler crabs abound.

Audubon (1840) describes the feeding habits, as follows:

The manner in which this bird searches for its food is very curious. The woodcock and the snipe, it is true, are probers as well as it, but their task requires ess ingenuity than is exercised by the white or the red ibis. It is also true that the white ibis frequently seizes on small crabs, slugs, and snails, and even at times on flying insects; but its usual mode of procuring food is a strong proof that cunning enters as a principal ingredient in its instinct. The crawfish often burrows to the depth of 3 or 4 feet in dry weather, for before it can be comfortable it must reach the water. This is generally the case during the prolonged heats of summer, at which time the white ibis is most pushed for food. The bird, to procure the crawfish, walks with remarkable care towards the mounds of mud which the latter throws up while forming its hole, and breaks up the upper part of the fabric, dropping the fragments into the deep cavity that has been made by the animal. Then the ibis retires a single step, and patiently waits the result. The crawfish, incommoded by the load of earth, instantly sets to work anew, and at last reaches the entrance of its burrow; but the moment it comes in sight, the ibis seizes it with his bill.

Oscar E. Baynard (1913) has shown that the feeding habits of ibises are much more beneficial than is generally supposed; he writes:

The ibis for their fondness of crayfish have about cleaned up the thousands of acres of flooded marshes around Orange Lake and the other known fact that crayfish destroy thousands of the spawn of fish and I have noticed that lakes and ponds that have lakes and ponds around them and no ibis are nearly always devoid of any great number of fish. Orange Lake has been fished with traps continually, but with the thousands of ibis and herons that use the lake as a reservation have kept the crayfish down to such an extent that there are more fish to-day in Orange Lake than in many years. There are several thousand acres of marsh around this lake and this has given the fish plenty of places to spawn. As young fish eat millions of mosquitoes it stands to reason that with ibis and herons we have more fish and less mosquitoes, and any bird that does so much good to a State is of very great value and should be protected for that reason alone.

He reported that the contents of the stomachs of 50 young white ibises contained 352 cutworms, 308 grasshoppers, 609 crayfish, and 42 small mocassins, an interesting bill of fare of a beneficial character.

Mr. Wayne (1922) says, of the feeding habits of the young:

Young white ibises, when able to take care of themselves, do not, as one would suppose, seek the principal food of the adult birds, which is crayfish, but hunt fiddlers in the canals and estuaries of the salt or brackish water marshes adjacent to the fresh-water reservoirs. The reason for this habit is obvious since fiddlers are easy to catch whereas crayfish would require more skill and dexterity.

Behavior.—The flight of the white ibis is strong, direct, and rather swift, with rapid strokes of the wings and varied with occasional shorter periods of sailing. When flying in flocks the birds flap their wings or scale in unison, but the scaling or sailing periods are much shorter than with pelicans or cormorants. On their morning and evening flight they usually fly very low and in large flocks, close to the water, over lakes, or along water courses, rising just over the tree tops when necessary. The long curved bill, the pure white plumage of the adults, with their black wing-tips, and the parti-colored plumage of the young, are all good field marks, by which the species can easily be recognized at any reasonable distance. Occasionally a flock of white ibises rises high in the air to indulge in interesting aerial evolutions for sport or exercise.

When frightened and forced to fly away from their feeding grounds or nests, they are apt to alight in large numbers on some convenient tree, preferably a large dead one with bare branches; they often perch for long periods on such favorite trees; preening their plumage or dozing, standing on one leg, in an upright attitude, with the head drawn down on the shoulders and the bill resting on the breast. A large tree full of white ibises is a pretty sight, especially if there are a few roseate spoonbills scattered among them, as is often the case.

The white ibis walks gracefully on the ground and is active in its movements; it also climbs nimbly among the branches of trees or bushes, where it is quite at home. It can swim well if it happens to fall into the water, but probably never does so from choice.

It is not a noisy bird and its vocal performances are limited to a few soft grunting notes.   One night, while waiting in my blind for the ibises to come to roost on the trees around me, I heard a peculiar conversational note which I recorded as sounding like *"walla, walla, walla."*   Audubon (1840) says that on their breeding grounds the females are silent, "but the males evince their displeasure by uttering sounds which greatly resemble those of the white-headed pigeon, and which may be imitated by the syllables *crool, croo, croo."*   And again he says that "if you disturb them when far away from their nests, they utter loud hoarse cries resembling the syllables *hunk, hunk, hunk,* either while on the ground or as they fly off."

Enemies.—Ibises are not generally regarded as game birds, but many are shot for food in the regions where they are plentiful and where they are locally called "white curlew."   That they have other enemies than man is illustrated by the following account by Audubon (1840):

The ibises had all departed for the Florida coasts, excepting a few of the white species, one of which was at length espied.   It was perched about 50 yards from us toward the center of the pool, and as the report of one of our guns echoed among the tall cypresses, down to the water, broken winged, it fell.   The exertions which it made to reach the shore seemed to awaken the half-torpid alligators that lay in the deep mud at the bottom of the pool.   One showed his head above the water, then a second and a third.   All gave chase to the poor wounded bird, which, on seeing its dreaded and deadly foes, made double speed toward the very spot where we stood.   I was suprised to see how much faster the bird swam than the reptiles, who, with jaws widely opened, urged their heavy bodies through the water.   The ibis was now within a few yards of us.   It was the alligator's last chance.   Springing forward as it were, he raised his body almost out of the water; his jaws nearly touched the terrified bird; when pulling three triggers at once, we lodged the contents of our guns in the throat of the monster.   Thrashing furiously with his tail, and rolling his body in agony, the alligator at last sank to the mud; and the ibis, as if in gratitude, walked to our very feet and there lying down, surrendered itself to us.   I kept this bird until the succeeding spring, and by care and good nursing, had the pleasure of seeing its broken wing perfectly mended, when, after its long captivity, I restored it to liberty, in the midst of its loved swamps and woods.

Bird Key in Pinellas County, Florida, is infested, during the breeding season, with a horde of Florida crows and fish crows, which are constantly hovering over the nests, looking for a chance to pounce upon and carry off any unguarded eggs.   The crows have a wholesome respect for the long, sharp beaks of the herons, but the soft, blunt bills of the gentle ibises are less dangerous weapons, and the crows work havoc among their eggs; every nest in the vicinity of my blind was cleaned out.   Large numbers of black vultures and a few turkey vultures live on this Key; and from the middle of April on a great many man-o'-war birds visit it; probably all three of these birds destroy some eggs and young birds.

DISTRIBUTION

Breeding range.—South Atlantic and Gulf coasts of the United States; Central America; Greater Antilles and northern South America. East to South Carolina (Mount Pleasant); Georgia (Alatamaha River); Florida (St. Johns River, Orange Lake, Indian River, Cuthbert and Alligator Lakes); Haiti (Sanchez). South to the coast of central Venezuela (Lake Valencia); and Peru (Santa Luzia). West to Costa Rica (La Palma); Nicaragua (Momotomba); and Lower California (La Paz). North to Texas (Nueces River and Victoria County); Louisiana (Bayou Sara and Point Coupee) and Mississippi (Natchez).

Migration.—The white ibis is resident throughout practically its entire range although a slight movement in spring has been detected in the United States. Early dates of arrival are Whitfield, Florida, March 17 (1903), and St. Marys, Georgia, also March 17 (1904). A nine years' average date of arrival at Bird Island, Orange Lake, Florida, is April 1.

Casual records.—Wanderers to the North have been recorded on several occasions: One near the mouth of the Colorado River in March, 1914; a few seen near Ogden, Utah, September 1 to October 8, 1871; a specimen was taken at Barr, Colorado in 1890; two were seen and one was secured in southeastern South Dakota in May, 1879; a flock of seven or eight, in immature plumage, were seen near Mount Carmel, Illinois, about May 8, 1878; one was taken near South Woodstock, Vermont, in the summer of 1878; one was seen near Milford, Connecticut, on May 23, 1875, by G. B. Grinnell; Giraud (1844) records two from Long Island, New York, one having been shot at Raynor South, in the summer of 1836 and the other at Moriches early in March, 1843; and Pearson (1899) reports taking a specimen in immature plumage from a flock of three, near Beaufort, North Carolina, July 26, 1898.

Egg dates.—Florida: 108 records, March 4 to August 17; 54 records, April 12 to May 11.

GUARA RUBRA (Linnaeus)

SCARLET IBIS

HABITS

Contributed by Thomas Edward Penard

The scarlet ibis is a neotropical species inhabiting the coastal and littoral areas of northern and eastern South America from Venezuela to eastern Brazil. Beyond its breeding range it has been observed as an irregular visitant in Jamaica and south as far as the State of São Paolo, where it is rare. Reports of its presence in Central

America and in Cuba require confirmation. Within the borders of the United States it is accidental and its claim to a place on our check list rests for the most part on questionable evidence.

Wilson (1832) states that it was found in the most southern parts of Carolina and also in Georgia and Florida, but he does not say upon what evidence his statements are based. He remarks that being a scarce species with us, a sufficient number of specimens had not been procured to enable him to settle the matter with certainty.

Nuttall (1834), adding Alabama to the range of the species, says "they migrate in the course of the summer (about July and August) into Florida, Alabama, Georgia, and South Carolina"; but he, too, is silent as to the source of his information.

Audubon (1840) remarks that he had seen only three in the United States, on the 3d of July, 1821, at Bayou Sara, Louisiana. He writes:

They were traveling in a line, in the manner of the white ibis, above the tops of the trees. Although I had only a glimpse of them, I saw them sufficiently well to be assured of their belonging to the present species, and therefore I have thought it proper to introduce it into our Fauna.

Dr. Elliot Coues (1865) mentions the scarlet ibis as being found on the Rio Grande, and later (1872) speaks of having examined a fragment of a specimen at Los Pinos, New Mexico. Many years afterward he assured Prof. W. W. Cooke (1897) that there was no question of this.

William Brewster (1883) found a specimen in the Museum of the College of Charleston, said to be from Florida, which he believed to be authentic, but the chain of evidence is hardly sufficient.

A record that has stood for many years is that of Willoughby P. Lowe (1894) who gave an account of a bird supposed to be a scarlet ibis, shot by one of a party that was duck shooting in May, 1876, at Grape Creek in Wet Mountain Valley, Custer County, Colorado. The specimen was preserved and later came into possession of Mr. Livesey. Prof. W. W. Cooke (1897) considered this account as trustworthy, but Alfred M. Bailey of the Colorado Museum of Natural History writes me that J. D. Figgins, who had occasion to trace the data on this bird, had secured the specimen from England and that it proved to be an unusually colored, white-faced glossy ibis. Mr. Figgins (1925) has recently published a statement to this effect. This specimen is now in the collection of the Colorado Museum of Natural History.

Walter Faxon (1897) considered the presence of a plate of the scarlet ibis among the drawings of Georgian birds by John Abbot as very good evidence of the species having occurred in that State; but the species could hardly be admitted to our check list on such testimony.

The records by H. E. Dresser (1866), H. B. Bailey (1881), W. E. D. Scott (1889), W. W. Cooke (1897a), and Beyer, Allison, and Kopman (1908) need not be considered here.

The most recent record is by R. A. Sell (1917) who saw a single bird at Corpus Christi, Texas, after the storm of August 18, 1916. He says:

On one of the drifts that contained 31 dead cattle besides the bodies of 215 birds of various kinds, there stood a solitary scarlet ibis. Like a garnet in the sands, or a rosy promise of the morning sun, it stood, gracefully poised above the terrible ruin—an encouragement, an inspiration, an unfailing hope—not as the rainbow suggesting the possibility of another destructive force, but as an animated symbol that life is immortal.

Later Mr. Sell (1918) gave an account of his investigations in Texas, quoting Prof. H. P. Attwater, W. N. Wilson, J. B. Sternberg, J. C. Carlson, H. E. Lea, J. G. Holman, J. H. Jones, Dr. F. H. Russell, J. W. Woods, I. N. Heibner, and C. E. Bainbridge, a taxidermist who had mounted a specimen as identified by him. He mentions nine specimens that have been preserved: Two in Houston, two in San Antonio, three in Galveston, one in Rockport, and one in Corpus Christi.

Words are wholly inadequate when it comes to describing the scarlet ibis in its native surroundings. "Once seen, never forgotten." (Dawson, 1917); "scarlet livery of dazzling beauty." (Edwards, 1847); "jets of flame." (Beebe, 1910); "glowing like the essence of rubies." (Beebe, 1918); "like a rose-colored cloud lighted by the morning sun." (Hagmann, 1907); "beautiful red stains on the green background." (Leotaud, 1866); "the mangroves as it were spattered with blood." (F. P. and A. P. Penard, 1908); these are some of the expressions used by writers who have seen this wonderful bird in life.

Picture an unfrequented spot on the "wild coast" of South America; a wave-scarred sandbar reaching out into the thick, muddy sea at the mouth of a mighty tropical river; unmapped beaches and treacherous mud flats bordered by dark-green mangroves. Suddenly from around a bend a flock of two score scarlet ibises break into view, flying abreast in a compact row. They approach swiftly passing almost within gunshot from where we stand and alight upon one of the inaccessible mangrove islets and the surrounding flats. Under the slanting rays of the morning sun these beautiful birds reflect the most dazzling scarlet, in sharp contrast with the dark-green foliage.

William Beebe (1910) gives the following description of such a scene in Venezuela:

The tide was falling rapidly, swirling and eddying past the boat, and the roots of the mangroves began to protrude, their long stems shining black until the water dried from them. Mud flats appeared, and suddenly, without warning, a living flame passed us—and we had seen our first scarlet ibis.

Past the dark green background of mangrove foliage the magnificent bird flew swiftly—flaming with a brilliance which shamed any pigment of human art. Blood red, intensest vermilion, deepest scarlet—all fail to hint of the living color of the bird. Before we could recover from our delight a flock of 20 followed, flying close together, with bills and feet scarlet like the plumage. They swerved from their path and alighted on the mud close to the mangroves, and began feeding at once. Then a trio of snowy-white egrets with trailing plumes; floated overhead; others appeared above the tops of the trees; a host of sandpipers skimmed the surface of the water and scurried over the flats. Great Cocoi herons swept majestically into view; curlews and plover assembled in myriads, lining the mud flats at the water's edge, while here and there, like jets of flame against the mud, walked the vermilion ibises.

Courtship.—Apparently very little is known of the courtship of the scarlet ibis. Charles L. Bull (1911) is the only one, so far as I know, who has had anything to say about it. He writes of a pair of captive birds:

He began bowing and shaking his wings, and dancing up and down before her with spread wings and fluffed shoulders and crest. For a few moments she paid no attention, then something stirred within her and she shyly pecked at him. At this he danced harder than ever, and soon she joined him, dancing as he danced, bowing as he bowed, shaking out her wings and yammering as he did.

Mr. Bull confirmed the above in a letter to me, in which he says:

The courtship antics are my own observation. There were a number of scarlet ibis in the Bronx Zoo when I lived for two years near its entrance. They were kept in the big flying cage and not long after they were put out in the spring I watched a pair going through the dancing and raising of the scapulars, bowing, etc. The male was most attentive, offering the other bits of food and making the curious yammering (I have no other words for it) sound, opening and closing the bill rapidly. They carried a few sticks about but to the best of my knowledge went no further; too many other birds trying to do the same thing.

Nesting.—The breeding season of the scarlet ibis does not come at the same time of the year in different parts of its range, but the choice is apparently the season of heavy rains.

In Surinam they breed during the so-called "big rainy season" which begins about the end of April and lasts until the middle of August. W. C. van Heurn (1912), however, also mentions February as the time.

Edwards (1847) says that they appear on the island of Marajo at the mouth of the Amazon in June and at once set about forming their nests. He also remarks that according to Captain Appleton the breeding season on Marajo is February.

August Kappler (1887) says that the scarlet ibis builds its artless nest of brush in inaccessible places on low trees (Kappler, 1854), that the eggs are laid in the rainy season in May and June.

Richard Schomburgk (1848) says that they use the nests several seasons in succession.

Scarlet ibises have definite nesting districts in unfrequented parts along the coast, particularly near the mouths of rivers. In speaking of these nesting sites in Dutch Guiana, F. P. and A. P. Penard (1908) say (translated):

Among the largest nesting colonies, or so-called "Flamingo-nissi," in Surinam, are those of the Hermina flats, Via-via flats, and the banks of the Motkreek. At Hermina flats there is a mangrove island of not more than two acres in extent, where scarlet ibises breed in such great numbers that the mangroves appear to be, as it were, spattered with blood.

They further say:

Old, blood-colored birds begin breeding first, after which the rest follow. Hunters and fishermen in Surinam are unanimous in declaring that the scarlet ibis builds no nests, but makes use of those of the sabakoes (herons and egrets) especially *Leucophoyx candidissima*, whose young of the second brood they throw out of the nest. Schomburgk also mentions this in his "Guiana Reisen," and D. E. Mackintosh asserts that he has on several occasions seen the scarlet ibis throw young herons out of their nest. After the victory the conquerors sometimes enlarge the nest.

C. A. Lloyd (1897), who records Mr. Mackintosh's observations, referred to above, writes:

D. E. Mackintosh, who has paid much attention to the coast birds of Surinam, asserts that the scarlet ibis or currie-currie, *Eudocimus ruber*, never builds a nest of any sort, but takes forcible possession of those of the small egret, *Ardea candidissima*, for the purpose of depositing its eggs. He states that he has often witnessed the ibis in the act of tumbling the young egrets out of the nest.

The small egret breeds in vast "rookeries" along the seacoast, and Mr. Mackintosh has seen several square acres of low courida bushes dotted with their nests. During the breeding season large numbers of young egrets fall a prey to the black carrion vulture, *Catharista atrata*, which may be seen hovering around the breeding grounds on the lookout for a chance to swoop down on some unguarded nest and carry off its contents. The old birds vigorously defend their nests against attacks of the vulture, but as the scarlet ibis appears on the scene they immediately desert their charges and fly away.

Of their breeding on the island of Cavianna at the mouth of the Amazon, Gottfried Hagman (1907) writes (translated):

Mexiana and the near-by island, Cavianna, certainly fulfill the requirements of an Eldorado for water birds. Unlike Mexiana, Cavianna possesses in its interior "aturiaes" (*Drepanocarpus-Bestände*), which, on account of the tangle of branches are almost inaccessible to man. Here nest in company big colonies of countless pairs of *Tantalus ajaja* and *Eudocimus*, which, owing to the absence of aturiaes, never build on Mexiana.

Edwards (1847) gives the following interesting description of a nesting colony near Jungcal, at the mouth of the Amazon:

Turning suddenly we left the bordering forest for a canebrake, and instantly broke full upon the rookery. In this part the scarlet ibis particularly had nested; and the bended tops of the canes were covered by half-grown birds in their black plumage, interspersed with many in all the brilliance of age. They seemed little troubled at our approach, merely flying a few steps forward, or crossing the stream. Continuing on, the flocks increased in size; the red birds became more frequent, the canes bent beneath their weight like reeds. Wood ibises and spoonbills began to be numerous. The nests of all these filled every place where a nest could be placed; and the young ibises, covered with down, and standing like so many storks, their heavy bills resting upon their breasts and uttering no cry, were in strong contrast to the well-feathered spoonbills, beautiful in their slightly roseate dress, and noisily loquacious. Passing still onward, we emerged from the canes into trees; and here the white herons had made their homes, clouding the leaves with white. Interspersed with these were all the varieties mentioned before, having finished their nesting, and being actively engaged in rearing their young. We had sailed above a mile, and at last, seeming to have approached the terminus, we turned and went below a short distance to a convenient landing, where we could pursue our objects at leisure. The boatmen at once made their dispositions for basketing the young birds; and soon, by shaking them down from the nest, and following them up, had collected as many as they desired. We wandered a long distance back, but the nests seemed, if anything, more plentiful, and the swarms of young more dense. At the sound of the gun the birds in the immediate vicinity rose in a tumultuous flock and the old ones circled round and round, as though puzzled to understand the danger they instinctively feared. In this way they offered beautiful marks to our skill; and the shore near the canoe was soon strewed with fine specimens. Evidently this place had been for many years the haunt of these birds. Not a blade of grass could be seen; the ground was smooth and hard and covered with excrement.

Eggs.—The number of eggs per clutch is usually two, sometimes three, and rarely four. F. P. and A. P. Penard (1908) describe the yolks as being very red, "peculiarly resembling blood," and the albumen as thinner than that of a hen's egg.

In size as well as in color the eggs resemble those of the white ibis, *Guara alba.* They vary in shape from oval and short ovate to elliptical ovate. The ground color is grayish, bluish, or greenish, rarely yellowish white, spotted, smeared, and blotched with dull blackish brown, red-brown, and paler shades of brown, chiefly around and at the large end, where the markings frequently form a blotch. Some eggs are almost entirely unspotted while others are covered all over with blotches, smears and spots. These markings can be almost entirely removed by washing. Naturally unspotted eggs are rare. Examples with a ring at each end, or at the small end only, are extremely rare. Occasionally runt eggs are found.

The measurements of 135 eggs in my collection, all taken at Hermina-flats near Coronie, Surinam, in June, 1902, average 56.4 by 37.3 millimeters; the eggs showing the four extremes measure **64.3** by 37.3, 59.2 by **41.7, 50.0** by 37.6, and 54.4 by **33.0** millimeters.

Young.—F. P. and A. P. Penard (1908) state that the period of incubation is 24 days and that both sexes incubate. The chicks are born helpless and remain in the nest where they are cared for by both parents. When old enough to shift for themselves the young birds form separate flocks, traveling apart from the adults. This habit has been observed by several writers. Schomburgk (1848) thought it remarkable that the young birds, up to the time they acquired the scarlet livery lived in companies by themselves. Léotaud (1866) added that the flocks generally consisted of individuals of the same age and were known in Trinidad as a "troupe de flamants gris," or "flamants roses," or "flamants rouges," according to the state of plumage. More recently F. P. and A. P. Penard (1908) and W. C. van Heurn (1912) have also commented upon this habit of segregation. Nevertheless mixed flocks are not uncommon.

On September 27, 1921, I watched a flock of about 30 scarlet ibises, a dozen of which were feeding on the exposed flats near a small mangrove island at Braamspunt at the mouth of the Surinam River. The rest were on the island or were perching on the mangroves. Among the scarlet adults were four in the juvenile brown plumage. There was nothing in the behavior of the members of this particular troop suggesting segregation.

Mr. Beebe (1909) who has seen great numbers of these birds in northeastern Venezuela. also makes mention of mixed flocks. He writes:

These birds were seen only on the Caño San Juan, from the very mouth up to a distance of several miles inland. Not a bird was visible at high tide but with the uncovering of the mud-flats, the scarlet ibises began to appear singly and in small flocks. They were, without doubt, the most abundant bird in all the mangrove region into which we penetrated. In every flock of 30 or 50, some 6 or 8 would be birds in the brown plumage.

Elsewhere Mr. Beebe (1910) speaks of a flock of seven of which two were in fully adult plumage, while the others while the others were only three-quarters grown and feathered wholly in brown and white. He judged from their actions that they were members of a single family.

Plumages.—Very little is known about the downy young. F. P. and A. P. Penard (1908) described it as blackish above and whitish below. Dr. Hermann Burmeister (1856) writes that the nestling is pale brown with whitish underparts, and Dr. H. Schlegel (1863) describes a very young bird, as having a brown bill with a wide yellow band.

In the young bird, soon after leaving the nest, the head, neck, mantle, wings, sides of breast, scapulars, and tail are grayish brown, over the darker feathers of which, particularly on the wings, there appears to be a greenish sheen under certain conditions of light; the lesser wing coverts obscurely edged with paler shades; some of the tail feathers edged with white at the base; feathers of head and neck edged with gray; entire lower back, rump, thighs, and under parts pure white, including the wing lining, tail coverts, and axillars, the latter finely and obscurely spotted with gray centrally along the basal half of the shaft.

When about 6 months old a few whitish or pale orange feathers appear in the lesser wing coverts; the under parts, lower back, rump, thighs, and tail coverts now have a decided salmon or rosy wash, but the axillars are still white; basal half of tail feathers white. A few months later we find conspicuous patches of salmon or rose in the lesser wing coverts and the interscapular region, and the under parts, rump, and thighs have become if anything a little rosier, but the axillars are still white, otherwise there seems to be no change in appearance.

The moult following this period is slow and ill defined. The bird passes gradually through every stage and condition of mixed brown, gray, white, rose, and scarlet, but through it all the outer primaries, particularly the first, and for a time the tail, remain dusky. The head and neck, and nape are the last to become uniformly scarlet.

The fully adult bird is deep scarlet throughout with the exception of the tips of the four outer primaries which are of a deep blue color almost black.

F. P. and A. P. Penard (1908) describe the changes of plumage of the Surinam bird as follows (translated):

During the breeding season the plumage of very old birds appears to have a blood tint. Only the ends of the first four primaries are black. It seems as if nature had, as it were, driven the colors of youth to the wing tips, of which a few vanes are sometimes scarlet, too.

After the breeding season the blood-red fades more or less to scarlet. The young birds differ entirely from the adults, the plumage consisting of brownish or whitish tints. Hunters say that the scarlet ibis requires at least three or four years to attain the fully adult plumage. The moulting or rather color change is a study in itself. We have seen moulting birds from January to December. As a rule the feathers of the back begin to change first, but these are also the last to attain the brilliant scarlet color. Generally we meet with scarlet ibises in adult plumage but with the feathers of the neck partly black, partly rose, or partly naked, washed with rose. Even during the breeding season this is the case. Birds in partly adult plumage, i. e., irregularly marked with blackish, white, and scarlet, look very odd.

Hunters assert that albinism also occurs in the form of a pale rose tint. The writers have never seen one of these abnormal individuals.

Food.—Scarlet ibises feed on the beaches and exposed mudflats or in the shallows, often in company with herons, spoonbills, curlews and other shore birds, walking or wading and prodding for hidden morsels. In feeding the flocks tend to scatter and single individuals or pairs may then be seen far from the main flock, sometimes many miles from the coast.

According to F. P. and A. P. Penard (1908) the food of the scarlet ibis consists of small fish, spawn, and insects. Léotaud (1866) also mentions soft mollusks, and Rev. Charles B. Dawson (1917) bivalves

and crustaceans.   Mr. Beebe (1910) found in the stomach of a young
female the chetae or claws of a small crustacean, each about one-third of
an inch in length.   Léotaud (1866) says that a scarlet ibis in captivity made itself useful in destroying the larvae of noxious insects.
He says that the bird never lost an opportunity of following anyone
who was spading the earth, in order to seize the morsels that were
uncovered.   Of another captive bird the Rev. Mr. Dawson says that
it ate banana but preferred a diet of bread and milk to anything
else.

The scarlet ibis feeds its young after the manner of the pelican.
F. P. and A. P. Penard (1908) state that the old birds gather the
food in the elastic gular pouches.   Arriving at the nest they open
their bills and allow the young to take out the fish and other food.
Edwards (1847) describes the habit of feeding in the following words:

We were amused by the manner of feeding the young scarlet ibises.   In the
throat of the old female bird, directly at the base of the lower mandible, is an
enlargement of the skin, forming a pouch, which is capable of containing about
the bulk of a small hen's egg.   She would return from fishing on the shallows
with the pouch distended by tiny fish, and allowed her young to pick them out
with their bills.

F. P. and A. P. Penard (1908) state further that if the parents
are killed at this time there are always others ready to take up the
duties of foster parents.

Behavior.—Scarlet ibises live in communities, sometimes very large
ones, the members of which scatter after the breeding season and
wander in small flocks, or in pairs, or singly, along the coast and
rivers. seldom venturing far from the coast.   The detached flocks
and stragglers return towards night to certain places to roost.   August
Kappler (1887) says that they pass the night perched close together
in high trees.   Individuals which I have seen sleeping (in captivity)
stood on one foot with the head and the long bill turned back and
resting on the back.

Hagmann (1907), speaking of the birds in Brazil, says that they are
to be seen on the coast in the evening in big flocks returning from Mexiana to their nesting sites in Cavianna.   According to F. P. and A. P.
Penard (1908) the males appear to be more numerous than the
females.

When traveling from place to place the flight of the scarlet ibis is
swift.   In flying the birds arrange themselves abreast in a line.   F. P.
and A. P. Penard (1908), Schomburgk (1848), W. C. van Heurn
(1912), and Edwards (1847) speak of this manner of flight, but Léotaud (1866) says that in flying the individuals follow each other in
single file, and when the flock is large form an interminable line.   On
September 28, 1921, I saw a flock at the mouth of the Surinam
River, the members of which flew swiftly, close together, in an irregular line, side by side, not one behind the other.   I did not notice

any leader, but the Rev. Mr. Dawson (1917) speaks of shooting "the captain of a red brigade as he led his troop to his evening feeding ground." William Beebe (1909), writing about a large flock he saw in northeastern Venezuela, says:

> On the evening of March 26 a flock of not less than 500 swung back and forth across the Caño ahead of us, in a series of graceful evolutions before rising and drifting out of sight over the dark-green mangroves, like a great cloud of living flame.

Charles L. Bull (1911) describes evolutions like these and in a letter dated December 27, 1923, writes me the following confirmation:

> I saw the big flock performing its evolutions, circling and wheeling in a very high development of the flock instinct. You asked me if I noticed any leader in the flock. No. It seemed to me that the entire flock would wheel as one bird, much as flocks of starlings I have seen, and some of the shorebirds, Sanderlings, I think.

Persecution has had its effect upon the scarlet ibis in making it watchful and retiring. Mr. Beebe (1909) says of birds in Venezuela: "they are quite wary and when feeding did not allow one to approach within gun-shot before flying." W. C. van Heurn (1912) has also noted this but remarks that young birds are much easier to shoot.

Hunters and fishermen in Surinam assert that scarlet ibises are more difficult to approach than they were about 20 years ago, and that the large flocks which at one time were to be seen at the mouth of the Surinam River, have moved eastward along the coast to the Motkreek, where they are much less liable to be molested.

Notwithstanding this shyness the scarlet ibis has a well developed trait of curiosity. A. E. Brehm (1871), in describing the nesting of *Porphyrio hyacinthinus* in captivity, says that it was necessary to protect the nest from inquisitiveness of a scarlet ibis.

In September, 1921, while on my way from Braamspunt to Paramaribo, a pair of adult scarlet ibises passed slowly side by side over our boat, as if they were watching us. One of this pair had a broken leg which dangled down loosely. Further up river, I saw a single bird, in brilliant plumage, dodging in and out of the mangroves, apparently following along in pure curiosity. Occasionally it would stoop to pick up something, but it seemed to me that inquisitiveness rather than search for food governed its action.

Scarlet ibises are attracted by any bright red object. I quote from F. P. and A. P. Penard (1908) (translated):

> Their partiality for anything red deserves mention. Hunters make use of this by waving a piece of red cloth or by laying a dead bird of bright plumage in some open place, sure of attracting passing ibises.

The vocal performance of the scarlet ibis is not very noteworthy. Indeed, its notes are so seldom heard that there are local proverbs relative to the bird's muteness. Rarely does it make any sound except in fear or excitement. F. P. and A. P. Penard (1908) describe the notes as harsh and disagreeable. In speaking of a large nesting colony at Hermina-flats, they say (translated):

A shot in their midst causes the whole flock to rise, like a red cloud, with a gurgling *gwe, gwe,* and fly to the higher trees. Feeling themselves safe there, each one seems to have something to say and does it with much hissing. Frequently there is a quarrel and then one chases the other away. In so doing they rattle their bills.

Rev. Mr. Dawson (1917) says that the only note he ever heard a captive bird utter was a low, harsh grunt.

Game.—As a game bird the scarlet ibis is in greater favor than the herons or egrets. I quote the following from F. P. and A. P. Penard (1908) (translated):

A few persons make their living in hunting the scarlet ibis during the breeding season. But this is a very cruel practice. Mercilessly the birds are shot while sitting on their eggs or standing beside their young, after which they are salted or dried, transported in barrels full to the city and sold at 25 cents (Dutch) each. Fresh or dried the meat has a somewhat oily flavor.

G. E. Bodkin and C. T. Matthey (1921) in their notes on shooting in British Guiana say:

It is not often possible to obtain a shot at these birds. Apparently they are getting scarcer than they used to be owing to continued persecution. They are certainly not so common on the inhabited parts of the coastlands as formerly.

The young birds—before they attain the scarlet plumage—occasionlly give sport, but to shoot them in any numbers it is necessary to go to out of the way places like the mouth of the Pomeroon River, Dauntless, or the mouth of the Waini River in the northwestern district most of them fearsome, mosquito-ridden spots.

Kappler (1887) says that the fat ibises, in comparison with the lean egrets, are well worth shooting. He speaks of shooting seventeen at one shot. Again he (1854) says (freely translated):

In the rainy season (May and June) the red ibises, here erroneously known as *flamingoes,* as well as other birds belonging to the order of herons, lay their eggs.

Eggs and young are particularly prized by Indians who occasionally make special expeditions to the nesting sites. One day my neighbors came in two big canoes to the post, on their way after eggs. After I had treated them to some brandy they promised to bring me a basket of eggs. A few days later both canoes returned, fully laden with eggs and emaciated young birds. They gave me about 100 of these eggs, which were green, spotted with black, and the size of a small hen's egg. Immediately I began preparations to make an omelet, but discovered to my disappointment that there was only one fresh egg in the lot. All the rest were addled or rotten or in an advanced state of incubation. I suspected a joke. But as my mind was set on an omelet I started in a canoe to the village, where I found the women cooking eggs. They were all like mine. In a soup of yelks floated birds in all stages of incubation, richly spiced with Spanish pepper, and this mess they ate gluttonously.

Captivity.—Young birds can be easily tamed, but never attain the deep scarlet plumage of the free bird.

Dr. Max Schmidt (1880) speaks of a bird which had been in captivity 10 years, 5 months, and 14 days, and was then still living. Pelzeln (1871) mentions another brought from Brazil by Spix and Martius, that lived 14 years. Adult birds soon lose their brilliant plumage, fading or rather moulting into the rose livery. This fact has been observed by many writers. Mr. Beebe (1909) gives the following account:

I obtained a bird from an Indian who had broken its wing and had cared for it until it recovered. It was in full adult plumage, scarlet from tip of beak to tip of toe. Shortly after placing it in the flying cage in the New York Zoological Park it moulted all the feathers on the head and neck, and a scattering through the scapulars, coverts, and back. The new plumage, with the exception of the lesser coverts, came in pale salmon instead of the original brilliant scarlet, and at the present date the contrast is striking. The salmon tint of the new plumage is exactly that of another individual, which has been in captivity since February, 1905, and has now, (December, 1909) passed through five annual moults. So in the case of my ibis, the loss of color was not gradual but sudden, and its cause was certainly not due to absence of sunlight, heat, or moisture. I am not yet prepared to say, however, that change in food alone was the cause.

Whether a diet of fish and frogs would prevent this fading as Dr. Th. Lorenz (1871) asserts has not, so far as I know, received conformation.

A. D. Bartlett (1866) records an instance of a female scarlet ibis that preferred to mate with a male white ibis rather than one of its own species. He writes:

A female of this bird has been in the aviary with other birds since March, 1864; and not withstanding that there were three of her own species in the same aviary, she paired with a white ibis in June last. These two birds built a nest upon the ground, composed principally of twigs, pieces of birch broom, sticks, etc., upon which was laid an egg of a pale green, thickly spotted and blotched with a dirty-brown color. The egg was constantly attended by both birds, and the nest was raised considerably under the egg by the constant addition of material, the egg being rolled from side to side as the sticks, etc. were placed under it. This raising the nest continued for about 10 days, after which time the birds began to incubate, taking turns on the egg. After setting four weeks, the egg was found to be addled, and was removed in order to save the specimen, which is now on the table.

Rev. Charles B. Dawson (1917) gives the following account of a wounded bird which he placed in an aviary with several other birds:

I turned him into a large aviary wherein were already established a few tame pigeons and wild doves, a bahama duck, a hanaqua, and a tinamou. Here his long beak gained for him a deference which its weakness and bluntness scarcely warranted. The pigeons would scatter at his awkward approach, but I soon protected their particular dominical with a few narrow strips of wood. In an aviary, birds soon settle themselves down in a particularly corner which they defend with all the sense of justice lying behind proprietary rights. And so in this case, for this ibis is an amiably-disposed bird, and having taken up a specially selected corner, he lived in peace with his novel associates.

But at first he would not eat, and simply ignored the choicest viands put before him. Then I had to resort to forcible methods and even so he persistently rejected food of all kinds, including fish and prawns. On the fourth day when I was on the point of considering the case hopeless, he, *mirabile dictu*, retained a piece of banana I had given him almost in despair. After that he retained nearly all the food I gave him and would even open his beak to submit to the process of feeding. On the twelfth day I saw him helping himself to bread and milk from the pan. Finally he seemed to prefer this diet to anything else. He was by this time quite accustomed to the altered conditions of his life; he would stand for hours in the trough of water, sunning himself and shaking his wings, or he would walk about prodding the sand for possible crabs.

DISTRIBUTION

Range.—Northern South America. East to the coast of Venezuela, (mouth of the Orinoco River); Trinidad; British Guiana (Waini and Berbice Rivers); French Guiana (Georgetown, Cayenne); eastern Brazil (Counany River, mouth of the Amazon River and Para). South to the southern coast of Brazil (Sao Paulo Iguape, and Paranagua). It apparently does not breed in the interior. North to the coast of Venezuela (Puerto Cabello, Lake Valencia, and Margarita Island).

Breeding range.—Northern and eastern South America from Venezuela to the mouth of the Amazon. Nesting has been reported from Trinidad (Léotaud); Surinam: Germina flats, Via-via flats, Motkreek (F. P. and A. P. Penard); Brazil; Marajo, Cavianna (Hagmann), and Jungcal (Edwards).

Casual records.—Probably it has occurred casually, when driven by severe storms, in the West Indies and on the Gulf coasts of Louisiana and Texas, but all of the records are more or less unsatisfactory and generally not substantiated by specimens with authentic data. The United States records are explained in the early part of the life history.

Egg dates.—Dutch Guiana: 52 records, May 2 to July 10; 26 records, May 2 to June 4.

PLEGADIS FALCINELLUS (Linnaeus)

GLOSSY IBIS

HABITS

The status of the glossy ibis, as a North American bird, is a puzzling problem, which it is difficult to solve with our present limited knowledge. It is widely distributed and well known in the tropical and subtropical regions of the Eastern Hemisphere, but in this hemisphere it seems to have a very limited breeding range, in which it is rare, and to occur elsewhere only as a straggler. It is known to breed in very limited numbers in Florida and Cuba, probably in Jamaica and possibly in some of the other West Indies. There are numerous casual records as far north as Nova Scotia and Quebec and as far west as Wisconsin and Colorado; it seems likely that these records were made by wanderers from Florida or Cuba and not by stragglers from the Eastern Hemisphere. The problem is complicated by the fact that the white-faced glossy ibis has been found breeding in Florida. Mr. William Brewster (1886) obtained a set of eggs of this western species from Mr. C. J. Maynard, who received them "directly from the collector, a young man by the name of Lapham—accompanied by the skin of the female parent, which was shot on the nest." The specimens were "taken April 18, 1886, at or near Lake Washington (near the head of the St. Johns River), Florida." Another very interesting, but puzzling, fact was discovered by Oscar E. Baynard (1913), who has given us the best account of the nesting habits of the glossy ibis in Florida. He collected one of the parent birds and thought at first that it was a white-faced glossy ibis, because the bare skin of the head was "pure white where the feathers join the skin for the full length across the front of the head extending down to the upper corner of the eye" and again "starting at the lower corner of the eye, the white streak extends down to the lower side of the lower mandible." This is well illustrated in his two photographs. This white *skin* might easily be mistaken for the white *feathers* in the face of the white-faced species and thus lead to much confusion. I can find no allusion to this character in any of the books on American or European birds and it seems hardly likely that all could have overlooked it, if it is a common character in normal birds. Mr. Baynard's bird may have been an abnormal bird; or this may be an overlooked character, perhaps present only during the height of the breeding season, in a distinct species found only in Florida and the West Indies, where it is a rare bird and seldom collected.

Nesting.—Mr. Baynard's (1913) observations in Florida give us about all the information we have on the home life of this species, in North America; he writes:

Glossy ibis bred on Orange Lake for four years of the five since I first saw it there; this year they did not nest there for some cause. I have seen glossy ibis once in 1912 in the month of November on the flats of the Miakka River and on two occasions on the canal that is the extension of the Caloosahatchee River leading into Lake Okeechobee. I have heard of it being seen by a hunter and trapper on the Kissimmee River, but it must be considered very rare in Florida. I have talked with scores of hunters and trappers, men who are observant and know their birds well, and but two have described the "black curlew" to me, and neither of them saw it in the nesting season, so no doubt the only nesting records for Florida are from Alachua County, where for four years I have found them nesting on Orange Lake. For the four years previous to 1909 I know it did not nest on Orange Lake, as I spent too much time there to miss seeing it. It must have bred there formerly though, as I understand a set was taken in that section about a dozen or more years ago by a gentleman who was staying in Micanopy.

The following observations were made during a period of eight weeks, during which time I had two pairs of these birds under daily surveillance. In looking for a suitable place to put up my photographic blind I stumbled onto these two pairs just beginning to build their nests, the second for the season, as all of the first built nests had been abandoned after being looted by the fish crows which swarmed in the rookery. Both parent birds aided in the construction of the nest, and I could not see that one bird did any more of the work than the other. I did note, however, that in one case the female selected the site and in the other the male did the selecting. Both nests were built at a height of about 10 feet in thick elder bushes, and about 3 feet from the tops of the bushes, as plainly shown in the accompanying photographs. The nests were ready for eggs at the end of the second day, although the nests were not finished by any means. Glossy ibis have the same characteristics as the white ibis in that they continue to add to their nest even up to the time that the young are able to leave it, so that by the time the eggs are ready to hatch the nest will be almost double the size that it was when the first egg was laid. An egg was laid each day until one nest contained four and the other three. Incubation did not start until after the last egg had been laid a full day. After the first egg was laid, however, the nest was never without one or the other of the pair close by, something that was very necessary in this rookery on account of the thieving fish crows. During the period of incubation, which lasted in each case exactly 21 days, I noticed that the female did most of the incubating; the male, however, put in about 6 hours out of the 24 covering the eggs. The female sat all night and until about 8.30 or 9.00 a. m., when the male came in from his morning hunt for food; on his approach to the nest he would give his call when about 50 feet away and his mate would immediately answer and spring up from the nest and pass him in the air sometimes 25 feet from the nest. The male would always fly directly to the highest twig above the nest and after about five minutes of careful preening his feathers he would give three or four calls in a medium tone and spring down to the nest, stand a few minutes examining the eggs and then go stalking through the bushes until he found a twig that suited him, break it off with his bill and take it back to the nest and after placing it on top settle down to a three hour job of incubating, getting off the nest, however, usually once during that time and getting another twig to add to the nest. The female would return and give her bleating note about 50 feet from the nest when the male would stand up and wait for her to alight in the bush over the nest, then would ensue about 15 minutes of as neat courting and billing and cooing as one will ever see being done by a pair of doves. This loving disposition toward each other seems to be characteristic of the glossy ibis, as every pair that I have observed have done it. The white ibis will occasionally do it, but not for any such length of time as the glossy. They will stand erect and seem to rub their bill against the other one, all the time making cooing (guttural, I must admit) notes of endearment, they will preen each others feathers and act just like a couple of young humans on their honeymoon; these loving scenes continued until the young were able to fly, never seeming to diminish at all. This trait I certainly admire, and while it is known to exist in birds that mate for life, is seldom seen in birds that are supposed to mate only for a season.

Eggs.—The glossy ibis lays three or four eggs, probably more often the latter. They are ovate, elliptical ovate or elongate ovate in shape. The shell is smooth or very finely pitted, with little or no gloss. The color varies from "Niagara green" to "pale Nile blue." The measurements of 75 eggs average 52.1 by 36.9 millimeters; the eggs showing the four extremes measure **57.8** by 38, 57.5 by **43**, **47** by 34, and 50 by **33.5** millimeters.

Young.—Mr. Baynard's (1913) notes on the behavior and feeding habits of young glossy ibises are well worth quoting in full, as follows:

After 21 days had elapsed three of the eggs hatched. The same routine was carried on, however, as when they were incubating; the female doing most of the covering, but both birds doing the feeding of the young. Until the young were 5 days old one bird always stayed at the nest and it was at this period that the last egg laid was hatched. I hardly expected it to hatch. This last hatched bird was considerably smaller than the three others were at time of hatching and always seemed to be more or less dwarfed until about time for them to leave the nest, when there was little difference to be seen in the size, but lots of difference in their activity, the last hatched one being the most active of the entire lot.

The disposition of the young at all times in both nests was fine. All were very active and restless after a week old, and at the age of two weeks would not stay in the nest at all but stray out to the ends of the limbs of the bushes in which the nests were placed, returning, however, to the nest to be fed, as I never observed on any occasion the old one feeding the young any place but on the nest. In this they differ from the white ibis, as they will feed the young wherever they find them and seem to let the youngsters tyrannize over them. On several occasions I noticed one or the other of the young when at the age of about 3 weeks try to make his parents come to him to feed him, but it never worked, as the old one would pay not the slighest attention to him, and when it looked as though the parent was through feeding and about ready to go away the young-ster would give in and come climbing down to the nest, where the old would treat him just as if he had been there all the time. I never noticed any of the young fighting among themselves, like the herons will sometimes do, but at all times they acted like well-behaved children, the only exceptions being that the three older birds would often take turns in trying apparently to swallow the last hatched baby. He was sure a hardy scamp or he would never have lived through the treatment he had to undergo. When the young are over 3 weeks old over half the food of these glossy ibis would be moccasins. I kept a record of the food by making the young disgorge after the old ones had fed them. This item-ized record will appear further along. The manner of the glossy ibis in feeding is to regurgitate the food up in the throat or mouth and for the young to put his bill, and many times head, down the old one's throat and take his portion. After one bird has been fed the second and third will get their turns, never longer than three minutes apart and usually immediately. I have seen the three young get two portions each in about seven minutes. Quick work this. They would each get four to five portions at each visit of the parent; when young, however, they would get as high as seven or eight turns. They would, of course, at this tender age, be unable to take on a very large quantity, and it would also be in a finer state of digestion, as many times I have seen the parent return from feeding and stand around and caress the young and not offer to feed until an hour had elapsed. This no doubt was to allow the food to digest to a point where the young would be able to eat it. But after the young had reached the age of 2 weeks and more this was never necessary, as they could at that age take anything from a portion of a half grown moccasin to a grown crayfish. At this age of the young the meal, if a moccasin, would be disgorged into the nest, and being half digested, be pulled into small enough portions to be capable of being swallowed by the young, who would take this up from the nest themselves. In no other instances did I ever see them pick up any food themselves until after they were quite large, when they would reeat the disgorged food that I had made them "cough up." In every case, however, the old bird fed from the throat, with the exception of the moccasins.

The old birds showed a great deal of intelligence in the feeding of the last hatched chick. They would feed the oldest three in every case three or four portions before they would ever notice the baby. This was no doubt due to the fact that it was unable to assimilate the food in as coarse a stage of digestion as its older brethern and apparently the parents knew this, because when they started to feed the baby they would give him as many meals as he cared to take and would never offer to give the older ones any more until another visit from the feeding grounds. As the young grew it necessitated many visits to the marshes for food because they were a hungry bunch all the time. I spent usually 8 to 10 hours a day in the blind photographing and making notes and no day during the four weeks after the young hatched did the parents make less than six trips each with food for the young and they made on some days as high as 11 trips each, the last ones being late, sometimes after dark. These last trips, however, were usually for their own food, as only on three occasions did I ever see the old ones offer to feed the youngsters when returning late.

After the end of the sixth week the young spent all their time flying down to the edge of the island and wading and feeding in the shallow water, returning, however, at night to roost on the old nest. The old ones, at this stage, will feed them wherever they can find them, and after the young are about 7 weeks old they will leave with the parents to their feeding grounds and stay with them returning at night to roost. At about this time all the ibis of both species are usually able to fly and it is not long then when some day they all leave as suddenly and mysteriously as they came in. They have probably pretty well cleaned up the hunting grounds of all the crayfish, etc., and move of necessity rather than choice. It is at this period that they are found in the Northern States. At what time they return south I am unable to state.

Plumages.—The plumages and molts of the glossy ibis are apparently similar to those of the white-faced species.

Food.—Mr. Baynard (1913) made a careful study of the food of the young glossy ibises; his itemized summary of 194 meals gives the following totals: 412 cutworms, 1,964 grasshoppers, 1,391 crayfish, and 147 snakes. He says that the adults feed "principally on crayfish, cutworms, grasshoppers, and other insects and young moccasins," from which it would seem that they are very useful birds. He figures it out in this way:

Total of 3,914 vermin in 194 meals, or an average of 20 to each meal. As the young would average seven meals apiece each day this would mean 28 meals, and 20 vermin to the meal would make 560 vermin for a day's feed for the young alone. The parents fed these young for about 50 days, making the total of vermin destroyed by this one nest of birds about 28,000, and this is saying nothing of what the old birds ate, which would be at least half of what the youngsters devoured, making a total of 42,000 vermin eaten while rearing one nest of young. When we stop to think that there were about 9,000 pairs of ibis, including both the white and glossy on this lake in 1912 that successfully reared nests of young, one can hardly conceive of the many millions of noxious insects and vermin of all kinds destroyed. The vast amount of good to any section of the country .where this vast army of ibis nest can hardly be reckoned in dollars. The cutworms and grasshoppers, we all know what great damage to growing crops they do; the crayfish destroys the spawn of fish, which in turn live off the eggs and young mosquitos. The deduction is self-evident to anyone when we consider the vast amount of territory in Florida that is covered with water. The crayfish also destroy levees on the rivers and cause the destruction of millions of dollars damage to growing crops.

Snakes, especially the moccasins, which, by the way, comprised 95 per cent of the snakes captured by the ibis, do lots of harm. Moccasins in rookeries destroy thousands of eggs and young birds, and even if they didn't they are so deadly poisonous that anything that helps to keep them down to reasonable numbers is welcome.

Behavior.—I must quote again from Mr. Baynard (1913) regarding the behavior of this species:

The disposition of the old glossy ibis towards the other ibis and herons is not good. I will have to admit that the glossy is pugnacious towards them, and one will never find an occupied nest of any other species as near as 10 feet to a glossy nest when they have reached the point where it is about time for the young to hatch. They will run off ibis and herons regardless of size and all the other birds seem to recognize their superiority and leave. Then happens a peculiar thing. The fish crows will, of course get the deserted eggs at once and then the glossy ibis will begin dismantling these old nests, pulling them apart and dropping the sticks down on the ground, or in the water, whichever happens to be underneath, saving any sticks that appeal to them and taking them back to their own nest. I noticed that it took six days for this pair to dismantle 14 white ibis nests and 3 little blue heron nests that they had made leave. The worst of it was that one of the white ibis had baby young in and when they died the glossies threw them out of the nest. It is barely possible, however, that the pair of white ibis that had used this nest were killed on their feeding grounds and failed to return, as this is the only instance where I ever noted the glossy dismantling a nest occupied by young.

The notes of the glossy ibis are very hard to explain so that any one would have the least idea how they sounded. The note of the white ibis is three grunting notes, sometimes uttered distinct, but more often sounding like a continuous note. The glossy starts off exactly like the white ibis with a grunting sound and then uttering four distinct notes resembling what to my mind best explains them, the bleating of a young calf or sheep. The ibis sounds as though there was something in the throat that gives a guttural sound. I became quite expert in imitating them, so much so that I could many times fool the young, but as for writing it, that is beyond me. This note is usually used in all cases when they approach the nest and when they are leaving and just as they take wing. They have another series of notes they use when caressing each other and caressing the young and the female has a very soft note, sort of cooing, that she uses when feeding the young when they are only a few days old. The young themselves never appear to make any notes except when trying to avoid a person, when they utter a squawking note of fear. The two nests in question were placed quite close to each other and as the young arrived at the age of two weeks and more they could always recognize their parents' notes even before I could distinguish them. I always knew which old birds were approaching by the actions of the young birds in the nest. They never in all the time I observed them made a mistake and put on the alert and expectant look for the parents of the other nest. I could not distinguish any material difference in the notes of the four adult birds, with the possible exception of the female of the nest photographed; she appeared to have a coarser tone to her calls. Glossy ibis appear to have less enemies than any other of the birds in the rookeries. Fish crows appear to be the only thing that bother them and they in nearly every case secured the first sets. Man, of course, is their next enemy, as is usually the case with any species but here in this rookery they were not molested by man at all.

DISTRIBUTION

Range.—Tropical and subtropical regions of both hemispheres.

Breeding range.—In the Eastern Hemisphere, east to China and Borneo, south to New Guinea and Australia, west to Egypt and Senegambia and north to Spain, Greece, and Persia. Definitely known as a breeder in America only in Florida (Micanopy and Bird Island, Orange Lake). It probably nests also in Louisiana and in Mexico.

Winter range.—Although generally resident in its breeding range, the glossy ibis has been taken at widely scattered localities. In America these have been mostly to the north while in the Eastern Hemisphere it apparently occurs regularly in South Africa. It is known as a straggler from Santo Domingo, Cuba, Jamaica (specimen in National Museum), and the Bahama Islands.

Casual records.—It has occurred casually northward along the coastal regions of the United States and southern Canada and is accidental in the interior.

There are two records for the District of Columbia (Washington, about 1817 and September, 1900); one for New Jersey (Great Egg Harbor, about May 7, 1817); one for Pennsylvania (near Philadelphia in 1866); several for New York (Grand Island, Niagara River, August, 1844, Cayuga Lake, 1854, and May 27, 1907, Tonowanda Swamp, May, 1884, Dunkirk, April, 1894, Seneca River, 1902; Howland Island, May, 1902, and also Southampton, Jamaica Bay, and Canarsie Bay); one for Connecticut (Middletown, May 9, 1850); a few for Massachusetts (near Cambridge, about May 8, 1850, Nantucket, 1869, Eastham, May 4, 1878, and Orleans, May 5, 1878); and one for New Hampshire (Lake Winnepesaukee, October, 1858). There is a specimen in the Thayer collection from the island of Montreal, Quebec, taken May 27, 1900; McKinley reported the occurrence of a specimen in Pictou County, Nova Scotia, about 1865, while Brewer reported one seen on Prince Edward Island in August, 1878.

In the interior the glossy ibis is known only as a straggler. One was taken from a flock of three in Marion County, Illinois, on February 27, 1880; two were seen and one was taken near Fairport, Ohio, in 1848; a pair were shot near Hamilton, Ontario in May, 1857; a specimen was secured at Lake Horicon, Wisconsin, on November 3, 1879; one was taken near Denver, Colorado, several years prior to 1900, another was secured on the Arkansas River near Salida, Colorado, April 12, 1898, while a third Colorado specimen was collected at Barr in June, 1905. Accounts of the occurrence of this species in other States have been either indefinite or have proved upon investigation to refer to the white-faced glossy ibis.

Egg dates.—Florida: 6 records, April 1 to May 25.   Continental Europe: 14 records, April 16 to June 13; 7 records, May 16 to 29.

PLEGADIS GUARAUNA (Linnaeus)

WHITE-FACED GLOSSY IBIS

HABITS

My first real aquaintance with this handsome bird was made in Texas in 1923, where we were told that there was a large breeding colony of "bronze ibises" to be found way off on the prairies of Refugio County.   During a drive of some 70 miles over the rough muddy roads through the "hog-wallow prairies," we had occasionally seen little bands of ibises feeding in wet places, or straggling flocks of them flying from the shores of ponds or banks of rivers, all heading in the same direction.   They had been spread out over many miles of country to feed and were now returning to their rookery; the direction of their flight helped us to locate it.   So we turned off the road and drove for some three miles across the prairie, picking our way through scattered clumps of mesquite and huisache, or dodging numerous prickly-pear cacti, until we came to the shore of a marshy lake.   The shores of the lake were lined with tules and the center of it was one great tule swamp, separated from us by 50 yards of open water.   Ibises were coming and going and over the tules a few of them were circling.   But it was not until we had partially stripped and waded out to it, in water nearly up to our armpits, that we realized what a large colony we had found.

Nesting.—Before we reached the tules the birds began to rise and soon there was a bewildering cloud of them circling overhead, uttering their peculiar cries of protest.   And looking through the more open spaces we could see the large brown birds leaving their nests, flopping off over the water or scrambling through the thicker tules.   Many of these were young birds, for at that date, May 19, most of the eggs had hatched and some of the young were able to fly.   As soon as we entered the tules, which grew far above our heads, we began to find nests. Many of them were in the more open places where they could be plainly seen, but many more were in dense clumps of tules where it was difficult to penetrate.   Progress was so slow and so difficult, in the deep water and dense tangles, that we did not attempt to explore the whole rookery; I could form no definite idea of its extent or how many birds it contained; but as far as we could see over the big expanse of marsh, birds were constantly arising and alighting; there must have been several thousands of them.   The nests were built in more or less open clumps of tules and attached to them; some were partially floating shallow platforms barely above the water; others were well made and built up of 10 or 12 inches above the water. They were all made of coarse pieces of dead tules, the last year's growth having been beaten down to form a foundation; they were often deeply cupped and were lined with finer pieces of tules and with grasses. Only a very few nests still held eggs, usually three.

The interesting colony, found near Brownsville, Texas, many years ago, described by George B. Sennett (1878) and Dr. J. C. Merrill (1879), had long since disappeared; the swamp has been drained and is now cultivated land. So far as I could learn there are now no ibises breeding in that section of Texas. Doctor Merrill's (1879) account of it is as follows:

On the 16th of May, 1877, Mr. G. B. Sennett and I visited a large patch of tule reeds growing in a shallow lagoon, about 10 miles from the fort, in which large numbers of this ibis and several kinds of herons were breeding. The reeds covered an area of perhaps 75 acres or less, growing in water 3 or 4 feet in depth Irregular channels of open water traversed the reeds here and there, but the bottom was comparatively firm, and there was little difficulty in wading in any direction. Besides the ibises, the great and little white egrets, Louisiana and night herons, and several other birds were breeding here. Often nests of all these species were placed within a few feet of each other, but there was a tendency toward the different kinds forming little nesting groups of 10 or 15 pairs. The reeds grew about 6 feet above the surface of the water, and were either beaten down to form a support for the nests, or dead and partly floating stalks of the previous years were used for that purpose. It was impossible to estimate the number of the ibises and different herons nesting here. On approaching the spot many would be seen about the edges of the lagoon or flying to or from more distant feeding grounds, but upon firing a gun a perfect mass of birds arose, with a noise like thunder, from the entire bed of reeds, soon to settle down again. Both nest and eggs of the ibises were quite unlike those of any of the herons, and could be distinguished at a glance. The nests were made of broken bits of dead tules, supported by and attached to broken and upright stalks of living ones. They were rather well and compactly built, and were usually well cupped, quite unlike the clumsy platforms of the herons. The eggs were nearly always three in number, and at this date were far advanced in incubation; many nests contained young of all sizes.

George Willett and Antonin Jay (1911) visited a large breeding colony of white-faced glossy ibises in San Jacinto Lake, in Riverside County, California, on May 28, 1911, which they describe as follows:

In nearly every patch of tules was a nest or two of this species, and in the patch farthest west which covered about a half acre, there must have been at least 200 nests. They were built on bent down tules, and were composed of tule stalks and lined with marsh grass. They were situated from 2 to 6 feet above the water, the average height being about 4 feet. About half the nests examined contained young and most of the others held badly incubated eggs. A very few fresh sets were found but the height of the nesting season was past. The sets almost invariably consisted of three or four eggs. In one or two instances sets of two incubated eggs were noted and three nests contained five eggs each, two nests six eggs each, and one nest had seven. It is probable that sets numbering more than five eggs were deposited by more than one bird. In fact they invariably showed two different types of eggs. The color of the eggs evidently fades with incubation, as the heavily incubated eggs are a much lighter blue than the freshly laid ones. This is probably the largest breeding colony of these birds in southern California west of the mountains.

A. O. Treganza writes to me that this ibis is not an uncommon breeder in suitable localities in Utah. There is a colony of about 100 pairs on the black sloughs about 8 miles from Salt Lake City, a colony at the mouth of the Jordan River of about 100 pairs and he knows of four colonies, two of about 75 to 100 pairs and two of about 150 to 200 pairs at the mouth of Bear River. They breed in company with snowy egrets and black-crowned night herons and in three cases with Treganza herons, nesting in tules growing in water about waist deep. In some instances the nests are made on the dead tules of the year previous, which have been broken and matted down by the winter snows, while in other cases they consist of entirely new nests attached to and on the new growing tules and reeds.

Eggs.—This ibis usually lays three or four eggs, but five, six or even seven have been found in a nest. They are ovate, elliptical vate or elongate ovate in shape. The shell is smooth or very finely pitted, with little or no gloss. The color varies from "Niagara green" to "pale Nile blue." The measurements of 46 eggs average 51.5 by 36 millimeters; the eggs showing the four extremes measure **55** by 37, 52 by **38**, **46** by 35.5 and 50.5 by **33** millimeters.

Young.—Incubation is said to last for 21 or 22 days and probably both sexes incubate, as is known to be the case with the glossy ibis. At the time we visited the rookery in Texas, referred to above, we found young of all ages from newly hatched to those which were able to fly. The youngest birds showed signs of fear, but remained in the nest or made only feeble attempts to leave it But the older birds, one-third grown or more, were very timid and very precocial; they left the nests as we approached and scrambled off through the tules with great agility and skill; the larger ones tried to fly and, if they fell into the water, they flopped over the surface or swam away.

Plumages.—The downy young of the white-faced glossy ibis is not a beautiful creature. It is scantily covered with dull black down, through which the pin-feathers soon begin to show; there is a white patch on the back of the crown; the bill is pale flesh-color, black at the tip and at the base, with a black band in the middle. This parti-colored bill is also characteristic of the juvenal plumage and does not disappear until September. In the juvenal plumage the rich chestnut hues are wholly lacking; the head, neck, and under parts are dull grayish brown; but the plumage of the upper parts, back, wings, and tail, is a rich, glossy, metallic green. A partial molt in September produces a head and neck plumage much like that of the winter adult, streaked with brown and dull white. I have been unable to trace the first prenuptial molt in young birds, but presumably a partial molt produces a body plumage approaching that of the adult. At the first postnuptial molt, which is complete, the young bird assumes the adult winter plumage. Winter adults have the head and neck streaked with brown and dull white, as in the first winter; but the upper parts are glossed with purple, green, and bronze reflections, but little duller than in spring, and the under parts are rich chestnut brown. Adults apparently have a partial prenuptial molt in early spring, March, and a complete postnuptial molt in July and August.

Food.—Like the white ibis, this species often makes long flights to its favorite feeding grounds, along the banks of rivers and on the shallow margins of muddy pools, ponds, and marshes. On the "hog-wallow prairies" of the coastal plains of Texas are many such pools, where we often saw this species feeding, walking about gracefully and probing in the mud; the crops of birds we shot here were crammed full of ordinary earthworms. Its food also consists largely of crawfish, various small mollusks, insects and their larvae, small fish and frogs, newts, leeches, and various other forms of low animal life. Probably a certain amount of aquatic vegetation is also eaten.

Behavior.—The name, "black curlew" has been well applied to this species, for at a distance in flight it certainly appears very dark colored; its long curved bill stretched out in front and its legs extended backward give it the shape of a curlew. It can be easily recognized at any distance. Its flight is strong, direct, swift and well sustained. When traveling in flocks, it flies in long, diagonal lines, sometimes with the birds abreast, usually with steady, rapid wing strokes, but varied occasionally with short periods of scaling.

Dr. Frank M. Chapman (1908) was priviledged to see flocks of from 10 to 40 of these birds perform a surprising evolution; he writes:

In close formation, they soared skyward in a broad spiral, mounting higher and higher until, in this leisurely and graceful manner, they had reached an elevation of at least 500 feet. Then, without a moment's pause and with thrilling speed, they dived earthward. Sometimes they went together as one bird, at others each bird steered its own course, when the air seemed full of plunging, darting, crazy ibises. When about 50 feet from the ground, their reckless dash was checked and, on bowed wings, they turned abruptly and shot upward. Shortly after, like a rush of a gust of wind, we heard the humming sound caused by the swift passage through the air of their stiffened pinions.

The same writer describes the note of this species as a "nasal *ooh-ick-ooh-ick.*" Dr. Joseph Grinnell (1918) records it as "a hoarse *ka-onk,* several times repeated."

Game.—Ibises can hardly be considered desirable game birds; yet, under the name of "brónze ibis" in Texas or "black curlew" in

California, this species has been persistently hunted and sold in the
market as game. Prior to 1915 there was an open season on it in
California, with a bag limit of 20 birds, but, as many of the birds
migrated out of the State during the open season, no great reduction
in its numbers was made by gunners.

DISTRIBUTION

Breeding range.—Western North America, including Mexico; South
America, south of the Amazon Valley. Range discontinuous; practically unknown from Central America (south of Mexico) and
northern South America. In North America, east to Louisiana
(Lake Arthur); Florida (one record, at Lake Washington). South
to Mexico (valley of Toluca, Mazatlan, and San Jose del Cabo).
West to California (near Escondido, San Jacinto Lake, Los Banos,
and Clear Lake). North to Oregon (Malheur Lake), Nevada
(Washoe Lake), Utah (Bear River marshes), and Minnesota (one
record for Heron Lake). In South America, east to Brazil (Rio
Grande do Sul), Argentina (Rozas, Cape San Antonio, and Estancia
Sta. Elena). South to Argentina (Rio Negro). West to Chile
(Santiago).

Winter range.—In common with other members of this family,
the white-faced glossy ibis is more or less resident in its breeding
range. It does, however, regularly withdraw from the northern and
southern extremes. In North America it winters north to California
(San Diego and Los Banos), Arizona (casually at Tombstone);
Texas (Corpus Christi and Brownsville), and Louisiana (Lake
Prieu). The winter range in South America appears to be regularly
south to Argentina (Cape San Antonio or Buenos Aires). In this
portion of the range there is a distinct movement north in the latter
part of September, indicating that the principal breeding areas may
be located along the rivers and marshes of the interior.

Spring migration.—Early dates of arrival are: California, San
Francisco, March 28, and Fresno, April 20; Oregon, Malheur Lake,
May 12; Arizona, Peck's Lake, Verde Valley, April 12; Idaho, Rupert, May 19; Colorado, Durango, April 7, and Barr, April 4; Minnesota, Wilder, May 27.

Fall migration.—Late dates of departure are: Oregon, Malheur
Lake, October 4; California, Dunlap, September 8; Colorado, Barr,
October 3, and Colorado Springs, October 10.

Casual records.—Stragglers have been noted in North America from
Washington (Clear Lake, about October 30, 1909); and British Co-
lumbia (Salt Spring Island in 1884, Sardis, fall of 1904, and also at
the mouth of the Fraser River). It also has been recorded from the
Straits of Magellan, Magallanes Territory, Chile, and from El Pozo,
Diquis River, Costa Rica.

Egg dates.—California: 92 records, May 20 to July 15; 46 records, May 28 to July 5. Texas: 35 records, April 15 to June 6; 18 records, April 22 to May 19.

Family CICONIIDAE, Storks and Wood Ibises

MYCTERIA AMERICANA Linnaeus

WOOD IBIS

HABITS

A striking and a picturesque bird is the wood ibis, also known in Florida as "gannet" or "flinthead," both appropriate names. It is a permanent resident in the hot, moist bottom lands of our southern borders and seldom straggles far north of our southern tier of States. To see it at its best one must penetrate the swampy bayous of Louisiana or Texas, where the big water oaks and tupelos are draped in long festoons of Spanish moss, or the big cypress swamps of Florida, where these stately trees tower for a hundred feet or more straight upward until their interlacing tops form a thick canopy of leaves above the dim cathedral aisles. One must work his way through almost impenetrable thickets of button willows, underbrush, and interlacing tangles of vines. He must wade waist deep or more in muddy pools, where big alligators lurk unseen or leave their trails on muddy banks, as warnings to be cautious, or where the deadly moccasin may squirm away under foot or may lie in wait, coiled up on some fallen log, ready to strike. If not deterred by these drawbacks, or by the clouds of malarial mosquitos or by the hot, reeking atmosphere of the tropical swamps, he may catch a fleeting glimpse of the big white birds or hear their croaking notes as they fly from the tree tops above. Probably he may see a solitary old "flint head" perched in the top of some old dead tree in the distance, standing on one leg, with his head drawn in upon his shoulders and his great bill resting on his chest. Perhaps there may be a whole flock of them in such a tree; but the observer will not get very near them, for the wood ibis is an exceedingly shy bird, and a sentinel is always on the lookout. One is more likely to see the wood ibis on the wing, flying in flocks to or from its feeding grounds, or circling high in the air above its breeding rookery. On the wing it shows up to the best advantage, sailing gracefully on motionless wings, a big white bird, with black flight feathers in its long wings and in its short tail.

Nesting.—My experience with the nesting habits of the wood ibis has been rather limited. In the big Jane Green cypress swamp, near the upper St. Johns River in Florida, we found a breeding colony in April, 1902. The cypresses here were the largest I have ever seen, measuring 6 feet or more in diameter at the base, tapering rapidly to about 3 feet in diameter, and then running straight up at about that size for 75 or 100 feet to the first limb. The nests were placed in the tops of the tallest cypresses and far out on the horizontal limbs; they were practically inaccessible by any means at our disposal, so we had to be content with seeing or hearing the birds fly off.

Near Cape Sable we were more fortunate, as the absence of cypress swamps in this region compelled the wood ibises to nest in smaller trees. We found a small colony of them breeding on an island in Bear Lake, about 2 miles back from the coast. The birds were very shy, leaving the island when we were about 100 yards away, and not coming within gunshot afterwards. There were about 20 nests in the tops of the red mangroves, from 12 to 15 feet from the ground; they were large nests, about 3 feet in diameter, made of large sticks, very much like the nests of the larger herons, and were completely covered with excrement. All the nests held young birds in various stages of growth.

Willard Eliot (1892) describes a typical nesting colony of wood ibises, found in southern Florida on March 23, as follows:

Out in the center of the lake was a small island about 100 feet in diameter, with about 3 feet elevation above the water. There were several large cypress trees besides a thick undergrowth of bay trees. What a sight met our gaze from the shore, the trees on the island were white with the ibises standing close together on the limbs, besides a number of American egrets, Florida cormorants, and anhingas. The ibises were nesting and we could see a number of the birds sitting on their nests. Most of the nests were on the island, but we found two trees near the shore, one had five nests and the other seven. After looking over the field I proceeded to climb the first tree, a large cypress, the nests were placed 50 feet from the ground and were saddled flatly on the top of a horizontal limb. One limb had four nests in a row and were so close together that their edges touched. A typical nest was 18 inches across by 5 inches deep outside, only slightly depressed inside, made of coarse sticks lined with moss and green bay leaves. The eggs were chalky white and nearly always blood stained; the average set is three but we found sets of two and four.

In the spring of 1913 F. M. Phelps (1914) visited a large rookery of wood ibises in the Big Cypress Swamp of Lee County, Florida, in which he estimated that there were not less than 5,000 pairs of these birds. He says:

Mr. Baynard, who visited this rookery in February, 1912, before the cypress trees had leaved out, gave it as his opinion that there were not less than seven or eight thousand nests of the wood ibis here. Tree after tree bore from 12 to 20 or more nests of this species, and in one I counted 32. Years ago before the egrets and spoonbills had become so sadly decimated, for they once bred here in large numbers, it must have been a spectacle so imposing as to defy an adequate description. The egrets, wood ibis, and spoonbills all nest high up in the cypress trees, very few under 50 feet and many 75 and 80 feet up. At this season, the middle of March, nearly all the nests contained young. A few of the wood ibis and egrets were still incubating eggs, but these were more than likely birds that had been broken up elsewhere.

Frederic H. Kennard has sent me some notes on a rookery fully as large, if not larger, which he explored in Okaloacoochee Slough in southern Florida. It was in some enormous cypress trees, 4, 5, 6, 7, and even 9 feet in diameter, grown well apart, so that most of them had good, spreading tops. It had been for years the place where the Seminoles came for their dugouts, as it contained the biggest and finest cypresses in the land. The rookery was perhaps from 100 to 200 yards across, and he followed it for about half a mile or more. Not all the trees were occupied, but most of the good ones held 4 or 5 to 20 nests apiece, clear way up on the tops of the trees. It was almost impossible to make any estimate of their number, even approximately, without spending a couple of days counting their nests, but there must have been several thousand flying about, or perched solemnly on the tops of the trees.

His guide, Tom Hand, estimated that there were 10,000 nests, for from a tree he climbed he could see the nests extending along the edge for a mile. At the other end of the rookery they all appeared to be building their nests. There was an almost steady stream of birds, perhaps 25 at a time, all flying to some live willows, breaking off twigs and flying back to the rookery with them. An old bird would fly up to the willows and alight, perhaps grasping several twigs in his feet, in order to get a firmer hold; he would then saw, pull, and yank at some twig with his bill; if unsuccessful, he would try another twig until, at last, he could break one off and fly away with it. In the rookery they frequently saw the birds flying overhead with long twigs or small branches, with the leaves still on them, or with long streamers of moss for nest linings.

Among the many courtesies extended to me by Oscar E. Baynard was an excellent opportunity to make an intimate acquaintance with a nesting colony of wood ibises; it was not as large as the one described above, but the nests were fairly accessible and the birds were rather tamer than usual. In the northern part of Polk County, Florida, lies a large tract of wilderness, unsettled and with no roads worthy of the name; it is largely flat pine woods with numerous large and small cypress ponds or swamps scattered through it. Here on March 7, 1925, after a 30-mile drive over some of the toughest trails I have ever driven, through woods, bogs, and cypress swamps, we camped near the edge of a long cypress swamp and visited the rookery in it the next day. We estimated that the colony consisted of between 200 and 300 pairs of wood ibises; no other species was nesting with them. We had not waded more than 75 or 100 yards into the swamp, where the water averaged about knee deep, when we began to see the ibises in the tree tops or on their nests. The cypress trees were of fair size, 12 to 18 inches in diameter, heavily festooned with Spanish moss, and the nests were mostly between 50 and 60 feet above us.   The birds were not shy at first and we had no difficulty in approaching near enough to photograph groups of them perched on the nesting trees or on other tall dead trees in the vicinity.   When we began climbing the trees they became more wary, but they perched on the tops of more distant trees and frequently flew over us.   Some of the trees held only two or three nests, but most of them held from half a dozen to a dozen.   The nests were in or near the tops of the trees, mostly well out on the horizontal branches and often beyond our reach.   They were surprisingly small and flimsy structures, not much larger than well made night heron's nests, ill adapted, it seemed to me, to the needs of such large, heavy birds.   The foundations of the nests were loosely made of rather large, dead sticks, on which more substantial nests were built of finer twigs and fresh, budding leaf stems of the cypress; some were also partially lined with green leaves of bay, oak, or maple.   Perhaps the nests would be added to, as incubation advances, as is customary with some of the herons.   Most of the nests contained three eggs, some only two, and at least two nests held four eggs.   All of of the eggs that we collected were fresh.

Eggs.—The wood ibis lays usually three, sometimes four, eggs and very rarely five.   The shape varies from ovate to elliptical ovate or even elongate ovate.   The shell is smooth, but finely granulated or finely pitted.   The color is dull or dirty white or cream white, without any markings, except occasional blood stains.

The measurements of 40 eggs average 67.9 by 46 millimeters; the eggs showing the four extremes measure **73** by 46.2, 64.7 by **54.9**, **60.8** by 46.8 and 70.9 by **34.3** millimeters.

Young.—George M. Sutton (1924) gives the following interesting account of his visit to a colony of wood ibises, in which the young birds were about ready to fly:

As evening came I noticed that from the hammock far to the westward issued forth strange sounds the like of which I had never heard.   I accredited them to alligators and bullfrogs, thinking at the time that Florida 'gators and frogs probably could, and perhaps usually did set up such a disturbance.   Although it was so far away, the penetrating quality of the racket made us believe that the sound would be very great close at hand.   It was so far distant that we heard but an incessant mumbling, varied occasionally with higher shriller, tones.

Although I constantly noticed wood ibises issuing in small flocks from this hammock, or returning to it, I never seemed to connect the strange sound with the birds; it hardly seemed credible that birds should make such a noise.   But when we visited the 'Gator Lake hammock on March 20, we found that the strange noises of the days before had come from a large "Flint-head" colony.   As we approached, the racket increased steadily, and soon we could detect individual grunts, loud and deep-throated; shrill squeals, incessant and angry; bellowing, coughing, deep wheezing, bleating—all in the most unbelievably hurried, earnest fashion, as though their fervor had to be kept at white heat all evening long. Even now we could not really see the birds, save those few which occasionally flew out to investigate us, or to search a feeding ground for the evening. But it was strangely exciting to listen, and to picture in our minds what might be going on in that dense hammock to the accompaniment of the weird notes we were hearing As we drew near, masses of the birds took wing and drifted about, soaring quite low for a time and gradually mounting higher and higher. Not until we had come very close did we realize that a large proportion of the colony was young birds, fully fledged but standing about on somewhat uncertain legs and very hesitant to fly. They were droll creatures. They seemed aware of our presence all the time but never turned their heads our way, seeming to prefer to listen intently and jump off with much flapping and squaking at what they considered the psychological moment. Many of them where standing on their large, flat, whitewashed nests; but I believe they had long since forgotten their own cradles and were standing about regardless of family relationships. Occasionally one very near us would lose his balance, and, hanging by his neck and toes, after much hideous noise and commotion would finally regain his perch or flap away. On the heads of the full-fledged young the juvenal feathering was still apparent. Many of them stood about with open mouths—whether bellowing or not.

Plumages.—The downy young wood ibis is partially covered with short, thick, wooly, white down; the front half of the head and the spaces between the feather tracts are bare. I have never seen any small juvenals, but Audubon (1840) says:

The young are dusky-grey all over, the quills and tail brownish-black. The head all covered with down, excepting just at the base of the bill. After the first molt, the bare space extends over the head and cheeks; the downy feathers of the hind head and neck are dusky; the general color of the plumage is white, the quills and tail nearly as in the adult, but with less gloss.

In the first winter plumage, which is worn without much change until the first postnuptial molt, the posterior half of the head and the whole neck is thinly covered with coarse, hairlike feathers, mixed dusky, brown and whitish, darkest and longest on the occiput. The body plumage is dull white. Some of the scapulars and tertials are extensively tipped with dull brown and the rectrices and remiges are brownish black with dull greenish reflections. Most of the immature birds that I have seen, taken from October to May fall into this class, hence I think that the fully adult plumage must be assumed at the first postnuptial molt in September and October, when the young bird is 15 or 16 months old. However, the young bird is not yet fully adult for some feathering still remains on the neck. The scaly, bare head and neck of the old "flint head" are probably not acquired for at least another year. Audubon (1840) says:

The wood ibis takes four years in attaining full maturity, although birds of the second year are now and then found breeding. This is rare, however, for the young birds live in flocks by themselves, until they have attained the age of about 3 years. They are at first of a dingy brown, each feather edged with paler; the head is covered to the mandibles with short downy feathers, which gradually fall off as the bird advances in age. In the third year, the head is quite bare, as well as a portion of the upper part of the neck. In the fourth year, the bird is as you see it in the plate. The male is much larger and heavier than the female, but there is no difference in color between the sexes.

The complete molt of the adult apparently occurs in September and October; I have seen no evidence of a molt in the spring or of any seasonal difference in plumage.

Food.—The wood ibis is mainly a fresh water bird and prefers to feed in shallow, muddy ponds, marshes and sloughs; but it also resorts occasionally, perhaps often to salt-water mud flats and shoals. I frequently saw them in winter, usually from two to four birds, feeding on the extensive mud flats of Boca Ceiga Bay in company with American egrets, little blue, Louisiana, and Ward herons. They must fly long distances to feed, for this locality, in Pinellas County, Florida, is at least 100 miles from the nearest known rookery. Two birds were seen occasionally in a little pond hole on Long Key beside a much frequented road, where they fed with the egrets, totally unconcerned with many passing automobiles. I once sat and watched them feeding within 20 yards of my blind and was much impressed by the loud clattering of their bills, as they walked about with long, deliberate steps, feeling for their food and scooping it out of the mud and water. A method of feeding, that I have never seen or read about, is described in some notes sent to me by Mr. Kennard, based on observations made by his guide. He reported watching a number of them at close range. They were in some open water with a very muddy bottom, walking back and forth, dragging their bills beside them, pointed downward and backward, opening and shutting them repeatedly, as if sifting the mud through them, after the manner of flamingos. He says that on moonlight nights numbers of them may be seen feeding in the sloughs; and on a cloudy, rainy day they could be seen all over the prairie, feeding, perhaps on grasshoppers.

Audubon's (1840) account of the feeding habits of the wood ibis is worth quoting, as follows:

This species feeds entirely on fish and aquatic reptiles, of which it destroys an enormous quantity, in fact more than it [eats; for if they have been killing fish for half an hour and have gorged themselves, they suffer the rest to lie on the water untouched, when it becomes food for alligators, crows, and vultures, whenever these animals can lay hold of it. To procure its food, the wood ibis walks through shallow muddy lakes or bayous in numbers. As soon as they have discovered a place abounding in fish, they dance as it were all through it, until the water becomes thick with the mud stirred from the bottom by their feet. The fishes, on rising to the surface, are instantly struck by the beaks of the ibises, and, on being deprived of life, they turn over and so remain. In the course of 10 or 15 minutes, hundreds of fishes, frogs, young alligators, and water snakes cover the surface, and the birds greedily swallow them until they are completely gorged, after which they walk to the nearest margins, place themselves in long rows, with their breasts all turned toward the sun, in the manner of pelicans and vultures, and thus remain for an hour or so. Besides the great quantity of fishes that these ibises destroy, they also devour frogs, young alligators, wood rats, young rails and grakles, fiddlers and other crabs, as well as snakes and small turtles. They never eat the eggs of the alligator, as has been alleged, although they probably would do so, could they demolish the matted nests of that animal, a task beyond the power of any bird known to me. I never saw one eat anything which either it or some of its fellows had not killed. Nor will it eat an animal that has been dead for sometime, even although it may have been killed by itself. When eating, the clacking of their mandibles may be heard at the distance of several hundred yards.

Grinnell, Bryant and Storer (1918) record the stomach contents of three wood ibises taken in Imperial County, California; one contained 3 tadpoles, 4 water beetles, 2 paddle bugs, and some moss and slime; another, 9 tadpoles, a water beetle, 9 dragon fly larvae, and a carp; and the third held 10 carp, a catfish, 2 bony tails (fish) and a water cricket. Another bird from the same region examined by Dr. Harold C. Bryant (1919) had in its stomach 10 seeds of the screw bean, 2 seeds of mesquite, parts of 4 water beetles and some finely comminuted vegetable material.

Behavior.—In flight the wood ibises are splendid birds and one never tires of watching them, as they fly along in flocks, high over the tree tops flapping their long wings or scaling at intervals, all in perfect unison. Even more interesting are the spectacular aerial evolutions in which these birds so often indulge. Rising in a flock, they soar in wide circles, mounting higher and higher, crossing and recrossing in a maze of spirals, until they are almost beyond vision in the ethereal blue. Then suddenly they dash downward and repeat the operation or else drift away on motionless wings until lost to sight. They are easily recognized at a great distance, great white birds with jet black flight feathers, with long necks and heavy bills and with long legs extended far beyond their short black tails.

Distance lends enchantment to this species; the sign of the cross, so boldly written in black and white on the distant sky, one stands and admires; but not so with the awkward, ungainly fowl that we see perched on a tree in a hunched-backed attitude of uncouth indolence. Its behavior on the ground is well described by Doctor Coues (1874) as follows:

The carriage of the wood ibis is firm and sedate, almost stately; each leg is slowly lifted and planted with deliberate precision, before the other is moved, when the birds walk unsuspicious of danger. I never saw one run rapidly, since on all the occasions when I have been the cause of alarm, the bird took wing directly. It springs powerfully from the ground, bending low to gather strength, and for a little distance flaps hurriedly with dangling legs, as if it was much exertion to lift so heavy a body.

Wood ibises are among the wariest of birds. Even on their breeding grounds it is usually difficult to approach them; when they first rise from their nests they may circle once around the intruder and then they disappear and do not return. When feeding or when perched on a tree resting and dozing there is always a sentinel on the watch; even when roosting at night they are difficult to approach; the crackling of a twig, the rustling of underbrush, the slighest sound or the glimpse of a man, which their keen ears or eyes can detect, will put them on the alert; it is then useless to attempt a closer approach; they are off and will not return.

The only note I have ever heard from an adult wood ibis is a hoarse croak, usually uttered when disturbed or frightened. It is generally a silent species. Young birds are very noisy, however.

Enemies.—The wood ibis has not suffered much from the hand of man; it is so wary that it is not easily approached and is generally well able to take care of itself; its plumage has never been much in demand, for it is not an attractive bird at close quarters; and it has never been considered a game bird, as its flesh is tough and un-palatable. It has few natural enemies and so it is likely to survive for a long time in its native wilderness.

Willard Elliot (1892) writes.:

A great pest of all rookery birds is the crow, and if an ibis leaves the nest for an instant down comes the black dare-devil with a scream of delight and grabs an egg by sticking his bill into it and flying away. The ibis seems to be very much afraid of them and I have seen a crow almost take an egg out from under one of them and they would croak and draw back their bills as if to strike, but never did.

Audubon (1840) says:

One of the most curious circumstances connected with this species is, that al-though the birds are, when feeding, almost constantly within the reach of large alligators, of which they devour the young, these reptiles never attack them; whereas, if a duck or a heron comes within the reach of their tails, it is immediately killed and swallowed. The wood ibis will wade up to its belly in the water, around the edges of "alligators' holes," without ever being injured; but should one of these birds be shot, an alligator immediately makes toward it and pulls it under water. The garfish is not so courteous, but gives chase to the ibises whenever an opportunity occurs. The snapping-turtle is also a great enemy to the young birds of this species.

Dr. Henry Bryant (1861), on a visit to a rookery in Florida, found the alligators very aggressive; he writes:

The moment the boat which I had had hauled there was launched, the alliga-tors assembled for the purpose of examining the new visitor; and before we had arrived at the breeding place there were more than 50 following the boat, the nearest almost within reach of the oars. On shooting a bird, the instant it touched the water it was seized by an alligator; and I was obliged to kill half a dozen of these creatures before I could secure a specimen, and even after this I was generally obliged to fire one barrel at the bird and the other at the nearest alligator.

Breeding range.—Southeastern United States, Central and South America south to Patagonia. East to South Carolina (Colleton County); Florida (Amelia Island, St. Johns River, St. Augustine, Orlando, Lake Kissimmee, Lake Okeechobee and Cape Sable); Cuba; British Guiana (Georgetown); Brazil (Monte Negro, Para, and Iguage). South to Brazil (Rio Grande do Sud); Uruguay (Rio Negro, and Sta. Elena); Argentina (Concepcion, Barracas al Sud and Cordoba). West to Argentina (Tucuman); Peru (Upper Ucayali River and Tumbez); Ecuador (Babahoyo, probably); Costa Rica (La Palma and Rio Frio); Nicaragua (Escondido River, probably); Guatemala (Coban); Mexico (southeastern Yucatan, Cozumel Island, Tepic, Mazatlan, and the Gulf of California). North to northwestern Mexico (Gulf of California); Texas (Corpus Christi); Louisiana (Cameron and Bayou Sara); and Mississippi (Rodney).

Postbreeding summer range.—After the breeding season there is generally in the United States, a distinct northward movement of both adults and immatures. At this time the species may be locally common in southern California (San Diego, Saticoy, San Bernardino Valley, Oceanside, Dagget, Bixby, Claremont, Dominguez, and Los Angeles); Arizona (Santa Cruz River, Yuma, Needles, Temple, and the valleys of the Colorado, Gila, San Pedro, and Bill Williams Rivers); northern Texas (Gainesville); New Mexico (Fort Fillmore and Fort Thorn); southern Illinois (across from St. Louis, Mo.); and southeastern Indiana (Lyons, Bicknell, near Brookville, and Terre Haute).

Winter range.—In winter the wood ibis withdraws only a short distance from the extremes of its breeding range. It is occasionally found wintering as far north as Royal Palm Hammock, Florida (Hurter, 1881) and Mount Pleasant, South Carolina (Wayne, 1910).

Spring migration.—Early dates of arrival: Florida, Orlando, March 5, Indian River, March 28, Smyrna, March 29; Mississippi, Biloxi, March 21; Texas, Corpus Christi, March 25.

Fall migration—Late dates of departure: Florida, Amelia Island, November 2, Indian Key Reservation, October 1; Mississippi, Rodney, September 25.

Casual records.—Stragglers have wandered much farther than the regular postbreeding summer range and have been taken or noted north to Montana (southwestern part of the State, June 18, 1911); Wyoming (Yellowstone, Grand Canyon, July 16, 1925); Colorado (two near Denver, August 30, 1902); Wisconsin (Racine, September 10, 1868; another at La Crosse and a third on Rock River between Janesville and Edgerton); Michigan (Monroe, June 19, 1910); Massachusetts (Georgetown, June 19 1880, Chilmark, Martha's

Vineyard, November 26, 1918; and Seekonk, July 17, 1896); Vermont (Burlington); and Ontario (Sincoe, November, 1892).

Egg dates.—Florida: 54 records, December 8 to April 30; 27 records, January 10 to March 21.

JABIRU MYCTERIA (Lichtenstein)

JABIRU

HABITS

This large, stately stork is a South American bird. Its scanty claim to a place on our North American list rests on the fact that the head of a specimen, that had been taken near Austin, Texas, was donated to the Philadelphia Academy of Sciences.

It must be a magnificent bird, when seen in the freedom of its native wilderness. W. H. Hudson (1888) has well described it, as follows:

> This is a majestic bird, the largest of the American storks; it stands 5 feet high, and the wings have a spread of nearly 8 feet. The entire plumage is pure white, the head and 6 inches of the neck covered with a naked black skin; from the black part extend two scarlet bands, the skin being glossy and exceedingly loose, and run narrowing down to the chest. When the bird is wounded or enraged this loose red skin is said to swell out like a bladder, changing to an ntensely fiery scarlet hue. The name "Jabiru" is doubtless due to this circumstance, for Azara says that the Indian word Zabiru signifies blown out with wind.

Nesting.—Gottfried Hagmann (1907) gives a good account of the nesting habits of the jabiru, which he calls the "tuyuyu"; Thomas E. Penard has kindly translated this, as follows:

> During my stay on Mexiana, 1901, I saw seven tuyuyu nests, of which six were on Mungubeiras and one on a Pao mulato (*Calycophyllum spruceanum*), of which the phonograph appears in the plate. In the year 1904 I again saw several nests but it was not until the end of July 1905 that I succeeded in obtaining the first eggs. Through a herdsman I obtained, on July 27, 1905, two clutches, one of two, the other of three eggs. All the eggs were slightly incubated. On August 3, 1905, I removed with the assistance of an old herdsman, a nest from a tall *Bombax munguba*. It was a difficult and hazardous undertaking. A whole half hour was spent in trying to throw the ropes in the right place over the lowest branch, about 10 meters from the ground. On this rope I climbed, and sitting on this first branch I had now to throw the rope over the next branch and so on since the trunk was still too great to embrace. Step by step I had to make my way, but the trouble was not in vain, because I found in the nest three eggs, had a splendid survey of the big nest and at the same time a comprehensive view of the almost endless Campo. The nest was built on a side branch, 15 meters from the ground and about 2 meters from the trunk. Since the wood of the *Bombax* is very treacherous every precaution had to be taken to reach the nest itself. Only with the greatest pains did I succeed in removing the eggs. Carefully packing the eggs in a tin box I lowered it with the rope to my companion who took care of them. Slowly and carefully I made the return trip which required just as much trouble and perseverance as the ascent.
>
> The nest was about 2 meters wide, and round. The under portion consisted of strong branches intertwined with smaller twigs, the inner part itself composed of a substantial bed of grass. There was no true cavity, on the contrary, the

nest was on top perfectly flat. All the nests I saw were so situated that they were comparatively difficult of access. The old birds do not defend either the eggs or the young but at the approach of man fly away and do not return until they feel quite safe. I was able to determine with certainty that the same nest is used several years. If the eggs are taken from a nest, the tuyuyus will not lay again in the same nest the same year.

Under the appropriate name, "negro cop," C. A. Lloyd (1897) describes the nest of the jabiru very well, as follows:

On the banks of the Awaricru the "negro cop" (*Mycteria americana*) breeds regularly. The nest, which is a rather bulky affair, consists of a bundle of sticks these varying from half to one inch in circumference. It much resembles a gigantic pigeon's nest and has but a very slight depression in the center for the reception of the eggs. These nests are generally placed on the large limbs of the silk-cotton tree (*Eriodendron anfractuosum*) parallel to the limb, and to avoid being blown down by the wind are cemented by a thick layer of mud mixed with grass, which on drying becomes hard and thus thoroughly secures the structure. The eggs, which are about the size of those of a goose and of a dirty white color, are laid in September, the usual number being four, but occasionally five are deposited.

A graphic picture of an interesting nest is given by Robert H. Schomburgk (1841), as follows:

Near the entrance to the valley, and rising from 60 to 80 feet above the plain, is a columnar group of trap rocks, the largest of which has been named by the Macusis, Canuye piapa, or the Guava tree stump. Half a mile further westward, and not quite so high, is another mass of rocks, which the traveler might mistake for the trunk of some large old tree, deprived of its leafy crown. It is a great object of wonder amongst the Indians far and near, who call it pure-piapa, "the felled tree." So complete was the illusion, that I almost doubted my guides when they told me it was the work of nature, and was composed of stone. The rock rises straight to a height of at least 50 feet, its sides are partly covered by a red Lichen, and in some places it is more acted upon by the weather than in others; the delusion being increased by the play of colors, the mind can scarcely divest itself of the belief that it is the gigantic trunk of a tree, the head of which, stricken by years, or shivered by lightning, lies mouldering at its foot. On its summit, a jabiru, a species of stork, had built its nest, above which we saw the head of a young one. On our approach its mother hastened from a neighboring savannah to its protection, and perched on one leg, on the summit of the rock, stood sentinel over the plain around.

The rock may be considered sacred by the Macusi Indians but it did not afford an asylum to the poor bird; for before I was aware of it, or could prevent it, we heard the report of a gun, saw the poor bird balance itself for a few moments, and, pierced by the ball fall at the foot of the column. One of the Indians had taken my rifle, and he being too unerring a marksman, even the height which the bird had selected for its nest could not preserve its life.

The nest shown in the photograph taken by Mr. J. R. Pemberton is described in the notes he sent me, as follows:

Only one nest was found although other unoccupied large nests which were seen in high trees may have belonged to this species. The nest, of which a photograph was taken, was situated fully 60 feet above the ground on a sloping branch of a giant dead tree. The nest was above the level of the tops of the surrounding living trees so that a commanding view obtained from the site.

The material consisted, so far as could be seen with glasses from the ground, of large sticks which formed a great mass and resembled pictures commonly shown of nests of the common white stork of Europe. Both parents remained standing on the nest while I was near and they kept up a continual snapping of their immense bills, plainly to be heard where I was. The date was October 31, 1912 and I do not know whether the nest contained eggs or young birds but imagine eggs because other forms of water birds such as herons, bitterns, etc., were found elsewhere with eggs at about this time.

Eggs.—In the Hagmann (1906) collection are eight eggs of the jabiru, two sets of three and one of two, of which he says (translated by Mr. Penard): "Two of the clutches were taken on July 29, 1905, all the eggs being slightly incubated. The third clutch I myself took on August 3, 1905, two eggs of which were still fresh, the third being decidedly incubated." He describes them as "short and wide, large end hardly distinguishable from the small end." The shell is "comparatively thick, finely enchased; in two eggs of the same clutch the pole-zones are strikingly coarse granular." The color is "dirty grayish-white, with some yellow, without any markings whatever." The measurements of the eight eggs average 73.4 by 58.2 millimeters; they vary in length from 75.3 to 71.5, and in breadth from 60.5 to 55 millimeters. An egg in the United States National Museum, from British Guiana, measures 71.7 by 54.8 millimeters; it fits the above description very well. Hagmann (1907) found four young in one nest. Two eggs in the Penard collection are larger than the above; one is rather pointed oval and measures 93 by 59 millimeters and the other is elliptical measuring 89 by 59 millimeters.

Young.—Richard Schomburgk (1848) says of the young (translated by Mr. Penard):

The number of young, which do not leave the nest until January or February, is usually two, seldom three. Both sexes incubate, taking turns, and as soon as one has satisfied its hunger it returns to the nearest branch on the nesting tree to keep its mate company, or in case of threatened danger which they frequently suffer from tiger-cats and monkeys, to give protection. Shy as we have found the bird on the Savanna, it was the more noticeable that it fearlessly watched our noisy doings under the tree on which its nest was built. Love for its eggs and young caused it to pay no attention to the threatened danger.

C. A. Lloyd (1895) writes:

The young birds make their appearance about the end of October and are then the size of young ducks, and covered with a grayish-white down. They are unable at first either to stand or squat up, but lie in the nest stretched at full length, with their heads on one side as if lifeless. The beak at this stage is perfectly straight, showing not the slightest indication of the upward curve at the tip characteristic of the adult bird. When the nesting tree is approached the mother bird stands upright in the nest as a signal to her mate, which is never far off. He hastens at once to her side and strutting up and down, claps his mandibles together with a loud defiant click that can be heard some distance away. The young birds grow rapidly and in a few weeks are nearly the size of their parents, but their bodies are still too heavy to be supported by their long weak legs, and not until the first plumage is complete are they able to stand upright in the nest. The quantity of fish the young birds consume is astonishing, and all day long the parents are constantly employed supplying them with food. For some time after leaving the nest the birds are of a light drab color, and they only assume the snow-white plumage of the adult after several molts.

C. Barrington Brown (1876) observes:

I was greatly amused with the appearance of two young but fully-fledged jabirus, which stood on their large flat nest, composed of sticks entwined together, on the branch of a large isolated tree, growing on the river's bank. They looked like two shipwrecked mariners on a rock in mid-ocean, waiting to be delivered from their lonely watch by a passing ship. They stood there as if scanning the horizon, apparently deep in thought, shifting their position now and then from one leg to the other, or taking a solemn and stately stroll round the confines of their nest. Thus we left them, to await the time when their powers of flight would be sufficiently developed, to enable them to go forth into the world and forage for themselves. They were fully feathered with a gray plumage, which on moulting would change to pure white.

Plumages.—In the Museum of Comparative Zoology, in Cambridge are two downy young jabirus, as well as birds in juvenal and adult plumages. In the downy young the lores and the spaces around the eyes are naked; and there is a naked space encircling the central part of the neck. Below this naked space the lower neck and the entire body is completely covered with short, thick, white down, locally tinged with yellowish; the top and back of the head are thickly covered and the sides of the head and upper neck are scantily covered with grayish white or yellowish white down.

I have not seen a bird in the full juvenal plumage, which is evidently wholly grayish brown, or "wood brown." Hagmann (1907) says of two young birds, taken from a nest in October 1901 (translated by Mr. Penard):

The birds were almost full fledged and were nearly full grown and defended themselves with their powerful bills. The otherwise naked head and neck were sparsely covered with a fine down; all the feathers were brownish, dirty white, without the slightest trace of the pure white adult plumage. During October, 1901, I obtained six more young birds which I placed in the same pen with the young *Euxenura.* Toward the end of October a few feathers appeared here and there; at our arrival in Para, at the end of November, 1901, the juvenal plumage was already half replaced, but toward the end of January, 1902, traces of it could still be seen.

This would seem to indicate that the adult plumage is acquired during the first year; but a note on the label of a specimen in the museum at Cambridge states that the bird changes to white at 2 years of age. This specimen was collected in Colombia on July 7 and is still in transition plumage; the crown, occiput, and cervix are scantily covered with dark brown, hairlike feathers, longest on the occiput, and tipped with yellowish; the mantle (back and wing coverts) is a mixture of pure white and "wood brown" feathers with darker tips ("buffy brown"); the wings and tail are white, tinged or washed with pale "wood brown"; all of the feathers of the upper parts have a silvery sheen; the under parts are white.

Food.—Mr. Pemberton refers in his notes to the feeding habits of the jabiru, as follows:

When feeding in the meadows the birds work singly. Fish are proably eaten least of all for never was a bird seen frozen after the fashion of a heron near water but they were always walking alertly, peering this way and that, with a frequent stab into the ground, often making great jumps after some rapidly moving prey. The only food actually seen eaten consisted of snakes and I suppose that these together with other reptiles and batrachians form the greater part of their diet. On one occasion a gigantic bird standing near me was seen to toss a writhing serpent fully 6 feet in length into the air, catch it, thrash it on the ground a few times, shake and generally maltreat it before finally placing it on the ground where it was doubtless then torn into segments, for it would be physically impossible to swallow entire such a large snake. A Maguari stork (*Euxenura maguari*) which I killed in Patagonia contained among other things a large rail intact in its gullet, in fact the plumage was scarcely ruffled and no apparent injuries could be found on its body. This leads me to believe that the jabiru, which is a larger bird even than the Maguari stork, will catch and devour almost any form of animal life which it can catch. Thus reptiles, batrachians, mammals, fish, and birds must form its principal diet because all of these live in abundance in the moist meadows where the bird was seen feeding.

Mr. Robert H. Schomburgk (1840) speaks of a captive bird which attacked a cage containing an opossum "and having seized the poor animal with its beak, drew it by force through the bars of its cage. and swallowed it without further hesitation." He also says:

A species of *Ampullaria* (*greyanensis*) is found in prodigious numbers in the lakes and swamps, as well as in the rivulets which meander through the savannahs, and it appears they constitute the chief food of the jabiru. In spite of their unshapely beak, they are able to remove the operculum most admirably, and to draw the mollusc out of its shell. I have found it difficult to procure perfect specimens of that *Ampullaria* for my collections, although shells partly broken or devoid of the operculum covered the low savannahs extensively while in other parts I found the opercula equally numerous, but no shells.

Behavior.—The same writer refers (1840) to the behavior of jabirus in the following interesting manner:

When the waters subside after the annual inundations, they frequent in small groups the sand banks of the river Rupunny in search of crustaceous animals. Nothing can surpass the gravity with which they stalk along; their measured step and upright bearing frequently amused my military companion while on our first expedition in the interior, who was forcibly reminded of the parade, so that he could not refrain while passing the beach from giving these feathered recruits the word of command, and they ever afterwards among ourselves went by the name of his recruits. Before they rise on the wing they prepare for their flight by taking two or three hops, by which they are better enabled to get on the wing. Their flight is light and graceful; and before they alight, or when rising, they first wheel round the place in gyral motions, either lessening or extending the circles according as it is their intention to do the former or the latter. They soar uncommonly high, and might vie with the eagle. Indeed they appear as a mere speck in the air. It is a beautiful sight to see a numerous flock on the wing. All appears confusion when they are first disturbed and rise in the air; they cross each other in the flight, and one would think from below they could not avoid coming in contact; but scarcely have they reached a height of 80 or 100 feet, when order is restored, and they begin flying in circles, rising with each circle higher and higher. When on a more extensive journey, they fly in a horizontal line, and change the leader like the cranes. When feeding on the savannahs, a party is always on the alert while the others seek for their food.

The haunts and habits of this species are described in Mr. Pemberton's notes, as follows:

During October of 1912, while traveling in the southern part of the State of Matto Grosso, central Brazil, jabirus were seen almost daily. The type of country preferred is the open grassy meadowland bordering the great Paraguay River. Due to tropical rainfall this region is wet most of the time and the meadows contain a succession of small ponds, lagoons, and marshes and even where these are lacking the ground itself is moist. Long winding narrow groves of trees which evidently follow old drainage channels separate the meadows into units. Unquestionably these meadows abounded in the usual food of the jabiru for they were only to be found here.

The bird is not gregarious to the slightest degree, at least, during this season of the year, and single birds or pairs were the only manner in which I saw them— usually single birds. While flying the bill is held close into the shoulders like that of the Pelican, the legs are held straight back. A few slow flaps are followed by a long glide after the fashion of the pelican also and in fact I know of no bird which this species so much resembles when on the wing. It gives the appearance of being a much larger bird on the wing than the pelican, however, and in fact the extent may be greater.

Hon. Hiram Bingham writes to me of his experience with the jabiru:

The first jabiru we saw in southwestern Venezuela was about 5 leagues south of Barinas, a town which flourished in the Colonial period. From Barinas we rode south in order to cross the Apure River at its junction with the Suripa. As I have said, about 5 leagues from Barinas we noticed a huge nest in the branches of a very tall tree. One jabiru parent and two chicks were perched on the nest and seemed to have no fear of us at all, although the parent kept up a continuous warning rattle with its long beak. We were impressed by the desolateness of this region. There was probably not a house within 10 miles of the jabiru's nest, perhaps more. There were many monkeys in the jungles near by. We saw the other jabiru parent flying back to the nest just as we were leaving the vicinity. The sight was a splendid one. His great white body glistened in the sun, in striking contrast to the red neck collar. He flew slowly and very gracefully. The next day we crossed the Paguei River, which has a jungle 2 miles wide on the south bank. A day or two later we crossed the Canagua, and on February 9, 1906, saw a large number of water fowl and perhaps a score of jabiru. I was so fortunate as to bring a jabiru down with my rifle. He measured, standing, 5 feet 10 inches from the point of his beak to his toes. The wing spread from tip to tip was 7 feet 10 inches. The beak was 12 inches long. The neck had almost no feathers, but a very tough, dark gray skin with a broad red band at its base. I took this skin with me as a trophy, but the red band soon faded out and the skin was finally lost during the course of the next three months of exploration. The body and wings were covered with beautiful white feathers, some of the wing feathers being 14 inches long. At that time these had a commercial value, so that the birds were exceedingly shy, quite as shy in fact as the egrets.   It was practically impossible to get within gunshot of them—hence the use of the rifle.   All the jabirus that I saw on the ground were standing on the low sandy banks of streams.   I was amused to notice that when the jabiru started to fly he was obliged to run along the beach for about 20 or 30 feet before taking off.   Later, when I learned to fly myself in Miami in 1917, I realized the necessity of running over the ground before taking off.   I also appreciated the difficulty the jabiru had in landing.   At the time, it seemed rather ridiculous to see this great big, beautiful flyer find it impossible to come to rest on the ground easily and gracefully, as small birds do.   Instead, he bumped and hopped along so that one got the impression his legs were about to break in pieces before he finally succeeded in stopping on the sandy shore.

DISTRIBUTION

Range.—Most of South America; accidental in the United States. A sedentary species that breeds generally throughout its normal range.   In South America the jabiru is found east to British Guiana (Georgetown) and northeastern Brazil (Para).   South to southern Brazil (San Paulo, Asuncion, and the lower Pilcomayo River) and central Argentina (Buenos Aires).   West to northwestern Argentina (Chiquinta and Chaco); Bolivia (Fortin Crevaux); Peru (Cerro de Pasco and the Ucayali River); Colombia (Meta River); and Costa Rica (La Palma, Nicoya, Rio Frio, and Miravalles).   North to Nicaragua (Escondido River); and Venezuela (Orinoco River). The species has been reported also from Mexico (Cosamaloapam in Vera Cruz); and the head of a specimen that had been taken near Austin, Texas, was donated to the Philadelphia Academy of Sciences.

Family ARDEIDAE, Herons, Bitterns, etc.

BOTAURUS LENTIGINOSUS (Montagu)

AMERICAN BITTERN

HABITS

Though nowhere especially abundant, the American bittern is widely and generally distributed over nearly all of the North American continent and adjacent islands, wherever it can find the secluded bogs and swamps, in which it leads a rather solitary existence.   It is less gregarious and more retiring in its habits than the other herons, hence less conspicuous and not so well known, even in localities where it is really common.   Doctor Coues (1874) has well described its character, as follows:

No doubt he enjoys life after his own fashion, but his notions of happiness are peculiar.   He prefers solitude, and leads the eccentric life of a recluse, "forgetting the world, and by the world forgot."   To see him at his ordinary occupation, one might fancy him shouldering some heavy responsibility, oppressed with a secret, or laboring in the solution of a problem of vital consequence.   He stands motionless, with his head drawn in upon his shoulders, and half-closed eyes, in profound meditation, or steps about in a devious way, with an absent-minded air; for greater seclusion, he will even hide in a thick brush clump for hours together. Startled in his retreat whilst his thinking cap is on, he seems dazed, like one suddenly aroused from a deep sleep; but as soon as he collects his wits, remembering unpleasantly that the outside world exists, he shows common sense enough to beat a hasty retreat from a scene of altogether too much action for him.

In spite of its peculiarities this recluse of the marshes has proved to be an interesting and an attractive object of study for many observers, perhaps on account of difficulties to be overcome in making only a slight acquaintance with it. There is a certain fascination in searching out and studying the home secrets of these shy denisons of the swamps. On a warm spring evening, when the waters are teeming with new life and the trees and shrubberies are enlivened by the migrating host of small birds, one loves to linger on its border and listen to the voices of the marsh. Many and varied are the sounds one hears at such a time. The air is full of twittering swallows, coursing back and forth in seach of their evening meal; the spirited, resonant trill of the swamp sparrow is heard in the long, tufted grass of the open spaces; the loud gurgling songs of the long-billed marsh wrens come from the cat-tail flags, where an occasional glimpse may be had of the lively little birds; from way off in the marsh the clucking, clattering voice of the Virginia rail alternates with the whinnying cry of the sora, only a few feet away. But above them all in intensity and volume are the loud, guttural pumping notes of the bittern, the weird, wild love notes of the "thunder pumper" or "stake driver."

Courtship.—The nuptial display of the American bittern, a remarkable and striking performance, has been well described by Mr. William Brewster (1911); I quote from his excellent paper on the subject as follows:

At morning and evening I have heard them pumping or have seen them flying to and fro, or standing erect with heads and necks stretched up on the watch for danger, but previous to to-day, (Apr. 17) I have paid little attention to them. Two, which I saw this morning, however, presented such a strange appearance and acted in so remarkable a manner that I watched them for half an hour or more with absorbing interest. When I first noticed them they were on the farther margin of a little lagoon where red-winged blackbirds breed, moving past it eastward almost if not quite as fast as a man habitually walks, one following directly behind the other at a distance of 15 or 20 yards. Thus, they advanced, not only rapidly, but also very evenly, with a smooth, continuous, gliding motion which reminded me of that of certain gallinaceous birds and was distinctly unheronlike. Occasionally they would stop and stand erect for a moment, but when walking they invariably maintained a crouching attitude, with the back strongly arched, the belly almost touching the ground, the neck so shortened that the lowered head and bill seemed to project only a few inches beyond the breast. In general shape and carriage, as well as in gait, they resembled pheasants or grouse much more than herons. But the strangest thing of all was that both birds showed extensive patches of what seemed to be pure white on their backs, between the shoulders.   This made them highly conspicuous and led me to conclude at first that they must be something quite new to me and probably because of their attitudes and swift gliding movements pheasants of some species with which I was unfamiliar.   Thus far I had been forced to view them with unassisted eyesight, but when I had reached the cabin and they the edge of our boat canal directly opposite it, I got my opera glass and by its aid quickly convinced myself that despite their unusual behavior and the white on their backs they could be nothing else than bitterns.

The white first appears at or very near the shoulders of the folded wings and then expands, sometimes rather quickly (never abruptly, however) but oftener very slowly until, spreading simultaneously from both sides, it forms two ruffs apparently almost if not quite equal in length and breadth to the hands of a large man but in shape more nearly resembling the wings of a grouse or quail held with the tips pointing sometimes nearly straight upward, sometimes more or less backward, also.   As they rise above the shoulders these ruffs spread toward each other at right angles to the long axis of the bird's body until, at their bases, they nearly meet in the center of the back.   Sometimes they are held thus without apparent change of area or position for many minutes at a time, during which the bird may move about over a considerable space or perhaps merely stand or crouch in the same place.   We frequently saw them fully displayed when the bitterns were "pumping" but not then more conspicuously, or in any different way, then at other times.   When the bird was moving straight toward us with his body carried low and his ruffs fully expanded he looked like a big, white rooster having only the head and breast dark colored, the breast often looking nearly black.   For in this aspect and and at the distance at which we viewed him (perhaps 200 yards) the broad ruffs, rising above and reaching well out on both sides of the back and shoulders, completely masked everything at their rear while the head and the shortened neck, being carried so low that they were seen only against the breast, added little or nothing to the visible area of dark plumage.   When he was moving away from us in the same crouching attitude the ruffs looked exactly like two white wings—nearly as broad as those of a domestic pigeon but less long—attached to either side of the back just above the shoulders.   When we had a side view of him the outline of the ruffs was completely lost and there seemed to be a band of white as broad as one's hand, extending between the shoulders quite across the back.   Thus whichever way he moved or faced the white was always shown. most conspicuously, however, when he turned toward us.

I was now joined by Miss E. R. Simmons, Miss Alice Eastwood, (the California botanist), and my assistant, R. A. Gilbert, all of whom became at once deeply interested in the birds which had stopped and were standing erect by the canal about 20 yards apart.   Suddenly both rose and flew straight at one another, meeting in the air at a height of 4 or 5 feet above the marsh.   It was difficult to make out just what happened immediately after this but we all thought that the birds came together with the full momentum of rapid flight and then, clinching in some way, apparently with both feet and bills, rose 6 or 8 feet higher, mounting straight upward and whirling around and around, finally descending nearly to the ground.   Just before reaching it they separated and sailed (not flapped) off to their former respective stations.   After resting there a few minutes the mutual attack was renewed in precisely the same manner as at first only somewhat less vigorously.   It was not repeated after this.   Although a most spirited tilt (especially on the first occasion), by antagonists armed with formidable weapons (the daggerlike bills), we could not see that any harm resulted from it to either bird. When we crossed the river in a boat some 15 minutes later both bitterns were them not infrequently placed between the bogs in the marshes that are devoid of all kinds of brush.   A rank bunch of grass that springs up in these places will most naturally be the place to look for them first, however."

R. C. Harlow writes me that he has found the American bittern "nesting regularly on the salt marshes of the coast from Cape May to Ocean County," New Jersey. William B. Crispin, of Salem, New Jersey, wrote me: "The only set I have taken contained three eggs built in a dry meadow amongst tall, blue, bent grass, with little or no nest material except a few dry grass stalks."

Several observers have noted that the bitterns usually make paths leading to and from their nests, using one as an entrance and one as an exit; and they say that the bird never flies directly from or to its nest, but runs out and flies from the end of one path in leaving and alights at the end of the other path and walks to the nest in returning.   Ira N. Gabrielson (1914) had an opportunity to watch a bittern making one of these paths which he describes as follows:

The paths were marked by a broken and trampled line of vegetation and ended in a small platform. Our boat was placed directly across the path for leaving, and we had an opportunity to watch the building of a new one. On the first visit she walked off through the wild rice to the east of the nest, grasping the upright stalks with her feet and climbing from one to another. Her weight broke numbers of them and made the beginning of the trail. After going about 25 feet, she commenced to break other stalks down and lay them in a pile. Some were already in the water and she soon had a platform capable of sustaining her weight. The reeds were seized in the beak and broken with a quick sidewise jerk of the head. When the platform was finished, she stepped upon it and stood there for a time before she flew away.

Eggs.—The American bittern lays from three to seven eggs; the set usually consists of four or five, but six eggs are often laid. The eggs are quite distinctive and are easily recognized. The shape varies from oval to elliptical ovate. The shell is smooth with a slight gloss. The color varies from "Isabella color" or "buffy brown" to "ecru olive" or "deep olive buff." The measurements of 43 eggs average 48.6 by 36.6 millimeters; the eggs showing the four extremes measure **54.2** by **38.6, 45.5** by 36, 48 by **33.5** millimeters.

Young.—The period of incubation is about 28 days and the young birds remain in the nest for about two weeks.   Mr. Gabrielson (1914) has made some very interesting observations on the behavior of young bitterns and their feeding habits, from which I quote as follows:

During the absence of the parents, however prolonged, no outcry was ever made by the young bitterns unless one of us went out of the blind and tried to touch one of them.   When we did this they backed away from us, uttering a curious hissing sound and pecking viciously at our fingers.   It was interesting to note the change in their actions after the parent left the nest.   For perhaps 10 minutes they remained in the position assumed after feeding, as described above· At the end of that time they commenced to raise their heads and look around.

still standing near the canal. Up to this time ʋoth had shown white cont
ously but it disappeared as we were approaching them. One took flight w
we were in the middle of the river. We got within 20 yards of the other bel
it moved, and then it merely walked off the marsh.

Nesting.—Strangely enough neither Wilson nor Audubon ever si
a bittern's nest. But much has been published on it since and ne:
ing bitterns have been favorite subjects for photographers. It h
often been said that the nest is hard to find, but I have never expei
enced any great difficulty in finding those for which I have looke(
I have even found as many as five in one day.

In Massachusetts the favorite nesting site seems to be in an exter
sive and rather dense cat-tail marsh, where the nest is at least pai
tially concealed among the tall dead flags (*Typha latifolia*) of th
previous year's growth. While incubation is progressing the nev
growth of green flags is going on, so that by the time the young ar(
hatched the concealment is complete. The nest consists of a practically flat platform of dead flags, a foot or more in diameter and raised
only a few inches above the surrounding water or mud. The color
of the eggs matches that of the flags almost exactly. Sometimes the
flags are arched together over the nest, but more often it is open above.
The nests are sometimes placed in other kinds of swamps or floating
bogs, where whatever nesting material is most easily available is used;
sometimes the eggs are laid on what is practically bare ground. I
once saw a nest at least 50 yards from a wet meadow; it was found
by mowing a grassy slope; the nest was concealed in the long grass,
but was on absolutely dry land, on which hay was regularly cut.

In the sloughs and meadows near Crane Lake, Saskatchewan, we
found the American bittern nesting among the cat-tail flags and
among the bulrushes (*Scirpus lacustris*). It was here that I found
the five nests in one day, referred to above, all of which were in one
slough less than a quarter of a mile square. This is at variance with
the statement I have seen in print that only one pair of bitterns
nests in a marsh. The nests were the usual platforms of dead flags
or bulrushes, to match their surroundings; the measurements of the
nests varied from 12 by 14 to 14 by 16 inches; they were built up 6
or 7 inches above the water, which was from 1 foot to 18 inches deep.
One of these bitterns sat on her nest contentedly while my companion,
Herbert K. Job, photographed her at short range. We also found a
bittern's nest here on the open meadow, near the slough, where the
grass was rather short and the ground nearly dry.

Dr. P. L. Hatch (1892) says that in Minnesota the nests "consist
of small sticks, coarse grass, with more or less leaves of sedge brush
and are placed directly on the ground in the most inaccessible bog
marshes and slough. Preferably a tuft of willowy sedge is chosen
that gives the nest a slight elevation, yet not uniformly so, for I find

For the next hour they sat contentedly on the shady side of the nest, occasionally dipping the tip of the beak into the water but never drinking anything. In the next half hour they began to grow uneasy and to keep watch for the parent. Every blackbird that flew above the nest caused each head to rise to its full height and silently watch his flight across their horizon. At times they seized each others' beaks in the same manner as the parent's was held. At other times they seized the reed stems crosswise and pulled vigorously on them, sometimes working the mandibles as if chewing. This continued until the return of the parent, when all would assemble on one side of the nest and watch her approach through the reeds. No sanitary measures were noted, and the nest became a rather unpleasant smelling place before our work was finished. At 9.55 a. m. I heard the flapping of heavy wings and the female settled down into the rushes about 20 feet from the nest. She consumed 10 minutes in covering that distance advancing a few steps and then remaining motionless for a time. When only 4 or 5 feet away, she stopped for five minutes, remaining, as far as I could see, absolutely motionless, and then, apparently satisfied, stepped up to the nest. She progressed by grasping the upright stems of the aquatic plants and when she stopped to listen looked as though she were on stilts. As soon as she reached the nest, the young commenced jumping at her beak, continuing this until one succeeded in seizing it in his beak at right angles to the base. A series of indescribable contortions followed, the head of the female being thrown jerkily in all directions and the muscles of the neck working convulsively. Finally her head and neck were placed flat on the nest for several seconds and then slowly raised again. As it came up the food came slowly up the throat into the mouth. As the food passed along the beak, the open beak of the young bird followed its course along until it slid into its mouth and was quickly swallowed. The young one then released his hold and the parent stood with the muscles of the neck twitching and jerking. The remaining young kept jumping at the beak until one secured a hold on it, when the process was repeated. By 10.30 all five of the brood had been fed. Each one after receiving the food staggered across the nest and lay down with the head and neck flat on the weeds and remained in this position for sometime before showing any signs of life again.

He says further:

An observation made in 1910 may be of some interest in this connection. While a piece of wild hay was being cut a nest of this species was uncovered and four of the five young were killed before the team could be stopped. A small patch of hay was left standing about the nest and the young one placed in it. At this time he was fully feathered out but was unable to fly. The next day the parent was noted flying into the patch of hay without anything in her beak. After she left I walked over and approached the young one, who immediately started to run. Seeing that he could not escape, he stopped and disgorged the contents of his stomach. An examination showed one garter snake about sixteen inches long, a meadow mouse and three crayfish, all partially digested. This observation seemed to prove that at this age the young were still being fed by regurgitation.

The following observation by Dr. Charles W. Townsend (1905) is of interest:

On June 26, 1904, while looking for sharp-tailed sparrows in a salt marsh reached only by the high spring and fall tides, I started a bittern that flew off with a complaining and frequently repeated quacking croak. Soon after I became conscious that a series of four stakes, projecting above the grass, was in reality the motionless necks and bills of four young bitterns. My companion noticed them too, but thought they were the remains of a shooting blind. The early age at which this protective habit was assumed is interesting, for the birds were entirely unable to fly, being only about two-thirds grown, and their scanty juvenal feathers were tipped with the fluffy natal down. When closely approached they abandoned this method of deception, snapped their bills loudly in anger, erected the feathers of their necks, spread their feeble pin-feather wings, and sprang defiantly at us, emitting a faint hissing snarl. One that I handled to examine closely, spat up great mouthfuls of small fish. The manner in which they attempted to escape was interesting. Crouching low, with necks drawn in and level with the back, they walked rapidly through the short grass, and we found one drawn up in a small bunch at the foot of the camera stand. Both the motionless and the crouching postures are the familiar protective methods used by the adults.

Plumages.—The young bittern, when first hatched, is covered on the head, back and rump with long fluffy, light buff down, "tawny olive" or "clay color"; the down on the under parts is more scanty and grayer or more whitish in color; the eyes are yellow, the bill flesh color and the feet and legs flesh color tinged with greenish.

The juvenal plumage appears at an early age, a week or 10 days, showing first on the back, scapulars and neck. By the time that the young bird is half grown it is practically fully fledged, except that the under parts are largely downy and a few shreds of down remain on the head. The juvenal plumage is much like that of the fall adult, but the crown is darker, the whole plumage is brighter colored and the black neck-ruffs are entirely lacking. The crown is dark "chestnut brown," variegated with dark "seal brown"; the back is "ochraceous tawny," tinged with "russet," sprinkled and barred with dusty markings; the buff in the wing-coverts is "yellow ochre" or "buckthorn brown." These bright colors soon fade and before the end of October the black neck-ruffs have appeared so that the young bird assumes, during its first winter, a plumage which is practically adult.

At the first postnuptial molt, the following summer and fall, the young bird becomes fully adult. This and all subsequent postnuptial molts are complete. There is little seasonal change in adult plumages; the spring plumage is grayer above and paler below, less buffy, than the fall plumage; this change is probably due to wear and fading.

Food.—The American bittern enjoys a varied diet and a large appetite, but it is no vegetarian; it will feed freely, even gluttonously, on almost any kind of animal that it can find in the marshes and meadows that it frequents or about the edges of shallow, muddy ponds. Its favorite food seems to be frogs or small fish, which it catches by skillfully spearing them with its sharp beak, as it stands in wait for them or stealthily stalks them with its slow and cautious tread. It also eats meadow mice, lizards, small snakes and eels, crayfish, various mollusks, dragon flies, grasshoppers, and other insects. Fish and other small creatures are gulped down whole, but the larger vertebrates and crustaceans are more or less crushed and broken before they are swallowed. Mr. Gabrielson (1914) describes its feeding habits as follows:

> The bittern soon came flying from the direction of the nest and dropped into the grass a short distance from me and immediately became stationary. The frogs, which were as thick here as on the other shore, soon forgot her presence and began to swim about or climb over the bogs. When one came within reach, out shot the long neck and beak and seized him. He was hammered against a bog a few times and swallowed. After securing a number in this fashion she stepped up onto a bog and went to sleep. After a short rest she flew a little way down the shore and went to hunting again. After her hunt and rest this time she flew heavily across the swamp toward the nest.

Behavior.—When disturbed at its reveries under the cover of its swampy retreat, the bittern surprises the intruder by a sudden but awkward spring into the air; with wings flopping loosely and feet dangling, it utters a croak of disgust, discharges a splash of excrement, and then gathers itself for a steady flight to a place of safety. When well under way its flight is firm and even, somewhat like that of the other herons, but stronger and with quicker beats of its smaller wings. Its flight is so slow that it is easily hit and easily killed, even with small shot; when wounded it assumes a threatening attitude of defense and is able to inflict considerable damage with its sharp beak, which it drives with unerring aim and with considerable force.

The bittern is not an active bird. It spends most of its time standing under cover of vegetation, watching and waiting for its prey, or walking slowly about in its marsh retreat, raising each foot slowly and replacing it carefully; its movements are stealthy and noiseless, sometimes imperceptibly slow, so as not to alarm the timid creatures which it hunts. When standing in the open or when it thinks it is observed, it stands in its favorite pose, with its bill pointed upward and with its body so contracted that its resemblance to an old stake is very striking; the stripes on its neck, throat, and breast blend so well with the vertical lights and shadows of the reeds and flags, that it is almost invisible. Professor Walter B. Barrows (1913) has noted an interesting refinement of this concealing action, which he has described as follows:

> The bird, an adult bittern was in the characteristic erect and rigid attitude already described and so near us that its yellow iris was distinctly visible. Then, as we stood admiring the bird and his sublime confidence in his invisibility, a light breeze ruffled the surface of the previously calm water and set the cat-tail flags rustling nodding as it passed. Instantly the bittern began to sway gently from side to side with an undulating motion which was most pronounced in the neck but was participated in by the body and even the legs. So obvious was the motion that it was impossible to overlook it, yet when the breeze subsided and the flags became motionless the bird stood as rigid as before and left us

wondering whether after all our eyes might not have deceived us. It occurred to me that the flickering shadows from the swaying flags might have created the illusion and that the rippling water with its broken reflections possibly made it more complete; but another gentle breeze gave us an opportunity to repeat the observation with both these contingencies in mind and there was no escape from the conclusion that the motion of the bittern was actual, not due to shadows or reflections, or even to the disturbance of the plumage by the wind itself. The bird stood with its back to the wind and its face toward us. We were within a dozen yards of it now and could see distinctly every mark of its rich, brown, black, and buff plumage, and yet if our eyes were turned away for an instant it was with difficulty that we could pick up the image again, so perfectly did it blend with the surrounding flags and so accurate was the imitation of their waving motion. This was repeated again and again, and when after 10 or 15 minutes we went back to our work, the bird was still standing near the same spot and in the same rigid position, although by almost imperceptible steps it had moved a yard or more from its original station.

The most characteristic performance of the bittern, for which it is best known and from which some of its names have been derived, is one in which it is more often heard than seen, its remarkable "thunder-pumping" performance. It is more frequently and more constantly heard in the spring, as a part of the nuptial performance, but it may be heard at any time during the summer and rarely in the fall. It is only within comparatively recent years that the mystery of this disembodied voice of the marshes has been thoroughly cleared up by actual observations; many erroneous theories had previously been advanced, as to how the sound was produced. Anyone who has ever skinned a male bittern in the spring, might have noticed that the skin of the neck and chest becomes much thickened and reinforced with muscular and gelatinous tissues, so that it can form a bellows for producing the loud, booming sounds. These notes have been likened to the sound made by an old wooden pump in action and to the sound made by driving a stake into soft ground; the fancied similarity of the bittern's notes to two such different sounds is not so much due to different interpretations by observers, as to the fact that there are two quite distinct renderings of the notes, by different birds or by the same bird under different circumstances. Mr. Bradford Torrey (1889) has published some valuable notes on this subject, from which I quote, as follows:

First the bird opens his bill quickly and shuts it with a click; then he does the same thing again, with a louder click; and after from three to five such snappings of the beak, he gives forth the familiar trisyllabic pumping notes, repeated from three to eight times. With the preliminary motions of the bill the breast is seen to be distending; the dilatation increases until the pumping is well under way, and as far as we could make out, does not subside in the least until the pumping is quite over. It seemed to both of us that the bird was swallowing air—gulping it down—and with it distending his crop; and he appeared not to be able to produce the resonant pumping notes until this was accomplished. It should be remarked, however, that the gulps themselves, after the first one or two at least, gave rise to fainter sounds of much the same sort. The entire performance, but especially the pumping itself, is attended with violent convulsive movements, the head and neck being thrown upward and then forward, like the night heron's when it emits its *quow*, only with much greater violence. The snap of the bill, in particular, is emphasized by a vigorous jerk of the head. The vocal result, as I say, is in three syllables; of these the first is the longest, and, as it were, a little divided from the others, while the third is almost like an echo of the second. The middle syllable is very strongly accented. The second musician, as good luck would have it, was a stakedriver. The imitation was as remarkable in this case as in the other, and the difference between the two performances was manifest instantly to both Mr. Faxon and myself. The middle syllable of the second bird was a veritable whack upon the head of a stake. I have no difficulty whatever in crediting Mr. Samuel's statement that, on hearing it for the first time, he supposed a woodman to be in the neighborhood, and discovered his error only after toiling through swamp and morass for half a mile. On this one point at least, it is easy to see why authors have disagreed. The fault has not been with the ears of the auditors, but with the notes of the different birds. During the hour or more that we sat upon the railway we had abundant opportunity to compare impressions; and, among other things, we debated how the notes to which we were listening could best be represented in writing. Neither of us hit upon anything satisfactory. Since then, however, Mr. Faxon has learned that the people of Wayland have a name for the bird (whether it is in use elsewhere I can not say) which is most felicitously onomato-poetic; namely, *plum-pudd'n'*. I can imagine nothing better. Give both vowels the sound of *u* in *full*; dwell a little upon the *plum*; put a strong accent upon the first syllable of *pudd'n'*; especially keep the lips nearly closed throughout; and you have as good a representation of the bittern's notes, I think, as can well be put into letters.

William Brewster (1902) writes:

Standing in an open part of the meadow, usually half concealed by the surrounding grasses, he first makes a succession of low clicking or gulping sounds accompanied by quick opening and shutting of the bill and then, with abrupt contortions of the head and neck unpleasantly suggestive of those of a person afflicted by nausea, belches forth in deep, guttural tones, and with tremendous emphasis, a *pump-er-lunk* repeated from two or three to six or seven times in quick succession and suggesting the sound of an old-fashioned wooden pump. All three syllables may be usually heard up to a distance of about 400 yards, beyond which the middle one is lost and the remaining two sound like the words *pump-up* or *plum-pudd'n* while at distances greater than a half mile the terminal syllable alone is audible, and closely resembles the sound produced by an axe stroke on the head of a wooden stake, giving the bird its familar appellation of "stake driver." At the height of the breeding season the bittern indulges in this extraordinary performance at all hours of the day, especially when the weather is cloudy, and he may also be heard occasionally in the middle of the darkest nights, but his favorite time for exercising his ponderous voice is just before sunrise and immediately after sunset. Besides the snapping or gulping and the pumping notes the bittern also utters, usually while flying, a nasal *haink* and a croaking *ok-ok-ok-ok*.

Winter.—The bittern migrates, as it lives, in seclusion, nor is it much more in evidence in its winter home in the Southern States and the West Indies, where its habits are similar to those of the summer and fall. It is said to be only of casual occurrence in Bermuda, but Capt. Saville G. Reid (1884) says:

A regular visitor in the autumn, and occasionally in March, frequenting the sedgy patches on the edge of the mangrove swamps. To show how plentifully they arrive in certain years, I may mention (though a cold shudder passes through me as I do so) that no less than 13 were shot by one officer, who shall be nameless, in the autumn of 1875.

Dr. Charles W. Townsend (1920) has found the bittern in Massachusetts in winter; he writes:

In the severe winter of 1917-18, on December 16, I flushed a bittern from the salt marsh near my house at Ipswich. It flew several hundred yards and alighted in a clump of tall grasses where I found it and again flushed it. There was snow on the ground and the temperature that morning was 2° Fahrenheit.

DISTRIBUTION

Breeding range.—North America from Florida and Southern California to Ungava and the Arctic Circle. East to Newfoundland (Humber River and St. Johns); Nova Scotia (Halifax); Maine (Bangor and Calais); Massachusetts (vicinity of Boston and Cape Cod); New Jersey (Trenton and Cape May); North Carolina (Raleigh); South Carolina (near Charleston); and Florida (Micanopy). South to Florida (Thonotosassa); Kansas (Witchita); Colorado (Barr and Alamosa); New Mexico (Lake Burford, probably); Arizona (Mormon Lake); and California (Alamitos, Los Angeles County). West to California (Buena Vista Lake and Stockton); Oregon (Klamath Lake, Salem, and Portland); Washington (Douglas County); and British Columbia (Vaseaux Lake, Okanagan Valley). North to Mackenzie (Willow River and Fort Rae); Manitoba (Fort Churchhill, York Factory, and the Severn River); Ungava (Fort George); and northeastern Quebec (Paradise).

Winter range.—Principally the southern and Pacific coast States, but also, Mexico and Central America, south to Panama. East to North Carolina (Pea Island and Fort Macon); Georgia (Savannah and St. Mary's); Florida (Gainsville and Kissimmee); the Bahama Islands (Nassau); and Cuba (Isle of Pines). South to Panama (Panama Railway); Costa Rica (Reventazon and Laguna de Ochomogo); Honduras (Swan Island); and Guatemala (Coban). West to western Mexico (Mazatlan); Lower California (San Jose del Cabo, Colnett, and La Paz); California (Santa Barbara, and Napa). North to Oregon (Klamath Lake); British Columbia (Pitt Meadows near Vancouver); and Idaho (Minidoka); in the Mississippi Valley (casually) to Illinois (Anna and Canton) and Indiana (Knox County and Greensburg); and on the Atlantic coast (rarely) to the District of Columbia (Washington) and Virginia (Virginia Beach). Stragglers or belated individuals from regions north of the usual winter range have been reported from New Jersey (Haddonfield, January 21, 1912); New York (Port Jefferson Harbor, January 26, 1912); and

Massachusetts (Attleboro Falls, January 16, 1901, and Ipswich, December 16, 1917).

Spring migration.—Early dates of arrival on the Atlantic coast are: Virginia, Tomsbrook, March 11; New Jersey, Norristown, March 20; Massachusetts, Boston, March 25; Maine, Deering, April 4; Nova Scotia, Pictou, April 15. In the spring in the Mississippi Valley bitterns have been reported from Missouri, Monteer, March 26; Illinois, Liter, March 28, and Chicago, March 29; Ohio, Oberlin, March 25; Wisconsin, Madison, March 30; Michigan, Detroit, March 12; and from Ontario, London, on April 12. In the Great Plains area bitterns arrive also in March and April; Kansas, Osawatomie, March 19; Nebraska, Dunbar, March 21; North Dakota, Bathgate, April 17; Manitoba, Greenridge, April 8; and Saskatchewan, Qu' Appelle, April 21. The advance through the Rocky Mountain region is a little later; Colorado, Fort Lyon, April 7, and Salida, April 16; Wyoming, Fort D. A. Russell, April 23; Montana, southwestern part, April 5, and Terry, April 23; and Alberta, Onoway, May 2.

Late dates of spring departure are: Louisiana, New Orleans, April 7; and Arkansas, Pike County, April 23.

Fall migration.—Early fall arrivals at the winter range are: South Carolina, Frogmore, August 26: Georgia, St. Mary's, September 12; Florida, Orlando, September 9; Texas, Swan, August 28, and San Angelo, September 4.

Late dates of departure on the Atlantic seaboard are: Nova Scotia, Pictou, October 24; Maine, Phillips, October 30; Massachusetts, Martha's Vineyard, November 1; New Jersey, Cape May County, November 19; and Pennsylvania, Chester County, December 8. In the Mississippi Valley: Minnesota, Minneapolis, October 6; Wisconsin, Milwaukee, November 4, and Elkhorn, November 8; Iowa, Emmetsburg, November 6; Ohio, Lakeside, October 29; Indiana, Goshen, November 1; Illinois, Rantoul, November 20; and Missouri, St. Louis, November 19. In the Great Plains area: Saskatchewan, Qu'Appelle, October 16; Manitoba, Treebank, November 6; North Dakota, Marstonmoor, November 9; and Nebraska, Long Pine, November 10. Bitterns leave the Rocky Mountain region also at late dates: Alberta, Whitford Lake, October 29; Montana, Terry, September 30; and Colorado, Mosca, October 23. An exceptionally belated individual was seen near Fort Morgan, Colorado, December 28, 1904 (Felger).

Casual records.—Stragglers from the normal range have been taken or reported from Porto Rico, Jamaica, Bermuda (Pembroke Marshes); Greenland (Egedesminde in 1809); while there are about twenty records of occurence in Great Britain. It also has been reported from Germany (near Leipzig).

Egg dates.—New England and New York: 30 records, May 12 to July 1; 15 records, May 23 to June 5. Illinois: 22 records, May 18 to June 16; 11 records, May 25 to 31. North and South Dakotas: 11 records, June 5 to July 21; 6 records, June 7 to 17. California: 11 records, April 21 to June 25; 6 records, May 23 to June 21.

IXOBRYCHUS EXILIS EXILIS (Gmelin)

LEAST BITTERN

HABITS

This pretty little bittern, the most diminutive of the heron tribe, is a summer resident in most of the United States and southern Canada. Messers. Dickey and van Rossem (1924) have recently given a new name, *Ixobrychus exilis hesperis*, to a larger race of this species inhabiting the western United States and Lower California. It is probably more widely distributed and commoner than is generally supposed, for, on account of its quiet, retiring habits it is seldom seen and less often heard by the casual observer. Like the Virginia and the sora rails, it sticks steadfastly to its chosen home in the inner recesses of the dense cat-tail and reedy marshes; even when some small piece of marsh is making its last stand against the encroachments of civilization, the bitterns and rails may still be found there, attending strictly to their own business, coming and going under the cover of darkness and unmindful of their outside surroundings. I can remember three such bits of marsh, near the centers of cities in Massachusetts, in which the rails and bitterns continued to breed until they were driven out as the marshes were filled.

Thus this quiet, retiring, and seemingly timid bird may live its listless life almost within our midst and without our knowledge, unless we choose to invade its home in the oozy bog, to wallow in mud and water and to push through the forest of cat-tails and reeds. There we may catch a glimpse of it, as it flops feebly away just over the tops of the reeds or, if we stand and watch, we may detect a gentle, swaying motion in the rushes, as a strange object appears which was not there before, like a dry and yellow flag, tapering to a long sharp point above and fading into the rushes below; now it stands stiff and still like the surrounding flags; but if we stare at it long and hard, we can see two bright yellow eyes watching us and can make out the distorted form of a bird, the hiding pose of the least bittern. How well it matches its surroundings, how well it knows that fact and how well fitted it is to survive among the tall, slender reeds and flags, one of nature's triumphs in protective mimicry!

Nesting.—The nesting habits of the least bittern vary considerably in various parts of its range, where it adapts itself to the conditions it finds in different kinds of swamps. The commonest type of nest found in Massachusetts is built in the tall, dense growths of cat-tail flags, which grow in water from 1 to 3 feet deep, rarely the latter. The nest is placed from a few inches to three or four feet, very rarely five feet, above the water. A foundation is made by bending down and interlacing the tops of the flags, on which a flimsy, flat nest of dry flags, grass, or reeds is built; this is so small, flat and apparently insecure that it seems as if it would hardly hold the eggs, but it usually proves to be quite sufficient to hold both eggs and young as long as necessary. The nest is usually placed where the flags or reeds grow very thickly and the tops are often interlaced above it for additional concealment; the nest is not conspicuous, but it can generally be recognized as a thick bunch in the reeds.

Dr. B. R. Bales (1911) gives a very good account of the nesting habits of the least bittern in an Ohio pond, as follows:

This pond, or swamp, is from one-fourth to one-half mile across and the water is from one to three feet deep. It is thickly dotted with buttonwood bushes. Wild rose thickets fringe the shores; saw grasses, tall water grasses, and calamus or sweet flag (from which the pond receives its name) are found in its shallower places and cat-tails further out. It is an ideal nesting place for this species; in June, 1907, I found 14 nests between the fourth and the twenty-first. The nests are mainly placed among the saw grasses in shallow water and are situated from 6 inches to 2½ feet above water; 18 inches is the average height. The nests are composed of saw grass blades, short lengths of smartweed stalks, slender twigs from the buttonwood, and about half the nests examined are lined with finer grasses; at the best the nests are very flimsy, frail, and loosely put together. Occasionally a nest is found composed almost entirely of a tall round water grass, but nests so composed are always built in a clump of this variety of grass. Saw grasses are usually bent over to form a platform on which to build the nest; these grasses are often bent over a small branch of buttonwood to give stability to the platform. An occasional nest is built among the diverging twigs of the buttonwood bush, much in the manner of a green heron nest, but nesting sites of this type are rare.

Dr. Clinton G. Abbott (1907) mentions a nest found in the marshes of New Jersey which "was situated in the top of a tuft of sedges which was growing on a large floating bog. It was open to the sky and almost surrounded by open water." Dr. Paul Harrington tells me of a nest, found near South Georgian Bay, which was composed entirely of small sticks, no rushes being used in its construction, and placed in a clump of rushes 3 feet above the water. I have seen nests in Texas which were made partially or wholly of fine twigs and similarly placed in cat-tail flags. Julian K. Potter has sent me several photographs of least bitterns' nests, taken near Camden, New Jersey; one of these was in a buttonbush (*Cephalanthus*) and was made of sticks, laid radially, like the spokes of a wheel; another was prettily situated in a clump of arrow head lily (*Sagittaria*).

In Florida we found the least bittern fairly common, nesting in the big saw-grass marshes and in the smaller bogs and sloughs, where the big, sleek boat-tailed grackles, in their glistening black plumage, were swinging on the reed tops and pouring out their curious half-musical notes, where the bubbling notes of the marsh wrens greeted us from the dense growth below and where the deadly moccasin lurked in the morass under foot. Had we cared to explore such places more thoroughly we doubtless could have found many more nests. In a small slough, about 30 yards square, on Merritt's Island, full of large tussocks of tall grass, as high as a man's head, we found two nests of the least bittern and five nests of the boat-tailed grackle. The bitterns nests were merely crude platforms or shallow baskets of coarse straws and grasses in the densest parts of the large tussocks. One was 24 and one 30 inches above the shallow water; the nests measured 7 by 4 and 7 by 5 inches, and held four eggs each on April 26.

Near Brownsville, Texas, we found several nests of the least bittern on May 23, 1923, in a marshy pond where the Mexican grebes were nesting. The bitterns' nests were in small clumps of tall cattail flags; some were the usual nests of dead flags and others were partially or wholly made of twigs of the water huisache, which was growing in the pond. George Finlay Simmons (1915a) describes another Texas nest, as follows:

The nest was supported by several rushes, dead reeds, and the broken stem of a small persimmon sapling growing in the pond. At this point the reeds and rushes were not so thick, and the nest and eggs could easily be seen at a distance of 15 or 20 feet. The bottom of the nest just touched the water, which was there about 18 inches deep. The nest itself was quite firmly built, with few loose ends projecting from the mass. It was built entirely of straight stems and twigs of a brushy reed which grows about the ponds, quite different from the flexible reeds and rushes used in the construction of the nests of the other water birds of the region. It measured about 6½ inches across the top and 5 inches high, being cone shaped and tapering towards the bottom. So flat was the top of the nest that it seemed the slightest jar would cause the eggs to roll off, for there were no rushes or grasses to guard the sides of the nest as in the case of the rails and gallinules.

Eggs.—The least bittern lays ordinarily four or five eggs, sometimes six and very rarely seven. Richard C. Harlow writes to me:

I have examined probably 50 of their nests; probably 70 per cent of the complete sets are five in number, though I have inspected seven nests holding sets of six and one of seven, all undoubtedly laid by the same bird.

The eggs are quite uniformly oval in shape, rarely showing a tendency towards elliptical oval or ovate. The shell is smooth but not glossy. The color is bluish white or greenish white. The measurements of 58 eggs average 31 by 23.5 millmeters; the eggs showing the four extremes measure **33** by **25**, **28** by 23.5 and 29 by **22.5** millimeters.

Young.—Both sexes incubate and the period of incubation is said to be 16 or 17 days. Ira N. Gabrielson (1914) gives a very good account of how the parents brood over and feed their young, which he observed from a blind, as follows:

One or the other of the parents kept the nest covered throughout the day and both assumed the same position. They sat on the nest with the wings spread in such a manner as to give the body a curious flattened appearance while the head and neck were extended to their full length with the beak pointing straight in the air. Occasionally the head was lowered for an instant to examine the young but almost immediately was raised again. Every bird that flew by was watched and every movement in the surrounding vegetation seemed to be noted by the bird on the nest. This position had the advantage of elevating the eyes some distance above the nest and gave the bird a better view of what was going on around. I was curious to see how these newly hatched young would get their food; to see if they were fed as the young American bitterns had been. At 10.50 the bright colored little male alighted on the platform behind the nest and stood there watching the female who was on the nest. From time to time he allowed the beak to hang open and shook his head in a comical way. After he had been doing this for 10 minutes, the female stepped from the nest and flew away. The male took her place and stood, still shaking his head. All of the brood, including the one just hatched, were jumping at his beak. Finally one of them succeeded in securing a hold on it and pulled his head down toward the nest. His beak was seized at right angles by that of the young as in the case of the American bittern. Instead of the violent contortions which preceded the act of regurgitation in the other species, a few convulsive jerks of the throat and neck muscles brought the food into the mouth, from which it passed into that of the young in the same manner as before. The food instead of being in a compact mass was more of a liquid containing pieces of small frogs and occasionally whole ones. These nestlings had not yet become proficient in their strange manner of feeding and more or less of the food material fell into the nest. When this happened, the young which were not receiving food at the time seized it and swallowed it. When two secured a hold on the same frog, an exciting tug of war followed until one or the other was victorious. All five young were fed at each visit, and it seemed to be as instinctive for them to jump at the beak of the parent as it is for other young birds to raise the opened beak. During the day the male and female alternated in the care of the nest but the brooding periods of the latter were much the longer. She seldom remained away any length of time. On the other hand the male did all the feeding, four times, during the day. The female evidently hunted only for her own food during her absences from the nest while the male foraged for both the nestlings and himself. Both parents did their hunting on an extensive mud flat about 200 yards from the nest.

Doctor Bales (1911) says of the behavior of young least bitterns:

Another nest discovered the same day contained six young in which the pinfeathers were showing. It is doutful if this nest would have been discovered, had I not seen one of the young birds clinging to one of the round water grasses fully a foot above the nest. While perched upon the slender, swaying water grass, they have a peculiarly pert and saucy look that is ludicrous in the extreme They are excellent climbers and use their long necks and bills in climbing by hooking the head over the perch and using it as a sort of hook to aid them in scrambling up, The feet are very strong. The young in this nest tried to peck my hand as I placed it above them; they acted like trained soldiers, all pecking at exactly the same time, as if at a word of command.

Plumages.—The downy young least bittern is well covered on the head and back with long, soft, buffy down, "ochraceous buff" to "light ochraceous buff"; the under parts are more scantily covered with paler, more whitish down.

In the juvenal plumage the sexes are much alike, but the crown is darker in the young male and the dusky shaft streaks on the throat, breast and wing coverts are more conspicuous in the young female. The juvenal plumage closely resembles that of the adult female; but the crown and back are somewhat lighter brown, the feathers of the back and scapulars are edged or tipped with buffy, and the buff feathers with dusky shaft streaks give the throat and breast a striped appearance; the buffy, lesser wing coverts also have dusky shaft streaks. The buffy edgings of the dorsal feathers generally wear away before October, leaving the back clear brown; but the juvenal wing coverts are more or less persistent, especially in females, until the first postnuptial molt the next summer. At this complete molt in August young birds become indistinguishable from adults. There is apparently no well-marked seasonal difference in the plumages of adults, but the sexual difference becomes apparent during the first spring and is well marked thereafter.

It now seems to be generally conceded that the dark form, known as the Cory least bittern, *Ixobrychus neoxenus* (Cory), is not a distinct species, but a case of melanism or erythrism, such as occasionally occurs in other species of birds and animals. Some 30 specimens have been recorded; the largest numbers have been taken in Florida and Ontario; but it has also been taken in Massachusetts, New York, Ohio, Illinois, Michigan, and Wisconsin. It is a striking case of high pigmentation which seems likely to turn up almost anywhere within the range of the least bittern, and it is sometimes combined with traces of albinism. It should not be called a color phase of a dichromatic species, as it occurs too rarely and irregularly. A dichromatic species, it seems to me, is one in which two color phases occur regularly, such as in the reddish egret, the parasitic jaeger, and the screech owl.

Since writing the above I have been much interested in what Oscar E. Baynard has told me about the Cory least bittern. He has had considerable field experience with it, has found several nests and is firmly convinced that it is a distinct species. He says that these dark colored birds never mate with ordinary least bitterns, but always with birds of their own kind, breeding true to color. He also says that the downy young are coal black, "as black as young rails," that all the young in the nest are also black and that he has never seen any buff colored young in the same nest with the black ones. If these facts hold true in all cases they are strong evidences of the validity of the species.

Food.—The least bittern is an active feeder, walking stealthily about in the marshes and bogs, and hunting for the various forms of animal life found in such places. One that Audubon (1840) had in captivity was "expert at seizing flies, and swallowed caterpillars, and other insects." He has also found "small shrews and field mice" in its stomach. Small fishes tadpoles, and small frogs probably make up a large part of its food; but lizards, snails, slugs, leeches, beetles, and other insects are included. One that C. J. Maynard (1896) had in captivity killed and devoured a pet humming bird.

Behavior.—When surprised or suddenly flushed the least bittern rises in weak and awkward, fluttering flight, with neck extended and feet dangling, usually dropping down into the marsh again at a short distance; but when going somewhere on a long flight, it draws in its head and extends its legs behind, after the manner of the herons, and proceeds with a strong, direct flight which may be quite protracted and rather swift. If not too much hurried, it seems to prefer to escape by walking, or climbing, through the reeds, at which it is very expert and makes remarkable speed. Where the water is too deep to wade and where the reeds grow close together the bittern walks, or even runs, through them at a height of 2 or 3 feet above the water, grasping a single upright reed or two or three of them together with each foot; often it is a wide, straddling gait, with many long strides; it is accomplished with so much speed, skill, and accuracy as to seem little short of marvellous; like a squirrel in the tree tops, or a marsh wren in the reeds, there seems to be never a slip or a missed step. When wading in shallow water, or walking on land, its movements are quick and graceful, its head shooting forward at each step. To facilitate its passage through the narrow spaces between the reeds, its has the power of compresing its body laterally; Audubon (1840) found by experiment that it would compress its body sufficiently to pass through a space 1 inch wide.

The well known hiding pose, or reedlike attitude, of the least bittern is well described by Dr. Arthur A. Allen (1915), as follows:

I parted the flags and counted the eggs before I finally perceived that there, on the back of the nest and in perfectly plain sight, stood the female bird less than 3 feet from my eyes. Under other circumstances, I should not have called it a bird, such was the strangeness of the shape which it had assumed. The photograph showing the "reed posture" gives one but a poor conception of the bird's real appearance at this time. The feathers were fairly glued to the body, and the head and neck appeared no thicker than some of the dried reeds that composed the nest. The bill, pointing directly upward, widened barely appreciably into the head and neck, and the feathers of the lower neck were held free from the body and compressed to as narrow a point as the bill at the other end. The neck appeared to be entirely separate from the body, which was flattened so as to become but a part of the nest itself. There was not a movement, not even a turning of the serpentlike eyes which glared at me over the corners of the mouth. Every line was stiff and straight, every curve was an angle. It mattered not that all about the vegetation was a brilliant green, while the bird was buffy brown. It was no more a bird than was the nest below it. I recalled the habit of the American bittern of rotating so as always to keep its striped neck towards the observer, and I moved slowly to another side of the nest. But this bird was not relying upon the color of its neck to conceal it. It was quite as unbirdlike from any angle, and it moved not a feather.

But this was not its only method of concealment, as was shown a few minutes later. I parted the flags directly in front of the bird, to see how close an approach it would permit. My hands came within 12 inches of it before it melted away over the back of the nest. Its movements were apparently very deliberate, and yet almost instantaneously it disappeared into the flags. It did not go far, and in a very few minutes it came back. Very slowly it pushed its vertical neck and upturned bill between the flags until it just fitted the space between two of the upright stalks at the back of the nest. No longer were the feathers drawn closely to the neck, which was at this time the only part visible. Instead, they were shaken out to their fullest expanse, and hung square across the base, instead of pointed. The dark feathers arranged themselves into stripes, and simulated well the shadows between the flags. Again I moved around the nest, and this time, instead of remaining motionless, the bird also rotated so as always to present its striped front to me and conceal its body. This was evidently a second and entirely different stratagem.

The same careful observer says of the notes of the male:

His notes were guttural and dovelike, or even froglike when heard in the distance, resembling the syllables, *uh-uh-uh-oo-oo-oo-oo-oooah*, similar to one of the calls of the pied-billed grebe. The call, when given close at hand, often drew a response from the female of two or three short notes, like the syllables *uk-uk-uk*.

Docter Chapman (1900) describes the notes of the least bittern as: "A soft, low *coo*, slowly repeated five or six times, and which is probably the love song of the male; an explosive alarm note, *quoh*; a hissing *hah*, with which the bird threatens a disturber of its nest; and a low *tut-tut-tut*, apparently a protest against the same kind of intrusion."

William Brewster (1902) writes:

Nor do we often hear its voice save during a brief period at the height of the breeding season when the male, concealed among the rank vegetation of his secure retreats, utters a succession of low, cooing sounds varying somewhat in number as well as in form with different birds or even with the same individual at different times. The commoner variations are as follows: *Coo, hoo-hoo-hoo* (the first and last syllables slightly and about evenly accented), *coo-coo, coo-hoo-hoo* (with distinct emphasis on the last syllable only), *co-co-co-co, co-co-ho-ho* or *co-ho-ho* (all without special emphasis on any particular syllable). These notes are uttered chiefly in the early morning and late afternoon, usually at rather infrequent intervals but sometimes every four or five seconds for many minutes at a time. When heard at a distance they have a soft, cuckoolike quality; nearer the bird's voice sounds harder and more like that of the domestic pigeon, while very close at hand it is almost disagreeably hoarse and raucous as well as hollow and somewhat vibrant in tone. Besides this cooing the least bittern occasionally emits, when startled a loud, cackling *ca-ca-ca-ca*.

Enemies——Young least bitterns have many enemies, birds of prey and crows overhead, predatory animals prowling through the marshes and crawling reptiles in the mud and water. From these enemies the young birds are partially successful in escaping by their ability in climbing and hiding among the reeds. Crows undoubtedly destroy a great many eggs and even the diminutive long-billed marsh wren punctures the eggs, perhaps maliciously. Docter Chapman (1900) found that some of the eggs, in two nests he was watching, had "been punctured, as if by an awl," and afterward saw a long-billed marsh wren puncture the remaining eggs; apparently the contents of the eggs were not eaten by the wren.

DISTRIBUTION

Breeding range.—Central America, the United States and southern Canada. East to New Brunswick (St. John); Maine (Portland); Massachusetts (Essex County); New York (Rockaway); New Jersey (Cape May); District of Columbia (Washington); North Carolina (Pea Island and Lake Ellis); South Carolina (Charleston and Frogmore); Florida (Titusville); and Porto Rico (San Juan). South to Porto Rico (San Juan); Jamaica (Port Henderson); southwestern Guatemala (Duenas); and central Mexico (Toluca and Lake Patzcuaro). West to western Mexico (Mazatlan); Lower California (Purissima); California (Santa Monica and Stockton); and Oregon (Tule Lake). North to Oregon (Tule Lake); North Dakato (Kenmare); Minnesota (White Earth and Minneapolis); Michigan (Grand Rapids and Detroit); southern Ontario (Mildmay, Coldwater, Toronto, and Ewart); and New Brunswick (St. John).

It has also been recorded in summer from Nova Scotia (Halifax); Panama (Lion Hill Station); Southern Saskatchewan (Crane Lake); Manitoba (Lake Manitoba and Shoal Lake) and from Quebec.

Winter range.—Florida, islands of the Caribbean Sea and Central and South America south to Patagonia. East to Florida (Micanopy); the Bahama Islands (Nassau); Cuba (Isle of Pines); British Guiana (Georgetown); and Brazil (Iguape). South to Paraguay (Asuncion); and Chile (Valdivia). West to Peru (Lima); central Mexico (Valley of Mexico and Lake Patzcuaro); to the west coast (Tepic). North to central Arizona (Fort Verde, Yavapai County); Florida (Micanopy); and Georgia (Athens).

Belated migrants or winter stragglers have been seen or taken at points much farther north: Rhode Island (Providence, March 1 and February 28, 1881); Nova Scotia (Halifax, March 16, 1896); Michigan (Detroit, November 6, 1919); and Ontario (Point Pelee, November 28, 1894).

Spring migration.—Early dates of arrival are: Georgia, Savannah, March 6; South Carolina, Frogmore, April 5; North Carolina, Manteo, April 20; District of Columbia, Washington, April 27; Pennsylvania, Limerick, April 22; New Jersey, Long Beach, April 1, and Camden, April 22; New York, near New York City, April 10, Rhinebeck, May 13, and Rochester, May 6; and Massachusetts, Essex County, April 15. In the Mississippi Valley: Louisiana, Rigolets, March 11, and New Orleans, April 9; Missouri, Jonesburg, April 20, and Alexandria, April 19; Illinois, Peoria, April 17, and Chicago, April 24; Indiana, Waterloo, April 7; Ohio, Painesville, April 9, Cleveland, April 13, Oberlin, April 25, and Sandusky, April 25; Michigan, Battle Creek, April 10, and Grand Rapids, April 17; Ontario, Point Pelee, May 13, and Guelph, May 17; Iowa, Cedar Rapids, April 28; Wisconsin, Berlin, April 1, and Sparta, April 11; Minnesota, Elk River, April 17, Wilder, May 2, and Heron Lake, May 9. In the Great Plains area: Texas, Corpus Christi, April 5, and Gainesville, April 25; Kansas, Elmsdale, April 26; Nebraska, Turlington, May 6; South Dakota, Sioux Falls, May 11.

In the Rocky Mountain region the spring arrivals are generally later: Colorado, South Park, May 14; Wyoming, Fossil, May 21; and Montana, Great Falls, May 16. The species arrives in southern California late in March and early in April (near Escondido, March 28); but it is not until after the middle of May that southern Oregon is reached (Klamath Lake, May 21).

Fall migration.-Late dates of fall departure on the Atlantic seaboard are: Quebec, Montreal, September 2; Massachusetts, East Templeton, October 27, and Newburyport, September 12; Rhode Island, near Middletown, September 14, and Providence, September 30; Connecticut, New Haven, September 22; New York, Verona, September 1, and Duchess County, September 11; Pennsylvania, Erie, September 25; District of Columbia, Washington, September 25; and North Carolina, Raleigh, September 11. In the Mississippi Valley the dates for departure are somewhat later: Ontario, Ottawa, September 1, and Point Pelee, September 2; Michigan, Ann Arbor, October 1, and Vicksburg, October 2; Ohio, Sandusky, October 3, and Cedar Point, October 17; Indiana, Waterloo, October 1; Illinois, Warsaw, October 10: Wisconsin, Madison, September 23, and North Freedom, October 10; Iowa, Indianola, October 18; South Dakota, Sioux Falls, October 8; Nebraska, Lincoln, September 20, and Belvidere, October 5; Texas, Corpus Christi, September 29; and California, Dunlap, September 24.

Casual records.—Stragglers north of the normal range have been reported from Manitoba (Oak Point, Lake Manitoba, October 20, 1907, Shoal Lake, June 1901, and York Factory, 1879).

The color phase of the least bittern that has been known as Cory's Least Bittern, *Ixobrychus neoxenus*, has been found breeding in southern Florida (Lake Okeechobee, Lake Flirt, and Fort Thompson) and in Southern Ontario (Toronto). It has been taken or reported in spring from Massachusetts, Scituate, May 18, 1901; Ohio, Toledo, May 25, 1907; Michigan, St. Clair Flats, May 14, 1904; and Wisconsin, Lake Koshkonong, May 22, 1893. The only fall record outside of the breeding area is from near Manchester, Michigan, August 8, 1894.

Egg dates.—Southern New England and New York: 30 records May 20 to June 23; 15 records, May 29 to June 11. Michigan and Wisconsin: 32 records, May 27 to July 1; 16 records, May 30 to June 12. Illinois: 35 records, May 22 to July 10; 18 records, May 30 to June 21. Florida: 22 records, March 25 to June 26; 11 records, April 26 to June 5.

ARDEA OCCIDENTALIS Audubon

GREAT WHITE HERON

HABITS

The Bay of Florida, including Barnes Sound, which is really a part of it, is a practically triangular body of water, approximately 35 miles long and 25 miles wide, bounded on the north by the southern coast of Florida, from Cape Sable on the west to the entrance to Blackwater Bay on the east, bounded on the south by the outer line of keys, and open on the west toward the Gulf of Mexico. Throughout its whole area the water is exceedingly shallow, averaging not over 3 feet in depth; the bottom is covered with white, soapy, slimy mud, which makes the water generally turbid and mostly opaque. At low tide many square miles of mud flats are exposed, leaving only an intricate maze of winding channels open to navigation in shallow draft vessels, and even at high tide a thorough knowledge of the channels is necessary to avoid running aground in a boat drawing over 2 feet of water.

The outer keys, forming the southern boundary, are mostly of coral formation and were probably the first to appear, inclosing an area in which mud and sand has accumulated and made possible the formation of the mangrove keys with which the whole interior of the bay is thickly studded. The inner keys are nearly all of the mangrove type, though many of the larger and older ones have now accumulated sandy beaches and considerable solid, dry soil. Their origin, however, is directly traceable to the agency of the red mangrove and all stages of their development can be seen in process of formation. The red mangrove drops its seed into the water, where it floats away until its long tail strikes root in some shallow place; as the tree grows, its spreading branches are constantly reaching outward and downward to take root again, until a dense thicket or "bush," as it is called, is formed; this increases steadily in size, soil is eventually accumulated in its center, where the red mangroves finally die out and are replaced by black mangroves growing in muddy soil; as the soil becomes drier by continued accumulation, the black mangroves are again replaced by other tree and shrubs, growing on dry land and often forming dense thickets; on some of the largest and oldest keys, open grassy plains have been formed with only scattering trees or clumps of bushes around their borders.

These mangrove keys or islands, particularly the larger ones, are favorite resorts of the great white heron, and here we found them in abundance. The broad mud flats covered with shallow water form their feeding grounds. As we cruised along the main channels we could see the great white birds standing in the water several miles away, often at a long distance from any land, dignified and motionless, until induced to move by the rise and fall of the tide or by our approach when they would leisurely depart for some more distant shoal. In such situations a near approach was impossible; 200 or 300 yards was about as near as we could come. Sometimes as many as a dozen or 15 birds were in sight at one time, generally scattered about, singly or in small groups, and often in company with brown pelicans, with which they seem to be on good terms.

Fish of various kinds are sufficiently plentiful in these shallow waters to support, in addition to the herons, large numbers of brown pelicans, Florida cormorants, man-o-war birds and royal terns, some of which were almost constantly in sight. When not fishing, the great white herons could be seen perched in small groups on the red mangroves which form the outer boundaries of nearly all the keys, their pure white plumage standing out in marked contrast against the dark green foliage, making them clearly visible at a distance of several miles, one of the most striking features of this mangrove archipelago. But the keenness of their vision and their extreme shyness afforded them all the protection necessary, for every attempt to sail up to them proved a failure; a fleeting picture of great white birds was all we ever saw, as, with slowly measured wing strokes, with heads drawn over their shoulders and long legs stretched out straight behind, they flew away to some far distant key.

Our chances of securing any seemed hopeless until we discovered their roosting place on one of the larger keys, to which we had traced their line of flight. I had been wading along through the outer strip of red mangroves in which I had seen them perched and had tramped through the black mangrove forest back of them where the crackling of sticks, as I picked my way through the tangled roots, had alarmed them, but not a bird had I seen through the dense foliage; the swish of their wings and their hoarse croaks of alarm were all that told me they had gone. That effort proving fruitless, I struggled through the tangled thickets toward the center of the island and came unexpectedly upon an open grassy plain surrounded by small trees and clumps of bushes. It was a beautiful sight that rewarded my efforts, for there were a dozen or more of the great white herons and a few Ward herons perched on the tops of the trees and larger bushes. They were on the alert and all took wing instantly, but I concealed myself and awaited their return. I had not long to wait before they began to circle back over me; two of them came dangerously near and I brought down one with each barrel, a fine pair of adult birds. But that was my last chance—they were too wary to return that day.

We found similar localities on other islands which proved equally attractive as roosting or nesting places for these herons and to which they seemed equally attached; and it was only in such places that we succeeded in securing any specimens. They are certainly the shyest of all the herons and are in no danger of extermination.

Nesting.—Scattering nests of great white or Ward herons were found on many of the larger keys or islands; most of them were empty, however, and so not identified. Only once, on April 29, 1903, did we find anything approaching a colony. This was on one of the Oyster Keys, a small mangrove key having a little dry land in the center on which a few black mangroves were growing with a dense thicket of underbrush, vines and small trees; it was surrounded by a broad belt of large red mangroves stretching away out into the water which was nearly waist deep under some of the trees.

We had seen the great white herons fly away as we approached, but not one came near us while we were in the rookery, though a Ward heron, which had a nest with young, frequently came within gunshot. Besides several empty nests scattered about the island, from which the young had probably flown, we found a little colony of four occupied nests of the great white heron and one of the Ward heron, all of which were grouped about a little inlet in rather large red mangroves. A nest, containing two addled eggs and one young bird recently hatched, was placed on the outer branches overhanging the center of the inlet; it was a large, flat, well-made structure of large sticks firmly interwoven, measuring 35 inches by 25 inches externally; the inner cavity measured about 15 inches in diameter and was smoothly lined with small twigs and dry mangrove leaves; the young bird, which was scarcely able to hold up its head, was scantily covered with white filamentous down. The young of this species are always pure white at all ages, by which they can be easily distinguished from the gray young of the Ward heron. Another nest, 15 feet from the ground in a red mangrove, contained two young birds about one-quarter grown and one egg; the young were covered with white down and hairlike feathers. Within a few yards of the first nest, across an open space in the inlet, were two more nests. One of these was about 12 feet above the water on the extremity of a red mangrove branch and was similar in size and construction to the first; it contained three very lively young birds, about half grown and well covered with white down and feathers; they protested vigorously at my intrusion, bristling up their plumage, squawking, snapping their bills and striking at anything within reach while their throats were vibrating as if panting from fear or excitement. The nest, the surrounding branches and the ground under it, were profusely whitewashed with the excrement of the young, as is generally the case with all of the herons.

The other nest illustrated the last chapter in the development of the young, which were nearly ready to fly. It was 20 feet above the water on the outer end of a leaning red mangrove and the two large white birds in it could be plainly seen from the ground; when I climbed the tree one of them stood up in the nest and posed gracefully for his picture. They were practically fully grown and fully feathered, pure white all over and lacking only the crest plumes and the plumelike feathers on the back of adult birds, which I believe are not acquired until the second nuptial season.

On March 27, 1908, I found, on Clive Key, in this same region, a nest of the great white heron placed within 3 feet of the ground on a low branch of a black mangrove near the center of the island; it contained three small young covered with white down. I was informed by the resident plume hunters that the great white herons raise two broods each season, one in January and one in April, but I am more inclined to think that the breeding season is prolonged over a period of four or five months and that only one brood is raised by each pair. We found a number of empty nests that showed signs of recent occupancy and saw plenty of immature birds on the wing in March. Ernest G. Holt found young birds as large as adults and nearly ready to fly on December 28, 1923; these eggs must have been laid in October.

Eggs.—The eggs of the great white heron are not readily distinguishable from those of the Ward heron in size or color; they are of the usual heron's egg color, pale bluish green, or "pale olivine." The measurements of 40 eggs average 61.1 by 42.4 millimeters; the eggs showing the four extremes measure 71 by 47, 66.5 by 48.8, 51.7 by 35.5, and 52.7 by 34.2 millimeters.

Plumages.—The young great white heron is clothed like the young great blue heron, except that its down and plumage is wholly white at all ages. The sequence of plumages and molts is also the same in both species. The plumage of the head, neck and body is acquired in about that order; these parts are fully feathered by the time the bird is two-thirds grown and before the wings are fully developed. Young birds remain in the nest until fully grown and by this time the wings are complete. The juvenal plumage, which is entirely devoid of plumes on the head, breast, and back is worn for about a year. During the second fall, when the young bird is over a year old, a plumage is apparently assumed which is much like the adults at that season; but the fully adult plumage is probably not acquired until the following spring or fall, at 2 years of age, or later. Adults have a complete molt in summer and fall and a partial molt, which does not include the wings and tail, in winter and spring. The prenuptial molt produces a higher development of the long plumelike feathers of the head, breast, and back in the spring than is seen in fall birds, but these plumes are more or less present at all seasons in adults.

Observations on this species would be incomplete without some reference to the hypothetical species which has been named Würdemann's heron (*Ardea wuerdemanni* Baird) and has been the subject of so much discussion and so many theories as to its status. This bird was first described by Baird in 1858 as a distinct species, but later developments suggested its relationship to *A. occidentalis* Audubon, or to *A. wardi* Ridgway, or to both. Later Mr. Ridgway (1880) published the following note based on observations made by Dr. J. W. Velie of the Chicago Academy of Sciences.

In his reply to my letter he makes this very interesting and, in view of certain curious facts which I have already brought to notice, very suggestive statement, that in two instances, once in 1872 and again in 1875, he found about half grown young, one each of *A. occidentalis* and *A. wuerdemanni*, in the same nest. This evidence is all that was needed to settle the question of the identity of the two forms in question, and there can now be no doubt that they represent two phases of one species, bearing to one another exactly the same relation as that between *Ardea rufescens*, Bodd., and *A. pealei*, Bonap.

While collecting in the Florida Keys with Dr. Frank M. Chapman and Louis A. Fuertes, we found on March 27, 1908, on Clive Key, a large heron's nest containing three young herons, two of which were apparently Ward herons and one a great white heron. Doctor Chapman photographed the nest and preserved all of the young, which are now in the American Museum of Natural History in New York. Near this nest Doctor Chapman shot a fine speciman of *Ardea wuerdemanni* and I shot typical specimens of both *A. occidentalis* and *A. herodias wardi*, as it is now called, as well as specimens in immature plumage which showed characters somewhat intermediate between the last two forms. I do not consider the finding of these young herons or those found by Doctor Velie conclusive evidence of dichromatism, for it is possible, and even probable that these two species occasionally lay in each others nests, or hybridize, as they are very closely related and on very friendly terms where their ranges overlap and where they nest in communites in close proximity to each other.

Ernest G. Holt made a very thorough study of this group of herons in the same region, during the winter of 1923–24, and has kindly placed his unpublished notes at my disposal. He summarizes the contents of the nests examined as follows:

A total of 40 nests were examined on Buchanan, Barnes, Bowlegs, Clive, and Oyster Keys, and an unnamed key near the last, and found to contain 48 young whites, 38 young blues, and 31 eggs. Forty-seven of the white nestlings were found on Buchanan, Barnes, and Bowlegs Key; one on east Oyster Key. Eighteen blue nestlings lived on Buchanan and Barnes Keys; 20 on the Cape Sable group. Among the adult birds was shown the same tendency of the great whites to predominate on the lower Keys, and of the big blues to be more numerous on the upper. Of the 40 nests examined, 3 held mixed broods of white and blue birds in the ratio of 2:1, 2:2, and 2:1. The first had a blue parent, the second a white parent; the parent of the last was not seen. The mixed broods were found on Buchanan and Barnes Keys, but all the adult blues, collected on any of the keys, showed admixtures of white blood.

It has been stated that the great white heron and the Ward heron are exactly alike in form, size and proportions, the only difference being in color. This generally accepted statement has strengthened the theory that they are merely color phases of one species. Mr. Holt has made a careful study and comparison of 24 great white herons, 24 Ward herons, and 10 Würdemann herons, all breeding adults, which throws considerable new light on this subject. He finds that a "noticeable feature of the white birds is the great reduction, often total absence, of the occipital plumes. Only 9 of the 24 birds have plumes over 100 millimeters in length, whereas more than half have no plumes at all. These plumes, when present; are wide at the base and taper to a fine point—a form perhaps best described as long acuminate—lanceolate—and are quite different from the two long ligulate occipital plumes of *Ardea herodias wardi*." Referring to his tables of measurements we find that the average length of these plumes in 24 specimens of *occidentalis* is 97.3 millimeters, the longest in any individual being 192 millimeters; the average length in 24 specimens of *wardi* is 177.8 millimeters, the longest in any individual being 230 millimeters; this leaves an average difference between the two species of 80.5 millimeters, or more than 3 inches.

The scapular and jugular plumes of the great white also show a tendency to reduction, when compared with similar structures of Ward's heron.

A small but distinct difference between *occidentalis* and *wardi* in absolute and proportionate size of bill is indicated by the measurements of the six fully adult *occidentalis* in hand, when compared with similar measurements tabulated by Oberholser (1912) for six entirely comparable Florida specimens of *wardi*. The average lengths of wing, tail, and tarsus in this series are greater for *wardi* than for *occidentalis*, whereas the bill averages longer and thicker. When the length of culmen is divided by the length of tarsus, the quotient gives an index of proportion that is very constant, and which quite sharply separates the two species, the index for *wardi* falling always definitely below that of *occidentalis*.

Referring to the specimens examined of the so-called *wuerdemanni*, he finds that the above characters are intermediate between the two species and show a tendency to approach the characteristics of the species to which the specimen seems to be the most closely related.

In the light of the above facts, there seems to be little, if any, evidence to support the color phase theory and much to support

that of hybridism.   Hybridism would seem to account satisfactorily
for the various specimens of *wuerdemanni* which have been taken,
especially if we assume, as seems reasonable, that hybrids between
such closely related species are fertile and might interbreed with pure-
blooded birds of either species, producing a great variety of intermediate specimens.   A parallel case can be seen in the hybrids between
the black duck and the mallard.

I can not understand how anyone who is familiar with the great
white heron in life can have any doubt that it is a distinct species.
It is a strictly maritime species, its habitat is decidedly restricted and
its behavior is quite different from that of the Ward heron, with which
it mingles in the Florida Keys and doubtless interbreeds.

Food.—The food of the great white heron seems to consist almost
entirely of fish, which it obtains in the shallow waters of the broad
bays and estuaries where it lives, always in salt water, I believe.   A
number of these stately birds are often in sight at one time scattered
about singly, or in groups, over the shoals and mud flats, often a long
distance from the shore.   I have never seen this heron walk about
when feeding as the others all do; it stands in patient, quiet dignity,
like a great white statue, waiting for its prey.   When its appetite is
satisfied, or when the tide drives it from the flats, it flies off to some
favorite roosting place on an island fringed with mangroves, where it
rests among the dark green foliage until it is time to feed again.

Probably other marine animal food is taken as well as fish.   It has
a voracious appetite; Audubon (1840) mentions that two captive
young birds "swallowed a bucketful of mullets in a few minutes, each
devouring a gallon of these fishes."   They also killed and swallowed
entire some young reddish egrets and Louisiana herons "although
they were abundantly fed on the flesh of green turtles."   Again he
says: In the evening or early in the morning, they would frequently
set, like pointer dogs, at moths which hovered over the flowers, and
with a well-directed stroke of their bill seize the fluttering insect and
and instantly swallow it."   They also killed and devoured young
chickens and ducks.

Behavior.—The experiences which Audubon (1840) and others have
had with great white herons in captivity show them to be always
wild, untamable, and vicious, quite different in disposition from great
blue herons which are gentle and easily tamed.   The white birds had
to be separated from the blue ones or the former would have killed
the latter.   Even then, one of the white herons thrust his bill between
the bars of the coop in which the blue herons were confined and killed
one of them.   "None of the sailors succeeded in making friends
with them."   Again he says: "Once a cat which was asleep in the
sunshine, on the wooden steps of the veranda, was pinned through the

body to the boards and killed by one of them.   At last they began to
pursue the younger children of my worthy friend, who therefore
ordered them to be killed."

Of the behavior of this species in a wild state, Audubun (1840)
writes:

These herons are sedate, quiet, and perhaps even less animated than the *A.
Herodias*.   They walk majestically, with firmness and great elegance.   Unlike the
species just named, they flock at their feeding grounds, sometimes a hundred or
more being seen together; and what is still more remarkable is, that they betake
themselves to the mud flats or sand bars at a distance from the keys on which
they roost and breed.   They seem, in so far as I could judge, to be diurnal, an
opinion corroborated by the testimony of Mr. Egan, a person of great judgment,
sagacity, and integrity.   While on these banks, they stand motionless, rarely
moving toward their prey, but waiting until it comes near, when they strike it
and swallow it alive, or when large, beat it on the water, or shake it violently,
biting it severely all the while.   They never leave their feeding grounds until
driven off by the tide, remaining until the water reaches their body.   So wary
are they, that although they may return to roost on the same keys, they rarely
alight on trees to which they have resorted before, and if repeatedly disturbed
they do not return, for many weeks at least.   When roosting, they generally
stand on one foot, the other being drawn up, and unlike the ibises, are never
seen lying flat on trees, where, however, they draw in their long neck, and place
their head under their wing.   I was often surprised to see that while a flock was
resting by day in the position just described, one or more stood with outstretched
necks keenly eyeing all around, now and then suddenly starting at the sight of a
porpoise or shark in chase of some fish.   The appearance of a man or a boat,
seemed to distract them; yet I was told that nobody ever goes in pursuit of them.
If surprised, they leave their perch with a rough croaking sound, and fly directly
to a great distance, but never inland.

The flight of the great white heron is firm, regular, and greatly protracted.
They propel themselves by regular slow flaps, the head being drawn in after they
have proceeded a few yards, and their legs extended behind, as is the case with
all other herons.   They also now and then rise high in the air, where they sail in
wide circles, and they never alight without performing this circling flight, unless
when going to feeding grounds on which so other individuals have already settled.
It is truly surprising that a bird of so powerful a flight never visits Georgia or
the Carolinas, nor goes to the mainland.   When you see them about the middle
of the day on their feeding grounds they "loom" to about double their size, and
present a singular appearance.   It is difficult to kill them unless with buckshot,
which we found ourselves obliged to use.

DISTRIBUTION

Range.—A nonmigratory species of greatly restricted range.   Breeds
only in the extreme southern portion of Florida and on some of the
Florida Keys.   North to Man-of-War Bush (Florida Bay), Cape
Sable, and Cape Romano.   East to Upper Metacumbe Key and Indian
Key.   South and west to Torch Keys, Cudjoe Key, Johnstons Keys,
and Marquesas Key.

The race described by Bangs and Zappey (1905) as *Ardea h. repens* (=*Ardea o. repens*) from Cuba (Isle of Pines) is probably the race that occurs also in Porto Rico (Gundlach); Jamaica (Marsh); and at the mouth of the Rio Lagartos, Yucatan (Brown).

Egg dates.—Florida Keys: 29 records, December 30 to June 16; 15 records, January 26 to April 4.

ARDEA HERODIAS HERODIAS Linnaeus

GREAT BLUE HERON

HABITS

The great blue heron, or "blue crane" as it is often called, is the largest, the most widely distributed and the best known of the American herons. Herons probably originated in the warmer climates, where they are certainly better represented in species and in numbers; but this species extends its range across the continent and well up into the cooler climate of Canada. It is a stately bird, dignified in its bearing, graceful in its movements and an artistic feature in the landscape.

In its native solitudes, far from the haunts of man, it may be seen standing motionless, in lonely dignity, on some far distant point that breaks the shore line of a wilderness lake, its artistic outline giving the only touch of life to the broad expanse of water and its background of somber forest. Or on some wide, flat coastal marsh its stately figure looms up in the distance, as with graceful, stealthy tread it wades along in search of its prey. Perhaps you have seen it from afar and think you can gain a closer intimacy, but its eyes and ears are keener than yours; and it is a wise and a wary bird. But even as it takes its departure, you will still stand and admire the slow and dignified strokes of its great, black-tipped wings, until this interesting feature of the landscape fades away into the distance. A bird so grand, so majestic, and so picturesque is surely a fitting subject for the artist's brush.

Courtship.—Throughout the northern portion of its range the great blue heron is migratory, but it returns to its breeding range early in the season. Its spectacular courtship is well described by Audubon (1840) as follows:

The manners of this heron are exceedingly interesting at the approach of the breeding season, when the males begain to look for partners. About sunrise you see a number arrive and alight either on the margin of a broad sand bar or on a savannah. They come from different quarters, one after another, for several hours; and when you see 40 or 50 before you, it is difficult for you to imagine that half the number could have resided in the same district. Yet in the Floridas I have seen hundreds thus collected in the course of a morning. They are now in their full beauty, and no young birds seem to be among them. The males walk about with an air of great dignity, bidding defiance to their rivals, and the females croak to invite the males to pay their addresses to them. The females utter their coaxing notes all at once, and as each male evinces an equal desire to please the object of his affection, he has to encounter the enmity of many an adversary, who, with little attention to politeness, opens his powerful bill, throws out his wings, and rushes with fury on his foe. Each attack is carefully guarded against, blows are exchanged for blows; one would think that a single well-aimed thrust might suffice to inflict death, but the strokes are parried with as much art as an expert swordsman would employ; and, although I have watched these birds for half an hour at a time as they fought on the ground, I never saw one killed on such an occasion; but I have often seen one felled and trampled upon, even after incubation had commenced. These combats over, the males and females leave the place in pairs. They are now mated for the season, at least I am inclined to think so, as I never saw them assemble twice on the same ground, and they become comparatively peaceable after pairing.

Miss Catherine A. Mitchell has sent me the following attractive sketch of the "morning love dance," a more peaceful courtship performance, of this species:

As I turned over in my sleeping bag, a glimpse of a rosy glow in the sky roused me to better appreciation of the world already awake around me. An old pine tree hanging from the mountain of sand back of us, was outlined against a gorgeous reflection in the peaceful waters of Lake Michigan; and in the smooth sands of the shore surrounding us. There! The Japanese picture was complete with a great blue heron in the foreground. But see! A little way farther down the beach are more great blue herons. A group of them together with outspread wings flapping slowly up and down, circling round and round. Eleven birds first, later 14, circling sometimes around each other and sometimes in the one large circle, somewhat as we used to do in dancing-school days. I watched the graceful motions perhaps half an hour, spellbound by the weirdness of the scene.

Nesting.—Many and varied are the nesting sites chosen by this species in the different portions of its wide breeding range, but certain characteristics are common to the species everywhere. It is, as most of the herons are, a sociable species, preferring to nest in closely congested communities, varying in size from a few pairs to several scores or even hundreds. Where trees are available it prefers to nest in trees and usually selects the tallest trees available; but it often nests in low trees, or bushes, or even on the ground. The location of the nesting rookery probably depends more on an available food supply for the young than on the presence of suitable nesting trees. But, as the main object to be gained is security for the eggs and young, a remote and more or less inaccessible locality is always chosen.

My first experience with the nesting habits of the great blue heron was in the Penobscot Bay region on the coast of Maine, where I have examined breeding colonies on the spruce-covered islands near Deer Isle. Bradbury Island, lying northwest of Deer Isle in Penobscot Bay, has long been known as a breeding place for great blue herons. It is a high island with open pasture land in the center, but heavily wooded at both ends with a dense forest of tall spruces and firs, with a few birches. I once counted nine ospreys' nests in the trees around its steep shores and found the bulky nest of a pair of northern ravens in the thickest part of the woods. When I first visited it, on June 10, 1899, the breeding season was well advanced. Most of the nests contained large young, but at least four nests examined held three, four, or five eggs, probably second layings of pairs that had been robbed previously. The nests were placed in or near the tops of the largest spruces or firs, at heights varying from 30 to 40 feet. They were large flat platforms of large sticks and twigs, only slightly hollowed, and smoothly lined with fine twigs; one that I examined was 30 inches in diameter and another was 40 inches. There were not over a dozen pairs of herons in this rookery at that time, but when I visited it again on June 20, 1916, the colony had increased to 30 or 40 pairs. Many of the nests were in dead trees, which probably had died since the nests were built; the damage done by the birds often kills the trees. I had long known of another colony of 25 or 30 pairs on White Island, east of Deer Isle, which I visited on June 25, 1916. Here the herons were nesting from 40 to 50 feet up in the tops of the tall spruces in a dense forest. The trees and the ground under them was completely whitewashed with the excrement of the young birds; but, by picking out and climbing to a nest under which the ground was clean, I succeeded in collecting a set of eggs for my companion.

In Alexander Wilson's (1832) time these herons nested in the primeval cedar swamps of New Jersey, which have long since disappeared as virgin forests; referring to their nesting haunts, he says:

These are generally in the gloomy solitudes of the tallest cedar swamps, where, if unmolested, they continue annually to breed for many years. These swamps are from half a mile to a mile in breadth, and sometimes five or six in length, and appear as if they occupied the former channel of some choked up river, stream, lake, or arm of the sea. The appearance they present to a stranger is singular. A front of tall and perfectly straight trunks, rising to the height of 50 or 60 feet without a limb, and crowded in every direction, their tops so closely woven together as to shut out the day, spreading the gloom of a perpetual twilight below.

More modern conditions in that region are thus described in some notes sent to me by R. P. Sharples:

Down back of Delaware City, near the Delaware & Chesapeake Canal, is a great swamp. It is many hundred acres in extent and is absolutely unfordable and impassable. In places are many trees growing out of the water and down below is a dense thicket shading the mud and ooze. It is such a place as snakes and frogs and slimy things inhabit. Crawfish in immense numbers make their homes in it. But above is a bird paradise, and the thickets and the grasses and the trees are alive with them. In a small patch of maples a colony of great blue herons have built their nests. There were 89 of the nests in the bunch and 35 of them were apparently in use when examined one day, the last of March, 1912. The birds had just begun to lay their eggs and were very wild. Seventeen of the nests were seen in one big tree. These structures are made of small twigs, in a thin layer, so thin that the eggs can be seen from the ground at the foot of the tree. The nests are shallow platforms, and instead of being close to the trunk are generally out on the tops of the higher limbs, often being from 85 to 100 feet from the ground. They are about 3 feet across and are very insecure nesting places.

William B. Crispin wrote me that near Salem, New Jersey, these herons build their nests in the forks of limbs of the largest trees, from 70 to 130 feet from the ground, in swampy, briery places. He said that the largest colony near Salem contained some 80 nests and that he has found nests in pines, pin oaks, white oaks, chestnuts, tulip trees, and swamp maples.

Richard C. Harlow mentions, in the notes he sent me, a colony of about 20 pairs, near Glassbow, New Jersey, nesting in tall pine trees from 70 to 90 feet high. The nests were all repaired from the remains of the preceding years, were made of oak sticks and were "lined with bunches of green pine needles."

Edwin F. Northrup (1885), in describing a large colony on the north shore of Oneida Lake, New York, says:

The timber in the swamp is all black ash and grows very high, branching at the top. The trees are slender, varying from 1 to 3 feet in diameter, and are readily climbed with spurs, that is if one is an adept at using them. Several hundreds of these nests, built in crotches of the limbs, are grouped together at one place in the swamp and cover a space nearly or quite half a mile across. Nearly every tree which rises to the general height of the rest and which has favorable crotches, contains from one to four nests. Two, however, is the more usual number in one tree, four being seldom found. The nests are constructed of sticks about one-fourth to half an inch in diameter. A large bundle is laid on a crotch and lined with finer twigs, making a flat nest from 25 to 40 inches in diameter.

Dana G. Gillett (1896) says that in Tonawanda Swamp in western New York:

The great blue heron also nests in large elm trees, selecting one with a very large trunk, and nearly always building at the extremity of a limb, generally a horizontal one, and many are not strong enough to bear the weight of a man, thereby making it exceedingly dangerous to try to approach the nest.

I have seen as many as eight nests in the top of one large spreading elm, and the old herons sitting on their nests, which would swing to and fro with every breeze. The nests are very large, usually about 4 feet across, and sometimes larger, being composed of sticks, some of them larger than a man's thumb, firmly stuck together, and lined with fine bark or moss, but sometimes composed only of sticks.

Perhaps the most interesting of all are the colonies in Michigan, where the herons build their nests in giant sycamores at heights varying from 50 to 90 feet above the ground. Eugene Pericles (1895) gives a thrilling account of egg collecting in such a rookery in Van Buren County. The smallest sycamore was only 7 feet in circumference, but it was 40 feet to the first limb and there were 12 nests in it, distributed over five large straggling limbs and either at or near their extremities. The largest sycamore in the heronry was over 10 feet in girth and held 16 occupied nests, as well as several old nests; the lowest nest was about 70 feet up and the highest was over 80 feet. Climbing the smooth trunks of these big trees and going out on the slippery limbs must test the nerve and strength of the best climber.

Walter E. Hastings has sent me some fine photographs and some interesting notes, including a map showing the locations of 18 Michigan rookeries of great blue herons. In the colonies that he has visited, the nests were usually placed in high elm trees, from 40 to 110 feet from the ground, near the tops of the trees or the ends of the branches; often the trees or branches are dead, making it dangerous to climb them. In building their nests the birds often break the twigs off the trees rather than pick them up off the ground. New nests of the year are often so frail that the eggs can be seen through them from below. The older nests, which have been added to each year, are much larger, thicker, and firmer; the accumulated filth helps to cement the material together. Mr. Hastings once sat in one of these nests, 110 feet from the ground, for a number of hours while photographing the birds.

On the plains and prairies of the interior the great blue herons have to be contented with the largest trees they can find, cottonwoods, poplars, and box elders, in the timber belts along the streams. We found a colony of about 15 or 20 nests on Skull Creek, near Crane Lake, Saskatchewan, on June 5, 1905. The nests were from 15 to 25 feet up in the tops of the largest box elders. At that date most of the nests contained young of various ages, but two nests held six eggs each and several others 4 or 5 each. We visited this colony the following year and found that it had been shot out; the dead bodies of the herons were lying on the ground under the trees and the nests were deserted.

A. D. Henderson writes me that there has been a small colony near Belvedere, Alberta, since 1920. He saw "two of the nests on an island in tall poplar trees in the fall of 1920." In the fall of 1922, he "saw six nests in a solitary spruce on another island about a mile distant." On May 15, 1923, he "visited this island and found five occupied nests and took one set of five eggs and one of six. The nests were all on the same spruce tree and those occupied had been newly built, the old nests being easily distinguished by the liberal coat of whitewash on them. The nests were large structures of dead sticks, lined with green alder twigs and weed stalks and a very little dry grass." This is the most northern colony of which I have any record.

Eggs.—Four eggs is probably the commonest number laid by the great blue heron, though full sets of three are not uncommon, sets of five are common, sets of six are frequently found, and sets of seven have been reported. The shape varies from ovate, or (rarely) oval to elliptical ovate, or (rarely) fusiform. The shell is smooth or slightly rough. The color varies from "pale Nigara green" to "lichen green" or "pale olivine." The measurements of 50 eggs average 64.5 by 45.2 millimeters; the eggs showing the four extremes measure **70.4** by 47.6; 67.9 by **49.2**; **56.9** by 42.7; and 59.2 by **42.2** millimeters.

Young.—The period of incubation is about 28 days. Mr. Hastings says that both sexes incubate. He once saw a bird with broken wing feathers leave a nest and very shortly another, with perfect wings, took its place. Also he has seen a great commotion around a heronry early in the morning, again about 10 a. m., and at about 2 p. m., and again just before dark, which he believes is due to the birds changing on the nests.

Young herons are far from attractive, either in appearance or behavior, at any age; at first they are feeble and helpless, but later on they are awkward, ungainly, and pugnacious. If undisturbed, they remain in the nest until as large as their parents and fully fledged; but when nearly grown they are easily frightened and leave the nest to climb awkwardly over the surrounding branches and perhaps fall to the ground or water below, which often results in death, as their parents do not seem to have sense enough to rescue or even feed them.

In the nest they are fed by both parents, at first on soft regurgitated food, later on whole fresh fish. With the youngest birds the soft soup-like food is passed from the bill of the parent into that of the young bird; but later on the more solid food is deposited in the nest and picked up by the young. The young birds usually lie quietly in the nest, crouched down out of sight, between feedings; but as soon as the parent is seen or heard returning (the senses of the young are very keen) there is great excitement, as they stand up to clamor and wrestle for their food. The old bird approaches with deliberate dignity and may stand on the nest for a few minutes with her head high in the air. Then with crest and plumes erected and with a pumping motion, she lowers her head and one of the youngsters grabs her bill in his, crosswise; the wrestling match then follows until the food passes into the young bird's mouth or onto the nest. The young are usually fed in rotation, but often the most aggressive youngster gets more than his share.

The young instinctively try to void their excrement by squirting it over the edge of the nest, but they are not eminently successful at it and the nest, the tree, and the ground under it are usually completely whitewashed with their profuse ordure before they are fully grown. This and the decaying fish which fall from the nests make a heronry far from pleasant and one has to expect an occasional shower bath from one or both ends of a frightened young heron.

Young herons are particularly noisy at feeding times and, as this is an almost continuous performance in a large rookery, there is always more or less chattering to be heard, which sounds like the barking of small puppies or the squealing of young pigs.

E. S. Cameron (1906) thus describes an interesting squabble caused by a young heron climbing into a nest where he did not belong:

Several times it seemed likely to fall into the water but managed to regain its balance with violent flapping of wings. Later, when all was quiet again, the four real owners of this nest stood erect indignantly protesting at this outrage on their rights, and one bolder than the rest endeavored to eject the intruder. The newcomer as valiantly resisted, and, being of the same size, a protracted and most extraordinary battle ensued which I witnessed through my binoculars. The birds would feint, and spar for a hold, until one was able to seize the other by the neck when, exerting all its strength, it endeavored to drag its antagonist over the side of the nest. Both in turn had the advantage and swayed backwards and forwards, while the three noncombatants crouched down in characteristic fashion, so that the battle was waged partly on their bodies and partly on the edge of the nest. The fight was continued until an old bird arrived with fish, when the five nestlings again stood erect, and, in the general scramble for food, the parent fed all without discrimination. As it became too dark for binoculars I saw no more that evening, but next morning the duel was renewed until the interloper became exhausted, and, being driven from the nest, scrambled down the branch to its rightful abode. As far as I could see, all the other young birds lived in perfect harmony.

Plumages.—In the downy, young, great blue heron, the top and sides of the head are thickly covered with long whitish and grayish plumes, one inch or more long, "light olive gray" to "pale olive gray," grayer, basally and whiter terminally; the back is thickly covered with long, soft down, "light mouse gray" basally to "pallid mouse gray" terminally; the flanks and belly are more scantily covered with soft, white down; and the throat is naked. The young bird begins to acquire its plumage at an early age; before it is one-third grown its head, neck, and body is well feathered and its flight feathers are growing, but the downy plumes persist on the crown, and the rump remains downy until the young bird is nearly fully grown.

In this first, or juvenal, plumage the crown is "dark mouse gray"; the cheeks, chin, and throat are white; the neck is variegated with grays and browns, and spotted with black and pale russet; the upper parts, back, and wing coverts are plain gray, "deep mouse gray" to "deep Quaker drab," without any signs of plumes anywhere; the feathers of the greater, median and lesser wing coverts are broadly edged with "russet" or "pinkish cinnamon" and there is at first a white spot on the tip of each greater covert feather; these spots and edgings gradually fade and wear off; the breast is streaked with dusky, and the thighs are "light pinkish cinnamon." All of the colors named above vary somewhat, as in the adults of the various subspecies.

The above plumage is worn through the first fall and winter without much change before February, when the first spring plumage begins to show advance toward maturity; at this season one or two occipital plumes may appear, but the crown remains black; rudimentary plumes appear on the breast and back; the buff edgings have worn away and some new feathers have replaced the old in the mantle; and the under parts are more like the adult.

At the first postnuptial molt, which is complete, the following summer and fall, further advance toward maturity is made; the forehead becomes partially white, some occipital plumes are acquired; the black shoulder tufts appear, somewhat mixed with white; many long, narrow plume-like feathers appear in the back and breast; the thighs are purer cinnamon; and the neck and under parts are more like those of the adult. This is the second winter plumage, which becomes nearly adult at the next prenuptial molt, when the young bird is ready to breed. After the next complete postnuptial molt, when the young bird is over two years old, the plumage becomes fully adult, though signs of immaturity are still to be seen, such as dusky markings in the white crown and white markings in the black shoulder tufts; these may not wholly disappear for another year or two.

Adults have a complete postnuptial molt in late summer and fall and a partial prenuptial molt of the contour feathers in late winter and early spring. There is little seasonal change in adults except that in spring the plumes of the head, breast, and back are more fully developed and perhaps the showy colors are a little more brilliant. The adult is a handsome bird at all seasons.

Food.—The principal food of the great blue heron is fishes of various kinds and it seems to be willing to accept whatever kind of fish is most easily available. Ora W. Knight (1908) says:

Frogs, eels, horn-pouts, pickerel occasionally, suckers, shiners, chubs, black bass, herrings, water puppies, salamanders, and tadpoles, are the items I have discovered among their rations. They do not frequent as feeding grounds the spots where trout usually congregate, and I have very strong doubts that they eat trout, except very rarely, let alone consuming them in the vast quantities certain persons have affirmed.

It fishes by night as well as by day and employs two very different methods, still hunting and stalking. The former is the best known and probably the commonest method. Standing as still as a graven image in shallow water, where fish are moving about, it waits patiently until one comes within reach, when a swift and unerring stroke of its well trained bill either kills or secures the fish. Usually the fish is seized crosswise between the mandibles; if it is a small one, it is tossed in the air and swallowed head first, so that it will slip down easily; but if the fish is a large one, the heron may walk ashore with it and beat it on the ground to kill it or may kill it by striking it in the water. I have never had the patience to watch a heron long enough to learn how long it would stand and wait for a fish to come to it. I have found it more interesting to watch it stalking its prey, a more active operation. Slowly and carefully, with stately tread, it walks along in water knee deep, its long neck stretched upward and forward; its keen eyes are scanning the surface and an occasional quick turn of the head indicates a glimpse of a fish; suddenly it stops, as if it had seen a fish, but it moves on again; at last comes its chance, as in a crouching attitude the long neck darts downward, quick as a flash; the stroke is not always successful, but sooner or later the heron secures a meal. Sometimes, in its eagerness, the heron may step beyond its depth and lose its balance, but a few flaps of its wings restores its equilibrium and its dignity.

Audubon (1840) says:

The principal food of the great blue heron is fish of all kinds; but it also devours frogs, lizards, snakes, and birds, as well as small quadrupeds, such as shrews, meadow mice, and young rats, all of which I have found in its stomach. Aquatic insects are equally welcome to it, and it is an expert flycatcher, striking at moths, butterflies, and libellulae, whether on the wing or when alighted. It destroys a great number of young marsh-hens, rails, and other birds; but I never saw one catch a fiddler or a crab; and the only seeds that I have found in its stomach were those of the great water lily of the Southern States. It always strikes its prey through the body, and as near the head as possible. Now and then it strikes at a fish so large and strong as to endanger its own life; and I once saw one on the Florida coast, that, after striking a fish, when standing in the water to the full length of its legs, was dragged along for several yards, now on the surface and again beneath. When, after a severe struggle, the heron disengaged itself, it appeared quite overcome, and stood still near the shore, his head turned from the sea, as if afraid to try another such experiment.

Wilson (1832) includes in its food grasshoppers, dragon-flies and the seeds of splatter docks. Mr. Hastings says that it eats great quantities of insects and mice. When the grasshoppers have been thick he has seen it feeding in the open meadow on these insects entirely, often for two hours at a time; it does not chase them but stands very still, allowing the insects to come within reach of its quick beak. Arthur H. Howell (1911) adds crustaceans to the list. Bartlett E. Bassett wrote me that a bird he shot for me was carrying a large black snake in its bill. Altogether the food habits of this species are decidedly beneficial. It may occasionally take a few trout, but it does not ordinarily frequent the streams where trout are found.

Behavior.—When forced to make a hurried departure, as when frightened, this heron makes an awkward start, as it scrambles up into the air with vigorous strokes of its big wings, with its long legs dangling and its long neck outstretched. When undisturbed it starts more gracefully; leaning forward, with extended neck, it takes a few steps and with a few long wing strokes it mounts into the air. When well underway its flight is strong and majestic, sustained by long, slow strokes of its great wings; its neck is folded back between its shoulders and its long legs are extended backwards, to act as a rudder in place of its tail, which is too short for this purpose. When about to alight the neck and legs are extended, a few flaps of the wings check the bird's momentum and it drops lightly to its perch.

The great blue heron is quite at home on dry land where it moves about with dignified ease and grace. M. P. Skinner writes to me that in Yellowstone Park it often walks "across the meadows from one pool to the next, with long, stately strides." It must spend considerable time on land in pursuit of such prey as field mice, shrews, grasshoppers, and other insects. It can also alight on the water or swim, if necessary. P. A. Taverner (1922) says that, while watching some of these herons flying across a lake, he "saw them drop to the lake level, hesitate a moment and then drop softly into the water. They remained perhaps half a minute there, and then, with an easy flap of wings, rose and continued their way." There was no shoal there and "nothing but deep water anywhere in the vicinity." Dr. John B. May has twice noticed a similar occurrence, about which he writes me, as follows

On the first occasion the bird was flying over the middle of Little Squam Lake, at Holderness, New Hampshire, where the lake is about 400 yards wide. It sailed down to the water, then flew to a raft of logs and was seen to swallow some object. Two years later, at the same spot, a similar event was witnessed more carefully this time. The bird closed its wings for about eight seconds, opened them slowly once and closed them again, then raising them flew away with a slender eel-like object dangling from its bill. The water was at least 25 feet deep at this place and the bird 150 to 200 yards from shore.

Dr. Charles W. Townsend, Dr. Daniel S. Gage, and Mr. Josselyn Van Tyne have told me of similar observations.

Illustrating the wariness and the sagacity of this species Wilfred A. Bretherton (1891) writes:

A mill pond some three-quarters of a mile from my home is a favorite feeding place for these birds. This pond, being just outside of the corporation in a very pleasant locality, is often visited, and hence the herons are often interrupted in their fishing. Past experience has made them very sagacious. One or two sentinels are always posted upon tall trees, usually at the upper end of the pond— if two, about 30 rods apart—and in such a manner that no one can approach the pond from any direction without being observed by one or the other sentinel, who will immediately give the alarm. The pond is so situated that the herons fishing can not be seen until the border is reached, and the sentinels, being high above the water, can see a man long before he gets to where he can see the fishers, unless he approach through the woods on the south side.

One day I thoroughly tested their sagacity, and found it greater than I had suspected. Stealthily moving through the woods south of the pond, I came near the steep bank of the pond, partly hidden from the pond, by dense shrubbery. However, the nearest sentinel, some 30 rods away, caught sight of my head above the bushes and uttered a harsh cry of alarm, which was repeated by the second sentinel, who was posted so far up that I would not have seen him had he not repeated the cry. Immediately four or five herons flew from the water between me and the nearest sentinel, one of them having been but a few rods from me, but invisible except from the water's edge. As they flew to the woods north of the pond they uttered hoarse cries, and soon all had disappeared save the two sentinels.

Moving back and eastward I crept up to a clump of bushes about 5 feet in height growing upon the very top of the bank. Lying close to the ground I kept silent for some time. The bushes entirely hid me from the watchful sentinels and they evidently supposed I had gone. Soon the one nearest me began to utter low and peculiar cries which the upper sentinel quickly answered. This style of conversation was kept up for several moments. This was shortly followed by the return of all the fishers, one coming quite near my locality. As soon as fishing had again gotten well under way I rose upon my feet. The instant my head appeared above the bushes the nearest sentinel uttered the harsh cry of alarm, immediately followed by the tumultuous flight of the fishers, most of which had been invisible from my hiding place.

The attitude of the great blue heron towards other species of herons with which it is associated on its breeding grounds or its feeding grounds is usually one of dignified indifference or haughty disdain. It never seems to molest the smaller herons, but apparently picks an occasional quarrel with other species. Dr. Charles W. Townsend (1920) once saw "a fine adult great blue heron flying high in the air pursued by a screaming common tern who darted at it from behind and from above. The heron screamed hoarsely, stretched out and around its long neck and partly dropped its legs. The feathers of its head were erected. The tern attacked again and again and the scene was repeated. It reminded one of an old hawking picture."

Audubon (1840) says he has—

seen the blue heron giving chase to a fish hawk, whilst the latter was pursuing its way through the air towards a place where it could feed on the fish which it bore in its talons. The heron soon overtook the hawk, and at the very first lounge made by it, the latter dropped its quarry, when the heron sailed slowly towards the ground, where it no doubt found the fish. On one occasion of this kind, the hawk dropped the fish in the water, when the heron, as if vexed that it was lost to him, continued to harass the hawk, and forced it into the woods.

Enemies.—There are very few birds or animals that dare to attack such a large and formidable antagonist as an adult great blue heron, for it is a courageous bird, armed with a powerful sharp bill that can inflict serious wounds. Even men must approach it with caution, when it is wounded and at bay. But great damage is done to the eggs, and probably also to the very young birds, by crows, ravens, vultures, and probably gulls. Once on Bradbury Island, referred to above, we flushed a heron from its nest and, on returning to it a few moments later, we found three eggs on the ground under it, which had evidently just been broken and sucked by a pair of ravens that were flying around and croaking. Crows and ravens often live in or near the rookeries and, as soon as the herons are frightened away from their nests, these black marauders pounce down on the nests and devour the eggs.

R. P. Sharples, in his notes, relates the following incident:

Once a red-shouldered hawk sailed over at great height. Presently he espied the unprotected heron eggs, and folding his wings he dropped down like a bullet right into the treetops amid the heron nests. Then the parent birds saw him and all came piling home in a hurry, no longer afraid of their human enemies. The hawk missed his dinner for the herons with their long daggerlike bills are well able to defend their nests.

In this connection it is interesting to note that both the red-shouldered hawk and the red-tailed hawk have been recorded as nesting in or near heron rookeries. In southern rookeries nests of turkey or black vultures are often found. Mr. Hastings once found a pair of great horned owls raising a brood in an old nest in the middle of a colony.

Fall.—Throughout the northern part of its range the great blue heron is migratory. Its fall migration is particularly well marked. Many individuals migrate singly, as solitary birds are often seen, but flocks of a dozen or 20 birds are not uncommon. I have several times seen such flocks in the fall, but none in the spring. Doctor Townsend (1920) says that "at Ipswich, on October 28, 1917, at 5 p. m. a flock of 20 of these great birds flew south high up over the marshes in a loose V or U formation." In some notes, sent to me by Harry S. Hathaway, from Miss Elizabeth Dickens, she writes that on November 12, 1910, a flock of 12 appeared about 8.30 a. m. on Block Island:

After circling awhile like gulls playing in air they dropped down on the edge of the bluff. I had never seen more than nine in a flock before. Of course, the gunners got after them and they had to depart, but that was only the beginning. All the forenoon they came from the west in flocks of from 2 to 60. I counted 40 in one flock and 60 in another that were in sight at one time. The life savers said these were all one flock until their shooting divided them.

I believe that there is a regular coastwise flight, over the water as well as over land, for we often saw them when off shore "coot" shooting.

Winter.—The great blue herons of the North mingle in winter with their near relatives of the southern Atlantic and Gulf States, adding materially to the heron populations of these congenial shores. There they live in peace and harmony with their neighbors, sharing with them the bounteous supply of fish and other foods. Many linger as far north as the central portions of the United States and stragglers are occasionally seen as far north as New England and Michigan. W. J. Erichsen (1921) says of their winter habits on the coast of Georgia:

The greater portion of its food is secured from the salt marshes and the banks and shallows of the numerous creeks that wind their way through them. It is often seen in company of the smaller herons, particularly the little blue species. At such times it is the first to take wing at the approach of danger, and usually is far away before the intruder has arrived within 100 yards of the spot where it stood. Upon stationing itself in a shallow creek to secure passing fish, if the latter are scarce the bird will remain motionless in one spot for a long period of time, apparently sluggish, and in an indifferent attitude; but when the fish are plentiful it becomes very active, spearing them right and left in rapid succession.

At sundown, or a little before, numbers of these stately birds can be seen slowly winging their way toward the forested portions of the islands, there to spend the night. They become much attached to these roosting places and will not desert them as long as their aspect remains unchanged and the birds are not greatly persecuted.

DISTRIBUTION

Breeding range.—Eastern United States and southern Canada. East to Nova Scotia (Halifax); New Jersey (New Providence and Cape May); Virginia (formerly Cobbs Island, Smith's Island and Cape Charles); North Carolina (Fort Macon and Brunswick County); and South Carolina (Waverly Mills and near McClellanville). South to South Carolina (near Charleston); eastern Tennessee (Athens); Indiana (near Indianapolis); Illinois (Peoria and Bernadotte); northern Iowa (Grinnell and Jefferson); and northeastern Nebraska (Omaha). West to South Dakota; North Dakota; and southeastern, probably British Columbia. North to northern Alberta (Edmonton, Belvedere and probably Birch Lake); southern Saskatchewan (Osler and Crane Lake); central Manitoba (Duck Mountain and Shoal Lake); northern Ontario (Moose Factory and Rat Portage); central Quebec (Lake Temiskaming); northeastern Quebec (Anticosti Island and Godbout); and New Brunswick (Woodstock and Chatham).

Winter range.—East to Massachusetts (Onset and Boston); Rhode Island (Point Judith); New York (Springs); New Jersey (Pine Barrens); Virginia (Cape Charles); Bermuda (probably); North Carolina (Raleigh); South Carolina (Charleston); Georgia (St. Marys); and Florida (Orlando and Micco). South to Florida (Micco); Alabama (Castleberry); Louisiana, probably; Texas, probably; and north-eastern Mexico (Camargo, Tamaulipas). West to Tamaulipas, Mexico (Camargo). North to eastern Pennsylvania (Philadelphia); and Massachusetts (Onset).

Spring migration.—Early dates of arrival are Nova Scotia, Yarmouth, March 31; Halifax, April 17, and Pictou, April 13; New Brunswick, Grand Manan, April 3, St. John, April 10, and Scotch Lake, March 30; Illinois, opposite St. Louis, February 13, and Chicago, February 28; Wisconsin, Milwaukee, March 20, Elroy, April 1, Winneconne,

March 10, Waupaca, March 29, and State Line, April 12; Minnesota, Wilder, March 31, and Hutchinson, March 21; Excelsior, March 15, Elk River, March 21, and St. Cloud, March 25; Manitoba, Reaburn, April 16 and Margaret, April 15; Saskatchewan, Indian Head, April 20, and Qu'Appelle, April 2; and Alberta, Brownfield, May 7.

Fall migration.—Late dates of departure are Nova Scotia, Pictou, October 11 and Yarmouth, October 12; New Brunswick, Scotch Lake, November 8 and St. John, October 30; Manitoba, Margaret, September 15; Minnesota, St. Vincent, October 4, Hutchinson, October 15, and Jackson, October 18; Wisconsin, Meridian, October 6, Shiocton, October 29, Westfield, October 2, and Milwaukee, October 26; Illinois, Lake Forest, November 22, Aledo, November 3, Canton, October 27, and Odin, October 14; Saskatchewan, Qu'Appelle, October 27; Alberta, Flagstaff, September 23; west in migration at least to British Columbia, Prospect Lake, September 18, 1896.

Egg dates.—New England and New York: 47 records, April 30 to June 25; 24 records, May 3 to 5. Michigan and Wisconsin: 22 records, April 19 to May 9; 11 records, May 1 to 3. Delaware and Virginia: 12 records, April 6 to June 10; 6 records, April 18 to May 3.

ARDEA HERODIAS FANNINI Chapman

NORTHWEST COAST HERON

HABITS

This well-marked, dark race of the great blue heron inhabits the humid coast belt from Washington to southern Alaska, the type locality being on the Queen Charlotte Islands. Being more strictly confined to the heavily timbered coast region, it adapts itself to its environment in nesting and feeding habits, and differs somewhat in these respects from the other subspecies. It is, however, just as picturesque a feature in the landscape as any other great blue heron. Maj. Allan Brooks tells me that "this heron is decidedly on the increase in British Columbia, especially in the interior, where, however, its numbers do not compare at any point to those seen on the coast or west of the Cascades."

Nesting.—J. Hooper Bowles has sent me some interesting notes on two breeding colonies of this heron in Pierce County, Washington, from which I quote, as follows:

The Puget Sound colony was visited about the third week in May and I was taken to it by a guide. It was a trip of a mile through virgin forest and undergrowth, which left me thoroughly lost from start to finish. How my guide knew his way has always been a mystery to me, well as I know wood hunting, but he traveled fast and without hesitation. Presently he said, "It is just ahead of us now," but I could not hear a sound and thought he must have missed his way, as I felt certain from the start he would. He was right, however, for soon the herons either saw or heard us and the silence was broken to a startling degree by their cries. At this late date the young had all hatched and many of them were fairly well grown, and the nests, nesting trees below them, and the ground and shrubbery beneath looked as if there had been a heavy fall of snow. This was due to their regardless depositing of excrement. The warm weather had dried it and every move in the heavy brush dislodged a cloud of it, making a handkerchief held over the nose and mouth a necessity. In spite of this, I have seldom had a more interesting experience. It is hard to say just how large the colony was, but from one spot I was able to count 39 nests. These were all built in a clump of immense cedar trees, at heights from the ground varying from 75 to 150 feet or more, sometimes five nests being built in one tree. Some years later I was told of the colony at Lake Tapps, which I determined to visit in time for eggs. The trip was made on April 20, 1905, but even that early date proved almost too late, zoologically, as only one of the nests held anything but newly hatched young. It was easy to tell this from the ground, as the birds had simply dropped the empty eggshells over the edge of the nest, evidently making no effort to carry them away. This colony had built in a clump of firs on a hill surrounded by other clumps of firs, and the same complete silence was noticed, as in the first one, until the birds knew we had found them. The trees were smaller here, being only about 100 feet tall, and the nests were almost invariably about 80 feet from the ground. The nest examined contained four "pipped" eggs, which required care in order to save for the collection. In size and color they are similar to what may be found in the eggs of any other form of this genus. The nest was composed of rather small twigs and branches, and lined with very fine twigs. In external measurements its main bulk showed a diameter of 3 feet, with a depth of 1 foot. The inside cup measured 10 inches in diameter by 3 inches in depth. This nest was so strong that my friend, who climbed to it, was able to stand in it and call down to me the conditions in the surrounding nests. These were 24 in number, all containing newly hatched young.

Kenneth Racey (1921) describes a well-known colony in Stanley Park, Vancouver, British Columbia, as follows:

It was situated in a very heavily timbered corner and the main nesting site was in a large spruce tree, this tree being about 250 feet in height. We counted 37 nests in this single tree, and about 15 young birds were in view, either sitting up in the nests, or perched on the branches of the tree. The young, which appeared to be half or three-quarters grown, kept up an incessant squawking, which increased fourfold whenever a parent bird appeared with food. The branches of this spruce tree, except for their tips, were devoid of foliage, and tree trunk, branches, and nests were of a greyish-white color from the birds' droppings. Much of the vegetation close to the ground under the tree was dead and everywhere the ground was littered with pieces of eggshells, filth, etc. I secured a number of eggshells, some of which were in excellent condition. Two nests and five young dead birds were found on the ground beneath the tree; two of these were about half grown, two about 3 weeks old, and the fifth about 1 week or 10 days old. All five birds were more or less decomposed. These nests with the young, had no doubt, been blown down by a recent heavy wind and rain storm. One nest was complete and unbroken, and proved to be a bulky affair and of solid construction, the outer part being constructed of coarse branches about half an inch in diameter, while the inside was well made with fine twigs securely plastered together with refuse and excreta from the young birds. From the size, the nest must have been in use several years, each year having had a little added to it. It was between 3 and 4 feet in diameter outside, while the bowl measured 11 inches wide by 5 inches deep; the whole nest was of a greyish-white color as if it had been whitewashed. The Stanley Park heronry has during the past few weeks become one of the points of interest in the park, and hundreds of residents of this city as well as visitors now stop to have a look at the curious bird colony, none of the members of which appear to be in the least disturbed, however many people gather about to watch them.

J. A. Munro has sent me a photograph of this interesting tree. He writes to me that there is another rookery at North Vancouver which is—

built in a giant, half-dead Sitka spruce, which is 6 feet in diameter at the base and is situated half a mile from the inlet, on a logged-off hillside, and nearly opposite the Stanley Park heronry. The nests, which numbered 18 on June 6, 1923, are 80 feet or more from the ground and can be seen only from a distance, as thick deciduous second growth completely hides the crown of the trees from one standing below.

Major Brooks writes to me:

The nesting is alway in large colonies, usually in heavy stands of Douglas fir or other conifers. Probably the largest heronry in the province is near Qualicum on the east coast of Vancouver Island, although the best known one is in Stanley Park, the playground of the city of Vancouver. Up to 1905 the only heronry that I could hear of in the Lower Fraser Valley was near the mouth of the Stave River; at present there is at least one other, a large one of recent occupation at Chilliwack some 30 miles further up the valley. This is notable also in being in a grove of large cottonwood trees instead of the usual conifers.

Eggs.—The eggs of this heron are not distinguishable in general appearance from those of other great blue herons. The measurements of 17 eggs average 57.4 by 38.3 millimeters; the eggs showing the four extremes measure **68.8** by 45; 65.7 by **48**; **50.7** by 35; and 57.9 by **29** millimeters.

Young.—Mr. Bowles's notes contain the following interesting observations on the behavior of the young:

I was surprised at first to see a number of dead young, in excellent condition of health, on the ground under the nests, but the reason for this soon became evident after we had seated ourselves out of sight. The young in each nest were seen to vary greatly in size, the largest one taking complete possession of the nest while the smaller ones stood around on the branches that supported it. Occasionally a small one would evidently get tired and try to get back into the nest for a rest, but he was promptly driven out by terrific jabs of the spearlike beak of his big brother, or perhaps sister. It was then that I had one of the most interesting exhibitions that has ever been given me in the pursuit of ornithology. Occasionally the younger one was hit so hard that he would be knocked completely off his balance, and would be hanging from the limb by one foot head downward. There he would hang for a few seconds, and then reach his head and long skinny neck up over the limb, by which means he would pull himself up until he could get a wing over. He would then draw himself back to his original position on the limb with a surprising degree of ease, making the observer think at once that they can not be so very far removed in relationship from the mammals.

Food.—Referring to the food of the northwest coast heron, Mr. Bowles says:

In regard to the food of these herons I believe that they will eat any living thing that they can swallow. In my collection of stomach contents I have one that contains the remains of a trout, a crawfish, and two dragon flies. Another bird found dead on the Nisqually Flats showed a large bulge about midway down its neck. Examination disclosed a saltwater bull head that was fully a foot long and so bulky that it ought to have seemed impossible for even a heron to try swallowing. Its side fins were set at right angles and their long, sharp spines had pierced clear through the neck of the bird on both sides. Thus it was impossible for the bird to swallow the fish or dislodge it in any other way, so that the death of both was inevitable. The two examples above mentioned are from the Tacoma region. In California I have seen sun-baked fields far from water where many herons of this genus were standing motionless at a distance from each other. This surprised me greatly, until I saw the head of one go down and come up with a small mammal speared on its beak. It seems probable that these birds are decidedly beneficial in ridding us of mice, gophers, and other similar forms.

D. E. Brown writes to me:

I think that the northwest coast heron feeds on most anything it can get on the tide flats and along the streams. I have never seen it feeding on dry land as J. H. Bowles has seen them. It eats fish, mice, shrews, and frogs mostly but I think that most anything that is alive is "fish when it comes to its net." I have seen this bird spear a flounder of surprisingly large size, much too large to be lifted from the water; it was landed by being shoved along the bottom to the shore. This was done at quite a rapid rate as though the bird knew it could not keep its head under water for any length of time. I have examined several of these fish after the heron had left it and was certainly surprised at the large size of the flounder, the bird being unable to swallow it or to reduce it in size.

Major Brooks says in his notes:

This heron differs very little in habits from the eastern bird except that it seems to affect tidal waters and inlets of the sea to a greater extent. On many portions of the British Columbian coast it is common, even abundant, its favorite fishing grounds are the shallow flats on which *zostera* grows plentifully; here it stands belly deep moving slowly, or not at all, its keen eye fixed on the small open spaces watching for the movement of any small fish that may be moved by the ebb or flow of the tide.

DISTRIBUTION

Range.—Pacific coast regions of North America from northwestern Washington to the Alaskan Peninsula. Permanent resident except perhaps in the northern part of its range. East and south from Alaska (Cook Inlet, Cordova Bay, Admirality Island, Mitkof Island, and Prince of Wales Island); British Columbia (Queen Charlotte Islands, Vancouver Island, Sooke Lake, Sumas, and Okanagan Landing); and Washington (Blaine, Cape Flattery, Nisqually Flats, Quiniault Lake, Seattle, Puyallup, and Fort Steilacoom). North to the Alaskan Peninsula (Portage Bay and Cook Inlet).

Egg dates.—British Columbia: 4 records, May 2 to 30.

ARDEA HERODIAS WARDI Ridgway

WARD HERON

HABITS

This larger, southern race of the great blue heron is much more abundant and more evenly distributed on the Florida and Gulf coasts than its northern relative is throughout its wide breeding range. It is also much less wary and suspicious and is therefore more often in evidence near the haunts of man and more easily studied. When I made my first trip down the east coast of Florida, especially where the train ran along for many miles close to the shore of the Indian River, I was greatly impressed with the abundance and the familiarity of this great heron. The shore seemed to be lined with these stately birds, standing sentinels at frequent intervals or flapping lazily away for a short distance; sometimes one would scale along close to the water on motionless wings until it could drop its long legs down and alight on some favorite sand bar or mud flat; but often it would stand its ground, heedless of the rushing train. The most casual traveler could hardly fail to notice such a conspicuous figure in the landscape.

Again in Texas, as I cruised along down the coast, these big "cranes," as they are called, were daily in evidence. The marshes and prairies of the coastal plains are dotted with little "mottes" or clumps of small trees or bushes, on which we often saw the long necks of these herons, raised above the tree tops and scanning us from afar. They were visible at a long distance and we could always tell which mottes or islands were inhabited by herons.

Nesting.—The breeding season of the Ward heron is much prolonged and one is apt to find either eggs or young in the nests at any time during the winter or spring. Mr. R. D. Hoyt (1905) says:

In its breeding habits Ward's heron is very erratic, and, with the exception of the bald eagle, is one of our earliest, or perhaps more properly speaking, the latest of our birds to begin nesting. It does not wait for the new year but a few individuals begin operations by the latter part of November and by Christmas time a few nests may be found with young. New nests are now more numerous, and by the middle of January many nests will contain fresh sets of eggs. Still the nest building goes on, but in diminishing numbers, until the latter part of February. I once took a set of two fresh eggs on April 4. This may have been a second set, but I am not aware that more than one brood is reared in a season. Here in Hillsborough County, Fla., the site selected for the colony is almost invariably a floating island in the center of a marshy spot. The growth on the island is usually bay, elder, and wax myrtle—low bushy trees all tangled up with bamboo briar. Some islands contain buttonwood only, and some have only willows. These islands are all small, from 20 to 100 feet in diameter, and the size of the colony is determined by the space it has; from half a dozen to 30 pairs occupy the ground. The nests in some instances are huge structures, having been renewed from year to year, presumably by the same pair of birds. They are placed in any situation that forms a good foundation—the entire top of a stout bush, or the horizontal limb of a tree if sufficiently strong, and some are within 2 feet of the ground, others 8 to 12 feet. One nesting place visited last season was a buttonwood island. During its years of occupancy the birds had broken off every limb and twig that could be used for nest building until now nothing but stubs remain. This island contained 11 nests, all of which were made of cypress sticks that had been brought at least 3 miles, that being the nearest cypress. Nests are usually from 30 to 40 inches in diameter, and 10 to 14 inches deep, of large sticks as a base, smaller ones toward the top, and a few twigs with green leaves, and some grass as a lining.

In Florida we found Ward herons breeding in small willow hammocks on the prairies of Brevard County and in the larger willows along the St. Johns River, where nests with newly-hatched young were found on April 21, 1902. The nests were bulky affairs, made of large sticks and were placed in the largest willows, about 10 or 12 feet from the ground. On the Florida Keys we found them breeding with the great white herons in small numbers. Here their nests were built in the red mangroves or on the tops of bushes, never more than half a dozen or so in a group.

In Texas, in 1923, we saw numerous small colonies scattered along the coast, in the live-oak mottes and in small clumps of bushes on the coastal marshes or prairies. On a small island in the Cedar Lakes, on the intercoastal canal, we found a colony of 13 pairs on May 7. It was a low island overgrown with grass, cow parsnip, sunflowers, clumps of other yellow flowers, and coarse herbage; the nests were all on the ground and were made of sticks, that must have been brought from a distance, and were lined with the rootlets of the island vegetation. The nests measured from 30 to 34 inches in outside diameter; in some nests the eggs or young were practically on the ground; other nests were built up as high as 14 or 16 inches. Two nests contained eggs, but the others held young of various ages. There was also a black vulture's nest, with two eggs in it, among the herons' nests. I imagine that the vultures counted on finding a convenient food supply.

As we passed Dressing Point Island, near the upper end of Matagorda Bay, on May 8, we saw the heads of some large herons above a clump of bushes in the center of the island, so landed to explore it. This is a large, flat, grassy island, mostly dry, covered with a rank growth of tall tufted grass and coarse herbage, with a few low bushes and prickly-pear cacti near the center. Mottled ducks and willets were nesting in the grass and a large flock of black-crowned night herons rose from their nests on the ground. A colony of about a dozen pairs of Ward herons had their nests in the center, built on the ground or on the low prickly pears. Some of the ground nests were low and flat, not much more than a rim of sticks; others were built up to 32 or 36 inches in height and and were from 28 to 32 inches in diameter. They were made of large sticks and were lined with fine twigs, rootlets, and grass. I collected a set of three and a set of four eggs that were nearly fresh, but most of the nests contained young of various ages, some of which were nearly as large as their parents. There was a black vulture's nest in this colony and another near it. We took the eggs from the first nest and killed the half grown young in the other.

At various other points along the coast we found small groups of Ward herons' nests in practically every heron rookery that we visited on the islands and on the mainland. They were nesting in close proximity to and in perfect harmony with American egrets, reddish egrets, snowy egrets, Louisiana herons, and black-crowned night herons. Nests were placed on the ground, on prickly pears, in low bushes, or in trees; but usually the commanding positions or the high spots. In the big white ibis rookery, described under that species, in Victoria County, the Ward herons' nests were in the tallest live oaks and elms, 40 or 50 feet from the ground. In all of these rookeries the Ward herons were not particularly shy; they frequently returned to their nests near my blind and did not seem to mind it much more than the smaller species did. Many of the rookeries were infested with swarms of great-tailed grackles; the trees and bushes were full of their nests; and many of the larger herons' nests, particularly those that had been used for several years and were built up quite high, held one or two grackles' nests in their lower stories. I believe that the same nests are used year after year, new material being added each year, until ultimately they become very large.

Dr. A. H. Cordier has sent me the following notes on some Ward herons' nests found by him in Texas:

Before visiting Big Bird Island in the Laguna de la Madre I had never seen a great blue heron's nest on the ground. Here I found several. They were huge affairs, built of coarse sticks and grasses carried from the main land a few miles away. The nests showed evidence of having been occupied for several seasons. Like an eagle's old nest the base showed evidence of decay, while the superstructure was made up of recently added sound sticks. One of the nests I measured was 4 feet high and 3½ feet across its foundation and 3 feet at apex. The nest cavity was 12 inches deep and 18 inches across. Some of the nests were mere shallow affairs with a layer of grass and weeds on the ground, surrounded with cacti, and in the midst of a colony of breeding brown pelicans. When one of these graceful long legged birds returned to its ground nest, it landed usually a few yards away. With majestic poise, dignified mien, it approached the nest with measured strides. Its crested head and streaming breast plumes stamped the bird as the aristocrat of Big Bird Island's bird population. To stand within a few feet of the threshold of one of these big birds as it strides leisurely toward its pleading, hungry young is an event ever to be pleasantly remembered.

Eggs.—The eggs are similar in appearance to those of the northern form. The measurements of 72 eggs average 65.4 by 46.4 millimeters; the eggs showing the four extremes measure **76.5** by 47, 67.7 by **51.5**, **59.7** by 45, and 60.3 by **43.5** millimeters.

Young.—I have described the process of feeding the young, as I have seen it, under the great blue heron, but Dr. Frank M. Chapman (1908) has given such a good account of it that I am tempted to quote his observations on the Ward heron, as follows:

The young herons were almost as easily alarmed as their parents, and, at the first sign of danger, squatted flat in the nest with close-pressed bills. It was not long, however, before the alert attitude of the young indicated beyond question the proximity of one of the parents and, following the direction of their eager, expectant look, I discovered the splendid creature perched on the higher growth to the left, clean-cut and statuesque against the sky. She stood there calmly, showing no trace of the intense excitement which now possessed her offspring, and quietly surveyed her surroundings. Assured that all was well, with erect plumes and partly expanded wings, she slowly walked downward toward the nest, with a dignity of motion and majesty of pose I have never seen excelled by any other bird. The young now were frantic with excitement and, in chorus, uttered their *cuk-cuk, cuk-cuk* feeding call. As the parent stepped slowly into the nest its bill was seized by one of the young. The young bird did not thrust its bill down the parental throat nor was the parent's bill introduced into that of the young. The hold of the young bird was such as one would take with a pair of shears, if one were to attempt to cut off the adult's bill at the base. In this manner the old bird's head was drawn down into the nest where more or less digested fish was disgorged, of which all the young at once partook. On one occasion the adult disgorged a fish at least a foot in length, and on discovering that it was too large for the young the parent reswallowed the fish and returned to a perch near the nest while awaiting for the processes of digestion to continue the preparation of the meal.

Young Ward herons have a peculiar habit, which is common to all the herons when exposed to the direct rays of the hot sun, of opening their mouths and vibrating their throats rapidly; this may be caused by fear or nervousness, but it seems more likely that it indicates distress from overheating and that it serves as a means of cooling their bodies by evaporation; a dog pants and hangs out its tongue when overheated; and probably young herons and young cormorants pant in this way for the same reason.

Young Ward herons are rather more precocial than their northern relatives, for their nests are usually closer to or even on the ground, which makes it easier for them to wander. I have seen young birds of all ages up to fully grown in the nests, and I believe that they prefer to remain in the nests, if undisturbed. But if frightened, they will readily leave the nests, particularly nests on or near the ground, when half grown or more. I have found it very difficult to photograph at close range any of the large young in ground nests. It is surprising to see with what speed the larger young can run, with the help of their wings which are then well grown.

Food.—The food of this subspecies does not differ materially from that of other great blue herons; it consists mainly of fish, but is varied occasionally with mammals, birds, reptiles, crustaceans, and insects. C. J. Maynard (1896) relates an interesting experience; he shot at a Ward heron carrying in its bill an unknown object, which "proved to be a fine specimen of that singular aquatic arviculine mammal, which had been recently described by Mr. True as *Neofiber alleni*, from a single specimen, which up to this time remained unique." A young bird which we frightened from its nest disgorged a mullet 10 inches long and a water moccasin 18 inches long.

Behavior.—There is very little difference in behavior between this and other great blue herons, but my experience with it, both in Florida and in Texas, has indicated that it is much less shy. It seems to have a decided antipathy toward the great white heron. Audubon (1840) took a pair of young Ward herons to Charleston with him, of which he says:

I had them placed in a large coop containing four individuals of the *Ardea occidentalis*, who immediately attacked the newcomers in the most violent manner, so that I was obliged to turn them loose on the deck. I had frequently observed the great antipathy evinced by the majestic white species toward the blue in the wild state, but was surprised to find it equally strong in young birds which had never seen one, and were at that period smaller than the others. All my endeavors to remove their dislike were unavailing, for when placed in a large yard, the white herons attacked the blue and kept them completely under.

Mr. Maynard (1896) had a somewhat similar experience. One that he kept in confinement in Florida was "constantly trying to get at some beautiful white herons," which he allowed to go at large. This bird managed, after a time, to kill one out of three of the white herons.

Enemies.—These large herons are well able to take care of themselves and the adults have few enemies; even man does not often molest them as they have no plumes of commercial value. But the eggs and small young are far from safe, if left unguarded by their parents. In Florida the crows and fish crows, which often live in or near the rookeries, pounce on the eggs of any of the herons at the first opportunity offered by the absence of the old herons, and many eggs are destroyed by them every year. In Texas the black vulture is the greatest scourge. One or more pairs of these rascals have their nests in practically every rookery and they must levy heavy toll on both eggs and young. This habit is so well known that the wardens make an effort to kill every vulture that they can and to break up their nests.

DISTRIBUTION

Breeding range.—Southeastern United States. East to southeastern South Carolina (Hiltonhead, Beaufort County); Georgia (Savannah and mouth of the Altamaha River); and Florida (St. Johns River, Mosquito Inlet, Indian River, and Hillsboro River). South to Florida Keys (Upper Matecumbe Key, Key West, and Marquesas Key); Alabama (Montgomery County and Greensboro); Mississippi (probably Biloxi); Louisiana (Houma and Cameron Parish); and the Gulf coast of Texas (Beaumont, Calhoun, Victoria, and Refugio Counties, Corpus Christi, and Brownsville). West to central Texas (probably Gurley, Waco, and Gainesville); central Oklahoma and Kansas. North to southeastern Iowa (Henry County); southeastern Illinois (Mount Carmel); southwestern Indiana (Knox County); and South Carolina (Hiltonhead).

Winter range.—Florida and the Gulf States, south to central Mexico. East to Florida (St. Johns River, Mosquito Inlet, Orlando, Micco, and Miami). South to the Florida Keys (Upper Matecumbe Key and Dry Tortugas, probably); Mississippi (probably Biloxi); Louisiana (Marsh Island and Vermilion Bay); Texas (Corpus Christi and Brownsville); and central Mexico (Ocotlan, Jalisco). West to central Mexico (Ocotlan) and Texas (Brownsville). North to Texas (Giddings); Arkansas (Fayetteville and Corning); Mississippi (Waverly) and Alabama (Greensboro).

Egg dates.—Florida: 44 records, December 8 to April 21; 22 records, February 7 to March 17. Texas: 35 records, March 8 to May 27; 18 records, April 3 to May 7.

ARDEA HERODIAS TREGANZAI Court

TREGANZA HERON

HABITS

The great blue heron of the western plains and the semiarid regions of the Southwest has been given the above name, as a pallid subspecies. In size it is but slightly larger than *herodias*, but the upper parts and neck are paler in color; it is like *wardi* in color but is decidedly smaller throughout.

Nesting.—Owing to the nature of the country it inhabits its nesting habits are somewhat different from those of the other subspecies. Coues (1874) gives us a vivid picture [of its breeding resorts, as follows:

The breeding places of the great blue heron on the Colorado River offer no such scenes as those of the same bird do in Florida, for instance. There may, indeed, be places along this river overgrown with low, dense woods, simulating a cypress swamp, where the birds may resort to breed, along with the wood ibises; but for the most part, the herons that wend their way along the Colorado are only screened by low, straggling mezquite, that scarcely hides them, or patches of arrowwood (*Tessaria borealis*), that they can overlook. Where the river flows deepest and swiftest, cutting its way through bold cañons that rise frowning on either hand like the battlements of giant castles—where the fervid rays of the sun heat the rocks till they almost crack, and sand blisters the feet—there the herons fix their nests, overhanging the element whence they draw subsistence. The face of the cliffs in many places is covered with singular nests of the eave swallow, breeding by thousands; while on the flat projecting shelves of rock we find, here and there, the bulky platforms of twigs and sticks, and perhaps see the sedate bird herself, setting motionless on the nest, hopefully biding her time, cheered during her long waiting by the joyous troops of the swallows that flutter incessantly around.

Referring to the same general region, Dr. Joseph Grinnell (1914) writes:

Nesting colonies were observed in trees at many points through the large valleys, and one group of nests was noted on a pinnacle of rock in the narrow canyon just below The Needles. Ordinarily nests were placed in the tips of the largest cottonwoods in the neighborhood. Special predilection was evinced for dead trees standing close to the river. This would seem to be because of the clear fly way afforded to and from the nests and because of the more extensive outlook possible. But there were in this region drawbacks to these advantages.

When Edward J. Court (1908) published his description of this subspecies he named it in honor of A. O. Treganza and published some of his notes on the breeding habits of this heron on certain islands in Great Salt Lake, Utah. The nesting habits here are so different from those of other great blue herons elsewhere, that it seems desirable to quote from Mr. Treganza's notes, as follows:

Hat Island, May 8, 1906.—Found a colony of 40 pairs. All stages of nidification existed, except nest building. There seems to be a decided difference in the disposition of the young. Some show signs of fight as soon as you make your presence known, while others pay little or no attention to your doings. The nests here are placed some on the rocks and some on top of the large thorny sage bushes which grow from 4 to 5 feet high. Some of the nests are very beautiful, being built out of sage branches that have been exposed to the elements until they have become a most subtle gray tone that fairly vibrates under sunlight. Some of the nests measure from 4 to 5 feet in diameter.

The nearest feeding ground for these birds is the mouth of the Jordan River, some 35 miles, almost due east of the island. The flight to the feeding grounds begins about 3 a. m., and by sunrise all the birds that are going for that day have left the island, except a few isolated cases which may be seen going and coming all day long, the main body returning so that they reach the island by sundown. Some of these birds travel 50 or 60 miles from the island for food. A certain portion of the birds always remain on the island during the day. Even were it not for the incubation of the eggs and the care of the young, this would be made necessary through the fact that as soon as a nest of eggs is left unprotected it is immediately pounced upon by the *Larus californicus*, who crack the eggs by pecking and feed on their contents. Here *Ardea herodias* is nesting in company with *Larus californicus* and *Pelecanus erythrorhynchos*.

Egg Island, May 11, 1906.—Here the *Ardea herodias* nests in company with *Larus californicus* and *Phalacrocorax dilophus*. This island contained about 50 breeding pairs. All stages of nidification existed except nest building. The nearest feeding ground for the birds on this island is about 15 miles. The nests on this island are all placed on the higher bowlders among the reef rocks, usually beside a large bowlder. The bowlder is used as a perch for the owner of the nest beneath. Apparently the birds consider this bowlder as much a part of their possession as the nest, for should another attempt to alight on a perch that is not his own, he is immediately and properly punished for his trespassing. Such an occasion as this is the only time I have ever seen the adult birds show any signs of quarreling. Some of the nests on this island are very handsomely and wonderfully made, two or three nests measuring each about 5 feet in diameter.

Most of the sticks used in constructing the nest are of the sage bush. Apparently these nests are very old and have been used for many years, a little bit being added each year in the way of rebuilding and house cleaning. It seems quite remarkable that the young do not injure themselves from the large coarse sticks which form the inner nest, if the same could be called an inner nest. The depression of the nests is very slight. The depression starts from the outer edge of the nest and very gradually sinks into the center.

General Remarks.—On first observation the nests of the great blue heron appear very flimsy, especially the edges, which seem to be very much frayed out and loose. One would think that the storms of a winter would entirely demolish these nests, but on close observation it is found that they are most compactly made, and it is quite evident that the same nests are used from year to year with but very little rebuilding in the spring. One can very easily tell where new sticks have been added, from the fact that they are not sun bleached, as are the old sticks in the nest. From seeing the size of the new nests that have been built this year and comparing them with the older nests, one would be very safe in saying that these large old nests are the pioneer homes of these birds and mark their first advent to Great Salt Lake, the date of which we shall omit.

Eggs.—The eggs are similar to those of the other great blue herons, The measurements of 44 eggs average 60.1 by 41.9 millimeters; the eggs showing the four extremes measure **68** by 47.2, 63 by **47.7, 51.9** by 35.1, and 52.4 by **34.8** millimeters.

Food.—Referring to the feeding habits of this heron in the lower Colorado Valley, Doctor Grinnell (1914) writes:

Along the whole course of the river, save in the rock-walled box canyons, blue herons were almost continually in sight. Their chief foraging grounds were the mud bars traversed by shallow diversions of the river. The habit of the river of having frequent periods of falling water, even when, as in the spring, the aggregate tendency is to rise, results in the stranding of many fishes in the shallow overflows as the water seeps away or evaporates. This frequently recurring supply of fish appears to be the chief source of food of all the species of herons occuring in the region. The stomach of one blue heron contained a semiliquid mass of fish, identifiable from the large-sized scales as carp; another contained a large catfish. One stomach was empty save for a single grasshopper leg; this gives a clue as to an emergency diet when the river is rising rapidly. It may be remarked that the opacity of the moving water of the main stream is so complete as effectually to prevent fishing here by piscivorous birds in the usual manner.

Behavior.—The tracts of curious, fluffy, buff-colored feathers found on the breasts of herons have long been subjects of speculation as to their function. A popular theory has been that the greasy powder, with which these tracts are filled, produces a phosphorescent light which serves to illuminate its surroundings when the heron is fishing at night. Several observers claim to have seen such phosphorescent illumination in living birds, but it has never been definitely proven that these feather tracts have any luminous qualities. Dr. Alexander Wetmore (1920) has made some interesting studies of this subject in a young Treganza heron, which lead to an entirely different conclusion. He writes:

In the young great blue heron powder-down tracts produced functional feathers soon after the contour and flight feathers had burst their sheaths and the bird began to preen and care for its plumage. The heron in question had been taken from the nest while still too young to know fear of man, and as I reared it by hand it became devoted to me, though fierce and truculent toward all others. As its plumage developed I noted that the bird constantly rubbed the bill in the powder downs, and on examination found that the heron was utilizing the greasy, powdery substance given off by the tracts to dress and oil the contour feathers. The bill was worked in among the powder downs until a small amount of the exuviae had gathered at the tips of the mandibles and then contour or wing feathers were pulled rapidly through the bill, anointing them with this oily substance. At once return was made to the powder downs after which other feathers were treated in turn until the whole of the body and wing plumage had been properly dressed. I had no difficulty in observing the process as, when permitted, the heron until practically grown delighted in standing upon my knee as I sat in a chair. I was able to place my fingers in beside the tip of the bill, in the powder downs, to feel the mandibles gently nibbling at the downy feathers and then to see the bill withdrawn with its sides covered with the grayish powder. Following this I observed as it was passed over other feathers. This process was repeated daily whenever I cared to see it. At the same time I discovered by examination that the uropygial gland, the usual source of oil for feathers, seemed undeveloped and remained in a nonfunctional condition until the heron was pratically grown. The bird in early life paid no attention to this gland, but worked in either pelvic or pectoral down patches. The actual development of the oil gland I did not observe as the heron at this stage became so vicious toward others that I was forced to discourage its tameness until finally it left the laboratory.

Parenthetically I may add that although on various occasions I examined powder-down tracts in living and in dead herons I was unable to observe that these tracts were luminous, in spite of numerous records on the part of others to the contrary.

DISTRIBUTION

Breeding range.—Western United States except the Pacific coast region. East to Montana (Damson County and Fallon); Wyoming (Sheridan and Fort Laramie); central Colorado (Crow Creek, Weld County, Brighton, and Arkansas Valley, probably); New Mexico (Carlsbad); and Texas (Kerr County, probably). South to central-western Texas (Tornillo Creek near Boquillas); Sonora (Guaymas); and northern Lower California (Salton River). West to Lower California (Salton River); southeastern California (Pelican Island, Salton Sea and the Colorado River near Riverside Mountain); Nevada (Truckee River and Pyramid Lake); and Oregon (Klamath Lake, probably). North to Washington (Yakima Valley, probably and Cheney); and Montana (Great Falls, probably and Dawson County, probably).

Winter range.—Mexico, and southwestern United States. North (rarely) to Idaho and Wyoming (Yellowstone Park). East to New Mexico (Dona Ana); and Texas (Fort Clark and Brownsville). South and west to the west coast of Mexico (Manzanillo). North to Arizona (Fort Verde); Utah (St. George); and occasionally to northern Idaho (Meridian, Neeley, and St. Joseph River).

Spring migration.—Early dates of arrival are: Colorado, El Paso County, April 2, Salida, March 19, Littleton, March 24, Denver, March 30, and Boulder, March 20; Wyoming, Cheyenne, April 3, Sheridan, April 13, and Yellowstone Park, May 3; Montana, Billings, April 11, and Terry, May 2.

Fall migration.—Late dates of departure are: Montana, Terry, September 24, Missoula, September 28; Wyoming, Yellowstone Park, October 5; Colorado, Greeley, October 15, Boulder, October 16, Denver, October 3, Littleton, November 3, and Teller County, November 27; west in migration to California, Sacramento Valley.

Egg dates.—Utah, Nevada, California and Arizona: 24 records, March 30 to May 30; 12 records, April 17 to May 9.

ARDEA HERODIAS HYPERONCA Oberholser

CALIFORNIA HERON

HABITS

The great blue heron of California and Oregon has been separated as a distinct subspecies under the above name. It closely resembles in color our bird of the Northeastern States, but it is said to be decidedly larger. Its habits are similar.

Courtship.—Mr. J. B. Smith (1894) has published an interesting account of the courtship of this heron, which I quote, as follows:

Just before mating time in the spring, the birds hie them to some secluded spot far from the madding crowd and there give themselves up to social amenities, at which times the male birds "show off" before the lady birds with a vanity almost human. On these occasions the birds form a circle, and when each has taken its position one of the older of the feathered frauds jumps into the ring and proceeds with the showing off act. This consists of a series of skips with wing-flapping accompaniment and curving of the neck. After any exceptionally striking display of agility the performer pauses and looks around with a most ludicrous "How's that for high?" expression; and, just like girls say, "O, ain't he sweet?" the lady herons sweetly *k-r-a-a-k* approval in the tones of the basso profundo bullfrog, while the envious male birds chip in dissonant remarks that rasp the atmosphere like the output of the horse fiddle. The performer having exhausted his repertory retires to the ranks and is succeeded by another; and thus the circus goes on until every male bird has made full display of his calisthenic accomplishments and the seance closes. The birds then shake the wing for home.

Nesting.—William L. Finley (1906) during the summer of 1904, made several visits to a large heronry in a swampy region not very far distant from San Francisco. He says:

This heronry was in the center of a narrow wooded belt reaching out into the swamp for about a mile. When we approached this thicket we saw the trees were well loaded with nests. We skirted the edge of the belt looking for an entrance, but to our surprise each place we tried to enter was barred with a perfect mass of tangled bushes and trees. I never saw such a tangled mass of brush. Fallen limbs and trees of alder, swamp maple and willow interlaced with blackberry briers, poison oak, and the rankest growth of nettles. All the while we were assailed by an increasing mob of starving mosquitos that went raving mad at the taste of blood. We pushed on, straining, sweating, crawling and climbing for a hundred yards that seemed more like a mile. We forgot it all the minute we stood under the largest sycamore. It was 7 feet thick at the base and a difficult proposition to climb. But this was the center of business activity in the heron village. The monster was 120 feet high and had a spread of limbs equal to its height. In this single tree we counted 41 blue heron nests and 28 night heron nests; 69 nests in one tree. In another tree were 17 of the larger nests and 28 of the smaller. We made the first trip to the heronry on April 21, and found most of the nests contained eggs. There were about 700 nests in the whole colony, of which the larger number were black-crowned night herons. The great blues and the night herons occupied the same trees, nesting side by side. The larger nests were built almost entirely in the tops of the sycamores, while the night herons set their platform nests at the very upturned tips of the sycamore's limbs and in the lower surrounding willows and alders.

When I first climbed in among the nests of a smaller tree with my camera, it sounded as if I were in the midst of a gigantic henhouse. Some of the birds were clucking over their eggs that were soon to be hatched; others were wrangling and squabbling, so that there was a continual clattering fuss, above which one had to yell his loudest to be heard. I sat straddling a limb, with my notebook in hand. About me, seemingly almost within reach, I counted 36 sets of blue eggs. I was high above the tops of the alders and willows. Set all about below, in the background of green, were the platforms each holding several eggs of blue. The trees were dotted with them in every direction. I counted over 400 eggs in sight.

Edward K. Taylor (1897) discovered an interesting colony of these herons in the southern marshes of San Francisco Bay, which he visited on April 30, 1897. He describes it as follows:

From the course of the creek it was evident that the herons have selected the highest spot on the salt marsh for a nesting place. The rookery is about 2 miles from the mainland and three-quarters of a mile from the bay shore, and here, within an area less than an acre in extent, are located more than 50 nests. I counted 36 from one point. The nests were constructed of smaller sticks than is usual in those found in trees, the birds securing twigs, none more than three-quarters of an inch in diameter, from bushes which grow to a height of about 3 feet on the marshes. They were from 6 to 18 inches in height. Some lined with dry grass. Depression was from 3 inches in the older nests to 9 inches in the more modern ones, the average being 4 inches. Most of the nests were bleached offal white and had apparently been in use for many years. All were remarkably neat and clean. They were ranged along the edge of the winding creek, about 8 feet apart, and another row of nests would be found on the opposite side. Three or four eggs or the same number of young herons were found in most of the nests but the older families were composed of but two or three young. Several sets were secured, and fresh eggs were taken from a few nests.

H. W. Carriger and J. R. Pemberton (1908) published an account of a colony which was forced to abandon its rookery in the tops of some eucalyptus trees, near Redwood City, California, and was later found established in a marsh with nests on the ground.

The colony consisted of 49 nests and covered an area of about 200 feet by 100 feet. The nests were built always upon the very edge of the little sloughs of 3 or 4 feet depth, and were sometimes within 5 feet of each other and as far as 20 feet apart; but usually about 10 feet was spaced between nests. All nests were constructed of the dried branches of the common marsh grass, and were quite serviceable structures. They varied in size from 2 feet in diameter flat on the ground to 4 feet across and 14 inches in height. Nearly all nests were built upon an old one, and probably in a few years quite high monuments will be erected. The contents of the nests varied from fresh empty nests to those containing young about big enough to find their way home again. Sets of eggs were two, three and four and both fresh and incubated eggs were plentiful.

John G. Tyler (1913) found a colony of nine pairs occupying a large lone cottonwood that stood on the bank of Fish Slough near New Hope in Fresno County. "All these nests were large, well-hollowed platforms strongly built of sticks and placed from 40 to 60 feet above the ground." A. B. Howell (1917) says that the herons that breed on the Santa Barbara Islands "build their nests in the niches of the cliffs." J. Eugene Law writes to me that he "found a colony of some size nesting in the tops of the giant native oaks in the vicinity of Visalia on the floor of the San Joaquin Valley of California. Some trees had 15 or 20 nests."

Eggs.—The eggs are similar to those of the eastern subspecies. The measurements of 40 eggs average 61.3 by 43.4 millimeters; the eggs showing the four extremes measure **71.5** by 47.5, 69.5 by **50.5**, and **51.3** by **34.8** millimeters.

Food.—The food of the California heron is, in the main, similar to that of the other subspecies. Mr. Tyler (1913) says:

The farmers of this county should do all in their power to afford protection to the blue heron, as it is one of the best gopher destroyers in existence. It is no uncommon sight to see a heron standing motionless for hours at a time in an alfalfa field waiting for a gopher to make its appearance. Small fish, frogs, and probably lizards, if they are obtainable, are eaten, and on many occasions herons have been observed in pairs on the dry barren hillsides along the San Joaquin River busily engaged in catching grasshoppers. Ability to adapt itself to changing conditions and a varied diet has caused this bird to become widely diffused throughout the valley, and has, no doubt, assisted materially in preserving the species.

Mr. W. Leon Dawson (1923) writes:

We dwellers by the southern sea oftenest descry this bird as a lone watcher far out in the kelp beds, and we are moved to call him the kelp heron. The same tactics of tireless patience and lightning speed evidently avail here to secure for him an abundant harvest of smelts and shrimps, for the bird will stand by the hour on a sinking raft of kelp fronds, though it leave him submerged to the belly. His sea legs are, therefore, considering their great length, rather best on earth, for their owner has to maintain his balance in the face of unceasing motion, and so nicely, that suspicious little fishes shall not be put to flight by a single false motion.

Behavior.—Dr. Alexander Wetmore's (1916a) experiments in ascertaining the speed of flight of certain birds, included two observations on this subspecies. The experiments were made in a moving automobile, driven at the same speed as a bird flying parallel with it, by keeping close watch of the bird and the speedometer. The two herons were about 70 yards away; they were observed separately; and they both traveled at exactly the same speed, 28 miles an hour.

DISTRIBUTION

Range.—"Pacific coast region of the United States, ranging east to San Gabriel, western California and Baird, central northern California; south to San Diego, southwestern California; west to Santa Barbara Islands and north to western Oregon. Apparently a permanent resident throughout most or all of its range but stragglers in winter have been detected west to the Farallon Islands, California and east to St. John, Glenn County, California." (Oberholser 1912a)

Egg dates.—California and Oregon: 91 records, February 18 to May 27; 46 records, March 30 to April 23.

ARDEA HERODIAS SANCTILUCAE Thayer and Bangs
ESPIRITU SANTO HERON

HABITS

The "very light colors" of the great blue heron of southern Lower California were first mentioned by Baird, Brewer, and Ridgway (1884); Brewster (1902a) enlarged upon this point and suggested recognition as a subspecies; but it was 10 years later when Thayer and Bangs (1912) actually named this local race. It is characterized as "a very large great blue heron, with all the colors very pale." In size it is nearly as large as *wardi* of Florida; and in color it is almost exactly like *cognata* of the Galapagos Islands.

Very little has been published regarding its habits, which are probably not essentially different from those of the other subspecies. The collector of the type series, W. W. Brown, jr., found a large colony breeding on Espiritu Santo Island, and another smaller colony in a mangrove swamp on San Jose Island. "The nests, well-made platforms of sticks, about 4 feet in diameter, were placed in the trees at about 40 feet from the ground." Six sets of eggs were collected here between February 15 and 18, 1909, of which the average measurements were 52 by 36.5 millimeters; the eggs showing the four extremes measure 59.4 by 42.1, 55.5 by 43.8 and 47.5 by 34.2 millimeters.

DISTRIBUTION

Range.—Known only from southern Lower California (Espiritu Santo Island and San Jose del Cabo) where it is probably resident.

Egg dates.—Southern Lower California: 12 records, February 15 to June 19; 6 records, February 18.

ARDEA CINEREA CINEREA Linnaeus

EUROPEAN HERON

HABITS

Contributed by Charles Wendell Townsend

While this heron ranges through Europe, Asia, and Africa, its only claim for recognition in North America is the fact that it is accidental in Greenland. A young bird has been found dead there and Hagerup (1891) says it is "an occasional visitor in south Greenland. In Benzon's collection there was a skin from Godthaab taken January 14, 1877."

Resembling closely our great blue heron in plumage and habits, the European heron, known in England as the common heron or simply as the heron—the *hearnshaw* of Shakespeare's day—differs from our bird in being somewhat smaller and paler, and in lacking the rich brown of the legs and bend of wing.

Nesting.—Where the birds are much persecuted and diminished in numbers, solitary nests are occasionally found, but the normal habit of this heron appears to be to nest in colonies of from 3 or 4 pairs up to 20 or 30 or even to 100 or more. As a rule the heron builds its nest near the top of a tall tree, a pine or fir or oak, often in open situations and on high ground, frequently at a distance from the water yet in some cases close beside it. Nesting colonies are also found on precipitous cliffs near the coast, the nest being placed on low bushes or amidst ivy. The nest is said on rare occasions to be placed among reeds and rushes on the ground. The excrements of the birds have a disastrous effect on the trees, as in all heronries, and, on this account, the attempt is sometimes made to drive the birds out, although as a rule a heronry is considered an interesting and desirable asset to an estate. Although heronries are not so large nor so numerous in England as in the old days of falconry when they were zealously guarded, they still exist in considerable numbers.

The nests are large flat structures made up of sticks and twigs, occasionally built up on old nests of cormorants, and lined with sheep's wool where this can be obtained on the moors, or with hair, dry grasses, moss, rushes or flags.

Eggs.—[Author's note: The European heron usually lays four or five eggs, but occasionally as many as six or even seven. They are practically indistinguishable in general appearance from those of our great blue heron. They are described in Witherby's (1290-24) Handbook as "dull light blue-green, frequently splashed with white-wash and sometimes stained with blood." The measurements therein given, of 101 eggs, average 60.2 by 43 millimeters; the eggs showing the four extremes measure **68.4** by 43.7, 61.5 by **49.7, 55.4** by 42.2 and 59.6 by **40** millimeters.]

Young.—According to Evans (1891), incubation is 25 or 26 days in length. Both parents feed the young which, helpless at first, later climb actively among the branches of the nesting tree and comport themselves in all respects like their near relatives in this country. A heronry resounds with the grunts, squeals, harsh screams, chattering, quackings, and barkings of the young birds eager to be fed.

Plumages.—[Author's note: The sequence of molts and plumages, from the downy young to the adult, which is fully described in Witherby's (1920–24) Handbook, seems to correspond with the sequence in our great blue heron. The juvenal plumage is worn for about a year. The second winter plumage is much like the adult, but the fully adult plumage is not complete until the young bird is 2 years old. Adults have a complete molt between July and November and a limited spring molt, especially of the crest feathers, between February and April.]

Food.—Fish of all sorts are the chief food of the European heron, but worms, water insects, newts, frogs, mice, water voles, and young birds are all welcomed.

Behavior.—The European heron like our great blue heron is shy and wary and well able to take care of itself, rarely allowing a human being to approach within gunshot. It is a striking figure as it stands motionless on its long legs in the marsh with its neck doubled up. Its keen eyes are on the watch for game, and, if a fish swims within striking distance, the heron's bill and long neck dart out with lightning speed and the prey is transfixed. Again it walks stealthily toward its prey, lifting and putting down its great feet with slow deliberation and holding its body horizontal. It rarely misses its aim and is a most successful fisherman. A. H. Patterson (1905) says: "I have seen a heron so replete with fish that it could swallow no more, yet continue to capture eels and let them go again, probably with regret, or possibly for the fun of the exercise."

When disturbed, the heron jumps into the air with quick, nervous wing flaps and with outstretched neck, the picture of awkward clumsiness, but it soon folds up its neck, extends its legs behind, and, with slow measured beats of its huge wings, it flies away in majestic grace and beauty. The cry of the adult, according to Hudson (1902), "is powerful and harsh, and not unlike the harsh alarm cry of the peacock."

Game.—The heron was formerly considered the most desirable quarry in falconry and on this account herons were protected by act of Parliament. It was royal game and the heronries were sacred. John Shaw (1635) gives the following quaint description of the sport: "The heron or hernshaw is a large fowle that liveth about waters * * * and hath a marvelous hatred to the hawk, which hatred is duly returned. When they fight above in the air, they labour both especially for this one thing—that one may ascend and be above the other. Now, if the hawk getteth the upper place, he overthroweth and vanquisheth the heron with a marvellous earnest flight." After one or two strikes, if the hawk is successful, the heron is borne to the ground where the attack is renewed, and the sharp, daggerlike bill of the heron and his great strength and quickness in striking make him a formidable antagonist. In later years it became a point of honor for the falconers to ride hard to the finish to make sure that the heron was uninjured. A copper ring was fixed to his leg with the date of capture engraved on it and the place of its liberation.

The heron was formerly considered a delicacy for the table. In the reign of Edward IV no less than 400 herons were served at the enthronement of the Archbishop of York, and there is the record of "6 hearnshaws" being served at the Hall of the Stationers' Company as late as 1812. Its fat, especially from the marrow of the thigh bones was believed to be especially attractive to fish and was much sought after as an ingredient in the pastes used as bait.

[AUTHOR'S NOTE.—Since the above was written, Julian S. Huxley (1924) has published some observations on the ceremonies of courtship, nest relief, stick presentation, and other expressions of emotion, as seen in the common European heron. The author would refer the reader to this interesting paper, which is well worth reading.]

DISTRIBUTION

Range.—Great Britain and most of continental Europe and Asia, south of 60° north latitude, and parts of tropical India and Africa, south to Cape Colony; replaced by a closely allied form in eastern Siberia, China, and Japan. Accidental in Iceland and Greenland (Godthaab, Jan. 14, 1877). Casual in the Faroes, Madeira, and Ascension.

Egg dates.—Great Britain: 10 records, February 28 to May 20; 5 records, March 26 to May 12.

CASMERODIUS EGRETTA (Gmelin)

AMERICAN EGRET

HABITS

The "long white," as it is called by the plume hunters of Florida, is well named. Its long, smooth, slender neck, so expressive in its varied poses, its long, graceful, flowing plumes, reaching far beyond its tail like a bridal train, and the exquisite purity of its snowy-white plumage make a picture of striking beauty when sharply outlined against a background of dark green foliage or when clearly mirrored on the surface of a quiet pool. Again, as it springs into flight with neck and legs extended, and as it flaps majestically away on its broad white wings, it seems to be the longest, the slenderest, and the most ethereal of the herons.

The beauty of its long, flowing plumes, which adorn its back only during the breeding season, has well-nigh proved its undoing; relentlessly pursued by avaricious plume hunters for many years, it has been driven from many of its former haunts and has been dangerously near extermination. But through adequate protection in certain places and by virtue of its own natural shyness, it has survived and is now increasing in many of its former haunts. It was never as numerous as its smaller relative, the snowy egret, and its numbers were proportionately less reduced. And now there is every reason to believe that it will continue to increase in favorable localities.

Courtship.—Audubon (1840) gives the only account I have seen of this interesting performance as follows:

As early as December I have observed vast numbers congregated, as if for the purpose of making choice of partners, when the addresses of the males were paid in a very curious and to me interesting manner. Near the plantation of John Bulow, Esq., in east Florida, I had the pleasure of witnessing this sort of tournament or dress ball from a place of concealment not more than 100 yards distant. The males, in strutting round the females, swelled their throats, as cormorants do at times, emitted gurgling sounds, raising their long plumes almost erect, paced majestically before the fair ones of their choice. Although these snowy beaux were a good deal irritated by jealousy, and conflicts now and then took place, the whole time I remained much less fighting was exhibited than I had expected from what I had already seen in the case of the great blue heron, *Ardea Herodias*. These meetings took place about 10 o'clock in the morning, or after they had all enjoyed a good breakfast, and continued until nearly 3 in the afternoon, when, separating into flocks of 8 or 10 individuals, they flew off to search for food. These maneuvers were continued nearly a week, and I could with ease, from a considerable distance, mark the spot, which was a clear sand bar, by the descent of the separate small flocks previous to their alighting there.

Nesting.—When I first visited Florida, in 1902, the egrets were probably at their lowest ebb, though they were still to be found in small numbers in all the localities we visited. In Brevard County we visited two localities, small cypress swamps, where the year before large breeding rookeries of egrets existed, but not an occupied nest was to be seen. On the upper St. Johns we saw a few egrets, but found no nests. In Monroe County in 1903, among perhaps 4,000 birds in the big Cuthbert rookery, we counted only 18 American egrets and found 7 nests. In the latter locality they increased decidedly during the following five years; when we visited the Cuthbert rookery in 1908, we estimated that it contained between 300 and 400 American egrets. Their nests were scattered all over the rookery and were mostly on the tops of the mangroves, where the birds could obtain a good outlook.

The largest rookery of American egrets that I have ever seen is now safely guarded in a United States bird reservation, locally known as Bird Key, in Boca Ceiga Bay, Pinellas County, Florida. It is well named, for it is a bird paradise, densely populated during the breeding season with many thousands of water birds, Florida cormorants, brown pelicans, white ibises, American and snowy egrets, Ward, Lousiana, and yellow-crowned night herons. I made a number of visits to this most interesting rookery during the spring of 1925, and became quite familiar with its varied bird population. At the time of my first visit, on March 11, the American egrets were already well along with their nesting and apparently all had eggs. They were grouped in a densely populated, but quite extensive area in the most heavily wooded portion of the island, where the trees were tallest and thickest, red and black mangroves, buttonwoods, bays and willows. They were intimately associated with Ward herons and Florida cormorants and apparently on good terms with them. The Ward herons had young in their nests, at that time, in the tops of the tallest trees. But the cormorants, the most numerous species on the island, were then busy with their courtships and were building their nests in the tops of all of the larger trees; these filthy, black creatures seemed out of place among the beautiful white egrets. The egret's nests were placed at various heights in the smaller and medium-sized trees, from 12 to 30 feet up; a few were in the larger trees, but usually not near the tops. The nests were frail and poorly made, as is usually the case with this species. The birds were very tame and it was an easy matter to watch them, even without a blind, at short range; but the foliage was so dense, with practically no open spaces, that it was almost impossible to get clear views for photographs. It was interesting though to watch the home life of these beautiful birds and see them standing or sitting on their nests all around us. Even when not alarmed they seemed none too anxiously to incubate, but spent much time standing on or near their nests in various attitudes of indolence or indifference; eventually they would settle down on their nests. Occasionally we saw the ceremony of nest relief, a spectacular performance; with much loud croaking, to which his mate replies, the male alights in the top of the nest-tree or one near it; with much display of plumage, raised wings and elevated plumes, he walks along or down the branches to the nest, where he greets and caresses his mate; she responds by lifting her head and raising the plumes above her back; in graceful attitudes they admire each others charms, a beautiful picture of conjugal happiness and a great display of purest loveliness; after a few moments she departs and he assumes charge of the nest. Settling down to incubate is a deliberate process; after standing over the eggs for awhile, the bird slowly crouches and finally settles down with the back plumes elevated and spread; gradually these are lowered, the head is drawn down between the shoulders and the long plumes extend beyond the nest like graceful white streamers.

The nests of the American egret are much like those of other herons, but are usualy not as well made; they are flat platforms of sticks rather loosely put together and not much larger than the better types of night herons' nests. Often there is little or no attempt at nest lining, but sometimes the nests are considerably hollowed and well lined with fine twigs, vines, or weed stems.

American egrets were not common on the coast of Texas in 1923, but we found three small colonies. On one of a chain of islands between Mesquite and San Antonio Bays we found a colony of five or six pairs nesting in a clump of small willows in the midst of a large breeding colony of reddish egrets, Louisiana herons, and snowy egrets; the island was low and rather swampy, overgrown with low bushes and herbage, in which the smaller herons were nesting; in the small clump of willows, the only trees of any size on the island, a few pairs of Ward herons were nesting with the American egrets. The egrets' nests were from 4 to 8 feet up in the small trees and all contained young of various ages on May 16.

In Victoria County, Texas, we found two colonies. One, in a button-willow swamp on Weed Prairie, had once been well populated; the nests were 8 or 10 feet above the water, which was 2 or 3 feet deep, in the willows; most of the nests had been abandoned when we visited it on May 21. The other, a colony of 25 or 30 pairs, was in a clump of willows in an open space among tall timber in a big rookery of white ibises, roseate spoonbills, Ward, and little blue herons. The nests were from 10 to 20 feet up in the willows and contained young of various ages on May 30.

W. J. Erichsen has sent me the following notes on a Georgia colony:

On May 11, 1915, a long-planned visit to the heron rookery on Ossabaw Island, 20 miles southwest of Savannah, became a reality. We began working our way through the rank vegetation toward the little colony of egrets which we determined upon as our first objective. Before we had penetrated the marginal growth many yards, egrets began to vacate their nests, most of the birds withdrawing entirely from the pond, alighting singly or in little groups on the branches of the tall pines at the far end of the pond where they stood out against the dark green foliage in statuesque beauty. As our stay in close proximity to their nests lengthened, some individuals were seen cautiously leaving their outposts and soaring overhead at considerable heights, their anxiety to return to their nests partly overcoming their wary nature. With snakelike necks drawn close in and legs extended straight behind they soared and circled lightly above our heads, mingling with the myriads of Louisiana and little blue herons whose homes were also in the willows here below.

Passing through the rank vegetation growing about the margin we find ourselves in more open water. Little islands of tall green saw-grass and cat-tail flags spring up here and there, between which are open spaces of water of various size. In some of these islands willows have taken root in the soft ooze, sometimes in clusters of two or three but more often singly. In the stoutest of these trees egrets had built their nests usually at a point where several stout limbs converged. Two or three pairs generally occupied a tree, but no nests of other species of herons were seen among the little colony, which occupied only a very small area. They seem to prefer living apart, at least they appear not to crave such close association with other herons as do the little blue and Louisiana. Although we made no very careful or accurate count of the number of pairs nesting here we estimated it not to exceed 15.

The nest is a very bulky platform of stout twigs substantially interlaced, nevertheless the structures can be pulled apart with suprisingly little effort. Any limb or crotch capable of supporting a nest was utilized, most of them being 8 or 10 feet above the surface of the water. We examined about 10 nests, all containing three eggs apparently only a few days incubated.

One of the most interesting rookeries of American egrets is still flourishing and probably increasing under the protection of a sportsman's club in South Carolina. This has been· visited and attractively described by Herbert K. Job (1905) and Dr. Frank M. Chapman (1908a). The latter writes:

For 2 miles we paddled thus in a bewildering maze of sunlit, buttressed cypress trunks with shiny, round-headed "knees" protruding from the water, and with every branch heavily moss drapped. The dark waters showed no track, the brown trunks no blaze. We seemed to be voyaging into the unknown.

Finally, the environs were passed and we now approached the most densely populated part of the rookery. Thousands of Louisiana and little blue herons left their nests in the lower branches and bushes, their croaking chorus of alarm punctuated by the louder more raucous squawks of hundreds of egrets, as they flew from their nests in the upper branches. It was a confusing and fascinating scene, an admirable climax to the passage through the weird forest. The little blue and Louisiana herons nested at an average height of 6 to 8 feet. One bush held no less than 32 nests, all of which contained eggs, few young of either species having yet been hatched. The egrets nested at an average height of 40 feet. Eggs were in some nests, while in others there were nearly fledged young. While far less shy than I had before found them, the birds were still abundantly wary, and obviously could be observed to advantage only from concealment.

Dr. T. Gilbert Pearson (1919) discovered a colony of "probably 20 pairs" of American egrets in Brunswick County, North Carolina, in 1898. This is probably the only colony in that State and Mr. Pearson says:

We have visited the birds during the nesting period seven different times within the past 12 years, and have found them just about holding their own in numbers.

Their nests were high up in tall cypress trees. The lowest one discovered was at least 40 feet and the others were fully 80 feet above the water.

George Willett (1919) describes an entirely different manner of nesting found in the marshes of Malheur Lake, Oregon. He writes:

On June 28, while rowing along the outer edge of the tules at the southern end of the lake, I finally located the colony in two small tule patches about 3 miles east of the mouth of the Blitzen River. Twenty pairs of the birds were nesting at this date, three nests containing eggs, apparently heavily incubated, and the other nests containing young of various ages, from newly hatched to half grown ones that were able to walk around among the tules. The nests were built on bent-down tule stalks much in the same fashion as nests of the ibis. Some were within 1 foot of the water and others nearly 4 feet up. They were large and rather well made of tule stalks and in two instances contained branches of greasewood that must have been carried at least a mile. The nest complement was from three to five in number, usually four.

A similar method of nesting was noted by George B. Sennett (1878) near Brownsville, Texas. The nests are described as "bulky, composed of the dead and broken down rushes, about 2 feet in diameter, and situated from 1 to 3 feet above the water."

Eggs.—The American egret lays from three to four eggs; I have never seen or heard of any larger sets. In shape they are usually oval with variations to elliptical oval. The shell is smooth with little or no gloss. The color is pale bluish green, varying from "pale Niagara green" to "pale olivine." The measurements of 53 eggs average 56.5 by 40.5 millimeters; the eggs showing the four extremes measure **68.5** by 41, 60 by **43**, **52.5** by 39.5, and 53.5 by **38** millimeters.

Young.—The period of incubation is probably about 23 or 24 days. In nests that are situated at considerable heights the young are inclined to remain until they can fly, but in the lower nests they are much more precocial and inclined to wander over the immediate surroundings of the nest. I have found them much more timid than other young herons and more inclined to leave the nest, to climb with surprising agility over the surrounding branches. I have experienced considerable difficulty in getting near enough to the half grown young to photograph them; they are lively travelers and generally succeed in keeping out of range.

It is interesting to watch the feeding of the young, as I have seen it from a blind at short range. The young have been crouching quietly in the nest, perhaps asleep or dozing; suddenly their keen eyes, or ears, detect the returning mother bird and they are all alert; excitedly they stretch their long necks and cry for food. At first she stands on or near the nest in a disinterested attitude until she is ready to regurgitate the semidigested food; they become impatient at the delay and peck at her plumage, or rise up and seize her bill shaking it vigorously and worrying her into action; at length she raises her beautiful plumes above her back, a token of her affection, lowers her head and delivers the coveted food. For the younger birds a more or less souplike food, fish chowder, is delivered into the mouth of the young bird; for older birds a fish only partially digested is deposited on the nest, where it is picked up and swallowed. I have seen two or three small young fed at one feeding.

Doctor Chapman (1908a) has described the feeding process very well, as follows:

Doubtless, the young birds were not a little puzzled by the unusual reluctance of their parents to administer to their wants. In vain they uttered their froglike *kek-kek-kek*, and stretched their necks hopefully. The old birds were not assured.

So the young resorted to their customary occupations of leg or wing stretching, or yawning or preening a brother's or sister's feathers, picking at imaginary objects here and there, all good exercises for growing birds. The larger ones made little journeys to the limbs near the nests, the neck taking a different curve with every movement, and expressing every emotion from extreme dejection to alert and eager expectancy. Finally, as the old birds were convinced that the blind was harmless, their reward came. With harsh, rattling notes and raised crest one of the parents alit near the nest. Its superbly threatening attitude was clearly not alarming to the young birds, who welcomed it by voice and upstretched, extended neck. Gravely the parent stood regarding its young, while its crest dropped and its pose relaxed. Then, as it stepped to the edge of the nest, it lowered its head, when its bill was immediately seized by one of the youngsters. The young bird did not thrust its bill down the parental throat, nor was the parent's bill introduced into that of its offspring. The hold of the young bird was such as one would take with a pair of shears, if one were to attempt to cut off the adult's bill at the base. In this manner the old bird's head was drawn down into the nest, where the more or less digested fish was disgorged, and at once devoured by the young.

Plumages.—The downy young egret is partially covered with long, pure white down, through which much light green naked skin shows on the neck and under parts; the bill and feet are light green and yellowish. On the forehead, crown and sides of the head the down is long and hairlike, an inch and a quarter long on the top of the head; the entire back is covered with somewhat shorter, softer down; the under parts are more scantily covered with coarser down; and the throat is naked.

By the time that the young bird is half grown it is practically fully fledged; the juvenal plumage appears first on the back, then on the wings, breast and crown; later the tail appears; and the last of the down is replaced on the neck and belly. This plumage is all pure white, without any trace of plumes. Young birds begin to acquire their first dorsal plumes, aigrettes, during their first prenuptial molt, which begins sometimes early in January, but sometimes not till February or later. The growth of plumes during the first year is always limited and sometimes omitted. At the first postnuptial molt young birds become practically adult.

The European egret is said to have two complete molts each year, but I can not find any trace of molting primaries in American birds during the prenuptial molt. The postnuptial molt is complete, the primaries being molted in August. The long, flowing train of decomposed feathers, known as plumes or aigrettes, is a nuptial adornment of breeding adults; it is acquired at the prenuptial molt in January and February and is shed soon after the breeding season is over, in June and July. I have counted as many as 54 long dorsal plumes in an extra fine specimen, but usually there are much fewer. The adult winter plumage, acquired by a complete postnuptial molt in July and August, is not always wholly devoid of plumes; but the plumes, if present, are fewer in number and much shorter than in spring. The plumage is, of course, all pure white at all ages and seasons.

Food.—Egrets obtain their food in the marshes and rice fields and around the marshy shores of lakes and ponds where their tall, graceful figures tower above the low vegetation or are reflected in the smooth waters as beautiful silhouettes in white. Their movements are stately and the strokes of their rapierlike bills are quick and sure. Their food consists only partially of small fishes and it includes frogs, lizards, small snakes, mice, moles, fiddlers, snails, grasshoppers, and other insects, as well as some vegetable matter. Oscar E. Baynard (1912) says:

Food of 50 young egrets that was disgorged by them at the nests immediately after being fed, running over a period of four weeks. The total of the 50 meals follows: 297 small frogs, 49 small snakes, mostly the water moccasin, 61 young fish, suckers, not edible, 176 crayfish.

Dr. Alexander Wetmore (1916) says of a bird taken in Porto Rico:

The single stomach available for examination contained 4 per cent of vegetable rubbish taken as extraneous matter with the animal food. Remains of one mole cricket (*Scapteriscus didactylus*) and seven entire grasshoppers, with fragments of many more, were found, as well as a moth and three large dragon flies. A small goby and seven entire frogs (*Leptodactylus albilabris*) with fragments of others, made up 69 per cent of the contents. Orthoptera amouted to 15 per cent, a surprising fact and one that should be given due weight in considering the status of this species.

Behavior.—The pose of the American egret in flight is not unlike that of the other herons; when well under way it carries its neck folded backward, with its head between its shoulders, and its long legs extended behind it as a rudder. But it seems to me that it is easily recognized at even a great distance by its more slender form and by its proportionately longer and broader wings; it is markedly different in these respects from the smaller white herons, and it is a much lighter bird with a more buoyant flight than the heavier great white heron.

It is much at home in the tree tops where it is very light, graceful and agile. A striking instance of its agility is related by C. J. Maynard (1896) who had made a pet of a young egret; he writes:

This bird was accustomed to sit on the prow of a canoe, which was towed astern of the yacht, and when hungry, the heron would walk deliberately along the rope, by which the smaller vessel was fastened to the larger, and which was some 10 feet long, and thus come on board. One day when it was making this trip, a sudden flaw struck the sail, causing the rope to sway, and the bird was thrown into the water. We were moving at the rate of 10 or 12 miles an hour, and the bow of the little boat swept past the heron in an instant, but it appeared to know just what to do, for, without making any usless struggles, it merely reached out and caught the edge of the rapidly passing stern with its bill, gave a flap or two, and in a moment regained its perch on the prow.

The only note I have heard uttered by the American egret is a loud, hoarse croak on a low key.   Doctor Chapman (1908*a*) refers to it as a "rapid *cuk, cuk, cuk* with the regularity and persistence of a metronome."

Unlike some other herons, the American egrets do not feed at night, but resort regularly to certain favorite roosting places where large numbers often congregate.   They gather at the roosting places just before dark, spend the night in the trees, and scatter out over the surrounding country early in the morning.   I once saw such a roosting place in Texas.   We had been hunting all day for a white ibis rookery and had driven down, just before dark, to look at a button-willow swamp where we thought it might be.   We were delighted to see that the trees, which were standing in about 2 feet of water and were surrounded by open water, were covered with birds, American egrets, snowy egrets, and little blue herons.   It was a wonderful sight when they all flew up, at our appoach.   It was too dark to investigate it further that night, but we had visions of some great chances for photographs the next day.   We were disappointed, however, on our return the next morning, to find it practically deserted; only a few scattering birds remained, which promptly flew away.   It was a night roosting place in an old rookery.

Audubon (1840), Maynard (1896), and Chapman (1892) all refer to this roosting habit.   Audubon (1840) writes:

The American egrets are much attached to their roosting places, to which they remove from their feeding grounds regularly about an hour before the last glimpse of day; and I can not help expressing my disbelief in the vulgar notion of birds of this family usually feeding by night, as I have never observed them so doing even in countries where they were most abundant.   Before sunset the egrets and other herons (excepting perhaps the bitterns and night herons) leave their feeding grounds in small flocks, often composed of only a single family, and proceed on wing in the most direct course, at a moderate height, to some secure retreat more or less distant, according to the danger they may have to guard against. Flock after flock may be seen repairing from all quarters to these places of repose, which one may readily discover by observing their course.   Approach and watch them.   Some hundreds have reached the well-known rendezvous.   After a few gratulations you see them lower their bodies on the stems of the trees or bushes on which they have alighted, fold their necks, place their heads beneath the scapular feathers, and adjust themselves for repose.   Daylight returns and they are all in motion.   The arrangement of their attire is not more neglected by them than by the most fashionable fops, but they spend less time at the toilet.   Their rough notes are uttered more loudly than in the evening, and after a very short lapse of time they spread their snowy pinions and move, in different directions, to search for fiddlers, fish, insects of all sorts, small quadrupeds or birds, snails, and reptiles, all of which form the food of this species.

Doctor Chapman (1892) refers to a roosting tree in Cuba as follows:

There was a flock of about 20 of these birds at San Pablo which came each night to roost in a tree at the border of the river.   They appeared in a body with much regularity just after sunset, and after circling about the tree once or twice alighted on its branches.   One now heard a low croaking chorus as the birds selected perches and settled themselves for the night.   This rookery was but 200 yards from the houses and mill of the estate, and not more than 60 feet from a well-traveled road.   The confidence thus displayed by the birds in their choice of a roost was in striking contrast with the habits of the shy, much-hunted egret of Florida.

Enemies.—Great damage is done in the breeding rookeries of this and all the smaller herons by crows and vultures, which devour all the eggs and young that they can find unguarded.   The bird photographer, who drives these shy birds from their nests and keeps them off for some time, is likely to find most of the nests in his vicinity rifled of their contents.

Man has always been the arch enemy of the egrets.   The destruction wrought by the plume hunters has been most cruel and wasteful; as the plumes are at the best during the breeding season, the birds were shot in their nesting rookeries, leaving the eggs to rot or the young to starve in the nests.   No thought was had for the future and whole rookeries were systematically annihilated.

The slaughter began in Aubudon's (1840) time.   He speaks of "a person who, on offering a double-barreled gun to a gentleman near Charleston for 100 white herons fresh killed, received that number and more the next day."   His friend Bachman brought home 46 from a single day's shooting and said that "many more might have been killed, but we became tired of shooting them."   And the slaughter continued with unabated fury in all parts of the world where egrets were to be found.   Herbert K. Job (1905), writing at a time when the egrets were at about their lowest ebb, published some interesting figures to account for their disappearance.   He writes:

When we know about the millinery plume trade, we understand the reason. In 1903 the price for plumes offered to hunters was $32 per ounce, which makes the plumes worth about twice their weight in gold.   There will always be men who would break any law for such profit.   No rookery of these herons can long exist, unless it be guarded by force of arms day and night.   Here are some official figures of the trade from one source alone, of auctions at the London Commercial Sales Rooms during 1902.   There were sold 1,608 packages of "ospreys," that is, herons' plumes.   A package is said to average in weight 30 ounces.   This makes a total of 48,240 ounces.   As it requires about four birds to make an ounce of plumes, these sales meant 192,960 herons killed at their nests, and from two to three times that number of young or eggs destroyed.   Is it, then, any wonder that these species are on the verge of extinction?

The absurd story was circulated by the millinery trade, as an argument in their defense, that the aigrettes were shed by the birds and picked up from the ground under the nests in protected rookeries; and many people believed the story.   I have explored many rookeries, looking for shed plumes, but can count on the fingers of one hand all I have ever found; and these were soiled and worn.

A few such plumes are picked up and sold, but they are known as "dead plumes" and bring in the market about one-fifth of the price of "live plumes." T. Gilbert Pearson (1912) published a long list of affidavits emphasizing the falsity of such propaganda, among which the following, from an old plume hunter, is most striking:

My work led me into every part of Venezuela and Colombia where these birds are to be found, and I have never yet found or heard tell of any *garceros* that were guarded for the purpose of simply gathering the feathers from the ground. No such a condition exists in Venezuela. The story is absolutely without foundation, in my opinion, and has simply been put forward for commercial purposes. The natives of the country, who do virtually all of the hunting for feathers, are not provident in their nature, and their practices are of a most cruel and brutal nature. I have seen them frequently pull the plumes from wounded birds, leaving the crippled birds to die of starvation, unable to respond to the cries of their young in the nests above, which were calling for food. I have known these people to tie and prop up wounded egrets on the marsh where they would attract the attention of other birds flying by. These decoys they keep in this position until they die of their wounds or from the attacks of insects. I have seen the terrible red ants of that country actually eating out the eyes of these wounded, helpless birds that were tied up by the plume hunters. I could write you many pages of the horrors practiced in gathering aigrette feathers in Venezuela by the natives for the millinery trade of Paris and New York.

Fortunately for this and the following species these conditions have now largely changed and plume hunting has become a thing of the past in most of the regions where it was formerly practiced. The vigorous educational and legislative campaign of the National Association of Audubon Societies, and other organizations and individuals interested in bird protection, have created a world-wide sentiment against it and have resulted in adequate laws to prevent it. Many colonies have been successfully protected. Charles J. Pennock wrote me in 1917 that egrets were more numerous in Florida than they had been for many years, since the days of plume hunting. In Texas in 1923 I traveled around with an old plume hunter who told me that no plume hunting had deen done in Texas for many years and that the egrets were increasing. Two beautiful species have been saved.

Fall.—This and several other species of herons are much given to northward wanderings in summer and fall; it is usually, if not always, the young birds that indulge in these erratic journeys after the nesting season is over. We do not know where they come from or how far they travel; perhaps systematic banding of young birds may throw some light on the subject. But they appear at frequent intervals, and sometimes in considerable numbers, as far east as New York, Connecticut, Massachusetts, and Vermont. I have seen the bird on Cape Cod as early as July 4 and it has been seen as late as September. Throughout the southern portion of its range, from Florida and the Gulf States, it is permanently resident; but it retires in the fall from the more northern portions of its breeding range.

Winter.—Thanks to the protection afforded it by the Audubon Society and by local sentiment, we found this beautiful egret to be ꝉ very common bird in Pinellas County, Florida, particularly in the vicinity of Boca Ceiga Bay, during the winter of 1924 and 1925. One day in November I counted 41 in sight at one time on a mud flat near Pass-a-Grille; they were in company with three white pelicans, four wood ibises, a number of little blue herons, and a few Lousiana herons. They were seen almost daily on the mud flats in the bay at low tide, and at high tide they resorted to the shallow lagoons or to fresh-water ponds. They could be easily recognized at a great distance by the long neck and slender body and at a considerable distance by the large yellow bill. A favorite resort of theirs was a small pond hole close to a much-traveled road on Long Key, where I lived; they were almost always there at high tide during November and December, sometimes as many as 15 or 20 of them; they paid no attention to passing automobiles, which were constantly buzzing by within a few feet, but, if one stopped for an instant, they were off immediately; any attempt to approach the pond on foot was utterly useless. Their confidence was well placed, for no one ever harmed them; but they showed wise discrimination in other places, for it was impossible to approach them anywhere else.

Before they began to resort to their breeding grounds on Bird Key, referred to above, they roosted at night on a small mangrove key in a secluded section of the bay, far from any human habitations. The black mangroves in the center were whitewashed with their droppings and the ground under them was littered with white feathers and a few plumes. I never saw any egrets there in the daytime.

DISTRIBUTION

Breeding range.—South America, Central America, and southern and western United States. North to Oregon (Silver Lake and Malheur Lake); Nevada (Truckee Valley); Utah (Bear River marshes and Salt Lake Valley); Wisconsin (Two Rivers); northern Indiana (Knouts, Wolf Lake, and Steuben County); Virginia, one record (Arlington); and southern New Jersey (Cape May). East to New Jersey (Cape May); Virginia (Arlington); South Carolina (McClellanville and Mount Pleasant); Georgia (Savannah and Cumberland Island); Florida (Orange Lake, Lake Jesup, Lake Harvey, Alligator Lake, Lake Gentry, Sebastian, Lake Okeechobee, Cuthbert Lake, and Cape Sable); Cuba (Manzanillo); Haiti; Porto Rico (Boqueron, Mameyes, and Pinero Island); Trinidad; Dutch Guiana (Maroni River); Brazil (San Paulo, Iguape, and Taguara); and Argentina (Buenos Aires and Cape San Antonio). South to Argentina (Cape

San Antonio, Carhue, and Chubut River); and Chile (Port Otway and Calbuco). West to Chile (Calbuco, Lake Aculco, Santiago, Coquimbo, Tarapaca, and Sacaya); Peru (Lima, Santa Cruz, and Junin); Ecuador (Babahoyo and Manto); Colombia (Meta River and Lake of Paturio); Costa Rica (San Jose, Miravalles, and La Palma); Nicaragua (Escondido River and Lake Nicaragua); Honduras (Tigre Island); Guatemala (Lake of Duenas and Chiapam); Guerrero, Mexico (Acapulco); Sinaloa, Mexico (Mazatlan); Lower California (San Jose del Cabo and Santa Margarita Island); California (Buena Vista Lake, Tulare Lake, Riverdale, formerly Stockton, and Sacramento); and Oregon (Silver Lake).

The account above given refers to the distribution of the egret before the plume hunters decimated their ranks. At the present time their breeding range in North America is restricted almost entirely to the States of the Gulf coast; Florida (Monroe County, Indian Key Reservation, Myakka River, Orange Lake, and Tallahassee); Louisiana (Delta of the Mississippi River and Cameron Parish); Texas (Karankawa Bay in Calhoun County, Mesquite Bay, Aransas County, and Guadalupe Valley, Victoria County); the States of the South Atlantic coast, Georgia (Okefinokee Swamp and Bird Pond, Chatham county); South Carolina (Mount Pleasant and Washoe Reserve near McClellanville); and North Carolina (Orton Lake, between Wilmington and the mouth of the Cape Fear River). Small colonies are also known in the Mississippi Valley; Arkansas (Walker Lake); and Tennessee (Reelfoot Lake); and also in California (Tulare Lake and Clear Lake); and in Oregon (Silver Lake and Malheur Lake).

Winter range.—South America, Central America, some of the islands of the Caribbean Sea and the southern and western United States. In North America the winter range of the egret extends north to California (Santa Cruz, formerly San Francisco, and Stockton); Oregon (formerly Fort Klamath); Texas (Giddings and Galveston); Louisiana (Marsh Island and Vermillion Bay); Florida (Gainsville); and South Carolina (Frogmore).

Spring migration.—Early dates of arrival are: Oregon, Silver Lake, April 14, 1913, and Malheur Lake, March 12, 1916; Arizona, Phoenix, March 30; Colorado, Denver, April 26, 1907; Louisiana, New Orleans, March 16, 1895; Mississippi, Rodney, March 19; Illinois, Canton, April 11, Peoria, March 20, and Grandridge, April 19; Iowa, Keokuk, April 17, 1894, and Wall Lake, March 22, 1912; Nebraska, Nehawka, May 2, 1905; Indiana, Bicknell, March 11, and Waterloo, April 22; Ohio, Sandusky, April 29; South Carolina, Charleston, February 23, 1913; District of Columbia, Washington, May 30, 1891 (only spring record); and Pennsylvania, Osceola Mills, April 22, 1893.

Fall migration.—Late dates of departure are: Oregon, Klamath Falls, October 31, 1912; California, Clear Lake, September 22, 1911, and Mona Lake, September 21, 1901; Louisiana, New Orleans, December 19, 1893 (possibly wintering); New Jersey, Audubon, September 4, 1912; District of Columbia, Washington, September 22, 1914; Maryland, Ocean City, September 23, 1894; and South Carolina, Charleston, November 6, 1913.

Casual records.—In common with many other species of herons, the egret frequently migrates in summer long distances north of its normal breeding range. Specimens have been collected at this season north to Manitoba (Lake Winnipegosis, summer of 1888); Minnesota (Lanesboro, July 21, 1884, and Wilder, June 16, 1894); Ontario (Rockliffe, spring of 1883, and Dundas County, August 3, 1916); Quebec (Montreal and Godbout); New Brunswick (Grand Manan, August, 1879); and Nova Scotia (Halifax, summer of 1867). In addition to these northernmost records there are numerous occurrences for Colorado, Kansas, Michigan, Ohio, New York, Massachusetts, Rhode Island, and the other New England States, including Maine.

Egg dates.—Flordia: 36 records, December 8 to June 14; 18 records, March 29 to May 1. Texas: 15 records, April 4 to May 20; 8 records, April 14 to May 16. Oregon: 8 records, April 16 to June 28.

EGRETTA CANDIDISSIMA CANDIDISSIMA (Gmelin)

SNOWY EGRET

HABITS

This beautiful little heron, one of nature's daintiest and most exquisite creatures, is the most charming of all our marsh birds. The spotless purity of its snowy plumage, adorned with airy, waving plumes, and its gentle, graceful manners, make it the center of attraction wherever it is seen. While darting about in the shallow water in pursuit of its lively prey, its light curving plumes fluttering in the breeze, it is a pretty picture of lovely animation. The full display of all its glory is seen as it approaches its nest to greet its mate or its young with all of the glorious plumes of its head, breast, and back erected and spread, like a filmy fan. It seems conscious of its beauty and likes to show off its charms for the benefit of its loved ones. No wonder that lovely woman appreciates the beauty of the plumes and longs to appropriate them to add to her own charms.

Courtship.—The display of plumes, referred to above, is a part of the courtship performance, where it is seen at its best, but it is also used all through the breeding season as a greeting to its mate or its young. In the full display the body is bent forward and downward, the neck is held in a graceful curve, the feathers of the head are raised in a vertical crest, the breast plumes are spread forward and downward, the wings are partially open and raised, and the plumes of the back are elevated and spread, with their curving tips waving in the air. Such a picture must be seen to be appreciated; no written words or printed photograph can do it justice.

During the mating season the males are quite quarrelsome and many little combats are seen, involving two or three birds. Standing erect with wings spread and crest raised, they spar with half open beaks or strike heavy blows with their wings, until one has enough and retires. Audubon (1840) describes the courtship, as follows:

At the approach of the breeding season, many spend a great part of the day at their roosting places, perched on the low trees principally growing in the water when every now and then they utter a rough guttural sort of sigh, raising at the same moment their beautiful crest and loose recurved plumes, curving the neck, and rising on their legs to their full height, as if about to strut on the branches. They act in the same manner while on the ground mating. Then the male, with great ardor, and the most graceful motions, passes and repasses for several minutes at a time before and around the female, whose actions are similiar, although she displays less ardor. When disturbed on such occasions, they rise high in the air, sail about and over the spot in perfect silence, awaiting the departure of the intruder, then sweep along, exhibiting the most singular movements, now and then tumbling over and over like the tumbler pigeon, and at length alight on a tree. On the contrary, when you intrude upon them while breeding, they rise silently on wing, alight on the trees near, and remain there until you depart.

Nesting.—During the first decade of this century, when my earlier visits to Florida were made, the numbers of this pretty little egret were about at their lowest ebb. We did not see any snowy egrets anywhere except in the breeding rookeries with other species and even there they were very shy. There were still a few left in the big rookeries on the upper St. Johns. Here we spent all of one day, April 20, 1902, and part of another in the largest of the rookeries at Braddock Lake, where hundreds of Louisiana herons and many little blue herons were breeding, among which were a few snowy egrets. We were unable to determine how many of this species were nesting there and I succeeded in positively identifying only two nests of the snowy egret. This rookery was on a small muddy island, in the middle of the great marsh, covered with a thick growth of small willows from 12 to 15 feet high. Although all three species of herons were very tame, alighting on the trees all about us, they were very careful not to settle down on any of the nests within sight of us; it was only by lying for hours carefully hidden under some thick clumps of large ferns that I was able to satisfactorily identify a few nests. The first nest of snowy egret, containing four eggs, was placed 8 feet up in a slender willow and was merely a flimsy platform of small sticks. The second nest held five eggs and was located only 5 feet up in a leaning willow; it was made of larger sticks and lined with fine twigs. Neither the nests nor the eggs of the snowy egret are in any way distinguishable, so far as I could determine, from those of either the Louisiana or the little blue herons. It is necessary to see the bird actually sitting on the nest to make identification sure; even then young little blue herons in the white phase are liable to lead to confusion and it is necessary to see the black legs and yellow feet or the graceful plumes of the snowy egret.

On both of my visits to the big rookery in Cuthbert Lake, in 1903 and 1908, there were a few pairs of snowy egrets among the hosts of other small herons; they were probably breeding there, but no nests were positively identified.

During the next two years conditions began to improve, as a result of protection and cessation of the plume trade. So that when I visited the coast of Texas, in 1923, I found snowy egrets quite common in many of the rookeries on the coastal islands. The best colony was found on Vingt-une Island in East Galveston Bay on May 5. We had seen many small white herons flying toward this island and were not surprised to find on it a flourishing colony, which we estimated to contain about 800 Louisiana herons, 400 snowy egrets, and 150 black-crowned night herons. It was a small marshy island, partly surrounded by shell beaches; on the boggy portions marsh grass was growing and extensive growths of tall canes separated the marshes from the drier portions; on the dry land were scattering clumps of low huisache trees and prickly pear cactus, together with thick tangles of vines, shrubbery, sunflowers, nettles, and other rank herbage. The snowy egrets' nests were mainly in the open places on the prickly pears or in the low huisache trees. They were mostly grouped in clusters by themselves; some were very close to the ground in the low cacti or underbrush and others were 5 or 6 feet up in the huisaches. They were rather flimsy structures made of sticks and pieces of dead canes and were lined with finer pieces of the same materials and rootlets; it seemed to us that the egrets used coarser material in their nests than the Louisiana herons. The nests all contained eggs, four or five in each, well advanced in incubation. I set up my blind in the center of this rookery and spent two or three interesting hours watching the home life of these beautiful birds. The nuptial display was often shown when a bird returned to greet its mate at the nest. I was greatly impressed with the tameness of these lovely birds.

Alexander Wilson (1832) gives us an idea of what conditions were in his day, when snowy egrets nested abundantly as far north as New Jersey; he writes:

On the 19th of May, I visited an extensive breeding place of the snowy heron, among the red cedars of Summers' Beach, on the coast of Cape May. The situation was very sequestered, bounded on the land side by a fresh water marsh or pond, and sheltered from the Atlantic by ranges of sand hills. The cedars, though not high, were so closely crowded together as to render it difficult to penetrate through among them. Some trees contained three, others four nests, built wholly of sticks. The birds rose in vast numbers, but without clamor, alighting on the tops of the trees around, and watching the result in silent anxiety. Among them were numbers of the night herons, and two or three purple-headed herons. Great quantities of egg shells lay scattered under the trees, occasioned by the depredations of the crows, who were continually hovering about the place. On one of the nests I found the dead body of the bird itself, half devoured by the hawks, crows, or gulls. She had probably perished in defence of her eggs.

An entirely different type of nesting was discovered by George B. Sennett (1878), in a marsh colony in Texas which no longer exists; he writes:

On May 15, I was delighted to meet with this, to me, the prettiest of all the herons in the salt marshes where it was breeding in innumerable numbers in company with others of the family. I otained numbers of birds, eggs, and young. It builds a flat nest of rushes, about 8 or 10 inches in diameter, with a depression of about 3 inches, and it is supported by broken-down, living reeds at a height above the water of from 6 inches to 3 feet. The young fresh from the egg are covered well with white down, and when a few days old are very pretty, compared with young herons. When I found them, the young were just hatching, and but few full families were out.

Similar nesting conditions in the tule marshes around Great Salt Lake have existed for many years; their history has been recorded by the Treganzas (1914); I quote from their notes of May 2, 1914, as follows:

This date found us in the marsh country destined for the rookeries. Within half a mile we noted a number of snowy herons rise at our right, whereupon we immediately secured a boat and set out to make investigation. We nosed into the dense tule growth to moor our boat, and had just started to break our way. With the first crackle of the reeds, head after head was seen to rise, long crane-like necks stretched up for inquiry, pure white birds, and in close proximity an iridescent black one; the ibis with their curved bills looking for all the world like quaint old Jews, lacking but spectacles and a skull cap. Another breaking of reeds and the whole colony rose en masse, a worrying confusion of wings and squawks and dangling legs; and for once we were actually convinced that white was black and black was white, so confounded were heron and ibis. This colony covered an area 20 yards wide by 100 yards long, and contained no less than 150 pairs of snowy herons, and about 100 pairs of white-faced glossy ibis. All of the ibis nests and many of the herons' were under construction, while some of the latter contained four to five fresh eggs. Having traversed this portion of the marsh at least once annually, we were surprised to find this new and larger colony, for previous years it contained only ducks and a very small colony of black-crowned night heron. All the nests were constructed of the growing reeds and rushes. Though quite dense, there was little matted down growth of years previous, thus much resembling the site of Black Sloughs, Salt Lake County.

Mr. Treganza writes to me that a colony which once numbered from 80 to 100 pairs, is now reduced to 50. He mentions also a colony of 50 or 60 pairs in the black sloughs and one of possibly 20 or 25 pairs at the mouth of the Jordan River. The other two colonies, at the mouth of Bear River and on Bear River Bay, numbered

75 to 100 pairs each when last visited in 1913. He says that the nests are in every way similiar to those of the white-faced glossy ibis, reeds, and rushes being used to form the platform which is attached to the growing tules; in some instances the nests have been built of small twigs and branches of the sage; and in other cases no nests have been made, the eggs simply being deposited in a well-defined depression in the broken and matted down tules of the previous year.

Eggs.—The snowy egret lays ordinarily four or five eggs, sometimes only three and rarely as many as six. These are ovate or oval in shape, generally near the latter. The shell is smooth with little or no gloss. The color is pale bluish green, varying from "pale Niagara green" to "pale glaucous green." The measurements of 46 eggs average 43 by 32.4 millimeters; the eggs showing the four extremes measure **48.4** by 33.3, 41.2 by **33.6, 40** by 31, and 42.5 by **30.5** millimeters.

Young.—Edward A. McIlhenny (1912) says that the period of incubation is 18 days. Both sexes apparently share in the incubation and the care of the young. William L. Dawson (1915) discovered a breeding colony of snowy egrets in Merced County, in California, in which he says that he established the fact that this species

deposits its eggs every other day, and the complementary fact that incubation begins with the deposition of the first egg. Indeed it could not well be otherwise, for a single day's exposure to that blazing interior sun would addle an egg however hardy. The youngsters showed, as the days passed, an exaggerated disparity in size and strength, yet even when a week old appeared amazingly small and helpless. Neither did they appear at all pugnatious as do baby squawks, but drew away timidly at the approach of the hand, and for the rest divided their time between panting lustily and scrambling about in search of shade.

Mr. McIlhenny (1912) **says** that the parent birds, at first during the warmer hours of the day shield the young birds from the sun under their drooping wings, as shown in one of his photographs. When 10 days old they show a marvellous appetite and are always clamoring for food. Either the father or mother bird watches the youngsters constantly, and when the absent mate returns they caress and coo, being a most loving pair, as if they had not seen each other for a week. In from 20 to 25 days the youngsters leave the nest and spend the day perched on the twigs of the home branch, going back to the nest at night. The young are fed on regurgitated food in the same manner as described under the previous species, in which the display of plumes is a pretty feature. How can any one who has witnessed such a picture of beautiful home life have the heart to break it up?

Plumages—The downy young snowy egret is much like that of the American egret, but smaller of course. The forehead, crown, occiput, and sides of the head are covered with long, hairlike plumes, long-

est on the crown, three-quarters of an inch; the back is covered more
scantily than the American egret, with long, soft, hairlike, white down;
the lower parts are very scantily covered with white down and the
throat is naked. The naked skin is light green, the bill and feet are
pale yellow, shaded with green on the upper surfaces.

The juvenal plumage, which is everywhere pure white with no
trace of plumes anywhere, is worn without much change through the
first fall and winter. Late in the winter or early in the spring, in
February or March, a partial molt produces rudimentary plumes on
the head, breast, and back. Young birds may breed in this first
nuptial plumage. The first postnuptial molt begins in June, is complete and produces a plumage indistinguishable from that of the
winter adult, when the young bird is less than a year and a half old.

Adults have a complete molt in summer, from June to September,
at which the beautiful nuptial plumes and aigrettes are shed and
replaced by the much shorter and straighter plumes of the winter
plumage. Beginning in January or February the partial prenuptial
molt produces the full perfection of the nuptial plumage, with its
beautiful, long, curving aigrettes.

Food.—Audubon (1840) has described the feeding habits of the
snowy egret so well that I can not do better than to quote his words,
as follows:

The snowy heron, while in the Carolinas, in the month of April, resorts to the
borders of the salt-water marshes and feeds principally on shrimps. Many individuals which I opened there contained nothing else in their stomachs. On the
Mississippi, at the time when the shrimps are ascending the stream, these birds
are frequently seen standing on floating logs, busily engaged in picking them up;
and on such occasions their pure white color renders them comspicuous and
highly pleasing to the eye. At a later period, they feed on small fry, fiddlers,
snails, aquatic insects, occasionally small lizards, and young frogs. Their
motions are generally quick and elegant, and, while pursuing small fishes, they
run swiftly through the shallows, throwing up their wings. Twenty or 30 seen
at once along the margins of a marsh or a river, while engaged in procuring
their food, form a most agreeable sight. In autumn and early spring they are
fond of resorting to the ditches of the rice fields, not unfrequently in company
with the blue herons.

Wilson (1832) adds: "It also feeds on the seeds of some species of
nymphae, and of several other aquatic plants." Oscar E. Baynard
(1912) found that 50 meals of young snowy egrets consisted of 120
small suckers, 762 grasshoppers, 91 cut-worms, 2 small lizards, 29
small crayfish, and 7 small mocassins, a most interesting collection,
which proves that this species is decidely beneficial. Dr. Alexander
Wetmore (1916) says of its feeding habits in Porto Rico:

Frequently the snowy egret feeds in lowland cane fields, especially when these
are wet or partly flooded. Often in flocks of three or four they feed in the dry
upland pastures. Two stomachs were available for examination, both of birds
which had been feeding in mangrove swamps. The main content of these is.

animal matter, vegetable remains occuring only as rubbish secured with other food and amounting to but 1 per cent. One bird taken near Rio Piedras had eaten two dragon-fly nymphs, a small crab, a lizard, and a small frog. The stomach of the other, secured, near Mameyes, was nearly filled with bones of small gobies, the remainder of the animal food consisting of fragments of flies of the family *Dolichopodidae* and bits of a grasshopper. In their excursions to drier fields the birds must secure other insects. They feed to a large extent upon fish, but the fishes taken are of no great importance and the birds are not abundant enough to become noxious.

Behavior.—Perhaps enough has been said above about its attractive behavior in its various lines of activity. In all of its movements it is light, airy, and active. It is very different in appearance and manner of flight from the American egret, besides being very much smaller. It is relatively much shorter and less slender, hence the plume hunter's name, "short white"; its wings are relatively smaller and its wing strokes are much quicker. From the white young of the little blue heron it is not so easily distinguished, unless one is near enough to see the plumes or the black legs and yellow feet of the snowy egret; in the little blue the legs and feet appear wholly dark. Audubon (1840) says:

While migrating, they fly both by night and by day in loose flocks of from 20 to 100 individuals, sometimes arranging themselves in a broad front, then forming lines, and again proceeding in a straggling manner. They keep perfectly silent and move at a height seldom exceeding a hundred yards. Their flight is light, undetermined as it were, yet well sustained and performed by regular flappings, as in other birds of the tribe. When they have arrived at their destination, they often go to considerable distances to feed during the day, regularly returning at the approach of night to their roosts on the low trees and bushes bordering the marshes, swamps, and ponds. They are very gentle at this season, and at all periods keep in flocks when not disturbed.

Dr. T. Gilbert Pearson (1922) writes:

At Orange Lake, Fla., they often approach the breeding island, flying at a height of only 4 or 5 feet above the water. When the colonies are in little ponds closely surrounded by high forests the birds must necessarily fly in over the tree-tops and then drop down to their nests. A situation somewhat similar to this exists at Avery Island, La., where Edward A. McIlhenny, by exercising ingenuity, based on a knowledge of the habits of the birds, has built up a colony of perhaps 2,000 nesting snowy egrets almost in his dooryard. Late in the afternoon these and other herons of the colony begin to arrive in numbers. Standing with Mr. McIlhenny on his lawn I have seen the birds arriving at a height of from 100 to 200 feet, until nearly over their nests, then with wings partly closed they volplaned almost to the bushes. A few vigorous wing beats and they would settle among the assembled hosts. Flocks of these snowy creatures dropping from the sky make a stimulating and most charming spectacle.

Enemies.—Much that I have already written about the ruthless destruction of the American egret applies with equal or greater force to this smaller species. The little snowy egret was slaughtered in much greater numbers than its larger relative, because it was originally much more numerous and more widely distributed, because it was much less shy and so more easily killed and because its short and delicate plumes were more in demand than the larger, stiffer plumes of the American egret. For these three reasons it suffered far more at the hands of the plume hunters and came much nearer being exterminated. But the same timely efforts stopped the slaughter before it was too late and saved the species, which is now increasing in protected localities.

The National Association of Audubon Societies in its campaign of education, circulated a great mass of literature on the subject. In its special leaflet No. 21 is a most striking picture of the horrors of the plume trade; it is a quotation from a paper by Mr. A. H. E. Mattingley, of Melbourne, Australia, published in The Emu; it reads as follows:

Notwithstanding the extreme heat and the myriads of mosquitos, I determined to revisit the locality during my Christmas holidays, in order to obtain one picture only—namely, that of a white crane, or egret, feeding its young. When near the place, I could see some large patches of white, either floating in the water or reclining on the fallen trees in the vicinity of the egret's rookery. This set me speculating as to the cause of this unusual sight. As I drew nearer, what a spectacle met my gaze—a sight that made my blood fairly boil with indignation. There, strewn on the floating water weed, and also on adjacent logs, were at least 50 carcasses of large white and smaller plumed egrets—nearly one-third of the rookery, perhaps more—the birds having been shot off their nests containing young. What a holocaust! Plundered for their plumes. What a monument of human callousness! There were 50 birds ruthlessly destroyed, besides their young (about 200) left to die of starvation! This last fact was betokened by at least 70 carcasses of the nestlings, which had become so weak that their legs had refused to support them and they had fallen from the nests into the water below, and had been miserably drowned; while, in the trees above the remainder of the parentless young ones could be seen staggering in the nests, some of them falling with a splash into the water, as their waning strength left them too exhausted to hold up any longer, while others simply stretched themselves out on the nest and so expired. Others, again, were seen trying in vain to attract the attention of passing egrets, which were flying with food in their bills to feed their own young, and it was a pitiful sight indeed to see these starvlings with outstretched necks and gaping bills imploring the passing birds to feed them. What a sickening sight! How my heart ached for them! How could anyone but a cold-blooded, callous monster destroy in this wholesale manner such beautiful birds—the embodiment of all that is pure, graceful, and good? The same scenes were enacted many, many times in this country. Picture the cost of a plume! The mother bird lies dead on the ground, the plumes rudely torn from her bleeding back, her reward for her maternal devotion. The fatherless and motherless young stand in the nest; there is no one to feed them and they are growing weaker day by day. At length, too weak to stand or cry for food, they sink down in the nest, awaiting the end; death will be a blessed relief.

But, happily, all this is now passed and we can look forward to better things. Plume hunting has been largely stamped out, the egrets are protected in many places and they are increasing. One of the most striking examples of their coming back is shown in the work accomplished by Mr. McIlhenny (1912) at Avery Island, La., as explained in his pamphlet.   Near his home "was a wet spot of a couple of acres between the hills," known as a Willow Pond, which "was partly covered with willow, buttonwood, and other water-loving trees, marsh grasses, and ferns.   In the trees and grass about this pond each spring a few green herons and least bitterns nested." With the idea of inducing other water birds to nest here and in the hope of saving a few of the remaining snowy egrets, he had a small dam built which raised the water level a couple of feet.   In the spring of 1895 he hunted up two nests of snowy egrets and took the eight young birds from them, just before they were large enough to fly, and put them in a large wire cage on the edge of his pond.   They became very tame, but, when liberated in November, they finally migrated south.   Six of these birds returned the following March, two pairs mated and they raised four young to each pair.   Thirteen healthy birds went south that fall and all returned the next spring. Five pairs nested that year, raising 20 young.   And so they kept on increasing year after year and other species joined the flourishing colony, until now its inhabitants number many thousands.   "The nesting water and marsh birds now include snowy heron, Louisiana heron, American egret, little blue heron, green heron, yellow crowned night heron, purple gallinule, Florida gallinule, American bittern, least bittern, King rail, anhinga, wood duck, blue wing teal, gadwall, and mallard."   This has proven to be one of the most remarkable and most successful experiments in conservation of which we have any record in this country.   It demonstrates what can be done under intelligent supervision and illustrates the great recuperative powers of wild life under favorable circumstances.

DISTRIBUTION

Range.—From southern South America, north through Central America, the West Indies, and the United States to southern Canada.

Breeding range.—South America, Central America, and southern and western United States.   North to California (Dos Palos); Utah (mouth of Bear River); Nebraska (Lincoln); Illinois (25 miles above Peoria); Indiana (Mount Carmel and Swan Pond); Long Island, New York (Sayville); and New Jersey (7-mile Beach and Cape May). East to New Jersey (7-mile Beach and Cape May); Virginia (Cobb's Island, Mochorn Island, and probably Back Bay); North Carolina (Pea Island and Orton); South Carolina (Washoe Reserve on the Santee River, Mount Pleasant, Buzzard's Island, and Frogmore); Georgia (Savannah, Darien, and St. Mary's); Florida (Braddock Lake, Ocklawaha River, Mosquito Inlet, Pelican Island, Brevard County, Hillsboro River, and Cape Sable); Cuba (Isle of Pines and

Manzanillo); Porto Rico (Pinero Island, Vieques Island, and Salinas);
Venezuela (Margarita Island and the mouth of the Orinoco River);
British Guiana (Georgetown); French Guiana (Cayenne); Brazil
(Counani, Parahyba, Bahia, Rio de Janeiro, and Taquara); and
Argentina (Buenos Aires, Cape San Antonio, and Carhue). South
to Argentina (Cape San Antonio and Carhue); and Chile (Valdivia).
West to Chile (Valdivia, Santiago, and Tarapaca); Bolivia (Reyes);
Peru (Santa Cruz, Ucayali River, and Tumbez); Ecuador (Manta
and Balzar Mountains); Colombia (marshes of Cauca River, Atrato
River, and Cartagena); Panama (Lion Hill); Costa Rica (Rio Frio
and Guanacaste); Nicaragua (San Juan del Sur); Colima, Mexico
(Rio Coahuayana); Tepic, Mexico (Acaponeta River); Sinaloa Mexico (Mazatlan); and California (Dos Palos).

Winter range.—Resident throughout most of its range in South
and Central America, and in the southern and western United States.
North to California (mouth of the Santa Clara River and Stockton);
Texas (Point Isabel and Galveston); and South Carolina (formerly
Charleston). East to South Carolina (formerly Charleston and St.
Mary's); Florida (mouth of the St. Johns River, Pelican Island, Or-
lando, and Lake Okeechobee); Cuba (Isle of Pines); and Argentina
(Buenos Aires). South to Argentina (Buenos Aires). West to Sina-
loa, Mexico (Mazatlan); and California (San Diego, San Pedro, and
the mouth of the Santa Clara River).

Casual records.—Like its larger relative (*Casmerodius e. egretta*) the
snowy egret migrates north of its normal breeding range although
not for such great distances nor in such large numbers. There are
many records for the State of New York (Brooklyn, August 15,1915;
Great South Bay, August 4, 1881; Sayville, Long Island, May 30,
1885; Fire Island, July 1, 1883, and others). In this general region
the species has been observed or secured in Connecticut (Groton Long
Point, early October; and Lyme, July 28, 1853, and August 16, 1853);
Massachusetts (near Boston, 1862; Northampton and Hummock
Pond, Nantucket, March, 1881); Vermont (2 secured at St. Alban's
Bay, in October, 1890); Nova Scotia (Windsor, 1872, and near Halifax, 1868); Ohio (Cleveland, August 25, 1889, also reported from
Lorain Lake and Ashtabula Counties); Michigan (Ann Arbor, April
9, 1872, August 17, 1874, April 20, 1895, and June, 1895, and Kala-
mazoo County, August 6, 1877); Ontario (Dunnville, May 18, 1884,
Mexican Point, Lake Ontario, July, 1888, and Combermere, August,
1892); Wisconsin (Lake Mills, fall of 1889, Lake Koshkonong, June,
1860, and August, 1886); Colorado (several records, the most northern being Fort Collins, and White River Post Office, 1905); and
Wyoming (Laramie, May 1, 1902, and May 23, 1913).

The specimen reported to have been taken at Burrard Inlet, British Columbia, May, 1879, has been reexamined and found to be the plumed egret, *Mesophoyx intermedia*.[1]

Egg dates.—Florida: 37 records, January 7 to July 15; 19 records, April 5 to May 6.   Texas: 15 records, April 29 to June 12; 8 records, May 5 to 16.   Utah: 21 records, April 22 to May 28; 11 records, May 2 to 25.

EGRETTA CANDIDISSIMA BREWSTERI Thayer and Bangs

BREWSTER EGRET

HABITS

This large subspecies of the snowy egret is known to inhabit the southern portion of Lower California, but its range is not well known and it may be considerably extended.   It was recognized and described by Thayer and Bangs (1909).   The following quotations from their paper tell us about all we know about it:

One of the important discoveries made by W. W. Brown, jr., while collecting birds in Lower California, for the Thayer Museum, was finding a large colony of snowy herons nesting at San Jose Island in the Gulf of California, about 60 miles north of La Paz.   From this colony Mr. Brown took several sets of eggs; he also made a dozen skins of the birds, then in full breeding plumage.   When unpacking these birds we were at once struck by their large size—especially by their long bills and huge legs—and upon comparison with an extensive series from the southwestern United States we found the differences to be so great that we propose to call the Lower California bird in honor of William Brewster, as a slight acknowledgment of the excellence of his "Birds of the Cape Region of Lower California."   *Egretta candidissima* (Gmel.) was named from Cartagena Colombia, and specimens from eastern South America are said to be even smaller than those from the southeastern United States; unfortunately we have seen no skins from near the type locality, and compare our new Lower California giant with birds from Florida, Georgia, etc.   The enormously heavy legs of the new form are enough to distinguish it; but in addition to this it is a much larger bird, the measurements of wing, tail, and bill only partially indicating the great difference in actual bulk between it and the form found in the southeastern United States.   In both forms females are rather smaller than males.   As to the range of the new form, we can say but little, though it is probable that it extends, or did extend, north to southern California and across the Gulf to western Mexico

In their tables of measurements it appears that the measurements of the smallest birds from Lower California and those of the largest birds from other places overlap; but the average difference is considerable.

Nesting.—W. W. Brown, jr., collected for Col. John E. Thayer, a series of eggs of this egret in San Jose Island, a small island near La Paz, Lower California, in June, 1908.   He supposed that they were the common snowy egret, as this new form had not been recognized at that time, so only a few notes were made.   Colonel Thayer tells

---

[1] See Kermode, F., The Canadian Field Naturalist, February, 1923.

me that there was a small breeding colony in a mangrove swamp on the island. The nests were described as "platforms of sticks, placed 8 to 10 feet from the ground, on the branches of the mangroves, overhanging the water." Evidently the nesting habits of this form do not differ materially from those of the other representatives of the species elsewhere.

Eggs.—There are eight sets of eggs in the Thayer collection, taken by Mr. Brown, on San Jose Island, from June 19 to 26, 1908, and by Manuel Cota, at the same place, between June 19 and July 5, 1909. There are six sets of three eggs and two sets of two eggs. The eggs are similar to those of the snowy egret. The measurements of the 22 eggs average 35.4 by 23.7 millimeters; the eggs showing the four extremes measure **43.5** by 28.4, 42.3 by **28.5**, **29.7** by 21.2 and 38.7 by **17.7** millimeters.

Very little seems to be known about the habits of this bird, but it probably does not differ materially in behavior from the snowy egret in similar surroundings.

DISTRIBUTION

Range.—Known only from Lower California, the adjoining mainland in western Mexico, and southern California. This egret has been found breeding only in Lower California (San Jose del Cabo), but is also reported from Guaymas, Sonora, and at Riverside, California.

Although this race may now be extinct there, it is possible that some of the records mentioned under *Egretta c. candidissima*, for Lower California and western Mexico might have been this bird had the specimens been available for critical examination.

Egg dates.—Southern Lower California: 8 records, June 19 to July 5.

DICHROMANASSA RUFESCENS (Gmelin)

REDDISH EGRET

HABITS

Although once abundant on the coast and islands of southwestern Florida, this interesting species had practically gone from that region before the time of my first visit in 1903, for we saw only a few scattering individuals in the Florida Keys and near Cape Sable. W. E. D. Scott (1887) has given us some idea of the former abundance of this species in Florida. Speaking of a locality in Old Tampa Bay he says:

Formerly I had seen birds breeding here in great numbers, and reddish egrets had been the most conspicuous feature of these breeding grounds in those days. But now how different! Not a single pair of birds of any kind did I find nesting, and only at rare intervals were any kind of herons to be observed. Not a reddish egret and only a few frightened and wary Louisiana herons were seen, and these were not breeding.

It was the same story with many other localities; and to-day I doubt if the reddish egret breeds anywhere in Florida.

To see the reddish egret at its best we must visit the coast of Texas, where it is really abundant from Matagorda Bay to Cameron County, reaching its maximum abundance on Green Island in Laguna Madre. The coast of Texas with its long string of bays and shallow inland waters, dotted with many low marshy islands, is well suited to the habits of this maritime species, which seldom strays far away from salt water. Here the reddish egret nests abundantly in the low vegetation on many of the islands and feeds in the shallow muddy waters in which small fishes are abundant.

Courtship.—The reddish egret in its nuptial display, in which it frequently indulges all through the breeding season to express its emotions, fairly bristles with plumes. The brownish pink plumes of the head, neck, and breast and the bluish gray plumes of the back stand out like the quills of a porcupine giving the bird quite a formidable appearance, terrifying to its enemies, perhaps, but probably pleasing to its mate. The males vie with each other in this spectacular display, the particolored bills pointed upward and the necks held in graceful curves, as they strut and bow before the lady of their choice.

Audubon (1840) describes the courtship as follows:

About the beginning of April, these herons begin to pair. The males chase each other on the ground, as well as in the air, and on returning to their chosen females erect their crest and plumes, swell out their necks, pass and repass before them, and emit hollow rough sounds, which it is impossible for me to describe. It is curious to see a party of 20 or 30 on a sand bar, presenting as they do a mixture of colors from pure white to the full hues of the old birds of either sex; and still more curious perhaps it is to see a purple male paying his addresses to a white female, while at hand a white male is caressing a purple female, and not far off are a pair of white, and another of purple birds.

He also refers to a display in flight:

The flight of this heron is more elevated and regular than that of the smaller species. During the love season, it is peculiarly graceful and elegant, especially when one unmated male is pursuing another, a female being in sight. They pass through the air with celerity, turn and cut about in curious curves and zigzags, the stronger bird frequently erecting its beautiful crest, and uttering its note, at the moment when it expects to give its rival a thrust. When these aerial combats take place between old and immature birds, their different colors form a striking contrast, extremely pleasing to the beholder.

Nesting.—On our trip down the coast of Texas in 1923 we found a few reddish egrets nesting in the mixed rookeries around Karankawa and La Vaca Bays near the lower end of Matagorda Bay. Near the entrance to Karankawa Bay we found, on May 9, a small but densely populated colony on a little motte of small trees and thorny bushes on a marsh; this contained perhaps 50 nests of Ward herons, reddish egrets, and Louisiana herons; the nests were on the tops of the thickly matted bushes and in the small trees; the bushes were also full of nests great-tailed grackles, some of which were also placed in the bases of the Ward herons' nests. The next day we ran up to the head of the bay to visit the great Wolf Point rookery, where we found a few reddish egrets breeding with thousands of Louisiana herons and lesser numbers of snowy egrets, Ward and black-crowned night herons. A very few reddish egrets were also seen in a large mixed rookery of the same species on Rose's Point, in La Vaca Bay, on May 12; this was in a dense and extensive forest of mesquite and huisache and the nests were mostly 10 or 15 feet from the ground. Both of these rookeries were also overrun with great-tailed grackles, which must destroy large numbers of eggs.

But when we reached the chain of islands between Mesquite and San Antonio Bays, on May 16, we really began to see reddish egrets in abundance. At least three of these islands were densely populated with large breeding colonies of herons; reddish egrets and Louisian herons were the most abundant; Ward herons were common; there were a few black-crowned night herons; and on one island there was a little group of half a dozen nests of American egrets and numerous snowy egrets were scattered among the other species. As if to add color to the scene, a large flock of roseate spoonbills, with a few cormorants as companions, frequented the islands, flying from one island to another and refusing to leave the chain. These islands were all small, low, shell reefs, inclosing flat marshy areas and surrounded by shallow muddy water; the drier portions supported a growth of low willows, huisache and other thorny bushes, sunflowers, prickly pear cactus, and a few Spanish daggers; the marshy portions, which were partially covered with water, were thickly overgrown with low bushes, grasses and rank herbage. Most of the reddish egrets nests were in the low bushes or on the thick growth of rank herbage, many of them in the wet places, with water under them; many nests were on the ground in the grass or herbage and some were in the clumps of sunflowers. They were usually between 2 and 3 feet above the ground or water and were often so close together that it was difficult to find room to set up a blind among them. The nests were well made of sticks and twigs, and were smoothly lined with finer twigs, rootlets, straws, and grasses. Nearly all of the nests contained the usual three eggs, but in a few nests we found newly hatched young.

Big Bird Island in Laguna Madre, with its wonderful colonies of skimmers, terns, gulls, pelicans, and herons, has been well written up and illustrated, for it contains one of the most interesting collections of breeding birds in North America. The pelican colony, mostly brown pelicans but sometimes a few of the big white pelicans, is located in the central and highest part of the island where the ground is hard and dry. In and around the pelican colony is an extensive growth of prickly pear cactus in more or less dense thickets, mixed with a few stunted mesquites and sunflowers. Here we found quite a large colony of reddish egrets and a few Ward herons with nests in the prickly pears, on the ground or 2 or 3 feet above it. At the time of our visit, May 29, most of the egrets' nests still contained eggs, but some held small young.

The largest colony of reddish egrets in Texas, probably the largest in North America, is on Green Island which lies 30 miles north of Point Isabel in Laguna Madre. I could not spare the time to visit this Island but Capt. R. D. Camp told me considerable about it and it has been well written up by others. Perhaps the best description of the island and its inhabitants is by Alvin R. Cahn (1923) who writes:

On the morning in question our investigations were confined to the outskirts of the vegetation, with excursions along the two paths which Mr. Camp had cut through the brush. It was this time that I learned the exact nature of the island to which I had come. I had been warned that the vegetation was thick, that there were cacti and "other things" with prickers; that I ought to wear leather trousers, leather gloves, and a leather coat—which would have been utterly impossible because of the heat. I was prepared, therefore, to find a tangled growth on the island, but down in the bottom of my heart I had doubted whether the brush could be as bad as reported. I had not been on the island five minutes, however, before I realized that the great problem in photographing the birds would be to get near them, for this mass of brush in which the birds nest is nothing but a huge pin-cushion armed with a million needle points, projecting in every direction, at every angle, and at every height. The bushes, some 8 or 10 feet high, are mostly a vicious species of *Condalia*, exceedingly branched and covered with short, very stiff, very sharp thorns that tear the skin painfully and cling to the clothing in a most annoying fashion. Amomg the *Condalia*, are scattered luxurant examples of the famous *Yucca*, or Spanish dagger, which grows about breast high, appearing as a great sheath of long, firm daggerlike leaves tipped with a thorny substance sharper than a Victrola needle. It was one of these villainous thorns that gently pierced my knee cap and made me a very stiff, sick, and unhappy mortal for three days. Beneath the *Yucca*, lies a substratum of *Opuntia*, the prickly-pear cactus, running vinelike over the ground, bristling like an angry porcupine and, porcupinelike, ready to shed hundreds of needles into anything that comes in contact with it. Under the cactus I believe was the ground, though I do not recall ever having seen it.

As far as the eye could reach the bush tops were alive with graceful forms. Reddish egrets and Louisiana herons were everywhere, the marvelous grace of their ever-changing postures exciting constant wonderment. In a far corner a few pair of black-crowned night herons had their nests hidden in a particularly dense thicket, and appeared for a moment only as they hurriedly escaped at our least approach. Ward herons sprang from their nests with a great squawk as we advanced, and disappeared on heavy wings over our limited horizon. Here and there in the heart of the tangle we could get a glimpse of a secretive form of won-drous white as some snowy egret or reddish egret in the immaculate plumage of the white phase slipped silently from a hidden nest. Through the underbrush we could see also the black sleek forms of the grackles as they slipped silently from nest to nest, making the most of the absence of incubating egrets and herons to ply their nefarious trade of egg eating. Frequently, too, one of these large blackbirds would come to the top of some conspicuous perch and there, with much ado, inflate and deflate himself, producing thereby not only a grotesque appearance but also a most peculiar song. From a nearby shrub a gray-tailed cardinal burst into a song of great richness, as if to ridicule the pathetic attempt of the grackle at vocal gymnastics. Everywhere there was life, and everywhere there was beauty and grace and a symphony of sound and color.

J. R. Pemberton (1922), who visited the island with Captain Camp, estimated that the heron population of the island consisted of about 4,000 reddish egrets, 2,000 Louisiana herons, 100 black-crowned night herons and 50 Ward herons. Captain Camp told me that in 1923 the total population had increased at least 20 per cent over the previous year. Mr. Pemberton (1922) said that "every individual bush appeared to have nests on it or in it," but that "nearly all the nests" of the reddish egrets "were on the top of the bisbirinda or the Spanish dagger. The mesquites had very few, although some of the stunted and more robust carried nests." In watching the egrets building their nests, he noticed that "the greater part of the material consisted of dry salt grass stems, which was placed as lining in old nests, but once in a while a bird carried a dead thorny twig found beneath a mesquite." Captain Camp told me that during the season of 1923 there had been a great increase in the number of nests built on the ground, where a more elaborate type of nest is built of dry grass, with a deeper cavity than in the tree nests. Perhaps the island is becoming overcrowded and building material is harder to find. Evidently the colony is flourishing under the able guardianship of Captain Camp and his assistant who lives on the island.

There are four sets of eggs of this species in the California Academy of Sciences collected on May 2, 1921, on islands in the Gulf of California. Three of the nests were on the ground under *Salicornia* bushes and one was on the lower branches of one of these bushes 16 inches above the ground. The nests were quite bulky and were well made of dry sticks and twigs of this plant; they measured from 20 to 26 inches in diameter outside, from 10 to 12 inches inside, from 8 to 10 inches in height and were hollowed to a depth of 3 or 4 inches.

Eggs.—The reddish egret usually lays from three to four eggs, occasionally five and very rarely six or even seven. The shape varies from ovate or oval to elliptical ovate or elliptical oval. The shell is smooth and not glossy. The color is pale bluish green, varying from "deep lichen green" to "pale Niagara green" or "pale olivine."

The measurements of 42 eggs average 51 by 37.6 millimeters; the eggs showing the four extremes measure **55.6** by 38.2, 53.5 by **41.7**, **46.5** by **36** millimeters.

Young.—Both sexes incubate. The period of incubation does not seem to be known, but it is probably between three and four weeks. Audubon (1840) says of the young:

Being abundantly and carefully fed, at first by regurgitation, they grow fast, and soon become noisy. When about a month old, they are fed less frequently, and the fish is merely dropped before them, or into their open throats; soon after they sit upright on the nest, with their legs extended foward, or crawl about on the branches, as all other herons are wont to do. They are now sensible of danger, [and when a boat is heard coming toward them they hide among the branches, making toward the interior of the keys, where it is extremely difficult to follow them. On one occasion, when I was desirous of procuring some of them alive, to take to Charleston, it took more than an hour to catch eight or nine of them, for they moved so fast and stealthily through the mangroves, always making for the closest and most tangled parts, that a man was obliged to keep his eyes constantly on a single individual, which it was very difficult to do, on account of the number of birds crossing each other in every direction. They do not fly until they are 6 or 7 weeks old, and even then do not venture beyond the island on which they have been reared.

Mr. Cahn (1923) writes:

The life of the young birds is anything but exciting. Day after day they lie on their shallow platform of sticks under the sweltering rays of a June sun, and the monotony of their lives is broken only by the coming and going of the old birds and, as the nestlings grow older, by innocent sparring matches among themselves. Long before they are able to fly, they leave the nest at the approach of danger and, using beak and wings and legs, climb unsteadily about in the brush, returning to the nest when the excitement is over. Before they are able to climb out of the nest, the babies make a valiant defense against an intruder by hissing and jabbing vigorously with their bills. They are so unsteady, however, that they very seldom hit what they are aiming at. They are a comical sight sitting on their heels, their great feet sprawling before them as they vainly endeavor to keep their balance during the violent exercise of defense. Once they become used to climbing about in bushes, they are safe, as then it is nearly impossible to capture them; they can go through the tangle much faster than you can.

The chief source of mortality among the young egrets and herons seems to be falling out of the nest, and a young bird is permitted to die of starvation or to be consumed by the red ants or a stray coyote that may reach the island during low water, right under the nest, without the old birds showing any sign or comprehending what is going on.

Plumages.—The downy young reddish egret has two distinct color phases, pure white and colored. In the colored phase, which is far commoner, the forehead, crown, and occiput are covered with long, hairlike plumes, an inch long, "light cinnamon drab" in color; the sides of the head and neck are scantily, and the back is more thickly, clothed with long, soft down of a "light mouse gray" or "drab-gray" color, the under parts are covered more scantily with down of the same color; and the throat is naked. The bill, feet, and naked skin are dark olive, darkest on the legs and feet.

The juvenal plumage appears first on the back, flanks, neck, and head, in about that order; then the flight feathers burst their sheaths, when the bird is from one-third to one-half grown; downy filaments still persist on the crown and the last of the down does not entirely disappear from the hind neck and rump until the bird is nearly grown. The fresh juvenal plumage, when it first appears, is brightly colored, "chestnut" or "auburn" on the head and neck, paler "auburn" on the under parts and grayish brown above; the browns fade out to paler colors later on. The first winter plumage, which is mainly a continuation of the juvenal, is chiefly gray, from "Quaker drab" to "light mouse gray" or paler, darkest on the wings and tail and lightest on the under parts; but it is everywhere more or less suffused with rufous shades, "fawn color," "vinaceous cinnamon" or "vinaceous tawny," brightest and almost solid "vinaceous tawny" on the throat and lesser wing coverts; the feathers of the crown, neck, and under parts are broadly tipped or streaked with dull "wood brown"; the back is largely dull "wood brown"; all the wing coverts have rufous edgings; and the bill is all black.

The above plumage is worn throughout the winter without much change, except that the rufous tints largely disappear by wear and fading. A first prenuptial molt takes place from March to May, involving mainly the head and neck and some of the body plumage, but not the wings and tail. The head and breast plumes are partially acquired at this molt, the new feathers being "vinaceous russet", "pecan brown," and "cameo brown." The juvenal wing coverts are all retained and are more or less edged with dull buff.

At the next molt, the first postnuptial, a complete change of plumage produces, some time in the fall, a second winter plumage which is much like the adult; all light edgings disappear; the crown and mantle become plain "Quaker drab" and the under parts plain "light mouse gray"; but the plumes of the head, back and breast are only partially developed. The following spring the young bird, when nearly 2 years old, becomes indistinguishable from the adult.

Adults have a complete postnuptial molt in late summer or fall and a partial prenuptial molt, involving mainly the display plumage, during the late winter. The winter plumage is much like the well-known nuptial plumage, except that the plumes are not so long and the plumage is darker and more richly colored, deep rich, chocolate brown on the head and neck, suffused with a purplish gloss.

It now seems to be generally conceded that the so-called Peale's egret is a white phase of the reddish egret, although the status of these white birds was a puzzling problem to some of the earlier writers. Peale's egret was included as a hypothetical species in the first and second editions of our check list, but was dropped in the third edition. Audubon (1840) supposed that Peale's egret was the immature plumage of the reddish egret.

Maynard (1896) still maintained, even in the latest edition of his book, that *pealei* was a good species; his theory was based on the fact that the two color phases seemed to be differently distributed; he found the white birds exceedingly common on the east coast of Florida, where he found only a single reddish specimen in two seasons; while on the west coast he found the reddish egret very abundant below Tampa Bay, but did not see a single white bird. In the Florida Keys and in the Bahamas he found both phases, as well as many birds of mixed plumage.

W. E. D. Scott (1881, 1887, and 1888) was always a firm believer in the color phase theory; he found both phases on the west coast of Florida, though somewhat differently distributed, where they were abundant in the early eighties; he also found a number of birds in mixed plumages. His assistant Mr. Devereux, "found young in both plumages in the same nest where the parents were both blue birds."

We found the white birds exceedingly scarce on the coast of Texas except on Green Island in the southern part of Laguna Madre. Here Capt. R. D. Camp has made a special study of the white phase problem for three years and he summarizes his findings, as follows:

I watched with a great deal of interest a pair of birds composed of a normal male and a white female, at least the white bird was the one which spent most of the time incubating. The three eggs laid in the nest were normal in every respect and produced three normal colored young. Out of the hundreds of pairs of reddish egrets breeding on the island, I have yet to find two white birds mated. Of about 15 nests which I have observed containing some white-phase young, never has there been a case where more than 75 per cent of the same clutch were white. In only one case where one of the parent birds was white have I seen a white young, and in this case three of the four were normal. In one instance a pair of normal birds produced three white and one normal young. In the majority of cases where there were white young in the nests, the number of white did not exceed one.

Although the irregular distribution of the white phase suggests the idea that it may be a distinct species; and although the mixed plumages suggest hybridism; the raising of white young, where both parents are reddish egrets, seems to clinch the color phase theory.

Although material for study is scarce in collections, white phase birds apparently pass through the same sequence of molts and plumages as the colored birds. They are pure white at all ages, but the full development of plumes and the parti-colored bill are not acquired until the second prenuptial molt, when the young bird is nearly 2 years old.

Food.—Being a bird of the seacoast the reddish egret probably obtains most, if not all, of its food in salt water. Large numbers of these birds may be seen at times standing in the shallow waters around their breeding grounds, or way off on the the mud banks or sand shoals in the lagoons, where they stand motionless watching for their prey or walk about slowly in search of it, until the rising tide forces them to leave. Mr. Cahn (1923), however, writes:

Just where the old birds went for food is a question. On a quiet evening hundreds of them would be seen standing in the shallow water that surrounds their island, but the birds remained almost motionless in the red glow of the setting sun, and there was little evidence that they caught their food so near home. On the contrary, with the approach of evening and the lessening of the intensity of the sun, the birds usually took wing and disappeared in small groups to the southwest, in which direction undoubtedly lay their feeding ground. The food consists of a small fish and frogs, tadpoles, and an occasional crustacean, which are probably caught in the marshes of the mainland coast. Before dark the birds were all back and at the nest, and there was relatively little night activity. With the daylight the birds would fly away once more to the feeding grounds, returning again before the heat of the sun was sufficiently intense to endanger their precious eggs or babies. Then followed another period of inactivity during which the birds remained close to the nest, preening their wonderful feathers or playing at repelling intruders.

Behavior.—In flight the reddish egret is very light, graceful and easy, as well as strong and rather swift. In the white phase, with its long plumes, it somewhat resembles the American egret, but it appears shorter and stouter and its wing strokes are not so long and slow. Its particolored bill is a good field mark, as it is conspicuous at quite a distance. On the ground it walks with deliberate grace and elegance. It is an adept on balancing itself on the insecure perches it finds on the slender tops of the bushes, where it nests. It is interesting to watch it swaying in the strong breeze, which generally prevails on the Texas coast, maintaining its balance by slight adjustments of its supple frame; only occasionally are its broad wings brought into play.

A curious habit is referred to by Mr. Cahn (1923) as follows:

They will stand at the very edge of the nest sometimes by the hour, simply for the purpose of warding off the supposed attacks of neighboring egrets that are likewise amusing themselves by repelling imagined intrusions. Bristling, with every feather erect, they jab viciously at the object of their attack, or simply endeavor, by a full display of plumage, to overawe the innocent offender. Thus they pass the time defending their nests against entirely theoretical attacks of their neighbors, whose one idea often is simply to slip back to their eggs as unobtrusively as possible.

I have never heard any notes from this species but the usual guttural croaks, but T. Gilbert Pearson (1922) refers to another, of which he says:

One very characteristic note of the reddish egret, which I noticed, both at the rookeries and on the feeding grounds, is a bugle like cry decidedly more musical in its nature than the ordinary heron squawk.

Enemies.—Evidently the reddish egrets of the Florida coast were exterminated by plume hunters. Their nuptial plumes are long and showy and those of the white phase must have been in good demand. The following statement by W. E. D. Scott (1887) is of interest in this connection:

We reached our destination—the island which Mr. Wilkerson had told me was the breeding place of reddish egrets—at about 4 o'clock, and at once came to anchor. A few herons were to be seen from time to time flying to the island, and presently I took the small boat and went ashore to reconnoiter. This had evidently been only a short time before a large rookery. The trees were full of nests, some of which still contained eggs, and hundreds of broken eggs strewed the ground everywhere. Fish crows and both kinds of buzzards were present in great numbers and were rapidly destroying the remaining eggs. I found a huge pile of dead, half decayed birds, lying on the ground which had apparently been killed for a day or two. All of them had the "plumes" taken off with a patch of the skin from the back, and some had the wings cut off; otherwise they were uninjured. I counted over 200 birds treated in this way. The most common species was the reddish egret, though there were about as many Louisiana herons; the other species were the snowy heron, great white egret, and the little blue heron in both phases of plumage.

In the Texas rookeries considerable damage is done by black vultures, which devour large numbers of eggs and young birds. We found one or more pairs of these black rascals living in or near almost every rookery that we visited. The wardens are well aware of the damage that these birds do and they kill them or break up their nests whenever they can. Prowling coyotes and wild cats kill a great many young birds that fall to the ground, but many of these would die anyway, as their parents do not seem to know how to care for them under such circumstances.

But the worst enemy of all the small herons in Texas is the omnipresent great-tailed grackle. These birds live in multitudes in nearly all of the rookeries and work great havoc among the unguarded eggs. Most of the eggs destroyed are in the incomplete sets, before incubation has begun, as they are less closely guarded at that time. Mr. Cahn (1923) says that "this destruction of the nest causes very little worry to the old birds; indeed I once watched a grackle break up an egret nest while the parent bird stood not 15 feet away, intently watching the performance and preening its feathers."

Captain Camp has lately been conducting a systematic campaign against the grackles on Green Island which has greatly reduced their numbers and lessened the destruction of eggs.

DISTRIBUTION

Range.—Florida and the Gulf coast of the United States; also the West Indies and Mexico.

Breeding range.—North to Lower California (San Jose Island); Sinaloa (Mazatlan); Texas (Cameron, Nueces, Calhoun, and Refugio Counties); Louisiana (Timbalier Island); formerly Florida (Suwannee River, Orange Lake and Pelican Island); and formerly Georgia (Chatham County). East formerly to Florida (Pelican Island and Dade County); the Bahama Islands (Great Bahama, Abaco, Nassau, Great Inagua, and probably the Caicos Islands); probably Santo Domingo; Cuba (Manzanillo); and probably Haiti. South probably to Haiti; Cuba (Manzanillo); Yucatan (probaby Cozumel Island); and Tepic (San Blas). West to Tepic (San Blas); Sinaloa (Mazatlan); and Lower California (San Jose Island).

The principal colonies now known are located on the islands off the coast of Texas.

Winter range.—The reddish egret is largely nonmigratory, except in the central northern part of its range. It has been found at this season north to Lower California (La Paz and San Jose del Cabo); Sinaloa (Mazatlan); and Florida (Fort Myers, Pinellas County, and Cape Florida).

Migration.—Early dates of arrival are: Corpus Christi, Texas, March 29, 1903; Orange Hammock, Florida, February 25, 1895; and Micanopy, Florida, March 20, 1909.

Returns from birds banded on the coast of Texas indicate a somewhat extensive southward migration from that region. A young bird (number 233333, Biological Survey), marked at Green Island, Cameron County on May 15, 1923, was killed about October 20, 1923, at Cuicatlan, Oaxaca, Mexico, about 600 miles south of the point of banding or at the southern extremity of the known range.

Casual records.—Few cases of wandering are known, as this species does not appear to indulge in the extensive postnuptial movements that characterize *Casmerodius* and *Egretta*. The collection of C. E. Aiken, at Colorado College, Colorado Springs, Colorado, is said to contain an immature specimen shot near that city about August, 1875; and during the period from August 17 to 31, 1875, it was reported as not rare in the vicinity of Cairo, Illinois.

Further evidence of late summer movements is afforded by the record of another bird (number 233347, Biological Survey), banded as a nestling in Cameron County, Texas, on May 15, 1923, and found dead near Galveston, Texas, on August 10, 1923.

Egg dates.—Texas: 45 records, April 6 to June 14; 23 records, May 16 to 27. Florida: 16 records, December 8 to May 16; 8 records, April 5 to May 9.

HYDRANASSA TRICOLOR RUFICOLLIS (Gosse)

LOUISIANA HERON

HABITS

My first morning in Florida gave me many delightful surprises and some charming new acquaintances. I had been wandering through a fascinating old hammock admiring the picturesque live oaks, with their festoons of Spanish moss, the stately cabbage palmettos, so suggestive of the Tropics, and here and there a Spanish bayonet in full bloom, shedding its fragrance from a pyramid of white blossoms; the thickets of saw palmettos, the various orchids and air plants on the old trees were all new and interesting to me. Finally I came to a little, muddy pool in an open glade and sat down behind some saw palmettos to watch a little flock of yellowlegs feeding in the pool. A passing shadow caused me to look up and there on silent wings a larger bird was sailing down to alight in the pool, my first glimpse of a Louisiana heron at short range. It was totally unaware of my presence and within a few feet of me. Soon another came and then another, until there were five of them. What beautiful, dainty creatures they were, their slender forms clothed in bluish gray, blended drabs, purples, and white, with their little white plumes as a nuptial head dress. How agile and graceful they were as they darted about in pursuit of their prey. With what elegance and yet with what precision every movement was made. For harmony in colors and for grace in motion this little heron has few rivals. I could have watched and admired them for hours, but the rattle of a dry leaf, as I moved, ended my reverie, for they were gone. But I shall never forget my first impression of this elegant "lady of the waters."

Courtship.—In its courtship this dainty little heron is most attractive; though it lacks the wealth of glorious white plumes displayed by the American and snowy egrets, and though it can not throw out the bristling array of plumage shown by the reddish egret, still it has a grace of action and beauty of plumage peculiar to itself. Perched on the topmost bough of some low tree or bush, the male bows to his mate, his long slender form swaying in the breeze, bending in long graceful curves and yielding to the pressure of the wind, as if he were a part of the tree itself. Like a "reed shaken by the wind" he bends, but does not break; and he never loses his balance. And now he dances along from branch to branch toward his mate, bowing and courtesying, with wings half spread. Many are the pretty attitudes that he assumes, with many graceful curves of his long slender neck. The plumes on his back are raised and lowered, like a filmy veil of ecru drab, and the pure white head plumes are raised and spread like a fan, in striking contrast to the blue and drab. It is a picture of irresistible beauty; his mate finally yields and the conjugal pact is sealed right there on the tree tops, without loss of poise.

Behavior, similar to that seen in courtship, is indulged in by the Louisiana heron, and by other herons, all through the nesting period, as a form of greeting between mates, in the ceremony of nest relief, and when approaching the young to feed them. Prof. Julian S. Huxley, who has made a special study of such sexual behavior, has sent me a number of photographs illustrating it and some very full notes on it, based on his observations made at Edward A. McIlhenny's preserve at Avery Island, Louisiana. I quote from his notes, substantially in his own words, as follows:

Migration is spread over a long period; some birds arrive at Avery Island early in March, the bulk come in mid-April and others not until May. On first arrival and for some time after, the birds are in flocks; mating then takes place (out on the feeding grounds, according to reports). The mated pairs no longer join the flock at its roosting place; but they jointly select a nest site. They may change their minds once or twice, but eventually, before building, they spend several days in a regular honeymoon. During most of this time they sit side by side, with one resting its head against the other's flanks. Now and again a special ceremony, which I have not seen at other times, is indulged in; with loud cries the birds face each other and lean their necks forward, partly or wholly intertwining them, each feverishly nibbling at the other's aigrettes.

One or the other appears to be on the nest site continuously. When one has been away feeding and returns to the other, a second type of ceremony occurs; this may be called the greeting ceremony and is the commonest seen in the species. In both birds (typically) the crest, neck feathers, and aigrettes are raised, the head is somewhat thrown up, revealing the patch of buff on the chin, the wings are spread and a special cry is uttered as the returning bird alights and walks through the branches to its mate. This, like most other ceremonies of the species, is a mutual one.

Nest building soon starts. It is my experience that the male usually, perhaps always, finds the sticks for the nest, and brings and gives them to the female, who then does the actual building. The giving of each stick is accompanied by a greeting ceremony.

After incubation has started, both birds take turns at sitting. The times of relief are somewhat irregular, though it appears that there are usually about four changes in the 24 hours, and that the female usually sits at night. Each time a nest relief occurs, there is normally a greeting ceremony, the attitude being kept up all the time the birds are changing places. This, however, does not close the performance. Almost invariably the bird which has been relieved goes and fetches one or (almost always) several sticks, which it presents to the sitting bird. The presentation is made in the greeting attitude. The sitting bird then builds the stick into the nest. I have seen as many as 11 sticks presented after one nest relief. The last one or two presentations are often characterized by a lower degree of emotional tension, as revealed in the degree of feather raising. Nest relief and stick bringing continue after the young are hatched and presumably until they leave the nest.

Another ceremony, which is much less commonly seen, appears to be performed by the male alone. In this the bird droops its wings, erects its neck vertically and its head almost so and gives vent to a groaning sound.

While brooding the bird often digs the angle of the wing into the contour feathers of the body, so that it is covered by a regular flap of these. If the bird is now slightly alarmed, it may stand up without opening its wings. This must push the flaps forward, for they then stand out at right angles to the body like epaulettes. So far as I could see, these epaulettes were never used in any display, although they were striking and gave the bird a bizarre appearance.

Nesting.—I have seen many breeding rookeries of Louisiana herons and have spent many pleasant hours studying them, for they are by far the most abundant of all the southern herons. My first experience with them was in the extensive marshes of the upper St. Johns River in Florida.   Here we found, on April 18, 19, and 20, 1902, some large colonies breeding on the willow islands in this great morass, which we could reach only by poling a skiff through many acres of dense, aquatic vegetation.   These little islands were thickly covered with small willows, averaging about 12 or 15 feet high.   In some cases the Louisiana herons nested in colonies by themselves, but in other cases they were associated with a few water turkeys, snowy egrets, many little blue herons, and a pair or two of yellow-crowned night herons.   The Louisiana herons far outnumbered all the other species and occupied the central portions of the rookeries.   Their nests were built in the willows in every available spot and at every height from 2 to 12 feet above the ground, often several nests in the same tree; they were neatly and well made of small sticks and smoothly lined with fine twigs.   Most of the nests contained four or five eggs and one held six.   There were no young at that date.

In Monroe County we found the Louisiana herons everywhere abundant, breeding in all the inland rookeries, as well as on many of the mangrove keys.   At the Cuthbert rookery they formed at least half of the colony, where we estimated that there were about 2,000 of them.   Their nests were found everywhere, all through the rookery, but they were especially abundant in the interior, often 4 or 5 and sometimes 10 nests in a tree; most of them were from 6 to 12 feet from the ground in the black and red mangroves, a few being in the buttonwoods.   At the time of our visit, on May 1, 1903, fully three-quarters of the nests held young birds of various ages.   The nests were small, irregular in shape, and loosely built of small sticks, but well lined with twigs.

On many of the islands off the coast of Louisiana we found breeding colonies of these herons.   Most of the young had hatched and many had flown away when I was there late in June, 1910; but Captain Sprinkle told me that, earlier in the season, he had estimated that the largest colonies contained from 500 to 1,000 birds.   One small colony, of about 50 pairs, still had eggs on Battledore Island. They were nesting in a row of low, black mangrove bushes which grew around the borders of a small marsh.   The nests were from 2 to 5 feet above the ground.   The mangroves were covered with white blossoms, among which the herons made a pretty picture.   And all around them were populous colonies of laughing gulls, black skimmers, Caspian, royal, Forster, and common terns; it was a great collection of noisy neighbors.

Along the coast of Texas, in 1923, we visited a number of colonies in which Louisiana herons were breeding and in which this species usually predominated, but in all cases two or more other species were breeding with them.   On Vingt-une Island, in East Galveston Bay, described under the snowy egret, we found a colony which, we estimated, contained about 800 Louisiana herons, 400 snowy egrets, and 150 black-crowned night herons. The Louisiana herons' nests were mainly in the tall canes which bordered the marsh, though many of them were in the small huisache trees and bushes, as well as in the prickly pear cacti. Some of the nests were on or close to the ground and others were at varying heights up to 6 feet. Besides the usual nests of sticks, there were many nests made wholly or in part of the dead and dry stems of the canes; fine strips or bits of cane were generally in use as nest linings.

One of the largest two rookeries seen was at Wolf Point, in Karankaua Bay, at the lower end of Matagorda Bay, which we visited on May 10, 1923. This was a densely populated rookery, on dry land, in a thick growth of willows, husiache, and other small trees, with dense thickets of thorny underbrush. The bulk of the population consisted of Louisiana herons, which arose in a great cloud as I entered; there were certainly several thousand of them. Among them were several hundred snowy egrets, a few pairs of reddish egrets and 15 or 20 pairs each of Ward and black-crowned night herons. Two or three pairs of black vultures were living in the rookery and the place was fairly alive with countless thousands of great-tailed grackles.

The other big rookery, visited two days later, was on Roses Point in La Vaca Bay. It was also on high dry land and was so well hidden in an extensive forest of mesquite and huisache that it took us sometime to find it. It was fully as large and perhaps much larger, as it was difficult to outline its limits. Besides several thousand, perhaps many thousand, Louisania herons, there were many snowy egrets, Ward, and black-crowned night herons, and some few reddish egrets. And, last but not least, I have never seen great-tailed grackles so thick as they were here; they fairly swarmed everywhere and the trees were full of their nests, sometimes scores of nests in a single tree. The herons' nests were mostly well up toward the tops of the trees, from 10 to 15 feet from the ground.

In the rookeries on the chain of islands, between San Antonio and Mesquite Bays, Louisiana herons were nesting abundantly among the reddish egrets and snowy egrets, in low bushes, 1 or 2 feet high, in the rank herbage and almost on the ground. On Big Bird Island, in Laguna Madre, they nested in a small colony by themselves in a tract of tall weeds. Here they had well made nests of dry weed stalks, straws, and grasses.

C. J. Pennock, under the name of John Williams (1918), describes an interesting colony, which he found near St. Marks, Florida, as follows:

In preparing to leave the island in a row boat, a landing was made across a small cove from the line of bushes that had formerly been used as nesting sites by these birds. On stepping ashore I was startled at seeing hundreds of Louisiana herons spring up from the open, treeless marsh and immediately settle down again as I sank to cover. A few steps into the thick matted rushes and again the birds arose on hurried wing beats almost directly upwards and drifted with much croaking farther down the island. A few steps more and I was in the midst of a nesting colony of these birds; every few yards a nest directly on the depressed rushes where a high tide had beaten down the tops of the tall rank growth. A hurried estimate of the number of these birds made approximately 500 individuals, but whether both sexes were in the marsh I could not determine, and no accurate count of the nests was attempted, as they extended to a considerable distance in at least two directions—just how far was not discovered—and an enumeration under the condition would have required more time than could be spared then, but enough was seen to convince me there were more than 150 nests, while there might have been two or three times that number. The nests contained from one to five eggs, but for the most part four, as far as examined all were freshly laid. The nests were but little more than the scratching aside of the tangled rushes and a few broken pieces of the same laid crossing one another to aid in retaining the eggs from working down.

Eggs.—The Louisiana heron usually lays four or five eggs, sometimes only three, occasionally six or very rarely seven. In shape they vary from ovate or oval to elliptical ovate or elliptical oval. The shell is smooth, not glossy. The color is pale bluish green, varying from "pale Niagara green" to "lichen green."

The measurements of 41 eggs average 44.1 by 32.3 millimeters; the eggs showing the four extremes measure 50 by 33, 48 by 34, 40.8 by 32, 44 by 30.5 millimeters.

Young.—Audubon (1840) gives the incubation period as 21 days. Both sexes incubate the eggs and guard the young; from the time that the nesting site is chosen until the young leave the nest one of the parents is always on duty. As one walks through a rookery it is easy to locate the nests containing young by their plaintive peeping notes. The young remain in the nests until they are half or two-thirds grown, probably longer if not disturbed; at this age or older they are easily frightened and readily leave the nest, climbing with great agility over the surrounding branches. They are quite expert at climbing, though apparently awkward, and can cling quite tenaciously with bill, wings, or feet. They sometimes fall, however; if they fall into the water they can swim quite well and may be able to reach their nests again; but occasionally they become entangled in the branches, or in the sticks of the nests, which usually proves fatal, as their parents do not seem able to help them in such situations; we saw a number of their dead bodies hanging where they were caught. The young are fed by regurgitation, after the manner of other herons, as long as they remain in or about the nests, and probably longer, until they learn to shift for themselves.

Plumages.—The downy young Louisiana heron is distinctively colored, quite unlike any of the others. The top of the head is covered with long hairlike plumes, nearly an inch long, shading from "army brown" basally to "fawn color" and "vinaceous fawn" terminally; the back is clothed in long, soft down, "fuscous" to "hair brown" in color; the under parts are scantily covered with coarse, white down; the bill, feet, and naked skin are light green, yellowish in the lightest parts of the bill and feet.

The juvenal plumage appears first on the back which is soon well feathered, then on the head, neck, and under parts, followed by the wings and lastly the tail; the flight feathers are not fully out until the young bird is fully grown. In full juvenal plumage, the head and neck are deep "chestnut" or bright "bay"; the throat, a narrow stripe down the front of the neck and the underparts are white; the mantle, wings, and tail are "dark Quaker drab," with "chestnut" tips on all the wing coverts, and more or less "chestnut" on the back. This plumage is worn through the winter with little change, except that bluish gray feathers gradually replace the brown ones and a partial prenuptial molt produces, by February or March, a plumage which somewhat resembles that of the winter adult; the white has increased on the underparts and there is more white and brown in the throat stripe; rudimentary plumes and long feathers have appeared on the back; but considerable chestnut still remains in the neck, shoulders, and lesser wing coverts; and the juvenal wings, with their chestnut edgings, have not been molted.

A complete postnuptial molt occurs during the following summer and fall after which the young bird is practically indistinguishable from the adult, at an age of 15 or 16 months.

Adults have a complete postnuptial molt in summer and early fall and a partial prenuptial molt in February and March, which does not include the flight feathers. The special adornments of the nuptial plumage are the long white head plumes, which form a part of the nuptial display and are lacking in the fall; but the "purple-drab" or "vinaceous purple" head plumes, the long feathers of the same colors on the neck, breast, and shoulders, and the "cinnamon-drab" back plumes are all much more highly developed in the spring than in the fall, though all but the white head plumes are present in fall adults to a limited extent.

Professor Huxley says, in his notes:

Although the sexes are qualitatively similar, it is my experience that there is normally a quantitive difference between the birds of each pair, in respect of brilliance and epigamic structures, the male having the brighter colors and the longer crest and aigrettes. In spite of this, the best adorned females are considerably above the level of the least brilliant males. This implies that assortive mating must occur, so that a well adorned male tends to mate with a well adorned female, and vice versa.

Food.—The Louisiana heron seeks its food to some extent in the shallow bays and estuaries along the coast, but more often around the shores of ponds, marshes, rice fields, and fresh-water meadows. It seldom stands and waits for its prey, but prefers to pursue it more actively. Stealing quietly along, with cautious and measured steps, its quick eye detects the presence of a school of minnows; then crouching low, with head drawn in, it takes a few rapid steps, its sharp beak darts swiftly outward and downward with unerring aim; sometimes it misses but often two or three of the small fry are caught before the school escapes. Its movements are so graceful, so swift and so accurate that it is a pleasure to watch them. Audubon (1840) has described its feeding habits very prettily, as follows:

See, it has spied a small fly lurking on a blade of grass, it silently runs a few steps, and with the sharp point of its bill it has already secured the prey. The minnow just escaped from the pursuit of some larger fish has almost rushed upon the beach for safety; but the quick eye of the heron has observed its motions, and in an instant it is swallowed alive. Among the herbage yet dripping with the dew the beautiful bird picks its steps. Not a snail can escape its keen search, and as it moves around the muddy pool, it secures each water lizard that occurs. Now the sun's rays have dried up the dews, the flowers begin to droop, the woodland choristers have ended their morning concert, and like them, the heron, fatigued with its exertions, seeks a place of repose under the boughs of the nearest bush, where it may in safety await the coolness of the evening.

He also says:

The food of this species consists of small fry, water insects, worms, slugs, and snails, as well as leeches, tadpoles, and aquatic lizards.

Oscar E. Baynard (1912) found in the stomach of an adult Louisiana heron the remains of about 200 grasshoppers; and he reported that 50 meals of young birds accounted for 2,876 grasshoppers, 8 small frogs, 17 cutworms, 6 lizards, and 67 small crawfish. Although this species probably eats more fish than the other small herons, its other food habits make it decidedly useful.

Behavior.—When starting to fly, this, and all the other herons, hold the neck extended in a long curve, with the legs dangling below but, when well under way the head is drawn in between the shoulders and the feet are extended behind to serve as a rudder. The wing strokes are deliberate, but steady and the flight is direct and strong. The morning and evening flights between roosting and feeding places are often made in loose flocks or long straggling lines, sometimes at a considerable height when traveling long distances. The white underparts serve as a good recognition mark. The graceful and elegant carriage of this heron has been referred to above. Quite a variety of croaking notes and squawks, some in soft conversational tones and some loud and vehement, are heard in the rookeries. Although it is more quarrelsome than the other small herons, it seems to get along well with its neighbors. However, I once saw a Louisiana heron alight on a little blue heron's nest and deliberately poke the eggs out of it onto the ground; no resistance was offered, as the owner was absent. The pilfering of sticks from the nests of others is a common occurrence in the rookeries, which often leads to a quarrel.

An interesting hiding pose, which suggests the usefulness of the stripe of brown, black, and white markings on the throat and neck of this and some other species of herons and bitterns, is thus described by William Palmer (1909):

The following interesting experience occurred in Florida. I had been walking among the pines with my gun and had slowly approached the backwater of the Kissimmee River where the water had overflowed the short grass well back of the usual shore line. Here I soon noticed a Louisana heron standing in a few inches of water near a small clump of scrub palmettoes and at once conceived the idea of trying to find out how near I could get to the bird. Using the clump as a blind I gradually moved to within about 60 feet. Waiting a while to notice the bird and to allay its fears, for it had evidently detected me, I sat down on the grass and slowly worked myself to one side of the clump in full view of the heron and not over 40 feet away. Here I sat for some time lounging, first on one side and then on the other, at the same time working myself gradually nearer to the water, the heron all the time standing upright and immobile with its breast toward me, the neck upstretched and the bill pointed skyward. I could plainly see the irides, but the bird, now about 25 feet off, stood absolutely still for perhaps 20 minutes until I arose and then it flew off.

Professor Huxley says in his notes:

The flight games of this species are interesting. They seem to be indulged in only when the birds have arrived over the nesting pond when flying back from the feeding grounds. They fly in at a steady rate, 100 or 200 feet up, and, when over the roosting place, they fold their wings and drop or volplane down. During the descent the aigrettes fly out like a comet's tail. Some birds volplane steadily down; others fall more rapidly and must skid from side to side before alighting. When thousands are thus performing at once, the sight is a very striking one.

Enemies.—Plume hunters have made no effort to hunt this species, as it has no marketable plumes—its plumes might have come on the market, if the demand had continued after the supply of white aigrettes had become exhausted. Many young birds and some older birds have been killed for food. There is, however, a human enemy, unconscious perhaps of his evil deeds, who causes considerable havoc whenever he indulges in his supposedly harmless sport in a heron rookery; and that is the bird photographer, who sets up his blind in a rookery and keeps the herons off their nests, often for long periods. I remember that, after we had spent parts of three days photographing birds in the great Cuthbert rookery, we left it in a sadly depleted condition. The crows and vultures had cleaned out practically all the nests anywhere near our blinds; the roseate spoonbills and American egrets had been completely broken up and driven away; hundreds of nests of the smaller herons had been robbed; and the ground was strewn with broken egg shells all over the rookery. The egg collector, who is constantly moving about in plain sight, frightens the crows away, as well as the herons, and is therefore much less destructive than the bird photographer. The safest time to practice bird photography, and the best time too to get good results, is when the young are partially grown, when there are no eggs for the crows to steal and when the young are too large for the vultures to swallow. Probably, when not disturbed by human beings, the herons' nests are constantly guarded by one of each pair. Otherwise, it is hard to conceive how many birds can be raised successfully, where fish crows are as common as they are in Florida or where great-tailed grackles abound as they do in Texas.

DISTRIBUTION

Range.—Southern and eastern United States, Central America, the West Indies, and northern South America.

Breeding range.—North to Lower California (Margarita Island and La Paz); Sinaloa (Mazatlan); Texas (Brownsville, Corpus Christi, Galveston, and Houston); Louisiana (Black Bayou, Jackson, and Lake St. John); Mississippi (near Natchez, Rodney, and probably Biloxi); Alabama (Petit Bois Island and Autaugaville); Florida (Tallahassee); and Virginia (formerly Clarkesville). East to North Carolina (Orton Lake, formerly Beaufort); South Carolina (Washoe Preserve on the Santee River, Charleston, and Frogmore); Georgia (Savannah, Darien, Blackbeard Island, and St. Marys); Florida (St. Augustine, Mosquito Inlet, and Titusville); Bahama Islands (Great Abaco, Berry Islands, New Providence, San Salvador, Mariguana, and North, Grand, and East Caicos Islands); Porto Rico; and probably the Islands off the coast of Venezuela (Aruba and Bonaire). South to probably the coast of Venezuela (Aruba and Bonaire); and Panama (Rio Sabana and Lion Hill). West to Nicaragua (San Juan del Sur and Momotombo); Oaxaca (Tehuantepec); Colima (Colima and Manzanillo); Tepic (Las Penas Islands); Sinaloa (Mazatlan); and Lower California (San Jose Island, La Paz, and Margarita Island).

Winter range.—North to Lower California (La Paz); Sinaloa (Mazatlan); rarely New Mexico (Gila River); Tamaulipas (Matamoros); rarely Louisiana (Vermillion Bay); Mississippi (Biloxi); and South Carolina (Charleston). East to South Carolina (Charleston); Georgia (Savannah and Darien); Florida (St. Augustine, Mosquito Inlet, and Titusville); the Bahama Islands (San Salvador and the Caicos Islands); and probably other islands of the West Indies. South probably to the Lesser Antilles; the northern coast of South America and Panama (Rio Indio). West to Guerrero (Acapulco); Jalisco (Ocatlan); Sinaloa (Mazatlan); and Lower California (La Paz).

Migration.—The Louisiana heron is only partially migratory as it winters plentifully as far north as South Carolina. On the coast of Louisiana and Texas, however, it is only seen there rarely at this season. It has been noted commonly at Breton Island reservation, Louisiana, on February 3 (1914); and at Corpus Christi, Texas, late in March, 1878. At the Breton Island reservation it was common at times until November 10 (1913).

Casual records.—The Louisiana heron apparently is not much given to postnuptial northward wanderings, as it has not been many times detected north of its usual summer range. It has been recorded from California (La Punta, January 17, 1914, and San Diego Bay, March 22, 1925); Arizona (near Fort Verde, September 24, 1884); northeastern Texas (Texarkana); Missouri (Clark County, April 13, 1890); Kentucky (Franklin County, about July 15, 1917); Indiana (Knox County, summer of 1894, and Starke County, June 26, 1876); Virginia (Cobb's Island near Washington, D. C., August 25, 1922); New Jersey (Cape May, August 1, 1920); New York (Patchogue, summer of 1836); and Manitoba (Nettley Lake, 40 miles north of Winnipeg, September 7, 1924).

Egg dates.—Florida: 57 records, December 8 to June 26; 29 records, April 7 to 26. Louisiana: 10 records, April 9 to June 21. Texas: 21 records, April 21 to June 22; 11 records, April 27 to May 16.

FLORIDA CAERULEA (Linnaeus)

LITTLE BLUE HERON

HABITS

Although not as widely distributed and not as numerous as formerly, the little blue heron is still very common in many of our Southern States. As its plumes have not been in such demand for millinery purposes, it has suffered less at the hands of the plume hunters than the white egrets have. It is, however, a shy and retiring species and has retreated somewhat before the advance of civilization. Although it is frequently seen feeding in coastal estuaries and ponds it is more essentially a bird of the interior than the other small herons of the Southern States. It seems to prefer to feed in fresh water ponds and marshes and along the banks of inland streams. It breeds by preference farther inland than the other species and its rookeries are seldom near the coast except in fresh water ponds on coastal islands. Dr. T. Gilbert Pearson (1922) describes its haunts very well as follows:

This species inhabits much of the extensive marshlands in our Southland. When traveling through the pine barrens of our South Atlantic and Gulf States, one will often come upon shallow ponds or small lakes whose margins and shallow reaches are more or less grown over with various water plants and scattered bushes; farther out the leaves of the water lilies are usually much in evidence. About the pond the bare grasslands, or prairies, extend from 100 feet to many hundreds of yards. Here is the natural and favorite feeding ground of the little blue heron. Singly, or in small flocks, they may be seen wading slowly along in the shallow water or standing stationary with heads erect, watching the intruder from a distance. Sometimes these lakes contain islands covered with button-wood or willow bushes, and these frequently are chosen as nesting sites for various herons of the neighborhood. Other favorite breeding places of the little blue heron are the small ponds in dense hammock lands that surround many of the lakes. Here, in the heavy semitropical forests, one may find quiet little ponds thickly grown with bushes, and such places the herons love.

Nesting.—In Florida, in 1902, we found little blue herons breeding in large numbers on the willow islands of the upper St. Johns, in rookeries with the Louisiana herons, which were much more numerous. So far as we could judge, from what few nests we were able to identify and from watching the birds rise from their nests as we approached the rookeries, the little blue herons always nested in the smaller willows on the outer edges of the islands. The nests were placed low down, mostly from 2 to 4 feet from the ground, in small trees or bushes or on the lower branches. In Monroe County in 1903 we found them breeding in the big inland rookeries with other speices; here also their nests were confined to the outskirts of the rookeries, where they were bunched together in compact groups. We did not find them breeding on any of the Keys; I have never found them breeding any where near salt water. We found none breeding in any of the coastal rookeries in Texas, in 1923; but we found them common and breeding in the big inland rookeries of Victoria County.

C. J. Pennock has sent me some interesting notes on breeding colonies of little blue herons in the ty-ty pond region of Wakulla County, Florida. Here several hundred acres "low, level moor" extend from the banks of the St. Marks River to the Gulf, where the "many ty-ty ponds, with their rank border growth, lie dotted around like so many slands in a sea of grass." The ponds vary in size from 15 to 20 yards in diameter to several times that size, in which there is sometimes 3 or 4 feet of water and sometimes only dry mud, according to the season. The ty-ty bushes, for which the ponds are named, grow from 8 or 10 to 20 or more feet high and their close-growing stems prove a formidable barrier. In one of these ponds Mr. Pennock found a colony of 100 or more pairs of little blue herons established, with nests in the bushes from 5 to 8 feet above the water. Eight nests were found in a single clump of ty-ty only 15 feet in diameter. In another small pond 18 to 20 pairs were nesting in isolated clump of bushes, less than 20 feet in diameter, that grew almost in the center of the pond.

Near Mount Pleasant, South Carolina, on May 19 and 20, 1915, while I was visiting Arthur T. Wayne, he showed me a small colony of 8 or 10 pairs of little blue herons. After wandering for sometime through a grand old forest of tall pine, sweet gum, black gum, live oak, and water oak, with occasional thickets of myrtle and bay, overgrown with tangles of vines, we came to a wet section in the forest, where the large live oaks and water oaks were standing in shallow water; and beyond, where the water was from knee deep to waist deep, were thickets of willows and other small trees and bushes. The little blue herons, with a few black-crowned night herons, and green herons, had established a little rookery in the willow and other bushes around the edges of an open pond, overgrown with wampee lilies (*Pontederia cordata*). The little blue herons' nests were from 3 to 8 feet above the water in the small willows on the borders of the pond or in solitary trees in the open. The nests were very small, frail structures of fine twigs; fully half of them still contained 3 or 4 eggs; some young were just hatching and some others were a few days or a week old.

Doctor Pearson (1919) mentions a colony found by him in Hyde County, North Carolina, in which "the nests were built in cypress and willow trees, at distances varying from 15 to 40 feet from the ground," unusually high nests for this species. Also, another "unusual fact noted was that the trees were not standing in water, but on virtually dry land." My experience has been that the little blue herons build their nests very low down, usually over water or mud, and in dense groups. Dr. Frank M. Chapman (1908) counted 32 nests in one bush. The nest is not distinguishable from those of the other small herons; it is a loose, frail platform of small sticks or twigs, very slightly hollowed, and with no lining except that the finer twigs on top may be laid more smoothly. Dr. A. H. Cordier (1923) once watched one of these herons building its nest, of which he says:

Near a rookery in Florida I witnessed a little blue heron building its nest of fine twigs, gathered from a burned-over area. Each twig was carefully selected from the dead limbs of the same bush, and was broken off and carried to the nest. The trips were made on an average of every 7 minutes and the nest was completed and contained one egg at the end of 48 hours.

Eggs.—The little blue heron usually lays four or five eggs, sometimes only three, and occasionally six. The shape is usually ovate or oval, varying rarely to elliptical ovate or elliptical oval. The shell is smooth but not glossy. The color is pale bluish green, varying from "light Niagara green" to "lichen green." The measurements of 54 eggs average 44 by 33.5 millimeters; the eggs showing the four extremes measure **49.5** by 35, 45.5 by **35.5, 40** by 33, 40.5 by **30.5.**

Young.—C. J. Pennock contributes the following notes on the behavior of young little blue herons:

Most of the nests were now empty; the oldest birds were able to use their wings a little and when startled would fly from bush to bush, but I saw none leave the pond. Younger ones were traveling though the branches or were perched on the tops of the bushes. Other young were on the ground and a few were still too young to leave the nest; although at a very early age, when approached, they showed determination to abandon the nest and scramble over the bushes. Several nests contained single dead birds. A few young were found dead on the ground and in two instances dead juveniles were found suspended by the neck in narrow forks of branches, presumably having fallen and being unable to extricate themselves. One young bird was seen stalking over the ground with the dead body of a still younger bird of the same species dangling from its mouth. On catching this bird I found the head of the dead bird was well down the throat of the captor and on pulling it out discovered that digestion had progressed considerably.

The young are fed at first on regurgitated food; as thus described by Doctor Cordier (1923):

The actual act of feeding is, to say the least, a vicious and terrible affair. The parent bird stands by the nest in a seemingly indifferent mood, while the young are screaming and fighting for the best position. Each time the parent's bill is within reach, a young bird seizes it crosswise at the base and jerks violently, while there is much protesting noise from the other less fortunate youngsters. The old bird may, with stoical indifference, refuse to feed for some time, during which the young bird continues, with bull-dog tenacity, to pull and jerk at the parent's beak getting nearer and nearer to the tip. When the psychological moment for regurgitation arrives the partly digested fish is either forced down the throat of the nestling, or, perchance it may light on the interested photographer's head or camera outfit. When the young birds have been fed the parent frequently stands by the nest for an hour or more, all the while uttering a contented note, much like that of a barnyard hen as she struts around the yard with her half-grown brood following her. The owner of a nest near my tent had the habit of descending to the ground and eating billful after billful of the mud so abundant under the trees, continually dancing and jumping around as if enjoying the feast.

Plumages.—The downy young little blue heron is like the downy young snowy egret, all pure white. The body plumage is the first to appear and the back is well feathered before the young bird is half grown and before the flight feathers burst their sheaths; the wings and tail are not complete until the bird is fully grown. The primaries are tipped with bluish black when they first appear, but the rest of the juvenal plumage is all pure white. This plumage, wholly white except the wing tips, is worn during the first fall and winter without much change; I have seen it as late as May 1. But usually young birds begin to acquire some blue in the plumage by February, which increases during the spring. Young birds are often found breeding in this first nuptial, mixed, plumage, which has suggested the idea that they are adults in a white phase. The amount of blue in this first nuptial plumage varies greatly in different individuals. Usually it appears first as a bluish wash in the crown or a sprinkling of blue in the primaries or tertials; the color then spreads to the lores, neck, and back, until the latter becomes largely blue in April; at about this time some new scapulars, many new wing coverts, and occasionally some new remiges, wholly blue, are acquired by molt, in addition to those which are sprinkled with blue; these last suggest the possibility of color change. The above is the normal or commonest type of progress, but there are exceptions to the rule. Some advanced birds begin to show a suffusion of blue in the crown, neck, and primaries as early as November. Some remain nearly all white through the breeding season and acquire some rudimentary, white, plumelike feathers on the back. Some other parti-colored birds acquire many long, blue, plumelike feathers on the back, similar to those worn by breeding adults. Both of these last two are probably breeding plumages.

I spent the winter of 1924 and 1925 in the vicinity of Tampa Bay, Florida, where little blue herons were very common and constantly under observation. Up to the time of my departure, on May 1, I did not see, among the hundreds of birds examined, a single white bird which showed any appreciable signs of molting into the blue plumage, though I was always on the watch for them. Hence I infer that the normal time of molting is in May or later.

Apparently the first postnuptial molt begins in the spring; perhaps the solid blue feathers seen in April birds show the beginning of it but I have seen birds taken in July in complete fresh winter plumage. This molt is complete and removes all traces of immaturity. I can not agree with the two-color-phase theory; I have never seen a bird in wholly blue plumage that was not unquestionably an adult. I have never seen a white bird which was not unquestionably immature; the whitest birds are all fall birds; the parti-colored birds are all spring birds; and I have never seen a white bird in the fall that showed any considerable amount of blue. The change from white to blue is progressive throughout the first year and no trace of it is seen afterward.

Adults have the usual heron molts, a partial prenuptial molt beginning in February, and a complete postnuptial molt beginning in July; the wings are usually molted in August. The long, "slate-blue," plumelike feathers of the back, and the "Indian red" plumage of the head and neck are characteristic of the nuptial plumage. In winter plumage the head and neck are more purplish, with more or less whitish in the chin and throat, and there are only a few short, plumelike feathers in the back.

Food.—The little blue heron feeds to some extent in salt or brackish waters in estuaries and coastal marshes, where it catches minnows, fiddler crabs, and other crustaceans. But its favorite feeding grounds are in fresh-water marshes and meadows, around the marshy shores of ponds and lakes, and along the banks of inland streams. Its active method of pursuing its prey has been portrayed so well by the illustrious Audubon (1840) that I can not do better than quote his words, as follows:

There, and at this season, reader, you may see this graceful heron, quietl and in silence walking along the margins of the water, with an elegance and grace which can never fail to please you. Each regularly-timed step is lightly measured, while the keen eye of the bird seeks for and watches the equally cautious movements of the objects towards which it advances with all imaginable care. When at a proper distance, it darts forth its bill with astonishing celerity, to pierce and secure its prey; and this it does with so much precision, that, while watching some at a distance with a glass, I rarely observed an instance of failure: If fish is plentiful, on the shallows near the shore, when it has caught one, it immediately swallows it, and runs briskly through the water, striking here and there, and thus capturing several in succession. Two or three dashes of this sort, afford sufficient nourishment for several hours, and when the bird has obtained enough it retires to some quiet place, and remains there in an attitude of repose until its hunger returns.

Oscar E. Baynard (1912) found that 50 meals of young little blue herons consisted of 1,900 grasshoppers, 37 small frogs, 149 cutworms, 8 lizards, and 142 small crawfish. And in the stomach of an adult, he found 51 grasshoppers, 2 small frogs, 3 cutworms, 1 small lizard, and the remains of 3 crawfish. These were quite substantial meals and their contents show that these little herons are decidedly beneficial.

Dr. Alexander Wetmore (1916) made a study of the food of this species in Porto Rico, from which it appeared that over 97 per cent was animal and less than 3 per cent vegetable. The animal food consisted of mole crickets, grasshoppers, locusts, and other insects, frogs, crabs, shrimps, and lizards. Mr. Arthur H. Howell (1911) says of the food of the little blue heron in Arkansas:

The food of this heron consists chiefly of fish, frogs, lizards, crawfish, small crabs, and insects. The rice growers of southern Texas consider it very useful on account of its fondness for crawfish, which cause trouble in the rice fields by their depredations upon the crop and by burrowing into the embankments surrounding the fields. The stomachs of 4 specimens killed near Wilmot in June contained crawfish and aquatic beetles. One bird had eaten 35 of the crustaceans and 28 beetle larvae.

Behavior.—The flight of the little blue heron is light, graceful, and strong; it is performed in the usual heron attitude, with the head drawn in upon the shoulders and the legs extended in the rear; the wing strokes are quicker than in the larger herons. On the ground or in the shallow water where it seeks its food, its movements are quick, graceful, and elegant. On its feeding grounds and in its breeding rookeries it is usually intimately associated with the Louisiana heron, with which it seems to be on friendly terms, though I once saw a Louisiana heron deliberately poke the eggs out of a little blue heron's nest. These two small herons are daylight feeders; I doubt if they ever feed at night. They may be seen at all hours of the day walking daintily and actively about on the marshes or mud flats; but their principal feeding hours are early in the morning and late in the afternoon. They roost at night on the trees and bushes in their breeding rookeries or in other suitable places such as motes or clumps of trees on open marshes or on islands, where they feel secure; large numbers congregate in such roosts. Early in the morning they fly out in detached flocks and scatter over their feeding grounds; returning again at night, the flocks circle around the roost to reconnoiter and then come gliding down into the trees. When preparing to alight or when circling in a strong wind they sometimes scale along for some distance on set wings.

These little herons are usually silent; a low clucking or croaking note is occasionally heard while they are feeding or a louder, harsher croak when alarmed. Doctor Chapman (1908) calls them "noisy and quarrelsome, calling at each other notes which sounded strangely like *tell you what, tell you what.*" Doctor Cordier (1923) writes:

The feeding note of these birds as they approach the nest is much like that of a guinea fowl; the fighting, or quarreling note resembles the scream of a parrot when it sees a dog coming around a corner toward its perch.

Prof. Julian S. Huxley tells me that the behavior of the little blue heron on its breeding grounds appears to be essentially similar to that of the Louisiana heron, which is so well described in his notes on that species. The courtships, greeting ceremonies, nest-relief ceremonies, and emotional displays are much alike in all three of the small southern herons; they all have plumes or aigrettes which they love to display. Their flight maneuvers are also similar. Little blue herons often travel in loose flocks. A flock of 15 or 20 birds, blue adults and white young birds, frequented some small ponds near my winter home in Florida; when frightened away from the ponds they invariably flew to and alighted on one of two dead pine trees in the vicinity; if disturbed there, they all took to wing, circled around in an open flock a few times and then all set their wings, scaling in unison, and returned to one of the trees, where they all gracefully alighted. These trees were their favorite perches to which they returned again and again after a few turns in the air. I have seen all the herons set their wings and scale, at times, especially when returning to their rookeries or when about to alight.

Enemies.—The lack of marketable plumes has saved this species from much of the slaughter from which the more popular species have suffered. But, in many places in the Southern States and in the West Indies it has been quite extensively killed for food, the young birds being particularly palatable. Its worst natural enemies are crows and vultures, which destroy vast numbers of eggs and young. Fish crows, in Florida, are always sneaking around in the rookeries, looking for a chance to rob any unguarded heron's nests, and the large number of broken eggs seen under the nests shows that they are all too successful. Vultures, crows, and large grackles should be systematically shot by all wardens that guard rookeries.

Fall.—The little blue is another of our southern herons that wanders far north of its breeding range in summer and fall, from July to October. These wanderings have carried it as far as Nova Scotia, Quebec, Ontario, Michigan, Wisconsin, and Nebraska. It is mainly the young birds, in the white plumage, that indulge in these erratic journeys, which may be caused by overcrowding on their breeding grounds resulting in a desire to find new fields in which to search for food.   The little blue herons are much more often reported from northern localities than the egrets, and during some seasons they are really quite common in New England.   Throughout the southern portion of its range this species is a constant resident or, at least, always present; but it withdraws in winter from all but the southern tier of States.

DISTRIBUTION

Range.—South America, Central America, Islands of the Caribbean Sea and southern and eastern North America.

Breeding range.—North to Tepic (San Blas, Las Penas Islands, and the Acaponeta River); Texas (Kerrville, Waco, and Houston); Arkansas (Arkadelphia, Osceola, and probably Wilmot); Missouri (southeastern part); Kentucky (Bowling Green); North Carolina (Craven and Hyde Counties); Virginia (Hog Island); and formerly New Jersey (Cape May).   East to formerly New Jersey (Cape May); Virginia (Hog Island); North Carolina (Hyde and Craven Counties); South Carolina (Washoe Reserve on the Santee River, Mount Pleasant and Frogmore); Georgia (Savannah, Darien, Blackbeard Island, and St. Marys); Florida (St. Augustine, Mosquito Inlet, Micco, and Miami); the Bahama Islands (Andros and New Providence); San Domingo; Porto Rico (San Juan and Vieques Island); Carriacou Island; Tobago Island; Trinidad; British Guiana (Georgetown); Brazil (Counani River, Bahia, Sao Paulo and Iguape); and Argentina (Mercedes).   South to Brazil (Iguape); Argentina (Mercedes); and Peru (Tumbez).   West to Peru (Tumbez); Ecuador (Vinces); Colombia (Lake Paturia and Cienega); Panama (Castillo and Remedios); Costa Rica (Punta Arenas); Nicaragua (Escondido River and San Juan del Sur); Guatemala (San Jose and Chiapam); and Tepic (Las Penas Islands and the Acaponeta River).

Winter range.—North to Sinaloa (Mazatlan); Texas (probably Tom Green and Concho Counties, Brownsville, Refugio County, and probably Lee County); Louisiana (west side of Vermillion Bay, Marsh Island, and the State game preserve); South Carolina (probably Frogmore, Charleston, and probably the Washoe Reserve on the Santee River); and North Carolina (Currituck Sound).   East to North Carolina (Currituck Sound); South Carolina (probably the Washoe Reserve, Charleson, and probably Frogmore); Georgia (St. Marys); Florida (Alachua County, Fruitland, Micanopy, Mosquito Inlet, Lake Harvey, Titusville, Kissimmee, Miami, and Upper Matecumbe Key); the Bahama Islands; Haiti; Porto Rico; Cuba; an southwards through the breeding range where it is resident.   West to Jalisco (Ocatlan); and Sinaloa (Mazatlan).

Migration.—Although the little blue heron remains in winter throughout most of the breeding range, most of the birds withdraw from the northern areas. They have been observed to arrive at New Orleans, Louisiana, on March 11 (1894); at Andrews, North Carolina on April 4; at Beulahville, Virginia, on April 14 (1912); and at Miller, Virginia, on May 12 (1917).

Casual records.—Like the egrets and some other herons, this species has a habit of wandering far north of its normal breeding range, although in the present instance, this is done not only after the nesting season but also before. This is particularly true of the birds in the white plumage which are frequently mistaken for the snowy egret and the opposite. There are several spring and fall records of little blue herons in Pennsylvania, New Jersey, New York, Connecticut, and Massachusetts, and others north to Vermont (Newbury, August 16, 1912); New Hampshire (Amherst, April 28, 1897); Maine (Scarborough, September, 1881, Vinalhaven, April 1, 1902, Popham Beach, May 19, 1901, and Whitneyville, August 16, 1906); Quebec (Quebec, October, 1881 and Lance au Loup, May 23, 1900); and Nova Scotia (Lawrencetown, March 18, 1896). In the Mississippi Valley and contiguous territory the species has been many times detected in Iowa, Illinois, Indiana, and Ohio, with records of occurrence extending north to Michigan (Detroit, May 2, 1882); Ontario (Point Pelee, September, 1904, and Aylmer, August 15, 1901); Wisconsin (Lake Koshkonong, and Racine County, August 28, 1848); and Manitoba (Winnipeg, May 11, 1905). Farther west it has occurred north to Oklahoma (Redrock, summer of 1884, Copan, July 16 to August 2, 1906, and Ponca, April 7–10, 1918); Kansas (Winfield, May 2 and October 5, 1902, Wichita, May 2, 1917, Elmdale, April 18–26, 1916, and Manhattan, April 27–30, 1915); and Nebraska (Nebraska City, September, 11, 1900, Omaha, June 15, 1897, and August 15, 1903, and Butler County). The Colorado record for this species really refers to the snowy egret, *Egretta c. candidissima.*

Egg dates.—Florida: 89 records, December 27 to June 3; 45 records, April 1 to 25. Louisiana: 11 records, April 7 to May 16.

BUTORIDES VIRESCENS VIRESCENS (Linnaeus)

GREEN HERON

HABITS

Contributed by Charles Wendell Townsend

Familiarity with the habits of this well-known little heron explains its common or vulgar names such as "fly-up-the-creek," "chalkline," "shite-poke;" and "skeow." These names are of long standing and very expressive, for the bird is a familiar one to the country boy and to the fisherman by stream or pond, where the tameness or stupidity of this bird often brings it within close range.

Spring.—The migratory flights of the green heron are generally made at night and are described by Audubon (1840) with his usual picturesqueness. He says:

I have observed their return in early spring, when arriving in flocks of from 20 to 50 individuals. They would plunge downwards from their elevated line of march, cutting various zigzags, until they would all simultaneously alight on the tops of the trees or bushes of some swampy place, or on the borders of miry ponds. These halts took place pretty regularly about an hour after sunrise. The day was occupied by them, as well as by some other species especially the blue, the yellow-crowned, and night herons, all of which at this period traveled eastward, in resting, cleansing their bodies, and searching for food. When the sun approached the western horizon, they would at once ascend in the air, arrange their lines and commence their flight, which I have no doubt continued all night.

The chance to see such a flight is, however, rare. Generally on a day in early spring one discovers at the pond or stream margin the familiar bird that has been absent all the winter months and has arrived unseen in the night.

Courtship.—Audubon (1840) says:

During the love season they exhibit many curious gestures, erecting all the feathers of their neck, swelling their throat, and uttering a rough guttural note like *qua, qua,* several times repeated by the male as he struts before the female.

Mrs. Irene G. Wheelock (1906) describes the dance or "hornpipe of a solitary green heron" in June, "although," as she says, "possibly his mate may have been an unseen witness. Backward and forward, with queer little hops, he pranced first on one foot and then on the other. * * * The effect is as ludicrous as though a long legged, dignified D. D. were to pause in his learned discourse and execute a double shuffle."

Nesting.—The green heron nests singly or in colonies. Although it generally prefers for its nesting locality a region close to the water, it may choose dry woods or an orchard in the midst of cultivated ground. The height of the nest is also very variable, and although most nests are placed from 10 to 20 feet from the ground, they may be found in the tops of high trees, or, on the other hand, on low bushes or even on the ground. Hatch (1892) says: "Instances have occurred under my observation, where in the entire absence of trees or bushes of any size, they have placed the nest, composed of coarse dry weeds and reeds and cat-tails, on a tussock in a reed-hidden quagmire." And he mentions one that was built on the top of a muskrat house. Maynard (1896) says that in Florida, "among the keys, they often place their domiciles on the roots of the mangroves, frequently not over 6 inches above high-water mark." W. J. Erichsen (1921) in his observations in Chatham County, Georgia, says:

These birds breed in considerable numbers on Sylvans Island on the Herb River, some 3 miles from the town of Thunderbolt, placing their nests in the extreme tops of tall pine saplings. Probably the most populous colony in the county is near Lazaretto station on Tybee Island. Here the birds breed in a jungle of oaks difficult to penetrate. So numerous are they that every available nesting site is occupied, many new nests being built on the foundation of old ones.

In Massachusetts, I have generally found single nests, but on several occasions, small colonies. One at Magnolia, many years ago between the beach and a fresh water marsh, consisted of 20 or 30 pairs nesting in pitch pines about 20 feet from the ground. Another colony was on an island in the salt marsh at Ipswich in trees of gray birch, red oak, and hickory about 15 feet from the ground. A colony of about 20 nests at Westport on a salt marsh island was in cedars, sassafras, and hickories. In this case the nests varied from 3 to 20 feet from the ground.

The nest itself is a simple affair from 10 to 12 inches in diameter, ill-adapted, it would seem, to hold eggs when the tree branches wave in the wind, for it is a flat platform of sticks, destitute of any sort of lining and not cup shaped. Some at least of the twigs composing the nest are green. The nest is so thin and flimsy that one can sometimes look through it from below and see the eggs. In making the nest the herons must weave the twigs in and out to a certain extent, for if they merely laid the sticks one on top of the other, the nest would fall to pieces at the least disturbance. The nests on the ground made of course weeds, reeds, and cat-tails already mentioned are very unusual both in site and material.

The green heron does not nest with other species as a rule, but is occasionally found nesting in the same grove with little blue, Louisiana, black-crowned, and other herons. The boat-tailed grackle and the bronze grackle have also been found nesting in the same group of trees. Mrs. Wheelock (1906) says of the association with the latter birds:

The grackles were quarrelsome, thieving, noisy, and the only possible advantage the herons could hope to derive from them would be the loud alarm always given by them at the approach of danger.

Eggs.—[Author's note: Green herons have been known to lay from three to nine eggs, but the ordinary sets consist of four or five eggs; the larger sets are probably the product of two females. The eggs are ovate or oval in shape. The shell is smooth without gloss and the color varies from "pale glaucous green" to "pale olivine." The measurements of 43 eggs average 38 by 29.5 millimeters; the eggs showing the four extremes measure **41** by 28, 40.5 by **30.5, 36** by **27.5** millimeters.]

Young.—The incubation according to Burns (1915) is 17 days. The young at an early age are expert climbers among the branches of the nesting tree, long before they are able to fly and while the natal down still adheres to the juvenal feathers and forms a halo around their heads. In climbing they make use of their feet, wings and bill, or, rather of the neck, hooking their bills and chins over the branches and pulling themselves up. The bastard wing is extended during the climbing process, suggesting an ancestral, reptilian use, but whatever power it may have had in the past, this was long since lost. I have never seen any attempt to use the bastard wing in grasping. If the ornithologist climbs the tree in order to observe the half-grown young in the nest, these almost always leave in haste and scatter to the outermost tips of the branches.

Another ancestral trait, which is suggested in the adult by the persistence of a distinct web between the middle and outer toes, is an ability on the part of the young to swim, an inheritance which must be of distinct value in many cases where the young fall from the nesting tree or bush into the water below. I once placed a vigorous half-grown young green heron in the water below its nest and was delighted to see it sit erect like a little swan and paddle gracefully off, using its feet alternately. It seemed perfectly at its ease, dabbed at the water occasionally with its bill, swam a creek 20 yards broad, and threaded its way among the grass stalks until it disappeared from sight. The grace and ease with which it swam contrasted forcibly with its movements on land. The adult also is able to swim.

When the young are approached too closely, they regurgitate the contents of their crops to the discomfort of the seeker after knowledge, although this action gives the latter an opportunity to learn the character of their food. Mrs. Irene.G. Wheelock (1906), who has made some interesting and valuable studies of several families of these birds in southern Wisconsin says:

As soon as the little ones were fairly out of the shells and before the down was dry on their heads we had taken several pictures of them. One of these revealed a remarkable heron trait, for the brand new baby, who had never been fed, and who had scarcely opened his eyes on this queer world, yet attempted to protest against our meddling by the characteristic heron method of defense. In his case the action was merely a nervous "gagging" and would seem to indicate that this act is involuntary rather than intentional on the part of all herons. * * * When first hatched the herons stretched up to a height of 3¼ inches, and when 7 days old, 11 inches.

She found that they "gained one-half ounce in weight every day for 6 days, weighing three-fourths of an ounce at the beginning and 3¾ of an ounce on the seventh day." These young were fed only in the early morning and in the late afternoon, and the periods of greatest activity were from 4 to 6 in the morning, and from 5 to 7 in the evening. One record taken when the young were a week old, showed that they were fed 7 times in the morning and 7 times in the afternoon. The food was given by regurgitation but was not predigested.

Plumages.—[Author's note: The downy young green heron is
scantily covered with "drab" down, thickest on the back and
longest on the crown; the color varies to light gray on the under
parts and to "hair brown" on the crown. The juvenal plumage is
acquired in the usual heron sequence and is complete before the
young bird reaches the flight stage, when fully grown.

The sexes are distinguishable even in the juvenal plumage. In
the young male, in August, the crown is solid, glossy, greenish black;
the sides of the head and neck are solid "chestnut"; the chin, throat,
and neck stripe are yellowish white, spotted with black; the back is
solid, glossy, dark green; the wing coverts are the same color as the
back, but the lesser coverts are edged with chestnut and the median and greater coverts are rounded (not pointed, as in the
adult), edged with pale buff and have a triangular buffy white spot
at the tip of each feather; these spots soon fade out to white and
then wear away; the remiges and rectrices are glossy, greenish black;
the secondaries and primaries are tipped with white in decreasing
amounts from the inner to the outer; the under parts are buffy
white, streaked with dusky. The young female differs from the
juvenal male in having chestnut streaks in the crown and having the
sides of the head and neck streaked with chestnut, buff, and dusky.

The juvenal plumage is worn during the fall and early winter,
without much change until the partial prenuptial molt begins in
February; this involves mainly the head, neck, and body plumage,
which, by May, is much like the adult plumage, except that there
is more white in the chin, throat, and under parts, with more broad,
dusky stripes in the fresh plumage of the lower neck and upper
breast than in the adult; some new, fresh back plumes, scapulars,
and wing coverts, similar to those of the adult, are acquired at this
molt; but the flight feathers are old and worn and some of the
juvenal wing coverts are retained. The complete postnuptial molt
begins earlier in young birds than in adults; I have seen a young
bird molting its primaries as early as April first; at this molt, when
the young bird is but little over a year old, the adult plumage is assumed. The adult wing is easily recognized by the coverts; the
lesser coverts are narrowly edged with rufous buff and the median
and greater coverts are pointed (not rounded as in the juvenal) and
narrowly edged with pale buff; only the inner primaries and the
secondaries are very narrowly tipped with white.

Adults apparently have a partial prenuptial molt in late winter
and early spring and a complete postnuptial molt from July to November. I have seen an adult male molting its primaries as late
as January 16, which suggests the possibility of a complete prenuptial molt, but this may be only a case of delayed molt. There is
very little seasonal difference in adult plumages.]

Food.—The food of the green heron varies somewhat with the locality. In birds taken in salt marshes, I have found the stomach contents to consist of the minnows common in the little creeks together with a variable amount of sand. Live stomach worms are also common, a fact mentioned by other observers. In regions of fresh water, tadpoles, water insects and their larvae, crayfish, and small bony fishes are common articles of diet. Food is also gathered in the uplands by these birds and their stomachs have been found to contain earth worms, crickets, grasshoppers, snakes, and small mammals. Grasshoppers in very large numbers have sometimes been found. B. S. Bowdish (1902) says of the food of the green heron in Porto Rico: "Several stomachs examined contained respectively, remains of lizards and crabs, and one whole fish about 6 inches long; a kind of water beetle about three quaters of an inch long, many entire; crawfish and grasshoppers; 11 crawfish; small live worms." Oscar E. Baynard (1912) reports that the stomach of an adult green heron taken in Florida contained 6 small crayfish, 16 grasshoppers, 2 cut worms and the remains of small frogs.

Behavior.—William Brewster (1906) said of the green heron:

Like the crow and black duck, it is at once a wary and venturesome bird, endowed with sufficient intelligence to discriminate between real and imaginary dangers and often making itself quiet at home in noisy, thickly settled neighborhoods where food is abundant and where it is not too much molested.

The green heron is equally at home in the salt water marshes and in the regions of fresh water. It is a day feeder but prefers the early morning and late afternoon, often taking a nap at midday. One of the familiar sounds and sights by salt creek or by river or pond is the frightened cry of this bird and its awkward flight over the water. The names "skeow" and "fly-up-the-creek" are expressive of these attributes. The classic names "chalk-line" and "shite-poke" express the commonly observed physiological effect of fright. This effect must incidentally serve a useful purpose in blinding the stealthily creeping pursuer, be it carnivore or savage.

The length of the neck of the green heron in life is a most variable one and this bird well deserves to be called "rubber neck." Early one May morning I watched unseen one of these birds with its neck drawn in creeping along the branches of a spruce. In the dim light it looked more like a mammal than a bird. Suddenly it elongated its neck and seized with its bill a twig of a near-by elm, but was unable to break it off. It tried another and another and finally succeeded in tearing the green twig off from its base. I watched another bird as it awoke from its morning nap and, as it stretched its neck to an equal length with its body and shook out its feathers, the general form and appearance of the bird went through a marvelous change. In short flights this heron may retain the elongated pose of the neck, but in longer ones it folds up and retracts that member.

When walking about, especially if it knows it is watched, the green heron nervously twitches its tail downwards and erects and depresses its crest. It is also able to remain perfectly still, especially when on the watch for game. A common posture assumed on the margin of a pond or sand flats at low tide is with the back and neck horizontal and the tarsi so nearly flat on the ground that the body is close to the same. The bird under these circumstances is easily mistaken for a log of wood. In this position it waits patiently, ready to pounce on the little fish that swim its way and it rarely misses its aim. At other times it approaches stealthily, putting down each foot with care and secures its prey with a quick stroke. That this stroke must be quick and accurate is evident when we consider the nature of some of its food, frogs, fish, and grasshoppers.

That green herons in some cases jump or even dive into the water after their prey, is shown in the following account by Samuel H. Barker (1901) who saw an individual plunge from a plank after fish into a pond 3 to 6 feet deep.

Although he missed his aim, the effort was well meant and, to judge by appearances, not the first of its kind. Turning about in the water, he rose from it with little difficulty and with a few flaps was back on the plank. * * * That this one instance of an individual green heron plunging into deep water after food proves such to be a natural habit of the species can hardly be said. I would add, however, that further study of the feeding habits of the green heron, with a view to settling this question, convinces me that a quite usual method of fishing is for it to watch from a stand a few inches above the water and from there to jump quickly down upon its prey.

W. Sprague Brooks (1923) watched a green heron walking stealthily along the stone rim of the Public Garden pond in Boston.

After a while it turned cautiously until facing the water, toes at the rim of the stone, its neck stretched out at full length, and suddenly, as a swimmer in a race plunges from the marble rim of a tank, it plunged into the water, completely submerged, came to the surface with a goldfish which it immediately swallowed, and raising its wings, flew back, only a matter of two wing strokes, to the stone border. Twice I watched it do this.

The note commonly emitted by this bird as it flies from the intruder can, perhaps, best be represented by the syllables *peu-ah*. It generally resembles very closely the sound made by blowing a blade of grass stretched tightly between the thumbs side by side. When much startled the green heron croaks hoarsely but soon returns to the usual *peu-ah*. Sometimes, especially about the nesting tree, it may be heard to give a short cackle or cluck. Early one morning, when I was lying concealed in a grove of trees, a green heron alighted among them nearly over my head.   Thereupon it emitted a series of low double groans at irregular intervals.   If I had not seen the bird, I should have been puzzled as to the source of the sounds.

The small size of this heron, somewhat smaller than a crow, its short cut-off tail, its general greenish-black color with a chestnut-colored throat and bluish-gray primaries make its recognition in the field easy.

The green heron is too interesting a bird to be used for a pot hunter's target as is often the case.   He who is so fortunate as to have a breeding place for this bird near him should zealously guard it and he will learn many interesting and amusing traits and will be well rewarded.

DISTRIBUTION

Range.—Central America north and west of Honduras, with the United States and southern Canada east of the Rocky Mountains.

Breeding range.—North to South Dakota (Vermilion and probably Sioux Falls); Minnesota (Minneapolis and Lanesboro); Wisconsin (Elkhorn, Kelley Brook, and Sturgeon Bay); Michigan (Grand Rapids); Ontario (Guelph, Yarker, and Loughboro Lake); Quebec (Montreal); Maine (Pittsfield and Calais); and probably New Brunswick (St. John and Grand Manan).   East to New Brunswick (probably Grand Manan); Maine (Calais); Massachusetts (Essex, Barnstable, and Dukes Counties); Rhode Island (Newport and Haversham); New York (Long Island); New Jersey (Elizabeth, Red Bank, Tuckerton, and Sea Isle City); Virginia (Cobb's Island, Wallops Island, and Dismal Swamp); North Carolina (Pea Island and Beaufort); South Carolina (Charleston and Frogmore); Georgia (Savannah, Blackbeard Island, St. Marys, and Okeefinoke Swamp); Florida (Palatka, Micco, and Cape Sable); Yucatan (Cozumel Island); British Honduras (Belize); and Guatemala (Lake Yzabel and Duenas). South to Guatemala (Lake Yzabel and Duenas); Oaxaca (Tehuantepec); and Colima (Colima).   West to Colima (Colima); Tamaulipas (Tampico); Texas (Brownsville, Del Rio, Kerrville, and Waco); Oklahoma (Chattanooga and Fort Reno); Kansas (Wichita, Ellsworth, Hays, and Onaga); Nebraska (Gibbon probably, and Alda); and South Dakota (Vermilion, and probably Sioux Falls).

Winter range.—Principally Mexico and Central America.   Distribution during this season severely circumscribed as this race is not found south of the southern limits of the summer range.   North to Sinaloa (Mazatlan); Texas (Brownsville, Aransas Bay, and Waller County); Florida (Lake Iamonia, Gainesville, St. Augustine, and Mosquito Inlet); and South Carolina (Capers Island).   East to South Carolina (Capers Island); Florida (Mosquito Inlet and Kissimmee);

Yucatan (Cozumel Island); and Honduras (Ceiba). South to Honduras (Ceiba); and Colima (Manzanillo). West to Colima(Manzanillo); and Sinaloa (Mazatlan). Accidental at this season in Porto Rico (Fajardo). Twice reported from Indiana in the winter months, Indianapolis, January 3, 1916 (Wilson), and Goshen, March 18, 1918 (Eby).

Spring migration.—Early dates of arrival are North Carolina, March 29, 1893; District of Columbia, Washington, April 9, 1905; Pennsylvania, Holmesburg, April 1, 1900, Philadelphia, April 16, 1884, and Renova, April 24, 1899; New Jersey, Englewood, April 1, 1913; New York, Brooklyn, April 17, 1884; Connecticut, Fairfield, April 15, 1920 and Meriden, April 12, 1919; Massachusetts, Needham, April 9, 1905, and Dennis, April 8, 1920; Maine, Portland, April 25, 1905; Quebec, Montreal, April 30, 1895; Louisiana, New Orleans, March 21, 1894, and Lake Catherine, April 2, 1918; Missouri, Monteer, April 10, 1905; Kentucky, Bowling Green, April 8, 1918, and Guthrie, April 16, 1918; Indiana, Bloomington, April 10, 1903, and Waterloo, April 13, 1905; Ohio, Oberlin, April 6, 1913, Scio, April 14, 1918, and Youngstown, April 16, 1919; Michigan, Vicksburg, April 25, 1908; Ontario, London, April 20, 1917; Iowa, Keokuk, April 21, 1893, and Bentonsport, April 22, 1920; Illinois, Chicago, April 11, 1908; Wisconsin, Delavan, April 20, 1896; Minnesota, Red Wing, April 18, 1919, and Lanesboro, April 23, 1885; Texas, Beaumont, April 4, 1887, and Kerrville, April 7, 1906; Oklahoma, Ponca City, April 15, 1918; Kansas, Manhattan, April 16, 1883; Nebraska, southeastern part, April 15, 1899.

Fall migration.—Late dates of departure are: Quebec, Montreal, September 2, 1897; Maine, Pittsfield, October 2, 1898; New Hampshire, Durham, October 13, 1900; Massachusetts, North Truro, October 5, 1889; Connecticut, Meriden, October 20, 1919; New York, Rochester, October 23, 1917, and Rhinebeck, October 11, 1921; New Jersey, New Providence, October 10, 1894; District of Columbia, Washington, October 2, 1910; North Carolina, Raleigh, October 5, 1916, and Weaverville, October 10, 1891; South Carolina, Frogmore, October 4, 1886; Ontario, Ottawa, September 20, 1918, and Port Dover, September 24, 1916; Michigan, Detroit, September 14, 1919, and southern part, October 4, 1903; Ohio, Waverly, October 1, 1898, Scio, October 4, 1919, and Oberlin, November 13, 1897; Indiana, Greensburg, October 7, 1894, and Crawfordsville, October 9, 1919; Kentucky, Bowling Green, September 23; Tennessee, Athens, October 10, 1902; Wisconsin, Elkhorn, September 30, 1916, and Madison, September 20, 1919; Minnesota, Lanesboro, September 25, 1891; Nebraska, Dunbar, September 24, 1904; Kansas, Onaga, October 10,

1917; Oklahoma, Copan, October 14, 1916; and Texas, Bonham, September 20, 1889.

Casuals.—Accidental in Colorado (Loveland, July 23, 1895) and in Porto Rico (Fajardo, February 16, 1899).

Egg dates.—Southern New England and New York: 58 records, May 8 to June 25; 30 records, May 22 to June 1.   New Jersey and Pennsylvania: 25 records, April 30 to June 11; 13 records, May 20 to June 2.   Georgia and Florida: 24 records, March 29 to July 9; 12 records, April 6 to May 10.   Indiana and Illinois: 15 records, May 12 to June 18; 8 records, May 19 to June 4.   Louisiana and Texas: 11 records, April 4 to June 28; 6 records, May 2 to 23.

BUTORIDES VIRESCENS FRAZARI (Brewster)

FRAZAR GREEN HERON

HABITS

The green herons of the American species, *Butorides virescens*, have been split by Dr. H. C. Oberholser (1912) and others into some eighteen subspecies, only three of which come within the limits of our check list.   This form, which is restricted to central and southern Lower California, was described by William Brewster (1888) and named in honor of M. Abbott Frazar, who collected the type specimen.   It is slightly larger than *virescens* and its general coloring is darker, duller, and more uniform.   "The deeper, more purplish maroon of the neck with its decided glaucous tinge, is perhaps the best character of the new form," according to the describer.   Mr. Brewester (1902a) does not tell us very much about its habits, in which it probably does not differ much from its eastern relative. He says that it "was discovered in 1887 by Mr. Frazar, who found it only at La Paz.   His notes state that it frequented mangrove thickets about the shores of the bay, where it was common during February and March, but as he mistook it for our eastern bird he preserved only two specimens."

Eggs.—The eggs of this subspecies are not distinguishable from those of our common eastern bird.   The measurements of 10 eggs average 30.8 by 29.4 millimeters; the eggs showing the four extremes measure **39** by 29.2, 37.5 by **30.5, 37** by 29.5, and 37.5 by **28.7** millimeters.

DISTRIBUTION

Range.—Lower California, from San Ignacio and Magdalena Bay southward to La Paz, where it is resident.

Egg dates.—Lower California: 10 records, May 11 to June 27; 5 records, May 24 to June 5.

BUTORIDES VIRESCENS ANTHONYI (Mearns)

ANTHONY GREEN HERON

HABITS

This is the large, pale race of the green heron which inhabits California and the arid regions of the Southwest. It was described by Dr. Edgar A. Mearns (1895) from specimens collected by him in the Colorado Valley, near the Mexican boundary, and named in honor of A. W. Anthony. It is described as similar to the green heron "of the eastern United States, but slightly larger, and paler throughout, with the light markings of the wings, neck and throat much less restricted, and whiter." It is not nearly so abundant anywhere as our eastern bird is in many places, and is restricted to comparatively few favorable localities, particularly the irrigated valleys.

Nesting.—In the arid, desert regions of Arizona, water birds are scarce, but many species of ducks visit the lakes and irrigation reservoirs on their migrations and shorebirds of various kinds are frequently seen along the river beds, where in the dry season the water is restricted to a narrow shallow stream meandering through broad expanses of mud or sand flats. Here too an occasional heron may be seen flapping lazily along searching for some pool deep enough to contain a few fish. In the well irrigated valley of the San Pedro River, where numerous ranches have cultivated and watered land, conditions are markedly different. Every ranch has its reservoirs, driven wells, and system of irrigating ditches, which have produced abundant crops and fertile conditions. Along the banks of the ditches vegetation is luxuriant, with large willows and cottonwood trees and often with a dense undergrowth of shrubbery and vines. On May 27, 1922, we were wandering along one of these irrigation ditches, exploring the thickets of small willows and wild gooseberry bushes, and looking for nests of Sonora redwings, Abert towhees and other small birds, when we saw the familiar figure of a green heron watching us from a tree top. Pushing on through the thick tangle of underbrush we soon found its nest, about 12 feet up in a slender willow. It was a typical green heron's nest, no different from those of our eastern birds, made of small sticks and lined with finer twigs. It held five fresh eggs. My companion, Frank C. Willard, was not surprised, for he had often found nests of the Anthony green heron along this and other similar ditches in the San Pedro Valley, where it finds a congenial home together with a host of small birds not found in the arid regions.

In other portions of its breeding range the nesting habits of this little heron are generally similar to those of its eastern relative, but sometimes it builds its nest at rather high elevations. John G. Tyler

(1913) mentions a nest near Fresno, California, which was 30 feet from the ground; there is a set in the California Academy of Sciences, taken at Napa, California, from a nest, at the same height, in a maple tree; and Laurence M. Huey (1915) records a nest found near San Diego, "situated in the top of a willow tree about 50 feet high."

Eggs.—The eggs of this heron are not distinguishable from those of our eastern green heron. Two rather remarkable sets of eggs have been taken in San Diego County, California, by Mrs. May Canfield and Messrs. D. R. Dickey and L. M. Huey. They were taken on May 11 and 30, 1915, and contained eight and nine eggs, respectively. In writing to me about these two sets, Mr. Dickey says:

The presumption is that the two sets were laid by the same birds and the interesting possibility of polygamy, or at least of two females laying in one nest, suggests itself. In former years, several pairs had nested in that general vicinity, but with the thinning out of the bottom-land timber, only these two nests were located in 1915. Of course, the actual cause of these large sets is purely speculative, but—as I say—the thought that possibly the scattered colony had been reduced to two females laying in one nest, with one male as the mate of both, is not beyond the realm of such pure speculation.

The measurements of 51 eggs average 39 by 29.7 millimeters; the eggs showing the four extremes measure 42 by 29.8; 40.7 by 31.5; 36.5 by 28.7; and 39 by 28.2 millimeters.

Plumages.—A. J. van Rossem writes to me regarding the molts and plumages of the two western subspecies of green herons, as follows:

We have exceptionally good series of various subspecies of the green heron, particularly *anthonyi* and *fraseri*, and the following notes are based principally upon these two races. There is a complete post juvenal body molt in most individuals. The new plumage is very similar to that of the adult, but as the juvenal remiges and their coverts are retained, there is no particular difficulty in separating the adults from birds of the year. The white-tipped primary coverts of the juveniles are subject to little wear, and retain their character until lost at the first postnuptial molt. One juvenile of *anthonyi* at hand has skipped the post-juvenal molt entirely and is, in April, still in pure juvenal plumage. Such circumstance is probably rather rare, although some October juveniles show no traces whatever of any post juvenal plumage. The spring prenuptial molt is a very limited one, particularly in adults, and amounts to little more than the taking on of some additional plumes on the back. In the first spring birds, there are also a few new feathers in evidence on the shoulders. By far the majority of the long, lanceolate feathers of the back are taken on with the fall plumage, and therefore cannot be properly classed as "breeding plumage." Some fresh post juvenal birds have plumes fully as long as the average adult of the same sex.

DISTRIBUTION

Range.—California, southern Arizona and Mexico to (rarely) Costa Rica; north rarely to southern Oregon.

Breeding range.—North to California, (Ukiah, Lower Lake and Colusa). East to California (Colusa, Grafton, Murphy, and probably Little Owens Lake); Arizona (Big Sandy Creek, Verde River and San Pedro River), and Sonora (San Pedro River). South to Sonora (San Pedro River); Arizona (Tombstone and Yuma); and Lower California (Gardners Laguna and Los Coronados Islands). West to Lower California (Los Coronados Islands); and California (San Diego, Whittier, Santa Barbara, Buena Vista Lake, Alcalde, San Benito, Gilroy, Alameda, Gloverdale, and Ukiah). Has occurred in summer north to Yreka, California, and Fort Klamath, Oregon.

Winter ranges.—North to California (Old Fort Tejon, and San Bernardino). East to Jalisco (Ocotlan); Michoacan (Zamora); the Valley of Mexico; Guerrero (El Limon); Oaxaca (Tehuantepec); and Costa Rica (San Jose). South to Costa Rica (San Jose); and Oaxaca (Tehuantepec). West to Guerrero (El Limon); the Plains of Colima; Sinaloa (Mazatlan); Lower California (San Jose del Cabo and Miraflores); and California (San Bernardino and Old Fort Tejon). Casually north to Oakland and Stockton (Belding).

Migration.—Early dates of arrival in California are: Santa Barbara, April 3, 1920; Gilroy, April 21, 1916; Palo Alto, April 13, 1919; Stockton, April 4, 1885, and Redbluff, May 9, 1884.

Late dates of departure in California are: Stockton, early October, 1878; Gilroy, Septmber 19, 1914; Santa Cruz, September 8, 1895; Clovis, September 7, 1905, and Santa Barbara, September 17, 1909.

Egg dates.—California: 22 records, April 16 to June 17; 11 records, May 12 to 25. Arizona: 13 records, May 5 to July 16; 7 records, May 11 to June 27.

NYCTICORAX NYCTICORAX NAEVIUS (Boddaert)

BLACK-CROWNED NIGHT HERON

HABITS

The familiar night heron or "quawk" is one of the best known and most widely distributed of our herons. Closely related forms of the same species are found throughout much of South America, Europe, Asia, and Africa. Throughout its wide North American range it is practically homogeneous. It is decidedly different in many ways from our other herons; its short, stout figure is easily recognized; and it well deserves the name of night heron. How often, in the gathering dusk of evening, have we heard its loud, choking squawk and, looking up, have seen its stocky form, dimly outlined against the gray sky and propelled by steady wing beats, as it wings its way high in the air towards its evening feeding place in some distant pond or marsh! And how often, as we walked along the reedy border of some marshy creek or pond hole, have we been startled by its croak of alarm, as it rose unexpectedly from behind the reeds and flew deliberately away, a wide band of black supported by broad gray wings! The young birds are particularly unsuspicious in such situations and often spring up almost under our feet; their peculiar shape and speckled plumage are easily recognized.

The name, night heron, immediately suggests to my mind Sandy Neck and the famous rookery that has flourished and struggled alternately for over a century on that long chain of sand dunes that separates Barnstable Harbor from Cape Cod Bay. Many ornithologists have visited it and I have seen it many times in spring, summer, autumn, and winter. Several times it has been "shot out" and it has, within my memory, occupied three different parts of the neck a mile or more apart. Sandy Neck is about 6 miles long. Its northern or bay side is the continuation of a broad, flat, sandy beach, which extends for many miles along the north side of Cape Cod and terminates in a wide point of bare sand. On its southern or harbor side it is bordered by extensive salt meadows or marshes, covering several square miles and intersected by numerous creeks, channels, and ditches. The central portion consists of a series of picturesque sand dunes, some low and rolling hillocks and some high mountains of sand with steep sides and narrow crests, from which one may gain a comprehensive view of the long succession of barren, wind-swept peaks, protecting sheltered hollows filled with luxuriant vegetation. Some of the older hills are heavily wooded with oaks and pitch pines and many of the hollows contain little forests of oaks, pitch pines, maples, sassafras, and wild cherries, beneath which are often impenetrable thickets of scrub oak, alder, sumac, and other underbrush, interwoven with tangles of cat-briar, woodbine, and poison ivy. There are also numerous clusters of beach plums and bayberry bushes in the hollows or on the sand dunes and several small cranberry bogs and swampy pond holes. Altogether it is an ideal location for a heron rookery, with plenty of suitable nesting sites in secluded spots and with abundant food supplies, on the broad sand flats off the beaches, along the many miles of tidal creeks on the marshes, and around the marshy pond holes and bogs in the hollows. Here the largest colony of night herons, at least the largest of which I can find any record, in North America makes its summer home.

Courtship.—On April 30, 1924, I made a special trip to the Barnstable rookery to study the courtship of this heron. I found the breeding season well under way; many nests were in process of construction and some already held from one to three eggs. The birds were rather shy, but several times I was able to observe the rather simple courtship ceremony. The male alights in the tree top beside the female, or a little above her; he bows low, leaning down toward her, erecting his crest and the feathers of his neck, breast, and back in a rather striking display; she responds in much the same way; their red eyes glow with sexual excitement; they caress each other with their bills and then assume a quiet pose, side by side, the plumage as smooth as usual. Or perhaps the female alights in a tree where the male is standing; with plumage erected, she courts his attention with a squawk of invitation; he responds in the same manner, comes to her and mounts her, holding her head with his beak, spreading his wings and erecting his plumage. Thus the conjugal pact is sealed. If another male alights near them, the female urges her spouse to drive him away; and he does so, with much squawking and ruffling of plumage, and with many savage bill strokes and wing blows.

Similar plumage displays are seen all through the breeding season, in this as in all other herons, as mutual greetings, in the ceremony of nest relief and when feeding the young. They seem to be expressions of love or sexual emotion.

Nesting.—My acquaintance with the Barnstable rookery began in 1897. It then occupied a heavily wooded area near the southern edge of the sand hills; the center of abundance seemed to be in a large deep hollow where the red oak, sassafras, and maple trees grew to a height of 25 or 30 feet. I remember standing in this hollow one day in the winter when the leaves were off, and counting 275 nests in sight from one spot. The herons were still occupying the same nesting site in 1908, but the colony had increased greatly in size; my impression was that it had nearly doubled, and it had spread out over a much larger area, nearly half a mile long and an eighth of a mile wide. The nests were placed in pitch pines, red oaks, maples, scrub oaks, and sassafras, mainly in the oaks, often two or three nests in a tree and sometimes as many as four or five. The so-called sportsmen of the neighborhood found the herons useful as targets on which to practice, and their constant persecution forced the herons to move to a new nesting site about a mile farther out on the neck. Here we found them in 1910, occupying a mixed tract of pitch pines and oaks on the borders of a cranberry bog in a hollow among the sand dunes. We estimated that the colony contained from 1,500 to 2,000 pairs of herons. The main portion of the colony was closely concentrated in a grove of small pitch pines, from 15 to 20 feet high, with a dense undergrowth of scrub oak and an almost impenetrable tangle of cat brier and other vines.

Three years later, in 1913, we found that the colony had moved again and was located still farther out on the neck, near the extreme end of the wooded areas, in an extensive grove of pitch pines, with comparatively few oaks. Here it has remained ever since and is still in a flourishing condition. During the summer of 1920, Dr. Alfred O. Gross (1923) camped on the neck for two months and made an intensive study of these birds; the published results of his exhaustive study would make an excellent life history of this species. I shall use his data freely, but would refer the reader to his excellent paper for many details which space will not permit me to publish. On June 22 and 23 he made a detailed census of the rookery, marking each tree as it was counted and recording the number of nests in each. The count showed 2,536 nests in 854 trees, the largest number of trees, 282, contained only 1 nest each; and the largest numbers of nests were recorded in 13 trees which held 8 nests each, 5 trees which held 11 nests and 1 tree each which held 13 and 14 nests, respectively.

About 90 per cent of the nests of this colony were built in low pitch pines and the remainder were in scrub oaks, maples, and a few in the bayberry and alder bushes which grew in the lower swampy portions of the grove. The height of the nests varied from one in a bayberry bush 2 feet above the water to one 42 feet high in one of the larger pines. The average height of 100 nests, which were carefully measured, was 22 feet, four inches. These nests, unlike those in the spruce groves of Maine were generally located on the forked tips of the large branches and a considerable distance from the main trunk of the tree.

The nests in this rookery vary greatly in size, stability, and composition. Many of them are crude, loosely-built platforms, made of coarse sticks, and scantily lined with finer twigs. Some are so small and so insecurely placed that the eggs or young are shaken out of them by heavy winds and the nests are blown out of the trees during the winter storms. Others are large, well-built structures, securely located in some firm crotch or supported by two or three flat branches; such nests usually survive the winter storms and are used year after year. These better types of nests consist of substantial foundations of sticks and twigs of pine, oak, cedar, beach plum, and bayberry, lined with fine twigs, roots, vines, grasses, and pine needles. Doctor Gross (1923) says:

A large percentage of the nests were lined in part or wholly with the long flexible roots of beach grass. It puzzled me to know how it were possible for the birds to secure some of the very long roots, some of which were more than a meter in length, until I chanced upon a score of adult herons tugging at the roots which had been left unearthed in the wake of a traveling sand dune. The numerous footprints in the sand evidenced that such places were the common source of their supply. The roots provided an unusual but admirable nesting material and some of the nests lined with them represented the finest types built by the herons at Sandy Neck. Both the male and the female actively concern themselves in the work of building the nest which usually requires from two to five days, but, in the case of one nest, construction work and alterations were going on for a period of more than a week.

A rookery quite similiar to the Sandy Neck colony, formerly located on Plum Island, Massachusetts, is well described by S. Waldo Bailey (1915). On July 5, 1903, I examined a fair-sized colony on Chappaquiddic Island, adjoining Martha's Vineyard; the rookery was located on the highest land in the center of the island in an extensive tract of dry woods, principally black and red oaks with some sassafras and beech; the nests were all in the oaks from 7 to 15 feet from the ground.   On June 8, 1919, I found a colony of from 200 to 300 pairs probably the same olony, nesting in an extensive patch of low cedars near the shore, a mile or more away; even at that date most of the nests contained young, some of which were fully grown and were climbing out on the branches.   Dr. Charles W. Townsend showed me, on July 19, 1913, a somewhat different type of rookery in Hamilton, Massachusetts, which he had previously described; it was in a mixed swamp of larches, black spruces, white pines, and maples in which the nests were from 20 to 30 feet up; the young were nearly all on the wing, but there were still a few in the nests.

I have seen several night heron rookeries on the coast of Maine, where this species nests in colonies by itself or in company with the great blue heron.   Referring to some of these colonies Doctor Gross (1923) says:

In Maine, spruce-covered islands or dense groves of conifers on the mainland near the salt water are the places where one is most likely to meet with success in locating the largest breeding places and roosts.   Mr. A. H. Norton of the Portland Natural History Society visited Allens Island in June, 1921, and found a rookery comprising about 100 great blue herons, and nearly 400 black-crowned night herons.   The nests on Allens Island were built at an average height of 25 feet in the low spruce trees which there do not exceed 30 to 40 feet in height.   The majority of the nests were supported by the lower branches of the green conical tops so that they were in plain view to an observer standing on the forest floor. Several ravens were seen at this colony and Mr. Norton thinks some of the dead half-eaten young that were lying on the ground represented the work of these black marauders.   The colony at Whaleboat Island which contained only 30 pairs of herons in 1915 has increased to a thriving community of more than 250 birds, not including about 50 great blue herons which regularly nest there.   The nests seen here were without exception built in the tall dead spruces, those of the night heron at an average height of 34 feet from the ground.   None of them were lower than 10 feet and one was built near the top of a tall spruce more than 60 feet in height.   At this place there seemed to be a rough correlation between the height of the trees and the position of the nest.   The majority of the nests were nearly the same distance from the top of the respective trees, a place where the densely branched limbs were best adapted for holding the nest. They were built near the trunk and were usually supported by the bases and smaller lateral branches of two or more horizontal limbs.

In other parts of the country night herons nest under widely different conditions.   Where suitable trees can not be found in favorable localities the herons are often found breeding in marshes or sloughs, where their nests are concealed in some secluded spot. Robert B. Rockwell (1910) found a particularly interesting colony of this type near Barr, Colorado, of which he writes:

As we approached the spot where the colony was supposed to be located, not a sign of the birds was to be seen—save the monotonous expanse of cat-tail marsh, flanked by a small rush-bound lake on one side and the sunburned prairie on the other.   We had worked well into the cat-tails, which towered some distance above our heads, when as if by a given signal the breeding birds rose from their nests in a cloud, and with much squawking, scolding, and flapping of wings, rapidly retreated to a place of safety in the marsh half a mile or more distant. Fifty yards farther on we came to the spot from which the birds had risen, and here in the dense cat-tails were the nests, probably 150 in all, large, clumsy, yet withal well built structures of coarse sticks and weed stalks, ranging in height from 6 inches to 3 feet above the ground, which was wet and boggy and in many places covered with several inches of water. On May 11, while working over a small lake about half mile below the marsh which harbored the nesting colony of the preceding year, we found two nests of these erratic birds, built just above the surface of water almost waist deep and fully 50 yards out from the shore of the lake. These nests—the bottoms of which were just level with the surface of the water—were supported by masses of floating, dead vegetation, and were anchored in place by a few upright dead cat-tail stalks. They were beautifully built affairs of slender twigs and weed stalks, very large, bulky, deeply cupped and quite symmetrical; and lying far out from shore upon the open water they were very conspicuous, being easily discernible at a distance of 100 yards. The parent birds were very wild, and it was impossible to approach anywhere near the nests without flushing the birds.

In Florida we often found black-crowned night herons nesting in small numbers in the rookeries with other herons. Many of the rookeries examined on the coast of Texas contained a few pairs of this species, nesting in low situations in the shrubbery. On one island, in Galveston Bay, they were nesting in tall canes, where their nests were made wholly of the stems of dead canes. On Dressing Point Island, in Matagorda Bay, we found a fair-sized colony nesting on the dry ground among tufts of tall grass.

Doctor Gross (1923) refers to a number of different colonies nesting in a variety of situations, among which he mentions a colony which "selected an old apple orchard for their nesting site," which they occupied for 10 years, near Atwood, Illinois.

W. L. Finley (1906) found a colony of about 200 pairs in a fir forest south of Portland, Oregon, in which none of the nests were less than 130 feet up and some were 160 feet above the ground. In a colony which he found at the lower end of San Francisco Bay, California, in the summer of 1904, he noted 41 nests of the great blue heron and 28 nests of the black-crowned night heron in a single giant sycamore, 7 feet thick at the base, 120 feet high and with a spread equal to its height. In another tree there were 17 great blue and 28 night heron nests. In this large colony of 700 nests those of the night heron were placed at the very upturned tips of the sycamore limbs or else in the willows and alders at a relatively short distance from the ground. Mr. Finley counted 400 eggs from a single point in a giant sycamore tree which gives some idea of the density of the heron homes at this unusal rookery. In other localities in California, such as Merced and San Diego Counties, night herons have also been found nesting in tule swamps, sometimes in company with white-faced glossy ibises.

Eggs.—This night heron usually lays from three to five eggs, sometimes only two or even one, occasionally six and very rarely seven or even eight; the larger sets may be the product of two birds. In shape they vary from ovate or oval to cylindrical ovate. The shell is smooth with no gloss. The color is pale bluish green, varying from "glaucous green" to "pale fluorite green." The measurements of 48 eggs average 51.5 by 37 millimeters; the eggs showing the four extremes measure **58** by 35.5, 50 by **39.5**, **48** by **35.5** millimeters.

Young.—Doctor Gross (1923) found that the period of incubation varied from 24 to 26 days and that both sexes take an active part in it; he "frequently had nests under observation when the shift from one sex to the other took place. Sometimes the shift involved a domestic quarrel in which there resulted a vigorous interchange of sharp, rebuffing shrieks accompanied by violent thrusts." He says it is customary to start incubation after the first egg is laid, although it may take a week to complete the set; this accounts for the inequality in the sizes of the young. He describes the hatching process in detail; a young bird which had pipped the shell at noon was not entirely free from it until 4.20 p. m. the next day.

Young night herons are fed by their parents until they are large enough to learn to fly and fish for themselves. Doctor Gross (1923) says:

The first food received by the downy young consist of juices of predigested material. In the examination made at Sandy Neck, this food was so completely liquified that it was practically impossible to determine the kind of animals composing it. In delivering the food to the downy young the adult seemed to insert the tip of her beak into the wide open mouth and the transference of the juices was made with comparatively little effort. The parent bird usually delivers small amounts at rather short intervals and I have frequently seen, from my blind, the downy heads of day old birds appear between the feathers of the parent to receive their ration of fish extract. By the third day, more substantial food, such as semidigested fish and shrimp, were given to the young. Among 20 regurgitations of nestlings 3 to 10 days old 16 were made up entirely or largely of shrimps present in pieces ranging from a few millimeters to one and in some instances three centimeters in length. When the young became more than three weeks old the food was made up chiefly of fish, which were often delivered without any predigestion.

I have several times watched the old birds feeding their young; the method varies with the ages of the young. The old bird approaches cautiously, climbing over the branches towards the nest and giving a few warning calls, soft guttural croaks, at which the young rise up in eager anticipation, or, if they are large enough, scramble over the branches toward her; she may keep them waiting for several minutes, but, when ready to feed them, she raises her crest, fluffs out her plumage, half spreads her wings and lowers her head to regurgitate the food. If the young are small, she inserts her bill into the mouth of the little one and pours into it the liquid, semidigested food; if the young are older they may seize the parent's bill and struggle with her until she delivers a good sized fish: sometimes the food is too large to be swallowed entirely and the tail is left protruding from the young bird's mouth until the lower end of it is digested. Often, with large young, the fish is deposited on the nest to be picked up, which frequently results in its falling to the ground and adding to the delightful odors of the rookery. The young have a very bad habit of voiding their excrement and vomiting the contents of their crops, when frightened; the investigator is quite likely to receive some very unpleasant shower baths under such circumstances. It would be well for the observer to wear an old hat and an old suit of clothes, which can be thrown away or better still a complete suit of oilskins or overalls, which can be washed as soon as he comes out of the rookery, else he may carry home some unpleasant reminders.

Provided one can stand the nauseating odors or does not mind the filth, the briars and the insect pests, flies, mosquitos, and wood ticks, it is an exceedingly interesting experience to visit the Sandy Neck rookery in July. As he climbs to the crest of some commanding sand dune, he looks down upon a broad expanse of pines, mingled with oaks and thickets of underbrush and vines. The scene becomes a lively one, as hundreds of the gray, black-backed birds rise in great clouds, circle over the rookery in a bewildering maze and then drift away to settle in the tops of distant trees. The tops of the trees in the rookery are dotted with hundreds of young birds in the brown juvenal plumage, clearly outlined against the dark green of the pines; they are not yet able to fly but have climbed up out of the nests to bask in the sunshine and see the outside world. As he walks down into the rookery the excitement increases, the air is full of birds overhead, the trees are full of scrambling and fluttering young and the din of many voices adds to the pandemonium; the shrill piping notes of the youngest birds, the "*yip, yip, yip*," or the "*yak, yak, yak*" of the older young, and the various croaks and squawks of the adults create a volume of sound that is not soon forgotten. Alexander Wilson (1832) has well likened it to 200 or 300 Indians choking or throttling each other.

The young birds remain in the nest, where their parents brood them, or stand over them with wings partly spread to protect them from the sun, until they are two or three weeks old; I believe that they would remain in the nests a week or two longer, if they were left undisturbed. But at the age of two or three weeks, or when about half or two-thirds grown, they are easily frightened from their nests and climb out on the branches or even scramble and flutter from tree to tree. They are awkward and ludicrous in appearance, but they are usually quite successful in their efforts and more expert at climbing than they appear to be. They make good use of all five of their extremities in climbing, clinging with their feet, supporting themselves on their wings, hooking the neck over a branch or seizing it with the bill. I have seen one do what we used to call the "giant swing," clinging to a branch with bill and feet. But, even with all these safeguards and aids to climbing, accidents sometimes happen and I have seen many a dead young heron, hanging by wing or foot, where it was caught and was unable to free itself. Often one falls to the ground where its parents can not find it, where it must starve unless some prowling fox or cat finds it and ends its misery.

Plumages.—The small downy young of this heron is partially covered on the upper parts with long soft down, varying in color from "dark mouse gray" to "deep neutral gray"; the crown is covered with long, rather coarse, whitish filaments an inch or more long; the under parts are covered more sparsely with soft down, varying from "dark mouse gray" on the neck to "pallid neutral gray" on the belly. These colors all fade out paler with advancing age.

Doctor Gross (1923) has described the development of the juvenal plumages, as follows:

The first papillae of the juvenal plumage make their appearance in the region of the flanks and scapulars on the fifth or sixth day after hatching. These are closely followed by the papillae of the wing coverts and of the ventral tracts. By the seventh day the papillae of the alar tracts (primaries and secondaries), show through the integument but those of the rectrices (tail) do not appear until the bird is about 10 days old. At this age the tips of the feathers of the scapular region and flanks are unsheathed. The primaries and secondaries present their unsheathed tips about the fifteenth day, but no unsheathing takes place in the rectrices until the bird is about three weeks old. The unsheathing when once started proceeds rapidly and by the time the bird is four weeks old it has the smooth contour possessed by an adult bird. The complete growth of the juvenal plumage is not accomplished, however, until the bird is about 50 days old.

He describes the juvenal plumage, of an unfaded specimen 28 days old, as follows:

Crown and back glossy olivaceous black, neck Chaetura drab, the feathers with median streaks of varying shades of buff. The median streaks in the feathers of the back are of a richer and deeper color approaching very nearly that of cinnamon. The apices of the crown feathers have filaments of natal down but the remainder of the juvenal plumage is entirely free of vestiges of this first plumage. The throat with an elongated median patch of white tinged with ivory yellow which extends posteriorly to the neck. Sides of chin, head and neck streaked with Chaetura drab, fuscous-black, and various shades of buff. Feathers of the breast, upper belly, and flanks white tinged with light cartridge buff, each feather with broad lateral streaks or bands of light fuscous or hair brown. Lower belly and crissum white and not streaked. Tail feathers deep mouse gray, primaries and secondaries fuscous black, tipped with white and with outer veins tinged with cinnamon. The white tips of the secondaries are much reduced and the outer veins have less of the cinnamon than have the primaries.   The feathers comprising the wing coverts and tertials have large conspicuous terminal spots of white or light buff.

I have several young birds in my collection in which the colors are richer and more rufous than those described above; the feathers of the mantle are largely "auburn" and "hazel" and the buffy central streaks and tips are "ochraceous buff."   However, these colors soon fade; in one bird, taken in July, the streaks and spots have all faded out to white and there is no rufous anywhere and very little pale buff.   This plumage is worn until the middle of winter or later.   The molt into the first nuptial plumage begins in January with the acquisition of clear brown plumage in the back, varying in color from "bister" to "snuff brown," which gradually replaces the streaked and spotted juvenal plumage; this molt spreads during the spring until the entire mantle, back, scapulars, and wing-coverts, become clear, dark, rich brown, with a purplish or greenish gloss when fresh; the crown becomes much darker, "clove brown"; the streaking becomes less conspicuous on the sides of the head and neck; and the breast and belly become clearer gray and white, with hardly any signs of streaking; the tail is molted, in April or May, in which the new feathers are clear drab; but the wings are not molted until July or August.   There is great individual variation in the time and progress of this prolonged molt.

Almost continuous with the above molt, beginning in July, or even earlier in some individuals, comes the first complete postnuptial molt. This produces, by September or later, a second winter plumage, in which the crown is glossy, greenish black and the mantle becomes "mouse gray," darkest on the back, with a greenish gloss.   During the late winter or early spring, a partial prenuptial molt, involving only the contour plumage, produces a second nuptial plumage, which is nearly adult; but the white space in the forehead is washed with drab, instead of being clear white; the black areas of the crown and back are less brilliantly glossed; the wings are darker and more brownish gray, "mouse gray" or "neutral gray"; and there is much more gray in the neck and breast, "light drab" to "drab-gray." One or two of the long, slender, white occipital plumes are acquired at this time.   At the next postnuptial, complete molt, which begins usually in June or July and lasts sometimes until December, the young bird assumes the fully adult plumage, when about 2½ years old.

Adults have a partial prenuptial molt, in late winter or early spring, and a complete postnuptial molt from August to October.   In the spring adult the forehead is pure white; the crown, and particularly the back, are brilliantly glossed with green; the wings are "pale mouse gray" or "pallid mouse gray"; and the neck and underparts vary from "pallid mouse gray" to pure white. The white occipital plumes are often present in the fall, but less highly developed.

Food.—As its name implies, the night heron feeds largely at night, or during the dusk of evening and before sunrise. It is a common experience to hear its familiar croaking notes, as it flies overhead during the evening, to or from its feeding grounds. During the nesting season, when the young demand an extra amount of food, it is necessary for their parents to spend more time in search of food and they are kept busy all day and probably most of the night. But the night heron is by no means wholly nocturnal in its feeding habits at any season. It may be flushed at any time during the day, even late in the fall from favorable feeding grounds around the marshy borders of ponds or along the reedy banks of streams. On the sea-coast it is largely influenced by the tides and may be seen at low tide out on the mud flats or around the fish weirs; and it knows at just what stages of the tides it can fish to best advantage in the shallows of the tidal creeks.

Audubon (1840) says that "it is never seen standing motionless, waiting for its prey, like the true herons, but it is constantly moving about in search of it." This active method may be the one employed when in search of the less active aquatic animals on which it feeds; but when fishing, I believe, it usually stands still, in shallow water, on the shore, or on some convenient perch. I once saw a young night heron given a lesson in still fishing by, presumably, one of its parents. Both birds had been standing as motionless as statues, for some time in the shallow water of a tidal creek; the young bird began to show its impatience by moving its head slightly from side to side; then it took a few steps forward, slowly and stealthily, with its neck stretched out and crouching close to the water; whereupon the adult, which had stood immovable, flew at the young bird, with loud, scolding croaks, and struck it some hard blows on the back with its bill. The young bird was forced to fly, but it settled again a few yards away and did not attempt to move again ; perhaps it had learned its lesson.

Doctor Gross (1923) determined that at Sandy Neck about 80 per cent of the night herons' food consists of fish, the commonest species being "whiting (*Merlucceus bilinearis*), herring (*Clupea harengus*), and cunners (*Tantogolabrus adspersus*)." "Many of the whiting and some other fishes were picked up dead on the beaches. Among the other fish taken were a few small flounders, an occasional mackerel and even sculpins, sea robins, and puffers. Many of these were taken from the fish weirs. Other kinds of fish, such as perch, carp, pickerel, and eels, have been reported by other observers. Probably fish consti-tute the bulk of the food everywhere and whatever species are easily available are taken.

Dr. Alexander Wetmore (1920) observed that, at Lake Burford, New Mexico, the night herons fed on waterdogs (*Ambystoma*) and frogs, where they acted as scavengers by eating the dead Axolotls which they found floating on the water.   Doctor Gross (1923) says:

The remains of animals in the food which could be identified comprised marine annelids, chiefly *Nereis virens*, crustaceans, represented by numerous shrimp, sand-hoppers, and a few small crabs; insects, chiefly beetles, flies, and dragon-fly nymphs, all present in negligible quantities.

Of the mollusks he found only squids, which were probably picked up dead; and the only fresh water animals found were tadpoles and adults of Fowler's toad.   Oscar E. Baynard (1912) found that 50 meals of young night herons in Florida consisted of 60 crayfish, 610 small catfish, 31 small pickerel, and 79 dragon flies.   R. P. Sharples wrote me that he found in the stomachs of this species a frog and a snake about a foot long.   Other observers have also noted crabs, lizards, salamanders, leeches, moths, and even mice.   Doctor Gross (1923) refers to a case, reported by Mr. S. F. Denton, "in which a partly fledged young swallowed a downy nestling which had been placed in the same cage."   Referring to vegetable food, which is seldom eaten, he cites authorities to show that sea lettuce, algae, and similar aquatic plants are sometimes eaten and fed to the young.

Behavior.—The flight of the night heron is very different from that of the other herons; in flight and in appearance on the wing it is more like a gull than a heron.   It holds itself much like a gull or a crow; its neck is shortened, but not folded back in true heron fashion; and its appearance is that of a short, stout bird.   Its flight is strong, direct, and swifter than that of other herons, with usually quicker wing strokes.   Sometimes it flies with the graceful ease of a large gull and sometimes it soars or scales almost as well as a hawk; often it sets its wings and scales down into the tree tops or onto the ground.   When not too busy with its search for food, it spends much time, especially during the middle of the day, in idleness, perched on some tree or on the shore in its characteristic pose, a short necked, round shouldered bird.   Its periods of greatest activity are from dawn till sunrise and from a little before sunset until after darkness has settled; but it is never quiet, day or night, in a night heron rookery.

The characteristic note of the night heron is well expressed in its popular names.   Doctor Gross (1923) notes variations which may be crudely represented by "*Qua*," "*Quak*," "*Quark*," or "*Squawk*." He has described the varied vocabulary of the species so well, that I can not do better than to quote his words, as follows:

When one approaches the colony he invariably disturbs first the outpost sentinels who seem ever ready to give a warning note which sounds like, "*Woc, woc, wock! a-woc, woc, woc.*"   This call usually results in a number of herons rising from the neighboring tree tops, who take up the call and repeat it until a virtual cloud of birds is flying about in great confusion. After you have entered the rookery, the notes of the adults are drowned out by the incessant clatter of the young birds which during July and August are represented by birds of all ages. The call of the downy young resembles a faint "*Tet! tet! tet!*" or "*Yip-yip-yip*" the half-grown nestlings utter a sound more like "*Yak! yak! yak!*" and the older young utter a harsher, coarser sound resembling roughly the words "*Chuck, chuck-a-chuck, chuck, chuck.*" These various calls of the young all mingled together sound like the deafening clatter and hum of an infinite number of machines in a great factory, and, indeed, it is a heron factory. During the course of the day the intensity of the calls of the young varies directly as the keenness of their appetites. These calls could be heard at all hours of the day or night, but just before the bulk of the adult birds came in from the feeding grounds, a time which varied with the tide, the number of young calling and the volume of sound was at a maximum. At such times the rookery resounded with a deafening monotonous clatter. When the young were hungry, they were also irritable, and the least disturbance by a neighbor would cause them to render a defensive thrust accompanied by a ghastly, sharply accented "*Sque-e-e-e-e-ak.*" In uttering this squeal the beak is thrown wide open, during the "*Sque-e-e-e-e*" and then suddenly snapped together at the termination of the much accented "*ak.*" Doubtless it is these weird sounds which have led some observers to compare the noises of a colony of night herons to the war whoops of a band of Indians.

A similar note is uttered by adults when they are defending their nests against intruders. When the parent bird arrives with food she often utters a series of low guttural tones, some of which resemble very much the sounds made by an old hen when she is brooding her chicks. At other times, she would give a series of loud calls resembling "*Oc-oc-goc-goc-goc-oc, oc-oc-oc*" or "*Woc-a-woc, woc, woc, Wock-a-woc, woc,*" which, judging from the actions of the young, conveyed a definite unmistakable meaning.

Enemies.—Audubon (1840) says that:

Crows, hawks, and vultures torment the birds by day, while raccoons and other animals destroy them by night. The young are quite as good for eating as those of the common pigeon, being tender, juicy, and fat, with very little of the fishy taste of many birds which, like them, feed on fishes and reptiles. In the neighborhood of New Orleans, and along the Mississippi as far up as Natchez, the shooting of this species is a favorite occupation with the planters, who represent it as equaling any other bird in the delicacy of its flesh.

Grackles often nest in or near the rookeries and may do some damage to the eggs. Ravens are destructive in the Maine rookeries. Foxes are very common on Sandy Neck and probably pick up many young birds that have fallen from the nests; Doctor Gross saw one in the rookery one night. Undoubtedly nest-robbing crows are the worst enemies of all herons.

Fall.—Young night herons, like the young of several other herons, are somewhat inclined to wander northward after the close of the breeding season. By September first, or soon after that, the Sandy Neck rookery is practically deserted, the herons having scattered in all directions, either to find new feeding grounds or to satisfy the lust for wandering, and the same seems to be true of other rookeries.

Systematic bird banding has thrown considerable light on this subject and given us a number of positive records, some of which Doctor Gross (1923) has published. Young birds, banded at Sandy Neck, have been taken at Goat Island, Maine, 120 miles north, at Seabrook, New Hampshire, 90 miles northwest, at Kennebunkport, Maine, and at Fryeburg, Maine, 200 miles north. Birds banded by Dr. Paul Bartsch, near Washington, D. C., were taken at Abington, Maryland, at Pennsville, New Jersey, and at Leesburg, Virginia. Herons banded by Dr. John C. Phillips, at Wenham, Massachusetts, were taken at Masonville Station, Quebec, and at Seabrook, New Hampshire.

Winter.—A few night herons occasionally spend the winter as far north as New England, but most of the birds which breed in the northern States migrate south in the fall to join the resident heron population of the Southland, where they can lead an indolent life of luxurious ease, grow fat, and prepare for the next breeding season.

DISTRIBUTION

Range.—South and Central America, and North America to southern Canada.

Breeding range.—North to Oregon (Willow Junction and Pendleton); Idaho (Midvale, probably, and Deer Flat Bird Reserve); Utah (Bear River Marshes); Wyoming (Sheep Mountain); Manitoba (Oak Lake and Shoal Lake); Wisconsin (Oak Center); Michigan (Rochester and probably Lake St. Clair); Ontario (Toronto and Ottawa); Quebec (Montreal and near Quebec); Maine (Houlton); and New Brunswick (Woodstock). East to Maine (Calais, Bucksport, and Saco); Massachusetts (Essex, Barnstable, and Dukes Counties); New York (Shelter Island and Gardiner Island); New Jersey (Tuckerton, 7-mile Beach, and Cape May); Virginia (Dismal Swamp); North Carolina (Mattamuskeet Lake and Newbern); South Carolina (Waverly Mills, Santee, Mount Pleasant, and Frogmore); Georgia (Savannah, Darien, Blackbeard Island, and St. Marys); Florida (Palatka, Titusville, Indian River, Kissimmee, and Bassenger); Cuba; Haiti; Porto Rico; Venezuela (Angostura); Brazil (Corumba, Rio de Janeiro, Curytiba, and Taguara); Argentina (Buenos Aires); and the Falkland Islands (Hope Place). South to the Falkland Islands and Chile (Valdivia). West to Chile (Valdivia, Santiago, and Valparaiso); western Argentina (Tucuman and Salta); Peru (Tumbez); Ecuador (Quito); Colombia (Medellin); Costa Rica (La Palma and Rio Frio); Honduras (Fonseca Bay); Chiapas (Comitan); Guerrero (Acapulco); Sinaloa (Esquinapa and Mazatlan); the Hawaiian Islands; Lower California (mouth of the Colorado River); California

(Escondido, near Long Beach, Santa Barbara, Del Monte, Alameda, Colusa, and Chico); and Oregon (Fort Klamath, Silver Lake, and Willow Junction).

Winter range.—Resident in Central and South America. In North America the winter range extends north to Oregon (Pendleton and probably Malheur Lake); Utah, rarely (Provo); Colorado, one record (Ft. Lupton, December 20–24, 1902); Texas (Matagorda and Lake Surprise); Louisiana (Cameron Parish and the Mississippi Delta); Pennsylvania (Philadelphia); Rhode Island (Providence); and Massachusetts (Boylston and Cambridge). East to Massachusetts (Cambridge); New York (Brooklyn and Shelter Island); New Jersey (Pensauken and Trenton); District of Columbia (Washington); North Carolina (Pea Island); South Carolina (near Charleston and Frogmore); Georgia (Blackbeard Island); Florida (Mosquito Inlet); and the Bahama Islands (Abaco, Andros, and Great Inagua Islands). West to Lower California (San Jose del Cabo, La Paz, Margarita Island, and the mouth of the Colorado River); California (Escondido, Santa Barbara, Tulare Lake, and San Geronimo); and Oregon (Pendleton). Accidental in winter at St. John, New Brunswick, and at Ann Arbor, Mich.

Spring migration.—Early dates of arrival in the north Atlantic areas are: Vermont, Woodstock, April 10, and Middlebury, April 26, 1888; New Hampshire, Monadnock, April 11, 1902, and Hanover, April 13, 1917; Maine, Bucksport, April 12, 1890, and Portland, April 18, 1906; Quebec, Montreal, April 19, 1890, and Quebec, April 10, 1904; and New Brunswick, St. John, April 20, 1888. In the Mississippi Valley: Arkansas, Jonesboro, April 17, 1913, and Osceola, April 20, 1886; Missouri, Stillwell, April 1, and Corning, April 10, 1907; Illinois, Urbana, March 26, 1904, Fernwood, March 27, 1886, Elgin, March 29, 1914, and Chicago, March 30, 1904; Iowa, Charles City, March 29, 1918; Indiana, Richmond, April 6, 1911, Hanover, April 7, 1910, and Indianapolis, April 8, 1884; Ohio, Hamilton, March 22, 1897, Garrettsville, March 31, 1888, and Sandusky, March 28, 1907; Michigan, Ann Arbor, April 25, 1910, and St. Clair Flats, May 5, 1904; Ontario, Todmorden, April 9, 1891, and Ottawa, April 18, 1894; Wisconsin, Beaver Dam, April 4, 1897, Janesville, April 7, 1888, Clinton, April 9, 1886, and Delavan, April 19, 1896; and Manitoba, Margaret, April 25, 1917, and Shell River, May 16, 1885. On the Great Plains, Kansas, Wichita, April 8, 1916, Richmond, April 17, 1885, Manhattan, April 19, 1885; and Lawrence, April 21, 1906; Nebraska, Dunbar, April 2, 1904, Vesta, April 2, 1882, and Lincoln, April 5, 1900; and South Dakota, Forestburg, March 23, 1913, and Vermilion, April 17, 1911. In the Rocky Mountain region: Colorado, Colorado Springs, April 9, 1913, Boulder, April 7, 1912, and Greeley, April 17, 1911.

Fall migration.—Late dates of departure on the Atlantic coast are: Quebec, Quebec, October 15, 1894, and Montreal, October 11, 1895; Maine, Portland, September 16, 1907; New Hampshire, Durham, October 1, 1900, and Vermont, Bennington, October 2, 1914, and Rutland, October 2, 1912. In the Mississippi Valley: Manitoba, Margaret, September 4, 1910; Wisconsin, North Freedom, September 10, 1903, Madison, September 8, 1915, Milwaukee, September 24, 1887, and Delavan, September 24, 1894; Ontario, Ottawa, October 27, 1894, Kingston, September 6, 1905, Modoc, September 15, 1913, and Point Pelee, October 14, 1909; Michigan, Detroit, September 20, 1912; Ohio, Waverly, November, 18, 1898, and Columbus, November 26, 1876; Indiana, Lebanon, October 10, 1894, and Carroll County, November 24, 1884; Illinois, Lake Forest, October 20, 1906, Kensington, October 16, 1892, Rantoul, October 22, 1912, and Canton, October 27, 1894; Iowa, Emmetsburg, October 31, 1919; Missouri, Forest City, October 25, 1915; and Arkansas, Turrell, November 19 (McAtee). On the Great Plains: South Dakota, Huron, October 18, 1887, Forestburg, November 12, 1905, and Sioux Falls, November 20, 1910; Nebraska, Lincoln, October 27, 1900; and Kansas, Richmond, October 15, 1885. In the Rocky Mountain region: Colorado, Greeley, October 18, 1912, and Littleton, October 11, 1908, and New Mexico, November, 1908.

Complementary to the fall southward flight is the northward post-breeding wandering, which in no species is more strikingly illustrated than with these birds as indicated by the returns from young banded on June 16, 1923, at the colony at Sandy Neck, Barnstable, Massachusetts. Data from these birds have been secured from points in New Hampshire, Vermont, Maine, Ontario, and Quebec, through the months of August and September while one (Biological Survey number 233871) was recovered at Amherst Island, Ontario on November 1, 1923. Several returns have come from points on the St. Lawrence River, the most northerly being number 233847, recovered on September 9, 1923, within a few miles of the city of Quebec.

That all birds from any colony do not undertake these wanderings to the North is illustrated by returns from other birds, banded at the same time and place and which evidently moved directly south. Thus number 233601 was returned from Napanoch, New York, on August 27, 1923; number 233764, from New Holland, Pennsylvania, on August 22, 1923, and number 233845 from the mouth of the White Oak River, North Carolina, on October 9, 1923. The wintering grounds of the bulk of the New England birds may possibly be indicated by the return record of number 233845, which was killed in the cypress swamps in northern Lee Country, Florida, on December 25, 1923, and by number 233743, which was killed in Hanover County, Jamaica, early in November, 1923.

Egg dates.—Southern New England and New York: 55 **records,** April 30 to July 19; 28 records, May 13 to 20.   California: 30 **rec**ords, April 2 to July 15; 15 records, May 3 to 23.   New Jersey **and** Pennsylvania: 14 records, April 10 to June 12; 7 records, April 17 to May 8.   Florida: 6 records, March 1 to April 17.

NYCTANASSA VIOLACEA (Linnaeus)

YELLOW-CROWNED NIGHT HERON

HABITS

This handsome and conspicuously marked heron has always been associated in my mind with the fresh-water swamps and bayous of our tropical and semitropical regions, where the deadly mocassin lurks under leafy shadows and the lazy alligator slumbers on muddy banks.   We found it in Florida in the extensive marshes of the upper St. Johns, living with the Louisana and little blue herons on the willow islands and on the borders of the big cypress swamps; there were at least one or two pairs of these herons in nearly every rookery we visited.   In Texas we found the yellow-crowned night heron common in the swamp and bayou forests along the banks of the Guadalupe River, in Victoria County.   Its favorite haunts seemed to be in the bayous and stagnant backwaters, where the stately cypress grows, along with a heavy mixed forest of swamp tupelo, sweet and black gums, water oak, magnolia, and various willows.   I understand that it lives under similar conditions in Louisiana and other Southern States.

But it has been found living under strikingly different conditions in other places.   Mr. B. S. Bowdish (1902) "found it common on Mona," an island near Porto Rico, which seemed rather remarkable, as it is a dry, hot rock, with no sign of lagoon or swamp."   Col. A. J. Grayson (1871) found it on Socorro Island, one of the Revillagigedo Islands, of which he writes:

Upon this remote island, where there is a scarcity of fresh water, I was surprised to find this well-known species.   Here its natural haunts are entirely wanting. Here there are no lagoons or mangrove swamps to skulk in during the day; and the croaking of frogs, its favorite prey, is not heard.   All is dry and destitute of such localities suited to the nature of fresh-water birds.   I saw solitary ones in the daytime perched upon the rocks in the interior of the island, and on one or two occasions were started from the dry grass, where they were concealed. Hardly a night passed that I did not hear the well-known *quak* of this heron as they came to our spring to drink.   From the appearance of the male bird on examination and the presence of the young one shot they doubtless breed here to some extent.

E. W. Gifford (1913) found it along the shores of many of the Galapagos Islands, while on two of them it was seen in the interior as well.   It frequented rocky and cliff-bound coasts, as well as those fringed with mangroves.   On Tower Island, two or three were noted a quarter of a mile inland among the rocks and bushes. On the east side of Cowley Mountain, Albemarle Island, the tracks of these birds were noted in the dust of the donkey trails at an altitude of about 2,400 feet, and an immature bird was seen.

Nesting.—My first experience with the nesting habits of the yellow-crowned night heron was in the marshes of the upper St. Johns, in Florida, on April 21, 1902. We saw one or two pairs of this species in nearly all of the rookeries of small herons, found on the little willow-covered islands scattered over the marsh, but found only two nests. The first nest was on the outer edge of one of these islands in a leaning willow, about 4 feet above the water; it was made of large sticks and lined with smaller twigs; it measured 20 by 16 inches and contained five eggs which were on the point of hatching. The other nest was similarly made and was 8 feet above the ground in a clump of willows on dry land; it was within a few yards of an occupied Ward heron's nest; it contained two eggs and two young birds. The old birds were quite tame in both cases and remained near the nests watching us.

We found no nests in Texas, but in Florida, in 1925, we found two colonies. The first was a small mixed colony of yellow-crowned and black-crowned night herons, little blue and Louisiana herons and a few Ward herons in a small willow swamp on the prairie in Charlotte County, found on March 5. The Ward herons had small young, but the other species were building nests and had not laid at that date. The water was waist deep or more, but the trees were all small and none of the nests were over 9 or 10 feet above the water in the slender willows.

The other colony, on Bird Key, in Boca Ceiga Bay, Pinellas County, was much larger, but it was very difficult to determine its limits, as the foliage was very dense and the birds were very shy; they sneaked off their nests when they heard us coming and kept out of sight; all we saw were fleeting glimpses of departing birds, or an occasional individual flying over. The nests were grouped in a grove of the largest black-mangroves, where there were no other species nesting except a few Louisiana herons; they were placed at moderate heights, 15 to 20 feet, in these trees, on the larger limbs and mostly under the shade of the upper branches. When I first visited the colony, on March 11, these herons were building their nests, but in April they all had eggs. The nests could usually be distinguished from those of the smaller herons; they were larger, thicker, and more substantially built of heavier sticks; but occasionally an especially well made nest of a Louisiana heron could be recognized only by the smaller eggs.

Audubon (1840) says:

This species places its nest either high or low, according to the nature of the place selected for it, and the abundance of food in the neighborhood. In the interior of swampy woods, in lower Louisiana, I have found the nests placed on the tops of the loftiest cypresses, and on low bushes, but seldom so close together as those of many other herons. On the Florida Keys, where I have examined more of these tenements than in any other part, I found them either on the tops of mangroves, which there seldom attain a greater height than 25 feet, or on their lowest branches, and not more than 2 or 3 feet from the water. In the Carolinas, they usually resort to swamps, nestling on the bushes along their margins. The nest is similar to that of other herons, being formed of dry sticks loosely put together, and a few weeds, with at times a scanty lining of fibrous roots.

C. J. Maynard (1896) says that, in the Bahamas, "the nests are generally placed low, in some instances not over a foot from the ground. They are usually huge stick-built structures, well hollowed, and remind one strongly of the nests of hawks, and they are often lined with leaves." Arthur T. Wayne (1906) found a nest that was built in a short-leaf pine, 40 feet from the ground, on the high land and half a mile from water, in South Carolina. John G. Wells (1886) says that, in the Lesser Antilles, "they sometimes build in the mangroves, but generally resort to the rocky islets during the nesting period, in April and May. There they build in the prickly-pear bushes a large platform of dry sticks."

Eggs.—The yellow-crowned night heron usually lays three or four eggs, rarely five. Those that I have seen are ovate in shape and the shell is smooth but not glossy. The color is pale bluish green, varying from "pale glaucous green" to "pale olivine." The measurements of 40 eggs average 51.3 by 36.9 millimeters; the eggs showing the four extremes measure 57 by 36.8, 50.5 by 39.5, 46 by 35 millimeters.

Plumages.—I have no specimens of the downy young of the yellow-crowned night heron, nor any partially fledged young; and I can not find any descriptions of them in print. In the full juvenal plumage in August, the crown and occiput are black, with whitish shaft streaks, and a few long whitish, hairlike plumes remain on the tips of some feathers; the sides of the head are streaked with "fuscous" and whitish; the mantle is "bister," or "warm sepia," with terminal, buffy arrowheads on the feathers of the back and wing-coverts; the chin and throat are white; the neck and under parts are pale buff and white, broadly striped with "olive brown," "hair brown" and "fuscous"; the remiges and rectrices are "dark grayish brown," or "fuscous," very narrowly tipped with white when fresh; the white tips soon wear away.

This juvenal plumage is worn through the first fall and winter, until February or March, when a complete first prenuptial molt begins; by the time that this molt is finished, in May, the entire plumage has been changed, except perhaps a few old, juvenal wing-coverts, showing a decided advance towards maturity; the head pattern suggests that of the adult, but the crown is brownish, black tipped, and white basally on the forehead, with short whitish plumes; the auriculars are grayish, but mottled; the black areas in the head are streaked with white and the chin and throat are white; the neck is drab; the new plumage of the mantle is a mixture of brown and blackish and sometimes there are a few long, plumelike feathers in the back; the under parts are striped, much as in the juvenal plumage. This is the first nuptial plumage, but it is probably not a breeding plumage.

Summer and fall specimens are so scarce in collections that I have been unable to trace what takes place during these seasons, but there is probably another complete molt, perhaps two molts, between the first nupital and the second nuptial plumages. I have, however, seen a small series of specimens, taken in March, which show various stages of a complete prenuptial molt into the second nuptial plumage, which is probably a breeding plumage. This plumage is nearly adult, but the crown is more or less brown and the chin and throat are partially black, but centrally grayish and whitish; the upper parts, particularly the wing coverts, are tinged with brown, instead of being clear gray and black; the under parts are tinged with brown; and the occipital plumes are nearly as in the adult.

A complete postnuptial molt, beginning in July or August, produces the fully adult plumage, with the wholly black throat, the white crown and the clear grays, blacks, and whites, without any tinges of brown. The young bird is then about 2½ years old. For lack of material, collected at the proper seasons, I can not trace the molts of the adults.

Food.—The yellow-crowned night heron is not quite so nocturnal in its feeding habits as the black-crowned night heron; it feeds more or less during the night, but it also feeds commonly at all hours of the day, chiefly, however, in the morning and evening hours. Fish seem to constitute a comparatively small portion of its diet, which is largely made up of crabs and crawfish; this may account for its more diurnal habits. Audubon (1840) says that it is not at all delicate in the choice of its food, but swallows "snails, fish, small snakes, crabs, crays, lizards, and leeches, as well as small quadrupeds, and young birds that have fallen from their nests." He also says that it appears to seize its food "with little concern, picking it up from the ground in the manner of a domestic fowl."

Mr. Maynard (1896) says:

The food of the yellow-crowned night herons is mainly land crabs, which they are very expert at catching, killing and breaking to pieces. They will eat all kinds, excepting possibly the large white crab, a species which often measures 14 inches across the body and claws, and which weighs about 1 pound. This animal appears to be too strong and bulky for the herons to manage, but they will kill the black crab, a crustacean which measures nearly or quite a foot across the body and claws. But a favorite crab with this heron is a smaller species, which resembles the black crab in form, which is, on account of its being a favorite with the herons, called the galden crab by the Bahamans. This crab is very abundant. Another crab, or rather group of land crabs, which I think is exempt from the attacks of the galden is the hermit crab, for they retreat within their borrowed shells, and guard the entrance with their large claws.

Mr. Bowdish (1902) found in the stomachs of birds, taken in Porto Rico, fiddler crabs, two fresh-water eels about 6 inches long and two crawfish. Mr. Wayne (1906) says that in the breeding season the food of these birds is chiefly crawfish, but that after the breeding season they "resort to the salt marshes, and feed chiefly upon fiddlers and fish."

Behavior.—The appearance of the yellow-crowned night heron in flight is midway between that of the black-crowned and that of the other small herons, hence it is quite distinctive; it is a more slender bird and has a longer neck and longer legs than the black-crowned; its flight is slower and its neck is folded, after the manner of other herons, rather than contracted. The color is distinctive and the large, black bill is conspicuous. Its appearance on the ground is also characteristic, as it walks gracefully and slowly about on its long legs, with its long neck extended and its orange-red eyes searching for its prey. I have found immature birds very tame and easily approached, but the adults are rather shy, as a rule.

Audubon (1840) writes:

This species is by no means entirely nocturnal, for I have seen it searching for food among the roots of mangroves at all hours of the day, and that as assiduously as any diurnal bird, following the margins of rivers, and seizing on both aquatic and terrestrial animals. Whilst at Galveston, I frequently saw a large flock similarly occupied. When they had satisfied their hunger, they would quietly remove to some safe distance toward the middle of an island, where, standing in a crouching posture on the ground, they presented a very singular appearance. That they are able to see to a considerable distance on fine clear nights, I have no doubt, as I am confident that their migratory movements are usually performed at such times, having seen them, as well as several other species, come down from a considerable height in the air, after sunrise, for the purpose of resting and procuring food. When in numbers, and surprised on their perches, they usually rise almost perpendicularly for 30 or 40 yards, and then take a particular direction, leading them to some well-known place. Whenever I have started them from the nest, especially on the Florida Keys, they would sneak off on wing quite low, under cover of the mangroves, and fly in this manner until they had performed the circuit of the island, when they would alight close to me, as if to see whether I had taken their eggs or young."

Enemies.—Audubon (1840) notes that the yellow-crowned night heron was "watched and shot with great eagerness, by the Creoles of lower Louisiana, on account of the excellence of its flesh" but it can not now be regarded as a game bird. According to Mr. Maynard (1896) it was also much hunted as a game bird by the inhabitants of the Bahamas.

Range.—Southeastern United States, Central America, and the northern half of South America.

Breeding range.—North to Kansas (formerly Coffee County); Illinois (formerly the Illinois River and Mount Carmel); Indiana (formerly Bicknell and Wheatland); Alabama (Autaugaville); and South Carolina (Washoe Reserve on the Santee River, and Charleston). East to South Carolina (Washoe Preserve, Charleston, and Frogmore); Georgia (Savannah mouth of the Altamaha River and St. Marys); Florida (St. John's River, Micanopy, Kissimmee, Bassenger, and the Hillsboro River); the Bahama Islands (Little Abaco, Abaco, Eleuthera, Watling, and Great Inagua Islands); Porto Rico (Guanica Valley); the Lesser Antilles (St. Thomas, Virgin Gorda, St. Croix, St. Bartholomew, Guadeloupe, Martinique, Santa Lucia, St. Vincent, the Grenadines, Grenada, Tobago, and Trinidad Islands); British Guiana (Georgetown); French Guiana (Cayenne); and eastern and southeastern Brazil (Cajutube Island, Bahia, Sapitiba, Cape Frio, Paranagua, and Santa Catarina). South to southeastern Brazil (Paranagua and Santa Catarina); and Peru (Santa Lucia). West to Peru (Santa Lucia and Tumbez); Ecuador (Babahoyo); the Galapagos Islands; Panama (San Miguel Island); Costa Rica (San Jose); Nicaragua (San Juan del Sur); Mexico, Guerrero (Papayo); Tepic (San Blas); Sinaloa (Mazatlan); Lower California (Magdalena Bay); Texas (Lomita, Laredo, Corpus Christi, mouth of the Colorado River, and Gurley); Oklahoma (Fort Reno and Copan); and Kansas (Coffee County).

In the United States most of the colonies are now located in the South Atlantic and Gulf coast regions.

Winter range.—The yellow-crowned night heron appears to be resident throughout its breeding range in the islands of the Caribbean Sea, and in central and South America, remaining north at this season rarely to Florida (Upper Matecumbe Key, Tampa, and near Fort Myers): Louisiana (Vermillion Bay): Texas (Giddings); and Lower California (La Paz).

Spring migration.—Early dates of arrival are Florida, Polk County, February 14, 1901, and Orange Springs, March 19, 1910; Alabama, Barachias, April 15; Georgia, Darien, April 3, 1890, and Savannah, March 12, 1905; South Carolina, Mount Pleasant, March 24, 1891; Louisiana, New Orleans, February 19, 1914; Mississippi, Rodney, March 20, 1890; Missouri, St. Louis, April 10; and Kansas, Wellsville, March 27, 1920.

Casual records.—The yellow-crowned night heron occurs with fair regularity both spring and fall in North Carolina and has been taken or noted at other points much farther north. These are: District of

Columbia (Washington, one taken in August 1901); New Jersey (Elizabeth, August 16, 1922 and Woodbine, May 23, 1891); Pennsylvania (near Philadelphia, Ten-mile Creek, Glenolden, April 23, 1922 and Berwyn, May 14, 1916); New York (Freeport, Long Island, April, 1893, Wading River, April, 1901, near Orient about 1892 and May 4 and 7, 1905); Rhode Island (Newport, August, 1892 and June 15, 1778, and Tiverton, April 23, 1886); Massachusetts (Provincetown, March 8, 1891, Lynn, October, 1862, and Somerville, July 30, 1878); Maine (Back Cove, April 13, 1901, and Portland, April 11, 1906); Nova Scotia (Cape Sable Island, April 13, 1904, and one previously at the same place); Ontario (near Toronto, August 15, 1898); Iowa (Council Bluffs, May 2, 1843, Lee County, June 2, 1883, Omaha [Iowa side], May 1, 1892, Florence Lake, August 23, 1903, and Jackson County, September 15, 1892); Nebraska (Beatrice, July 19, 1901); and Colorado (Salida, May 1, 1908 and Byers, May 3, 1914).

Egg dates.—Florida: 25 records, March 25 to May 15; 13 records April 4 to 26. Texas: 8 records, April 13 to May 23.

Order PALUDICOLAE, Cranes, Rails, etc.

Family MEGALORNITHIDAE, Cranes

MEGALORNIS AMERICANUS (Linnaeus)

WHOOPING CRANE

HABITS

This magnificent species, one of the grandest and most striking of North American birds, is supposed to be on the verge of extinction. In its former abundance, its great migration flights, its curious conventions, in which it indulged in grotesque dances, and its interesting aerial evolutions must have formed some of the most spectacular performances in American ornithology. This is the tallest and most stately of all our birds and, as Coues (1874) says, when seen on the prairies, "its immense stature is sometimes singularly exaggerated by that quality of the prairie air which magnifies distant objects on the horizon, transforming sometimes a weed into a man." He knew of a person who mistook a sandhill crane for one of his stray mules and went in search of it. Once he himself mistook a whooping crane for an antelope feeding with its broad white stern toward him, and attempted to stalk it, until the "antelope" spread its broad, black-tipped wings and flew away.

Like many of our larger birds and mammals, particularly those that lived on the broad plains of the interior, the whooping crane has been steadily reduced in numbers and has become entirely extirpated in much of its former range. It has retreated before advancing civilization, farther west and then farther north, for it is one of our wildest birds, it can not stand human companionship and it loves the great open spaces in primitive solitudes.

Dr. E. W. Nelson (1877) wrote, half a century ago, that "a few pairs breed upon the large marshes in central Illinois." Dr. R. M. Anderson (1907) found it breeding in Hancock County, Iowa, in 1894; and it was found breeding, according to Prof. W. W. Cooke (1914), at Yorkton, Saskatchewan, in 1900. Having heard that whooping cranes had been seen recently around Quill Lake, Saskatchewan, I spent considerable time there in May and June, 1917, chasing up various clues; several men told me that they had seen white cranes there that spring and that they bred there regularly; though I did not succeed in finding them, I have no doubt that a few pairs still breed in northern Saskatchewan and Manitoba. M. P. Skinner writes me that he saw five of these cranes in Yellowstone Park, Wyoming, on August 4, 1914; after circling about high in the air, they flew off towards the southwest. George Lang, of Indian Head, Saskatchewan, "a reliable observer of long standing," reported to Fred Bradshaw, that he "saw 15 whooping cranes pass over that town on April 15, 1920"; and J. R. Garden, 20 miles east of there "got within 50 yards of six whooping cranes in the fall of 1921. In the spring of 1923 even larger numbers were reported from Qu' Appelle and Tynan." Under date of October 1, 1923, C. E. Boardman writes to me that, for the past 10 days, a flock of five adult and one young whooping cranes have been seen in the vicinity of Long Lake, south of Steele, North Dakota. Harry L. Felt, of Findlater, reported to Mr. Bradshaw that he saw nine whooping cranes passing over, on May 3, 1924. From the above records and from recent Texas records, to be referred to later, it would seem that the whooping cranes are not all gone yet. Let us hope that the few survivors will long continue to outwit their relentless pursuers.

Courtship.—Mr. Ernest Thompson Seton sends me the following notes on what is probably a courtship performance:

While the lowlands were their chief haunts, they had always not far away some high knoll on which one or more pairs would meet in the early morning and near sundown during spring and summer, and indulge in a sort of stately dance with much bowing, capering, flapping, and trumpeting. Fragments of this dance are sometimes rendered by the captives in zoological gardens. In some sort, it is the practice of many, if not all, cranes. It bears much resemblance to the mating dance of the prairie chicken. While dancing on the knoll, the cranes were visible for a mile or two. This with their raucous and daily trumpeting, called attention to the fact that a pair were nesting near. The result, alas, has been the extermination of the cranes in most of the Northwest.

Nesting.—Our knowledge of the nesting habits of the whooping crane is mostly past history, about which very little has been published. Nor have we much definite knowledge as to the exact limits of its former breeding range, which occupied a comparatively narrow belt in the interior of the continent; perhaps it once included much or all of the prairie regions from Great Slave Lake to Illinois.

J. W. Preston (1893), writing of conditions "years ago, when northwestern Iowa was a vast prairie, out into which few settlers had ventured, thus describes the nesting of this species in that State:

One memorable afternoon in early May I left the tent in kindly shelter of the fringe of woods on Crystal Lake, Winnebago County, Iowa,'the lakelet in whose sparkling waters classic Iowa River finds birth. Following the stream as it wound about through flat meadows or by low, gravelly hills, I reached the immense marsh lying north from Eagle Lake. Here were secured a number of the large, drab-and-spotted eggs of the white crane. They had chosen the center of the marsh for a nesting place, and there, a mile from the higher shores, the mother birds could be seen upon the nests, which were formed of soft grass gathered together in a firm heap about 1½ feet high, and placed on firm sod, out of water, but very near it. In the top of this heap was a very slight depression for the eggs. Upon these nests the birds sit in the same posture that a goose assumes, the legs protruding behind. They often let the head and neck lie down along the side of the nest in a wearied way, which is usual for the Canada goose, especially if the hunter is near. Upon my approaching the marsh these birds moved away with stately tread, walking much faster than I cared to do, yet apparently taking it easy. The white crane is certainly a strikingly handsome bird in its wild retreats. One does not tire of watching their peculiar movements. When walking at a distance they appear almost as tall as a man. They are far more alert and much wilder than the brown cranes.

Dr. R. M. Anderson (1894) gives us another good account of what was probably the last nesting of the whooping crane in that same region as follows:

On May 24, 1894, a boy offered to sell me two sandhill crane's eggs, which he had found about a week previously. The next Saturday, May 26, I started out to his place to try and collect some eggs. In the afternoon we started for a marsh, which a pair of white cranes had frequented all spring. The boy said that quite a number of white cranes had been seen around there in the early spring, but only one pair had remained over. As we came up over the top of a hill we saw in the middle of a large marsh two white objects, which looked like large rocks, but they began moving, and had evidently seen us as soon as we saw them, for they soon rose up with slow, heavy flaps of their great wings and flew over to the further side of the marsh, where we could see them stalking along with long strides as fast as a man could walk. In fact, when they stood straight up they looked almost as tall as a man. Occasionally one would utter a whoop that could be heard for a long distance. We waded along the whole length of the slough finding some masses which looked like crane's nests, but securing nothing but a Grebe's egg, which I dug out of a wet, floating mass of rotten vegetation. While wading through the slough we scared up several small flocks of mallards, pintails, blue-winged teals, and saw Wilson's phalaropes and black terns by the dozen. When we got near the west end of the slough, I started to wade down a branch that went off toward the south. I saw several cranes' nests or muskrat houses, I could not tell which, only a few rods apart. As I stood up on one and looked around I saw two great eggs on the next one. All this while the two cranes had been stalking along on the hill quite a ways off, keeping close together, and seemed trying to attract our attention by holding their heads down, dragging one leg, and sometimes spreading their wings. I yelled to the boys to come over, as I had found a crane's nest. While they were coming up, the cranes were approaching nearer until they were about 20 rods away. They would stand perfectly still for a minute at a time, with the wings widespread and held out from the body, and made a beautiful picture with their graceful snowy white bodies and great black-tipped wings. On our coming toward them they flew a short distance and lighted again. My companion and I went around in opposite directions to try and get a shot at them, but the cranes were too wary to be outwitted by such maneuvers and before we could get within 40 rods of them they flew up again and lighted over in the slough nearer the nest. My brother, who was sitting on the nest while we sneaked around, said they then came up within about 10 rods from him, and would hop on one leg, stretch out one wing, and try to decoy him after them. We could see the cranes far out on the prairie for the hour or two we were around there, and even after we were out of sight we could hear their loud singing whoops. The whooping crane's note seems to be louder and has a more ringing and resonant tone than the sandhill crane's voice, which has a rougher, rasping sound. But, let us speak of the nest. It was a mass of grass, rushes and reeds about 2 feet across and 8 or 10 inches above the water, which at this place was about a foot and a half deep. The water was open for a few feet around the nest, but in most places was grown up with rushes and saw grass. The nest was so solid that I sat down on it without sinking it into the water.

In 1914 the keeper at Buffalo Park, Wainwright, Alberta, told Mr. Seton "that at least one pair of white cranes breed each year on the west part of the Park." A. D. Henderson writes to me that a friend of his, C. E. Mills, saw a pair of whooping cranes, about the end of April, 1922, about 10 miles west of Birch Lake, Alberta. The residents told him that they were breeding and were being protected.

The latest information regarding the nesting habits of the whooping crane comes from the Game Commissioner of Saskatchewan, Fred Bradshaw, who has sent me the fine photographs illustrating the home life of this rare species and his notes made in regard to it. He has also sent me a copy of a very full and interesting report by Neil Gilmour, a provincial game guardian, relating his experience in searching for a nest, which he finally located on May 19, 1922, in western Saskatchewan. I quote from Mr. Gilmour's report as follows:

This marsh is approximately 3 miles long and from 1 to 2 miles in width and comprises an area of upwards of 3,000 acres. It is a shallow marsh, the water at no part being of a depth of more than 3 feet, and much of it being only about knee deep. The entire marsh is covered by a heavy crop of grass growing to a height of about 2 feet above the level of the water. As the marsh does not dry out, the hay, or grass, is never cut, and at the time of my visit, the previous season's growth everywhere covered the marsh with a carpet of brown. Over toward the west end of the marsh there is a small irregular strip of land of possibly 10 acres extent that forms an island elevated, at the time of my visit, about 1 foot above the level of the water. Failing to see anything of the birds at the east end of the marsh, I traveled westward along the south shore for a distance of a mile and half, pausing from time to time and with the aid of my field glasses, searching the surface of the marsh for evidence of the cranes. Suddenly, I saw a single bird where a moment before I thought no bird had been. I sat down upon a mound, the creation of some badger, and through the glasses studied this bird, which appeared to be strolling about gathering its breakfast. Chancing to elevate the glasses a little I picked up in the distance, perhaps a half mile beyond the north shore of the marsh, a white object which proved to be the second crane feeding in a stubble field. Watching this bird through the glasses I had the satisfaction, in a little time, of seeing it spread its great wings, and with slow, and apparently, effortless strokes of these mighty pinions, glide out over the marsh and alight within a short distance of its mate, where both strolled, seemingly, aimlessly about picking from time to time some morsel of food as they strolled.

Being myself inclined by nature to leisure, and further influenced by the delightful warmth of this day in early summer, I stretched myself upon the ground, yet in such a position that with the aid of my field glasses, I could see without being seen, and follow the movements of the cranes. No sooner had I thus rendered myself invisible to the birds, than I noticed a change in the actions of one of the pair. Instead of continuing to wander in an easterly direction as both had been doing, this one, the smaller of the two, and the one which had flown in from the wheatfield, turned and began drifting westward, and in the direction, apparently, of the point in the marsh where I had first observed the other bird. Finally it came to a place where it seemed to rise higher above the level of the dead grass or hay of the marsh. After preening the feathers of its breast for a time, it gradually settled down until only the top of its head was visible. At once I was filled with interest and rose to my feet the better to study what I had witnessed. But almost as soon as I arose the bird also, rose up and again drifted off aimlessly in the direction of its mate. A very natural conjecture was the possibility that the point where the bird settled down out of sight in the grass was where the nest was located; on the other hand the squatting of the bird in the water might very well be some natural habit of the crane. If the former were the correct deduction then I had to deal with an exceedingly wary bird, if the sight of a man standing at a distance of fully a mile was enough to alarm it and cause it as a matter of precaution to move away from the nest. I spent the next two hours playing hide and seek with this bird. Each time I lay down, thus concealing myself from its view, the bird would slowly drift back and again settle down, until only the tip of its head was visible, and exactly at the same spot so far as I could judge. I remained hidden for 20 minutes at a time and as long as I did not expose myself the bird remained in the one spot. The nest was there I felt assured, but how to locate it was the problem. I crawled to the left until I had the head of the hidden bird and a building some miles distant across the lake in line. I figured that if I could rise and walk in a perfectly straight line in the direction of the building, I must come to the nest, if nest there were. I arose and immediately the bird did the same, and tramped off to the eastward. Fixing my eyes upon the distant building, and keeping them steadily upon it, I started forward; but when I entered the marsh, I found that the bottom on this side was boggy, and at each step growing worse, so that I had difficulty in withdrawing my feet, and I feared, was in danger of being engulfed. I was glad to get back in safety to the shore and, my hope of locating the nest began to wane. I determined to have a try at it from another point of the compass. I traveled for another mile or better turning the west end of the marsh, and for a distance up that end. During the time I was thus visible the pair of cranes continued to wander about although at such a distance from me that it seemed remarkable they should be concerned by my presence on the shore. Selecting my proposed point of attack I again concealed myself in the tall grass and very shortly was rewarded by observing one of the birds separate itself from its mate and stroll for some distance in a different direction to a point where, after preening the feathers of the breast as before, it settled down until only the top of the head was visible through the waving grass. Donning my waders, I again set forth, and this time to my great relief I found the bed of the march fairly firm so that I had no difficulty in proceeding.

If, however, the reader has ever tried the experiment of wading through a muskeg with uneven bottom, without once daring to drop his eyes in the direction of his pedal extremities, he will have some idea of the task I had set myself. Time and again when one foot or the other would drop into a bit of a pothole, threatening a spill with its inevitable result, it was with the utmost difficulty I kept my eyes raised, and steadfastly fixed upon the distant lodestone. After plunging along for what appeared like miles, I stopped and without moving a step, looked all around me. I saw nothing of the nest, but the two birds, a few hundred yards to my left, appeared uneasy I thought and were making manifest efforts to attract me to themselves. Again sighting my beacon and getting my bearings I trudged on, and when next I paused and looked about me, I could scarcely believe my eyes when about 10 feet to my right I beheld the object of my two day's search, the nest of the whooping crane. In the center of an open sheet of water about 30 feet in diameter, there arose out of the water a mound of coarse grass and reeds that just resemble the upper part of a two-thirds submerged coil of hay. It arose about one foot above the level of the surface of the water, was flat on top being just slightly concave. In this depression were placed the two large grayish cream colored eggs. They were about 4 inches in length, and only slightly larger at one end than the other. The distressed whooping cries of the birds, as I tarried at the nest, I shall never forget. They were the most remarkable calls I had ever heard. They boomed out and floated over the marsh, until the whole air seemed to vibrate, and for a time I was not at all sure that an attack was not imminent.

Mr. Bradshaw's experience with the birds was almost exactly similar. The nest contained three eggs when found on May 28, 1922. One egg hatched the next day and one was infertile. He says in his notes:

After a long tiresome tramp through 2 feet of water in a heavy marsh, I located a nest and three eggs despite the efforts of the birds to lead me off the track, one went to the left and the other to the right, and when I found the nest they came closer and closer, feigned many times to be on the nest and went through antics of covering eggs; one bird circled within 100 yards radius twice while I was taking a photograph. The nest was made of rushes, three-sided sedge grass, pulled up by the roots. I found it very difficult to uproot, it having adventitious roots. These rushes were nipped from 1 to 5 inches from the root and I am of the opinion that this is done when the birds are gathering material for the nest. The nest was from 4 to 5 feet in diameter and about 15 or 18 inches above the water, dry on top and lined with the finer outside covering of the old dry grasses, the seed of which is a brownish color and pear-shaped. A very slight depression formed the top of the nest. The gathering of material for the nest clears the water surrounding the nest of rushes and forms an island home for the birds, as shown in the photograph.

Eggs.—The whooping crane lays ordinarily two eggs, occasionally only one and very rarely three; in the set of three, referred to above, one egg proved to be infertile. The shape is elliptical ovate. The shell is smooth, but more or less pimpled and slightly glossy. The eggs are usually, if not always, darker colored and more heavily marked than those of the sandhill crane. The ground color varies from "cream buff" to "olive buff." This is clouded and blotched, quite heavily near the larger end and more sparingly elsewhere, with dull browns, "wood browns" or "buffy brown," overlaid with blotches of darker and brighter browns, "Verona brown" or "hazel." The measurements of 38 eggs average 98.4 by 62.4 millimeters; the eggs showing the four extremes measure 107.5 by 63.5, 98 by 67.5, and 87.4 by 50.2 millimeters.

Young.—Mr. Bradshaw while near the nest "heard a strange piping whistle," which he discovered to be "that of a young crane just breaking through the shell. The call was very vigorous for an unhatched bird." After hatching the young bird called "almost constantly, by a whistle resembling that of the red-winged blackbird, but fainter; occasionally it would be louder or more pathetic." On the day after hatching he was surprised to see the young bird leave the nest at his approach and start swimming toward the rushes.

Plumages.—I have never seen a downy young whooping crane, but Mr. Bradshaw describes, in his notes, one that he found in a nest, apparently recently hatched on May 30, as follows:

The young bird for the most part is of a buff color; from the neck to the rump on the back it is somewhat darker, while the under parts are much paler than the color of the head. The bill is about three-fourths inch long, upper half flesh color, lower half darker or horn color, a small white spot on the upper mandible.

Specimens of immature birds are too scarce in collections to give any definite idea of the time required to reach maturity. A young bird collected in October probably represents the juvenal or first winter plumage. The head is wholly feathered, including the forehead and lores. The plumage is mainly white, but it is heavily mottled on the head and neck with "pinkish cinnamon" or "cinnamon buff," almost solid color on the crown; the back and wing coverts are variegated with the same colors, due to a mixture of white feathers and colored feathers in varying amounts, the colored feathers being thicker in the back and scapulars and more scattered in the wings; the colored feathers are darkest in the scapulars, some as dark as "sayal brown"; the primaries are dull black.

Apparently a partial molt of the contour feathers occurs in winter and spring, producing an advance toward maturity. A young bird, taken February 16, has the head and neck still mottled and the larger scapulars, wing coverts, rectrices, and upper tail coverts more or less extensively washed at, or near, the tips with cinnamon. Another young bird, taken April 10, has less cinnamon in the head and neck and the crown and malar regions are becoming blacker. Unfortunately we do not know the ages of these young birds. At the seasonal molts of adults we can only guess, for lack of material.

Food.—The whooping crane is not at all fastidious in its diet; it is quite omnivorous and eats a great variety of both animal and vegetable food. Audubon (1840) supposed that the sandhilll cranes were the young of the whooping cranes, so some of his remarks may apply to either species; but he says that—

Both old and young may be seen digging through the mud before the rains have begun to cover the shallow ponds with water, for during summer they become almost dry. The birds work very assiduously with their bills, and succeed in uncovering the large roots of the great water lilly, which often run to a depth of 2 or 3 feet. Several cranes are seen in the same hole, tugging at roots and other substances, until they reach the object of their desire, which they greedily devour.

His plate illustrates a whooping crane killing young alligators. Nuttall (1834) writes:

In the winter season, dispersed from their native haunts in quest of subsistence, they are often seen prowling in the low grounds and rice fields of the Southern States in quest of insects, grain, and reptiles; they swallow also mice, moles, rats, and frogs with great avidity, and may therefore be looked upon at least as very useful scavengers. They are also at times killed as game, their flesh being well flavored, as they do not subsist so much upon fish as many other birds of this family.

In the fall whooping cranes resort to the grain fields and feed among the stubble, with the sandhill cranes, on various kinds of grains. They are also said to eat vegetables, plants, bulbous roots, snakes, frogs, mice, tadpoles, snails, slugs, worms, grasshoppers, and sometimes a few fish.

Behavior.—Col. N. S. Goss (1891) says:

These birds are very wary and ever upon the lookout, rising over every suspicious spot when on the wing, and when on the ground spring into the air at the first sight or appearance of danger, with a warning note to others. In flight, their long necks and stiltlike legs are stretched out in line with the body to their full extent, moving strongly, with slowly beating wings, but not swiftly; I say strongly because they they are able to face a strong wind, and to sustain themselves for a long time in the air, often circling spirallike to a great height. They occasionally bunch up, and I have seen them in a triangular form, but, as a rule, they travel in single file, following their leader in a wavy line, croaking as they go, like hounds upon a cold trail.

A writer in Forest and Stream over the pseudonym, Picket (1883), writes as follows:

The whooping crane is, to say the least, a fantastic fowl. When marching about on *terra firma* he appears awkward to the last degree. Judging from the length of his stiltlike legs, one would suppose he was made to run rather than fly; but in spite of his clipper build and striding abilities, he is only a moderate pacer. His manner of taking flight is peculiar. Spreading his wings and stooping down, he apparently runs up an inclined plane of air until his feet no longer touch the earth, then stretching them out behind him, he floats away as gracefully as a racing yacht before a steady breeze. In fine, calm weather he delights to mount up, in great undulating spirals, to the height of a mile or so, and take a quiet float, while he whoops at neighbors in the adjoining counties. After airing himself to his heart's content, he descends, sometimes spirally as he arose, at other times with great plunges and wild, reckless dives, until within about 50 feet of the earth when he hangs himself upon the air with his long, spindling legs down, gently settles and alights.

Dwight W. Huntington (1903) refers to this interesting flight performance as follows:

I was once shooting mallard on the margin of a western lake, with an Army officer. The day was warm and bright, and, after a short morning flight, the ducks ceased to move about, and we retired to a slight elevation, ate our luncheon, and reclined in the grass to smoke our pipes and tell tales of shooting game of all sorts. A large flock of white cranes arose from the marsh and flew directly toward us, ascending, however, as they came, far beyond our range. When quite overhead, in the azure sky, their white feathers gleaming in the sunlight, they proceed to go through many graceful evolutions, flying about in a circle, forming sides and crossing over and back and dancing in midair to their own loud music. We were much entertained by their performance, and observed them until the exhibition was ended and they continued their flight until quite out of sight.

The whooping crane is a dangerous antagonist when wounded, striking with great force and with unerring aim with its powerful and sharp bill. Many stories have been told of men being severely wounded by its savage thrusts. Picket (1883) says:

At another time I crippled one of the large white species by breaking a wing. As it was marching off rather rapidly, I sent a little rat terrier to bring it to bay. No sooner did the dog come up with it than it turned about, and quick as lightning drove its long sharp bill clean through him killing him on the spot.

Mr. Seton writes to me:

An extraordinary tragedy was much talked of in my earliest days in the North. About 1879, there was a young Indian living near Portage la Prairie, Manitoba. In the spring, he went out shooting among the famous wild-fowl marshes of that section. A white crane flew low within range and fell to a shot from his gun. As it lay on the ground, wounded in both wing and leg, crippled and helpless, he reached forward to seize it. But it drove its bill with all its force into his eye. The brain was pierced and the young hunter fell on the body of his victim. Here next day, at the end of a long and anxious search, the young wife found them dead together and read the story of the tragedy.

Doctor Coues (1874) once measured the windpipe of a whooping crane and found it to be about 58 inches long, "quite as long as the bird itself"; about 28 inches of this is "coiled away in the breast bone." This is the trumpet through which the bird produces the loud sonorous notes for which it is named and which are said to be audible at a distance of 3 miles Nuttall (1834) writes:

At times they utter a loud, clear, and piercing cry that may be heard to a very considerable distance, and which, being not unaptly compared to the whoop or yell of the savages when rushing to battle, has conferred upon our bird his peculiar appellation. Early in February, Wilson met with several of these cranes in South Carolina; at the same season and in the early part of the following month I heard their clamorous cries nearly every morning around the enswamped ponds of west Florida and throughout Georgia, so that many individuals probably pass either the winter or the whole year in the southern extremity of the Union. It is impossible to describe the clamor of one of these roosting flocks, which they begin usually to utter about sunrise. Like the howling monkeys, or preachers of South America (as they are called), a single individual seemed at first as if haranguing or calling out to the assembled company, and after uttering a round number of discordant, sonorous, and braying tones, the address seemed as if received with becoming applause, and was seconded with a reiteration of jingling and trumpeting hurrahs. The idea conveyed by this singular association of sounds so striking, quaint, and ludicrous that I could never hear it without smiling at the conceit. Captain Amidas (the first Englishman who ever set foot in North America) thus graphically describes their clamor on his landing on the isle of Wokokou, off the coast of North Carolina, in the month of July: "Such a flock of cranes (the most part white) arose under us, with such a cry, redoubled by many echoes, as if an army of men had shouted all together."

According to Mr. Bradshaw's notes, the whooping crane can "rise against the wind with no run to speak of; sometimes one or two steps are taken; at other times it simply crouches down and seems to spring from the feet and tarsi." In flight the wings are in motion most of the time and average, approximately, one beat per second; there is a very slight curve in the neck when flying and the legs are held slightly down from the horizontal. The birds are very graceful when planing. Previous to alighting, there is a "slight downward curve in the wings" and the legs are spread apart and "thrust well forward." While walking through the marsh the tibiae are held "horizontal with the body" and there is a "kink in the neck." The reddish patch on the crown is very prominent in the sun and the plumes are conspicuous.

Fall.—Nuttall (1834) witnessed a great fall flight of this species, of which he says:

In the month of December, 1811, while leisurely descending on the bosom of the Mississippi in one of the trading boats of that period, I had an opportunity of witnessing one of these vast migrations of the whooping cranes, assembled by many thousands from all the marshes and impassable swamps of the North and West. The whole continent seemed as if giving up its quota of the species to swell the mighty host. Their flight took place in the night, down the great aerial valley of the river, whose southern course conducted them every instant toward warmer and more hospitable climes. The clangor of these numerous legions passing along high in the air seemed almost deafening; the confused cry of the vast army continued with the lengthening procession, and as the vocal call continued nearly throughout the whole night without intermission, some idea may be formed of the immensity of the numbers now assembled on their annual journey to the regions of the south.

Audubon (1840) unquestionably referred to this species when he wrote:

The variegated foliage of the woods indicates that the latter days of October have arrived; gloomy clouds spread over the heavens; the fierce blasts of the

North, as if glad to escape from the dreary regions of their nativity, sporting dreadful revelry among the forests and glades. The ducks and geese have already reached the waters of the western ponds; here a swan or two is seen following in their train, and as the observer of nature stands watching the appearances and events of this season of change, he hears from on high the notes of the swiftly traveling but unseen whooping crane. Suddenly the turbid atmosphere clears, and now he can perceive the passing birds. Gradually they descend, dress their extended lines, and prepare to alight on the earth. With necks outstretched, and long bony legs extended behind, they proceed, supported by wings white as the snow but tipped with jet, until arriving over the great savannah they wheel in their circling flight, and slowly approach the ground, on which with half-closed wings, and outstretched feet they alight, running along for a few steps to break the force of their descent. Reader, see the majestic bird shake is feathers, and again arrange them in order. Proud of its beautiful form, and prouder still of its power of flight, it stalks over the withering grasses with all the majesty of a gallant chief. With long and measured steps he moves along, his head erect, his eye glistening with delight. His great journey is accomplished and being well acquainted with a country which has often been visited by him he at once commences his winter avocations.

Mr. Seton, in his notes for October 11, 1907, made on the Athabaska River, writes:

This morning, besides honkers (Canada geese) and waveys (snow geese), we heard the glorious trumpeting of the white crane. It is less of a rattling croak and more of a whoop or trumpet call than the note of the brown crane. Belalise (the Indian guide) says that every year a few come to Fort Chipewyan, then go north with the waveys to breed. In the fall, they come back for a month and linger on the great marshes about Fort Chipewyan. They are usually in flocks of three or four, two old ones and their offspring of the year. If you get the two old ones, the young are easily killed, as they keep flying about low over the place where the parents fell.

Winter.—The winter range of the whooping crane formerly extended east to Florida, but the remnants of the race, now left, spend the winter in the great wild fowl sanctuaries of the Louisiana coast, on the open coastal prairies of Texas or in Mexico. It is a very rare bird even here and is restricted to a few favored localities where it is not disturbed.

On the King Ranch, in Kleberg County, Texas, about 30 miles southwest of Corpus Christi, is a large shallow lake, known as Laguna Larga. This is a famous resort for wild-fowl in winter, particularly snow geese and Hutchins geese. Every winter for a number of years a few whooping cranes have frequented this vicinity and have been observed by several good ornithologists. Mr. Richard M. Kleberg, one of the owners of the ranch, an educated gentleman and a student of natural history, told Herbert W. Brandt, in 1919, "that there are now 16 whooping cranes on the place and they grew from a flock of 3, all breeding here in the wild stretches along the coast." Apparently there is no positive evidence of their breeding there, but some of the birds remain there all through the year and I was told that they were still there when I visited Texas in 1923. It is of interest to note that they have apparently increased in numbers. Mr. Kleberg says that they are the most wary creatures he has ever tried to approach; one does well if he can come within 300 yards of them; so, as they frequent country which is flat and entirely open, there is not much danger of their being shot. In their winter resorts they can probably survive, but, as they require immense wild tracts of open country in which to breed, it will be necessary to set apart some very large reservations within their breeding range in order to save these magnificent birds from extinction.

Charles L. Broley writes to me that on September 13, 1925, he saw a whooping crane "at fairly close range at Shoal Lake, 40 miles north of Winnipeg. He flew over us leading 28 sandhill cranes." Thus this remnant of a vanishing race, once the proud leader of a mighty host, still retains his place at the head of the trumpeting column. May he lead them on in safety! And may he long survive to perpetuate a noble race of birds!

DISTRIBUTION

Range.—Formerly the central Canadian Provinces, the United States, and Mexico, east rarely to the Atlantic coast. At present the species is almost extirpated and probably breeds only locally in south central Canada.

Breeding range.—North to Mackenzie (probably Fort Simpson and Fort Resolution); Alberta (Fort Chipewyan, Whitford Lake and stony Plain); and Saskatchewan (Qu'Appelle and Yorkton). East to Mackenzie (Fort Resolution); Manitoba (near Moose Mountain, Shoal Lake, Winnipeg, and probably Fort Churchill); North Dakota (probably Larimore); Minnesota (probably Herman and Mille Lacs); and Iowa (Eagle Lake, Dubuque and Midway). South to Iowa (Franklin County, Spirit Lake and Midway); probably Nebraska; eastern Montana and Alberta (Whitford Lake). West probably to Nebraska and eastern Montana; Alberta (Whitford Lake, Birch Lake, and Wainwright); and Mackenzie (probably Fort Simpson).

Winter range.—Gulf coast of the United States and central Mexico. Florida (Hastings and Lee County); Alabama (Dauphin Island and probably Prattville); Louisiana (Avery Island and Vermillion Bay); Texas (Harris, Brazoria, Refugio, and probably Tom Green Counties); and Mexico (northern Tamaulipas, Guanajuato, and Jalisco).

Spring migration.—Early dates of arrival are: Arkansas, Corning, April 22, 1914; Missouri, Stotesbury, March 9, 1894, St. Louis, March 17, 1884, and La Clede, March 20, 1889; Illinois, Mount Carmel, March 6; Indiana, Waterloo, April 4, 1907; Iowa, Indianola, March 18, 1901, Wall Lake, March 21, 1904, Storm Lake, March 22, 1886, Gilbert, March 22, 1891, Emmetsburg, March 23, 1885, Ferry, March 23, 1890, and La Porte, March 30, 1885; Minnesota, Heron Lake, March 26, 1891, North Star, March 28, 1890, and Waverly, March 28, 1889; Kansas, Richmond, March 7, 1887, and Baldwin, March 18, 1904; Nebraska, Falls City, March 16; 1890, Gibbon, March 19, 1890, and Doss, March 21, 1890; South Dakota, Harrison, March 25, 1890, and Grand View, April 6, 1888; North Dakota, Menoken, April 5, 1885, Larimore, April 8, 1893, and Devil's Lake, April 11, 1903; Manitoba, Aweme, April 6, 1900, Reaburn, April 9, 1900, Margaret, April 12, 1913, and Shell River, April 16, 1890; Saskatchewan, Qu'Appelle, April 20, 1901, and Indian Head, April 26, 1905; Mackenzie, Hay River, May 12, 1908, Fort Anderson, May 25, 1865, and Fort Simpson, May 28, 1861; Colorado, Loveland, April 8, 1889; Montana, Billings, April 8, 1918, and Big Sandy, May 1, 1903; and Alberta, Whitford Lake, May 21, 1909.

Fall migration.—Late dates of departure are: Alberta, Fort Mc-Murray, October 16, 1907; Montana, Terry, October 5, 1904; Saskatchewan, Indian Head, October 2, 1904; Manitoba, Aweme, October 12, 1904, and Margaret, October 20, 1909; North Dakota, Inkster, October 18, 1904, and Chase Lake, October 11, 1913; South Dakota, Harrison, November 1, 1891, and Huron, October 13, 1887; Nebraska, Gresham, October 11, 1896, Cherry County, October 16, 1912, Lincoln, October 27, 1899, and Doss, November 12, 1890; Kansas, Onaga, October 20, 1907; Minnesota, Heron Lake, November 13, 1885; and Iowa, southern part, November 12, 1871.

Casual records.—In addition to the range above outlined, the whooping crane has been taken or reported from: Ontario (Yarker, September 27, 1871, and Emsdale, 1895); New York (Cayuga Lake); New Jersey (Beesley's Point, 1857, and Cape May); South Carolina (Waccamaw River, 1850); Georgia (St. Simons Island); Alabama (Dauphin Island and Prattville, November or December, 1899); New Mexico (Fort Thorn); Colorado (Loveland, April 8, 1889, and April 16, 1890, and Fort Collins); Wyoming (Yellowstone Park, August 4, 1914); and California (Butte and Sutter Counties). Some of these records that are unsupported by specimens, may apply to either *M. canadensis* or *M. mexicanus.*

Egg dates.—Central Canadian Provinces: 11 records, May 9 to June 2. Iowa: 8 old records, April 25 to May 15.

MEGALORNIS CANADENSIS (Linnaeus)

LITTLE BROWN CRANE

HABITS

The little brown crane is brown only in its immature plumages and the sandhill crane is brown at the same ages; both birds begin to breed in the brown plumage; the only good field mark is the difference in size; and size is often very deceptive. For these reasons much confusion of the two birds exists in the literature of ornithologists, egg collectors, and sportsmen. The little brown crane breeds only far north in the Arctic regions well across the continent; it spends the winter mainly in southern Texas and Mexico; but it is very abundant on migrations in the Western part of the continent, mainly west of the Rocky Mountains. It is now generally conceded, I believe, that this and the sandhill crane are only subspecifically distinct.

Spring.—Dr. E. W. Nelson (1887) has had abundant opportunities for studying this crane in its summer home in Alaska and gives us the best account of its habits; of its arrival in the spring, he says:

At Saint Michaels it sometimes arrives by May 7, when there is yet scarcely a bare spot of ground, and one season these early comers had to endure some severe weather, and several inches of new snow, over which they stalked glum and silent, showing little of their usual roystering spirit. As a rule they are not seen until from the 10th to the 15th of the month, when the ground is usually half bare and the cranes can search every hillside for last year's heathberries, which, with an occasional lemming or mouse, constitute their food at this season. They come from the south toward the lower Yukon, and on mild, pleasant days it is a common sight to see the cranes advancing high overhead in wide circuits, poised on motionless wings, and moving with a grace unexpected in such awkwardly-formed birds. As the weather gets warmer they become more and more numerous, until the drier parts of the wide flats and low, rounded elevations are numerously populated by these odd birds. The air is filled with the loud, hard, rolling *k-r-roo, kr-r-r-roo, ku-kr-r-roo*, and either flying by, with trailing legs, or moving gravely from place to place, they do much to render the monotonous landscape animate.

Courtship.—Of this interesting performance, he goes on to say:

The end of May draws near, and the full tide of their spring fever causes these birds to render themselves preeminently ludicrous by the queer antics and performances which the crane's own book of etiquette doubtless rules to be the proper thing at this mad season. I have frequently lain in concealment and watched the birds conduct their affairs of love close by, and it is an interesting as well as amusing sight. Some notes jotted down on the spot will present the matter more vividly than I can describe from memory, and I quote them. On May 18, I lay in a hunting blind, and was much amused by the performance of two cranes, which alighted near by. The first comer remained alone but a short time, when a second bird came along, uttering his loud note at short intervals, until he espied the bird on the ground, when he made a slight circuit, and dropped close by. Both birds then joined in a series of loud rolling cries in quick succession. Suddenly the newcomer, which appeared to be a male, wheeled his back toward the female and made a low bow, his head nearly touching the ground, and ending by a quick leap into the air; another pirouette brings him facing his charmer, whom he greets with a still deeper bow, his wings meanwhile hanging loosely by his sides. She replies by an answering bow and hop, and then each tries to outdo the other in a series of spasmodic hops and starts, mixed with a set of comically grave and ceremonious bows. The pair stood for some moments bowing right and left, when their legs appeared to become envious of the large share taken in the performance by the neck, and then would ensue a series of stilted hops and skips which are more like the steps of a burlesque minuet than anything else I can think of. Frequently others joins and the dance keeps up until all are exhausted.

Dr. Joseph Grinnell (1900) observes:

The peculiar and often ludicrous performances of these birds during the mating season have been well described by Nelson, but these antics do not seem to be confined to the courting season only for late in June I observed a pair of cranes which I knew to have a set of eggs in the near neighborhood already laid, accomplishing a series of hops, skips, and profound bows, though these were mainly participated in by one of the birds, the male I presume. Possibly such belated demonstration is analogous to the singing of smaller birds even long after the courting season.

I find another phase of this curious performance described by F. Seymour Hersey in his field notes for July 5, 1915, made near St. Michael, as follows:

To-day I watched two cranes for about 20 minutes. They were walking about over the tundra some half mile from where I lay concealed. As they drew near together they turned facing one another and first one and then the other would jump into the air to a height of about 3 or 4 feet. They would do this six or seven times with half-open wings, then run along side by side for a few yards, again wheel and face each other and resume their odd dance. This was repeated until both birds passed out of sight.

Herbert W. Brandt, in his notes, sent to me in advance of publication, relates his experience with a pair of dancing cranes in the vicinity of their nests, as follows:

Both parent birds were very much agitated, striding back and forth past each other, when suddenly they bowed gravely to one another a few times and began their picturesque dance. This was a series of hops and jumps, and of bowing low to the left and right, with the wings limply extended, as if loose jointed, and nearly touching the ground. Their movements were those of ease and rhythm, while they arched their necks in graceful curves that moved in perfect unison with their bodies. We had drawn the kyak up alongside the nest, and one of the Eskimo boys now removed a blunt bird arrow from its place. With this he began to beat the tightly drawn sealskin deck of the boat so as to produce the only native instrumental music. Then both boys chanted their crane song accompanied by rhythmic beating of their improvised drum. As they sang the two cranes continued their dance and seemed to keep perfect time with the strange music. Their movements were not continuous, but were punctuated by a slight pause at the end of each motion, giving to them thus all the grace for which the famous Spanish minuet dancer is noted. This continued for perhaps 10 minutes and was to me one of the most entrancing, as well as one of the most novel, experiences that I enjoyed while in the North.

Nesting.—Doctor Nelson (1887) describes the nesting habits of the little brown crane, as follows:

The site for the nest is usually on the grassy flats, where the drier portions or the slight knolls afford them suitable places. The spot usually has an unobstructed view on all sides, and it is common to see the female's long neck raised suspiciously at the appearance in the distance of anything unusual. If one approaches, the head sinks lower and lower to avoid being seen, but if the person, even though 150 or 200 yards away, should stop and look toward the bird, she will generally rise and skulk away, her neck close to the ground, wings hanging loosely by the sides, and legs bent, so as to avoid being seen. When she is 100 yards or more from the nest she straightens up and stalks anxiously about, uttering her loud call note incessantly, and is generally joined by the male; but it is rarely that either can, even then, be approached within gunshot. In one case the female was about 75 yards from the nest, and as we drew near she staggered from side to side with trailing wings, looking as if in death agony. The nest is frequently a mere hollow in the ground and is commonly lined with more or less coarse grass stems and straws. In one instance a nest was found on a bare flat, and was lined with a layer of straws an inch deep, all of which must have been brought for some yards; this is unusual however.

MacFarlane (1908) who found this species breeding at Franklin and Liverpool Bays and on the lower Anderson River says "the nest is usually a mere cavity in the sandy soil, thickly lined with fine dry grasses and a few feathers."

Doctor Grinnell (1900) says:

Doctor Coffin found a set of two eggs of the little brown crane in the Kowak delta on the 14th of June. They lay about 6 inches apart on the level ground of the tundra near a willow bush. For a diameter of 2 feet the ground was sprinkled with finely broken twigs; otherwise there was nothing to mark the spot as a nest.

George G. Cantwell sent me a photograph and some notes on a nest he found on Kalgin Island, Cook Inlet, Alaska, on June 10, 1913. The nesting site was a wild grass marsh of several miles extent, completely surrounded by small spruces, probably a partly dried up lake in the center of the island. The nest was made of dead grass, wet and soggy. The bird was flushed from the nest and returned several times, trying to entice him away; it kept up a continual bugling, which finally attracted its mate.

Mr. Brandt says in his notes:

The little brown crane nests on the grassy lowland flats that are just above high tide. Through these meander tidal sloughs, and scattered about are many ponds mostly very irregular in shape. The grass that grows long and dense on the flats is in early June dead and still matted down from the snow of the previous winter. Here on the ground the crane makes of this dead grass a nest about 3 feet in diameter and 4 to 6 inches high with an inner depression from 12 to 15 inches across. Some of the birds, however, merely tramp the matted grass down and place their eggs upon this. On May 27 a nest with two eggs, perhaps five days incubated, was found by an Eskimo, and after this date many others were discovered. The male and female share in the duties of incubation, changing places often, and at such times each bird calls, the one as it approaches the nest, the other as it departs. The nest-changing call is different from the regular notes and gives the natives a clue to the location of the nests, of which they are quick to take advantage, for the eggs as well as the birds themselves are considered among the finest delicacies of Eskimo home life. One native brought in six fine fresh eggs for which he refused a considerable sum, preferring to serve them to his family, as they are supposed to render those who eat them immune from disease.

Eggs.—Two eggs is the usual set laid by the little brown crane. These vary in shape from ovate to cylindrical ovate. The shell is smooth or slightly pimpled, with little or no gloss. There are many wrongly identified eggs of this crane in collections. All authentic eggs of the little brown crane that I have seen average much darker in color than those of the sandhill crane. The ground color varies from "buffy brown" or "Saccardo's umber" to dull "clay color" or "deep olive buff." This is spotted and blotched, generally more profusely around the larger end, with various shades of brown. The underlying markings are of dull browns, such as "fawn color," "wood brown," or "army brown." The overlying markings are of darker and brighter colors, "walnut brown," "russet" or "chestnut," and often there are a few small spots of "blackish brown" near the larger end.

Doctor Grinnell (1900) describes his two sets of eggs as follows:

The eggs of these two sets are quite similarly colored. The general effect is rather pale. The ground color is olive-buff, over which are evenly distributed spots and longitudinally extending dashes of clay color, Vandyke brown, vinaceous, and lavender. These spottings are rather more numerous at the large end of the eggs, but not so pronouncedly so as to form a wreath. The longitudinal tendency of the markings easily reminds one of the pattern of coloration on the eggs of *Myiarchus*.

Doctor Nelson (1887) says:

The eggs vary in ground color from pale greenish clay color to buffy brown or warm brownish, and the entire surface is irregularly marked with spots and blotches of chocolate brown, rather sparsely distributed at the small end, but numerous about the large end of the egg, chiefly at the very apex.

The measurements of 25 eggs average 89.5 by 55.1 millimeters; the eggs showing the four extremes measure 101 by 56.5, 83 by 60, 77.4 by 46.5 and 79.2 by 44 millimeters.

Young.—H. B. Conover writes to me:

The first newly hatched young were seen June 21, when a nest with one chick and a badly pipped egg was found. The nest was visited several times during the day to see if the other egg had hatched. At each visit the two old cranes would fly off to a little side hill where a cock ptarmigan was always stationed, evidently standing guard over his mate and her nest. Immediately the big birds had alighted, the grouse would ruffle up like a game cock and make a dash at the male crane, who would jump into the air and strike out with his long legs. The ptarmigan always kept a safe distance away and no damage seemed to be inflicted by either side. After a little of this, however, the cranes would stalk solemnly away on their long legs, with the ptarmigan in hot pursuit, but badly put to it to keep up with his enemy.

Mr. Brandt says:

We helped one pair of chicks out of their eggs on June 21, and as soon as they became dry they were handsome sturdy little fellows, balls of golden-brown down. The strong legs were slatey red, rather short in proportion to the bird, and in great contrast to the long legs of the parent. The "knees" were thick and the legs fleshlike throughout. The reddish color in the legs and bill of the newly hatched chick was due, no doubt, to the fact that the blood could be seen

through the transparent covering. During the first day the legs of the little
cranes were large and soft, but by the next morning they had shrunken and
hardened considerably. The "knees" were visibly enlarged, the skin had lost
its reddish tinge and become of a shiny, slatey color. The young showed interest in food shortly after hatching, but they would not pick up boiled egg yolk
themselves until a tapping noise was made with the fingers on the floor, whereupon they at once began to eat. Their high pitched "*peep*" had a gurgle in it,
a miniature of the rolling "*r–r–r–r–*" in the trumpet note of the adult.

Plumages.—My remarks on this subject are based on a study of
a considerable series of little brown and sandhill cranes of various
ages and refer to the plumage changes of the two birds combined,
as the two are, apparently, exactly alike in this respect and are, probably, only subspecifically distinct. The small downy young crane is
completely covered with thick, soft down and is very prettily colored.
The color is deepest in the centers of the crown, hind neck and back
and on the wings, where it is "chestnut" or "burnt sienna"; it shades
off on the sides to "ochraceous tawny" and on the throat and belly
to dull grayish white. These colors fade somewhat as age advances.
I have seen no specimens showing the change into the juvenal
plumage.

In the juvenal plumage the crown, which at first is fully feathered,
is "tawny"; the head and neck are washed and mottled with "tawny"
and "cinnamon" and the under parts are mottled with the same
colors; the back is almost solid "hazel" or "tawny" and the scapulars
and wing coverts are heavily washed with these same colors.

This brown plumage is worn through the first fall and winter, but
the crown and lores become partially bare before spring. A partial
prenuptial molt, involving the contour feathers, scapulars and some of
the wing coverts, but not the flight feathers, produces a fresh, brown
first nuptial plumage, in which I think that some birds breed.

At the next complete molt, the first postnuptial, from September
to December, most of the adult gray plumage is assumed, but many
of the feathers in the neck, back, scapulars and wing coverts are still
brown. During the second winter, or at the second prenuptial molt,
most of the brown plumage is replaced by new gray feathers, "mouse
gray" to "pale mouse gray," on the head, neck, and body; but some
of the old brown wing coverts are still retained in the second nuptial
plumage. At the next, complete, postnuptial molt, which is not
finished until December, the young crane becomes fully adult, at an
age of $2\frac{1}{2}$ years.

Adults have a complete molt from August to December; the flight
feathers are molted in August, but the molt of the body plumage and
wing coverts is not finished until December. The prenuptial molt,
if any, must be very limited; it probably involves only a renewal of
some of the contour plumage.

Food.—Doctor Grinnell (1900), referring to the food of this crane in the Kotzebue Sound region, says:

Its food consisted largely of berries and grass, while a few insects and, I have reason to believe, mice, also entered into its diet. We found the cranes usually fat, and they proved very fine eating, in fact we esteemed crane above every other game except ptarmigan.

Doctor Nelson (1887) included berries, lemming, and mice. Mr. Brandt says that "they feed usually out on the drier parts of the marshes and the tundra, though I have often seen them grazing high up on the mountain sides more than 1,000 feet above their home in the valley." Dr. A. K. Fisher (1893) found in the stomach of one killed in Nevada "small bulbous rootlets, foliage of young plants, and a quantity of barley, which it had picked up from the place where the horses had been fed." Messrs. Grinnell, Bryant, and Storer (1918) write, regarding its food in California:

When feeding on the plains or in stubble fields these birds dig up the ground with their bills in such a way that it looks as though a pick had been used. In the tule country near Stockton, Belding states that they used to feed extensively on sagittaria bulbs. In the Imperial Valley, Van Rossem observed cranes visiting the grain fields to forage, going and coming from Salton Sea morning and evening and as regularly as though timed by a clock. In 1901 it was reported that cranes were so numerous in the wheat fields west of Tulare that they had to be scared away. The birds were seeking the newly sprouted grain, but no detailed account of the kind or amount of damage has been obtained.

Behavior.—In flight and in general behavior the little brown crane is much like its larger relative, the sandhill crane and can not be readily distinguished from it in the field. It flies with the neck and legs outstretched to full length and, when migrating, it flies at a great height. It is said to bear some resemblance to a turkey when walking about on the ground and feeding. Its loud and sonorous notes are described by Doctor Nelson (1887) as "hard, rolling *K-r-roo, Kr-r-r-roo, Ku-kr-r-roo.*" It is said to be a very shy bird and very difficult to approach, but Doctor Nelson (1883) writes:

They are not very shy, and I have frequently approached them within gunshot by merely appearing not to notice them but continuing in a narrowing circuit to walk round their position until within 60 or 75 yards; the bird continued to stare stupidly at me and uttering its long note and appearing as if doubtful whether it was worth while to take wing or not, until its thoughts were accelerated by a shot. They are extremely curious at this season, and I have frequently decoyed them within gunshot by lying upon the ground and waving a hand or some conspicuous article in the air. As the birds approach from a distance they will almost invariably turn and try to investigate the matter before passing on their way. In many cases they only make a slight detour from their course and pass on, but I have frequently had six or eight of the birds circling about until some would approach within 35 or 40 yards, offering an easy prize.

Mr. Hersey had a chance to see an exibition of its curiosity, which he describes in his notes as follows:

While lying in my boat in a narrow channel in the canal a crane came down close to the bank. Only his head could be seen, but after looking at me for awhile he ran along some 50 feet in a series of hops of about 6 feet in distance, stopping at each to raise his head and survey the boat. He then turned looked me over carefully and went back to about an equal distance the other side of his first position, examined me critically from that point of view and then returned to the point where I first saw him. I do not know how much longer he would have continued his antics had I not ended the interview with a charge of shot.

Doctor Grinnell (1914) relates the following incident, illustrating the caution displayed by this species in selecting a roosting place, which he observed in the lower Colorado Valley:

A large flock spent the night of March 9 on a mud bar in the river at the lower end of Chemehuevis Valley. This roosting ground was about midway between the high wooded banks of the river, and about 200 yards from either bank. The cranes had thus selected a place which could not be approached except in the open, and were evidently on their guard all night. They were just opposite our camp; every now and then something would disturb them and a chorus of sonorous calls and wing-flappings would ensue for a minute or more.

Fall.—Doctor Nelson (1887) says:

The last of July, and during August, the cranes frequent the hillsides, and feast upon the berries growing there, and early in September the small flocks, which have been trooping about from one feeding ground to another, join into larger companies, until toward the last of the month—from the 18th to the 30th—they pass to the south, making the air resonant with their guttural notes as they file away toward the Yukon.

Dr. Wilfred H. Osgood (1904) writes, of their migration at the base of the Alaska Peninsula:

Little brown cranes were first seen September 3, on the Malchatna River, a few miles above the mouth of the Yikchik, and from that point down to the vicinity of the mouth of the Nushagak, they were very abundant. The river for this distance abounds in islands and long sand bars and spits upon which large water birds spent much of their time. When not flying the cranes are seldom seen except on these sand bars, where they mingle with the more numerous gulls and geese. On fine days they stand for hours in small groups enjoying the sun, scarcely ever making a move. Their unmistakable rattling, metallic cry usually kept one informed of their whereabouts when they were flying anywhere within half a mile. They were quite wary and rarely came within gunshot.

E. S. Cameron (1907) says that the little brown crane is commoner than the sandhill crane in Montana, occuring in flocks of from 10 to 150. He writes:

In September, 1898, a regular invasion of southward-bound flocks took place at Terry. The inhabitants pursued them with every description of weapon but only one was shot—by J. C. Braley, with a rifle at 300 yards. When fired at with a rifle the birds would fly only about half a mile and again alight, so that the fusillade could be continued at intervals. The only possible way of obtaining specimens is from concealment in the corn fields which they frequent. The cranes always flew low, generally within shot from the ground of a heavy shoulder gun, and in a straggling manner, although during migration they rise to a great height. They continued to arrive in the neighborhood of Terry for three weeks (until October 10) when all had left excepting a small flock.

Game.—The little brown crane is just as good a game bird as its larger relative, but it is nowhere sufficiently abundant, except on the Pacific coast, to be of much interest to sportsmen. In California it seems to be much commoner than the sandhill crane. According to Grinnell, Bryant, and Storer (1918) cranes brought fancy prices in the San Francisco markets in the early days when turkeys were scarce:

More recently cranes were of regular appearance in the markets of San Francisco and Los Angeles. In the season of 1895–96, 385 cranes were sold, bringing to the hunter about 50 cents each, considerably more than any of the geese. All testimony agrees as to the edible quality of the flesh of the crane, and this is to be expected from its chiefly vegetable diet. * * * There are a few of our game birds which, because of their extreme wariness, may be expected to survive in spite of the increased efficiency of firearms and the increasing number of hunters. The little brown and sandhill cranes are to be included in this category. It is nowadays only by mere chance that the shotgun can bring one of these birds to bag. To get within range with a rifle, even, takes considerable ingenuity. This, with the protection afforded them by our closed seasons, should suffice to maintain cranes indefinitely, as far as California is concerned.

In this connection it is pleasing to note that Mr. Brandt learned from the Eskimos of Alaska that cranes have been increasing in numbers there during recent years; this may be due to better protection in their winter homes or to increasing wariness on the part of the birds.

DISTRIBUTION

Range.—North America to central Mexico.

Breeding range.—North to the coast of Siberia (Semiavine Strait); northern Alaska (Kotzebue Sound region, Colville River and Circle); northern Mackenzie (delta of the Mackenzie River, Liverpool Bay, Franklin Bay, and probably Cape Kellett, Banks Island); and Franklin (Mercy Bay, Melville Sound region, the Boothia peninsula, Igloolik, and Baffin Island). East to eastern Franklin (Baffin Island); southeastern Keewatin (Southampton Island and near Cape Eskimo). South to southeastern Keewatin (near Cape Eskimo); Mackenzie (Fort Resolution and Nyarling River); and Alaska (Nushagak and Cook Inlet). West to Mackenzie (region of Great Slave Lake); and western Alaska (Nushagak and St. Michael).

Winter range.—North to southern Texas (San Patricio and Corpus Christi). East to Texas (Corpus Christi); and San Luis Potosi (Rio

Verde). South to San Luis Potosi (Rio Verde); Guanajuato (Silao); and Jalisco (Ocotlan). West to Jalisco (Ocotlan).

Accidental in winter in California (near San Francisco).

Spring migration.—Early dates of arrival are: Missouri, Clark County, April 10, 1896; Iowa, La Porte, April 5, 1884, Whiting, April 6, 1886, and Holly Springs, April 8, 1887; Nebraska, Dunbar, March 28, 1904; Wisconsin, Johnstown, April 4, 1894; North Dakota, April 12, 1886, and Cutler, May 1, 1907; Manitoba, Dufferin, April 25, 1874, Reaburn, May 4, 1895, and Portage la Prairie, May 5, 1898; Franklin, Igloolik, June 25, 1823, Felix Harbor, June 4, 1830, and Cape Graham Moore, July 29, 1858; Colorado, near Colorado Springs, March 27, 1900; Wyoming, Albany County, April 3, 1912; Saskatchewan, Indian Head, April 14, 1915, and Carleton House, April 28, 1887: Alberta, Alliance April 19, 1917, Stony Plain, April 24, 1911, Fort Vermilion, April 24, 1906, Athabaska River, 40 miles below Athabaska Landing, May 7,1901, and Fort McMurray May 15, 1901; Mackenzie, Hay River, May 1, 1908, Fort Resolution, May 7, 1860, and Fort Simpson, May 9, 1904; Franklin, Mercy Bay, about May 15, 1852; California, Riverside, February 19, 1893, Needles, March 1, 1914, San Jacinto Lake, March 11, 1897, and Long Beach, March 24, 1912; Nevada, Ash Meadows, March 10, 1891; Oregon, Malheur Lake, April 17, 1915; British Columbia, Chilliwack, March 19, 1889, and Okanagan Landing, April 20, 1906; and Alaska, Bethel, May 14, 1915, and Beaver Mountains, May 12, 1917.

Fall migration.—Late dates of fall departure are: Alaska, Kowak River, September 4, 1898, St. Michael, September 15, 1889, Nome, September 17, 1899, and near Iditarod, September 18, 1915; Yukon, Russell Creek, September 30, 1903; British Columbia, Chilliwack, September 22, 1888; Washington, Pierce County, October 10, 1909; Mackenzie, Fort Reliance, September 14; Alberta, near Edmonton, September 17, 1911, 20 miles below Athabaska Landing, September 22, 1903, and Belvedere, October 5; Saskatchewan, Fort Pelly, September 16, 1881; South Dakota, Edmonds County, October 22, 1883; Montana, Terry, October 10, 1898; Wyoming, Yellowstone Park, August 4, 1917; Colorado, Fountain, September 29, 1913; and Oklahoma, Canadian River (at 98°), October 7, 1845.

Casual occurrences.—The little brown crane has been taken or noted at a few places east of its normal range: South Carolina (Mt. Pleasant, October 21, 1890); Rhode Island (Natick, October 9, 1889); and Prince Edward Island (Alexander, September 22, 1905, and Earnscliffe, October 23, 1905).

Egg Dates.—Alaska: 28 records, May 1 to June 17; 14 records, June 3 to 12.

MEGALORNIS MEXICANUS (Müller)

SANDHILL CRANE

HABITS

The sandhill crane has a very peculiar breeding range, or rather two distinct breeding ranges, separated by an area of more than 600 miles wide, in which it does not now breed. Its extensive breeding range in the Northwestern States and southern Canada and its more restricted breeding range in Florida, the Gulf States, and Cuba are probably the remnants of what was formerly a continuous breeding range.

Since this chapter was written James L. Peters (1925) has shown that these two separate ranges are occupied by birds which are probably subspecifically distinct, but, as their habits are doubtless similar, I prefer to let this stand as a life history of both forms.

The advances of civilization, the drainage of swamps and the cultivation of prairies have doubtless driven this wary, old prairie scout away from all the central portions of the United States; and they are still driving it farther west and north into the unsettled wilderness; the wilderness is fast disappearing and with it will go the cranes and many other interesting forms of wild life. According to Prof. Wells W. Cooke (1914):

Its numbers have decreased decidedly in the past 30 years, and it is now rare as a breeder in the southern half of the above-defined breeding range, although within the last 10 years it has nested in southern Michigan (1907), northern Indiana (1905), northern Iowa (1907), northwestern Nebraska (1904), and central Colorado (1903).

It nested in Ohio as late as 1897, in Louisiana in 1907, and in Alabama in 1911.

It is interesting to note that it still breeds commonly in Florida where it can still find large tracts of uninhabited, open plains; here it will perhaps make its last stand. While driving through the "flat woods," or pine barrens, and the extensive inland prairies of Brevard County in April, 1902, I was greatly impressed with the similarity of these plains to the prairie regions of North Dakota, Saskatchewan, and Manitoba. We first saw the cranes in the "flat woods," through which we drove for 6 or 7 miles, flat, level country with an open, parklike growth of large, long-leafed pines; among the scattered pines the ground was covered with a low growth of saw palmetto about knee high or with large areas of tall fine grass. Occasionally among the pines we found open spaces covered with prairie grass, or wet meadows, or saw-grass sloughs. Beyond the pines we drove for 8 miles over the open prairie to the marshes of the St. Johns River; the country here was as flat and level as any we had seen in North

Dakota, but not quite as boundless, for always there were some trees within sight in the distance. Roving bands of wild cattle, which we were told were dangerous, and an occasional mounted cowboy added a western tinge. The rich song of the southern meadowlark suggested, but did not equal, that of his gifted western relative, and the loud familiar whistle of a pair of upland plover added to the charm and made us dream of happy days on the northern prairies. Sandhill cranes flew over us in the "flat woods," making the air ring with their loud trumpetings and we saw several pairs of them walking about with stately tread in the wet meadows or around the sawgrass sloughs on the prairies. The cranes were undoubtedly nesting in or around these wet places but we did not succeed in finding a nest. Such is the congenial home of the sandhill crane in this and many other parts of Florida.

Spring.—Referring to its arrival in Manitoba, Ernest T. Seton (Thompson, 1890) says:

The first intimation that we usually have of the advent of the crane is the loud trumpeting or croaking that seems to shake the air for miles. But soon we begin to see the birds themselves, usually in pairs, even at this early season. Their food now is chiefly rosepips, and as they stalk over the bare plains gathering this manna of the feathered race, ample opportunity is offered for observation. At first one sees little to note beyond their excessive wariness, but as the warmer weather quickens their feeling, these majestic stalkers, these stately trumpeters, may often be seen so far forgetting their dignity as to wheel about and dance, flapping their wings and shouting as they "honor their partners," and in various ways contrive to exhibit an extraordinary combination of awkwardness and agility. This dance is no doubt one of the courting maneuvers for I have observed it only during the pairing season.

Stephen S. Visher (1910) writes:

The sandhill crane is one of the most conspicuous birds of the prairie region. Every farmer boy knows its call, and on fair days has seen large flocks soaring at great heights, slowly passing northward. Constantly their unsurpassed calls drift down to earth. When only a slight wind is blowing, these rich, buglelike notes can be heard farther than the bird can be seen. Several times I have examined, for some moments in vain, the horizon before the authors sailed in view. On windy or rainy days, the flocks fly low and swiftly in a direct line, and each individual croaks in turn. Thus slowly the music moves along the undulating, curving line.

Courtship.—Mr. Visher (1910) also gives us the best account of the curious courtship dance, as follows:

The mating habits of this bird are very interesting. In Sanborn County, South Dakota, I have often watched the mating dance; each time with increasing interest. In the early spring, just after the break of dawn, the groups that were separated widely, for safety, during the night, begin flying toward the chosen dancing ground. These flocks of six or eight fly low and give constantly their famous, rolling call. The dancing ground that I knew best was situated on a large, low hill in the middle of a pasture of a section in extent. From this hill the surface of the ground for half a mile or more in every direction could be seen. As soon as two or three groups had reached this hill a curious dance commenced. Several raise their heads high in the air and walk around and around slowly. Suddenly the heads are lowered to the ground and the birds become great bouncing balls. Hopping high in the air, part of the time with raised wings, and part with dropping, they cross and recross each other's paths. Slowly the speed and wildness increases, and the hopping over each other, until it becomes a blurr. The croaking, which commenced only after the dancing became violent, has become a noise. The performance continues, increasing in speed for a few minutes, and then rapidly dies completely out, only to start again upon the arrival of more recruits. By 7 o'clock all have arrived, and then for an hour or so a number are constantly dancing. Occasionally the whole flock of 200 or so break into a short spell of crazy skipping and hopping. By 9 o'clock all are tired and the flock begins to break up into groups of from four to eight and these groups slowly feed to the windward, diverging slowly, or fly to some distance.

Nesting.—The only nests of the sandhill crane that I have seen have been in Florida. Here the cranes nest in the shallow ponds in the open flat, pine woods, or on the prairies, though much more commonly in the prairie ponds. There are two types of ponds which they seem to prefer; these are well illustrated by two nests found on March 21, 1925, on the Kissimmee prairie, near Bassenger, in Okeechobee County. The first nest was in a small shallow pond, only about a foot deep, overgrown with an open, scanty growth of "pond cypress," a small plant with a woody stem and feathery leaves that grows only a foot or two above the water. The bulky nest was in plain sight from the shore of the pond; the crane had seen us and left it, as we approached. It was a large pile of dead reeds, rushes, tufts of grass and entire plants of pond cypress, torn up with the roots; it was built up 6 or 8 inches above the water and measured 38 by 33 inches in diameter.

The second nest was out near the middle of a large pond which was overgrown with a dense growth of pickerel weed (*Pontederia*) in water 2 feet deep or more. It was so well concealed that my guide walked within 10 or 15 yards of it, to the leeward, without seeing it or flushing the bird; but, as I walked by on the windward side considerably farther away from it, she flew off with the usual series of rolling, guttural croaks; the eggs were on the point of hatching, which may have caused her to sit more closely. The nest was a huge pile of dead reeds and rushes, built up 6 or 8 inches above the water, and measuring 60 by 45 inches. Ponds of these two types are numerous on the Florida prairies, the pickerel weed ponds being much commoner; but one must not expect to find a crane's nest in every pond. Much hard tramping is necessary which becomes very tiresome in thick vegetation and water knee deep. The most efficient way to hunt the nests is on horseback, which gives one a better outlook and saves much hard work. One day in Charlotte County we worked all day, seeing no less than 30 cranes, but did not find a single nest.

F. M. Phelps (1914) writes that the sandhill crane is still rated as a common bird in Lee County, Florida, and observes that:

The nesting of this bird is very uncertain. It may begin in late February or it may be deferred to April or May. Mr. Green told me of finding a nest early in June, 1912, with fresh eggs. I am inclined to think the amount of water in the nesting ponds is an important factor. The bird seems to require that its nesting site be surrounded by water. Twice after heavy rains I found them scratching up nests in grassy ponds which they abandoned without using when the ponds began to dry up. Three occupied nests were found, on April 4 and 8, with eggs far advanced in incubation, and on April 12 with fresh eggs. In this latter case the birds had scratched up no less than four nests in a small flag pond I could throw a stone across. Why the extra nests, two of which were only about half complete, is a question.

S. F. Rathbun writes to me:

On June 12, 1889, I was working over a very large marsh situated about 8 miles southeast of Eden, Manitoba. This marsh was a famous breeding place for many of the ducks and other water birds. As we were wading waist deep in the water some distance from the edge of the marsh, a sandhill crane arose some ways off and keeping our eyes fixed on the spot which was soon reached, after a short search the bird's nest was found. This was made of a very large mass of dead rushes placed on a somewhat elevated spot in an open space of the marsh, and far away from the dry land. The nest was lined with smaller strips of the dead rushes and contained one egg. This I left but on again visiting the spot a few days later, found it had disappeared. This nest was about 4 feet across its base and had a height of at least 2 feet. It was very substantial, as on my second visit to it I found that it would nearly sustain my weight. In 1889 the section in which the marsh was located was virgin country, there being hardly a dozen settlers in an area of several hundred square miles.

Dr. A. G. Prill (1922) has studied the nesting habits of this crane in Oregon and writes:

The region covered in my investigation, covered an area of 36 miles long by from 5 to ten miles wide, or about 180 square miles. Ten pairs of sandhill cranes were nesting in this territory, which would mean about one pair of birds to every 18 square miles of territory. Warner Valley has some half dozen lakes, surrounded by tules and flags, and wild meadow lands, all of which is covered with water, but here and there small islands were found, which were always above high water. The places selected for the nest of this crane were generally several miles out in the marshes, and the nests located were all on the tops of large masses of dried tules and flags, and grass, which had undoubtedly been piled up in this manner the year previous in harvesting the hay crop. These masses were generally 5 feet in diameter and at least 12 inches above high water mark, and in the center a slight depression is made upon which the two eggs or young are found.

A Colorado nest is described by Edward R. Warren (1904) as follows:

In the western part of Gunnison County, Colo., between the slope of Ragged Mountain and Muddy Creek, is a high, rolling plateau, of an elevation of 8,000 feet or more. In amongst the hollows of this plateau are many little lakes or ponds, varying in size from 50 to 60 feet in diameter to 100 yards or more. During the past three seasons I have been about this country very much, surveying, and every season have seen sandhill cranes (*Grus mexicana*) flying overhead and heard their melodious(?) notes, but did not find a nest until June 5, 1903, when, while chopping out a line across the top of a little knoll just south of a small pond, my assistant disturbed a crane. This kept flying about and croaking so anxiously as to make him think there was a nest there, and going to see he found it, with two eggs. When I came along he showed it to me. Out about 20 feet from the shore was the nest, on a bare space among some tussocks of grass which lay more or less in a line. The water was not very deep but the mud was and I could not get to the nest as there was nothing of which to make a bridge, so I had to content myself with a careful examination from the shore. The nest was irregular in shape, about 2 feet across and made of dead marsh grass. On this platform, such as it was practically, lay the two large eggs, looking, my man said, something like turkey eggs.

Eggs.—The sandhill crane usually lays two eggs, sometimes only one, and very rarely three. The shape varies from ovate to elongate ovate. The shell is smooth, with little or no gloss, but there are generally a few pimples on it and sometimes it is finely pitted. The eggs average much lighter in color than those of the other two cranes; and they are marked more sparingly with smaller blotches and spots. The markings are sometimes quite evenly distributed, but are often massed at the larger end. The underlying markings are in shades of "drab-gray," "ecru drab" or "pale vinaceous drab." These are overlaid with spots of "Isabella color," "Saccardo's umber," "snuff brown," and "brownish drab."

The measurements of 43 eggs average 96.2 by 61.4 millimeters; the eggs showing the four extremes measure **109.5** by 60.5, 98.2 by **66.3, 84** by **55** millimeters.

Young.—Nothing seems to be known about the period of incubation of any of the North American cranes; but we do know that both sexes incubate. Young cranes belong to the precocial class, but they probably remain in the nest for a day or so after they are hatched, perhaps for only a few hours however. Dr. Henry Bryant (1861) says:

The young remain with their parents until fully grown, and are fed for a long time by regurgitation. They do not fly until they are as large as their parents, but run with great speed, and hide like a young partridge.

Mr. Moore says in his notes:

No one here, and I have questioned many, has seen the young in the nest; many have, however, seen the young not much larger in the body than a turkey a week old, walking about with their parents; which seem to remain with them till they are several months, probably a year, old, as two pairs are often seen in company from April and May till January. The young are often seen, and sometimes caught by a person giving chase, on foot, and overtaking them, after they are quite large, but still unable to fly. At such times the parents remain at a safe distance, deserting their captive offspring, but expressing their anxiety by uttering their peculiar notes loudly, and walking hither and thither over the ground. They never attack the persons at such times.

The following interesting incident is related by George H. Mackay (1893):

Mr. Horace Thomson of St. Paul, slightly wounded with a rifle ball at long range an immature sandhill crane (*Grus mexicana*) which with several others was resting on the prairie. At the report they all flew away except the wounded bird and one other which apparently was its parent. The wounded bird, after a number of unsuccessful attempts to fly (assisting itself by first running, accompanied by the parent which kept beside it), finally succeeded in rising some 10 or 15 feet from the ground, but it evidently could not long sustain itself in the air. The parent bird, perceiving this, deliberately placed itself underneath the wounded one, allowing it to rest its feet on her back, both birds flapping away all the while. In this position she actually succeeded in bearing it off before our eyes for quite a distance to a place of safety, where we would not follow it. It was one of the most touching examples of parental affection in a bird tha has ever come under my observation.

Plumages.—The downy young of the sandhill crane, its sequence of plumages to maturity and its subsequent molts and plumages are all, apparently, exactly like those of the little brown crane, from which it is, probably, only subspecifically distinct.

Food.—Mr. Moore's excellent notes contain the following information as to the feeding habits of the sandhill crane in Florida:

They feed in ponds, in water 4 inches deep; along their wide margins that are drier, where only a little grass is seen, on the highest grounds, among the lowest palmettoes and grasses, and also over the lands that are blackened by the sweeping fires where no green thing is seen. In six stomachs, opened by me at varying times of the year, I was unable to designate any portion of the contents, but in no one did I discover any sign of animal food. In some instances in two birds, which were killed while feeding together in about 3 inches of water, I detected a mass so nearly entire and having a peculiar bulb attached to a fiber now and then, that, on proceeding to the spot where they fell, I was enabled to discover and identify it; I found it to be the roots of a small species of *Sagittaria*. Another one contained 10 or more seeds of an unknown plant, as large as that of coffee. All contained much sand, small white quartz, and larger brown pebbles. I have now the sand and pebbles taken from one, which weighed after drying 2 ounces, together with the 10 seeds just mentioned.

Wright and Harper (1913) found these cranes in Okefinokee Swamp, in southern Georgia, where "they are said to breed in the prairies, but at other times seem to prefer the pine woods with their growth of saw palmetto and ericaceous plants. Here they find vast quantities of huckleberries, and are doubtless attracted also to pools where killi-fishes and tadpoles have entered at high water."

The varied bill of fare of the sandhill crane, as reported by various observers in different parts of the country, includes much animal food such as rats and mice, frogs, lizards and snakes, worms, grasshoppers, crickets, beetles, and other insects. Dr. Amos W. Butler (1897) says that in Indiana this crane is very fond of white potatoes and sweet potatoes. On the fall migration it lives largely on grains, notably corn, wheat, and barley, which it gleans from the stubble fields. Here it becomes very fat and is much esteemed as a game bird. Hamilton M. Laing (1915) gives us a very good account of its feeding methods and its scouting tactics, as follows:

Judging by the time he takes to a meal, one might be led to think that the quantity of grain he can store away at a sitting is prodigious. His regular hours on the field are from 7 to 11 a.m., and from 2 or 3 p.m. till dark. But he is a slow eater; he has not learned to chew and guzzle a whole wheat head at a time, as the geese do, but must pick it to pieces with his dagger bill. Yet before he leaves for the South he gets enough grain below his gray coat to round and plump his angularity, and 15-pound "turkeys"—as they are usually called by the plains folk—are not uncommon. The main moves in his system are simple. Night is spent usually in the shallows of marsh or grassy pond hole, morning and evening upon the grain fields, noon and early afternoon aloft or at a pond hole or on the prairie. His plan is the reverse of that of the geese. The goose is a water bird that comes to the uplands and fields to feed; the crane is a land bird that goes to the water merely to drink and secure a safe night roost. But, though simple, these movements have been modified in so many ways that the tyro hunter who attempts to solve the combination and outguess his quarry finds that he has tackled a knotty problem. First to the feeding ground at dawn go the scouts, the wise ones—it may be a ground used the previous evening, or it may be an entirely new one—the others follow when the coast has been declared safe. In feeding, the several units scatter widely; every unit has one or more scouts on high-headed guard; eyes are pointed at every angle, and approach by a foe is almost impossible.

Behavior.—Referring to the flight of this species Doctor Coues (1874) writes:

Thousands of sandhill cranes repair each year to the Colorado River Valley, flock succeeding flock along the course of the great stream, from their arrival in September until their departure the following spring. Such ponderous bodies, moving with slowly-beating wings, give a great idea of momentum from mere weight—of force of motion without swiftness; for they plod along heavily, seeming to need every inch of their ample wings to sustain themselves. One would think they must soon alight fatigued with such exertion, but the raucous cries continue, and the birds fly on for miles along the tortuous stream, in Indian file, under some trusty leader, who croaks his hoarse orders, implicitly obeyed. Each bird keeps his place in the ranks; the advancing column now rises higher over some suspected spot, now falls along an open, sandy reach, swaying meanwhile to the right or left. As it passes on, the individual birds are blended in the hazy distance, till, just before lost to view, the line becomes like an immense serpent gliding mysteriously through the air.

Its powers of locomotion on foot or awing are well described by Mr. Laing (1915), as follows:

Mounted on his long, strong shanks, he covers the ground easily and thinks nothing of a little jaunt of a mile from water hole to feeding ground, or vice versa. He is as ready to walk away from lurking danger as he is to fly from it. His stride is like that of a man, and when he runs hard it is a fleet foot that overtakes him. Though his shanks are trim, his thighs are thick and powerful; they have the resiliency of steel, and the owner can spring and bounce 10 feet in air when he takes to dancing or reconnoitering. But if he is strong and able afoot, on the wing he is superb. Though apparently slow in flight, it is necessary only

to time him over a mile or see him fan by at close range to realize that his huge
wing-planes, though slow in action, really propel him forward at a goodly speed.
Owing to his far-extended frame he has not the same aerial fighting powers as
the more solidly built gray goose, and thus can not combat a gale so sturdily.
Nevertheless it is in the wind that one sees him at his best—a display of aerial
skill surpassed by but few birds indeed.

Like most feathered navigators of the air that hover or circle much, the crane
matches one opposition against the other to his own profit.   Gravity tends to
drag his huge bulk down; the strong air current, striking the under side of his
upward-slanting planes and body, tends to lift him kitelike.   Thus matching
one force against the other enables him to hang almost suspended in midair.
His long rudder-legs trail far astern, his slender neck is far outthrust ahead (not
crooked back after the manner of the heron or the stork); so he rocks back and
forth, changing the angle of his planes to suit the air current and performs prod-
igies of flight.   In swinging spirals, with scarce a wing motion to indicate the
power of his flight muscles, he ascends or descends airily, easily.   He is the original aeroplane; the man-made product, in spite of its motor, is an infringement.
Almost equally wondrous are his sky-chasing flights on calm days.   Daily in
August and early September, when his clans are gathering, it is his custom, if the
day is hot and clear, to rise about noon and circle dizzily at a vast height—so
high that often his figure is lost to view, and even his trumpet croak faint to the
ear.   On the spiralled ascent he swings around and around, after the manner of
the hawks, apparently getting power from some mysterious source; on the descent
he arches his wings downward and sweeps back and forth in short circles.

As to its powers of vison, the same writer says:

His great stature gives him the range almost of that of a man; his eye is won-
drously keen, telescopically so; it is so near the top of his head that he can peer
over the crest of a knoll and see without being seen, and its clear amber yellow
suggests an owllike vision at night.   Though he is big and tall, he is really not
easily seen, for his coat is one of nature's triumphs of protective coloration.   Blue-
gray in tone, it is obscure always; it fades into the gray-green of the prairie even
in the brightest sunlight; it melts into the dusk of twilight or is swallowed in the
blue dome of the heavens at midday.   A sentry on the alert at all times, his
trumpet throat gives warning of danger to his kind far and near and all instantly
pay heed.

The voice of the sandhill crane is most remarkable; its loud, ringing, and sometimes musical trumpetings have great carrying power
and often can be heard long before the bird can be seen.   For a good
account of its vocal performance I must again quote from Mr. Laing
(1915):

It is a hoarse, unnatural croak that rips from the throat, a vibrant puttering
that seems to suggest something prehistoric—such a call as one might expect that
our far-gone ancestors heard in the days when pterodactyls and their kind flew
about the marshes.   His vocabulary is limited to a code of signals, but it is all
sufficient for his needs.   A few of his more common calls might be syllablized
as:

"Gar-oo-oo-oo-oo!   Gar-oo-oo-oo!"—the fair-weather, sky-scraping call uttered
in the heavens.

"Hur-roo-oo-roo-roo!"—a broken, three-word call of inquiry when one flock on
the wing seeks another far below.

"Kit-er-roo-oo-oo!"—"Danger!   Look out for yourself!"

"A-rook-crook-crook! A-rook-crook-crook!"—"Come on; safe feeding here"—the invitation call uttered in stentorian tones on the field in the morning.

Then also there are short guttural croakings and putterings, conversational exchanges while the birds are feeding; and, in addition, the youngsters have a plaintive, absurd little whistle.

Fall.—According to Seton (Thompson 1890):

The young cranes are apparently strong on the wing in August, for at this time small bands of the species may be seen sailing high over the prairie, apparently strengthening their wings before they are compelled to journey southward for the season. As September draws nigh their numbers are increased, and the long array of the grand birds present a most imposing spectacle as in serpentine lines they float away after the sun.

W. Leon Dawson (1909) writes:

Prior to leaving the breeding grounds for the winter season, the cranes are aid to assemble for a stately promenade, which is the "swell" function of the year. When the clan is fully assembled, and after much preliminary sociability, the great company takes to wing and rises in majestic circles. These spirals are continued until a considerable height is attained with a great ado of sonorous croaking, a solemn leave taking of the happy scenes of youth, after which the birds move southward.

Doctor Coues (1874) says:

Late in September and early in October numbers of this species and *G. americana* together were migrating through the same region; they appeared to journey chiefly by night. Often, as we lay encamped on the Mouse River, the stillness of midnight would be broken by the hoarse, rattling croaks of cranes coming overhead, the noise finally dying in the distance, to be succeeded by the shrill pipe of numberless waders, the honking of geese, and the whistle of the pinions of myriads of wild fowl that shot past, sounding to sleepy ears like the rushing sound of a far away locomotive.

The sandhill cranes that breed in Florida are permanently resident there and to what extent their numbers are increased in winter by migrants from the North is an open question. Now that this species has been so thoroughly extirpated in the eastern prairie regions, the birds which breed in the Northwest may all migrate to Louisiana, Texas, and Mexico, rather than to Florida. Mr. Moore says in his notes:

I do not believe the migrators ever extend their southern sojourn so far south as this bay (Sarasota), as no increase in numbers occurs during that time among those seen here, and no movement is observed among them to excite such a presumption. These birds are never seen to soar high in the air in flocks, at any time of the year, as the migrators may be seen frequently to do in their southern winter home in Louisiana, Texas, and other States; one or a pair only have I ever seen moving thus, not intent on travel, but simply circling for "an airing," as it were.

Game.—The sandhill crane combines many of the qualities of a fine game bird. There is pleasure to be derived in the pursuit of what is difficult to obtain, and certainly the cranes give plenty of opportunities to practice patience, skill, and ingenuity in outwitting them. In the open places where they live they can exercise to the best advantage their keen eyesight and acute sense of hearing. They are constantly on the alert to detect the slighest movement or sound and are suspicious of everything new or strange. In proportion to their size their flight is slow and steady; so they are not difficult to hit; but it is a real problem to get them to come near enough to shoot. For a good account of the difficulties to be encountered I would refer the reader to Mr. Laing's (1915) interesting paper, referred to above, relating his adventures while hunting cranes with a camera, in which he was finally successful.

The best places for hunting cranes are the big grain fields of the prairie regions, after the crops have been harvested in the fall, to which the cranes resort at certain hours during the day, early morning, and late afternoon, to feed on the fallen grain, wheat, barley, or corn among the stubble. Sometimes a pit is dug in the ground, such as is used for goose shooting, but this must be artfully concealed to escape detection. Better success can be had by utilizing, as a blind, one of the numerous corn shocks left standing in some corn field which the cranes are frequenting. The hunter must be well concealed in his blind long before daylight and wait quietly and patiently for his best chance, for he is not likely to have more than one. The crafty, old scouts are sure to inspect the field critically before reporting that it is safe for the main flight to come in. Their system of sentinels and patrols is most complete and very efficient. If the hunter succeeds in outwitting them all and brings to bag one or two of the big birds, fattened on ripe grain, he will be rewarded with a feast worthy of his efforts.

DISTRIBUTION

The ranges of the two forms proposed by Mr. Peters (1925) are given separately below, under the new names used by him. Both are here treated as subspecies of the little brown crane, which is probably correct.

MEGALORNIS CANADENSIS MEXICANUS

Range.—Southern Canada, the United States, and Mexico.

Breeding range.—North to British Columbia (158-mile House and Lac la Hache); Alberta (Innisfail); Saskatchewan (Big Quill Lake, Balgonie and Kutanajan Lake); Manitoba (Shell River, Oak Point, Crescent Lake, and Ossawo); Minnesota (Herman, Elk River, and probably Lake Minnetonka); Wisconsin (Plover, Marquette, and Peshtigo); Michigan (Taquamenou River, Vans Harbor, Sheldrake Lake, Morrice, and Petersburg); and Ontario (Rond Eau). East to Ontario (Rond Eau); and Ohio (near Toledo). South to Nebraska

(Alda and Omega); Colorado (Loveland, Middle Park, Gunnison, and San Juan County); Arizona (Mormon Lake); Nevada (Independence Valley and Carson); and California (Fort Crook). West to California (Fort Crook and Tule Lake); Oregon (Fort Klamath, Malheur Lake, and Camp Harney); Washington (Fort Simcoe, Fort Steilacoom, Coulee City, and near the Strait of Juan de Fuca); and British Columbia (New Westminister, Lac la Hache, and 158-mile House).

The above outline indicates the former breeding range of this species for at the present time its habitat is greatly restricted. It is now known to breed in only southern Canada, Minnesota, and the western and Rocky Mountain States south to northern Colorado.

Winter range.—North to California (Modesto, Fresno, and San Jacinto Lake); Arizona (near Avondale); and Texas (Eagle Pass and Fredericksburg). East to Texas (Fredericksburg, Corpus Christi, and Brownsville); and probably Yucatan (Tizimin). South to probably Yucatan (Tizimin); San Louis Potosi (Angostura); Guanajuato; Jalisco (La Barca); Sinaloa (Mazatlan); and Lower California (Colorado River delta). West to Lower California (Colorado River delta); and California (Pilot Knob, San Jacinto Lake, Pasadena, Fresno, Salton Sea, and Modesto). Accidental in winter at the mouth of the Columbia River, Oregon (January 2, 1806), and at Alda, Nebraska.

Spring migration.—The sandhill cranes usually leave the vicinity of San Antonio, Texas, by February 21, the last birds passing Fredericksburg by April 10.

Early dates of arrival are: Arkansas, Delight, March 12, 1911, and Newport, March 19, 1884; Kentucky, Eubank, March 8, 1894; Missouri, Gilman City, February 28, 1911, St. Louis, March 4, 1882, Bolton, March 5, 1895, Fayette, March 19, 1888, and La Clede, March 20, 1889; Illinois, Odin, February 19, 1890, Mount Carmel, March 1, Tampico, March 8, 1887; Florida, March 19, 1888, and Griggsville, March 24, 1884; Indiana, Rochester, March 4, 1891, and Bicknell, March 18, 1906; Ohio, Alliance, March 23, 1886; Michigan, Locke, February 19, 1857, Petersburg, March 9, 1898, and Ann Arbor, March 24, 1911; Iowa, Jefferson, March 8, 1889, Wall Lake, March 8, 1907, Boone, March 10, 1887, Grinnell, March 11, 1890, and Storm Lake, March 12, 1887; Wisconsin, Milford, March 13, 1851, Westfield, March 24, 1914, Elkhorn, March 25, 1910, North Freedom, March 25, 1902, and Delavan, March 30, 1896; Minnesota, Waverly, March 22, 1889, Elk River, March 22, 1887, Fairmont, March 24, 1916, White Earth, March 27, 1881, Lake Wilson, March 28, 1910, Minneapolis, March 29, 1880, and Wilder, March 30, 1895; Texas, Grapevine, March 1, 1916, and Gainesville, March 2, 1887; Oklahoma. Caddo.

February 26, 1884; Kansas, Onaga, February 14, 1896, Girard, March 8, 1911, Richmond, March 11, 1885, North Topeka, March 16, 1891, Bucklin, March 21, 1907, Oswego, March 28, 1889, and Lawrence, April 2, 1906; Nebraska, Pullman, February 22, 1916, Long Pine, March 5, 1896, Gibbon, March 9, 1902, Turlington, March 12, 1898, Alda, March 14, 1884, Red Cloud, March 20, 1916, and Nenzel, March 23, 1920; South Dakota, Forestburg, March 12, 1913, Pitpodie, March 13, 1889, Harrison, March 26, 1890, Sioux Falls, March 29, 1908, Vermilion, March 31, 1912, Spencer, April 1, 1916, Lacreek, April 2, 1914, and White, April 3, 1888; North Dakota, Marstonmoor, March 21, 1910, Bathgate, April 5, 1894, Valley City, April 8, 1887, Argusville, April 8, 1895, Devils Lake, April 11, 1903, Chase Lake, April 12, 1913, Larimore, April 12, 1890, and Antler, April 12, 1907; Manitoba, Pilot Mound, March 23, 1905, Alexander, March 26, 1895, Margaret, April 2, 1918, Aweme, April 6, 1905, Reaburn, April 7, 1894, Killarney, April 7, 1912, Shell River, April 14, 1891, Oak Point, April 15, 1885, Neepawa, April 17, 1896, and Portage la Prairie, April 21, 1884; Saskatchewan, Indian Head, April 5, 1912, and South Qu'Applle, April 5, 1913; New Mexico, State College, March 11, 1915; Arizona, Tombstone, February 13, 1910; Colorado, Springfield, February 13, 1908, Monte Vista, March 16, 1889, Coventry, March 20, 1908, Durango, March 21, 1917, and near Denver, April 21, 1907; Idaho, Neeley, March 5, 1914, and Meridian, March 16, 1916; Montana, Fort Shaw, February 28, 1868, Great Falls, March 12, 1905, Big Sandy, April 6, 1905, Billings, April 8, 1918, and Deer Lodge, April 16, 1911; Alberta, Veteran, April 8, 1918, Alliance, April 9, 1918, Flagstaff, April 10, 1916, and Fort Vermilion, May 2, 1911; Oregon, Forest Grove, February 23, 1886, Malheur Lake, March 8, 1916, Narrows, March 9, 1914, and Klamath Falls, March 14, 1910; Washington, Puyallup, March 31, 1915, and North Yakima, April 7, 1915; and British Columbia, Okanagan Landing, March 30, 1907, Osoyoos Lake, April 19, 1908, Vaseaux Lake, April 26, 1917, and Metlakatla, April 30, 1907.

Fall migration.—Late dates of departure are: Minnesota, Wilder, November 1, 1894, Lake Andrews, November 8, 1890, and Heron Lake, November 9, 1885; Wisconsin, Delavan, October 23, 1892; Iowa, Washta, October 14, 1913, Emmetsburg, October 24, 1922, Fairfield, November 7, 1892, and Grinnell, November 22, 1887; Michigan, Unadilla, October 25, 1900, and Manchester, November 24, 1896; Ohio, Canton, November 5, 1911, Chardon, November 7, 1888, and Medina, November 8, 1920; Indiana, Waterloo, September 7, 1904, and Bicknell, October 27, 1894; Illinois, Bureau, October 27, 1906, and Rantoul, October 29, 1917; Missouri, Fayette, October 20, 1885, Waverly, October 25, 1890, Cape Girardeau, November 18, 1820; Saskatchewan, Eastend, October 11, 1910, and South Qu'Appelle, October 21,

1907; Manitoba, Killarney, October 8, 1913, Margaret, October 18, 1912, Aweme, October 31, 1900, and Alexander, November 5, 1894; North Dakota, Argusville, October 2, 1885, Antler, October 10, 1908, Keene, October 14, 1913, Westhope, October 16, 1910, Chase Lake, October 22, 1913, and Marstonmoor, October 25, 1909; South Dakota, Huron, October 11, 1887, Wall Lake, October 12, 1908, Sioux Falls, October 22, 1908, Forestburg, October 23, 1905, Harrison, November 3, 1891, and White, November 7, 1889: Nebraska, Long Pine, October, 10, 1898, Whitman, October 15, 1915, Red Cloud, October 20, 1903, Valentine, October 22, 1914, Lincoln, October 27, 1899, and Belvidere, November 3, 1891; Kansas, North Topeka, October 24, 1890, Onaga, October 30, 1897, Lawrence, October 31, 1905, and Richmond, November 3, 1885; Oklahoma, Caddo, November 11, 1884; British Columbia, Okanagan Landing, November 12, 1918; Oregon, Arlington, October 25, 1919, Klamath Falls, October 20, 1912, and Klamath Lake, November 8, 1914; Alberta, Veteran, October 16, 1918; Montana, Terry, November 10, 1903; Idaho, Meridian, November 1, 1914, and Rupert, November 11, 1911; Colorado, Beloit, October 9, 1889, Beulah, October 19, 1904, and West Mountain Valley, November 15, 1899, and New Mexico, near Socorro, December 16, 1846.

Casual records.—There is a record of the occurrence of the sandhill crane in the District of Columbia, sometime prior to 1861; one near Waynesburg, Pennsylvania, in May, 1902; one near Cohoes, New York, in October, 1892; one at Natic, Rhode Island, October 1, 1889; one at Buzzards Bay, Massachusetts, in October 1890; one at Lunenburg, Vermont; one at Wakefield, New Hampshire, in 1896 or 1897; and at Guelph and Beaumauris, Ontario.

Egg dates.—Manitoba and Saskatchewan: 14 records, May 5 to June 12; 7 records, May 27 to June 2. Iowa: 5 records, May 2 to 27. Oregon: 8 records, April 14 to May 30.

MEGALORNIS CANADENSIS PRATENSIS

Range.—The Florida sandhill crane is a resident subspecies confined to the southeastern United States, probably including the coastal regions of Alabama and Louisiana.

The range extends north to Georgia (Okefinokee Swamp). East to Florida (Micanopy, Lake Monroe, Lake Kissimmee, Micco, and Fort Pierce). South and west to Florida (Fort Myers, Charlotte Harbor, Miakka, Tarpon Springs, and Cedar Keys); probably Alabama (Perdido Bay); and probably Louisiana (Houma, Calcasieu Pass, and Cameron Parish).

In winter cranes have been noted at Waverly, Mississippi, Mer Rouge, Louisiana, and Sabine Pass, Texas.

Sandhill cranes formerly in the collections of the Charleston Museum and reported to have been taken on the Waccamau River, South Carolina, were probably wanderers of this race.

Egg dates.—Florida: 89 records, January 28 to August; 45 records, February 23 to March 21.

Family ARAMIDAE, Courlans

ARAMUS VOCIFERUS VOCIFERUS (Latham)

LIMPKIN

HABITS

"The voice of one crying in the wilderness" is the first impression one gets of this curious bird in the great inland swamps of Florida. While exploring the intricate channels, half choked with aquatic vegetation, that wound their way among the willow islands in the extensive marshes of the upper St. Johns, we frequently heard and occasionally caught a glimpse of this big, brown, rail-like bird; it peered and nodded at us from the shore of some little island, or went flying off with deliberate wing beats over the tops of the bushes; once one perched on the top of a small willow and looked at us.

The limpkin, or crying bird, as it has been called most appropriately, was once very abundant in Florida, but for the past 40 years or more it has been steadily decreasing in numbers. It is so tame and unsuspicious, almost foolishly so, and it flies so slowly, that it has been an easy mark for the thoughtless gunner who shoots at every large bird he sees, especially if it is good to eat. The flesh of the limpkin has been much esteemed as food and in many places it has been hunted as a game bird. It was decidedly scarce when I was in Florida, in 1902, and had practically disappeared from all regions within easy reach of civilization.

T. Gilbert Pearson, who has recently been investigating the status of the limpkin in Florida, writes to me:

In May, 1921, I left Leesburg, Florida, in a motor boat, crossed Lake Griffin and descended the Oklawaha River to its confluence with the St. Johns River. During this trip of three days, in which a constant lookout was kept for limpkins, only 11 individuals were seen and another was heard calling one morning near our camp. Three of the birds were so tame that it would have been very easy to have shot them from the boat with a .22 rifle. In one case we passed within 40 feet of a limpkin sitting on a dead limb. The noise of the motor boat did not even cause it to leave its perch. Natives along the river told me the bird was excellent for food and some years ago it was not an uncommon custom to shoot 20 or 30 before breakfast. On March 30, 1923, I secured a small boat at the town of Kissimmee and traveled southward through a series of three lakes until we entered Kissimmee River. This we followed to its mouth in the waters of Lake Okechobee River. Five days were spent on the trip. Limpkins were in evidence and very noisy. Although weather conditions as well as the surroundings and methods of our travel were very favorable for seeing the birds along the river and canals or streams connecting the lakes, only 41 were discovered. The bird is so easily killed, so highly esteemed as food, and is found in a State where so little attention is paid to the enforcement of the bird and game laws, the prospects of its long survival are not at all encouraging.

Nesting.—Audubon (1840) says of the nesting habits of the limpkin:

The nest of this bird is placed among the larger tufts of the tallest grasses that grow at short distances from the bayous, many of which are influenced by the low tides of the Gulf. It is so well fastened to the stems of the plants, in the same manner as that of *Rallus crepitans*, as to be generally secure from inundation; and is composed of rank weeds matted together, and forming a large mass, with a depression in the center. The eggs, which rarely exceed five or six, are large for the size of the bird. The young are hatched early in May, and follow their parents soon after birth.

Thomas H. Jackson (1887) gives a somewhat different impression; he writes:

For a nesting place this bird chooses a secluded spot where intruders are not likely to venture, on the bank of a river or a slough, often overhanging the waters and surrounded by a bottom of mud so deep that only a boat can give access to it. Several pairs often nest close together in the manner of herons, though isolated nests are frequently observed. The nest is composed of pieces of dead vines, dry leaves, and old vegetation of various kinds loosely constructed, and is generally bedded on a mass of vines and from 5 to 8 feet from the ground.

C. J. Pennock has sent me some extensive notes on his experience with the limpkin, from which I quote as follows:

During the latter part of March, 1924, the writer had an opportunity, for the first time, to form an interesting acquaintance, lasting but five or six days however, with individuals of this species in a vast marsh in southeastern Florida. We found probably eight or ten pairs of the birds scattered over different sections of what may be roughly estimated as 25 square miles of the marsh. Four days of this time, March 22, 24, 25, and 26, were spent traversing this area in a small boat propelled by poling, as oars were impossible in almost all places on account of the matted growths of water hyacinths, water lilies, yellow spatter docks, and various other forms of aquatic plants usually grouped in name as "bonnets" by natives of the district. So far as observed the limpkins confined their activities to the broad open reaches of marsh where we found numerous tracts of saw grass and clumps of myrtle. The nests, of which we found six or seven, were invariably in the tall saw grass. A bulky platform was lashed securely to the upright growing stems by interlacing the blades. On this were laid broken leaves and stems to make a secure receptacle which was but slightly depressed like a shallow plate. The whole quite in the form of the more common type of nest of the clapper rail, as I have noted it along the Gulf coast of Florida. All of the nests seen were in coarser, taller groups of saw grass growing in water 18 inches to 2 feet or more in depth and were placed only a step or two back from the open water. But three of the nests found contained eggs; one held five the others had four each, all others were about completed. Nesting did not appear to be communal. No two nests were nearer than a half mile of one another, but the scarcity of the birds might account for such happening. With birds as numerous as different persons related and saw grass in no greater abundance than was seen, the probabilities are that in former years these birds did nest in colonies or at least several pairs in close proximity. No bird was seen on the nest but three were flushed at different places as we approached the clumps of saw grass where we presently located nests. In one instance we had pushed our boat through a narrow deep channel by the side of great bunches of saw grass 10 to 12 feet in height and a limpkin flew with raucous calls from 15 to 20 yards back in the pond. Passing that way later we discovered the nest directly alongside of the channel and so near we could reach into it from the boat. This nest was nearer the water than any other we saw and was scarcely a platform-built structure but placed low down among the stems of the saw grass about a foot from the surface of the water.

Frederic H. Kennard has sent me the following notes on a nest he found, near the north shore of Lake Okeechobee, on April 4, 1914, in an unusual location:

While coming out of a creek called Limpkin Creek, Tom spied what looked like a nest, about 15 feet up, among some vines in a myrtle tree beside the stream. I thought it was no nest until I could see the tail of a bird protruding from the edge of the possible nest. We returned to the place and flushed a limpkin crying from the nest. I climbed to the nest and found it a frail structure of fresh twigs, containing one fresh egg. The female was flying about, crying and perching on neighboring bushes and trees, and evidently in great distress of mind. The nest was about 15 feet or more from the ground, placed in a thick clump of what looked like matrimony vine (I don't know that matrimony vine grows in Florida) in the crotch of a black gum sapling that was growing right up through the myrtle tree, all of which grew at the very top of a high bank bordering the creek. The vines were so thick and the nest so thin that it made no showing at all, and only the bird's tail revealed it.

Oscar E. Baynard, who has probably had more experience with the nesting habits of the limpkin than any other living collector, made two unsuccessful attempts to show me an occupied nest of this species in Florida, in the spring of 1925. On March 30 we explored some 8 miles of the Wekiva River in Orange County. It is a beautiful river of clear spring water, winding its picturesque course through a splendid swampy forest of large cypress, maples, water oaks, hickories, ashes, magnolias, and a few cabbage palmettos and pines; the banks are lined with dense shrubbery and are overgrown with tangles of morning glories, cat briars and poison ivy; and the stream is partially choked with water hyacinths, "bonnets," and "lettuce." He pointed out several ideal nesting sites for limpkins, but we saw only one bird and found no nests.

On April 19 we explored the Weekiwachee River, in Hernando County, a similar river, but not so heavily forested and bordered in places with open saw-grass marshes. Here we saw only three birds and found two or three old nests. One of these was placed on an old stump and the others were on low bushes, in dense tangles of morning glory vines; large quantities of Spanish moss had been used in building the nests, which were close to the bank of the stream or on a little islet in it.

Eggs.—The limpkin lays from four to eight eggs; the larger numbers are comparatively rare. The shape is ovate, somewhat rounded, and the shell is smooth with a slight gloss. The ground color varies from "deep olive buff" or "cream buff" to "cartridge buff." Some eggs are splashed, chiefly near the larger end, with longitudinal blotches of drabs and dull browns, such as "vinaceous drab," "drab-grays," "buffy brown," and "wood brown." Others are more clearly spotted with the same colors; and some are boldly spotted or blotched at the large end with darker browns, "burnt umber," "warm sepia," or "bone brown." The measurements of 40 eggs average 59.4 by 43.8 millimeters; the eggs showing the four extremes measure **64** by 42.8, 62.5 by **47, 57** by 42, 57.5 by **40.5** millimeters.

Plumages.—The downy young limpkin is completely covered with long, thick, soft down; the color of the upper parts varies from "cinnamon brown" to "snuff brown"; it is paler on the sides of the head and belly and almost white on the chin. The body plumage is acquired first and the wings last; the bird is fully grown before the wings are half grown. The juvenal plumage is much like that of the adult, in general appearance, except that it is softer and looser in texture and the white markings on the back are smaller and more restricted. A complete molt during the first spring, when the young bird is about a year old, produces the adult plumage.

Adults have a complete prenuptial molt, from February to April, and a complete post-nuptial molt from August to November, with no great seasonal difference in plumage.

Food.—The limpkin seems to feed mainly on animal food, which it finds in the swamps where it lives, such as various mollusks, crustaceans, frogs, lizards, worms, and aquatic insects. Audubon (1840) says:

The Everglades abound with a species of large greenish snail, on which these birds principally feed; and, from the great number of empty shells which are found at the foot of the nest and around it, it is probable that the sitting bird is supplied with food by her mate.

Dr. Henry Byrant (1861) writes:

On the St. Johns it feeds principally on a species of *Natica*, which is extremely abundant, and also on the small Unios. The large green snail, so common in the Everglades, is not very often met with on the St. Johns. Its manner of feeding is to hold the shell in one of its feet, and then with a few blows of its powerful bill to detach the animal, which it immediately swallows. All the specimens I killed had the stomach filled with more or less digested remains of various mollusks—principally Unios.

It is easy to detect the presence of limpkins by looking for the deposits of the empty shells of these snails. The birds have favorite feeding places where they bring the snails; one can often find a number of empty shells around some old log or snag or on an open place on a bank.

Behavior.—Under the old name, courlan, which seems much more appropriate tnan the local nickname, limpkin, Audubon (1840) gives us a good account of the behavior of this species, as follows:

The flight of the scolopaceous courlan is heavy and of short duration; the concavity and shortness of its wings, together with the nature of the places which it inhabits, probably rendering it slow to remove from one spot to another, on wing, it being in a manner confined among tall plants, the roots of which are frequently under water. When it rises spontaneously it passes through the air, at a short distance above the weeds, with regular beats of the wings, its neck extended to its full length, and its long legs dangling beneath, until it suddenly drops to the ground. Few birds then excel it in speed, as it proceeds, if pursued, by long strides, quickly repeated, first in a direct course, along paths formed by itself when passing and repassing from one place to another, and afterwards diverging so as to ensure its safety even when chased by the best dogs, or other not less eager enemies inhabiting the half-submerged wilderness which it has chosen for its residence. When accidently surprised, it rises obliquely out of its recess, and the neck greatly bent downward, and although its legs dangle for awhile, they are afterwards extended behind in the manner of those of the heron tribe. At such times these birds are easily shot; but if they are only wounded, it would be in vain to pursue them. Although of considerable size and weight, they are enabled, by the great length and expansion of their toes, to walk on the broad leaves of the larger species of Nymphaea found in that country. They swim with the same buoyancy as the coots, gallinules, and rails.

William Brewster (1881) writes attractively about it, as follows:

But if our presence was a matter of indifference to the birds just mentioned we certainly were not ignored by the vigilant courlans, for any sudden noise, like the splash of a paddle in the water or the rapping of its handle against the boat, was sure to be instantly followed by a piercing *"kur-r-ee-ow, kurr-r-ee-ow, kurr-r-ee-ow, kr-ow, kr-ow,"* from the nearest thicket; or perhaps several would cry out at once as rails will do on similar occasions. For the most part the birds kept closely hidden but at length we discovered one feeding on the shore. His motions were precisely similar to those of a rail, as he skirted the oozy brink, lifting and putting down his feet with careful deliberation. Occasionally he detected and seized a snail, which was quickly swallowed, the motion being invariably accompanied by a comical side shake of the bill, apparently expressive of satisfaction, though it was.perhaps designed to remove any particles of mud that may have adhered to his unique food. Finally he spied us and walked up the inclined trunk of a fallen tree to its shattered end where he stood for a moment tilting his body and jerking up his tail. Then he uttered a hoarse rattling cry like the gasp of a person being strangled, at the same time shaking his head so violently that his neck seemed in imminent danger of dislocation. Just as we were nearly within gun range he took wing, with a shriek that might have been heard for half a mile. His flight was nearly like a heron's, the wings being moved slowly and occasionally held motionless during intervals of sailing. Shortly afterwards another, his mate probably, was detected under a palmetto leaf near at hand. In the shadow her form was dimly outlined and she stood perfectly motionless, evidently relying upon concealment for protection, but her quick eye took in every suspicious movement and at length, conscious that she was seen, she ran rapidly for a few paces and launched into the air, following the course taken by the first. He is perfectly at home in the tops of the tallest trees where he walks among the twigs with all the ease of a heron or stands motionless on some horizontal branch with one leg drawn up and the curved bill resting on his breast. These elevated perches are generally resorted to at daybreak. The people told us that when the country was first settled the "Limpkins," as they are called from their peculiar halting gait, were so tame that they could frequently be caught on their nests, but incessant persecution has had the usual result and they are now at all times among the most wary of birds.

Dr. Bryant (1861) says of its voice:

The common note of this bird is the most disagreeable of any of our native birds, and resembles more that of the peacock than that of any other bird I am acquainted with; it is if anything more powerful, and equally harsh and disagreeable. It is very fond of uttering it. Besides this, which I presume is the call note, it makes a number of other sounds, all of the most inharmonious description, but of which I can convey no correct idea.

Mr. Pennock says in his notes:

Our introduction to the bird was a self-announcement of his presence which came in no uncertain notes from afar across the open stretch. If this bird was located where the guide pointed out, he was at least three-quarters of a mile distant and at other times, by the same authority, they were heard at even greater distances. At any rate their notes are far-reaching, are strident, and have great volume— a prolonged wail "*curr-r-u-ck*" perhaps might give an idea of the call as we heard it most frequently, but the guide insisted I have not heard the "sure enuf" cry, nor did I until some days later; then a wounded bird which fell in the water near the boat sent forth repeated and most terriffic clarionlike screams, more prolonged and earpiercing than we had previously heard and which I was informed were the "sure enuf thing." Several of the birds seen were discovered by their loud calls and were found to be perched aloft in or near the tops of the myrtle clumps, usually so high up as to be seen for a long distance—not infrequently for a half mile—and several times when a bird was alarmed and flew up from the grass pond it made for such a refuge and gave close attention to our approach, as we came across open water in the boat. At times we could pole within 50 yards of one of these perching birds and again they flew while we were yet 150 yards distant. Always such birds sent forth their shrill, rolling calls from on high whether they were approached or not, perhaps an indication of nervous apprehension.

DISTRIBUTION

Breeding range.—The interior of the peninsula of Florida and southeastern Georgia (Okefinokee Swamp). The breeding birds of the West Indies and Central America are now considered subspecifically distinct.

Winter range.—The same as the breeding range. This is a nonmigratory species.

Casual records.—Has wandered in winter to the Florida Keys and the Dry Tortugas; and to South Carolina (Aiken County, October 18, 1890). The record for Brownsville, Texas, May 29, 1889, refers to the Central American form.

Egg dates.—Florida: 80 records, January 3 to August 2; 40 records, March 19 to April 20.

Family RALLIDAE, Rails, Gallinules and Coots

RALLUS ELEGANS Audubon

KING RAIL

HABITS

This large, handsome rail is an inhabitant of the freshwater marshes of the interior. It is never seen in the salt marshes of the coast except on migrations or in winter and even then it prefers fresh water. Audubon (1840) has well described its favorite haunts, in the words of his friend Bachman, as follows:

Wherever there are extensive marshes by the sides of sluggish streams, where the bellowings of the alligator are heard at intervals, and the pipings of myriads of frogs fill the air, there is found the fresh-water marsh hen, and there it may be seen gliding swiftly among the tangled rank grasses and aquatic weeds, or standing on the broad leaves of the yellow *cyamus* and fragrant *water lily*, or forcing its way through the dense foliage of *pontederiae* and *sagittariae*. There, during the sickly season, it remains secure from the search of man, and there, on some hillock or little island of the marsh, it builds its nest. In such places I have found so many as 20 pairs breeding within a space having a diameter of 30 yards.

Arthur T. Wayne (1910) says:

This fine species, which is locally known as the fresh water marsh hen, is abundant on abandoned rice plantations and in ponds of fresh water where there s a dense growth of reeds and water plants. It is a permanent resident, but during protracted droughts is forced to migrate from the ponds in order to procure food and water. On the freshwater rivers it is most numerous, and breeds in numbers.

C. J. Pennock tells me that in Florida, near St. Marks and about Punta Gorda, the habitats of the two large rails come together, or even overlap, in the marshes of the tidal rivers and creeks. The clapper rails fairly swarm, where the marshes are in wide open areas, even well up the rivers; but, at the first appearance of wooded tracts along these waterways, the clapper rails disappear and are replaced by the king rails. He found the latter nesting regularly in a small pond, near one of these creeks, which was usually fresh, but at high tides it became salty.

Nesting.—The only nest of a king rail that I have ever seen was shown to me by Oscar E. Baynard, near Plant City, Florida, on March 30, 1925. He had found it while investigating a colony of 80 pairs of boat-tailed grackles in an extensive swamp overgrown mainly with pickerel weed (*Pontederia*), a scattered growth of small "ty-ty" bushes and a few flags (*Typhus*). The nest was in the midst of the colony of grackles, which had nests in the bushes, and was not far from a least bittern's nest. It was beautifully concealed in a thick growth of pickerel weed, which grew all around and over it. It was well made of the dead, dry stems of pickerel weed, and flags and was deeply hollowed; it measured 8 inches in diameter and the rim was about 8 inches above the water, which was about a foot deep. It contained nine practically fresh eggs. The rail was heard, but not seen.

T. E. McMullen tells me that in New Jersey it nests in or near marshes in grass tussocks, sedge tussocks, or water arum, where the nests are built up from 6 to 18 inches above shallow water.

William B. Crispin wrote to me in 1913 that it was then a common resident of Salem County, New Jersey, and that it builds its nest in the tussocks or the thick grasses of a fresh water marsh or meadow; the nest is lined with a few dry grasses, arched over and well concealed by the green grasses about it.

Mr. Wayne (1910) says that, in South Carolina, "numerous nests" that he has "found have been invariably placed in rushes or button-wood bushes, 8 inches to a foot and a half over water."

Referring to the nesting habits of the king rail in Henry County, Illinois, A. C. Murchison (1895) writes:

Around the edge of the marsh are a number of large ponds, and on the side of these where the water was not over a foot or so deep, or any place in a shallow pond and even in the fields, we found the nests. The nests in the ponds were placed in clumps of coarse rushes or cat-tails, and from 3 to 8 inches above the water. Some of the dead rushes were bent down to form a slight platform in the middle of the clump, and on this the nest material of rushes and grass was laid to a thickness of from 1 to 4 inches, hollowed just enough to hold the eggs. The nests found on the ground were placed in slight hollows scratched by the birds in a thick clump of grass and lined with dead grass, forming a close mat from 1 to 3 inches thick. In all cases where the set was complete the rushes were very neatly interwoven to form a canopy that very often led to the detection of the nest. I think the grass canopy is usually the sign of a full set, as it is not often found over a small number of fresh eggs.

Eggs.—The king rail lays from 6 to 15 eggs, from 8 to 11 being the commonest numbers. They are ovate in shape and the shell is smooth and slightly glossy. The ground color averages lighter than in eggs of the clapper rails, but not so light as in those of the California species; it is pale buff, varying from "cream buff" to "pale olive buff." They are sparingly and irregularly spotted, mostly in small spots, with various shades of "vinaceous drab," "army brown" and "vinaceous brown" and sometimes with a few spots of brighter browns. The measurements of 56 eggs averaged 41 by 30 millimeters; the eggs showing the four extremes measure 44 by 32, 38.5 by 28 millimeters.

Young.—The period of incubation does not seem to be known. The hatching process is well described by W. F. Henninger(1910) as follows:

A fourth nest contained two eggs and one young and while looking at the third egg I noticed a small hole and soon had the chance to see a young rail chick's bill pecking away at its inclosure. The chick kept up a constant pecking and calling with a shrill voice *"peep, peep,"* till the one half of the egg, the more pointed end, dropped away. The blackish little creature showed some traces of blood and seemed to have a hard time to free itself from the membrane, and it took considerable time till it had extricated itself from the other half of the egg, the whole process occupying perhaps 16 to 20 minutes. Then it shuffled down to its brother and laid there gaping from time to time, where I left it after having seen one of the most interesting phases of wild bird life.

Audubon (1840) says:

The young, which are at first black, leave the nest as soon as they burst the shell, and follow their mother, who leads them along the borders of the streams and pools, where they find abundance of food, consisting of grass seeds, insects, tadpoles, leeches, and small crayfish. At this early period, when running among the grass, which they do with great activity, they may easily be mistaken for meadow mice.

Plumages.—In the king rail the downy young is well covered with short, thick, black down. The juvenal plumage appears first on the under parts, then on the back and still later on the head and neck; the wings appear last, when the young bird is nearly grown. In this plumage the upper parts are much like the adult, but darker; the upper back is nearly black with brown edgings; the under parts are dull white or buffy white, washed with pinkish buff or "light pinkish cinnamon" on the neck and sides; many feathers of the breast and belly are tipped with dusky; the wings are much like those of the adult, except for a few whitish tips on the median coverts, which soon wear away. During September and October progressive changes take place toward maturity, by continuous molt of the contour plumage. The pinkish buff on the under parts increases in extent and intensity during September; and the barred flanks, in dull tones, are acquired in October or a little earlier. By November the young bird is in practically adult plumage, though the colors do not attain their full brilliancy until the next molt.

Adults have a complete molt in August and September and a partial molt of the contour plumage in early spring.

Food.—Audubon (1840) says:

When grown they feed on a variety of substances, and it has appeared to me that they eat a much greater proportion of seeds and other vegetable matters than the salt-water marsh hens. It is true, however, that, in the gizzard of the latter we find portions of the *Spartina glabra;* but when that kind of food is not to be procured, which is the case during three-fourths of the year, they feed principally on "fiddlers," small fish, and mollusca. In the gizzard of the present species, besides the food already mentioned, I have always found a much greater quantity of the seeds of such grasses as grow in the places frequented by them. On one occasion I found the gizzard crammed with seeds of the cane (*Arundo tecta*); and that of another contained a large quantity of the seed of the common oat, which had evidently been picked up on a newly-sown field adjoining to the marsh.

W. Leon Dawson (1903) writes:

The food of the marsh hen consists of insects, slugs, leeches, tadpoles, and small crayfish, besides a goodly proportion of seeds from aquatic and palustral plants.   The last are obtained not only from the soft bed of ooze upon which they may have fallen, but from the seed pods themselves, since the bird can climb quite nimbly.   Like all birds of this class, the most active hours are spent just after sunset and before sunrise.   But in a region where they were in little fear of molestation, I have seen them deploy upon an extensive mud flat in broad daylight and go prodding about in company with migrant sandpipers, for the worms which riddle the ooze with their burrows.   At such times, too, I have seen a few standing stock still for a quarter of an hour at a stretch, evidently to catch a wink of sleep along with their sun bath, and trusting, perhaps, to their more vigilant neighbors to give warning of approaching danger.

Behavior.—Audubon (1840) writes:

The flight of this rail resembles that of the salt-water kind, but is considerably stronger and more protracted.   When suddenly flushed, they rise and go off with a chuck, their legs dangling beneath, and generally proceed in a straight line for some distance, after which they drop among the thickest grass, and run off with surprising speed.   In several instances they have been known to stand before a careful pointer.   They are less apt to take to the water than the *Rallus crepitans,* and are by no means so expert at diving.

Col. N. S. Goss (1891) says:

Its flights, when not suddenly started, are at dusk and during the night.   It springs into the air with dangling legs and rapid strokes of its short wings; but if going any distance, its legs, like its neck, are soon stretched out to their full extent, flying rather slowly and near the ground.   Its call note, " *Creek, creek, creek, creek,*" and of flight, " *Cark, cark, cark,*" can often be heard both night and day, and at times during the early breeding season they are almost as noisy as the guinea hens.   If it were not for its voice its presence would seldom be known, as it skulks and hides from its pursuers, and when hard pressed runs into the deeper waters within the reeds and rushes, preferring to swim (and can also dive) to taking wing, knowing well that it is safer within its watery, grassy cover, for which it is so well adapted.

Mr. Murchison (1895) refers to its notes as follows:

One of the very characteristic sounds of bird voices to be heard on the borders and nearby ponds of the large swamps in Henry County, Illinois, is the *"chuck-chuck"* of the king rail, or "stage driver," as he is called by the natives, from the almost exact imitation of the " chuck " of the plowboy to his plodding team.

Enemies.—The king rail is considered a game bird and is pursued to some extent by sportsmen.   Its flesh is said to be tender and juicy and to resemble that of the sora rail, as it is largely a vegetarian. But its flight is so slow and it is so easily killed that it is not much of a sporting proposition.

Audubon (1840) says:

These birds are rarely shot by common gunners, on account of the difficulty of raising them, and because they generally confine themselves to places so swampy and covered with briars, smilaxes, and rough weeds, that they are scarcely accessible.   But although they are thus safe from men they are not without numerous enemies.   My friend Bachman once killed a large moccasin snake, on opening which he found an old bird of this species, that had evidently been swallowed but a short time before.   Its feathers are frequently found lying on the banks of rice-fields, ponds, and lagoons, in places where the tracks of the mink plainly disclose the plunderer.   The barred owl and the great horned owl also occasionally succeed in capturing them in the dusk.   "On one occasion," says my friend Bachman, in a note addressed to me, "while placed on a stand for deer, I saw a wild cat creeping through a marsh that was near to me, evidently follow- ing by stealthy steps something that he was desirous of making his prey.   Pres- ently he made a sudden pounce into a bunch of grass, when I immediately heard the piercing cries of the marsh hen, and shortly after came passing by me the successful murderer with the bird in his mouth."

Mr. Wayne (1910) writes:

In the month of April, 1900, I was observing a nest of this species in a button- wood bush, which was in a pond of water, and, about every other day, I waded into the pond to see how many eggs were there.   About the 8th of May, I judged that the full complement of eggs would be completed, and upon visiting the nest in the afternoon which was very cloudy, I saw what I supposed to be the bird incubating.   But upon close inspection I was very much surprised to find that what I took for the bird was a huge moccasin (*Ancistrodon piscivorus*), which I promptly shot.   This snake had eaten all the eggs and perhaps caught the bird as the feathers were scattered around the nest.

DISTRIBUTION

Range.—Eastern United States, Mexico, and southeastern Canada. The Cuban bird has been separated as a new subspecies, *Rallus elegans ramsdeni* Riley.

Breeding range.—North to southern Minnesota (Jackson, Faribault, Waseca, and Minneapolis); southern Wisconsin (Madison, Janesville, Jefferson County, and Racine); southern Ontario (St. Clair Flats and Listowel); northern Ohio (Port Clinton, Middle Bass Island, and Cleveland); New York (Buffalo, Branchport, Ithaca, and near New York City); and Connecticut (Saybrook).   East to Connecticut (Saybrook); New Jersey (Avalon, Summit, Newark, and Repaupo); Pennsylvania (near Philadelphia); Maryland (Tolchester); Virginia (Wallops Island); North Carolina (Raleigh and Lake Ellis); South Carolina (Waverly Mills, Mount Pleasant, and Frogmore); Georgia (Savannah and Blackbeard Island); and Florida (Gainesville, Titus- ville, and Fort Myers).   South to Florida (Titusville, Fort Myers, Tarpon Springs, Tallahassee, and Whitfield); Alabama (Barachias, Autaugaville, Greensboro, and Mobile); Mississippi (Vicksburg); Louisiana (Calcasieu); and (rarely) Texas (Corpus Christi).   West to (rarely) Texas (Corpus Christi); Oklahoma (Wister); northwest- ern Arkansas (Eureka Springs); eastern Kansas (Wichita, Stafford County, and Manhattan); eastern Nebraska (Falls City, Lincoln, and Omaha); western Iowa (Wall Lake and probably Sioux City); and southwestern Minnesota (Heron Lake).

The king rail also has been observed or taken in South Dakota (Vermilion); North Dakota (Fargo, October 15, 1925); Minnesota (Lake Minnetonka in September 1911, and in Ottertail County); Ontario (Toronto, September, 1903, and Ottawa, May 7, 1896); Vermont (Bennington, May 1910); and Maine (several records in the vicinity of Portland).

Winter range.—Southern part of the breeding range and coast regions of Louisiana and Texas, rarely to east-central Mexico. North to Texas (Brownsville and Corpus Christi); southern Louisiana (New Orleans and Mandeville); Mississippi (Hancock County); Alabama (Greensboro); and South Carolina (Mount Pleasant). East to South Carolina (Mount Pleasant, Port Royal, and probably Frogmore); Georgia (Savannah and Blackbeard Island); and Florida (Titusville). South to Florida (Fort Myers); Louisiana (Octave Pass and Vermilion Bay); Texas (Brownsville); and rarely Mexico, Vera Cruz (Tlacotalpam).

There are also records of winter occurrence north to Virginia (Wallops Island, January 9 to February 3, 1921); Maryland (Pawtuxent River, December 16, 1889; Marshall Hall, December 2, 1914 and Cecil County, February 15, 1917); Pennsylvania (Philadelphia, December 12, 1909); New York (Greene, January 1891, and Ithaca, November 29, 1901); Connecticut (Meriden, October 14, 1914, Milford, December 15, 1892, and Saybrook, January 14, 1876); Massachusetts, Needham, October 10, 1907, Nahant, November 21, 1875, West Barnstable, December 30, 1909, Cambridge, December 30, 1896, and Ellisville, January 20, 1903); Michigan (Port Huron, December 13, 1902, Hudson, December 11, 1896, Monroe, December 12, 1908, and Detroit, February 6, 1907, and February 1909); Ontario (Point Pelee, December 31, 1906); and Wisconsin (Beaver Dam, December 19, 1906).

Spring migration.—Early dates of arrival are: Pennsylvania, Erie, April 17, 1902, and Berwyn, May 4, 1905; New Jersey, Salem, April 26, 1914, Cape May, May 6, 1880, and South Amboy, May 12, 1879; New York, Montauk Light, March 3, 1887, Geneva, April 19, 1908, and Buffalo, May 4, 1914; Arkansas, Brookland, April 29, 1914; Missouri, Fayette, April 2, 1887, Corning, April 4, 1913, and St. Louis, April 9; Illinois, Chicago, March 27, Rockford, April 3, 1887, Alton, April 5, 1894, Farina, April 10, 1897, Fernwood, April 10, 1887, Milford, April 13, 1909, Morgan Park, April 14, 1895, and Glen Ellyn, April 19, 1899; Indiana, Richmond, April 1, 1914, Worthington, April 10, 1908, Bicknell, April 7, 1921, Crawfordsville, April 12, 1921, and Indianapolis, April 15, 1916; Ohio, Medina, April 10, 1922, Circleville, April 11, 1917, Huron, April 16, 1912, Montgomery, April 18, 1895, Cleveland, April 19, 1880; Michigan, Petersburg, April 20, 1886, Vicksburg, April 23, 1911, Detroit, April 28, 1907, and Ann Arbor, May 4, 1910; Ontario, Point Pelee, April 22, 1908; and Ottawa, May 7, 1896; Iowa, Keokuk, March 27, 1894, Grinnell,

April 5, 1889, Sioux City, April 10, 1887, New Hampton, April 14, 1921, National, April 15, 1909, and Mount Vernon, April 22, 1907; Wisconsin, Burlington, April 4, 1919, Milwaukee, April 10, 1911, Madison, April 21, 1911, Whitewater, May 1, 1911, Delavan, May 3, 1896, Berlin, May 6, 1914, Elkhorn, May 8, 1909, and Racine, May 10, 1907; Minnesota, Waseca, April 15, 1893, Heron Lake, April 22, 1890, Fairmount, April 23, 1916, Hennepin County, April 27, 1890, Jackson, May 5, 1903, and Lanesboro, May 12, 1908; Kansas, Emporia, April 14, 1885, Onaga, April 23, 1891, Paola, April 28, 1918, and Wichita, May 9, 1916; and Nebraska, Falls City, April 13, 1889.

Fall migration.—Late dates of fall departure are: Nebraska, Nebraska City, September 20, 1900, Lincoln, September 22, 1890, and Gresham, September 24, 1896; Kansas, Lawrence, November 4, 1905; Oklahoma, Caddo, November 1, 1883; Minnesota, Jackson, August 25, 1902; Wisconsin, Delavan, October 22, 1894; Iowa, Keokuk, September 26, 1899, and McGregor, November 2, 1890; Ontario, Point Pelee, August 22, 1909; Michigan, Manistee, October 16, 1904, Detroit, October 30, 1904, and Ann Arbor, November 5, 1888; Ohio, Youngstown, October 7, 1916, Cedar Point, October 22, 1906, Oberlin, October 23, 1906, and Lakeside, October 30, 1918; Indiana, Indianapolis, October 4, 1914, and Richmond, November 11, 1916; Illinois, La Grange, September 28, 1914, Fernwood, October 13, 1885, Canton, October 27, 1894, and Warsaw, November 8, 1899; Connecticut, Portland, September 18, 1913, North Haven, September 26, 1905, and Meriden, October 4, 1914; New York, Amityville, September 7, 1891; New Jersey, Avalon, September 22, 1902, Camden, October 17, 1915, and Pennsville, October 20, 1914; and the District of Columbia, Washington, November 7, 1891.

Egg dates.—Illinois: 31 records, May 4 to June 26; 16 records, May 15 to June 10. Minnesota and Wisconsin: 8 records, May 21 to June 30.

RALLUS BELDINGI (Ridgway)

BELDING RAIL

HABITS

This little known species is confined, so far as we know, to the southern part of the peninsula of Lower California, from Magdalena Bay southward. It somewhat resembles the king rail, but is considerably smaller and is darker and richer in color. It is a very shy and retiring bird, living in the most inaccessible mangrove swamps in a remote region; consequently very little has ever been learned about its habits and still less has been published.

William Brewster (1902a) writes:

The type specimen of this rail was taken by Mr. Belding on Espiritu Santo Island, but Mr. Frazar found the bird only about the shores of the Bay near La Paz, where it inhabits mangrove thickets bordering mud flats or intersected by small tidal creeks. It is evidently rare here, for Mr. Frazar shot only two specimens, and saw or heard less than half a dozen in all. *R. beldingi* is probably resident wherever found, but as yet even this can not be positively asserted.

Col. John E. Thayer (1909) quotes from some notes sent to him by Wilmot W.Brown, jr., who has probably collected more of these rails than any one else, as follows:

As for the Belding rail, I found this species a most difficult one to collect on account of its retiring habits in the dense mangrove jungle, where the branches and long roots are interwoven and interlaced. You can not enter a foot without cutting with axe and machete. In my search for the nest and eggs of this rail I cut trails through various parts of the mangrove tangle, but was unable to find but an abandoned nest with two eggs which the mice had nearly destroyed. The collecting of this rail is a question of high tides. At low tide this rail can not be hunted. He keeps in the depths of the mangrove tangle where he feeds on small crabs, etc.; but when there is a very high tide the water forces him to seek his food more inland, along the shore outside of the swamp; then by careful and patient hunting you can occasionally shoot one, but it is very slow work and requires much time and patience. In fact, for a long time I thought I should be unsuccessful in. my search; for although I hunted faithfully for it over a month I was unable to find one until I thought of the high tide plan.

Eggs.—Mr. Brown found two eggs of this rail, badly eaten by mice, in a deserted nest on San Jose Island on June 28, 1908; the eggs are now in Colonel Thayer's collection. In comparing these eggs with several sets of *Rallus levipes*, Colonel Thayer wrote me that he "could see little or no difference." He describes the eggs as "oval, creamy white, and dotted and spotted sparingly with 'Hay's maroon, and 'pale mauve' markings." They measure 44.6 by 30 and 44 by 29 millimeters.

DISTRIBUTION

Range.—Cape region of Lower California. The Belding rail is a resident species, occupying both coasts of the southern part of Lower California, its range extending north (on the west coast) to Santa Margarita Island and (on the east coast) to San Jose Island.

Egg date.—Southern Lower California: 1 record, June 28.

RALLUS OBSOLETUS Ridgway

CALIFORNIA CLAPPER RAIL

HABITS

As its name implies this bird is a product of the Golden State and it never wanders far from the general vicinity of the Golden Gate. Messrs. Grinnell, Bryant, and Storer (1918) say:

No other game bird in California has so limited a distribution as has the California clapper rail. The salt marshes bordering the southern arm of San Francisco Bay and a few smaller nearby areas of the same character alone seem to afford the proper kinds of food and shelter necessary for its existence. It is found in small numbers on the marshes of Monterey Bay near Elkhorn, Monterey County, and individuals have been recorded from Tomales Bay and Humboldt Bay. The California clapper rail makes its permanent home on the salt marshes where the vegetation consists chiefly of pickleweed (*Salicornia ambigua*) and an evergreen shrub (*Grindelia cuneifolia*). Here it may easily be found at any time of the year skulking along the banks of the small muddy sloughs which penetrate the marsh in every direction.

Nesting.—The same authors refer to the nesting habits of the California clapper rail, as follows:

A high piece of marsh ground, usually on the bank of a slough, is selected for a nesting site. The nest may be concealed in salt grass or pickleweed, or under a small bush. It is a platform built up 3 to 6 inches above the ground, and measures about 10 inches across with a cavity in the center 1½ inches deep. Grasses or dead and living stems of pickleweed are used for building material. A well-marked trail leading off through the adjacent vegetation is usually discernible. A nest examined by the authors on May 7, 1914, was composed of closely matted *Salicornia* stems, some of the stems being bent over from the growing plants surrounding it. The structure was well saucered, the cavity containing the eggs being 5½ inches across and 1½ inches deep. The rim was 2½ inches above the ground which was still wet from a recent high tide. The nearest slough was 20 feet away. Like some other rails this one sometimes builds nests which it never uses. Three or four new nests, often uncompleted, apparently possessing all the advantages of the one used, are occasionally to be found in the near vicinity of an occupied nest. The female is a very close sitter and will sometimes remain on the nest until the intruder is within 2 feet of her. She will then jump from the nest and either fly away, or glide swiftly through the grass or along the edge of a slough.

Dr. Barton W. Evermann has sent me his notes on his experiences with the nesting habits of this species on Bay Farm Island, Alameda County. His records include observations on some 40 nests found during the month of April, which seems to be the height of the nesting season; he found a total of 13 nests with eggs on one day, April 9, 1916. In summarizing his notes, he says:

The dates given were probably those of the height of the nesting season. without exception the nests were under, or more or less protected by, clumps of *Salicornia* or *Grindelia*, or both. The birds would usually slink away from the nest when one came upon them cautiously. If one came upon the nest hurriedly they would leave with a rush, sometimes cackling. Bay Farm Island is, or soon will be, a thing of the past. It is being cut up into truck farms, thus destroying the best breeding grounds of this species in the State.

Eggs.—The California clapper rail lays from 5 to 14 eggs, but the usual set consists of from 8 to 10. The shape is ovate and the shell is smooth and glossy. The eggs of this and the next species are the lightest colored of any of the eggs in the clapper rail group, lighter even than those of the king rail. The ground color is pale "cartridge buff" or "ivory yellow." They are sparingly and irregularly marked with a few small blotches and spots, and a larger number of minute dots, of drab and brown, such as pale shades of "purple drab," "ecru drab," or "drab-gray," darker shades of the same colors, and various shades of dark browns, such as "chocolate" and "Vandyke brown." The measurements of 57 eggs average 44.1 by 31.3 millimeters; the eggs showing the four extremes measure **47.9** by 32.6, 46.9 by **33.4**, **41.2** by 31, 43.2 by **29.6** millimeters.

Young.—Ernest Adams (1900) says: "I have often seen two birds about a nest and I am certain that the male assists in incubation."

W. Otto Emerson (1885) has published the following interesting note regarding the young:

One nest of seven glossy jet black chicks was found, seemingly just out of the shell, one not quite dry. All but this one would hold their long necks out, moving them from side to side, and calling in a low plaintive tone *"pe–ee–ep, pe–ee–ep,"* very much like a weak young chicken. Putting these little fellows in my basket for further study at home, no more attention was paid to them until I got to my buggy, when I found two of them missing, knowing no doubt, the fate awaiting them. On skinning one I noticed a small claw sticking out from the second joint of each wing, not more than a sixteenth part of an inch long, claw part turning down, of a light horn color and comparing only to a little kitten's claw; it was found on all the chicks.

Plumages.—There are not enough specimens of the California clapper rail, in immature plumages, in eastern collections, to work out the sequence of plumages to maturity; but what material I have seen gives no reason to think that the molts and plumages are essentially different from those of the king rails and clapper rails, all of which are closely related. The downy young is black with a slight greenish gloss on the upper parts. Grinnell, Bryant, and Storer (1918) describe the juvenal plumage as "similar to that of the adult, but with streaking on back duller, less strikingly contrasted, lower surface very much lighter, more buffy in tone, and barring on sides and flanks scarcely or not at all in evidence."

Food.—According to Grinnell, Bryant, and Storer (1918), the food of the California clapper rail—

is made up almost entirely of animal matter—worms, crustaceans, and the like, as afforded on the salt marshes. In the gullet of a bird shot on a salt marsh, near an artesian well, W. E. Bryant (1893) found a good sized frog. Several stomachs from birds taken at Bay Farm Island, Alameda County, were found by us to contain only parts of crabs (*Hemigrapsus oregonensis*).

Donald A. Cohen (1895) says:

Their chief food is crustaceans, and the craws of those I shot were mostly empty. One contained bits of leaf of a plant common to the salt marsh and one bird had swallowed a mud crab the size of a quarter of a dollar and had discarded the legs and pincers, probably to prevent the crab causing trouble after being swallowed.

Behavior.—Referring to the behavior of the California clapper rail, Grinnell, Bryant, and Storer (1918) write:

Its very long and unwebbed toes make large chicken-like tracks spaced about 10 inches apart in the soft mud of the slough banks, and these are very easy to recognize. The voice, too, is characteristic. It is a harsh, mechanical cackling—"*chuck, chuck, chuck, chuck,*" or "*cheek-a-cheek-a-cheek*"—uttered rapidly for several seconds and sounding as if two or more birds rather than a single one were participating in its production. When flushed this rail jumps almost straight up into the air for 6 or 8 feet and then flies off in a clumsy manner, its short, narrow wings moving at the rate of two or three beats per second. These flights are usually short, the bird soon dropping down again into the protection of the marsh vegetation.

Like all rails, the clapper rail is, when need be, very skillful at keeping out of sight. Sometimes individuals appear shy, flushing at a distance, or running toward the denser vegetation at great speed, with lowered head and elusive mien; at other times they walk out into the open in bottoms of sloughs at close range and view the intruder seemingly with perfect equanimity. They have a long running stride, and the body is held close to the ground. The narrowly compressed body enables them to slip easily between the rigid upright stems of a sort of rush which grows in thick beds along the larger salt sloughs. If not thoroughly alarmed, rails will sometimes stop or hesitate on open ground, when the peculiar twitching movement of the tail may be clearly seen. This member is held vertically and the twitching of it is rendered conspicuous because of the white color flashed from the undertail coverts. When walking, the head and tail twitch forward in unison with each stride. When thoroughly alarmed this rail will take to water and swim considerable distances, as, in one observed instance, across a 30-foot slough.

Mr. Adams (1900) says:

During several seasons of collecting, I have noticed that some days I would kill nothing but males of this species, while at another place only females were shot. Again when two of us were separated on the marsh one would procure males and the other females only. This would indicate that in fall and winter at least, the sexes resort to different feeding grounds. The birds fly very heavily and only for short distances, but the fleetness of foot is as remarkable as it is ungainly. When wounded they make good use of their legs and claws as well as their bill. The rail rarely swims for the mere pleasure it affords, but it can often be seen crossing a large slough, and when injured is very agile in the water.

Game.—I must quote again from Grinnell, Bryant, and Storer (1918), regarding the game qualities of this species, as follows:

The California clapper rail has long been considered an excellent bird for the table, and formerly great numbers were sold on the markets of San Francisco. The weight of an adult bird, freshly taken by the authors, was three-fourths of a pound (340 grams); so that the food value of a clapper rail as regards size is not inconsiderable. The sport furnished in hunting clapper rails is of a rather tame sort; for the birds are ordinarily not wild, and, owing to their slow, or sluggish, straightaway flight, are easy to hit on the wing. Unlike many other game birds, this one seems to be but slightly endowed with effective means of self-preservation. When pursued, a clapper rail is said to sometimes hide its head, ostrich-like, in a tuft of grass; and it is not an uncommon thing for dogs to catch the birds alive. For these reasons, as well as for the fact that they are considered by many to be excellent eating, these rails have been slaughtered in great numbers.

Few game birds in this State were more surely on the road to total extinction than was this species just previous to the passage of the Federal Migratory Bird

Law. The reclaiming of much of their former breeding grounds was concentrating them into smaller and smaller areas, where they were still more easily sought out and killed. Ray (1902), speaking of the abundance of this bird in San Mateo County, says: " As late as 1889, I remember sportsmen returning with as many as 200 clapper rails, while now one would find it exceedingly hard to bag a dozen." Mr. Samuel Hubbard, jr., of Oakland, has stated to us that formerly during high tides as many as 40 clapper rail could easily be killed along Oakland Creek. None of these birds are to be found in that locality at the present time. Accounts generally agree that the California clapper rail is much less abundant now than it once was. Even the extended annual close season, in force for a few years and now replaced by total protection, was not sufficient to protect this bird; for its haunts are so readily accessible to the Bay cities that hunting remained excessive. In 1913, the Federal Migratory Bird Law was passed, and within two years a marked increase was observable locally on the Alameda County marshes—proof that adequate protection long enough continued will restore the species. The worst enemy of the rail now remaining is the Norway rat, which infests many parts of the salt marshes, and whose depredations during the nesting season have come to our personal notice.

The California clapper rail is truly a native of the Golden State, being found nowhere else in the world. It deserves protection on esthetic grounds, if not on economic ones. It is entirely within possibility that at the expiration of the present closed term of years, hunting can again be safely allowed—with of course, a small bag limit and short season.

Mr Cohen (1895) writes:

Rail hunting at flood tide is not the highest sportsmanship, as the rail take refuge on high ground, and, when very little of that is exposed your dog is sure to put up a bird almost every few yards. Occasionally these birds will climb into a thick, short bush, common to the salt marsh, or sit contentedly on a pile of drift or a floating log, and at such times can be hit with an oar, but the birds to-day, with the exception of one, were flushed before I saw them, and this one was standing partly concealed among some salt grass in several inches of water, and tipping his body quickly up and down; a common habit. Again, the rail is not a swift flyer, flying in a straight line, and when hunters are numerous one of them will get the bird you miss if it flies his way, or mark it down and flush it again and keep Mr. Rail on the hop-skip-and-jump until he is shot or has presence of mind to sink into the water and keep his head out by holding to a stem by his bill. This is a favorite trick of theirs when wounded.

Enemies.—Besides the sportsmen and the rats, this poor rail has other enemies to contend with, of which W. Leon Dawson (1923) says:

According to Mr. Chase Littlejohn, still another enemy has arisen to make the life of this bird miserable—a certain mussel once imported from the East. This thrifty bivalve flourishes and increases enormously in just that range which has been from time immemorial the peculiar province of the rail; viz, the mud strip just below the line of vegetation on the banks of the tide channels. Now the bird must seek its living here or change its habits entirely. But the mussel is a sensitive, not to mention a supercilious creature, and when our native son steps carelessly it closes its doors with a bang—and often seizes the hapless rail by the toe. So common is this that many specimens with maimed feet or missing toes have been taken, and a few have been captured right where they were being held captive by the mussels. Others, more fortunate in escaping, are nevertheless condemned to drag about a ball on the foot, a mass of dried mud and trash of which the mussel is the unyielding nucleus. The bivalve apparently never releases its hold, and even in death, which must soon occur, does not relax its deathly grasp upon its victim.   In one instance at least, a bird was seized by the bill, and although it was able to wrest the bivalve free from its anchorage, the creature had closed upon its beak with such a grip that the bird was unable to get food, and was found in a famished and attenuated condition. This specimen Mr. Littlejohn has in his collection, a mute reminder of one knows not how many scores of similar tragedies.

DISTRIBUTION

Range.—A nonmigratory species, inhabiting the coast region of California from Humboldt Bay south to Monterey Bay. At present restricted largely to the region of San Francisco Bay (Petaluma, Tomales Bay, Alameda, Haywards, San Mateo, Redwood City, and Menlo Park) and Monterey Bay (Elkhorn). Accidental on the Farallon Islands.

Egg dates.—California: 107 records, April 1 to July 13; 54 records, April 10 to 25.

RALLUS LEVIPES Bangs

LIGHT-FOOTED RAIL

HABITS

For many years the clapper rails of the coastal marshes of California and northern Lower California were all supposed to be one species, *Rallus obsoletus*, until Outram Bangs (1899) separated the southern bird as a distinct species and named it *Rallus levipes*.   It is similiar to *obsoletus*, but is slightly smaller, the back is darker and more olive in tone, the breast is a richer tone of cinnamon and there is a whitish, instead of a rusty stripe from the bill over the eye. Grinnell, Bryant, and Storer (1918) suggest that "it might be considered merely a southern race of '*obsoletus.*'   Neither of them is migratory, and there is a strip of coast nearly 200 miles in extent between the southern limit of the California clapper rail and the northernmost station for the light-footed rail."   They also observe that "there are no essential differences in the general habits of the two species.   The light-footed rail, however, has been found breeding in an inland brackish marsh though, to be sure, this was not far from the seacoast."

Nesting.—W. Lee Chambers has sent me the following notes:

On April 13th 1917, I visited a salt-water marsh near Long Beach, Calif., and found an island fairly well inhabited by the light-footed rail. This was the only piece of land not used in cattle grazing, and was probably because of its being so low and not large enough to be of any grazing value. The total area was approximately five acres and in any kind of a storm it must have been completely covered by water. On this date I noticed three sets with eight eggs in each, one nest with two eggs and another nest which had just been finished and about ready for eggs. One fresh egg was found washed up on the beach. The island was practically covered with salicornia and the birds would waddle over this grass in their search for food, forming regular well-defined trails leading to the water's edge. I visited this island during several successive years and found that by following up these runways from the water's edge, they would invariably lead up to a feeding ground or a nest. The nests were generally on the highest piece of ground in that immediate vicinity that happen to be covered with salicornia. The bird would evidently waddle under a clump of salicornia and form a nest on the bare ground. A very poor nest was generally the result, for apparently the only lining was what happened to be on the ground at the spot chosen for the nest. A line of power poles ran across this island, and in digging the holes for the poles some little piles of dirt were left. On these hillocks the salicornia seemed to grow very rank and two of these clumps were selected for nesting sites. In summing up the nest sites, it seemed that every available bit of high ground near the water was occupied by its nest. These nests would be not over 100 feet from a body of water, and generally only a few feet. The birds were very quiet and the only time I saw them was when they would flush from immediately under my feet, and then they immediately took to the water and dove out of sight.

A. M. Ingersoll writes to me that the—

nests are generally well hidden on a dry portion of a salt marsh, but are sometimes placed over water of a foot or more in depth. In one instance a nest was placed against the back of a dead hog on a dry sandy beach several hundred feet from any marsh vegetation, certainly an unusual place for any rail.

Harold M. Holland contributes the following notes:

Since 1918 I have not been in the marshes around Los Angeles, but understand the rails have decreased and become rather scarce. On the other hand, having collected near San Diego last year (1922), it was my impression that the light-footed rails, in favorable places thereabout, were not especially uncommon. It is recalled there were a few marshy tracts in which cattle had been turned loose, and it was quite noticeable that no rails were therein encountered, although just across a narrow ditch, serving as a barrier to the cattle, they might be found. Occasionally one met with distinct runways from one ditch or channel to another, or a runway, often of surprising length and clearly defined, extending from a ditch to a clump of particularly thick or high salicornia in which would be hidden the nest. I think in some instances the same clump of salicornia is used season after season, and the worn appearance of the runways would bear this out. Across the marsh on the way from Los Angeles to Seal Beach, near the latter place, there was an electric line, and the heavy growths of salicornia at the bases of the trolley poles were favorite nest locations from year to year. Then there would be a little pool, almost round, encircled by a somewhat prominent growth of salicornia, and in this from one season to another a rail nest could be counted upon at almost the same identical spot. Often the fresh runways could easily be distinguished and would be mud spattered for a short distance near the ditch. The light-footed rail likes the salicornia in which to hide its nest and doubtless generally uses it, but at times does nest in other marsh vegetation.

George Willett (1906) found a nest of this species in a bunch of reeds growing in about three inches of fresh water, on the edge of Nigger Slough, near Los Angeles, on May 29, 1906.

The nest and eggs, which are now in my collection, are typical of the species. The nest is a very loose affair, the foundation being composed of decayed tules and reeds and the upper part, containing the cavity, of broken bits of tule stalks. It measures 11 by 7 inches on the outside, with the cavity 5 by ½ inches.

A. J. van Rossem writes me that he once—

Found a nearly completed nest, from which the bird was flushed, in a clump of spear grass (*Scirpus*). Because of the dense growth of the stems, the nest was about 18 inches from the ground. This is the only occasion which has come to notice where the nest was off the ground.

Eggs.—The eggs of the light-footed rail are practically indistinguishable from those of the California clapper rail. The measurements of 40 eggs average 44.6 by 31 millimeters; the eggs showing the four extremes measure **49.1** by 31, 44.9 by **32.3, 41.5** by 30.9, 48 by **29.7** millimeters.

Young.—A. M. Ingersoll has sent me the following notes:

Both sexes incubate. I have seen young when alarmed by my presence seek concealment by placing their heads in crab holes and cavities on a rather steep mud bank, also under pieces of driftwood and other rubbish. Young light-footed rails are able to swim on the day of birth. On one occasion an old rail with swaying head and quivering wings stood some 25 feet from me, and about the same distance from a nest with six babies, facing me; a few rapid notes were uttered, evidently family instructions, for the young scrambled from their nest and five of them slowly made their way over several yards of oozy mud, across water of a tide stream and up the bank to a patch of weeds. The anxious parent did not take wing or apparently cease to look at me until the five young were safely concealed. One frail baby only got a few inches away from the nest; and two of the swimmers were so exhausted that the tidal current carried them some distance away from their companions.

Plumages.—The molts and plumages of the light-footed rail are apparently similar to those of the California clapper rail, to which it is closely related.

Behavior.—I also have the following interesting notes from J. Eugene Law:

The secretiveness of this species renders it hard to find but when the annual highest tides come it is literally floated up out of its cover and becomes conspicuous. I collected specimens on such a tide on December 7, 1915. When I arrived the water was already over most of the salicornia leaving only thin patches of cover. Perhaps 50 or more light-footed rails were seen in the course of two hours. As I rowed about they swam frantically toward such cover as was in sight, and would "freeze" along side any projecting grass or weed, but their bodies silhouetted conspicuously on the glassy water. They swam with awkward, chickenlike movements of the head, forward and back, and when pressed too hard rose into the air and flew some distance before dropping heavily into the water. As this rarely happened until the boat was within gun range, they were at the mercy of the gunner. They could not swim so fast quite as I could row a small flat bottomed skiff.

The clear water only a foot or so deep over the salicornia afforded a splendid opportunity to observe two which were wing-tipped, and which dove when pressed too closely. They went straight down, poking their head into the salicornia where they apparently held on by means of their beaks, for their bodies were in plain sight with legs and feet sticking up. Here they invariably stayed until unconscious, when their hold would relax and they would come to the surface feet first, to lie for a moment before regaining consciousness. One of them got partly under a weed in one of its dives, and its toes became entangled so that it stuck there, and I believe would have drowned. When I thought it was drowned I retrieved it, leaving it on the surface of the water, beak partly submerged, but it gradually regained its faculties and soon started swimming off again at full speed.

W. Leon Dawson (1923) describes the vocal performances of this species as follows:

Eventide, also, is the time for that discursive song which won for our hero the name "clapper." In a populous marsh one may hear six or seven birds at once uttering these peculiar, strident, iterative calls. The tones are very hard to characterize. Some one, I suppose, must have likened them to the sound of a fence board struck by a stick. To me they sound more like the cheep of a baby blackbird greatly exaggerated. With head and neck stretched vertically, the bird delights to roll out 10 or a dozen of these notes in a series, *rallentando sostentuto* or *rallentando et diminuendo*, as the case may be.

Enemies.—A. B. Howell, who has had considerable experience with these rails, writes to me:

They used to be common on our marshes, and during the unusually high December tides, we would collect as many as we wished, rowing about over the submerged flats and flushing the rails from almost every little grassy clump, in the cover of which they would be paddling about. They were thus hunted by local pothunters as well, until now they are decidedly rare where they were abundant half a dozen years ago. They are certainly less well protected, and much less numerous, than the northern bird about San Francisco Bay. In addition, their range is being restricted by reclamation of the marshes, and the future of the subspecies is not at all bright.

DISTRIBUTION

Range.—A nonmigratory species, occuring in the coastal marshes of southern California and the northern part of the western coast of Lower California.

In California the light-footed rail is found north to Santa Barbara and south along the coast to Wilmington, San Pedro Bay, Long Beach, Newport and San Diego. There is one record of a set of eggs taken in the fresh water marsh of Nigger Slough, Los Angeles County (Willett, 1906). In Lower California the species has been observed or taken principally in the region of San Quintin Bay.

Egg dates.—California: 56 records, March 18 to June 11; 28 records, April 9 to May 3.

RALLUS YUMANENSIS Dickey

YUMA CLAPPER RAIL

HABITS

To Donald R. Dickey (1923) belongs the honor of discovering and the privilege of naming a new rail from a new and unexpected locality. He writes that:

Field work carried on during the spring of 1921 in the Colorado River Valley, Imperial County, California, by Laurence M. Huey and Mrs. May Canfield, in behalf of the author's collection, resulted in the utterly unexpected capture of three individuals of a distinct new species of clapper rail.

For the characters on which the species is based he gives the following:

Nearest in appearance to certain examples of *Rallus levipes*, but instantly separable from typical *levipes* by duller and more olivaceous outer superior wing-coverts and alula, by paler coloration of underparts and more slender tarsus and bill.

The characters are rather slight on which to base a species, especially when he admits that his—

Own examination of 29 specimens of *levipes* has disclosed two individuals from National City, San Diego County, California, which superficially seem to bridge the gap between these species both in measurements and in general coloration. However, the outer superior wing-coverts and alula, even in these unusual specimens, are distinctly brighter than the same areas in the three specimens of *yumanensis* examined.

It would seem as if a subspecific designation might have been wiser, in view of the small series examined and our very limited knowlege of its distribution. He is justified in saying, however, that "it is interesting to note that we here have a true clapper rail inhabiting for the first recorded instance a purely fresh-water environment."

Eggs.—Laurence M. Huey has sent me, for description in this work, the only known egg of this rail, which was kindly loaned for this purpose by Mrs. May Canfield. It was taken from the oviduct of a bird, collected on May 27, 1921, by a boy named Edward Heiser, and presented to Mrs. Canfield. The parent is one of the series on which Mr. Dickey's description was based. The egg resembles certain eggs of *Rallus levipes* in a general way. It is ovate in shape, rounded at the small end; the shell is smooth and rather glossy. The ground color is between "pale pinkish buff" and "cartridge buff"; it is sparingly spotted, chiefly around the larger end, with underlying drab spots, varying in color from "vinaceous drab" to very "pale ecru drab," and a few small spots and dots of dark browns, "chestnut brown" and "chocolate." It measures 41.8 by 28.8 millimeters.

Behavior.—Mr. Huey has sent me a little additional information, as follows:

On May 18, 1924, Mrs. May Canfield and I were collecting about a mile north of Potholes, Imperial County, California, when suddenly the clacking of clapper rails was heard in three different directions. At the time the Colorado River was commencing to overflow its banks in the annual spring flood, and many low places were filling from the river and muddy streams were flowing through the willow bottom in many directions. It was along these streams that the rails were clacking. I pursued a pair of clacking birds whose voices seemed to issue from a large pond nearby, while Mrs. Canfield followed another pair nearer the river. I never again heard my pair of birds, nor did I see them, but Mrs. Canfield had the good fortune of getting within 20 feet of her pair. Both were swimming in the running water at the time, and appeared by their actions, to be getting in line. As she has but a single-shot collecting gun, the thought struck her that possibly both rails could be obtained at the same shot. Unfortunately the rails observed her before the time to shoot occured, and she got neither.

In regard to the voices of these birds—I had, but a few weeks before, been on the rail marshes in the vicinity of San Diego Bay and had heard *Rallus levipes* clacking. I was therefore quite surprised at the thinner, higher note of the voice of *Rallus yumanensis*, which is pitched at least three notes higher. However, it descends the scale as do the voices of other clapper rails of my acquaintance.

It is my opinion that the center of abundance of this rail is in the delta of the Colorado River, but that, during the flood time, which usually occurs in May and June of each year, the lower reaches of the river are made uninhabitable for the nesting of this bird and they annually come up the river seeking suitable localities in which to nest. It so happened in 1921 that the water was unusually high and hence the rails that formed the type series, now in the Dickey collection, were obtained unusually far up the river. Again, in 1924, the river was above normal, and rails were observed in the marshes above Potholes. It appears that these birds only come as far from the delta each summer as suitable nesting grounds are to be found. Hence their occurrence at these northern stations during periods of excessively high water. This phenomenon might well be responsible for the bird's extending its range into the vast tule marshes now growing in Imperial Valley, California, though as yet no definite records of this species have been forthcoming from that region.

DISTRIBUTION

Range.—"So far as known, the fresh water riparian strip along the Colorado River above Yuma, and adjacent irrigation canals in the vicinity of Laguna Dam" (Dickey 1923).

RALLUS LONGIROSTRIS CREPITANS Gmelin

CLAPPER RAIL

HABITS

In the salt water marshes of the Atlantic and Gulf coasts, from southern New England to Texas, the clapper rail, in its various forms, has been a widely distributed,well known, and conspicuous feature, though more often heard than seen; its loud clatter is still often heard in many places, but its popularity as a game bird and as an egg producer has greatly thinned its ranks; it no longer exists anywhere in anything like the astonishing abundance described by the earlier writers. Audubon (1840) boasted of having collected as many as 72 dozen eggs in one day. He says further:

In the Jerseys, it forms almost a regular occupation to collect the eggs of this bird, and there I have seen 20 or more persons gathering them by thousands during the season; in fact, it is not an uncommon occurrence for an egger to carry home 100 dozen in a day; and when this havoc is continued upwards of a month, you may imagine its extent. The abundance of the birds themselves is almost beyond belief; but if you suppose a series of salt marshes 20 miles in length and a mile in breadth, while at every 8 or 10 steps one or two birds may be met with, you may calculate their probable number.

Nesting.—Clapper rails were still common on the coast of Virginia when I was there in 1907, though in nothing like their former abundance. On Cobb and Wreck Islands, and on other large islands along the coast, the outer shore line is protected by long, high beaches of broken shells and sand and by great piles of oyster shells thrown up by the surf; behind these barriers are extensive tracts of low, flat, salt marshes and meadows, intersected by numerous, winding tidal creeks. At low tide broad mud flats are exposed to view in the estuaries and along the creeks, where the rails find suitable feeding grounds. At ordinary high tides the marshes and meadows are more or less covered with water; and at spring tides they are flooded, so that only a few of the highest spots are above water and only the tops of the grasses are visible in the low places.

During the few days that we spent in these marshes, from June 24 to 28, we found a large number of nests of the clapper rail, which must have been second layings, for it was late in the season for them and yet most of them were not heavily incubated. Perhaps the spring tides had destroyed many of the first layings. Practically all of the nests that we found were on the higher and drier portions of the marshes, which are only partially covered at high tide with a few inches of water. The nests were mostly built in the little clumps of coarse, green, marsh grass, which was then about 18 or 24 inches high, growing principally along the banks of the creeks in the soft, wet mud. They varied in height, above the mud, from 8 to 12 inches and were evidently intended to be high enough to escape the ordinary high tides; but they were not all high enough to avoid the high course of spring tides. The nests were usually more or less arched over, with pretty little canopies of green grass interlaced above, through which the eggs could be plainly seen, making a very pretty picture; these little canopies were often conspicuous at a long distance, making it easy to locate the nests. But in many cases the nests were entirely open and uncovered, in plain sight in the shorter grass. The nests were well made of dry sedges and grasses, and were lined with finer and shorter pieces of the same material; they were usually well cupped and measured from 7 to 10 inches in outside and from 5 to 6 inches in inside diameter. Many of the nests had well-defined runways leading to them and some were provided with pathways or stairways, made of dry grasses, leading up to them. One nest was concealed almost perfectly under a bunch of drift seaweed, which had lodged on top of a thick clump of coarse, green grass; there was an entrance left open on one side which was the only point from which the eggs were visible. Another nest was hidden similarly under a bunch of drifted dead sedges. One nest was found in a colony of Forster terns, within 3 feet of a tern's nest.

Eggs.—The clapper rail lays from 6 to 14 eggs, but the usual numbers run from 9 to 12. The shape is ovate and the shell is smooth and more or less glossy. The ground color varies from warm, yellowish buff to pale, greenish buff, or from dull, "cream buff" or "pinkish buff" to "ivory yellow" or "pale olive buff." The eggs are irregularly marked with small blotches and spots of various shades of browns and drabs. Some eggs are richly colored with bold markings, others are finely speckled and some are very sparingly spotted. They average darker in color and are usually more heavily marked than the eggs of the king rail. The measurements of 50 eggs average 42.5 by 30 millimeters; the eggs showing the four extremes measure **48.5** by 31, 44 by **31.5**, **37.5** by 28, and 41 by **27.5** millimeters.

Young.—The period of incubation is said to be 14 days and it is probably performed by both sexes. The young are precocial and leave the nest soon after they are hatched, to follow their mother through the marshes and learn to procure their own food. Under her guidance they soon learn to swim and to run and hide in the great jungle of marsh grass, where they are comparatively safe from most of their enemies.

Plumages.—The downy young clapper rail is wholly covered with soft, thick, jet black down, glossy above and dull black below. The juvenal plumage appears first on the sides of the breast, where it is "mouse gray" or "pale mouse gray" in color; whitish feathers then invade the ventral region, a central strip of black down being the last to disappear from the breast; the back then becomes feathered with "hair brown" and "mouse gray" plumage; the young bird is fully half grown before the head becomes feathered or the wings start to grow; the latter are not fully grown until the young bird is completely feathered and has reached its full size.

In the full juvenal plumage some of the races can be recognized by their characteristic colorings. In *crepitans*, from Virginia, the upper parts are mainly olive drab with broad edgings of "Quaker drab"; the under parts are mostly dull whitish, washed with pale buff on the neck and variegated with "pale Quaker drab" on the sides. In *scotti* from Florida, the upper parts are much darker, nearly black with "clove brown" edgings; the sides of the head and flanks are lighter "clove brown"; and the throat and under parts are buffy white with dusky tipped feathers. In *saturatus*, from Texas, the juvenal plumage is darker and more richly colored than in *crepitans*, but not nearly so dark as in *scotti*.

The juvenal plumage is short lived, for almost as soon as it is compelted a molt of the contour plumage begins to produce the first winter plumage, which is practically indistinguishable from that of the adult, the barred flanks are acquired in September and the change is completed in October.

Adults have a complete postnuptial molt in August and September, the wings being renewed first and the body plumage last; they apparently have a partial prenuptial molt of the contour plumage in early spring.

Food.—Audubon (1840) writes:

During ebb, the clapper rail advances toward the edge of the waters as they recede, and searches, either among the grasses, or along the deep furrows made by the ebb and flow of the tides, for its food, which consists principally of small crabs, a species of salt-water snail attached to the rushes, the fry of fishes, aquatic insects, and plants. When the tide flows they gradually return, and at high water they resort to the banks, where they remain concealed until the waters begin to retreat. This species is by no means exclusively nocturnal, for it moves about in search of food during the whole of the day, in this respect resembling the gallinules.

Behavior.—The same gifted author, who evidently studied the habits of this rail quite thoroughly, describes its various activities very satisfactorily, as follows:

The salt-water marsh hen swims with considerable ease, though not swiftly or gracefully. While in this act, it extends its neck forward, and strikes the water with its feet, as if unwilling to move far at a time, the motion of its neck resembling that of the gallinules. It dives well, remains a considerable time under water, and in this manner dexterously eludes its pursuers, although it certainly does not possess the power of holding fast to the bottom, as some persons have alleged. When hard pressed, it often sinks just below the surface, keeping the bill above in order to breathe, and in this position, if not detected, remains for a considerable time. If perceived and approached, it instantly dives, and uses its wings to accelerate its progress, but rises as soon as it comes to a place of safety.

Their movements on the ground, or over the partially submersed or floating beds of weeds, are extremely rapid, and they run swiftly off before a dog, the utmost exertions of which are required to force them on wing. Such an attempt by man would prove utterly futile, unless he were to come upon them unawares. When not pursued, and feeling secure, they jerk the tail upwards, although by no means so frequently as gallinules are wont to do. On the least appearance of danger, they lower the head, stretch out the neck, and move off with incomparable speed, always in perfect silence. They have thousands of paths among the rank herbage, crossing each other so often that they can very easily escape pursuit; and, besides, they have a power of compressing their body to such a degree as frequently to force a passage between two stems so close that one could hardly believe it possible for them to squeeze themselves through. When put up, they fly slowly and generally straight before you, with their legs dangling, so that they are very easily shot by a quick sportsman, as they rarely fly far at a time on such occasions, but prefer pitching down again into the first tuft of rank grass in their way. When on their migrations, however, they pass low and swiftly over the marshes, or the water, stretched to their full extent, and with a constant beat of the wings.

From about the beginning of March to that of April, the salt marshes resound with the cries of the clapper rail, which resembles the syllables " *cac, cac, cac, cac, ca, caha, caha.''* The commencement of the cry, which is heard quite as frequently during day as by night, is extremely loud and rapid, its termination lower and protracted. At the report of a gun, when thousands of these birds instantaneously burst forth with their cries, you may imagine what an uproar they make. This bird seems to possess the power of ventriloquism, for, when several hundred yards off, its voice often seems to be issuing from the grass around you.

Game.—The clapper rail has long been pursued as a game bird and countless thousands have been shot by, so-called, sportsmen. But it seems to possess few of the qualities of a good game bird. Its flight is slow, weak and direct and it is so tame that it usually rises at close range; it is consequently one of the easiest of birds to shoot. When the marshes are covered with water, at high tides, the rails gather in large numbers in the few available high spots where there is grass enough above water to conceal them; it is then a simple matter to pole a boat up to one of such spots and pot them, as they fly slowly away in the open. The flesh of this rail will not compare in flavor with that of the sora, especially when the latter has been fattened on wild rice; it is said to be insipid and sedgy, but is undoubtedly tender and fairly palatable, as is the flesh of most birds, particularly young birds. Audubon (1840) has given us a graphic account of clapper rail shooting, as follows:

About Charleston, in South Carolina, the shooting of marsh hens takes place from September to February, a few days in each month during the springtides. A light skiff or canoe is procured, the latter being much preferable, and paddled by one or two experienced persons, the sportsman standing in the bow, and his friend, if he has one with him, taking his station in the stern. At an early hour they proceed to the marshes, amid many boats containing parties on the same errand. There is no lack of shooting grounds, for every creek of salt water swarms with marsh hens. The sportsman who leads has already discharged his barrels, and on either side of his canoe a bird has fallen. As the boat moves swiftly towards them, more are raised, and although he may not be ready, the safety of the bird is in imminent jeopardy, for now from another bark double reports are heard in succession. The tide is advancing apace, the boats merely float along, and the birds, driven from place to place, seek in vain for safety. Here, on a floating mass of tangled weeds, stand a small group side by side. The gunner has marked them, and presently nearly the whole covey is prostrated. Now, onward to that great bunch of tall grass all the boats are seen to steer; shot after shot flies in rapid succession; dead and dying lie all around on the water; the terrified survivors are trying to save their lives by hurried flight; but their efforts are unavailing—one by one they fall, to rise no more. It is a sorrowful sight after all; see that poor thing gasping hard in the agonies of death, its legs quivering with convulsive twitches, its bright eyes fading into glazed obscurity. In a few hours, hundreds have ceased to breathe the breath of life; hundreds that erstwhile revelled in the joys of careless existence, but which can never behold their beloved marshes again. The cruel sportsman, covered with mud and mire, drenched to the skin by the splashing of the paddles, his face and hands besmeared with powder, stands amid the wreck which he has made, exultingly surveys his slaughtered heaps, and with joyous feelings returns home with a cargo of game more than enough for a family thrice as numerous as his own.

Enemies.—The gentle rail has many enemies which Audubon (1840) refers to, as follows:

Their courage is now and then brought to the test by the sudden approach of some of their winged enemies, such as a hawk or an owl, especially the marsh hawk, which is often attacked by them while sailing low over the grass in which they are commonly concealed. On such occasions, the rail rises a few yards in the air, strikes at the marauder with bill and claws, screaming aloud all the while, and dives again among the grass, to the astonishment of the bird of prey, which usually moves off at full speed. They are not so fortunate in their encounters with such hawks as pounce from on high on their prey, such as the red-tailed and red-shouldered hawks, against which they have no chance of defending themselves. Minks, racoons, and wild cats destroy a great number of them during the night, and many are devoured by turtles and ravenous fishes; but their worst enemy is man. My friend Bachman has shot so many as 60 in the course of four hours, and others have killed double that number in double the time.

Wilson (1832) adds:

These birds are also subject to another calamity of a more extensive kind: After the greater part of the eggs are laid, there sometimes happen violent north-east tempests that drive a great sea into the bay, covering the whole marshes; so that at such times the rail may be seen in hundreds, floating over the marsh in great distress; many escape to the mainland; and vast numbers perish. On an occasion of this kind I have seen, at one view, thousands in a single meadow, walking about exposed and bewildered, while the dead bodies of the females, who had perished on or near their nests, were strewed along the shore. This last circumstance proves how strong the ties of maternal affection are in these birds; for of the great numbers which I picked up and opened, not one male was to be found among them; all were females. Such as had not yet begun to sit probably escaped. These disasters do not prevent the survivors from recommencing the work of laying and building anew; and instances have occurred where their eggs have been twice destroyed by the sea; and yet in two weeks the eggs and nests seemed as numerous as ever.

DISTRIBUTION

Range.—Salt marshes of the Atlantic coast from southeastern Maine to northeastern North Carolina.

Breeding range.—The clapper rail breeds north to Connecticut (Saybrook) and south to North Carolina (Pea and Brodie Islands). The east and west limits of its range are, of course, determined by the width of the salt-marsh belt.

Winter range.—North, casually, to New York (Far Rockaway, L. I.) and south to Georgia (Savannah and St. Marys). The species has also occurred in winter in Connecticut (Stamford, February 9, 1900).

Casual records.—Specimens have been taken or observed in Massachusetts (East Orleans, Springfield, Ipswich, Kingston, Boston, and Plymouth); New Hampshire (Portsmouth); and Maine (Popham Beach and Sabattus Pond).

Egg dates.—Virginia: 46 records, April 16 to July 17; 23 records, May 27 to July 3. New Jersey and Long Island: 21 records, May 24 to June 21; 11 records, May 30 to June 5.

RALLUS LONGIROSTRIS SATURATUS Ridgway

LOUISIANA CLAPPER RAIL

HABITS

A somewhat more richly colored race of the clapper rail inhabits the Gulf coast regions from Alabama westward to Corpus Christi, Texas. It does not differ materially in its habits from the Atlantic coast races, except that in some places in Texas it is found quite far inland in brackish swamps. We found this rail common on the low marshy islands and mud lumps off the coast of Louisiana near the delta of the Mississippi, where it was doubtless breeding in the long salt-marsh grass. The coast of Texas, from Bolivar Peninsula, which separates part of Galveston Bay from the Gulf of Mexico, to Neuces Bay at Corpus Christi, is lined with salt marshes and brackish meadows, which often extend many miles up the rivers. Many of the islands are low and marshy, covered with long grass. And scattered all over the broad, coastal strip are numerous sloughs and marshy ponds, overgrown or bordered with rank growths of marsh grass and sedges. Throughout all of this region, which we explored more or less hurriedly, we found the Louisiana clapper rail living under ideal conditions. These marshes are so extensive that it is a hopeless task to attempt to explore them thoroughly; the rails did not seem to be particularly abundant anywhere, so we made only spasmodic efforts to hunt for nests in a few places and did not succeed in finding any.

My companion on the Texas trip, George Finlay Simmons, has made quite an extensive study of the history and habits of this rail in Texas and has published two interesting papers (1914 and 1915) on the subject. The following passages, taken from his first paper (1914) will give a good idea of the haunts of this bird:

From the timber of the Brazos River bottoms northward and eastward along the coast is the low, nearly level coast prairie of Texas. The only vegetation of this prairie is the tall grass, usually burned brown by the hot summer sun and killed by the cold "northers" which sweep over Texas in winter; here and there a huisache (*Vachellia farnesiana*) and an occasional "motte" of three or four scrubby oaks serve to break the monotony. A few slowly winding bayous cross this plain, but the water in them rarely ever flows; these bayous are generally skirted by timber, but many of them contain marshy spots overgrown with tall grass, reeds, and sedge. At the mouths of these bayous the country is usually so flat and low that the water spreads over a considerable area, forming innumerable marshy flats and salt-water marshes, where tall grass, reeds and sedge grow in abundance. In winter large numbers of ducks and other waterfowls attract the hunter, but in summer these marshes are abandoned to the rails, mottled ducks and herons.   Farther inland from the coast, throughout this strip of coast prairie, are numbers of shallow ponds overgrown with reeds and sedge, and spots where tall grass and reeds grow over several inches of water.

My favorite spot for the Louisana clapper rail is a small red-wing blackbird colony about 6 miles south of the courthouse in Houston, being a mere damp spot on the prairie covering about two acres, and overgrown with tall grass and sedge.   Two small clumps of persimmon trees grow in this marsh, one at either end.   Though fully 22 miles from Galveston Bay and 50 miles from the Gulf of Mexico, this salt marsh might be termed a typical salt marsh, for here nested a pair of Texas seaside sparrows, and not a mile off to the south a nest of the mottled duck with 11 eggs was found in another such marsh.

Nesting.—Mr. Simmons (1914) gives more or less detailed accounts of a number of nests of the Louisiana clapper rail, found by him and by E. F. Pope, from which it appears that its nesting habits do not differ materially from those of its eastern relatives, except that the nests seem to be more widely scattered.   His notes on one nest are well worth quoting, as follows:

On my way home I stopped at the red-wing colony again to try to get a look at the rail on the nest.   Slowly I drew nearer and nearer to the nest, but I could not tell whether there was a bird on it or not, so still did she sit and so perfectly did she blend into the background that I was unable to see her until I was within about three feet of the nest.

Sitting on one heel while using the opposite knee as an improvised table, I checked down a few descriptive notes and sketches in my note book, although I feared she would leave the nest while I was doing so.   However, she did not, but remained on the nest eyeing me askant, her slightly curved bill nearly sidewise to me.   Dropping my note book and other paraphernalia, I arose until I was half over the bird on the nest; I could easily have caught her and might have stroked her as she sat on the nest, had I not been so slow.   But as I remained in that position for several minutes without moving, she began to get nervous, and while I stood there watching her she stepped off the nest into a well-defined little runway or path leading away from it.   So slowly did she go and such time did she take to lift her feet at each step that I could have counted a second or two between each stride.   About 12 feet away she stopped and half turned to watch me as I examined the nest and eggs.

The nest was 8½ inches across the top from rim to rim; the cavity was 2¼ inches deep, being a gradual slope from rim to rim, with the reeds firmly and smoothly packed inside.   For the most part the nest was composed of reeds and fragments of reeds or marsh grass from 1 inch to over a foot in length; a few were somewhat longer, being the standard blades of grass which had been bent flat against the ground and folded back again.   The lining was of small fragments of the same buffy, broad-bladed marsh grass, and packed flat against the body of the nest.

Eggs.—The eggs of the Louisiana clapper rail are not distinguishable from those of the other subspecies.   The measurements of 40 eggs average 42 by 29.3 millimeters; the eggs showing the four extremes measure **46** by 30, 41.2 by **31.6**, **39.5** by 28.5, and 40 by **28.4** millimeters.

Food.—Mr. Simmons (1914) says that the food of these rails " consists of small crabs, slugs, snails, aquatic insects, grasshoppers, and occasionally a few seeds." He quotes some interesting notes made by Mr. Pope, as follows:

At one point I squatted on my heels and remained stationary for a few moments and was rewarded by seeing a rail walk out of the grass into the mud and begin feeding, which it did by thrusting its bill into the soft mud and feeling around and stirring its food to the top, now and then securing a shrimp or a small minnow. I was advised by an old fisherman who lives on the bay shore about 3 miles from Flake, that he had often seen these birds feeding on young diamond-backed terrapin, which were once quite plentiful in this part of the bay and which deposited their eggs in the shell banks along the shore, the eggs hatching and the young taking to the adjacent marsh and bayous, probably to escape their numerous enemies in the bay. There they fell before the rails.

On warm days the "fiddler" or fighting crabs would crawl out of their holes around the old schooner and were eagerly devoured by the rails. After catching one of the crabs they would usually remove the large claw before swallowing the victim. This was often accomplished with the assistance of a neighbor who would hold the crab in his beak while the other wrenched off the objectionable limb; but this method was not always satisfactory to the bird that removed the claw, as the one that held the crab usually proceeded to bolt it while the other was left to hold the claw, or rather to drop it. On one occasion when the crabs were not plentiful, a rail found and tackled an unusually large "fiddler," which it mauled around in the mud for some time without apparent effect. Suddenly, as if getting an idea, it left the crab and disappeared on the other side of the schooner, to return a moment later with a companion, the two soon disarming Mr. Crab. Now, I presume the same rail came back; they are so much alike it is impossible to tell one from the other under such conditions, but from the way the birds went straight to the spot where the crab was left, I did not doubt the bird in the lead being the one that found the crab. Which one got the crab I can not say, as after scuffling over him, they disappeared from my sight in the tall grass.

Behavior.—I once saw a good demonstration of the swimming ability of this rail, while collecting off the coast of Louisiana; I flushed a rail from a small grassy island and was surprised to see the bird fly off and settle on the water about 100 yards offshore, where it swam about as unconcernedly as a duck.

Mr. Simmons (1914) makes the following observations on behavior:

Doubtless the reader will be suprised that the rail has ever been known to perch; indeed, I was more than surprised. On one occasion, in August, 1912, I was surprised to see a clapper rail flap up out of the marsh and light on a flat-topped post of the barbed wire fence, where it remained for some few minutes, standing there on the small flat surface as unconcerned as if on its marshy home ground.

The voice of the clapper rail is peculiar indeed, its loud, harsh cackling resembling that of a Guinea fowl or the sound produced by some automatic toys. This harsh cackling might be likened to the sound of: "*chack-chack-chack-chack-chack-chack-chack-chack,*" rapidly repeated. This call is usually heard about the break of day and again about dusk; sometimes, however, it is heard during the daytime or at night, though rarely. On Bolivar Peninsula Mr. Pope says that he could always tell when a "norther" was due by the clatter of the rails, as they invariably heralded its approach several hours before its arrival.

During the mating season in March, at which time they congregate in small flocks, Mr. Pope says that the birds became very noisy, especially late in the afternoon and about dusk. At the start of the nesting season, however, they quieted down. While I was examining nest No. 2 the parent bird now and then uttered a note which resembled the "*keck*" of the red-winged blackbird. At times during the early part of the breeding season I have stopped to watch adult rails which appeared very ill at ease. The note uttered under these conditions is a hoarse grunting noise sounding like "*bruck*" or "*gruck*." The newly hatched young have a constant, but very faint twitter, and a note reminding me, as stated before, of the "*cheap*" of a tiny domestic chick.

Enemies.—Evidently the clapper rails of Texas are disappearing, owing to the same causes as prevail elsewhere, for Mr. Simmons (1914) writes:

Once common, the birds are rapidly becoming scarce. If protection is not afforded them at once they will soon be wiped out entirely. Hunters kill numbers of them during the hunting season. In fact, it is one of the easiest of the water birds to secure on the wing, and therefore is one of the first to be shot by the amateur marksman. Mr. Pope observed that numbers of them fell victims to steel traps which he had set in the pathways of the mink in the marshes near Flake. These rails caught in the traps were usually devoured by mink if caught in the night, and most of those caught were taken then. The majority of the nests located by Mr. Pope in the Bolivar marshes in 1912 were usually found destroyed before the sets of eggs were complete, probably by mink, raccoon, or opossum, as tracks of these animals were in evidence in the immediate vicinity of the several nests. The eggs remaining in the nests or on the ground nearby had the appearance of having been sucked.

Probably the greatest factor the rails have to contend with in their fight for existence is the flooding of the marshes, both from high tide and from heavy rains. At such times the birds are much exposed and bewildered and many drown. In the seaside marshes they build their nests on the banks of the sloughs or bayous instead of the higher parts of the marsh, and in rainy spells numbers of nests are destroyed. They are naturally very delicate birds and sensitive to the cold of the more severe winters; many freeze to death where they are unable to secure shelter. During November and December 1913 Texas was visited by one of the most destructive floods of its history, two of the largest rivers of the State rising and overflowing miles and miles of the lowlands towards the coast. During that time numbers of the rails left the marshes and took to higher ground until the waters receded. One of these birds was caught in a bewildered condition in Mr. Farley's yard in Port Aransas in October.

Winter.—Of the winter habits of these rails, he says:

In the colder weather they haunt drifts of logs or trash in the marshes, where they take shelter from the cold north wind and from rains. But as the thermometer rarely falls below freezing in this semitropical coast country, the birds are rarely forced to seek shelter, and their actions and habits then are not noticeably different from other times of the year. In winter in the marshes on Bolivar Peninsula Mr. Pope says that the birds were fully as common in winter as in summer, if not more so. In traveling through the grass the birds had well-beaten paths about 6 inches wide, and from the way these paths were beaten out in the vicinity of the bayous, it would appear that the birds were much more common.

DISTRIBUTION

Range.—The Louisiana clapper rail is confined to the salt marshes of the Gulf coast extending east to Alabama (Perdido Bay) and probably western Florida (Pensacola); and west through Mississippi (Biloxi); Louisiana (New Orleans, Grand Island, and Vermilion Bay); and Texas (Galveston, Port Lavaca, Corpus Christi, and Brownsville). So far as is known it is nonmigratory.

Egg dates.—Mississippi to Texas: 15 records, April 13 to June 28; 8 records, April 30 to June 8.

RALLUS LONGIROSTRIS SCOTTI Sennett

FLORIDA CLAPPER RAIL

HABITS

This is the dark colored race of the clapper rail which is found on the Gulf coast of Florida, from Charlotte Harbor to the mouth of the Suwanee River and perhaps beyond both points, where it seems to be confined to the salt-water marshes, particularly about the mouths of rivers. At the mouth of the Suwanee River, Messrs. Brewster and Chapman (1891) found these rails to be "the most common and characteristic birds"; they say of their haunts:

The marshes and small islands at the mouth of the river were covered with a tall grass, each blade of which ended in a very sharp point or spine. Beneath the upright grass there was a mat of dead grass representing probably the growth of previous years. This formed a dense mass—a foot or more in thickness—and raised 15 or 20 inches above the ground. Beneath this mat the rails had their runways from which it was almost impossible to dislodge them. At intervals of 15 or 20 minutes one would call out when another would answer, and then still another, until the call was taken up by dozens of birds in succession. We did not observe that these outcries were at all stimulated or excited by any sudden noise, such as the report of a gun, as in the case with the Carolina rail. After a vain attempt to flush these birds by wading in the marshes, we were obliged to resort to firing the islands in order to obtain specimens.

Dr. Louis B. Bishop (1904) describes a similar haunt, as follows:

At the mouth of the Anclote River stretches a wide marsh overgrown with a cylindrical, sharp-pointed rush, stiff and sharp enough to bring blood after passing through several thicknesses of cloth. As these rushes die and bend over new ones take their place, resulting in a breast-high tangle through which it is difficult to force one's way, and even dangerous on account of one inhabitant of this marsh with which I became acquainted. Channels of varying width intersect the reeds, becoming at low water small stretches of sand flat. This is the home of Scott's rail, and he clings closely to it, not flying unless driven to cross some narrow opening, and then burying himself rapidly in the tangle beyond. Even these open spaces he prefers, under ordinary circumstances, to cross by running.

Courtship.—W. E. D. Scott (1889) says:

They begin to mate in February, and the breeding season is at its height by the 1st of April. During the mating season the male birds are very pugnacious and resent any intrusions from others of the species. At such times I have seen them have pitched battles, and finally, one giving in and taking to flight, the victor would pursue the vanquished on the wing for several hundred feet and then return to the neighborhood of the particular tuft of grass that sheltered the nest. At such times, on alighting, the peculiar rattling notes so characteristic of the bird are indulged in with more than ordinary vigor.

C. J. Pennock has sent me the following notes on the courtship of this rail:

Regarding the mating of Scott's rail, I have found these birds at St. Marks and also about Punta Gorda quite silent throughout the winter season. Only when considerably alarmed, at that period will they utter more than a hasty alarm. As nesting time approaches or by early March, they may be heard even with little or no cause, so far as the observer can determine. When mating is at the flood, one and not rarely two birds may be seen making short flights above the tops of the reeds. Only once did I hear one of these flying birds call out, and then two birds were in close company. On April 16, 1923, as I stood in a much-traveled roadway bordered on either side by a tidal ditch and small marshes and but 75 yards from the bay shore, what proved to be two males and a female Scott's rail came in sight. One and then quickly a second bird crossed the roadway and disappeared into a small clump of scrub palmettos. The smaller, the female, promptly came out onto the open sand near the ditch, walking slowly and frequently stopping, the characteristic jerking of body and tail much exaggerated; two other birds now appeared near the palmettos and for two or three minutes they were in full chase in and out of different small covers. When this encounter ceased, with the running off of one bird, the other came toward the yet visible female and approached her by short runs, with turns and gestures of body and wings, at times half open; the female meanwhile moved slowly toward a small patch of reeds, and finally dropped with body quite flat and head stretched well forward, but not quite to the ground, when the male came to her and the mating was complete.

Nesting.—Doctor Bishop (1904) describes a nest of this rail, as follows:

Although I looked for nests of Scott's rail on each trip that we made to this and other marshes, as it was evident they were laying, it was not until March 31 that I found my first and only nest. This was on a small mangrove island in the Anclote River near its mouth. Surrounding the mangroves was a narrow belt of the same rushes that composed the marsh, and the nest was situated on the ground in the rushes about 10 feet from shore, where they jutted into the mangroves, one of which shaded the nest. The nest was a mass about 1 foot in height composed of small pieces of dead rushes carelessly piled together, lined with fragments of the same, and only slightly hollowed. There were seven eggs in the nest and the same number on April 2, when I collected them, so, although fresh, they were doubtless a full set. On neither occasion did I see or hear the parent, but there can be little doubt of the identification, as Scott's is the only large rail I found near Anclote.

Eggs.—Except for the fact that they average slightly smaller, the eggs of this rail are not distinguishable from the eggs of the other eastern clapper rails. The measurements of 13 eggs average 40.4 by 29.9; the eggs showing the four extremes measured 43.5 by 31.4; and 37 by 27.7 millimeters.

Behavior.—Mr. Scott (1889) writes:

They are confined, so far as I am aware, to the salt-water marshes, and about Tarpon Springs are abundant the year around. They do not appear to be as retiring in their habits as are their congeners, and are frequently to be seen feeding at low tide on the exposed banks of mud and sand. At such times they are very tame and unsuspicious, and may be approached within a few feet. If alarmed they run to the neighboring shelter of coarse grass of the salt water marsh but presently return to feed, even though the intruder remains close at hand. Now and then one or two may be seen swimming some narrow arm of the bayou, and several times I have found pairs at least 300 or 400 feet from shore, swimming about and apparently feeding on some small fish or crustacea.

N. B. Moore says in his notes:

I once measured the footprints of the clapper rail, made on a smooth and naked sand bar, over which it had passed at night. I found the interval between them for several steps to be 19 inches. It would be fair to suppose that these were impressed when the bird ran at its utmost speed. Even then this extent of reach is suprising when the shortness of the tarsus is called to mind, it being in the largest birds only 2¾ inches; besides, I do not think this species uses its wings in running, as some birds are known to do.

This length of stride is rather remarkable for so small a bird; Mr. Moore found that the longest stride of a sandhill crane measured 19½ inches and the average was about 15 inches; and the longest step he could find of the great blue heron was only 19⅞ inches.

During the winter and spring of 1924 and 1925 we found these rails very common in all the numerous salt-water marshes that we visited on the Gulf coast of Florida from Tarpon Springs to Tampa Bay, living in the localities so well described above. They were more often heard than seen, but occasionally one would show itself on the open mud flats near the edge of the reeds, or, more rarely, one could be flushed from the dense tangles of sharp pointed reeds. I believe that they live, at certain seasons, among the red mangroves, where on several occasions I saw them feeding on the muddy shores of small ponds, far from any reedy marshes. I never succeeded in finding an occupied nest, though I spent considerable time in exploring suitable marshes.

Mr. Pennock writes to me:

Along the St. Marks River, for 7 miles up its length, to the confluence with Wakulla River, 1½ miles below the little village of St. Marks, such conditions of marsh, as are above described, do prevail and continue along the main stream close up to the fish houses. On both sides of these two rivers the open marshes maintain from one-half to over a mile in width, with numerous wide draining creeks which under ordinary weather conditions have wide, bare mud flats on either shore at low tide. In such localities the "salt-water" rail can be observed most readily. The brooding bird, from late March until June or later, hurries along the border of the reeds or scurries out toward the water's edge, pecking here and there for a tidbit or tarrying long enough to probe successfully for a burrowing fiddler crab and then hustling along for further repast, all quite in the manner of a barnyard "setting hen." Later the brood of sable chicks tag along behind the adult, their numbers usually lessening rapidly as days go by, from toll levied by their numerous predatory neighbors, which include fish crows, some of the smaller hawks, snakes, and turtles. While the old bird at this time is solicitous for her charge, she is not hurried in her actions. At other seasons of the year and under normal feral conditions the movements of the adult bird are stately, graceful, and attractive.

DISTRIBUTION

Range.—Nonmigratory. The range of the Florida clapper rail extends from extreme southeastern Alabama (Perdido Bay), along the Gulf coast of Florida (St. Marks, mouth of the Suwanee River, Cedar Keys, Anclote Keys, Tarpon Springs, Clearwater, Tampa Bay, Charlotte Harbor to near Fort Myers). It probably breeds throughout this range although the occurrence in Alabama is based upon a single specimen (Howell) and was possibly a wanderer.

Egg dates.—Florida: 18 records, April 18 to July 30; 9 records, May 6 to 26.

RALLUS LONGIROSTRIS WAYNEI Brewster

WAYNE CLAPPER RAIL

HABITS

The clapper rails of the Atlantic coast, from North Carolina to Florida, have been designated as a subspecies under the above name. This subspecies seems to be of doubtful value; the characters on which it is separated are a generally darker color, more ashy under parts and under tail-coverts with fewer markings; at best it seems to be only intermediate between *crepitans* and *scotti;* and if we are to recognize intermediate races in nomenclature there will be no end of splitting.

Dr. Louis B. Bishop (1904) describes the haunts of this rail, as follows:

With this bird I have become well acquainted at Pea Island on the coast of North Carolina. Pamlico Sound is separated from the Atlantic by a belt of drifting sand and mud flats, that broadens in places sufficiently to support trees and bushes, and narrows in others to but the ocean beach backed by a mile of sandy flats, where may frequently, be seen in position the stumps of trees that grew there in past centuries. The sound side of this belt is bordered here and there by meadows of salt marsh, some of these quite similar to the wetter marshes of the New England coast, and covered like them with a coarse grass or sedge, while others are densely grown with rushes evidently closely related to those that compose the salt marshes of western Florida. These marshes are the home of Wayne's rail, and at evening or in cloudy weather you will hear their harsh cackle, and occasionally see one of the birds walking along the margin of an inlet, ready to run quickly to the grass at the slightest sign of danger. In winter apparently the great majority go farther south, the true clapper rail occurring at this season in about equal numbers; but in May the marshes are filled with these birds and the clapper rail is rare.

C. J. Maynard (1896) writes—

The coasts of South Carolina and Georgia are low, and many sounds make in
to the land, which receive the contents of numerous rivers. Between these
sounds, are islands, back of which are creeks of varying widths, in which the tide
rises and falls; while between these bodies of water and the mainland, are extensive marshes, many miles in width. These level tracts are scarcely elevated
above low water mark, consequently are overflowed by every flood tide, and during the extreme high water that occurs at the full of the moon even the grass
tops of all but some of the more elevated spots are submerged. As remarked,
these marshes are widely spread, extending from the islands to the westward, as
far as eye can reach, and stretching from the extreme northern confines of the
State of South Carolina, quite to Florida. Many aquatic birds find a home in
this lonely reach of country, but by far the most abundant, at all seasons are the
clapper rails, and their harsh voices may be heard at all hours of the day and
night, as they skulk through the grass or run along the margins of the creeks in
search of food. Like all the members of this genus, these rails are difficult to
tart, and the only way in which they can be secured in numbers, is to watch the
occurrence of a spring tide which, overflowing nearly everything, forces the birds
to take refuge in the few clumps of grass left uncovered, or they will sit upon the
floating débris and quietly await the falling of the water.

Nesting.—The nesting habits of this subspecies do not differ materially from those of its more northern representative, as the following
account by Doctor Bishop (1904) will illustrate:

Although I have taken incubated eggs by May 2, the greater number of rails
do not begin to lay until about this date, and some postpone this duty until the
latter half of the month. The nests are scattered everywhere over the marshes,
the bases of some resting in the water, and of others on dry ground. In the
rushes a spot is selected under a thick mass of semiprostrate stems; in the coarse
marsh grass as thick a clump as possible is chosen, and the tips of the grass seem
to be bent over as a canopy to the nest. This bending over of the tops of the
grass is sometimes sufficiently evident to draw one's attention to the spot. The
nest is a slightly hollowed heap of small pieces of dead rush or grass stem.

Troup D. Perry writes to me that this rail does not always breed
in wet places, as he has found it nesting in Beaufort County, South
Carolina, on high, dry land, where the nest was a slight hollow in the
ground, lined with bits of dry grass, and 30 or 40 feet from a creek.
He once found a nest on the top of a sand dune 15 feet high and
about 200 feet from any water; the nest was a slight hollow, lined
with dry grass, among the lavender bushes that covered the sand dune.

Eggs.—The eggs of this subspecies are indistinguishable from those
of the other clapper rails. The measurements of 40 eggs average
41.5 by 29.1 millimeters; the eggs showing the four extremes measure
46.2 by 28.8, 41.3 by 30.6, 36.6 by 27.9, 37.8 by 27.8 millimeters.

Behavior.—Doctor Bishop (1904) says of this bird;

At all times Wayne's rail is a shy and secretive bird, never flying if it can help
it, but an adept at running, dodging and hiding, and can seldom be forced from
the grass without the aid of a dog. Against the wind it can not fly, and even
with the wind its progress is slow and seldom sustained for more than 100 yards.
With a fresh breeze blowing I have seen a rail roll over and over when it attempted
to alight on the hard sand.

Enemies.—Mr. Arthur T. Wayne (1910), for whom this bird was named, writes:

This bird is well known to all the inhabitants along the coast, and during the spring tides in September, October, and November, countless thousands are annually killed, yet there is no diminution in its numbers, as the birds are vigorous and very prolific, and two broods are annually raised, each pair being able to raise 24 young under favorable circumstances. These birds, however, have innumerable enemies to contend with during the breeding season, as crows take their eggs at every opportunity, crabs catch the young, and the mink is ever on the alert; while spring tides often wash away the nest and eggs. Yet with all these vicissitudes there is absolutely no diminution of their numbers. From the last of February until November the notes of this bird can be daily heard, and I have often heard it shriek when the marsh hawk (*Circus hudsonius*) was attacking it. These birds are generally very quiet at high water, but as soon as the tide begins to recede, their notes can be heard all through the marshes.

DISTRIBUTION

Range.—Atlantic coast of the United State from southeastern North Carolina to the central part of the east coast of Florida. The breeding range extends north to North Carolina (Beaufort) and south along the coast to South Carolina (Mount Pleasant and Frogmore); Georgia (Savannah, St. Katherine's Island, Blackbeard Island, Darien, St. Simons Island, Cumberland, and St. Marys); and Florida (Fernandina, Pilot Town, Matanzas Inlet, Sea Breeze, and Mosquito Inlet). In winter it is found somewhat farther south (near the head of Indian River, Florida).

Egg dates.—South Carolina: 18 records, March 9, to June 24; 9 records, May 6 to 16. Georgia: 23 records, March 23 to June 25; 12 records, May 3 to June 3. Florida: 12 records, May 19 to July 25; 6 records, May 24 to 28.

RALLUS VIRGINIANUS Linnaeus

VIRGINIA RAIL

HABITS

Contributed by Charles Wendell Townsend

The Virginia rail, like most of its family, is rarely seen except by those who know its ways, and, even when heard, its strange noises are often attributed to frogs or other creatures. One who has seen only the usual short and feeble flights of this bird would receive with astonishment, if not with incredulity, the statement that some individuals migrate annually many hundreds of miles. Such, however, must be the case, for the Virginia rail winters but sparsely north of North Carolina and it breeds as far north as Quebec and even Manitoba.

Spring.—Audubon (1840) describes the arrival of this bird as follows:

The males usually arrive at the breeding places a week or 10 days before the females. They travel silently and by night, as I have ascertained by observing them proceed singly and in a direct course, at a height of only a few feet, over our broad rivers, or over level land, when their speed is such as is never manifested by them under ordinary circumstances. Their movements can be easily traced for 50 yards or so during nights of brilliant moonshine, when you see them passing with a constant beat of the wings, in the manner of a green-winged teal.

This low flight in migration accounts for the fact that their dead bodies are sometimes found under telegraph lines or under wire fences.

Courtship.—Audubon (1840) was fortunate in witnessing the courtship dance of the Virginia rail, and thus describes it:

The notes of the rail came loudly on my ear, and on moving toward the spot whence they proceeded, I observed the bird exhibiting the full ardor of his passion. Now with open wings raised over its body, it ran around its beloved, opening and flirting its tail with singular speed. Each time it passed before her, it would pause for a moment, raise itself to the full stretch of its body and legs, and bow to her with all the grace of a well-bred suitor of our own species. The female also bowed in recognition, and at last, as the male came nearer and nearer in his circuits, yielded to his wishes, on which the pair flew off in the manner of house pigeons, sailing and balancing their bodies on open wings until out of sight. During this exhibition, the male emitted a mellow note, resembling the syllables "*cuckoe, cuckoe,*" to which the female responded with the kind of lisping sound uttered by young birds of the species when newly hatched.

The courtship song of the Virginia rail suggests at a distance the sounds made by striking an anvil with a hammer which rebounds. If the bird is near at hand the sound suggests the clicking of a telegraph instrument. The song has a peculiar vibrant, metallic quality and may be written down "*kid-ick, kid-ick, kid-ick,*" or again "*cut, cut, cut-ah, cut-ah.*" It is sometimes repeated many times and may be heard at night as well as by day, for this bird, although largely diurnal in its habits, is often abroad during the night hours.

Nesting.—The nest of the Virginia rail is cunningly concealed and is almost always built in a fresh-water marsh or near fresh water. Occasionally, however, it is found in the upper reaches of salt marshes that are sometimes overflowed by storm tides. Although it usually selects a dryer place in the marsh than the sora, yet it not infrequently builds its nest over water. One such nest I found in an extensive growth of cat-tails in water 6 inches deep on the edge of a pond. The nest was slung a foot from the water, was 8 inches in diameter and was composed of coarse grasses and cat-tails. Often, even in water, the nest rests on the mud and is composed of a great mass of grasses and reeds, forming sometimes a towerlike structure 7 or 8 inches high. J. A. Weber (1909) describes such a nest that was—

in the center of a circular bunch of growing cat-tails. It consisted of a mass of cat-tail blades and stems, placed layer upon layer, the foundation resting on the mud, so that the rim of the nest was 7 inches above the surface of the water. The inside of the nest was rather shallow, 4¾ by 4½ inches in diameter, and lined with cat-tail blade chips ½ to 2 inches in length.

F. S. Hersey in his notes describes a nest that—

was built up in a tussock of grass in a rather dry spot bordering a cat-tail marsh. One end of the nest was somewhat depressed—in fact, so much that the eggs rolled dangerously near the edge—and from the depressed side a narrow runway sloped down about 2 feet to the level of the ground.

P. L. Hatch (1892) noticed that when the first egg was laid there was only a slight depression in the nest and he thinks that this becomes deeper as egg laying and incubation progress. He supposes that the male continues to build up the structure around the female, in which work she assists, and he also thinks that the weight of her body helps to deepen the excavation.

Eggs.—[Author's note: The Virginia rail lays from 7 to 12 eggs; I have never heard of any larger sets. The eggs are easily distinguished from those of the sora rail, which often breeds in the same marshes, as they are lighter colored, less heavily marked, and less glossy. In shape they vary from ovate to elongate ovate. The shell is smooth with very little or no gloss. The ground color is pale buff, varying from "pinkish buff" to "cartridge buff" or nearly white. They are sparingly and irregularly spotted, often chiefly around the larger end, with "hazel," "russet," "cinnamon-brown" and "army brown"; some specimens have a few spots of light shades of "drab-gray." The measurements of 73 eggs average 32 by 24.5 millimeters; the eggs showing the four extremes measure 35 by 24, 34 by 25.5, 29 by 22.5 millimeters.]

Young.—The exact length of incubation has not been recorded, but it is known to be not less than 15 days. The young come out of the egg with their eyes open and are so active that they leave the nest even before the coal-black down in which they are clad is dry. The first chicks often leave the nest before the rest of the eggs are hatched. In a few days, at the latest, the nest is deserted, in all cases observed, although it is possible that when undisturbed by visitors, human or other, the young may remain in the nest a little longer. As the female begins incubation before all the eggs are laid, several days may elapse between the hatching of the first and the last egg. Bowdish (1891) says that the young are conducted away by one parent as fast as hatched, while the other parent continues to incubate.

From the beginning, the downy young are good swimmers and divers, and are well able to run over the ground and to climb about in the reeds and grasses, making use of their large feet and claws and of their little wings, each of which is provided with a tiny claw on the outer digit.

Verdi Burtch's (1917) observations of the young and their parents are of much interest. He says:

On May 11, 1908, the eggs were just beginning to hatch in a nest that I had found some few days before, and, as I approached, the female slipped from the nest and away through the cat-tails. She was quickly followed by the two little ones, although they were but a few hours old. The nest was surrounded by water so that the birds had to swim, but even then they managed to elude me. Hoping to get a picture of the nest and eggs I set up my camera, and, while focusing, the mother appeared, carrying one of the little ones in her bill, dropped it into the nest, went on, and settled down to brood.

In another nest on—

June 17 the eggs were beginning to hatch, and there were six silky little ones in the nest. Three of them followed the mother when she left the nest and hid in the flags around its base. The three others were not yet dry and with their bright eyes shining lay kicking and struggling to get out of the nest. Soon the mother came back calling softly "ka-ka-ka-ka-ka," and the young ones left their hiding place and ran to her. One of them fell into one of my foot tracks, and the mother came quickly and taking it up, ran off into the flags, carrying it dangling from her bill as a cat carries her kittens. The male now showed himself for the first time.

On the next day all but one were hatched and that one appeared a few minutes later. Whereupon all left the nest and hid. When the mother appeared and called softly "kiu-kiu-kiu-kiu," ending with a grunting noise, they all ran to her.

Late in July both parents and young will be found on the muddy shore where they feed and dodge back into the flags at the least sign of danger. At this time the young are about half grown and still keep their downy appearance. When feeding, the mother comes out on the mud, a young one following, and when she finds a choice morsel it is there to receive it. Back in the flags the other young are following, uttering plaintive peeps. As soon as one is fed it returns to the flags and another one comes out to take its place.

While the parent birds usually slip unseen from the nest before the young are hatched, they are much bolder when the chicks are about. J. A. Weber (1909) relates a case where the female, flushed from her nest, remained in the immediate vicinity—

strutting about with her feathers puffed up and wings spread like a turkey cock, giving her a rather formidable appearance; at the same time she uttered a low grunting sound which I had never heard from a rail before and quite unlike their characteristic notes. The male showed his interest by his sharp " keck-keck-keck-keck " calls, evidently trying to lead me away from the nest.

Verdi Burtch (1917) was almost attacked by a female bird with wings drooping and feathers ruffled, and when he attempted to photograph her, she actually struck the lens of his camera with her bill.

J. H. Bowles (1893) relates a curious and unusual case where after the discovery of a Virginia rail's nest with nine eggs, the bird was seen three minutes later to return to the nest and, standing among the eggs, to deliberately spear them with her long bill. The question has been raised whether this destructive bird may not have been a rival and not the owner of the nest.

Plumages.—[Author's note: The downy young Virginia rail is completely covered with long, thick, rather coarse, black down, glossed bluish on the head and greenish on the back. It can be distinguished from the young sora by the much longer bill, which is yellowish at the base and tip and crossed by a broad black band in the middle; there are also no orange bristles on the chin.

The down is soon replaced by the juvenal plumage, early in July or earlier, as soon as the young bird is fully grown. In this the head, neck, and upper parts are mostly dull black, with brown edgings on the back; the under parts, particularly on the breast and flanks, are more or less dull black, in some mostly black, in others only mottled with black; the throat is white or grayish white; the central breast and belly are more or less mottled with white and sometimes, particularly in males, suffused with pinkish buff; the wings are much like those of the adult, but a little duller.

A partial and gradual molt of the contour plumage, beginning sometimes as early as the middle of August and usually completed in October or November, produces the first winter plumage which is practically adult, I have been unable to recognize young birds after this postjuvenal molt.

Adults have a complete postnuptial molt, in July and August, and probably a partial prenuptial molt in the spring. In fresh fall plumage adults are rather darker and more richly colored than in spring.]

Food.—With its long curved bill the Virginia rail probes the mud and extracts many a fat earth worm and the larvae of insects. It also eats slugs and snails, small fish, caterpillars, beetles, and other insects, and it is said to eat occasionally the seeds of grasses.

Alvin R. Cahn (1915) tried some interesting feeding experiments on a Virginia rail that was captured when exhausted by an early snowstorm in October in Madison, Wisconsin. The bird recovered and became remarkably tame and developed an insatiable appetite, but at the same time, showed great discrimination in its feeding habits. These were strictly carnivorous. It refused to swallow rice or corn or bread. Even finely chopped liver was refused. Sunfish, sticklebacks, bullheads, and crayfish when captured by this bird were at once removed from the water of its tank and taken as far from it as the limits of its cage would permit before they were eaten, a proceeding evidently intended to eliminate the possibility of their escape. Crayfish were pecked and shaken until all their legs fell off and the creature rendered helpless before they were eaten. The legs were afterwards sought out and swallowed. Amphipods and other small aquatic forms were captured with great skill and eaten on the spot. Caterpillars were taken to the water and their bristles softened and broken before they were eaten, while frogs were pounded into insensibility in the water. Small snakes were eaten with avidity. The largest snake given this bird was a garter snake 12 inches long. It was attacked at once with vigorous thrusts of the bill, and, after half an hour's efforts, the bird began to swallow it head first. The snake, however, soon looped its body about the bird and was hastily unswallowed. Renewed thrusts with the bill and further unsuccessful swallowing trials ensued and not until the end of two strenuous hours was the reptile finally disposed of. After an hour's sleep, the rail was ready for new worlds to conquer.

Behavior.—It sometimes happens that in walking through a marsh one almost steps on a Virginia rail that springs into the air and, with dangling legs, flies on feeble wings for 5 or 10 yards and drops, apparently exhausted, to the grass. If one runs at once to the spot, the bird seems to have vanished—it can not be flushed again. It has run swiftly through the grass, its thin body enabling it to pass among thickset reeds, while its muscular legs soon carry it beyond our reach. In these tactics it can generally escape from a dog. That it was flushed in the first place was a rare happening. In the migrations or when on long flights, the Virginia rail extends its legs horizontally behind like all water birds, and wings its way with considerable speed and power.

While the Virginia rail is able to run with agility through the grass and over the mud and even on the broad leaves of the water lilies floating on the water, it is also able to cling to the grass stalks and rushes or to the ascending branches of bushes and to climb to their summits. It also swims gracefully.

The best way to observe these shy birds is to take up one's station near a pond or marsh frequented by them and watch patiently, silently, and immobile, and in so doing the watcher is often well rewarded. In pursuance of this plan I once concealed myself in the low branches of a willow and made the following observations (Townsend, 1920):

I heard an ear-piercing *"Spee"* or *"See"* from near at hand and saw a Virginia rail threading its way in and out among the rushes, thrusting continually its long curved bill into the water and mud. It ran within 10 feet of me up onto the bank, so near that I could see its dark red eyes, and, as it disappeared in the cat-tails, another one appeared. Their frequently emitted notes were as sharp as those of a red squirrel, at time suggestive of the squeak made by the grass-blade stretched between the thumbs, at times a low guttural chattering or grunting or moaning; now a mild *"cut-ta, cut-ta"*, then a loud and disdainful *"eh-eh"*. The one that had passed me soon popped out of the cat-tails with a long worm hanging from its bill, but, disturbed by my presence, turned back to reappear a little farther off and returned to the rushes as before. It then flew out over the pond with weak, feeble wing beats, legs dangling close to the water, and the worm still in its bill. It landed feebly and awkwardly, sitting down in the water before scrambling to its feet and elevating and depressing its short tail.

The courtship song and many of the calls have already been described, but the vocabulary of this bird is so extensive that it would be impossible to include it all here. Brewster (1902) describes a common call as a "rapid succession of low yet penetrating grunts not unlike those of a hungry pig," and he states that the grunting is emitted by both sexes. He also says that, "The female when anxious about her eggs or young also calls '*ki-ki-ki*' and sometimes '*kiu*' like a flicker."

W. E. Saunders (1918) says:

The tone of the calls of the young resembled the squeaking of a door hinge and the vocal sound was "*kee-a*" the final syllable being very short, while in the case of the old birds, the first syllable was so short as to be inaudible at any considerable distance.

The small size of this rail, its long curved bill and its rich brown wings and underparts make its recognition in the field comparatively simple.

Game.—While the sora is shot in great numbers for sport, the Virginia rail is rarely sought for this purpose. Its flight is so feeble that no skill is required to kill it, although a few are occasionally picked off by snipe shooters. In former days this bird was sometimes to be seen exposed for sale in the markets.

In their southern migrations in the autumn with ranks recruited by the summer's broods, the Virginia rails are more easily seen than in the spring and their course is a more leisurely one. At this time of the year I have occasionally found them in the salt marshes of the coast.

DISTRIBUTION

Range.—Southern Canada, the United States, and Central America south to Guatemala.

Breeding range.—North to British Columbia (Beaver Creek, Chilliwack, probably 158-mile House and Okanagan); Montana (Columbia Falls and Great Falls); Saskatchewan (Indian Head); Manitoba (Shoal Lake, Chemawawin, Reaburn, and Winnipeg); Minnesota (Leach Lake and Millelacs Lake); Wisconsin (Madison, Kelley Brook, and West Depere); Michigan (Douglas Lake, Bay City, Pontiac, and Detroit); Ontario (Wellington and Waterloo Counties, Kingston, and Ottawa); Quebec (Montreal and Quebec); New Brunswick (Scotch Lake and St. John); and Nova Scotia (Kentville). East to Nova Scotia (Kentville); Maine (Fryeburg); Massachusetts (Boston); Rhode Island (Newport and Quonochontaug); New York (Shelter Island and New York City); New Jersey (Ocean County and Cape May);

Virginia (Wallops Island); and North Carolina (Gull Shoal). South
to North Carolina (Gull Shoal); Ohio (Lewiston Reservoir); Indiana
(Bluffton); Kentucky (Henderson); Illinois (Mount Carmel and
Vandalia); Missouri (Clark County); Iowa (Newton and Boone);
Nebraska (London, Lincoln, and Valentine); Colorado (Clear Creek
[near Denver], Fountain, and San Luis Lakes); probably New Mexico
(Lake Burford); Mexico (Lerma); Lower California (San Ramon);
Utah (Salt Lake City); Nevada (Carson City); and California (Lone
Pine and Escondido). West to California (Escondido, Fullerton,
Los Angeles, Tulare Lake, Paicines, Haywards, Eagle Lake, and Fort
Crook); Oregon (Klamath Lake, Newport, and Beaverton); Wash-
ington (Tacoma, Waldron Island, and Bellingham Bay); and British
Columbia (Victoria, Beaver Creek, and probably 158-mile House).

The Virginia rail was found at Tizimin, Yucatan, on June 23 (specimen in British Museum). It is casual in summer in Newfoundland (Reeks) and there is a record of one in 1891 from Hamilton Inlet,
Labrador.

Winter range.—North to British Columbia (Chilliwack and Okana-
gan); Utah (Provo); Colorado (Clear Creek [near Denver], and Barr);
Arkansas (Stuttgart); Illinois (Mount Carmel); and North Carolina
(Pea Island). East to North Carolina (Pea Island); rarely Bermuda;
South Carolina (Charleston and Sea Islands); Georgia (Blackbeard
Island and Darien); Florida (mouth of St. Johns River, Orlando,
Titusville, and Fort Myers); Cuba (Isle of Pines); Mexico, Vera Cruz
(Jalapa); and Guatemala (Antigua and Duenas). South to Guate-
mala (Duenas); State of Mexico (Lerma); Sinaloa (Mazatlan);
Lower California (probably San Jose del Cabo and San Quentin);
and California (Riverside and Tomales Bay). West to California
(Tomales Bay); Oregon (Salem); Washington (Walla Walla and pro-
bably Port Townsend); and British Columbia (Chilliwack).

Casual in winter north to Virginia (Virginia Beach, January 6,
1912); Maryland (Easton, January 20, 1891); New Jersey (at a warm
spring near Trenton, during January, 1869); New York (Long Island,
February 6 to 13, 1885); Massachusetts (Barnstable, December 31,
1894, Cape Cod, December, 1892, and Worcester, January 1, 1891);
and Montana (Helena, February 22, and March 12, 1911).

Spring migration.—Early dates of arrival are: South Carolina,
Charleston, April 1, 1912; North Carolina, Raleigh, March 7, 1891,
and Highlands, April 6, 1910; West Virginia, Scott Depot, April
24, 1907, and Winfield, April 14, 1908; District of Columbia, April
2, 1903; Pennsylvania, State College, April 19, 1916; New Jersey;
New York, Bear Mountain near Stony Point, March 13, 1920,
Branchport, April 7, 1905, Ithaca, April 11, 1910, Geneva, April 15,

1911, East Otto, April 19, 1888, Lockport, April 22, 1890, Canandaigua, April 27, 1905, and Shelter Island, April 28, 1887; Connecticut, Middleton, April 6, 1912, Portland, April 11, 1913, and Bethel, April 13, 1890; Massachusetts, Dennis, March 14, 1921, Rehoboth, April 17, 1884, Jamaica Plain, April 18, 1891, and Harvard, April 20, 1909; Quebec, Montreal, April 25, 1913; Kentucky, Bowling Green, April 6, 1902; Missouri, Marionville, March 24, 1920, and St. Louis, March 31, 1887; Illinois, Englewood, April 3, 1889, Knoxville, April 9, 1896, Hennepin, April 14, 1885, and Rockford, April 15, 1893; Indiana, Vincennes, March 28, 1921, Waterloo, March 31, 1907, Frankfort, April 1, 1897, Indianapolis, April 7, 1916, and La Porte, April 17, 1892; Ohio, Hillsboro, March 13, 1918, Sandusky, March 27, 1902, Lakeside, April 3, 1917, Huron, April 14, 1913, Oberlin, April 14, 1913, and Canton, April 16, 1911; Michigan, Albion, April 11, 1899, Vicksburg, April 12, 1905, and Ann Arbor, April 11, 1918; Ontario, Dunnville, April 23, 1889, and Toronto, April 30, 1901; Iowa, Sioux City, April 22, 1916, and Keokuk, April 14, 1889; Wisconsin, Milwaukee, April 8, 1900, New Cassel, April 16, 1884, Delavan, April 19, 1896, and Madison, April 19, 1917; Minnesota, Elk River, April 25, 1915, Heron Lake, April 27, 1890, and Minneapolis, April 28, 1911; Nebraska, Lincoln, April 28, 1900, and Red Cloud, May 1, 1920; North Dakota, Grafton, May 12, 1916, and Grand Forks, May 14, 1903; Manitoba, Margaret, May 7, 1910; Saskatchewan, Dinsmore, May 10, 1911, and Indian Head, May 19, 1910; and Alberta, Stony Plain, May 24, 1908.

Late dates of spring departure are: Lousiana, New Orleans, April 7; and Mississippi, Bay St. Louis, April 19, 1902.

Fall migration.—Late dates of fall departure are: Manitoba, Margaret, October 10, 1912; Nebraska, Valentine, October 7, 1893, and Long Pine, October 10, 1898; Minnesota, Hutchinson, October 25, 1915; Wisconsin, Delavan, October 16, 1894, and Madison, October 21, 1913; Iowa, National, October 17, 1908; Ontario, Ottawa, October 14, 1889, and Toronto, November 10, 1906; Michigan, Livonia, September 9, 1894, Charity Island, September 11, 1910, Ann Arbor, October 17, 1918, Manchester, November 2, 1894, and Vicksburg, November 24, 1912; Ohio, Youngstown, October 1, 1914, Oberlin, October 7, 1907, Huron, October 16, 1912, Cleveland, October 18, 1915, Chillicothe, October 26, 1904, and Circleville, November 23, 1880; Indiana, Waterloo, October 17, 1905; Illinois, Chicago, November 5, 1904; Quebec, Montreal, October 23, 1897; Massachusetts, Boston, October 5, 1909, and Harvard, November 29, 1914; Connecticut, Portland, October 20, 1890, and New Haven, October 29, 1904; New York, Canandaigua, October 3, 1905, Montauk Point, October 30, 1900, and Mayville, November 19, 1903; New Jersey, Atlantic

City, November 6, 1891, and Dennis Creek, December 30, 1895; and
Pennsylvania, Erie, October 28, 1893, Chester County, November 7,
1879, and Harvey's Lake, November 18, 1911.

Early dates of fall arrival are: South Carolina, Mt. Pleasant, September 21; and Louisiana, southern part, October 1.

Egg dates.—Southern New England and New York: 62 records,
May 14, to August 6; 31 records, May 24 to 31. New Jersey and
Pennsylvania: 12 records, May 17 to July 17; 6 records, May 23 to
June 10. Michigan and Wisconsin: 18 records, May 21 to June 24;
9 records, May 30 to June 9. Utah and California: 12 records,
April 3 to June 22; 6 records, May 20 to June 3. Washington: 6
records, April 1 to June 10; average May 1.

PORZANA PORZANA (Linnaeus)

SPOTTED CRAKE

HABITS

Contributed by Charles Wendell Townsend

The spotted crake, according to Dresser (1871) inhabits Europe
generally during the breeding season, ranging further north in the
eastern than in the western part. In the autumn it migrates southward, and is found commonly in winter in northern Africa; and in
Asia it is met with as far east as eastern Siberia. Its only claim to
inclusion here is that it occasionally visits Greenland. Hagerup (1891)
says it is "A rare visitor in South Greenland, Benzon's collection
contains a skin from Julianeshaab, dated 1878."

Nesting.—It generally selects a wet place for its nest which is sometimes surrounded by water. Dresser (1871) says: "The nest of the
spotted crake, resembling that of the water rail, is a careless,
bulky structure of flags, dried reeds, and leaves of aquatic plants,
lined with finer material." Selby (1833) says: "Its nest is built
amongst the thick sedges and reeds of the marshes, and from the foundation of it being frequently placed in water, is composed of a large
mass of decayed aquatic plants interlaced, with the hollow neatly
formed and comfortably lined."

Eggs.—The eggs are from 8 to 12, or even 15 in number and, according to Dresser, " are oval in shape, the surface of the shell being smooth
and rather glossy. In ground color they are warm ochraceous, or
dull ochraceous marked with fine dots, with violet-grey shell markings
and reddish brown spots and blotches, which are tolerably regularly
scattered over the surface of the shell." Witherby's Handbook (1920)
gives the measurements of 100 eggs as averaging 33.62 by 24.57
millimeters; the eggs showing the four extremes measure 37.5 by 24.8,
33 by 26.8, 29.1 by 23 and 32 by 22.2 millimeters.

Young.—The young are clothed in black down and are able to follow their parents and swim well soon after they are hatched.

Plumages.—The sexes are alike. Ramsay (1923) describes the plumage as follows:

Above olive brown, streaked white and with some black feathers; forehead, sides of crown, throat and chest slaty, spotted white; inner web of inner secondaries reddish brown, outer web like the back; abdomen whitish, flanks, under wing coverts and axillaries brown barred white, under tail coverts buff. Iris brownish red. Bill olive yellow, orange at base below. Legs and feet yellowish green.

Food.—The food of the spotted crake consists of worms, aquatic insects, slugs and snails, grass seeds and the tender shoots of water herbage.

Behavior.—Dresser (1871) says:

It frequents swampy localities where aquatic herbage is abundant, and where it can find good shelter; and it is extremely difficult to force it to take wing when it is in the dense cover of the reeds, through which it creeps and glides with the greatest ease. When followed by a dog, it invariably seeks to escape by running and hiding; and it is only when hard pressed that it will take wing, to fly only a short distance, and again seek shelter amongst the reeds. On the wing it does not by any means appear to advantage; for it flies heavily, like a young bird that has not yet attained to the full use of its wings and its legs hang down clumsily unless it flies to some distance, when they are stretched out behind. * * * Its call-note is a clear loud *"kweet,"* which is seldom heard during the daytime, but most frequently in the evening or at night. * * * It swims with grace and ease, jerking its head as it paddles along.

Bonhote (1907) calls it "a very skulking species and its only note is a low '*kwit, kwit*', so that it is seldom either seen or heard." For these reasons, probably, the ornithological accounts of this bird are generally very brief.

Game.—Yarrell (1871) says:

In the autumn these birds are considered to be in the best condition for the table, and, as an article of food, are in great estimation, particularly in France. The flesh is said to be of a fine and delicate flavor.

DISTRIBUTION

Range.—The breeding range of the spotted crake is confined mainly to continental Europe, from Norway and Finland to the Mediterranean, and also east to western Siberia and Turkestan. It winters in India, Africa, Madeira, and the Canary Islands.

Its inclusion in the American list of birds rests on several accidental occurrences in Greenland (Frederickshaab, Godthaab, Nenortalik, and Julianshaab).

Egg dates.—Central Europe: 12 records, May 10 to June 18; 6 records, May 21 to June 15.

PORZANA CAROLINA (Linnaeus)

SORA RAIL

HABITS

The sora or Carolina rail is unquestionably *the* rail of North America. It is the most widely distributed and the best known of its tribe. Throughout its wide breeding range its cries are among the most characteristic voices of the marshes. During some part of the year it is more or less common in practically every Province in Canada, every State in the United States, and in much of Central America and the West Indies. It is the most popular of the rails among sportsman and, when one speaks of rail shooting, he generally refers to this species. Being a prolific breeder, it is astonishingly abundant in favored localities during the fall migration.

The sora, like the other rails, is a denizen of the oozy marsh; and for this reason it has continued to live and breed in the midst of civilization long after so many of the wilder and shyer birds have been driven away. Man clears away the forests, cultivates the prairies, cleans up the bushy hillsides and mows the meadow hay, forcing the birds that live there to move elsewhere; but he dislikes the quaking bog, which is perhaps too low to drain, and so he leaves it until the last, when the land becomes valuable enough to fill in for houselots. Many such little swamps and bogs, which had long persisted near the heart of some big city, have been filled in within my memory. And the rails, Virginia and sora, have stuck to them to the last; so well hidden were they in the seclusion of the marsh, that they little cared for the activities of civilization so close around them; the marsh was their world and supplied all their needs.

In my college days, in the late eighties, such a bog still existed near the center of Brookline, where a friend and I used to wade around in the mud up to our waists, collecting rails eggs; then, dripping with mud and water, we would return to his house, jump into the bath tub with our clothes on and wash off the mud, much to his mother's disgust. In those days the Fresh Pond marshes in Cambridge were an oasis of wilderness in a desert of civilization and both the Virginia and sora rails nested there in abundance. Both of these marshes were filled in and obliterated by human "improvements."

As late as 1908, Mr. J. A. Weber (1909) found both Virginia and sora rails nesting on the northern portion of the Manhattan Island in New York City. He writes:

The marshes inhabited by the rails are situated at the northern portion of Manhattan Island and extend northward and eastward from the foot of the hill at Fort George (One hundred and ninetieth Street and Amsterdam Avenue). These marshes formerly lined the shore of the Harlem River, but through street· improvements have been separated from the river and cut up into small areas

The water in these marshes no longer rises and falls with the tide and the only connection with the river is through drain pipes under the streets; consequently the water is more or less fresh.

I discovered another nest of the Virginia rail on June 6, 1908, in a small marsh bordering on Dyckman Street, with two baseball fields adjoining it on the east and south. The nest was placed within 20 feet of the street where hundreds of people as well as vehicles pass daily and large crowds often assemble to witness the speedway trotting races or the baseball games. Yet the little mother rail quietly sat on her 10 eggs, apparently unconcerned about the civilization around her. Within an hour after finding the above nest, I discovered a nest of the sora (*Porzana carolina*), containing 14 eggs. The marsh in which this nest was built is situated on the south side of Two hundred and seventh Street between the foot of the new bridge across the Harlem River at this point and the Two hundred and seventh Street subway station. The marsh is so close to the subway station that some of the passengers noticed and watched me from the station platform while I was floundering about among the rushes. Yet strangely enough the noise of the numerous passing trains did not deter these shy birds from nesting in such close proximity.

Spring.—Audubon (1840) throws some light on the spring migration of the sora rail, which he describes in some detail, as follows:

This bird, which I think might have been named the Pennsylvanian or Virginian rail, enters the Union from the shores of Mexico, early in March, when many are to be seen in the markets of New Orleans. Some reach their northern destination by ascending along the margins of our western streams, or by crossing the country directly, in the manner of the woodcock; while those which proceed along the coast shorten their journey as much as possible by flying across the headlands of the numerous inlets or bays of our southern districts, retiring or advancing more slowly according to the state of the weather. Thus, those which cross the peninsula of Florida, through the marshes and lagoons that lead to the headwaters of the St. Johns River, instead of traveling around the shores of Georgia and South Carolina, fly directly across toward Cape Lookout. It is nevertheless true, that a certain number of these birds follow the sinuosities of the shores, for I found some in the markets of Charleston, in the month of April, that had been killed in the immediate neighborhood of that city, and I obtained others in various parts; but the number of these is very small compared with that of those which cross at once. When their passage takes place, either during calm weather or with a favorable wind, the fortunate travelers pursue their journey by entering Pimlico Sound, and following the inner margins of the outward banks of this part of the coast until they reach Cape Henry. From thence some ascend the Chesapeake, while others make for the mouth of the Delaware, and these perhaps again meet on the borders of Lake Ontario, or the waters of the St. Lawrence, after which they soon enter those portions of the country in which they breed, and spend a short but agreeable season.

Nesting.—The nests that we used to find in the Fresh Pond marshes, and in other places in Massachusetts, were usually well hidden in the dense growth of cat-tail flags (*Typha latifolia*) where the water and mud was quite deep, were generally well-made baskets of dead flags built up a few inches above the water and supported by the surrounding and growing flags. A nest found on Martha's Vineyard on May 27, 1900, illustrates a more open type of nesting. It was near the edge of a marshy island in a muddy pond, much overgrown with cat-tail flags. We had to push our boat a long way into the low, dead flags to find water shallow enough to wade in, but did not discover the nest until we returned later and happened to see it within a foot of the boat. The nest contained 12 handsome eggs and was placed in a little hummock among low, open, dead flags, where the water was about knee-deep; it was built of dead flags, arranged in a solid mass and dry on top; it was raised about 4 inches above the water, and measured about 6 inches in diameter; the inner cavity was about 3 inches wide by 2 inches deep. It was a typical cat-tail nest in which some of the eggs were arranged in a second layer, as they almost always are in a large set, so that the small body of the bird can cover them all.

In the prairie regions of North Dakota, Manitoba, and Saskatchewan we found numerous nests of both Virginia and sora rails, around the borders of the sloughs or in wet, grassy meadows. The nests of the sora were generally in deeper water and were more substantially built than those of the Virginia rail. They were sometimes found in meadows where the grass was not very tall, but more often they were better concealed in clumps of bulrushes (*Scirpus lacustris*) or flags. The nests were built up from 3 to 6 inches above the water and were made of dead flags, bulrushes and dry grasses.

A nest found by F. Seymour Hersey near Lake Winnipegosis, Manitoba, on July 2, 1913, was placed in a clump of grass in a grassy marsh; it was made entirely of green grass, with which the center of the clump was entirely filled, and the rim of the nest was 10 inches above the wet ground; it appeared to have been built upon the remains of an old nest. The nest of the sora is usually more or less concealed by a canopy of grass, reeds, or flags arched over it, especially if it is in an open situation, and there is often a runway, made of the nesting material, leading up to it.

Eggs.—The sora rail lays from 6 to 18 eggs, the extremes being very unusual and the average numbers running from 10 to 12. The shape is ovate and the shell is smooth and glossy. The eggs are more richly colored, more heavily spotted and more glossy than those of the Virginia rail, with which this species is often associated. The ground color is a rich buff, varying from "chamois" or "cinnamon buff" to "cream buff," "ivory yellow," or even "pale olive buff." They are irregularly spotted with browns and drabs, "auburn," "chestnut brown," "russet," "snuff brown" and shades of "cinnamon-drab" and "ecru drab." The measurements of 96 eggs average 31.5 by 22.5 millimeters; the eggs showing the four extremes measure 34.5 by 23.5, 31 by 24.5, 28 by 22, and 30 by 20.5 millimeters.

Young.—The period of incubation is said to be 14 days; it is shared by both sexes and is nearly continuous from the time that the first few eggs are laid, as is shown by the protracted period of hatching; nests often contain young birds just hatched, others hatching, and eggs in various stages of development. The birds stick to their nests very closely and hatch the eggs even when they are partially submerged. It is inconceivable how so small a bird can successfully cover and hatch such large numbers of eggs, even when they are arranged in two layers, as is generally the case; but it is accomplished somehow, probably by frequently shifting the eggs and by close sitting. One seldom sees a rail leave its nest, but always finds warm eggs; the bird slips quietly off and disappears.

The young rails are very precocious. They leave the nest soon after they are hatched, or immediately if necessary. W. Leon Dawson (1903) says:

I once came upon a nestful in a secluded spot at the critical time. Hearing my distant footsteps most of the brood had taken to their new-found heels, leaving two luckless wights *in ovo*. At my approach one more prison door flew open. The absurd fluff ball rolled out, shook itself, grasped the situation, promptly tumbled over the side of the nest, and started to swim across a 6-foot pool to safety.

Dr. Morris Gibbs (1899) writes:

It is but natural to suppose that the male Carolina rail assists in the care of the young as the mother sets and brings the little fellow out slowly; and this is found to be true, as I have seen the black animated fluffy bunches of down pattering after the old man. The young leave the nest about as soon as they are hatched and run among the grass and rushes. A large number of them must become prey for their enemies in the marsh, for notwithstanding the large sets of eggs laid by all of the members of this family, none of them appear to increase to any extent.

Edward H. Forbush (1914) observes:

The young of this bird have often been mistaken for those of the little black rail. They are certainly both small and sable. When they once leave the nest, they are constantly in danger. Most of the larger animals and birds of the marshes, from the sandhill crane down to the mink, devour the eggs and young of rails wherever they find them. In the water, snakes, frogs, fish, and turtles lie constantly in wait to swallow them. They soon become experts in climbing and hiding. They can clamber up and down the water-plants, or run through them over the water by clinging to the upright stems. They swim more like a chicken than like a duck, nodding their little heads comically as they advance. Necessity soon teaches them to drop into the water and dive like a stone to safety.

In some notes sent to me by Miss Althea R. Sherman she mentions seeing a brood of young soras in which the birds were of different ages; "one was still covered with black down, one was quite well feathered, and one midway between them," indicating that they were hatched at different dates. She says that they "ran about in a lively fashion and fed like the adults from seeds and insects picked from the surface of the water."

Plumages.—The downy young sora is completely covered with thick, glossy, black down, except on the chin, which is ornamented by a small tuft of stiff, curly hairs of a "deep chrome" color. The natal down is replaced, during July and August, by the juvenal plumage, in which the sexes are alike. In this the upper parts are much like the adults, but the browns are paler, more olive, there is less black, and there are fewer white spots and edgings; there is no black on the head, except a central black stripe on the crown and forehead; the throat is dull white; the breast and under parts are pale grayish and buffy; and the flanks are barred with brownish black and buffy white, instead of clear black and white, as in the adult. A nearly complete molt of the contour plumage, in varying amounts in different individuals and at various times between August and December, produces the first winter plumage, in which the sexes begin to differentiate. I have seen this molt in progress as early as August 20 and as late as December 24. In this plumage a few black feathers or restricted black areas are acquired on throat and face, with varying amounts of slate gray on head and breast. Some birds become much like adults, while others remain in a decidedly juvenal plumage all winter, and even through March. Usually a first prenuptial molt of the contour plumage produces, in March or even earlier, a nuptial plumage which is nearly adult. A complete molt, between July and September, makes the young bird indistinguishable from the adult.

Adults have an incomplete prenuptial molt, involving only the contour plumage, between January and March, and a complete postnuptial molt of all the plumage in summer, between July and September. The two seasonal plumages are alike, except that in spring the black stripe down the throat is broader and unbroken. The female is much like the male, but the black in the head is duller and more restricted; the mantle is usually more spotted with white; and all the colors are less intense.

Food.—Referring to the food of this species Doctor Gibbs (1899) writes:

The ortolan or sora rail feeds largely upon the small mollusks of the marsh. and at times many of these minute shells may be found in the crops of the birds. Neuropterous insects, those belonging to the order in which the dragon fly is embraced, form a good share of their food. These insects are aquatic, like the mosquito, in their earlier forms of development. This rail, like the others, also feeds to a limited extent on vegetable substances, and especially on a particular kind of seed in late summer, which I have been unable to identify. One authority, Cook, in his "Birds of Michigan," gives reptiles as the food of the rails. This is undoubtedly incorrect, as I have yet to learn of reliable instances where rails feed on reptiles, and my readers may readily see that the make-up of these birds does not admit of their tearing snakes, frogs, and turtles to pieces. The nearest that these marsh birds come to feeding on reptiles is when an occasional small tadpole is gobbled up. A captive rail of this species, which I once owned, fed greedily on hashed meat and earthworms.   The bird came readily at my approach and after three days in confinement exhibited no signs of fear, and quickly learned to feed from my hand.

The foregoing remarks refer to the food of these rails on their breeding grounds or during the spring and early summer.   Later in the summer and early in the fall, when the seeds of various aquatic plants are ripening, their food is more largely vegetable.   They are especially fond of the seeds of wild rice (*Zizania*) which grows profusely along the banks of sluggish streams and in fresh-water marshes.   In these wild-rice marshes they congregate in enormous numbers in August and September, in company with bobolinks, and feast on the seeds of these and other plants until they become very fat.   Both rails and reed birds are then easy marks for the embryo sportsmen and tempting morsels for the table.   Probably most of the seeds are gleaned from the surface of the water or mud, where they have fallen, but, as the rails are good climbers, they undoubtedly pick some from the stalks above.

Behavior.—When flushed in a marsh the sora usually rises from almost underfoot, flutters feebly along just over the tops of the reeds for 40 or 50 yards, with a slow and apparently labored flight and with feet awkwardly dangling, and then, with uplifted wings, suddenly drops down out of sight again.   Perhaps it can be flushed again but it is more likely to escape by running.   When making a long flight across a river or pond, its flight is much stronger; its neck and legs are extended and its wings are making strong steady strokes.   Audubon (1840) says:

The flight of this little bird while migrating is low, and performed with a constant beating of the wings, as in the coot and other birds of its kind.   They pass swiftly along in compact flocks of from 5 to 100 or more individuals.   At times you see them rise in a long curve, as if they had perceived some dangerous object beneath them; then resume their ordinary direct flight and are soon out of sight.

However weak this rail may appear on the wing, its appearance when seen on foot is one of strength and activity.   Owing to its shy and retiring habits, it is seldom seen, but, if the observer lies concealed near some open place in the bog, he may catch a glimpse of it as it comes out to feed, stepping daintily over the bog, flirting its short tail up and down or spreading it out in display, and nodding its head back and forth with a graceful dovelike motion.   Its toes are so long and its body is so light, that it is easily supported on the lily pads or on a few floating reeds.   It takes long steps when walking, but when running its tracks may be a foot apart.   If alarmed by a sudden movement or sound, it runs to cover with lowered head and outstretched neck and with wings and plumage closely pressed against the narrowed body, as it slips out of sight in the narrow aisles between the reeds. Robert J. Sim (1911), who kept a sora rail in captivity until it became quite tame, says:

A rail which is quite at ease is very different in appearance from one that is frightened or at all nervous. Most birds of this kind to be seen in taxidermal collections look as if they had been "scared stiff"—a state of things which is, perhaps, consistent enough. But a live, comfortable rail going about his own business is as graceful a bird as you could find, and plump like a guinea hen or a Hubbard squash. The tail is carried in a horizontal position or droops slightly. On the other hand, when filled with apprehension the bird is very slim, the head is lowered and extended, and the tail is cocked up or is twitched up at every step.

The sora, like other rails, can swim well or even dive, if necessary. It often swims across narrow strips of water, rather than fly. C. J. Maynard (1896) writes:

All the rails swim and dive well but I think the Carolinas rather excel them all in this respect, for they will not only take readily to the water, but will pass beneath it with great facility, and I once saw one run nimbly along the bottom of a brook, the water of which was about a foot deep, by clinging to aquatic plants, and crossing it obliquely, emerged on the other side, thus passing over some 15 feet while submerged.

William Brewster (1902) has described the various notes of this rail remarkably well, as follows:

In the more open, grassy stretches of meadow, as well as among the beds of cat-tail flags but seldom, if ever, in thickets of bushes, we also hear, after the middle of April, mingling with the notes of Virginia rails and the din of countless frogs, the love song of the Carolina rail, a sweet, plaintive "er-e" given with a rising inflection and suggesting one of the "scatter calls" of the quail. Such, at least, is its general effect at distances of from 50 to 200 or 300 yards, but very near at hand it develops a somewhat harsh or strident quality and sounds more like "ka-e," while at the extreme limits of ear range one of the syllables is lost and the other might be easily mistaken for the peep of a Pickering's hyla. This note, repeated at short, regular intervals, many times in succession, is one of the most frequent as well as pleasing voices of the marsh in the early morning and just after sunset. It is also given intermittently at all hours of the day, especially in cloudy weather, while it is often continued, practically without cessation through the entire night.

Equally characteristic of this season and even more attractive in quality is what, has been termed the "whinny" of the Carolina rail. It consists of a dozen or 15 short whistles as sweet and clear in tone as a silver bell. The first 8 or 10 are uttered very rapidly in an evenly descending scale, the remaining ones more deliberately and in a uniform key. The whole series is often followed by a varying number of harsher, more drawling notes given at rather wide intervals. Although it is probable that the "whinny" is made by both sexes I have actually traced it only to the female. She uses it, apparently, chiefly as a call to her mate, but I have also repeatedly heard her give it just after I had left the immediate neighborhood of her nest, seemingly as an expression of triumph or rejoicing at the discovery that her eggs had not been molested. When especially anxious for their safety and circling close about the human intruder she often utters a low whining murmur closely resembling that which the muskrat makes while pursuing his mate and sometimes a "*cut-cut-cutta*" not unlike the song of the Virginia rail, but decidedly less loud and vibrant. In addition to all these notes both sexes have a variety of short, sharp cries which they give when startled by any sudden noise.

Rev. J. H. Langille (1884) gives it as "*queep-eep-ip-ip-ip-ip-ip-ip*, or *quaite, peep, peep, kuk, kuk, kuk*—the first two or three syllables in long-drawn, coaxing tones, and the remaining syllables shorter and more hurried." I have seen this rail utter a plaintive note, which sounded like "*peet-it-wheet*," or a sharper call note, like "*peek* or *puck*."

Both soras and Virginia rails often breed in the same marsh and in close proximity, but Miss Sherman's notes indicate that they are not always as friendly as they might be. In a marsh where both species were under daily observation, she saw the soras drive the Virginias before them and frequently, but not always, the latter fled upon the approach of the former.

Fall.—During the late summer and early fall, when the seeds of the wild rice, wild oats, and other aquatic plants are ripening and falling, the soras, greatly increased in numbers with their large broods of young, desert their breeding grounds and gather in great multitudes in the more open marshes on the rice-covered borders of the lakes and streams, where they feast and fatten on their favorite food. At such times a sudden noise, such as the report of a gun or the splash of a paddle or a stone thrown into the grass, will start a chorus of cries ringing from one end of the marsh to the other. In such places they remain until driven farther south by the first frosts. They are very sensitive to cold and are good weather prophets. After a frosty night, in late September or early October, a marsh, which was teeming with rails the day before, may be found entirely deserted, every bird having departed during the night. They have started on their autumn wanderings, their fall migration.

Mr. Forbush (1914) says:

The little wings which erstwhile would hardly raise the birds above the grass tops now carry them high and far. Some cross the seas to distant Bermuda, and they occasionally alight on vessels hundreds of miles at sea. They have been taken on the western mountains even as high as 12,500 feet, in the sagebrush of the desert, and on the cliffs of Panama.

This really remarkable migration is thus described by Prof. W. W. Cooke (1914):

The flight of the sora is slow and labored but some individuals travel more miles between the summer and winter homes than almost any other rails in the Western Hemisphere. The birds breeding in the Mackenzie Valley do not winter farther north than the Gulf coast and hence must travel at least 2,500 miles during their fall migration. The species passes in winter to about latitude 5° S., and as none of these South American birds nest south of latitude 35° N. the migration route can not possibly be shorter than 3,000 miles and may be much longer.

The autumnal flight to Bermuda is even more remarkable. Baird, Brewer, and Ridgway (1884) write: "Its movements and the irregular character of its visits to Bermuda are interesting features in its history. Maj. J. W. Wedderburn[2] states that it regularly visits Bermuda, arriving early in September. The first specimen, obtained September 3, 1847, was settling on a branch of a mangrove-tree—a very unusual action for this species, as it very rarely alights on a limb, and this one was 4 feet from the ground. A few remained throughout the winter. In October, 1849, it arrived in immense numbers, and one was killed January 17, and another April 26. J. L. Hurdis, in some supplementary notes [p. 82] added to Major Wedderburn's paper, states that however heavy and sluggish this bird may appear when disturbed in its marshy retreat, there can be no doubt that it possesses great strength of wing, and the fact that it never fails to visit Bermuda in its great southern migrations is sufficient proof of its powers of flight. A single instance was noted of its being met with as early as August 24. In September it had become rather numerous, but was more abundant in October than at any other time. In some seasons these birds all disappeared about the end of October, while in others a few remained to the 25th of November, and some even beyond that time. In 1849 and the three following years this bird visited Bermuda in its spring migrations, appearing in the latter part of February, and remaining through the months of March and April. Ten specimens were shot and three taken alive. During a southwest gale which prevailed on the 9th of October, 1849, thousands of this bird suddenly appeared in the marshes of Bermuda, and on the 29th of the same month not one of this species was to be seen. The whole immense flight had departed on some unexplained journey. This departure could not have been occasioned by any want of food, for the marshes were abundantly supplied, and the prevailing temperature was between 70° and 80° Fahrenheit. Mr. Hurdis states that this bird is also found in its migrations in the Island of Barbados, and thinks that there is little cause to doubt that the rivers and marshes of South America are its southern haunts during the winter months. It is very fat when it arrives in the Bermudas—evidently a provision of nature to sustain it in its long and arduous flight from one region to some distant point, as it probably traverses the Atlantic Ocean for 30 or 35 degrees of latitude without food."

Game.—The sora, or Carolina rail, has always been a popular game bird. It is exceedingly abundant at times in certain places; its flight is so slow and steady that it is easily killed; and when fattened on the succulent grains of the marshes its flesh is excellent food. But, to my mind, it is too small, too tame, and too easily

---

[2] Naturalist in Bermuda, p. 45.

killed to afford really good sport, in which the bird should have a
sporting chance for its life. My experience with rail shooting has
been limited to one day on the marshes of Essex, Connecticut, as
the guest of Dr. L. C. Sanford. It was the opening day of the
season and we each shot the legal limit, 35 birds, in a very short
time. His description of it is so much better than anything I can
write, that I prefer to quote from Doctor Sanford (1903), as follows:

When the wild oats along the tidal rivers of our coast begin to turn yellow
with the first touch of fall, the time for rail has come, and the high tides of September give the sportsman his first chance. The Connecticut River, where it
broadens into the Sound, is one of the favorite haunts of these birds. Here Essex
is the usual destination. Some 3 miles up the river from Saybrook, the little town
of Essex, with its one hotel and old-fashioned houses, looks now pretty much as
it did a hundred years ago. Rail tides generally come toward the middle of the
day, and the pusher is waiting for you at the landing; you stand for a minute
looking up and down the broad expanse of river. Everywhere along the shore
are wavy patches of high grass reaching far out into the water. These are the
wild oats, and here live the rail. A strong tide is running in, and you step into
a flat-bottomed skiff, which is rigged with a high stool firmly tied to the front
seat. The only task now is to sit still on this stool and be shoved. A short
row up the river and you are in the midst of thick wild oats, so high it is
difficult in many places to see over the tops, even from your exalted position.
A flutter just ahead, and a rail rises, shot almost before it cleared the grass; a
few feathers alone are left to tell the fate of the first bird of the season. The
next is given a chance to get in range, and the score is two; three or four more
straight exalt a man's idea of his shooting ability—without reason, though, for no
easier mark ever flew in front of a gun. Now a rail runs among some broken grass
ahead of the boat, and a whack from the pusher's pole starts him; at the shot
half a dozen teal jump within range, and the last one is feathered but not
stopped. Presently several rail start in quick succession; you fire, and load,
and fire again—not a miss yet, but all idea of definite direction is lost and the
last bird is the only one marked. Here a clever pusher shows his skill, and
after you have given up all thought of retrieving he picks them up in order.
Under these circumstances painted blocks can be used and tossed out to mark
the dead birds before the position of the boat is changed. The time of high tide
is short, but sufficient; every few seconds a bird rises, its slow flight affording a
sure mark; generally in front or to the side, occasionally behind, when you are
startled by the pusher's yell "Hi, rail!" in time to try a long shot. Sometimes
a larger bird, of the same general appearance and similar flight, starts up.
This is a clapper rail, known by many of our gunners as marsh hen. About
Essex they are rare. Sometimes, too, a mud hen flops out over the tops. In
some instances mud hens are quite common on the rail grounds. The Florida
gallinule is also a straggler here. Rail keep fluttering from the grass, less often
now, though, than an hour ago, but you have some time since reached the
limit—as well, for a falling tide makes the pushing hard and the birds refuse to rise.
Most of the birds are soras; occasionally the longer bill and darker coloring
mark a Virginia rail. An occasional chattering note tells of the presence of a rail,
secure in the high grass, until the next high tide. A lone bittern wings his way
to some safer spot, and this is our last glimpse of the marsh.

Before there were any bag limits on rails, much larger numbers
were killed; as many as 195 rails have been killed by one man on a

single tide, which usually includes about two hours before and two hours after high tide. Edward H. Forbush (1912) writes:

Doctor Lewis gives a record of the bags of Sora rails killed by a few men on the Delaware River, below Philadelphia, in 1846. The 34 records of consecutive days show an average of about 100 rails per man per day. He states that over 1,000 rails were brought into Chester in one day. Doctor Brewer (1884) says that it is not uncommon for an expert marksman to kill from 100 to 150 rails per day, and such scores were made on the Connecticut River in Connecticut in olden times, when there was no legal limit to the bag. This slaughter has made some inroads on the number of the birds in Massachusetts. Robert O. Morris writes that it is said that about 1,000 were killed at Longmeadow near Springfield, in 1908.

DISTRIBUTION

Range.—North America, Central America, the West Indies, and northwestern South America. Accidental in Great Britain.

Breeding range.—North to British Columbia (southern Cariboo district and Vanderhoof); Mackenzie (Fort Simpson, Fort Rae, and Fort Resolution); Manitoba (Chemawawin, Fort Churchill, and York Factory); Ontario (Severn House, Moose Factory [probably] and Bracebridge); Quebec (Montreal, Quebec, and Godbout); and Prince Edward Island. East to Prince Edward Island; New Brunswick (Grand Manan); Maine (Pittsfield and Norway); New Hampshire (Monadnock); Massachusetts (Boston and Ponkapog); Connecticut (Norwich and Westville); New York (Shelter Island); New Jersey (Princeton); and Pennsylvania (Philadelphia). South to Pennsylvania (Philadelphia, Carlisle, and Dubois); Ohio (Salem and Lewiston Reservoir); Indiana (Bluffton); Illinois (Springfield); Missouri (Independence); Kansas (Osawatomie); Colorado (Barr, Denver, Blue River, and Lay); probably Arizona (Mormon Lake); Utah (Provo); Idaho (Rupert); Nevada (Quinn River and probably Pyramid Lake); and California (San Bernardino and Escondido). West to California (Los Angeles and Eureka); Oregon (Klamath Lake and Portland); Washington (Tacoma and Seattle); and British Columbia (Chilliwack, Ashcroft, and Cariboo District).

Winter range.—North to California (Gilroy and Marysville); Arizona (Pecks Lake in the upper Verde Valley); Texas (Corpus Christi); Louisiana (Hester and Dimond); Mississippi (Biloxi and Bay St. Louis); Florida (Royal Palm Hammock, Whitfield, and Amelia Island); and Bermuda. East to Bermuda; Florida (Amelia Island and Titusville); Bahama Islands (Little Abaco, New Providence, Watlings Island, and Great Inagua Island); Porto Rico; St. Croix; Dominica Island; Santa Lucia Island; Grenada Island; Tobago Island and Trinidad. South to Trinidad; Venezuela (Caracas and Lake Valencia); Colombia (Medellin); and Peru (Sarayacu and Tumbez). West to Peru (Tumbez and Sarayacu); Ecuador (Quito);

Guatemala (Lake of Duenas and Lake Atitlan); Jalisco (La Barca); Sinaloa (Escuinapa and Mazatlan); Lower California (San Jose del Cabo, La Paz, and Colnett); and California (Escondido, Los Angeles, Santa Barbara, Gilroy, and Marysville).

The sora also has occurred in winter at more northern latitudes; Montana (Corvallis, March 30 and 31, 1910); Minnesota (Lanesboro, November 30, 1893 to January 25, 1894); Illinois (Rantoul); Pennsylvania (Kresgeville); New York (Rochester and Flushing): Connecticut (Hartford); and Massachusetts (Salem).

Spring migration.—Early dates of spring arrival are: Alabama, Greensboro, March 11, 1893; Georgia, Savannah, February 21, 1912, Cumberland, March 7, 1902, and Darien, March 24, 1890; South Carolina, Mount Pleasant, March 4, 1895, and Columbia, April 9, 1909; North Carolina, Raleigh, April 8, 1886, and Weaverville, April 30, 1894; Pennsylvania, Coatesville, March 30, 1888, and Swarthmore, March 30, 1914; New York, Buffalo, March 5, 1900, Ithaca, April 14, 1908, Branchport, April 17, 1914, Lockport, April 22, 1890, and Canandaigua, April 27, 1905; Connecticut, Hadlyme, April 2, 1910, Middleton, April 5, 1914, Northford, April 11, 1894, and East Hartford, April 18, 1888; Rhode Island, Quonochontang, March 2, 1900; Massachusetts, Lynn, April 19, 1911, and Cambridge, April 23, 1897; Maine, Pittsfield, May 4, 1899, Quebec, May 27, 1892; Kentucky, Bowling Green, April 5, 1902; Missouri, Jonesburg, March 31, 1917, Kansas City, April 17, 1902, Monteer, April 20, 1909, St. Louis, April 22, 1909, and Independence, April 30, 1903; Illinois, Milford, March 30, 1909, Chicago, April 1, 1894, Lebanon, April 4, 1876, Carthage, April 7, 1882, Alton, April 10, 1894, Carlinville, April 11, 1890, Rockford, April 12, 1893, and Glen Ellyn, April 14, 1899; Indiana, Frankford, March 6, 1895, Middletown, March 23, 1907, Waterloo, March 30, 1907, Bloomington, April 3, 1893, Terre Haute, April 8, 1890, Lyons, April 9, 1915, Worthington, April 14, 1907, and Indianapolis, April 16, 1916; Ohio, Sandusky, March 8, 1910, Franklin County, April 2, 1916, Cleveland, April 9, 1883, Oberlin, April 11, 1914, Canton, April 13, 1913, and Huron, April 14, 1913; Michigan, Ganges, April 5, 1893, Vicksburg, April 11, 1904, Ann Arbor, April 13, 1908, Greenville, April 16, 1896, Hillsdale, April 17, 1894, Albion, April 17, 1896, and Battle Creek, April 20, 1888; Ontario, Dunnville, April 20, 1885, Todmorden, April 23, 1891, Ottawa, April 23, 1908, London, April 26, 1915, and Windsor, April 28, 1898; Iowa, Keokuk, April 1, 1893, Dubuque, April 3, 1897, La Porte, April 16, 1884, Iowa City, April 18, 1916, and Sioux City, April 22, 1916; Wisconsin, Milwaukee, March 30, 1911, Wauwatosa, April 11, 1889, Madison, April 18, 1904, Delavan, April 20, 1896, North Freedom, April 26, 1902, and Stevens Point, April 28, 1897; Minnesota, Minneapolis, April 11, 1906, Heron Lake, April 13, 1894, Elk River, April 24, 1915, Hallock, April 27,

1897, and Redwing, April 29, 1907; Kansas, Emporia, April 11, 1885, Onaga, April 29, 1893, and Wichita, May 1, 1917; Nebraska, Peru, May 5, 1889, and Badger, May 7, 1903; South Dakota, Brown County, April 17, 1891, Pitrodie, April 25, 1889, and western Lyman County, April 25, 1907; North Dakota, Antler, May 3, 1908, Cando, May 10, 1890, and Devil's Lake, May 13, 1903; Manitoba, Aweme, April 30, 1902, Margaret, May 9, 1910, and Reaburn, May 12, 1894; Saskatchewan, Indian Head, May 11, 1912; Mackenzie, Fort Simpson, May 19, 1904; Arizona, Tucson, April 2, 1909; Colorado, Barr, May 2, 1917, Salida, May 8, 1908, and Boulder, May 8, 1910; Wyoming, Jackson, April 26, 1911; Idaho, Rathdrum, May 11, 1902; Montana, Terry, May 9, 1906; Alberta, Flagstaff, May 1, 1915, Carvel, May 8, 1915, and Onoway, May 14, 1912; Oregon, Fort Klamath, March 28, 1887; and British Columbia, Chilliwack, April 9, 1889, and Okanagan Landing, April 26, 1906.

Fall migration.—Late dates of fall departure are: Saskatchewan, Indian Head, October 25, 1904; Montana, Terry, September 13, 1901, and Fallon, September 17, 1908; Idaho, Rupert, September 16, 1911; Wyoming, near Hatton, September 14, 1911; Colorado, Hillside Lake, Gunnison County, September 23, 1900, and Boulder, October 22, 1910; Manitoba, Reaburn, September 15, 1903, Aweme, October 5, 1914, and Margaret, October 20, 1912; North Dakota, Grafton, October 5, 1914, and Antler, October 12, 1908; South Dakota, Sioux Falls, October 17, 1909; Nebraska, Gresham, October 10, 1896, and Badger, October 11, 1899; Kansas, Osawatomie, October 9, 1897, and Topeka, October 18, 1902; Minnesota, Minneapolis, September 24, 1906, Hallock, October 2, 1899, and Lanesboro, October 10, 1887; Wisconsin, Shiocton, October 9, 1883, Madison, October 16, 1910, Delavan, October 22, 1896, Milwaukee, October 23, 1886, and North Freedom, November 2, 1903; Iowa, Hillsboro, October 10, 1899, Indianola, October 18, 1902, and Keokuk, November 19, 1893; Ontario, Todmorden, October 12, 1891, Point Pelee, October 14, 1909, Toronto, October 29, 1898, and Ottawa, October 30, 1895; Michigan, Palmer, October 6, 1894, Detroit, October 18, 1907, Neebish Island, November 9, 1893, and Vicksburg, November 17, 1902; Ohio, October 1, 1914, Waverly, October 2, 1897, South Webster, October 13, 1894, Cedar Point, October 17, 1909, Huron, October 19, 1912, and Oberlin, November 11, 1890; Indiana, Greensburg, October 1, 1894, and Brookville, October 14, 1890; Illinois, Chicago, October 5, 1907, Morgan Park, October 13, 1894, Glen Ellyn, October 17, 1897, and Oak Point, October 17, 1914; Missouri, Kansas City, October 8, 1902, and Monteer, October 14, 1908; Arkansas, Pinnacle Mountain 800 feet above Clinton, September 18, 1896; Quebec, Godbout, September 14, 1891, and Montreal, October 7, 1893; Maine, Pittsfield, October 9, 1895, and Westbrook, October 26, 1904; Vermont, Bennington, November 11, 1904; Massachusetts, Monomoy Island, October 2, 1887, Harvard, October 19, 1907, and North Truro, October 20, 1889; Rhode Island, Black Island, November 22, 1912; Connecticut, Middletown, October 18, 1914, East Hartford, October 19, 1888, and Portland, November 5, 1894; New York, Branchport, October 1, 1905, Canandaigua, October 3, 1905, Shelter Island, October 5, 1893, Geneva, October 10, 1914, Sing Sing, October 16, 1885, Phoenix, October 17, 1885, and Ithaca, November 9, 1907; New Jersey, Pennsville, October 23, 1914; Pennsylvania, Renovo, October 4, 1894, Berwyn, October 16, 1909, and State College, October 25, 1916; Maryland, Patuxtent River, October 24, 1916; North Carolina, Raleigh, October 30, 1891; South Carolina, Charleston, October 26, 1911; Georgia, Kirkwood, October 14, 1899; Alabama, Coden, December 2, 1916.

The earliest arrivals in Porto Rico were noted on October 8, 1922, and the last to leave in the spring were observed on March 25, 1921.

Casual records.—The sora also has been observed or taken at several points beyond its normal range. A specimen was found dead at State College, New Mexico, on August 27, 1912; another was found on the ice at the terminal moraine of Arapahoe Glacier, Colorado, at an altitude of 12,000 feet, in September, 1903; it has occurred in summer at Massett on the Queen Charlotte Islands, at Anticosti Island and St. Joachim, Quebec. It has been reported from Newfoundland and there are several records of occurrence in Greenland, Avigait, September 30 (year?), Sukkertoppen, October 3, 1823, and Umanak. It also has been detected in England, near Newbury, Berkshire, in October, 1866; Wales, Cardiff, in 1888; and in Scotland, Tiree Island, October 25, 1901.

Egg dates.—Southern New England and New York: 50 records, May 7 to July 26; 25 records, May 24 to 30. Quebec: 8 records, May 29 to June 26. Michigan and Wisconsin: 27 records, May 16 to June 28; 14 records, May 26 to June 6. Manitoba, Saskatchewan, and Alberta: 19 records, May 31 to July 23; 10 records, June 9 to 23. California, Utah, and Nevada: 11 records, April 23 to June 25; 6 records, May 23 to June 9.

COTURNICOPS NOVEBORACENSIS (Gmelin)

YELLOW RAIL

HABITS

This beautiful little rail, perhaps the handsomest of all our rails, is a most elusive bird. Although it has a wide distribution at certain seasons, ranging from Nova Scotia to California, it is seldom seen and is one of the least-known of this elusive group. Most of its life history is shrouded in mystery and even its voice is not too well known. Probably it is much more abundant than is generally supposed, but its secretive habits cause it to be overlooked.

Spring.—The yellow rail is undoubtedly an abundant migrant, both spring and fall, throughout the United States, east of the Rocky Mountains at least. Spring records are not as numerous as fall records, probably because there are fewer men out with guns and dogs at that season. It is an early migrant in the spring, one having been taken near Detroit on March 26, 1908, and one caught alive in a snow bank during an early April blizzard near River Forest, Illinois. On the other hand there are some late records, which may indicate a more southern breeding range than is generally supposed. F. B. McKechnie (1906) reported a female taken in Massachussetts on May 26, 1906, in which an egg was found that would probably have been laid in three or four days. S. T. Danforth writes to me that he has seen the yellow rail in Porto Rico as late as April 1, 1922, and C. J. Pennock's notes contain a record of one at St. Marks, Florida, on May 22, 1915. Audubon (1840) was firmly convinced that this species bred in the Southern States, but no recent positive records have confirmed this view.

Courtship.—We know little or nothing of the courtship of the yellow rail, except that the clicking or "kicker" notes form an important part of it. Rev. P. B. Peabody, in his extensive notes sent to me on this species, says:

While the clicking which constitutes the nuptial song of the yellow rail may be fitfully heard at various times of the middle day, both its frequency and its duration are greatly accentuated as day wears on to its final close. From mid-June observations, the writer has sometimes believed that the nuptial ardor of the male may wane after incubation begins, as indicated by the fact that under this circumstance the clickings are sometimes more irregular and less frequent, in some cases altogether ceasing during the greater part of the day. But that this may not be indicative appears to be proven by Mr. Preble's experience. This observer speaks of the calling of the yellow rails as being frequent, and apparently persistent, in the middle of July.

Nesting.—No one has had anywhere nearly as much experience with the nesting habits of this elusive little rail as this same enthusiastic observer; therefore I can not do better than to quote from some of his writings. Mr. Peabody (1922) has well described its familiar breeding grounds, in the "Big Coulee," in Benson County, North Dakota, as follows:

One must give reasons why this bed of an ancient river should have been chosen as a summer home by that rarest of inland water birds, the yellow rail. The winding coulee, deep-set among the hills, is reached by steep ravines. These are clothed with partridge berry, rose, willow, aspen, and the silver-leafed buffalo berry. Rarely on these ravine sides are found huge boulders of yellow sandstone, under the edges of which at times a turkey vulture may place her eggs; and often beside them are the nests of the ferruginous roughleg. On top of the morainic buttes are scattered granite boulders of varied colors, all enriched by wonderfully varied lichens. Amid all these boulders, blossomed vetches, coneflowers, and puccoons, in glowing tapestries. Here, in this most radiant setting, was the paradisic home of the yellow rails. The faunal conditions in the coulee itself were rarely fine for the yellow rails. Everywhere were wide 'areas of salt grass, alive with appetizing snails. There were great expanses of soft, fine grass, unburned and unmown year by year. Better still as will appear later, there were great expanses of soft, fine grass that were annually mown leaving in spots just the sort of matted flotsam that the yellow rail so dearly loves for its nesting.

One unusual condition has, I am sure, determined the fitness of the Big Coulee as a breeding place for the yellow rail. Far up on the top of a butte, rising out of a boggy spring pool, there flows a tiny stream of clear, sweet water. Down the slopes the streamlet flows, now losing itself to view amid lush grasses, and, again, pouring itself with noisy babbling over some buried boulder. Across the reach of narrow, coarse-grass meadow it quietly flows among the cowslips and sedges. Onward it meanders into the coulee; here it enlarges by intake; then spreads wideningly and sluggishly into the broader expanses. Now there appears a stretch or two of clean sand amid the alluvial muck. Onward, at last, the stiller waters flow, out into one of the lagoons. No one element of that wonderful coulee is more delightsome than this little stream of clear, cool water, and right here, throughout many of the years of my observation, has been the focal point of the nesting domain of the yellow rail in that famous coulee. Nowhere else in all that region, during many years, was the yellow rail ever found.

After the above excellent account of the breeding haunts of the yellow rail, he gives us, in the same paper, the following description of the nests:

The first-found nests of the yellow rail on the Big Coulee were all of them placed among coarse grasses. In such cover, then, did I first seek. It is amusing to recall how, although repeatedly warned that one should work his way through the meadow growth with care, lest he crush precious eggs, I should still, near the close of the first day's search, and weary with the unusual exertion, have allowed my feet to drag a bit. Then, just at the despair point, I happened to see an egg lying on a bare spot. Stooping to pick it up, I saw that it was what I had been seeking. Assured that a nest was near at hand, I faced about, only to find that the toe of my boot had drawn away the canopy from the cosiest possible nest of a yellow rail. In this case, it was plain that the nest canopy was incidental. It was just a mat of dead and partly prone grass, perhaps somewhat moulded by the rail as her nest making went on. Of this character were most of the nest canopies afterward found, in whatsoever sort of matrix the nest proper may have been placed. And yet, the coarse-grass *locus* is hardly the norm. Of two distinctive types of nest matrix appearing (with water of the same depth in both), I have found the fine-grass type to have been the prevailing one. My second nest, found next morning, was the only one of the entire series in which there has been any evidence of a built-in canopy. This nest was in a fine-grass area, some rods from the former, amid rather scanty grasses. Water was of about the usual depth favored—4 inches. The canopy was very slight and the surrounding herbage quite thin. Only two other nests that I now recall were so poorly hidden. In every other case, all nests have been utterly concealed, there being no trace whatever of any artificial moulding of the standing or the prone herbage. Herein lies the supreme cunning of yellow rails. In the majority of cases noted, then, the nesting sites of this rail have been where the hayrake of the previous year has dropped a small wisp of hay. This fact has led to success in the nest finding, when once the trick has been learned. One had only to traverse the cleanmown areas and examine every likely wisp of dead grass; and ultimately the nest would be found. Under some one of such, and that, usually, the most unlikely one of a hundred or more, would be the place where has lurked a most neat and elaborate nest. The most wonderful fabric of all was found, on June, years ago, after both skill and insight had become evolved. Amid coarse-grass bogs, 100 feet and over from the springstream, there stood one bog, a bit apart from the rest. The water about it was rather deep. On top of this grass tussock was a bit of the dead grass of the previous year. This I tore away, finding beneath a nest of unusual perfection. It was of the usual diameter—about 5 inches—but thicker—an inch and a half. Most wonderful the structure of it. Every blade of the fine grasses that composed it had been brought from far, and carried upward, from the side of the tussock into the top, through a small hole but little larger than a mouse hole. Every yellow-rail nest of my finding has been of this general character: About 1 inch thick; made of the finest possible grasses; and between 4 and 5 inches in diameter. The cupping of the nests is never so broad as with other rails; just because, one must presume, fewer eggs are to be placed within it.

Two nests, out of a dozen, found by Fred Maltby (1915), are somewhat different; he describes them as follows:

Nest No. 8 which I found on June 24 was out in the Big Coulee. I was crossing a little hay meadow from which the hay had been removed in 1899, when I caught sight of egg shells lying on the ground. Examination showed them to be those of the yellow rail from which the young had hatched. In another moment I spied the nest. There was no dead grass here and the green blades had been pulled down and fastened about the nest, thus forming a green screen over it. The nest was a rather thin affair of dead blades, placed on the damp ground. I had been under so strong an impression that the nests of these birds would be found only in places where there was plenty of dead grass to afford concealment that I hadn't thought of searching the "cleaner" areas.

Nest No. 11 was my lucky find. After I had about given up hope, in the outskirts of the meadow, outside the damper, soggier portion, I suddenly found myself looking down upon a beautiful set of nine eggs. The nest was of coarse, dead blades mostly, and placed upon the ground in a rather thick bunch of growing grass. There was no dead grass about and no canopy over the nest, the ends of the green blades simply hanging loosely together a foot or more above it.

A most surprising discovery was the finding of a yellow rail's nest in Long Valley, Mono County, California, on June 6, 1922, by W. Leon Dawson (1922); he relates the experience, as follows:

We were dragging a rather thin stretch of marsh grass when a Jack Snipe flushed and I called Stevens to my assistance, leaving Bobby, who was more remote, standing listlessly by his rope-end. Returning from a fruitless quest we were about to resume operations when Bobby exclaimed, " Well, look at this!" He had been standing all the while within 3 feet of a low-lying cushion which held, in a compact and perfect circle, eight fresh eggs. The cover of marsh grass was scanty, not over 18 inches high, and the water shallow—an inch or so—yet there was no trace of a bird about. The eggs were different—no doubt of that; much smaller than those of a sora, which we had, fortunately, just examined; of a dark, old-ivory color, heavily sprinkled almost capped at the larger end, with rich reddish brown spots.   The nest itself was noncommittal, a wellrounded and rather deep bowl of coiled grasses, 3½ inches across by 2 in depth inside, built up to a height of three inches clear of the water.   Notably, there was present a leaning and overshadowing wisp of dead grass.   I considered the exhibit long and carefully, too sobered, for once, to render snap judgment.   The boys became impatient and pressed for an expression of opinion.   Finally I said, "Well, boys, to the best of my knowledge and belief, these are eggs of the yellow rail (*Coturnicops noveboracensis*), the first breeding record for California, and the first set ever taken west of the Rocky Mountains."

Eggs.—I quote the following from Mr. Peabody's notes:

As might be expected *noveboracensis* parallels *jamaicensis* in the fewness of the eggs normally laid.   Enough nests have been found to establish the norm beyond dispute.   My field notes involve 5 sets of 8, 3 of 9, and 3 of 10.   No sets numbering more than 10 have ever been found.   The ground color of the eggs of the yellow rail is usually of a rich, warm buff, as rich as the richest-colored eggs of Asiatic fowl.   This color fades, rapidly, with time, even when hidden from the light.   The dominant shape of these eggs is a decidedly-pointed ovate. Rounded-ovate specimens are not infrequent.   In any case, there is a remarkable uniformity in the eggs of any one set, not only in shape but in the markings.   No other eggs of North American birds could be confused with the eggs of this rail. It is rarely, indeed, that an egg bears any marks, however small, below the upper-height of the apex.   Of extra-typical character, in this respect, was a nestless incomplete set of six eggs that were marvelously like eggs of *jamaicensis*, except for one fairly-typical specimen.   The dominant style of markings is the dense, floriated, or stippled cap.   This is borne, often, on the extreme apex.   The ordinary color type is a pale sepia or bright cinnamon, with a slight tendency toward pale vinaceous.   Thus, the eggs of the yellow rail are of very remarkable beauty. Where markings occur on the body of the egg they are very small, often mere specks.   If wreathings occur they are usually near the *apices;* and they are generally rather loose.   In this type, also, spots, and specks predominate.   It is not so very infrequently that one finds an egg capped at the small end.   Two such did I find in one set.   Rarely do more than two or three eggs in a set bear any body markings whatever.   A single very dark and unusually handsome egg (Maltby), was marked as follows: On a very dark surface was found a loose and streaky cap, somewhat "bedaubed."   The markings were of light and dark cinnamon with little of lilaceous tint.   The markings extended well down toward the middle of the egg.   There were a few streaky body spots.   Another egg in the same set bore three cinnamon spots, near the small end.   A third egg in this set was the most peculiar egg of the entire Benson County series, faintly and scatteringly specked, all over, with a marked tendency toward a capping with the brighter markings.

The measurements of 32 eggs average 28.3 by 20.7 millimeters; the eggs showing the four extremes measure 29.7 by 21.3; 27.2 by 22.3; and 26.3 by 19.5 millimeters.

Plumages.—The downy young of the yellow rail seems to be entirely unknown, but it is probably black like the young of the other small rails.   The youngest juvenals I have been able to find are October birds, which probably represent a first winter rather than a juvenal plumage.   These differ from adults in being more plainly colored below, in having a different color pattern on the head and neck and in being lighter colored and more buffy generally. The breast is "light ochraceous buff," unmarked with the dusky tips seen in adults, paling to buffy white on the throat and to pure white on the belly; the flanks are as in the adult, but more brownish and less blackish; the crown, hind neck, and upper back are less blackish, more brownish and buffy, with a striped effect, each feather being centrally dark brown, "bister" or "warm sepia," broadly edged laterally with "light ochraceous buff"; the small white spots, so conspicuous on the head and neck of the adult, are entirely lacking in the young bird; the back, scapulars, and rump are much as in the adult, but with rather less of the white, transverse barring and with decidedly more and wider buff edgings, especially on the scapulars; the wing coverts are browner and more buffy than in the adult, "snuff brown" to "sayal brown."

This plumage is worn, with practically no change, during the first winter and spring; April birds are like October birds. Apparently a complete postnuptial molt takes place during the next summer and fall, which produces the adult plumage. Specimens showing the beginning of this molt are lacking, but several September and October birds show the final stages of it.

Material is lacking to show the annual molts of adults. Adults are much darker colored above than young birds, with more white bars and spots, especially on the forward parts, and the breast is marked with little dusky crescents, the tips of the feathers. Audubon's (1840) plate illustrates an adult.

Food.—Very little is known about the food of this species. Mr. Peabody's notes say:

We have seen that the feeding habit which carries the yellow rail out of its favored *penetralia* into the short-grass areas would seem to indicate a fondness for insect food. Personally, I am inclined to believe that fresh-water snails constitute a large part of this bird's diet. Most of the nests in a colony visited by me for many years, lay not over 100 yards from a sluggish little stream of fresh water that meandered across a meadow largely alkaline, and the bed and margins of this stream were swarming with little snails. In June of 1923, as I passed along this stream whose margin was narrowly fringed with grasses, left by the mower, I twice flushed a yellow rail within a few minutes, one of these dashing into the water, in his haste to escape me, withal the scanty covert. To corroborate this thesis comes Mr. Wayne (1905a) to say that the yellow rails dissected by him all contained snail remains in their stomachs.

Behavior.—The flight of the yellow rail is said to resemble that of the sora. It usually makes rather short, feeble flights just over the tops of the grasses and drops down suddenly with uplifted wings and dangling legs. But, when thoroughly aroused and intent on going somewhere, its flight is strong, direct, and rather swift. It can be recognized easily in flight by the large amount of white in the second-

aries. But it is seldom seen in flight and most observers agree on
its secretive and skulking habits. Audubon (1840) seems to have
been more fortunate in seeing it than more recent observers, for he
says:

> In the course of my stay at the Silver Springs in East Florida, I observed a
> good number of these birds along the margins of the lakes and swampy bayous,
> and had ample opportunities of assuring myself that this species is far from being
> nocturnal, as authors have alleged, at least when in places where they are under
> no apprehension of danger. In those sultry solitudes I have at times seen them
> following the margins of the muddy shores, with delicate and measured steps, until
> attracted by something worthy of their attention, when they suddenly jerked
> their tail upwards and for a moment disappeared. Again, they would gracefully
> leap upon the slender twig of some low shrub or bush, apparently in search of
> small snails or other objects, jerking their tail at every movement. There it was
> that I again saw the extraordinary power of contraction which their body is able
> to assume while they are pushing forward between two or more stubborn branches.
> They were all so gentle that I at times approached within a few yards of them,
> when they would now and then look cunningly at me, rise more erect for a
> moment, and then resume their occupations.

On the other hand, Mr. Peabody, after his many years of experience with it, says in his notes:

> But once in 20 years did I ever flush a yellow rail from her nest. I have
> several times approached a nest previously discovered, with slow caution, mak-
> ing then a quick run to the spot. Yet never did I succeed in finding the bird
> at home. Once, after discovering a nest where surrounding herbage was wholly
> beaten down by horses, making unnoticed escape by skulking fairly impossible, I
> left the spot, after examining the eggs, amid pitiless cold rain. Ten minutes
> later I returned, against the wind, and cautiously; no rail appeared; yet the eggs
> were warm. Never but once, in the 20 odd years, did I ever actually *see* a yel-
> low rail come out into the open. In this case, as I approached a small area of
> smoothly beaten-down fine grass, a yellow rail ran out, some feet ahead of me;
> ran swiftly for about fifteen yards; then stood for just an instant in statuesque
> pose; and then vanished, in an instant. For all the world like a 10-day, brown
> leghorn chicken did it look.

The voices of the marsh are often veiled in mystery; the vocalist
is seldom seen, almost never by the average observer; and among
the many, varied calls that one hears it is often difficult, if not impossible, to identify positively the author of any one. Fortunately
for us, J. H. Ames (1902) has positively identified the notes of the
yellow rail from a bird he had in captivity; he records the notes as
"kik-kik-kik-kik-queah"; sometimes the *"kik"* note was repeated
seven or eight times. His published note on it is entitled "Solution
of the 'Ornithological Mystery,' " assuming that the *"kicker"* notes
referred to by William Brewster (1901), as probably made by the
black rail, were really referable to the yellow rail. I am inclined to
agree with Mr. McKechnie (1906) that Mr. Ames has solved the
mystery and that the yellow rail may yet be found breeding in
Massachusetts.

I quote again from Mr. Peabody, as follows:

Right here one should emphasize the marvelous acoustic of the clicking of the yellow rail. When heard at a fair distance it seems decidedly nonresonant; but when one listens only a few feet away, this sound has all of the hollow, throaty quality so characteristic of the Virginia rail. This note may be almost perfectly imitated by tapping a hollow beef bone with a bit of iron. The usual rhythmic form of the call is, — —, — — —/— —, — — —/— —, — — —, etc. Thus, the ordinary motif is in double time, with triplets in the second measures. These iterations are very uniform, though with occasional variations. Now and then a male may break into quadruplets toward the end of his half-minute series; while an occasional bird may break the rhythm altogether. But the sound of this clicking carries far. More than once, after toiling the meadow reaches until after dusk, have I set out for my own roosting place a mile away, only to stop, on renewed occasion, to listen to my yellow rails. With a keen wind blowing in the opposite direction, I have distinctly heard the calls, not only from the butte crest, 200 feet above the meadow, but from the prairie, a full quarter-mile away.

Fall.—Much more is known about the autumnal migration of the yellow rail than about its movements in the spring, probably because more gunners are afield in the fall. Walter H. Rich (1907) says that it is more common in Maine than the Virginia rail; he writes:

Within the last three years I have known of the capture of possibly 50 specimens of the yellow rail near Portland, Maine, and have myself taken at least half that number, while of the Virginia rails scarcely 20 have been killed in the same time. The yellow rail seems to be quite hardy, staying here after the other species have deserted us and the ice has made in the pond holes of the marsh. The writer has shot them when there had been severe cold for November and after a snowfall of 3 or 4 inches.

Robert O. Morris (1905) has taken a number of yellow rails near Springfield, Massachusetts. He says:

The place where they were found was wet meadow land covered with wild grass, which in October stood, in places where it had not been harvested, to the height of 2 or 3 feet and harbored many Virginia rails and soras. The grass upon the other part of the land was cut in the summer, and by the middle of October the second growth reached the height of 7 or 8 inches, and in this portion the yellow rails are to be found, they apparently not desiring so thick a cover as do the common kinds. I have flushed all by the aid of a dog, except one, and that rose about 20 feet ahead of me, evidently frightened by my approach. The earliest date in any autumn that I have found them was the 17th of September, and I think that the latest was the 22d of October. In this part of the Connecticut valley I have been in many meadows of the same character as the one in question, accompanied by a dog educated in such a way that the scent given out by any kind of rail would so attract his attention that he would be likely to make known the presence of such a bird, if any were there, but in these places I have never found a yellow rail, and it seems worthy of note that this species should be a regular autumn visitor to a certain piece of meadow land, containing perhaps three acres, and to be found nowhere else in this vicinity at any time.

Winter.—Very little has been published since Audubon's time on the winter habits of the yellow rail. Arthur T. Wayne (1905a) once showed me a meadow near his home in which he had taken a number of these birds, of which he writes:

On February 3, 1904, while out partridge shooting, I saw my dog pointing in a low, wet piece of open land with a dense growth of short, dead grass, and being unable to flush anything myself, although I trampled the grass down in every direction, I told her to take it. She at once caught a yellow rail, which was the first one I had ever seen alive in South Carolina. I then made her hunt the entire field, and in less than 10 minutes she caught two more. These three yellow rails were caught near sunset. The next morning, February 4, I again visited the field, in company with my dog, and in less than five minutes she had caught another; while a second specimen was flushed and shot. On February 5 and 8, two more were taken, which make seven in all. On November 19, 1904, my dog again captured another one alive. These rails would not flush, although in every instance I tried my utmost to make them fly, and the only one that did elude the dog by flying, was due to the dog's failure to seize it in a very thick growth.

DISTRIBUTION

Range.—United States and Canada north to latitude 60 degrees.

Breeding range.—North to Mackenzie (Fort Resolution, Little Buffalo River, and Salt River); Manitoba (York Factory); Ontario (Fort Severn); Quebec (Fort George); and Maine (Calais). East to Maine (Calais). South to Ohio (Circleville); Illinois (Chicago and Winnebago); Wisconsin (Jefferson County and Racine); North Dakota (Devil's Lake and Esmond); and Saskatchewan (Fort Qu'-Appelle). West to Saskatchewan (Fort Qu'Appelle); Alberta (Red Deer); Mackenzie (Salt River, Little Buffalo River, and Fort Resolution); and California (Mono County).

Summer occurrences for this species, some of which may possibly represent breeding birds, extend the range southeast to New Hampshire (Hampton); Massachusetts (Salem, Boston, and Plymouth); Rhode Island (Westerly); Connecticut (New Haven and Milford); and the District of Columbia. South to the District of Columbia; Pennsylvania (Erie); Ohio (Hamilton); Indiana (Brookville, Bloomington, and Vincennes); Missouri (St. Louis and Independence); Kansas (Lawrence); and Colorado (Barr).

Winter range.—North to California (probably Suisun Marshes); Arizona (Sacaton); Louisiana (Belle Isle and New Orleans); Mississippi (probably Bay St. Louis and Biloxi); Alabama (Barachias and Greensboro); Georgia (Darien); and South Carolina (Mount Pleasant). East to South Carolina (Mount Pleasant); Georgia (Darien); and Florida (upper St. Johns River and probably Cape Sable). South to Florida (probably Cape Sable); Louisiana (Diamond and Belle Isle); and California (Riverside County). West to California (west central counties).

Winter occurrences have also been noted from more northern points: California (Humboldt Bay); Oregon (Scio); northern South Carolina (Chester); North Carolina (Weaverville, Newbern, and

Fort Macon); Maryland (Prince Georges County); and New York (Seaford and Ithaca). It has also been listed as a probable visitor to Cuba at this season; and two were reported from Bermuda in October, 1847.

Spring migration.—Early dates of arrival are: District of Columbia, March 28, 1884; Maryland, Patapsco Marsh, April 27, 1893; Pennsylvania, Erie, April 23, 1904; New Jersey, Princeton, April 10, 1895; New York, Murray, April 21, 1894, and Long Island, April 27, 1887; Connecticut, Gaylordsville, March 24, 1888, and Milford, April 17, 1880; Missouri, St. Louis, March 27, 1876, and Sand Ridge, Clark County, April 21, 1889; Illinois, Madison County, March 27, 1876, Lebanon, April 5, 1877, Odin, April 5, 1892, Normal Park, April 12, 1888, Fernwood, April 14, 1888, and Chicago, April 18, 1896; Indiana, Muncie, May 12, 1890; Ohio, Barnesville, April 2, 1916, Cleveland, April 24, 1880, and Oberlin, April 30, 1917; Michigan, Detroit, March 28, 1908; Ontario, Toronto, April 24, 1899; Iowa, Clinton, April 10, 1879, Iowa City, April 18, 1916, and Keokuk, April 22, 1888; Wisconsin, Sumpter, April 23, 1908, Barrow, May 5, 1911, Whitewater, May 5, 1911, Madison, May 13, 1911, and Stoughton, May 18, 1885; Minnesota, Lake Wilson, May 3, 1909; Kansas, Lawrence, April 18, 1885; Nebraska, Lincoln, April 30, 1909; and Manitoba, Margaret, May 9, 1913. A late spring record is a specimen from Dedham, Massachusetts, on May 26, 1906.

Fall migration.—Late dates of fall departure are: Manitoba, Aweme, September 10, 1901; Kansas, Lawrence, October 1, 1885; Minnesota, Lanesboro, September 24, 1891: Wisconsin, Delavan, October 13, 1901; Michigan, Ann Arbor, September 30, 1908, Kalamazoo, October 19, 1890, and Vicksburg, October 20, 1912; Ontario, Toronto, October 15, 1895, and Ottawa, October 22, 1895; Illinois, Chicago, September 20, 1879; Maine, Portland, October 1, 1905; New Hampshire, Seabrook, October 15, 1871; Vermont, Windsor, October 20, 1913; Massachusetts, Springfield, October 16, 1894, and Chatham November 25, 1911; Rhode Island, South Auburn, October 15, 1911; Connecticut, New Haven, October 1, 1902, Hadlyme, October 10, 1903, Quinnipiac Marshes, October 15, 1894, and Milford, November 10, 1876; New York, central, September 20, 1872, Geneva, September 20, 1911, Orient Point, October 4, 1898, and Canandaigua, October 6, 1883; New Jersey, Palmyra, October 13, 1886, and Salem, October 24, 1908; Pennsylvania, Erie, October 19, 1894, and Carlisle, October 16, 1844; Maryland, Dorchester County, November 17, 1920; District of Columbia, November 13, 1843; and Virginia, Blacksburg, October 19.

Egg dates.—North Dakota: 10 records, May 20 to June 18; 5 records June 4 to 8.

CRECISCUS JAMAICENSIS (Gmelin)

BLACK RAIL

HABITS

Although the little black rail was discovered in Jamaica in 1760 and received its scientific name in 1788, it was not discovered in the United States until 1836, when Audubon (1840) described and figured it from specimens given him by Titian R. Peale. Practically nothing was known about its distribution and habits in North America for 100 years after its discovery in Jamaica. For a full account of the early history of this species I would refer the reader to Dr. J. A. Allen's (1900) interesting paper, in which is told about all that was known about it up to that time. Much has been learned about it since and many of its nests have been found, but its distribution and life history are still imperfectly known and specimens of the bird are still rare in collections. Owing to its secretive habits, it is seldom seen, and it is probably much commoner and more widely distributed than is generally supposed. William Brewster's (1901) interesting paper on the "Kicker" furnishes some food for thought and some suggestions for solving "an ornithological mystery." I have no doubt that the black rail breeds in some of the marshes of southeastern Massachusetts; in fact, a nest is said to have been found in Chatham; but though I have explored many miles of marshes and spent many hours in the search, I have never seen a trace of this elusive little bird.

Nesting.—Dr. E. W. Nelson (1877) was the first to discover and describe a nest of the little black rail in the United States, of which he writes:

During the spring of 1875 I saw three specimens in the Calumet Marshes. The first was observed early in May. On the 19th of June, the same season, while collecting with me near the Calumet River, Frank DeWitt, of Chicago, was fortunate enough to discover a nest of this species containing 10 freshly laid eggs. The nest was placed in a deep cup-shaped depression in a perfectly open situation on the border of a marshy spot, and its only concealment was such as a few straggling *carices* afforded. It is composed of soft grass blades loosely interwoven in a circular manner. The nest, in shape and construction, looks much like that of a meadow lark. The following are its dimensions in inches: Inside depth, 2.50; Inside diameter, 3.25; outside depth, 3.50; outside diameter, 4.50.

Next came the discovery of two nests in Connecticut, near Saybrook, by Judge John N. Clark (1884). The first nest was brought to him by a neighbor, who had decapitated the rail on her nest and 9 eggs while mowing in a meadow. Of the second nest he says:

On the 6th of June, 1844, I made a trip to "Great Island"—a tract of salt meadow near the mouth of the Connecticut River, on its eastern shore—in search of nests of *Ammodrami* which abound in that locality. During a very successful hunt for them I observed a tuft of green grass carefully woven and interlaced together too artificially to be the work of nature. "Merely another Finch's nest," I mused, as I carefully parted the green bower overhanging it. But wasn't there an extra and audible beat to my pulse when before my astonished gaze lay three beautiful little black rail's eggs? Recovering from my surprise I carefully replaced the disarranged curtain that excluded the sun from the precious eggs, fixed some permanent ranges, and quietly departed to await the completion of the set. A week later, on the 13th of June, I again visited the nest and found therein the full complement of nine eggs. This nest was situated about 40 rods back from the shore of the river, on the moist meadow, often overflowed by the spring tides. The particular spot had not been mowed for several years, and the new grass, springing up through the old, dry, accumulated growths of previous years, was thick, short, and not over 8 or 10 inches in height—a fine place for rails to glide unseen among its intricacies. The nest after the complement of eggs were deposited in it resembled that of the common meadow lark, it consisting of fine meadow grasses loosely put together, with a covering of the standing grasses woven over it and a passage and entrance at one side. I must add an account of my efforts to secure the little black rail with the set. I devoted the whole day to this special end, and visited the nest about every half hour through the day, approaching it with every possible caution, and having a little tuft of cotton directy over the nest to indicate the exact spot; but although I tried from every quarter with the utmost diligence and watchfulness, I was never able to obtain the slightest glimpse of the bird—never perceived the slightest quiver of the surrounding grass to mark her movements as she glided away, and yet I found the eggs warm every time, indicating that she had but just left them.

Since that Judge Clark has "met with eggs of the species from four different nests," one of which he (1897) describes, as follows:

One was found on the salt meadow near the west shore of the Connecticut River near its mouth in Old Saybrook. The situation was on the bank of a small ditch which was partially grown up with sedges and nearly dry at the time of the find. The meadow was a tract which had not been mowed in some years and on the ditch bank was a large growth of old dry blue grass, of previous years, partially prostrated by winter's ice and snow and held up from the ground by the new growth sparsely working its way through to the light. As I lifted a bulging tuft of it I was startled to find a nest beneath with a beautiful set of six eggs of the little black rail. Carefully smoothing back the drooping grasses I left them hoping for an increase which however failed to develop. Four days later I again gently lifted the covering and found the bird sitting closely on her treasures. At a motion on my part she darted from the nest across the ditch and stopped without taking flight in a little tuft of grass within an inch of my boot; at a slight movement on my part she darted into another tuft a few feet behind me, and as I essayed to turn she darted back to her former position by my boot. I say darted, for I can think of no other word that so nearly expresses her every movement, which was so swift that the eye could scarcely follow it. I wanted that bird greatly for still I have no representative of the species in my collection, though it is quite complete of that class found in Connecticut otherwise, but vain was every effort to get a stroke of my staff at it. Its next movement was to spring into the air and take flight, dropping into a patch of cat-tails a few rods away. Its flight was after the manner of the rail family and I could easily have shot it on the wing had my gun been with me. This is the only bird of the species I have ever seen.

Richard C. Harlow (1913), who has probably found more black rails' nests than anyone else in North America, thus describes the first two nests seen by him in New Jersey, one of which was collected for him—

on the edge of the marshes back of Brigantine, on June 20, 1912. On the 29th I visited the nest from which the set had been taken. It was built in a low marshy meadow, overgrown with salt grass and sedge and very skillfully concealed in a thick mass of mixed green and dead grass, so that it was completely hidden from above. In composition, it was better built and deeper cupped than the nests of the Virginia, sora, king, and clapper rails that I have seen. In size the nest was little larger than the average structure of the robin, but deeper-cupped and built entirely of the dry, yellowish stalks of the sedges, and there in the lining, clung several black feathers. Thinking that there might be other nests in the vicinity we began searching every thick clump of marsh grass that we saw, and presently came upon another also containing seven eggs. It was placed among thick clumps of marsh grass and was quite invisible until the grass was parted from above. It was an inch above the salt meadow and was interwoven on all sides with the surrounding stalks.

On June 10, 1903, a small negro boy showed to Arthur T. Wayne (1905) a nest he had found on the ground in an oat field, near Mount Pleasant in South Carolina. "The nest contained eight eggs, and was built among the oats on high ground, and made entirely of the dry oat leaves arranged in a circular manner, but not arched over."

George H. Stuart, 3d, has sent me the following notes:

On July 4, 1919, Julian K. Potter and the writer flushed a small rail in a marsh an acre or two in extent beyond the sand dunes immediately back of the ocean beach on an island below Beach Haven, N. J. Searching for the nest in the belief that the bird was a little black rail, we were rewarded by finding it placed in the long grass, the tops of which were so drawn over as to almost completely hide the eggs from view. The nest, which was composed entirely of the same rather fine grass, was placed about one inch from the damp ground and contained eight eggs, very heavily incubated. On returning several times at intervals of 10 minutes we had opportunities of observing the female on the nest, her bright red eyes being the most prominent feature. On each occasion when leaving the eggs it darted from the nest into the surrounding grass never raising and with such celerity that it was impossible to observe her movement, the action resembling more that of a mouse than a bird.

Donald J. Nicholson sends me the following notes on the breeding of this species in Florida:

It was on the 13th of July, 1926, that I discovered the two sets of black rail, on Merritt's Island, in the Dusky Seaside colony. I had just about given up hope of finding any more sparrow nests when I heard a pair singing and thought I would take one more last search for them before going home. I got out of the car and was going over to where they were when, under my feet, a small black bird rose feebly and flew wabbly and weakly, low over the salicornia, and dropped into the dense growth 20 feet away. At first I thought it was a young bird of some kind, but the thought struck me that it might be the rare species of which we had no breeding record, so I began a search and almost immediately upon parting the grass 7 feet from where it rose I looked upon a cozy small nest with six fresh eggs of the black rail. I knew the eggs as soon as I saw them, as I had just received a set from Henry W. Davis a few days before, a set of eight taken in June, 1926, in New Jersey.

The nest was made of dead Bermuda grass placed on damp ground among a thick growth of the same under a sparse growth of salicornia, or pickleweed, with the green grass bent over to form an arch, with an entrance on the east side, giving a view to more open growth, with a background of a heavy dense tangled patch of salicornia growing to the river's edge, 100 yards away. The nest was completely and entirely concealed and could be seen only by parting the grass. The bird made no sound and was not seen again.

Eggs.—The black rail lays usually from 6 to 10 eggs, but as many as 13 have been found. They are ovate in shape and the shell is smooth with little or no gloss. The ground color is buffy white or pinkish white and they are spotted rather evenly with fine dots of bright browns and pale drabs. The measurements of 92 eggs average 25.6 by 19.8 millimeters; the eggs showing the four extremes measure **27.5** by **20.5**, **23.5** by 18.5, and 25.5 by **18** millimeters.

Plumages.—I have never seen a downy young black rail, but Mr. McMullen tells me that it is black, like all other young rails, but smaller of course. The young birds referred to below by Mr. Pennock, taken on September 11, probably represent the juvenal plumage. They resemble adults, but are grayer below and blacker above, with less brown in the wings; the throat is grayish white; there is very little brown on the back and hind neck; and the white spots are duller and smaller. This plumage is worn but a short time, as it is replaced during the late fall, November and December, by a plumage which is practically adult. As to the molts and plumages of the adults, very little can be learned from the limited material available. Black rails are difficult to collect at any time, but during the molting season they are more secretive than ever.

Food.—Very little is known about the food of the black rail. It probably consists largely of insects and other small bits of animal life, with perhaps some seeds of aquatic plants. P. H. Gosse (1847) says that the gizzard of one taken in Jamaica "contained a few hard seeds." One that Stanley Cobb (1906) had in captivity for a few days showed himself to be insectivorous. "Peeping timidly about the ferns, he saw a little insect on the underside of a leaf, and quickly snatched it." He ate earthworms eagerly, but died on the fourth day "after eating several hard bugs."

Behavior.—The black rail is not fond of flying and is seldom seen in flight. Ludlow Griscom (1915), who had a good opportunity to observe one, says that "the flight is much more feeble than that of any other rail with which I am familiar; the bird seemed barely to sustain its weight in the air, while its legs dangled down helplessly behind." But when on the ground it runs swiftly and disappears under the nearest cover as quickly as a mouse. Mr. Cobb (1906) relates the following interesting experience with a black rail in Milton, Massachusetts: "An extract from my log of May 16, 1904, reads":

As I was standing by the B-s spring to-day, I heard something among the branches of a small pine near by. On looking up, I saw a small bird come tumbling down through the soft pine tips, now and then clinging to one for a second. Finally he landed on the ground. Here he stopped for a minute on the wet pine needles as if to recover his balance and then made for cover. While this was going on I had stood watching the proceedings with interest, but as soon as the bird started to run I saw at once, by his diminutive size and peculiar shape, that he must be something unusual. I quickly gave chase, and, with the help of my terrier, soon cornered the bird in some underbrush; but, after getting close enough to touch him with my hand, he escaped to another hiding place. Knowing now that he was the rare black rail, I redoubled my zeal, and, at last after an exciting quarter of an hour, I caught the little fellow. The strange thing about the chase was that he never attempted to fly more than a few yards. If chased into the open, he would take wing and flutter into the nearest cover, but never once did he try a prolonged flight. In running on the ground he was very skillful, and, had it not been for the open character of the piney hillside on which he fell, I never should have seen him an instant after he struck the ground. The only explanation that I can give of the little rail's strange appearance is that, tired out by a long migration and bewildered in the fog, he had lost his way and fallen to earth exhausted. This theory complies well with weather conditions. There was a northeast breeze driving in a fog from the ocean, and, whenever the fog lifted, hurrying clouds could be seen passing across the sky.

T. E. McMullen writes to me that he has seen them fly out of the marsh and alight on horizontal limbs of bayberry bushes and remain there until he was within 6 feet of them, just like sparrows. H. L. Stoddard (1916), who collected a black rail near Chicago, says:

The specimen was first flushed in a small cat-tail growth, and flew rather strongly at a good height for 5 or 6 rods before dropping back into the scant vegetation, which here stood in a foot or so of water. On going to the spot the bird flushed again, nearly underfoot, and was secured. The flight of this individual was fully as strong as that of sora and Virginia rails seen a short time previously.

Mr. Wayne (1905) took special pains to identify the notes of both sexes, which he explains as follows:

As soon as she entered the standing oats she began to call, which notes resembled the words " *croo-croo-croo-o*," and then again almost exactly like the commencement of the song of the yellow billed cuckoo. This was answered at once by the male but his song was very different and the notes may best be described by the words, "*kik, kik, kik, kik*," or even "*kuk, kuk, kuk, kuk*." As the birds were rare, and the field would be plowed as soon as the oats were harvested, I determined to make every effort to capture both parents, after listening to the song of both birds for more than one hour. I walked into the standing oats, and little did I dream of ever flushing one of the birds, but to my great surprise one flushed almost immediately and with a squib charge of dust shot I killed it, which proved by dissection to be the female. I then tried to flush the male knowing the one I had was the female by the coloration), so as to be positive of the song of both sexes. After hunting for more than 40 minutes I failed to flush the mate, so went home and skinned the one which I had secured. At 3 p. m. o'clock I went in search of the male, accompanied by a friend, Lieut. J. D. Cozby, who brought with him his fine pointer dog. Although we heard the notes of the bird incessantly, which never changed from *"kik, kik, kik, kik"* or *"kuk, kuk, kuk, kuk,"* it was absolutely impossible to flush him but once in two hours' careful search when he flew into the oat stubble, but ran like a phantom into the standing oats. It was nearly 7 o'clock p. m. and I was fast losing hope of obtaining the male, when I saw the dog pointing, but the bird ran between Lieut. Cozby and myself, then flushed as it passed me. I quickly requested my friend to shoot and by a fortunate shot he succeeded in killing it. When it is realized that it required four hours' constant search in order to secure the male it can be understood how secretive the rail is in its environment.

The descriptions of the notes of this rail, as given by others, are not sufficiently different from the above to warrant quoting them. It seems likely that the notes described by Mr. Brewster (1901) as coming from the mysterious "kicker," were referable to the black rail; but there is a bare possibility that they may have been made by a yellow rail, which is known to produce similar notes. Mr. T. E. McMullen tells me that the call of the black rail sounds like *"did-ee-dunk,"* three times repeated, with the accent on the last syllable.

Winter.—Mr. C. J. Pennock, writing from St. Marks, Florida, has sent me the following notes:

The presumption seems probable that they occur here regularly in considerable numbers during the fall and winter. Being so extremely elusive, and I believe silent while here, their presence is most difficult to establish unless they are forced from the dense cover of our extensive marshes by an unusually high tide. During such occurrences two birds were taken by hand on September 4, 1915, and six were captured from a boat by hand on September 11, 1919. Two of these latter birds were birds of the year and showed some down while the primaries were but just pushing from the sheaths. The indication being certain that they had been reared on the marsh where they were found. A third one of the six was a bird of the year but older than the two tiny ones.

DISTRIBUTION

Range.—Eastern United States to Central America.

Breeding range.—North to Kansas (Garden City, Finney County, probably Beloit and Manhattan); Iowa (Linn County); Minnesota (Hennepin County); Illinois (Chicago); probably southern Ontario (Dundas); Connecticut (Saybrook); and Massachusetts (Chatham). East to Massachusetts (Chatham); Connecticut (Saybrook); New Jersey (Mount Holly, Camden, Brigantine, and Beasley's Point); probably Virginia (Wallops Island); North Carolina (Raleigh); South Carolina (Mount Pleasant); and Florida (Alachua County and Merritt's Island). South to Florida (Alachua County, Merritt's Island and Wakulla County); western North Carolina (Statesville and Weaverville); Illinois (Philo); and Kansas (Princeton). West to Kansas (Garden City).

The black rail also has been reported as occurring in summer from Wisconsin (Lake Koshkonong); and Ohio (Grand Reservoir). A specimen believed to be this species was reported as seen near Tucson, Arizona, on April 23, 1881 (Brewster).

Winter range.—The black rail is known to winter in Jamaica and Guatemala (Duenas); and it appears to occur rarely at this season north to Louisiana (New Orleans) and Florida (the Tortugas Islands, Key West, St. Marks, and Daytona). It has been reported in winter from Tybee Island, Georgia (Hoxie), but this case lacks subsequent confirmation.

Spring migration.—Early dates of arrival are: District of Columbia, Woodridge, May 14, 1923, and Washington, May 29, 1891; Massachusetts, Boston, May 5, 1913, and Milton, May 16, 1904; Illinois, Canton, April 15, 1895, and Rantoul, May 11, 1914; Ohio, Medina, April 14, 1921, and near Carthage, May 17, 1890; Texas, Houston, April 21; and Kansas, Neosho Falls, March 18, 1886.

Fall migration.—Late dates of fall departure are: Kansas, Lawrence, September 26, 1885; Illinois, Chicago, October 15, 1903, and Canton, October 27, 1894; Iowa, Iowa City, October 11, 1885; Maine, Scarboro, October 4, 1881; New Jersey, near Camden, September 22, 1887; Maryland, Piscataway, September 25, 1877, and Mount Calvert, October 19, 1906; District of Columbia, near Washington, September 25, 1877; and South Carolina, Mount Pleasant, November 9, 1906.

The typical form of this rail (*Creciscus jamaicensis jamaicensis*) is now said to occupy Jamaica, Cuba, and Porto Rico; and the bird found in the eastern United States has recently been named *Creciscus jamaicensis stoddardi* Coale, as a distinct subspecies.

Egg dates.—New Jersey: 26 records, May 30 to August 12; 13 records, June 12 to 23.

CRECISCUS COTURNICULUS (Ridgway)

FARALLON RAIL

HABITS

The above name was given to this rail because the type, an immature bird, happened to be taken on the Farallon Islands, where, of course, it was only a straggler, as there is no suitable habitat for rails on these rocky islands. The type specimen was taken on October 18, 1859, and remained for many years unique. Mr. Ridgway (1890), who described the bird as a subspecies in 1874, reviews the matter and expresses some doubt as to its status, as follows:

Whatever doubt there may be, however, of the present occurrence of the bird on the Farallons, or even of the type specimen having really been obtained there, there can not, I think, be any question as to its distinctness from *P. jamaicensis.*

That it is not an "abnormal specimen" of the latter is almost certain, from the fact that specimens of *P. jamaicensis* from the mainland of California do not, apparently, present any difference either of size or coloration from those from the Atlantic States, the West Indies, or Chili, notwithstanding numerous examples have been compared.

Some years later William Brewster (1907), who had accumulated a series of black rails from the mainland of California, called attention to certain characters which convinced him "that the black rail of California is at least subspecifically distinct from that of the eastern United States." He treats it, however, as merely a subspecies of the eastern bird, though it now seems to masquerade as a full species. Recent California writers have called it the California black rail, which seems to be a most appropriate name, as its connection with the Farallones was purely accidental.

Nesting.—It was just 50 years after the type specimen was taken on the Farallones that Frank Stephens (1909) gave us the first information as to its only known breeding grounds near San Diego. He writes:

Many years ago Mr. H. W. Henshaw told me that he had been informed that California black rails (*Creciscus coturniculus*) were sometimes common in the salt marshes around San Diego Bay. In our conversation Mr. Henshaw seemed to be under the impression that these rails were but migrants at San Diego and that they were most likely to be found very late in the autumn. Last spring the manual training teacher here told me that one of his pupils had found the eggs of the California black rail in a marsh near National City. This boy gave me considerable information about the habits of these rails which I will summarize. He had done much hunting for the nests and thought he was lucky if he found a nest in half a day's steady search. The nest seems to be usually situated in very thick marsh vegetation (*Salicorn a*, etc.) near the highest limits of the high tide. He carefully turned over all the upper part of the mass of plants foot by foot. He said the nests were always covered, but were usually from an inch to several inches above the ground. I understood him to say that he had found several empty nests, some not yet used, and some which the young birds had left. He said that he had never found any bird at the nest, which might be expected from the nests being so well hidden and the ease with which the bird could slip off and keep out of sight. He said he found eggs about the middle of March and about the 20th of April. Five and six seems to be the usual number but he knew of one set that contained eight eggs. All the eggs he knew of had been found in the last four years in a tract of less than 100 acres. He said that he had heard notes that he believed were made by this rail and described them as a sort of clicking sound. He thinks that at low tide the rails hide in crab holes, at times.

A. M. Ingersoll (1909) then published the results of his own experience with the nesting habits of this elusive rail, from which I quote, as follows:

While searching for the undiscovered eggs of the large-billed sparrow, May 4, 1908, I took a few high steps to break my way through a tangled mass of weeds and was surprised to see rise near my right knee, a California black rail. Examination of a dense growth of *Salicornia ambigua* brought to light a well concealed nest with one whole and three smashed eggs. An egg-smeared boot explained the unfortunate destruction of what would have proved a valuable addition to any zoological collection. Incubation had commenced in each egg of this small set. This nest as well as an empty one found in a similar location at a distance of a few hundred feet, was placed from 10 to 12 inches above the mud. Having flushed birds directly from two nests, I imagined I should have no difficulty in securing a series of specimens if searched for diligently; time has shown the fallacy of that idea. Extensive field experience throughout this and several other States, warrants the writer in claiming that there is no bird whose nest is more difficult to find than an occupied nest of this species under consideration. Some of our small feathered denizens of the forest effectually conceal their homes in bewildering foliage of tall trees, but the nesting site can usually be located by a sharp-eyed and patient collector watching the birds during building operations. The California black rails inhabit such dense vegetation, in which an abundance of nesting material is close at hand, that work could be carried on at a distance of 6 feet without one's being aware of the fact. Twenty-five special collecting trips to this colony by the undersigned, has resulted in only one bird and three sets of eggs; on each occasion two to six hours was spent in a most painstaking search for specimens. I have seen but 10 birds. Five of them were flushed by a young man and his dog; one was captured by the same party seizing it with his hand as it endeavored to escape from the dog by running, and the others were flushed by myself. The salt weeds of this marsh are of an evergreen character and perennial, varying little from season to season. Old clumps of Salicornia become more or less matted down, forming an ideal retreat for this secretive little bird. A favorite nesting site is one formed by an old top-heavy weed falling over a growth of previous years in such a way as to leave a shelf-like space between the layers of stems and foliage. Away from the glaring sun on such a platform, is concealed a flimsy nest of fine dry weed stems. These weeds are too brittle to admit of weaving, and fall apart on being lifted from the sustaining platform. Nests that are built on the ground are sometimes as much as 2 inches thick in the center. Even the best constructed nests partially fall away on removal from the supporting weeds and earth. To Mr. Park Harris, a former resident of San Diego, is due the credit of discovering the first eggs of the California black rail. Mr. Frank Stephens killed a California black rail on May 28, 1908, and recorded the fact in March–April, 1909, Condor. This is the earliest known summer record. All previous records are of birds taken out of breeding season. Most of these birds have been recorded from points 500 miles north of National City.

Laurence M. Huey (1916) adds the following information:

With these birds there is a noticeable lack of uniformity in their nesting dates, as well as a great variation in the nests themselves as constructed by different pairs of birds. Sometimes the nests are raised well off the ground, but this is unusual. The more typical ground nests are greatly affected by the tides. Some that I have seen were fully 5 inches thick, with as many as three distinct layers, showing how often reconstruction has been necessary. One thing is interesting as a side light on this bird's shyness, a habit that is a constant aggravation to the collector. This is the astonishing ease with which the birds bring themselves to abandon incomplete sets when they are discovered. Although I have found several incomplete sets, I have in no instance succeeded in collecting a full set from the nest at a later date. In every case the bird had deserted when

I went back. Of course, with the method of search employed, one is bound to kick into some of the nests and disturb the surrounding marsh weed before discovering them.   That a naturally retiring bird should desert under these conditions is, of course, not surprising.   On at least two occasions, however, I have found nests containing incomplete sets by a lucky glimpse of the eggs through an opening in the protecting growth above them, while I was still at a considerable distance from them.   In these cases, I have turned aside without apparently noticing the nests, and have left the vegetation absolutely untouched in their vicinity, and yet the result has been the same—desertion!

An impression has prevailed during recent years that these rails have disappeared from the limited area in which they were known to breed, the salt marshes of San Diego Bay between National City and Chula Vista. But Griffing Bancroft writes to me that he took a set of their eggs there on May 21, 1922; so it seems that the rails were not entirely wiped out by the flood of 1919.

Eggs.—The Farallon rail lays from four to eight eggs. They are ovate in shape and the shell is smooth and slightly glossy. The ground color is creamy white or nearly pure white. They are sparingly marked, chiefly at the larger end, with minute dots of browns and drabs. The measurements of 54 eggs average 25.1 by 18.9 millimeters; the eggs showing the four extremes measure 27.5 by 18.5; 25.5 by 20.6, and 22.5 by 17.2 millimeters.

Plumages.—The sequence of plumages to maturity and the seasonal molts and plumages of adults are apparently the same as in the eastern black rail.

Food.—We don't know very much about the food of this rail, but Mr. Huey (1916) has published the following:

The nature of the food of these birds remained unknown to collectors for many seasons, until the fall of 1912, when the stomachs of a small series were saved for examination. On close inspection, I found the remains of a species of small "bug" that lives very abundantly on the salt marshes where the birds were taken. I then gathered a number of these animals and sent them to Joseph Grinnell of the Museum of Vertebrate Zoology, to whom I am indebted for forwarding them to the United States National Museum for identification. The reply was as follows: "They are Isopod crustaceans belonging to the species *Alloniscus mirabilis* (Stuxberg)." Appearances to the contrary notwithstanding, it's really just a small bug. I believe this to be the chief food of the rails living in the salt marshes of this region, and as nearly all the tidal sloughs abound with these small creatures, the food problem can not be a serious one for the birds.

Behavior.—These little black rails are so secretive in their habits that they are seldom seen and we know very little about them. Mr. Stephens (1909) "when passing along a broad tide creek * * * saw one crouched in the mud a few feet from the bank. It stood perfectly still, with head lowered, as if expecting to be overlooked." Again he says:

A few days later I hunted a part of the marsh at high tide late in the afternoon. On my way to camp at dusk in a place where the marsh lay at the foot
of a bluff one flushed almost under my feet and lit a dozen yards away among
the débris lodged at the foot of the hill and stood there in the open, though not
to be seen distinctly, because of the gathering darkness. I fired at it without
effect. The bird flew out over the water and then turned around the point,
where I failed to flush it again. This is the only long flight I have seen and it
reminded me of the flight of a water ouzel. The other two flights I have seen
were short and raillike. The birds seem to lie very close and must be nearly
stepped on before they will flush. I fancy that the species will be found fairly
common in many localities when they are looked for carefully in the right places.

Mr. Ingersoll (1909) observed a bird in flight, of which he writes:

While packing the eggs a tuft of cotton was blown from my fingers; on making a quick grab, my hand was thrust into a clump of weeds, causing one of
the elusive birds to rise and fly feebly 30 to 40 feet, then with a sort of boomerang flight, hover and return to within 16 feet (actual measurement) of the
starting point. The bird flew so slow it seemed to have difficulty in keeping in
the air; this appeared to be a flight of observation. The bird turned its head and
scrutinized me with one of its red eyes while flying off. The legs were hanging
down until the turning point was reached. They were then drawn up to the body
and dropped as she settled out of sight in a tangled mass of weeds.

Mr. Huey (1916) refers to the voice of this rail, as follows:

I have spent hours and even days on the rail marshes at all times of the year,
and find that even as early as February, on clear mornings, the *"clee-cle-clee-ee"*
(accent falling on first syllable of last word) may be heard in many places on the
marsh. This is particularly true when one has walked about the marsh enough
to disturb the birds. This call is chiefly used during the early mating season,
and also as a protest against intruders in their domain. Occasionally, however,
I have heard it even in the late fall.

DISTRIBUTION

Range.—Pacific coast of the United States.

Breeding range.—Imperfectly known. Eggs have been collected
only from the marshes in the vicinity of San Diego, California, in
which area the species is resident. Summer occurrence records take
the Farallon rail north to central California (Suisun, the Farallon
Islands, and Martinez), with casual records in Oregon (Malheur Lake)
and probably Washington (Tacoma). The range extends south
through coastal California (Santa Cruz, Santa Barbara, Ballona,
Hueneme, Riverside, and Orange) to northwestern Lower California
(San Quintin).

Winter range.— This rail appears to have the curious habit of
wintering north of its principal breeding area, a conclusion that seems
warranted from the numerous winter records from the vicinity of
San Francisco Bay. It probably also winters on the Farallon Islands
and southward to San Diego.

Egg dates.—California: 19 records, March 12 to May 23; 10 records, March 30 to May 12.

CREX CREX (Linnaeus)

CORN CRAKE

HABITS

Contributed by Charles Wendell Townsend

The corn crake, or land rail, as it is also called, breeds throughout Europe and western Asia. It appears to be an enterprising, wide-ranging bird, extending its migrations on the south to Africa, even to Cape Colony, while on the north its breeding haunts reach nearly to the Arctic Circle. On this side of the Atlantic it has been recorded as an accidental visitor to Greenland and there is a record for Nova Scotia, and one each for Falmouth, Maine; Saybrook, Connecticut; Cranston, Rhode Island; Salem, New Jersey; Cape May, New Jersey, and also from Bermuda. The first part of its name it owes to the fact that it frequents and often nests in fields of grain, called in England corn, while the second part of its name is derived from its call which sounds like *creak* or *crake*.

Nesting.—Morris (1903) says that the nest of the corn crake is placed among long grass or corn, in a furrow or some slight hollow, and is lined with a few of the leaves and stalks of the neighboring herbage.

Eggs.—The eggs are 7 to 10 and occasionally 12, 14, or even 18 in number, of a pale reddish-brown or yellowish-white color, spotted, blotched, and speckled with ashy gray and warm reddish brown. Witherby's Handbook (1920) gives the measurements of 100 eggs as averaging 37.26 by 26.75 millimeters; the eggs showing the four extremes measure **41.6** by 25.9, 38.3 by **29, 34** by 25 and 34.3 by **24.1** millimeters.

Young.—The duration of incubation, according to Evans (1891), is three weeks. Only one brood is raised unless the first nest is destroyed. Bonhote (1907) says:

The male, who takes no part in the incubation, is very attentive to his mate, bringing her delicate tid-bits and accompanying her when she leaves the nest. * * * When the young are hatched the "craking" ceases, and both parents brood and tend the young. These when first hatched are jet black, and become fully feathered in about a month or five weeks, their wing feathers being the last to grow. Although they can run and leave the nest as soon as hatched, they do not feed themselves for some days, but take all their food from their parents' beaks.

Plumages.—Bonhote (1907) says:

In winter the sexes are practically identical, the upper parts being dark brown, with rufous edges to the feathers; wing coverts chestnut; throat and abdomen white, breast pale brown; flanks barred with brown and buff. After the spring molt the male has part of the head, throat and breast gray. The female is grayer than in winter, but much browner than the male, especially on the breast. The young resemble the adults in winter, but the rufous margins are much broader.

The downy young are jet black. The adult is about the size of the bobwhite.

Food.—The food of the corn crake is chiefly animal, consisting of worms, slugs, snails, small lizards, and insects, but occasionally of grain and other seeds.

Behavior.—Dresser (1871) says:

Owing to its secretive habits, and being at the same time a rather noisy bird than otherwise, the land rail is much better known by its harsh, grating note than by anything else. It is essentially a frequenter of cultivated districts and of the lowlands, though seldom of really wet, swampy ground; for it prefers meadows and cornfields, where the ground is open and there are but few bushes or trees. It does not, however, effect very dry soil, but fields where it is neither very wet nor yet very dry, and especially, it would seem, where a few flowers are intermixed with other herbage; and it evinces a partiality for clover fields. In most parts of Europe it is a migrant, or, rather, a summer resident, arriving in the spring and leaving again for the South in the autumn, migrating, it would seem, altogeher at night, and when on passage flying at a considerable altitude. * * * As soon as it arrives in the spring it gives notice of its presence by its well-known call. It appears to move about at night, and more especially in the early morning and late evening; and though it is not infrequently seen about during the day, yet it prefers, as a rule, to remain quiet then. Its form enables it to run about with ease amongst the grass and corn, and it always evinces a dislike to taking wing, prefering, if possible, to seek security by running; and a dog will sometimes spring on and catch one on the ground, so close will they at times crouch before the dogs. Its cry, resembling the syllables "*crek, crek, crek,*" may be heard at all times of the day, but more especially early in the morning and late in the evening; and it appears to possess considerable power as a ventriloquist, as it is most difficult to judge where the bird is by its note, which is now loud, now low, as if close or at a considerable distance. When uttering its cry the bird usually stands still, the neck rather drawn in; but sometimes it calls as it moves leisurely along * * * Its movements when not alarmed are graceful and elegant. It moves sedately, lifting its feet rather high, jerking its tail, and moving its head backwards and forwards. When alarmed it stops, crouches, and then starts off with extended neck and body thrown forward, and is soon out of danger.

Yarrell (1871) says the male is the caller and that "this call-note may be imitated by passing the edge of the thumb-nail, or a piece of wood, briskly along the line of the points of the teeth of a small comb, and, so similar is the sound, that the bird may be decoyed by it within a very short distance."

Game.—Yarrell (1871) says: "Land rails are considered most delicate as articles of food, and in such high estimation, that two land rails are said to be a present for a queen." They are occasionally picked off by snipe shooters.

DISTRIBUTION

Range.—Europe and Asia, from the Faeroe Islands, Scandinavia, Russia, and western Siberia to the Pyrenees, northern Italy, Macedonia, Arabia, northern India, and Africa; accidental in Greenland, North America, and Australia.

The corn crake has been taken in Greenland on several occasions; one was obtained in Newfoundland about 1859 and there are the following records for the Atlantic coast of the United States and Canada: Nova Scotia (Pictou, October 1874); Maine (Falmouth, October 4 1889); Rhode Island (Cranston, 1857); Connecticut (Saybrook, October 20, 1871); New York (Amagansett, about August 15, 1885, Montauk Point, November 1, 1888, Green Island, November 6, 1883, Sag Harbor and Oakdale, November 2, 1880); Pennsylvania (Philadelphia); New Jersey (Bridgeton, Salem, fall of 1854 and Dennisville, November 11, 1905); Maryland (Hursley, November 28, 1900); and Bermuda, (October 25, 1847).

Egg dates.—Great Britain: 16 records, May 5 to July 26; 8 records, June 5 to 24.

IONORNIS MARTINICUS (Linnaeus)

PURPLE GALLINULE

HABITS

The extensive marshes which border the upper waters of the St. Johns River in Florida gave us, among other thrills, our first glimpse of the purple gallinule in its chosen haunts. Here the marshes were about 3 miles wide, through which the river wound a meandering course. Except in the river channel the water was only 2 or 3 feet deep with a muddy botton of decidedly uncertain depth. There were numerous permanent islands, overgrown with willows, which served as rookeries for herons, extensive tracts of tall saw grass, almost impassable and with very uncertain ground beneath, and innumerable small floating islands of grass, small shrubs and marsh vegetation, treacherous to walk upon with imminent danger of breaking through to unknown depths. The, so called, open water through which we had to pole our skiff, wound in tortuous channels among the islands and through the saw grass; it was completely filled with a rank and luxuriant growth of yellow pond lilies, or spatter docks (*Nymphaea advena*), locally known as "bonnets," through which we were constantly pushing the skiff with two long poles, the pointed prow making a passageway between the thick, fleshy stalks and great broad leaves. It was still more difficult to push through the patches of "lettuce," a small floating plant, not unlike a small head of lettuce in appearance, which grows in rather deep water and so thickly as to be often impenetrable. Common, white pond lilies were quite numerous in the open places; and among the "bonnets" they were in full bloom. Water turkeys, wood, and white ibises, and various herons were seen flying over or found nesting in the willows. Least bitterns, sora rails, and boat-tailed grackles were breeding in the saw grass and the loud notes of the grackles and redwings were heard all over the marshes. And in the larger open spaces, where the "bonnets," "lettuce" and pond lilies grew we saw the purple gallinules, together with their more common relatives the Florida gallinules and coots. We were thrilled with the striking beauty of this handsome species, as we saw for the first time its brilliant colors in its native haunts. One can not mistake it as it flies feebly along just over the tops of the "bonnets" with its long yellow legs dangling. And how gracefully and lightly it walks over the lily pads, supported by its long toes, nodding and bowing with a dovelike motion and flirting the white flag in its tail.

Arthur T. Wayne (1910) says of this species in South Carolina:

This beautiful and graceful summer resident is locally abundant during the breeding season on abandoned rice plantations, and also on fresh-water rivers where the wampee (*Pontederia cordata*) grows in profusion. This plant bears purplish blue flowers which act as a protective coloration to this species. Where the plant is growing in profusion the gallinules are always most abundant, but where it is absent scarcely more than one or two pairs can be found. The birds generally arrive between April 10 and 17, and are common by the 25th.

Nesting.—We failed to find the purple gallinules' nests in the St. Johns marshes because we did not know where to look for them; but in 1925, with the help of Oscar E. Baynard, I learned something of its nesting habits, for we found it breeding in two places. He taught me to look for the nests on the floating islands, with a high, dense growth of herbaceous vegetation rather than in the pickerel weed or "bonnets." They seem to like to have the nesting site surrounded by deep water. In a marshy pond in Pasco County, while we were watching some Florida gallinules, we saw a pair of purple gallinules near some patches of rank vegetation that looked promising. The pond looked shallow enough to wade, for it was overgrown with pickerel weed around the borders and covered with "bonnets" in the center, with numerous clumps of cat-tails, willows and "ty-ty" bushes scattered over it. But we soon found that it was too deep to wade; and so we made another visit to it with a boat on April 25. We examined several empty nests on the larger, boggy, or floating islands of cat-tails, pickerel weed, grasses, and other rank vegetation, one of which was 2 feet above the water in a small bunch of the flags. And we finally found a nest containing six nearly fresh eggs; it was in a small bunch of isolated cat-tail flags in an open place surrounded by deep water, overgrown with "bonnets" and white pond lilies; the nest was a floating mass of dead flags, soggy and wet below, but dry above and well hollowed in the center, which was only a few inches above the water, exceptionally low for this species; the flags were arched over the top of the nest, which only partially concealed it.

The following day, April 26, we found two nests, each with six eggs, in which incubation had begun, in an arm of Lake Apopka, in Lake County. This arm of the lake is about a mile or more long and perhaps half a mile wide; much of it is open water, but around the shores is a broad strip of marsh with a rank growth of flags, pickerel weed, and other aquatic vegetation; and at the upper end of it, farthest from the lake, it is full of boggy or floating islands, surrounded with water 8 to 10 feet deep, covered in the open spaces with "bonnets" and white pond lilies. It is an ideal place for both species of gallinules. Our first nest was on one of the floating islands, far too treacherous to walk on, overgrown mainly with a rank growth of wild parsnip, conspicuous with its white blossoms, together with *Pontederia, Hydrocotyle,* flags and sedges, the whole being tied together with a tangle of morning glory vines. The nest was made of the dried leaves and stems of *Pontederia,* firmly interwoven with the growing plants and well concealed. Its rim was about 20 inches above the water, it measured 8 by 10 inches in diameter, and was hollowed to a depth of about 3 inches; the whole structure was about 8 inches in depth. The other nest was similar, but slightly smaller and placed 2 inches lower, on a larger and firmer island, but not strong enough to walk on, where the principal growth was *Pontederia.*

Audubon (1840) writes:

The nest is generally placed among a kind of rushes that are green at all seasons, round, very pithy, rarely more than 5 feet high, and grow more along the margins of ponds than in the water itself. The birds gather many of them, and fasten them at the height of 2 or 3 feet, and there the nest is placed. It is composed of the most delicate rushes, whether green or withered, and is quite as substantial as that of the common gallinule, flattish, having an internal diameter of 8 or 10 inches, while the entire breadth is about 15.

A nest found by Herbert W. Brandt, in Bexar County, Texas, on June 8, 1919, is described in his notes as—

a shallow platform located among the cat-tails and rushes near the shore in shallow water and in an isolated clump. The cat-tails were bent down and woven together in the manner of our least bittern and the nest would easily be taken for one. The nest was about 30 inches above the water and a shallow but well made platform of live flat leaves.

Messrs. Quillin and Holleman (1918), referring to the same general locality, say:

Nests of this species are better built than those of the Florida gallinule, and are placed at a greater elevation from the water. The majority are rarely under 2 feet, and in a few cases, where the exceptional growth of the reeds permitted, they were found 4 or 5 feet from the water. Some are placed on the densely matted boughs in thickets of willows growing in shallow water, but these are always placed lower than those found in the reeds.

Alexander Sprunt, jr., has sent me the following notes on the nesting of the purple gallinule in South Carolina:

This species is a much handsomer bird than the Florida gallinule, and in my experience, much shyer. It is a summer resident of South Carolina, and frequents the old rice plantations in large numbers. They are very partial to growths of wampee (*Pontederia cordata*) rarely placing their nests anywhere except in clumps of this water loving plant. The materials used are decayed leaves, and stalks of the same plant, and the nests securely fastened to stems of the growing clumps. Mr. A. T. Wayne in his Birds of South Carolina, mentions the fact that there are always three or four half completed nests in the vicinity of the one which holds the eggs. This seems to be an invariable rule, as all the nests I have examined in late years have had others in various degrees of completion scattered about within a radius of several feet.

The locations are generally in a more exposed place than those used by the Florida gallinule; I have found nests placed on top of piles of drift weed, almost totally exposed to the sun. Mr. Wayne also mentions that he thinks incubation is aided by the decomposition of vegetable matter in the nest. I consider this highly probable. Crows must do great damage to these exposed nests, as there are many about the rice fields, and little escapes their eyes. The high spring tides also cause damage by flooding the nest locations. This last May, I found perhaps, 15 nests, in rice fields that showed every indication of having been torn loose from their holdings by the high tides, which inundate the fields at this season.

Eggs.—The purple gallinule lays from 5 to 10 eggs; from 6 to 8 are the usual numbers and larger sets are uncommon or rare. They are ovate in shape and the shell is smooth with little or no gloss. The ground color varies from "pale cinnamon-pink" or " pale pinkish buff" to "cartridge buff." They are lightly and unevenly marked with very small spots and fine dots of bright browns and pale drabs. The measurements of 56 eggs average 39.2 by 28.8; the eggs showing the four extremes measure 42.7 by 30.2; 39 by 30.2; and 34.6 by 26.2 millimeters.

Plumages.—In the downy, young, purple gallinule the head is scantily covered with black down, mixed with silvery white hairs on the crown, cheeks, and throat; the base of the bill is yellowish, the outer half black, with a white nail; the body is thickly covered with long black down, glossy on the back and sooty black on the belly.

In the juvenal plumage, in July and August, the head, neck, and breast are dull brownish, shading from "bister" on the crown to "cinnamon buff" on the neck and breast and to whitish on the chin and central abdomen; the back is glossy olive bronze; the wings are glossy olive green of varying shades and reflections; the rump and tail are "Prout's brown" or "mummy brown." This plumage is worn for only two months, or less, when a postjuvenal molt begins. This molt seems to be very variable in its progress, or much prolonged, for various stages of it can be seen all through the fall and winter. It involves a complete renewal of all the contour plumage and in some cases the flight feathers also. I have seen birds showing a complete molt in February and others which still retained the old, worn wings and tail in April. Generally by February, at the latest, the juvenal plumage has been replaced on the head and breast by new purple feathers, tipped with whitish on the breast; these white tips soon wear away; the new plumage on the back is glossy green, much as in the adult.   Traces of immaturity remain through the spring, such as some old brown feathers in the head and neck and some whitish feathers in the throat.   The first postnuptial molt, which is complete and probably earlier than in the adult, produces the adult plumage.   Adults have a complete postnuptial molt, in late summer and fall, and a slight, partial prenuptial molt in early spring.

Food.—Very little has been published about the food of the purple gallinule.   Mr. Wayne (1910) says that it "feeds largely upon rice during the autumn."   It certainly frequents the rice fields at that season and is said to do much damage to the rice crop, for it not only picks up grains from the ground but bends down the stalks to reach the seeds.   Mr. J. G. Wells (1902) says that, in the West Indies, "they are caught in fish-pots baited with corn" and that "they do damage to the Indian corn, as they climb up the stalks and eat the ears; they also climb and eat plantains and bananas."   Probably they live chiefly on grains, seeds, and other vegetable food, but there is some evidence that they also eat snails, and perhaps insects.   Baird, Brewer, and Ridgway (1884) say:

"Worms, mollusks, and the fruit of various kinds of aquatic plants are its food.   It gathers seeds and carries them to its beak with its claws, and it also makes use of them in clinging to the rushes where the water is very deep."

Behavior.—The purple gallinule is easily recognized in life by its brilliant colors and by its bright yellow legs, which hang down in flight.   Its flight is weak and raillike, slow, and not long protracted; it hovers feebly along, just clearing the tops of the vegetation, and then suddenly drops down out of sight.   It cackles almost constantly while flying, the notes sounding much like the cackling of a hen or the syllables "Kek, Kek, Kek, Kek."   Mr. Wayne (1910) says that it has "very peculiar call notes.   One, which is very guttural, is to be heard incessantly."

Audubon (1840) writes:

The jerking motions of the tail of this bird, whenever it is disturbed, or attracted by any remarkable object, are very quick, and so often repeated as to have a curious appearance.   It runs with great speed, and dives with equal address, often moving off under water with nothing but the bill above.   The lightness and ease with which it walks on the floating plants are surprising, for in proceeding they scarcely produce any perceptible disturbance of the water.   When swimming in full security, they move buoyantly and gracefully, throwing the head forward at every propelling motion of the feet.   The flight of this species is less swift than that of the common gallinule, or of the rails, unless when it is traveling far, when it flies high, and advances in a direct course by continued flappings; but when it is in its breeding or feeding grounds, its flight is slow and short, seldom exceeding 30 or 40 yards, and with the legs hanging down; and it alights among the herbage with its wings spread upwards in the manner of the rails.   It often alights on the low branches of trees and bushes growing over the water, and walks lightly and gracefully over them. The purple gallinule not infrequently alights on ships at sea. While at the Island of Galveston, on the 26th of April, I was offered several live individuals by the officers of the Boston frigate, which they had caught on board. My friend John Bachman once received three specimens that had been caught 300 miles from land, one of them having come through the cabin window.

P. H. Gosse (1847) has drawn a good word picture of this bird, which he calls the sultana, as he has seen it in Jamaica, as follows:

I was struck with the remarkable elegance of one that I saw by the roadside, about midway between Savanna le Mar and Bluefields. It was at one of those pieces of dark water called blueholes, reputed to be unfathomable. The surface was covered with the leaves and tangled stems of various water plants, and on these the sultana was walking, supported by its breadth of foot; so that the leaves on which it trod sank only an inch or two, notwithstanding that the bird, according to its usual manner, moved with great deliberation, frequently standing still, and looking leisurely on either side. As it walked over to where the water was less encumbered, it became more immersed, until it seemed to be swimming, yet even then, from the motion of its legs, it was evidently walking, either on the bottom, or on the yielding plants. At the margin of the pool, it stood some time in a dark nook overhung by bushes, where its green and purple hues were finely thrown out by the dark background. I could not help thinking what a beautiful addition it would make to an ornamental water in an English park; and the more so, because its confiding tameness allows of approach sufficiently near to admire its brilliancy. Nor are its motions void of elegance; the constant jerking of its pied tail is perhaps rather singular than admirable, but the bridling of its curved and lengthened neck, and the lifting of its feet are certainly graceful.

DISTRIBUTION

Range.—Southern United States, islands of the Caribbean Sea, Central and South America; casual in southern Canada.

Breeding range.—North to Texas (Harris and Orange Counties); Louisiana (Cameron County, Avery Island, and Houma); probably Mississippi (Natchez); probably Alabama (Chuckvee Bay, Baldwin County); Florida (Tallahassee and Oldtown); and South Carolina (Yemassee, and probably Charleston). East to South Carolina (Yemassee, Frogmore, and probably Charleston); Georgia (probably Okefinokee Swamp and Savannah); Florida (Oklawaha River, Lake Harris, Lake Okeechobee, and Caloosahatchie River); Cuba (Isle of Pines); Haiti; formerly Porto Rico; the Lesser Antilles (Guadeloupe, Dominica, Santa Lucia, Carriacou, Grenada, Tobago, and Trinidad); British Guiana (Georgetown); French Guiana (Cayenne); Brazil (Pernambuco, Bahia, Espiritu Santo, Cantagallo, and San Paulo); and Argentina (Barracas əl Sud). South to Argentina (Barracas al Sud and Santiago del Estero); western Brazil (Caicara); and Colombia (Gorgona Island). West to Colombia (Gorgona Island, Medellin, and Lake of Peten); Colima (Rio de Coahuayana); Tepic (probably

San Blas); Tamaulipas (Matamoras); and Texas (Brownsville and Harris County).

Winter range.—The purple gallinule is resident throughout most of its breeding range, withdrawing at this season, only from the northern portion. At this season it is found north to Florida (Tallahassee, Royal Palm Hammock, and probably Lake Harris); and Texas (Brownsville).

Migration.—An early date for their arrival in South Carolina is Charleston, April 21, 1908.

Casual records.—The species has on numerous occasions been taken or observed at points far outside of its normal range. Several were recorded in Bermuda in April 1849, April 1850, and one on May 30, 1851, and one on October 22, 1851. Continental North American records include North Carolina (Currituck Sound, November 12, 1919, and Raleigh, June 3, 1887); Virginia (Cobb Island, May 1891); Pennsylvania, (Cumberland County, February 19, 1895); New Jersey (Cape May, May 10, 1907, and May, 1892, Tuckerton, prior to 1894, Longport, May 23, 1898, and Ventnor, May 1902); New York (Middle Island, summer of 1879, and near Flatlands); Connecticut (Middletown about 1855, and again in 1877, Stamford, spring of 1884, and Bridgeport, June 26, 1903); Rhode Island (Westerly, about 1857, and Seaconnet, June 8, 1900); Massachusetts (Randolph, May 24, 1904, near Rockport, April 12, 1875, Boxford, June 1897, Chatham, April 1890, Sandwich, April 1902, Worcester, May 30, 1887, Swampscott, April 22, 1852, Plymouth, April 9, 1892, and Cape Cod, April 1870); New Hampshire (Rye, and Dover); Maine (South Lewiston, April 11, 1897, Winter Harbor, November 7, 1899, Calais, 1869, and Boothbay, September 1877); New Brunswick (St. John, April 6, 1881, and Gagetown, September, 1880); Nova Scotia (Halifax, April, 1889, January 30, 1870, January 19, 1896, February 1870, and May 23, 1880); Quebec (near Quebec, about September 15, 1909); Missouri (St. Charles, April 22, 1877); Illinois (opposite St. Louis, April 18, 1877, Chicago, May 1866, near Coal City, April 24, 1900, and Wilmington, April 26, 1909); Indiana (Richmond, March 27, 1918); Ohio (Big Miami River, March 31, 1877, Sandusky Bay, April 28, 1896, Cedar Point, September 2, 1894, Lakeside, November 10, 1917, and Circleville, May 10, 1877); Michigan (Ann Arbor, August 12, 1879, and St. Clair Flats, about 1883); Ontario (Guelph, about 1894 and the mouth of the Rouge River, April 8, 1892); Wisconsin (Milwaukee, about 1860, also at Racine and near Janesville); Kansas (Douglas County, April 26, 1896, and April 18, 1909, and Manhattan, April 14, 1893); Arizona (near Tucson, October 20, 1887, and Tombstone, June 1904); Colorado (Florence, June 17, 1911); and Utah (Haynes Lake, November 23, 1924).

Egg dates.—Florida: 32 records, April 10 to June 26; 16 records, May 6 to 30. Louisiana: 11 records, April 15 to June 2; 6 records, April 29 to May 19. Texas: 16 records, April 27 to July 6; 8 records, May 19 to June 8.

GALLINULA CHLOROPUS CACHINNANS Bangs

FLORIDA GALLINULE

HABITS

The Florida gallinule is unfortunately named, for it is by no means confined to Florida, nor is it any more abundant there than elsewhere; if anything, it is less common there. It enjoys a wide distribution over the American continent, ranging as far west as California and as far north as Minnesota, Ontario, and New England, as a regular breeding bird. Where it can find congenial swampy resorts, it may be found by one who is familiar with its notes or is willing to explore such unattractive places; often it continues to frequent and breed in the last remnants of swampy hollows, close to civilized centers, until driven out by the filling in of such places. William Brewster (1891) describes such a resort in the Fresh Pond marshes in Cambridge, Massachusetts, as follows:

Their chosen haunt was a swamp about five acres in extent, covered with dense beds of cat-tail flags and thickets of low willows, among which were many pools and ditches of open water 3 or 4 feet in depth connected by a network of muskrat run ways. The only really dry places were the tops of the numerous large tussocks and scattered houses of the muskrats, for among the willows and cat-tails the water was everywhere from 6 to 12 inches deep. The swamp was bordered on one side by a railroad, on the next by a high knoll, on the third by partially submerged woods of dead or dying maples, while on the fourth side an expanse of marshy ground stretched away for hundreds of yards to the shores of a pond. The area covered most thickly with flags and willows was separated from the maple swamp by a ditch, broad, straight, and practically free from all vegetation save duckweed, which formed an emerald carpet on the surface of the brown, stagnant water.

Courtship.—I have seen the courtship display in Florida, in which the white undertail coverts perform a conspicuous part; with head held low, wings partly raised and opened and tail greatly elevated and spread, like a great white fan, the male swims about in a swanlike attitude, uttering his love notes. An open bit of water in the marsh forms the stage and the female watches the performance from the seclusion of neighboring reeds.

C. J. Pennock has sent me the following notes on the courtship of this species, as observed by him in a marsh near Wilmington, Delaware, on June 6, 1925:

Our attention was attracted to a pair of Florida gallinules swimming in one of the larger open tracts and we tarried for an inspection. It quickly became evident that this pair of gallinules were amorously intent; at least while the one appeared to the spectators as supremely indifferent to all extraneous affairs and placidly bobbed about within a quite restricted area the other bird was most intent on creating a responsive thrill or in convincing his lady love that he alone was the gayest, handsomest, and most infatuating Lothario in that muddy pond! While his movements were never rapid he was ever alert and continually in motion, paddling to one side of the female and across in front of her, then back and forth, close by, or veering he might get 5 or 6 yards distant, rarely farther away; now he would serenely sail toward her with brilliant, flaring figurehead or frontispiece, the red of shield and scarlet bill making a vivid mark as viewed against the dark background of water and reeds; again with quite as much seeming aplomb he would reverse his course when within perhaps but a foot or two of the female, and now it became evident that he considered his greatest charm was centered in the white feather patches of the undertail coverts, border of wings, and upper flanks, for these were flashed in display for her benefit in short or longer intervals, but usually well shown, as he bobbed off from her or tacked, now right, now left, with tail apeak and wings one-third or one-half open. At such times the three tracts showed to the greatest advantage, not quite as a single white area continuously, but when we had a direct stern view there was quite as much, probably more, white to be seen than of the dull plumbeous tint of upper wings and body. When swimming toward his mate, the male swam quite erect, head well up, evidently to make the brilliant face and bill most conspicuous, while on the reverse course, usually, I am not sure it was always so, the head and neck were inclined well forward and at this time the erected tail was often opened and closed, fanlike, which brought the white in greater evidence.

Nesting.—Mr. Brewster's (1891) careful description of his Cambridge nest is worth quoting in full; he writes:

It was in the midst of a low, half-submerged thicket of *Spirea salicifolia*, intermingled with a few wild-rose bushes and alders, 4 or 5 feet in height. The foliage was scanty, and the tops of the bushes withered. Among their stems the water was from 12 to 15 inches deep, quite free from grass, flags, tussocks, or any floating vegetation save a thin coating of duckweed over the surface. The uniform light color of the nest—a pale bleached straw, nearly that of dead grass—thrown into relief against the background of dark water, rendered it so conspicuous an object that it caught my eye at a distance of fully 25 feet. Obviously the birds had disregarded, either deliberately or unconsciously, all considerations of protective coloring, and then, with apparently studied boldness, had rejected the safe shelter of tangled wild-rose thickets, dense beds of cat-tail flags, and clusters of bushy topped tussocks with which the marsh abounded, to build their home among scattered bushes in the center of a nearly open pond. With the exception of a little dry tussock grass which formed a lining, the nest was composed wholly of cat-tail flags of last year's growth, all of which must have been brought by the gallinules a distance of at least 25 yards, much of the way through bushes where the water was too deep for the birds to get any firm footing. As some of the stalks were nearly 2 feet in length, an inch thick at the base, and very heavy, the labor involved must have been great. About the rim and outer edges of the nest the flags were broken or doubled in lengths of 3 to 6 inches, the ends of which, projecting upward and outward, formed a fringe of blunt but bristling points that prevented the eggs from rolling or being crowded out. On one side this fringe was wanting for a space of 2 or 3 inches where a pathway about 6 inches in length led from the edge of the nest down a gentle incline to the water. This pathway was composed of broad flags from 20 to 23 inches long drawn out straight, with the slender tips firmly woven into the nest and the heavy water-soaked butts resting some distance away on the bottom. It was evident that these flags had been carefully selected and adjusted to form a sort of "gangplank" by means of which the bird might enter and leave the nest without disarranging or breaking the brittle material which formed its rim. The whole structure was saved from danger of submersion in case of a sudden rise of water by the buoyancy of its materials, but it derived its chief support from the stems of the bushes, among which it was firmly wedged. It certainly did not rest on the bottom, for I ran my hand under it and found everywhere a clear space of several inches in depth. The measurements of the nest *in situ* were as follows: Greatest external diameter, 20 inches; least external diameter, 13 inches; height of rim above the water, 4 inches; total height about 8 inches. The egg cavity was symmetrical but shallow (2⅜ inches in depth), and measured 7 inches across.

Another flourishing colony was well established in the Hackensack Meadows, New Jersey, close to civilization, between two large cities, Clinton G. Abbott (1907) and his companions were surprised at the numbers of the gallinules in this marsh, as they saw at least 50 separate birds in the open, and counted as many as 28 in a single pool. He says:

The water in the swamp was found to be about thigh deep, that is to say the wader sank that distance, but fully half the apparent depth was caused by the soft mud under the water. Occasionally, one would step into a hole up to his chest, but this was unusual, and for the most part the ground under the mud was solid and trustworthy. The area searched consisted of a broad tract of open, water containing a few islands, and bordered on one side by the railroad track and on the other by a luxuriant growth of cat-tails into which many arms and bays extended. In addition there were among the cat-tails a number of isolated ponds unconnected with the main tract. All water, with the exception of the center of the open tract, was covered with a solid scum of duckweed so thick that swimming birds left no path in it, as it closed immediately in their wake. The cat-tails often extended at least 2 feet above the wader's head, so that in a thick bed it would have been easy to lose one's bearings were it not for the tall chimney of a bluing factory close by—evidence in itself of the proximity of civilization to the marsh birds' haunt. Mr. Hann and I found no less than seven inhabited nests the first afternoon and at least three times as many empty ones. The inhabited nests contained anywhere from 10 eggs to one young bird. The nests themselves, which are composed entirely of dead rushes with but a shallow cup, are usually placed in an isolated tussock or else at the edge of a cat-tail bed, so that the bird when leaving may have immediate access to open water. A notable exception, however, was a nest found in a dense growth of cat-tails, at least 12 feet from open water. In the majority of cases the bed of the nest was 4 to 6 inches from the surface of the water, but several, perhaps built by birds whose first nests had been flooded, were higher. Almost every nest had a sort of sloping runway to the water's edge by which the bird probably always entered and left the nest. One nest was especially worthy of notice for its unusual height above the water, as we could barely see into it when standing on tiptoe in the mud. It was placed high on a mass of cat-tails tangled by the wind. Occasionally the tips of the rushes were drawn together to form a sort of arch over a nest, as is done by rails, but this was by no means universal.

A similar colony near Philadelphia is described by Richard F. Miller (1910). Dr. Thomas S. Roberts (1879) found several nests of this species in a large, reedy slough near Minneapolis.

They were placed in patches of old, wild-rice stubble, and were built up on a floating foundation of reed and rice stems, so as to be high enough to keep the inside of the nest dry. Coarse rushes and reeds were used in building, much of the material being so long that only one end entered into the construction of the nest, the remainder hanging in the water.

Alexander Sprunt, jr., writes to me that he finds the Florida gallinules breeding, about May 1, in two localities near Charleston, South Carolina.

One of these is a large fresh-water reservoir about 17 miles to the northwest of Charleston. A large expanse of about several hundred acres is flooded, and has a rank growth of various water plants, some of these tracts forming veritable floating islands, some hundreds of yards in length and width. There are also numerous floating logs which have a growth of weeds and grasses springing from the exposed sides, and floating almost stationary in the masses of duck-weed which cover the water for large areas. The Florida gallinule abounds here. I make the trip to this locality each year, and have always been rewarded by the finding of several nests. The large majority are placed very near the water, sometimes under a growth of weed on the floating islands, or saddled upon one of the semisubmerged logs, usually near one end. This situation is rather a favorite one. At times the log may change its position by a distance of several rods, making the nest a traveling one, to a certain extent. All the nests I have found are composed of dried, half-decayed leaves, and stalks of aquatic plants, sometimes the bottom of the nest being quite damp, so close is it to the water.

A rather unusual type of nest was found on May 2, 1914 in this same reservoir. It was placed on the top of a dead stump, about 2 feet from the water, and surrounded by a growth of willows. In the rice field sections this species seems fully as partial to wampee (*Pontederia cordata*) as does the purple gallinule, and I have found many nests, about 1 foot from the water, made of decayed leaves of wampee, and attached to the stems of the growing clumps of the same plant. The graceful arrowhead leaves of this plant, the beautiful green color, and the general setting of such a nest makes a wonderful picture. However, other situations are chosen. Sometimes one finds the nests along the banks of the rice fields, amid a thick tangle of briars, grasses, and vines, but always within a few feet of the water.

Snakes take toll of both the eggs and the young, and are a constant menace. Crows, too, rob the exposed nests at frequent intervals. One thing that always interested me is the complete indifference with which this species regards an investigation of its nest. Time and again have I had the adults within a few feet of me while photographing the nest, and examining the eggs. This would not be so strange if it were not for the air of utter unconcern on the part of the bird. Walking about on the decayed vegetation, picking up food here and there, within 6 and 8 feet at times, clucking and chuckling in its peculiar way, they stroll about as if there was no enemy, human or otherwise, within miles.

My own experience with the nesting of this species has been rather limited. In Texas we found it breeding on some of the deep ponds near Brownsville, while we were hunting for nests of the Mexican grebe, on May 23, 1923, wading in water waist deep or more. These ponds are more or less overgrown, especially around the borders, with water huisache bushes and scattered clumps of cat-tail flags. Some of the nests were in the flags and similar in construction to those described above. One nest, found by Mr. Simmons, was in a low crotch of a huisache bush, close to the water.

In Florida we found Florida gallinules breeding in all the ponds where we found purple gallinules breeding, rather more numerous than the latter, but nowhere very abundant. They had eggs during the last week in April. The ponds frequented by gallinules have been described under the foregoing species. The Florida gallinules' nests were usually placed in the shallower parts of the ponds, around the borders, where the water was often not over one or two feet deep. They seemed to prefer the extensive tracts of pickerel weed (*Pontederia cordata*), but they often nested among the "bonnets" (*Nymphaea advena*) mixed with a lower growth of water pennywort (*Hydrocotyle ranunculoides*). The nests were placed just above the water, or practically floating, and usually they were more or less wet. They were made of the dead stems and leaves of the pickerel weed. There were generally three or four empty nests in the vicinity of every occupied one.

N. B. Moore says, in his Florida notes, that an interval of one or two days often occurs between the layings of eggs. He also states that the birds add to the material in the nest during the egg laying period, placing new green leaves of *Pontederia* under, as well as around, the eggs; most of the material was probably within reach, as the bird stood on the nest; and it was probably added, as the leaves dried and shrunk, to keep the nest high and dry. He ascertained these facts by visiting a nest daily from the time nest building began until the young left the nest.

Verdi Burtch (1917) mentions a case where, after a heavy rain, the birds raised a nest, eggs and all, at least 10 inches by the addition of new green flags.

Eggs.—The Florida gallinule lays from 6 to 17 eggs, both of which extremes are unusual; probably 10 or a dozen would be nearly the average number; the smaller sets are often incomplete. The eggs are ovate in shape and the shell is smooth, with little or no gloss. The ground color varies from "cinnamon" or "cinnamon buff" to "cartridge buff" or "pale olive buff." This is irregularly marked with spots, mostly fine dots, of various shades of brown, from "Vandyke brown" to "russet," and occasionally with a few spots of "wood brown" or various shades of drab. The measurements of 105 eggs average 44 by 31 millimeters; the eggs showing the four extremes measure **49.5** by **33**, and **39** by **28** millimeters.

Young.—Incubation is said to begin with the laying of the first egg, to last for about 21 days and to be shared by both sexes. The young gallinules are able to leave the nest soon after they are hatched and are well able to take care of themselves at an early age. There is a sharp spur at the bend of the wing, which the young bird uses to assist it in climbing among the reeds and lily pads. Audubon (1840) gives the best account of the early life of the young birds, as follows:

The females are as assiduous in their attentions to their young as the wild turkey nens; and, although the young take to the water as soon as hatched, the mother frequently calls them ashore, when she nurses and dries them under her body and wings. In this manner she looks after them until they are nearly a month old, when she abandons them and begins to breed again. The young, which are covered with hairy, shining, black down, swim beautifully, jerking their heads forward at each movement of their feet. They seem to grow surprisingly fast, at the age of 6 or 7 weeks are strong, active, and perhaps as well able to elude their enemies as the old birds are. Their food consists of grasses, seeds, water-insects, worms, and snails, along with which they swallow a good deal of sand or gravel. They walk and run over the broad leaves of water lilies as if on land, dive if necessary, and appear at times to descend into the water in search of food, although I can not positively assert that they do so. On more than one occasion, I have seen a flock of these young birds playing on the surface of the water like ducks, beating it with their wings, and splashing it about in a curious manner, when their gambols would attract a garfish, which at a single dart would seize one of them and disappear. The rest affrighted would run as it were with inconceivable velocity on the surface of the water, make for the shore, and there lie concealed and silent for a quarter of an hour or so. In the streams and ponds of the Floridas, this species and some others of similar habits, suffer greatly from alligators and turtles, as well as from various kinds of fish, although, on account of their prolific nature, they are yet abundant.

Plumages.—The downy young Florida gallinule is nearly bald, the crown being very scantily covered with black hairlike down; the skin at the base of the bill is bright red; the black down on the chin and throat is tipped with curly whitish hairs; and the rest of the body is covered with thick, soft, black down, glossed with greenish above and dull sooty black below.

The body plumage is acquired at an early age, but the young bird is fully half grown before the wings and tail have even started to grow; these are not fully developed until the bird is fully grown, in September. In the full juvenal plumage, of late summer, the throat and chin are white, mottled with blackish; the remainder of the head and neck varies from "hair brown" above to smoke gray below; the mantle is much like that of the adult, "Prout's brown" to "cinnamon brown;" the under parts are "neutral grays," mixed with white; and the central belly is all white. This plumage is worn through the fall with a gradual progress, by molt, towards maturity. By December the young bird is much like the adult; but traces of immaturity, chiefly white in the throat, persist until spring and the frontal shield remains rudimentary all through the first year. At the first postnuptial molt, the following summer, the fully adult plumage is assumed. Adults have a complete postnuptial molt in the late summer and a very limited prenuptial molt in the spring, with no well-marked seasonal differences in plumage.

Food.—Gallinules seek their food among the aquatic vegetation where they live. Their long toes enable them to walk with ease over the lily pads, where they may be seen picking up their food from the surface; they can also swim and dive, if necessary to secure it, or travel and climb with ease among the denser vegetation. Their food consists of seeds, roots, and soft parts of succulent water plants, snails and other small mollusks, grasshoppers, and various other insects and worms. Dr. Alexander Wetmore (1916) found that, in Porto Rico, 96.75 per cent of their food was vegetable, grass and rootlets forming 90.75 per cent and the other 6 per cent consisting of seeds of grasses and various weeds, much of which must have been picked up on dry land. The remaining 3.25 per cent was made up of insects and a few small mollusks.

Behavior.—On its migrations to and from its more northern breeding resorts the Florida gallinule shows greater powers of flight than are apparent at ordinary times; when making such a long flight, or when flying from one pond to another, it travels at a reasonable height with a direct and fairly swift flight the head and feet being extended. But when seen on its breeding grounds, or in the ponds where it feeds, its flight seems weak, labored, and awkward; it flutters along, barely skimming the surface, half flying and half running on the water, as if unable to rise: or, with a feeble, raillike flight, it just clears the tops of the swamp vegetation, into which it suddenly drops again, as if exhausted.

It swims with ease, in spite of its lack of webbed feet, punctuating its foot strokes with a graceful dovelike motion of its head; while swimming the forward parts are depressed and the hind quarters are raised, the white under tail coverts serving as a conspicuous signal. It can dive to obtain its food or to escape its enemies, often hiding under water, with its head or bill concealed among the water plants.

It seems most at ease, however, and its movements are most graceful, when walking lightly about over the lily pads, picking up its food with quick, nervous strokes, much after the manner of a barnyard fowl. It is equally at home on land where most of its food is obtained. If disturbed it runs swiftly to cover and disappears in the reeds, where it can travel with all the skill of a rail and can even climb to the tops of the tall stalks. It can easily be distinguished from the coot by the absence of the white bill, so conspicuous in that species, and by its [more slender form; its color and its green legs will distinguish it from the purple gallinule. The red frontal shield is conspicuous only at short range and the white under tail coverts are present in all three species.

Mr. Brewster (1891) heard what he thought was the wooing note of the male, uttered while in active pursuit of the female; it sounded like "*ticket-ticket-ticket-ticket* (six to eight repetitions each time)."
He also writes:

The calls of these gallinules were so varied and complex that it seems hopeless to attempt a full description of them. I certainly know of no other bird which utters so many different sounds. Sometimes they gave four or five loud harsh screams, very like those of a hen in the clutches of a hawk, only slower and at longer intervals; sometimes a series of sounds closely resembling those made by a brooding hen when disturbed, but louder and sharper. Then would succeed a number of querulous, complaining cries, intermingled with subdued clucking. Again I heard something which sounded like this: "*kr-r-r-r-r, kruc-kruc, krar-r; kh-kh-kh-kh-kea-kea*," delivered rapidly and falling in pitch toward the end. Shorter notes were a single, abrubt, explosive *kup*, very like the cry given by a startled frog just as he jumps into the water, and a low "*kloc-kloc* or *kloc-kloc-kloc*." Speaking generally, the notes were all loud, harsh, and discordant, and nearly all curiously henlike. At intervals of perhaps half an hour during the greater part of the day the two birds called to one another from various parts of the swamp, evidently for the purpose of ascertaining each other's whereabouts. They were occasionally answered by a pair in a neighboring swamp and these in turn by a third pair further off. In the early morning and late afternoon their calls were frequent and at times nearly incessant. They ceased almost entirely after nightfall, for the Florida gallinule is apparently much less nocturnal than any of the rails, if not so strictly diurnal as most of our birds.

Fall.—The Florida gallinule is a summer resident only in the northern portions of its range. Birds which breed in the Northern and Central States migrate south in the fall to the southern tier of States and perhaps farther. The species winters regularly as far north as South Carolina and southern California, but even there it is much less common than in summer. Its flesh is good to eat and it is probably shot to some extent by gunners out after other game; but it has never been considered much of a game bird. Doctor Wetmore (1916) says that in Porto Rico it ranks as a game bird and that its eggs are persistently hunted for food.

DISTRIBUTION

Range.—Southeastern Canada, the United States, islands of the Caribbean Sea, and South and Central America.

Breeding range.—North to California (San Francisco Bay and near Sacramento); probably Arizona (Tucson); Nebraska (Omaha); Minnesota (Heron Lake and Minneapolis); Wisconsin (Madison, Milton, and Kelley Brook); Michigan (Kalamazoo and Detroit); southern Ontario (Hamilton, Toronto, Pictou, Kingston, and Ottawa); Quebec (Montreal); Vermont (St. Albans); and Massachusetts (Belmont, Provincetown, and Truro). East to Massachusetts (Cambridge and Truro); New York (Long Island City); Pennsylvania (Philadelphia);

Delaware (Odessa); North Carolina (Lake Ellis); the Bermuda Islands; South Carolina (Charleston and Frogmore); Georgia (Savannah and probably Blackbeard Island); Florida (Fernandina, St. Augustine, Titusville, Kissimmee, and Lake Okeechobee); the Bahama Islands (New Providence, Watling Island and Great Inagua); Porto Rico; St. Croix; the Lesser Antilles (Anguilla, St. Thomas, Guadeloupe, Dominica, Martinique, St. Lucia, formerly Barbados, Grenada, Tobago, and Trinidad); Brazil (Caicara, Cantagallo, Piracicaba, and Iguape); and Argentina (Parana River and Buenos Aires). South to Argentina (Buenos Aires); and Chile (Concepcion). West to Chile (Concepcion Lake, Aculco, Sacaya, and Sitani); Peru (Chorillas and Valley of the Tambo); the Galapagos Islands; Colombia (Antioquia); Nicaragua (Los Sabalos); Honduras (Lake Vojoa); Guatemala (Lake Duenas and Lake Amatitlan); Mexico, Oaxaca (Tehuantepec); Tepic (Tepic); and California (Escondido, Los Angeles, Santa Barbara, Stockton, and Sacramento).

Spring or summer occurrences north of the known breeding range are Colorado (Colorado Springs, May 9, 1882); South Dakota (Vermilion, April 15, 1899); Ontario (Beaumauris); Quebec (Quebec); and Maine (Calais).

Winter range.--The Florida gallinule appears to be resident throughout its breeding range in South and Central America. At this season it has been found north to California (Los Angeles); probably Arizona (Tucson); Texas (Aransas Bay, Lake Surprise, and Port Arthur); Louisiana (Vermilion Bay and New Orleans); Florida (St. Vincent Islands Tallahassee and Gainesville); and South Carolinia (Ashepoo River and Cooper River).

The species has a few curious northern winter records as, Pennsylvania (Richmond, February 12, 1913); Massachusetts (Ware, about December 15, 1909 and Palmer); and Minnesota (Minneapolis, January 23, 1915).

Spring migration.—Early dates of arrival are; District of Columbia, Washington, April 19, 1892; Pennsylvania, Waynesburg, April 26, 1894 and Germantown, May 2, 1888; New Jersey, Camden, April 25, 1914; New York, Canandaigua, April 12, 1905, Cruger's Island, April 16, 1922, Branchport, April 18, 1914, Phoenix, April 26, 1891 and Rochester, April 27, 1919; Massachusetts, Cambridge, April 30, 1896; Vermont, Little Otter Creek, April 28, 1879; Quebec, Montreal, April 26, 1913; Kentucky, Versailles, April 11, 1905; Illinois; Quincy, April 3, 1889, Elgin, April 21, 1914 and Morgan Park, April 24, 1902; Indiana, Richmond, March 17, 1917, Waterloo, March 30, 1907, Greencastle, April 6, 1894, Irvington, April 16, 1888 and Indianapolis, April 23, 1916; Ohio, Columbus, March 25, 1917, Sandusky, March 28, 1908, Oberlin, April 11, 1921, Lakeside, April 15, 1917, Wooster, April 19, 1890 and Youngstown, April 30, 1917; Michigan,

Albion, March 31, 1896, Vicksburg, April 19, 1912, Ann Arbor, April 23, 1916 and Bay City, May 2, 1891; Ontario, near Toronto, April 8, 1892, Todmorden, April 17, 1891 and Queensborough, April 19, 1906; Iowa, National, April 18, 1909, Hillsboro April 18, 1896 and Grinnell, April 28, 1890; Wisconsin, Milwaukee, April 12, 1914, Whitewater, April 5, 1914 and Madison, April 26, 1908; Minnesota, Goodhue, April 2, 1918; Kansas, Lawrence, April 19, 1907 and Nebraska, Dunbar, April 27, 1899.

Fall migration.—Late dates of fall departure are: Minnesota, Hutchinson, October 25, 1914; Wisconsin, Milwaukee, October 3, 1914, and November 25, 1886; Iowa, Marshalltown, October 17, 1914; Ontario, Toronto, October 1, 1898, Point Pelee, October 9, 1906, Ottawa, October 19, 1910, and Todmorden, October 10, 1891; Michigan, Detroit, Octoder 9, 1907, and Vicksburg, November 16, 1910; Ohio, Cleveland, October 4, 1885, Lakeside, November 11, 1916, Oberlin, November 11, 1910, and New Bremen, November 16, 1909; Indiana, Richmond, October 15, 1912; Illinois, Calumet, October 23, 1876; Quebec, Montreal, October 29, 1895, and November 5, 1898; Maine, Falmouth, September 30, 1894, and Portland, October 15, 1907; Vermont, Rutland, September 20, 1915; Massachusetts, near Springfield, October 1, 1884, Sudbury, October 2, 1880, Essex County, October 3, 1903, and Cambridge, October 6, 1912; Rhode Island, Point Judith, November 29, 1900; Connecticut, New Haven, September 30, 1902, Norwich, October 2, 1907, Quinnipiac Marshes, October 10, 1913, and Lyme, October 16, 1897; New York, Rochester, October 4, 1919, Geneva, October 10, 1914, Rhinebeck, October 16, 1921, Shelter Island, October 28, 1898, and Sayville, November 28, 1886; Pennsylvania, Erie, October 7, 1891, and Carlisle, October 18, 1841; and Virginia, Surrey County, October 21, 1915, and Quantico, October 29, 1882.

Casual records.—Florida gallinules also have been observed or taken in New Brunswick (St. Johns, September, 1880); Nova Scotia (near Kentville, September 20, 1886); and Newfoundland (one reported in a newspaper as captured at Colinet in the fall of 1911).

[Author's note: The above distribution is for the entire species, formerly known as *Gallinula galeata*, including all the American forms. Two new forms have been described from the West Indies and others may be found there. There are at least three other forms in southern and western South America. But apparently the ranges of the different forms can not yet be definitely outlined.]

Egg dates.—New York: 23 records, May 9 to July 5; 12 records, May 23 to June 10. Pennsylvania and New Jersey: 25 records, May 22 to July 19; 13 records, May 30 to June 22. Michigan and Wisconsin: 29 records, May 20 to July 4; 15 records, May 30 to June 12. California: 24 records, May 5 to July 9; 12 records, May 22 to June 15. Texas: 8 records, May 16 to July 25.

FULICA ATRA Linnaeus

EUROPEAN COOT

HABITS

Contributed by Charles Wendell Townsend

The European coot is accidental in Greenland. It closely resembles the American coot, from which it differs in being slightly larger, in having the frontal shield white, and in lacking the white on the crissum. From a study of the accounts of its habits by European ornithologists, it is evident that in these respects it also closely resembles our bird.

Nesting.—Saunders (1889) says "the nests are strong and compact structures of dry flags, and are usually raised from 6 to 12 inches above the water on foundations of reeds or tufts of rushes, some of them being so firm as to support the weight of a man seated."

Dresser (1871) quotes Stevenson as follows:

The outside of this ingeniously formed basket usually consists of dried flags, reeds, and other withered plants; but I have occasionally known young reeds and rushes used in part, when the contrast of the fresh green has had a very pretty effect. The interior is lined with rather finer substances, chiefly with portions of the dead leaves of the reed. Though not infrequently placed in dry situations, on the sedgy bank of an island, or the rushy margin of a pond or lake, I have more commonly found them on the broads, built over the water amongst the reed stems, in shallow spots resting on the weeds at the bottom, in others well raised over the surface, but so fastened to the reeds themselves as to rise with the tide, though with but little danger of getting adrift.

Cases have been reported where the birds continued to incubate after the nests had been torn from their moorings by storms.

Eggs.—[Author's note: The eggs of the European bird are similar in every way to those of our American coot. According to Witherby's Handbook (1920), the usual numbers are from "6 to 9, occasionally up to 13, while still larger numbers, up to 17 and 22, have been recorded, probably by two females."

The measurements of 38 eggs average 53.6 by 37.1 millimeters; the eggs showing the four extremes measure **57.9** by 36.6, 53.6 by **39.3**, **50.1** by 36.3, and 51.9 by **35.7** millimeters.]

Young.—The incubation period, according to Evans (1891), is from 21 to 22 days. Both parents incubate and the young are able to leave the nest and follow their parents soon after they are hatched.

Plumages.—[Author's note: The downy young, the sequence of plumages to maturity, and the seasonal molts of adults are apparently similar to those of the American coot, to which it is very closely related.]

Food.—The food of the European coot consists of aquatic insects, molluscs, slugs, worms and small fish, seeds, buds, and the tender shoots of aquatic plants. It also eats meadow grass and berries and, according to Selby (1833), "in a state of confinement it will greedily devour grain and other farinaceous diet."

Behavior.—Dresser (1871) says:

It frequents marshes, pools, and lakes which are overgrown with or skirted by reeds, sedges, water lilies, or other aquatic plants, amongst which it can secure hiding places should danger threaten. It is generally to be seen swimming, if it feels itself quite safe, out in the open water, or otherwise close to or amongst the reeds, and but seldom coming on shore to open places, though it often wades about in wet marshy places which are well covered with aquatic herbage. On land it is but an awkward-looking bird; for its legs being placed so far aft it is compelled to walk very erect, and its feet, though excellently adapted for swimming, render its progress on land rather clumsy; but it runs almost as well as the moor hen, and with tolerable ease when disturbed and forced to run to shelter. On the water it floats very bouyantly, and swims with ease, though not very swiftly, jerking its tail and moving its neck to and fro. It dives extremely well, and when closely pursued will pass along some distance under the water, and then catching hold of the stem of a stout plant will keep its body immersed, the bill and fore part of the head to the eyes only being left above the surface.

Saunders (1889) says:

The coot may occasionally be seen perched in trees, and it sometimes ascends them, leaping from branch to branch with as much ease as a gallinaceous bird. It sometimes roosts in trees, and has been known to repair to them to feed on berries. It generally sleeps on the water * * *. On many sheets of ornamental water the coot lives in a semidomesticated state, and will allow an observer to approach it quite closely; otherwise it is an exceedingly wary bird, ever on the alert for danger, and giving the alarm to the other waterfowl with which it often congregates.

And he quotes Hawker, who says, "If a gentleman wishes to have plenty of wildfowl on his pond, let him preserve the coots, and keep no tame swans."

Hudson (1902) quotes Lord Lilford on an interesting habit of the coot as follows: "I have several times observed the singular manner in which a flock of these birds defend themselves against the white-tailed eagle. On the appearance over them of one of these birds they collect in a dense body, and when the eagle stoops at them they throw up a sheet of water with their feet, and completely baffle their enemy." A similar habit has been observed in our American coot.

The European coot like our own is slow at taking wing, splashing along the water for some distance before it can rise in the air. On migrations or when going a distance its flight is strong and swift.

Of the cry of the coot, Seebohm (1884) says it is "loud and plaintive, sometimes a single note, but frequently repeated several times. It is a clear, bell-like *"ko,"* not unlike the cry of the golden plover." Dresser (1871) says "Its call note is a clear, loud, almost trumpet-like cry, uttered abruptly; but heard at night, when several are calling, it is not unlike the shrill barking of a small dog."

While the American coot displays prominently the white terminal line on the under tail coverts in elevating the tail, this field mark is lacking in the European coot.

Winter.—Seebohm (1884) says: "In winter coots collect into immense flocks in the low-lying counties and frequent the fresh water as long as it remains unfrozen, only quitting it for the sea when absolutely compelled by the long-continued frost. They appear to migrate to the coast under these circumstances in large flocks, quitting their fresh water haunts to a bird."

DISTRIBUTION

Range.—Great Britain and greater part of continental Europe, Asia and northern Africa, from 70° north latitude in Scandinavia and 60° north latitude in Russia southward and eastward to China, Japan, India, the Philippine Islands, and the Azores. Rarely wanders to Iceland and casually to Greenland.

Egg dates.—Great Britain: 17 records, April 20 to June 23; 9 records, May 1 to 18.

FULICA AMERICANA Gmelin

AMERICAN COOT

HABITS

Except in the Northeastern States and Provinces, where it occurs only as a migrant and not very commonly, everybody who knows birds at all is familiar with the plainly dressed, but exceedingly interesting, coot or "mud hen" or "blue Peter." For it enjoys a wide distribution over most of the North American Continent, in which it is very abundant at some seasons of the year in all suitable localities, breeding from the "fur countries" to the West Indies and resident the year round in the southern part of its range.

I first became acquainted with this curious bird in the North Dakota sloughs, those wonderful wildfowl nurseries of the western plains, teeming with a varied bird life in which the coot played a prominent part, as a conspicuous, noisy, and amusing clown. Among the flocks of ducks, floating on the open water, a few of the somber, gray birds, with black heads and conspicuous white bills, were always in evidence; they were constantly startling us by splashing and spattering off over the water, as we started them from the reedy borders; and to the ceaseless din made by the rythmic notes of countless yellow-headed blackbirds, the loud, guttural voices and varied calls of the coots played a fitting accompaniment. They were never quiet and their antics were often entertaining.

Spring.—The coot is a hardy bird and an early spring migrant, pushing on northward as fast as advancing spring melts the ice in the ponds, often arriving while there is still some ice. M. P. Skinner tells me that, in Yellowstone Park, "they come just as soon as the ponds begin to melt"; he has seen them there as early as April 11. A. D. Henderson has known them to reach northern Alberta, Lac La Nonne, as early as April 16. He has seen them at Bear Lake when "the lake was still full of ice, but there was a narrow strip of open water along the shore on which were thousands of ducks with the coots and a few Canada geese."

Courtship.—The best account of the courtship of the coot is given by Dr. Alexander Wetmore (1920) as he observed it at Lake Burford, New Mexico, as follows:

Many were in pairs on the date of my arrival, but until June 5 small flocks of unmated birds remained feeding in the open bays or rested in little bands on open beaches. Toward the latter part of this period these flocks at short intervals presented a scene of great animation as the birds displayed and fought savagely with one another. A little later on the companies broke up entirely. Each male selected an area of shore line in the tules and remained near this constantly, guarding it jealously, taking frequent occasion to drive away ducks and eared grebes who might chance to trespass, and having many fights with neighboring males. In these encounters they drove at each other with heads extended on the water and wing tips elevated. When near they began striking viciously with their bills and then, lying back, struck heavily first with one large foot and then the other, a most effective means of fighting as their claws were long and sharp, and their leg muscles powerful. Each tried to guard against these blows by seizing the feet of his antagonist so that often the two held each other by means of their feet, while they thrust savagely with their bills. The females frequently took part in these squabbles also, so that sometimes three or four birds were engaged, at one time, while neighboring males came rushing up also seeming minded to interfere. When they separated the males sometimes rested for several minutes with heads down on the water and wing tips raised, eyeing each other like two game cocks.

Their mating actions were interesting. Males frequently rushed after females, paddling over the surface of the water with flapping wings, while the females made off in the same manner, 10 feet or so ahead. Frequently the females made merely a pretense at escape, striking out with their feet and making a great splashing but traveling slowly, but if too closely pressed they dove, leaving the males looking about for them on the surface. In the most common act of display the male came paddling out with head and neck prostrate on the water, wing tips raised high above the tail, and the tail spread and elevated so that the white markings on either side were very prominent. As he came near the female usually assumed the same attitude. When 2 or 3 feet away the male turned and presented the prominently marked tail to the female, swimming off slowly and returning to repeat the performance. This action was seen constantly whenever coots were under observation. Paired birds often swam toward one another from a distance of several feet with heads extended on the water calling "*kuk kuk kuk kuk.*" As they met they assumed a more erect attitude and then as they brushed against one another and turned about they dabbled in the water with quick jerks of the open bill that threw drops of water from side to side. Frequently the female reached over and worked her bill gently through the feathers on the male's head and then lowered her head while he preened her feathers in return.

Nesting.—The same observer says in regard to nest building:

In building, the female arranged the dead stems of the round stalked *Scirpus occidentalis* to form a platform, bending them over and striking them repeatedly with her bill to make them stay in position, causing a peculiar knocking, hammering noise that at this season was to be heard in the rushes on all sides. Frequently the first one or two eggs of a set were laid on a mere platform and the completed nest built up later, depending perhaps upon the need of the female for a place to deposit her eggs. A complete set of seven eggs with incubation begun was seen on June 7 and after this sets were common. The males seemed to take no part in nest building, but stood about in the rushes a few feet away. This guard continued as the eggs were laid and incubation began. When the females were on the nest it was amusing, as I approached slowly in the boat, to see the males stalk truculently down and slide into the water, eyeing me closely all the while. Frequently at this season they rose on the surface of the water, treading heavily for a few strokes, making a loud turmoil in the water and driving themselves backward for a foot or more with the force of the effort, apparently a threatening act intended to frighten away an intruder.

I made my first acquaintance with the nesting habits of the coot in Nelson and Steele Counties, North Dakota, in 1901; since then I have seen many coots' nests, for it is an abundant bird in all suitable prairie sloughs. The nests are usually partially, or well, concealed in the bulrushes (*Scirpus*) or flags (*Typhus*) about the borders of the sloughs or marshy ponds; sometimes the nests are in plain sight near the edge, or in an isolated clump; occasionally one is seen in an entirely open situation with no concealment whatever. The nest is usually a floating structure, under which one could pass the hand without obstruction, but it is generally firmly attached to growing reeds or flags, to prevent drifting. Whatever material is most readily available, bulrushes, flags, reeds, or grass, is used and firmly woven into a substantial basket; the inner cavity, which is hollowed just enough to hold the eggs, is neatly lined with pieces of dry flags or other smooth material. An average nest, well concealed in a thick clump and containing 10 eggs, measured 14 inches in outside and 7 inches in inside diameter, the rim being 8 inches above the water. A larger nest, in a more open situation and containing 15 eggs, measured 18 inches outside and 7 inches inside, but the rim was only about 4 inches above the water. The largest nest I ever measured contained only 9 eggs but it was 20 by 15 inches in outside diameter and built up 7 inches above the water. These are normal types.

John G. Tyler writes to me that he found about 15 pairs of coots nesting in a shallow pond of about 40 acres, near Fresno, California, on June 18, 1917; the nests were "all built of green wire-grass stems and anchored in patches of grass in water averaging a foot deep."

Robert B. Rockwell (1912) describes several other types of nests found in the Barr Lake region, Colorado, as follows:

In the large number of nests examined were found wide variation in construction and location. Most of the nests were built well out toward the edge of the cat-tails over water 3 or 4 feet deep, others were built in close to shore in very dense cat-tail thickets.   One nest was found built on dry ground, another fully 2 feet above the ground on a platform of dead cat-tails, with a neat runway leading up to it; and still another nest fully 4 feet above ground in the lower branches of an apple tree, the water of the lake having receded that much after having inundated the orchard.   Two nests were seen far out on open water that were readily visible at a distance of 100 yards.   One nest was found that looked exactly like a grebe's nest; another was built entirely of weed straws; still another entirely of freshly cut green cat-tails and one over deep water was made entirely from green moss brought up from the bottom of the lake.

Eggs.—The number of eggs in a coot's nest varies from half a dozen to two or three times that number; normal sets usually run from 8 to 12 eggs; as many as 16 even 22 have been recorded, probably the product of more than one bird.   The shape of the eggs varies but little from ovate, but they are often quite pointed.   The shell is smooth with a very slight gloss.   The ground color varies from dull "pinkish buff," rarely, to "cartridge buff," which is the usual color.   It is thickly and evenly covered with very small spots and minute dots of very dark, or blackish, brown.   The measurements of 122 eggs average 49 by 33.5 millimeters; the eggs showing the four extremes measure **53** by 32.5, 52 by **36**, and **41.5** by **30** millimeters.

Young.—The period of incubation is 21 or 22 days.   It is shared by both sexes and the male often stands on guard while his mate is sitting.   The eggs are apparently laid on successive days and incubation is continued more or less regularly during the laying period, for one, or sometimes two, young birds hatch each day during the hatching period.   The young are decidedly precocial, leaving the nest soon after they are hatched and swimming about in the vicinity; they can swim and dive almost as well as their parents and their ability to remain under water is astonishing.   Grinnell, Bryant, and Storer (1918) say: "In two instances youngsters not more than a day old were observed to remain under water nearly three minutes as timed by a watch.   They could be seen clinging to vegetation beneath the surface until apparently forced to come up for air."

Dr. Joseph Grinnell (1908) writes:

A quite significant and interesting fact was noted in that the feet of the young grew far more rapidly in proportion than the rest of their body.   A half-grown mud hen has astonishingly large feet, and after observing the ease with which the youngsters swam and dived (apparently just as well as the adults), the relative importance of those members to the early success of the individual seemed plain.   The young of a family near camp returned with both parents to the old nest each evening at dusk, but much squabbling and jostling, accompanied by various toots, grunts, and cries, took place before they were all finally settled for the night.

Plumages.—The downy young coot is a grotesque but showy little chick; a black ball of down with a fiery head.   The almost bald crown is but thinly covered with hairlike black down; the upper parts are thickly covered with glossy black, long, coarse down, mixed with long, hairlike filaments, which vary in color from "orange chrome" on the neck and wings to "light orange-yellow" on the back; the lores, chin, and throat are covered with short, stiff, curly hairs, varying in color from "flame scarlet" to "orange chrome"; the bill is "flame scarlet," with a black tip; the under parts are thickly covered with dense, furlike down, very dark gray to almost black, with whitish tips.

While raising young ducks and coots from the eggs in Manitoba we had a good chance to study their development. The young coot grows rapidly, especially the feet and legs, which soon seem out of proportion; but it is slow in assuming its plumage. The first, light grayish plumage appears on the breast when the bird is about 4 weeks old and about one-third grown; it is still covered with dark, sooty gray down and the orange hairs have not wholly disappeared. The wings do not start to grow until the young bird is 6 weeks old and the plumage is not complete until it is at least 2 months old. In this full juvenal plumage the upper parts vary from "hair brown" to "chaetura drab" more brownish on the back; the chin, throat and neck are "deep neutral gray," mottled with grayish white; and the under parts are mottled with neutral grays and whitish.

During the fall and winter a gradual molt of the contour plumage produces steady progress towards maturity; but traces of immaturity persist all through the first year; young birds have much more white in the under parts, chin, throat, and belly, and they have not yet developed the white bill and frontal shield. The young bird becomes practically adult after the first postnuptial molt, when over a year old. Adults have a complete molt in August and September and a very limited, partial prenuptial molt in the early spring.

Food.—The coot is quite omnivorous, living on a varied bill of fare at different seasons. Most of its food is obtained on, under, or near the water of its marshy haunts; but it is no uncommon sight to see it walking about on the marshy shores or even on dry land picking up its food in a lively fashion after the manner of domestic fowl. Sometimes far from the water it may be seen in flocks clipping off the green grasses in the meadows or pulling up the sprouting grain on cultivated land. It feeds largely on the leaves, fronds, seeds and roots of aquatic vegetation, such as pond weed (*Potamogeton*), the tops of water milfoil (*Myriophyllum*) and the seeds of bur reed (*Sparganium*). Much of this food must be obtained by diving to moderate depths, at which it is an expert. It is very fond of wild celery, some of which it steals from the canvasbacks and other ducks. In the great duck shooting resorts of Virginia and North Carolina coots congregate in enormous numbers in winter to feed on wild celery and the foxtail grass, both favorite duck foods. In California, according to John G. Tyler (1913), it still further annoys the duck hunters by eating the grain thrown out to attract the ducks. In some duck clubs coots have become such a nuisance that mud-hen shoots have been inaugurated, at which sometimes as many as 5,000 coots have been killed in a day. Dr. Alexander Wetmore (1920) has seen a coot, at Lake Burford, "eating algae and slime that had collected on dead tule stems floating in the water. It fed eagerly on this material, seizing and stripping one piece after another."

Its animal food includes some small fishes, tadpoles, snails, worms, water bugs and other insects, and their aquatic larvae. It has even been known to pluck the feathers off and partially eat dead ducks. A bird, dissected by Doctor Wetmore (1916) in Porto Rico, had eaten "a number of small crustaceans, and a large mass of eggs belonging probably to other crustaceans"; another "had eaten a large quantity of grass or sedge, with a few small roots."

Behavior.—There is much that is interesting in the behavior of the coot, characteristic of and peculiar to this curious bird. The name of "spatterer" has often been applied to it on account of its well-known habit of rising noisily from the water; running along the surface, it beats the water with wings and feet, splashing alternately with its heavy paddles and making the spray fly, until it gains sufficient momentum to fly; it has been suggested that this and other noisy splashing antics are of use to frighten its enemies or warn its companions. When well under way its flight is strong and direct, much more vigorous and swifter than the flight of gallinules; the neck is extended, with the conspicuous white bill pointing slightly downwards, and the feet are stretched out behind, with the toes pointing upwards, to serve as a rudder in place of the useless little tail. The white tips of the secondaries show up well in flight as a good field mark. It flies usually near the water, or 10 or 15 feet above it, and seldom makes long high flights except when migrating. It is much more likely to escape by swimming or by scurrying off over the surface than by rising and flying away as the ducks do. It is ordinarily not a shy bird, unless persistently hunted.

It is a strong rapid swimmer, floating higher in the water than the ducks or the gallinules, with the back more level, less submerged forward. When either swimming or walking it nods its head in step with its foot movements, like a dove or a hen. Its white bill, in contrast with its black head, fairly gleams in the sunlight, an excellent field mark.

On land the coot walks about actively, often in a hunched-back attitude suggestive of the guinea fowl; its lobed feet give it a firm footing on soft ground, but do not impede it on firmer soil. Dr.

Charles W. Townsend has noted that it folds its toes as it lifts its foot. Audubon apparently had never seen it dive, but it is now well known to be a good diver. to obtain its food and to escape its enemies. Dr. Townsend (1905) says that it "often goes under water with very little effort; at other times it leaps clear of the water like a grebe, with its wings pressed close to its sides, its body describing an arc, and the head entering as the feet leave the water."

I have often observed the peculiar antics of a coot when its nest is approached; with head lowered until the bill almost touches the water and with wings elevated behind like a swan's, it paddles about splashing loudly and grunting a loud guttural *"kruk, kruk, kruk"*; it often "backs water" vigorously with both feet, raising the body backwards out of the water. Sometimes it stands upright on its hind quarters, flapping its wings and splashing with both feet. Such noisy demonstrations may be due to nervous excitement or may be intended to scare us away.

Coots associate on their breeding grounds and in their winter quarters with various species of ducks, with which they mingle freely and never seem to quarrel. But with members of their own species they are often very pugnacious and sometimes murderous. F. W. Henshaw (1918) tells the following remarkable story:

Our boathouse rests in a cut opening out on Butte Slough, in Calusa County. California. Between the end of the boathouse and the current of the slough, there are 60 or 80 feet of still water; three mud hens (*Fulica americana*) have taken possession of this spot. They have grown quite tame; not only do they come up to the boathouse for their food, but when hungry swim up and are clamorously insistent with their "put-put-put." The men have frequently told me that they were murderous fighters against their own kind, and one day I was a witness of such a fight. A strange mud hen swam from the creek into the quiet water. The first of the three to see him attacked the stranger at once, "putting" harshly, and the intruder gave battle without the slightest attempt to retreat. They pecked at each other savagely. The other two boathouse mud hens swam up to the fray, one of them joining in, the other, the smallest of the three and probably the female, simply looking on. In time they pecked the strange mud hen into a state of exhaustion. It was manifestly too weak to fly, but tried to make its escape by swimming. They followed it up, and one actually stood on its body while the other held its head under the water until it was dead. When satisfied of this, they left it.

Coots indulge in quite a variety of grunting, croaking, and squawking notes and are responsible for most of the noise coming from the innermost recesses of a slough or tule swamp. Rev. J. H. Langille (1884) says:

It is decidedly a noisy bird, its *"coo-coo-coo-coo-coo"* being heard both day and night, the first note being prolonged on a much higher key, while the rest are somewhat accelerated. It will often *squack* similar to a duck, and has other notes too unique and difficult of description to be given here.

Mrs. Florence Merriam Bailey (1910) gives a very good idea of the notes as follows:

As we walked along behind the tule hedge a confusion of most remarkable sounds came from the tules where invisible coots were swimming about—coughing sounds, froglike plunks, and a rough sawing or filing *"kuk-kawk-kuk, kuk-kawk-kuk,"* as if the saw were dull and stuck. Often there was just a grating *"kuk-kuk-kuk-kuk-kuk-kuk."* But all the mixed medley had the sound of good fellowship, and, too, as open fearless disregard of who might be passing the other side of the tule screen—for who wanted coots?

Enemies.—On the Atlantic coast and in Florida, where bald eagles are common, these cowardly birds of prey seem to be the coots' worst enemies. C. J. Maynard (1896) writes:

The eagle hovers over a bunch of coots and endeavors by diving down towards the flock to make them scatter. The eagle will never attack a coot when surrounded by its fellows, but the instant one is separated from the flock his life is in jeopardy, for, no matter how expertly he dives, his untiring enemy is above him whenever he comes to the surface, and drives him further and further from his friends, who will never attempt to protect him, but who swim away as fast as their lobated toes would propel them. But the chase, unequal in the outset, soon ends— the exhausted coot rises for the air which it must have, when like a thunderbolt falls the eagle and the lifeless waterfowl is borne away to satisfy the hunger of the eaglets who are waiting, expectant, in their stick-built home in the high top of some neighboring pine. I have never seen the coots attempt to defend themselves even when in a body, in fact, they always dive and scatter somewhat when the eagle comes swooping downward toward them, but quickly gather again as soon as they rise. The reason why the eagle tries to separate one coot from its fellows must be that he can then trace that particular bird, and by chasing it until it is exhausted, effect its capture, whereas it would quite easily elude him if it kept among its fellows. Among coots, their safety lies in numbers, even if all be cowards, but the wonder is, not that the eagles know this, but that the coots themselves do.

But the eagle is not always successful. The following incident is related by Moses Williams, jr., in a letter to Dr. Charles W. Townsend:

An eagle after putting a large flock of ducks and geese to flight in the usual way, approached a flock of some 200 coots. They crowded together so that from our boat they appeared to be a solid black mass. When he came over them, he dropped from a height of about 25 yards to within a few feet. He did not swoop, but rather, comparatively slowly, pointed his flight downward. Immediately the coots set up such a splashing that the black spot was converted into a mass of white spray. The eagle hovered over them for a moment, apparently looking for an individual to strike at and then passed on. The splashing ceased only to begin again as he turned and again stooped and the same thing happened three more times and then the eagle gave it up and in two minutes the coots were again in open formation and swimming about and feeding in their usual animated way. We were all quite sure that the flock made no attempt to get away, but did their splashing throughout on the same spot. It seemed to me a very intelligent performance on the part of a bird, which could not escape by flying or diving as the other fowl can.

Fall.—The hardy coots not only arrive early in their northern homes, but they are loath to leave in the fall, lingering often until they are driven out by the freezing of the lakes. They gather into immense flocks before leaving and hold noisy conclaves, as if discussing the propriety of departure. On the morning after such a caucus the lake is usually deserted, all having gone during the night. Sometimes they linger too long and may be seen crowded in a dense black mass, perhaps mingled with the hardier ducks, in some unfrozen water hole in the ice. The fall migration takes the coots to southern lakes and even to brackish estuaries near the coasts where they mingle with the ducks and are often shot as game. But they are hardly worthy to be classed as game birds; they are too easy to kill and their flesh is not highly regarded. "Blue Peters," as they are called, are good game for boys and they help fill the pot when other game is scarce. While camping in Florida we often found them a welcome addition to our larder, as they are clean feeders and quite palatable.

Winter.—Below the frost line, from California to Florida, coots are very abundant in all suitable lakes, ponds, bayous, marshes, and marshy rivers, all through the winter, where they are highly gregarious. But they are seldom seen on salt water. Mr. Maynard (1896) writes:

The coots are remarkably abundant in the little ponds and lagoons on the marshes which lie to the eastward of Indian River, Florida. Here they have the habit of gathering together in a nearly solid mass in the middle of the body of water on which they float and it is exceedingly difficult to make them leave one of these chosen resorts. Even when shot at those that are uninjured will frequently remain while those which do fly, generally circle around about and after a time return. I remember once of walking along the margin of a narrow creek near Mosquito Lagoon, with my assistant, when we encountered a large body of coots. At the point where we found them the creek was only about 10 yards wide, and as we could walk faster than the birds could swim, we were soon abreast of them, but although we were so close to them none of them attempted to fly, but as we passed the first portion of the flock, the coots of which it was composed turned and swam back, then, sheeplike, all followed, and we stood still while hundreds of them swam past us. As the birds were crowded together, somewhat, their ranks were quite wide so that the nearest birds were only a few feet away.

Back Bay, Virginia, is a favorite winter resort for coots where they find an abundant food supply in the seeds and tops of the foxtail grass and other duck foods and where they steal the wild celery from the canvasbacks and redheads. I thought I had seen coots in Florida, but that was as nothing compared with the countless thousands that I saw here in November. There were acres and acres and acres of them spread out over the smooth waters of the bay in vast rafts. They were much tamer than any of the ducks and geese; even these big flocks allowed our power boat to approach almost within gunshot; and then they only pattered or flew away for a short distance and then settled down again, thus making a pathway for us through the vast flocks.

Range.—North and Central America.

Breeding range.—North to British Columbia (Quesnal, Kamloops and Okanagan): Mackenzie (Fort Simpson, Hay River, Fort Resolution, and Fort Smith); Saskatchewan (Prince Albert and Cumberland House); Manitoba (Moose Lake and Chemawawin); Minnesota (White Earth, Leech Lake, and Millelacs Lake); Wisconsin (La Crosse, Kelley Brook, and Green Bay); Michigan (Lansing, Saginaw, and Rochester); Ontario (Sudbury and Beaumaris); and Quebec (Montreal and Quebec). East to Quebec (Quebec); Vermont (Hyde ville); Massachusetts (formerly Boston); New York (probably Long Island City); New Jersey (Newark and Morristown); Pennsylvania (formerly Philadelphia); formerly District of Columbia (near Washington); North Carolina (Pamlico Sound); probably South Carolina (near Charleston); formerly Florida (Monticello); Mexico, Vera Cruz (Tampico); and Yucatan (Cozumel Island). South to Guatemala (Duenas); Mexico, Michoocan (Lake Patzcuaro); Jalisco (Guadalajara); Tepic (Tepic); and Lower California (Comondu). West to Lower California (San Pedro Martir Mountains); California (San Diego, Los Angeles, Santa Barbara, Santa Cruz, Gridley, and Crescent City); Oregon (Bandon, Dayton, and Portland); Washington (Tacoma, Seattle, and Bellingham Bay); British Columbia (Quesnal); and Mackenzie (Fort Simpson).

The breeding of the coot anywhere in the eastern United States is of rare or accidental occurrence as the species is not common as a nesting bird east of Indiana (Kewanna, Lafayette, and Terre Haute); southern Illinois (Mount Carmel); western Kentucky (Hickman); western Tennessee (Reelfoot Lake); eastern Arkansas (Big Lake); and central Texas (Decatur, Giddings, San Antonio, and Brownsville). The status of the coot as a breeder in the West Indies also is somewhat disputed as another form, *Fulica caribaea* Ridgway, described from the Lesser Antilles, is resident in this region and to this probably most, if not all, West Indian records are referable. Until adequate specimens are available, this problem probably can not be solved. A larger form of this has been described from Porto Rico.

The coot also has been noted in the Bermuda Islands in April, May, November, and December but is not known to breed.

Winter range.—North to British Columbia (Sumas and Okanagan;) probably Nevada (Carson); probably Idaho (Deer Flat Bird Reservation); Arizona (Salt River Bird Reservation, near Whipple and Tucson); Colorado (Barr); Texas (Mason, San Angelo, and San Antonio); southern Illinois (Anna and Mount Carmel); western Kentucky (Hickman); and Maryland (Miller's Island). East to Maryland (Miller's Island); Virginia (Cobb Island); North Carolina (Raleigh); South Carolina (Cooper River and Charleston); Georgia (Blackbeard Island and Savannah); Florida (Palatka, Fruitland Park, and Titusville); the Bahama Islands (Abaco, New Providence, Rum Cay, and Great Inagua); and Panama (Calobre). South to Panama (Calobre); Costa Rica (Juan Vinas and Las Corcovas); Honduras (Lake Yojoa); Guatemala (Lake of Duenas and Lake Atitlan); Mexico, Sinaloa (Escuinapa); and Lower California (San Jose del Cabo and La Paz). West to Lower California (San Jose del Cabo); California (Los Angeles, Point Pinos, and San Francisco); Oregon (Klamath Lake, Corvallis, and Netarts Bay); Washington (Seattle); and British Columbia (Sumas).

Winter occurrences of the coot outside of its normal range at this season include: West Virginia (Buckhannon); New York (Montauk Point, February 22, 1921, Mastic, Long Island, February 12, 1916, Geneva, December 13, 1913, and January 11, 1914, Branchport, January 1, 1914, and Oswego, January 17, 1904); and Rhode Island, (Point Judith, December 20, 1900); and one was taken in Connecticut, December 26, 1913. One wintered at Jamaica and Leverett Ponds, Boston, Massachusetts, during 1907–8 and another remained on Lake Maxinkuckee, Indiana, until it froze over January 10, 1901. The species also has been noted in winter from Clipperton Island, west of Mexico.

Spring migration.—Early dates of arrival are Pennsylvania, Renova, March 5, 1900, Cumberland County, March 16, 1894, Erie, March 28, 1898, Westtown, March 30, 1913, and Coatesville, April 14, 1887; New Jersey, Camden, April 2, 1916, and Audubon, April 12, 1914; New York, Geneva, March 14, 1909, Oswego, March 16, 1890, Rhinebeck, March 18, 1903, and Rochester, April 1, 1902; Connecticut, West Haven, April 2, 1910, and Portland, April 22, 1888; Massachusetts, Harvard, March 23, 1911, Sandwich, March 29, 1890, and Boston, April 2, 1910; Maine, Castine, March 23, 1904, Phillips, April 2, 1908, and Farmington, April 12, 1910; Quebec, Montreal, April 28, 1893, and Quebec, May 14, 1890; New Brunswick, Chatham, April 10, 1914; northern Illinois, Odin, February 26, 1890, Chicago, March 14, 1920, Alton, March 15, 1894, Rockford, March 19, 1891, and Forest Park, March 21, 1916; Indiana, Indianapolis, March 5, 1884, Goshen, March 6, 1918, Frankfort, March 8, 1895, Vincennes, March 10, 1922, La Porte, March 16, 1894, Waterloo, March 17, 1907, Fort Wayne, March 15, 1918, and New Castle, March 19, 1911; Ohio, Columbus, March 10, 1906, Youngstown, March 13, 1918, Circleville, March 15, 1884, and New Bremen, March 21, 1911; Michigan, Battle Creek, March 12, 1885, Sandhill, March 18, 1884, Vicksburg, March 19, 1904, Ann Arbor, March 23, 1912, Detroit, March 28, 1905, and Grand Rapids, April 8. 1890; Ontario, Dunnville, March 15, 1885, Port Rowan, March 16,

1884, Yarker, April 13, 1890, Queensboro, April 16, 1912, and Ottawa, April 27, 1892; Iowa, Cedar Rapids, February 23, 1889, Council Bluffs March 11, 1916, Indianola, March 12, 1904, Keokuk, March 13, 1900, La Porte, March 16, 1886, Mason City, March 19, 1921, Sioux City, March 20, 1916, Burlington, March 20, 1884, Emmetsburg, March 21, 1916, Marshalltown, March 25, 1913, Spirit Lake, March 25, 1892, and Grinnell, March 26, 1886; Wisconsin, Elkhorn, March 1, 1911, Eau Claire, March 17, 1918, Beloit, March 18, 1916, Portage, March 19, 1914, Madison, March 22, 1907, Delavan, March 24, 1894, La Crosse, March 25, 1910, Milwaukee, March 26, 1911, and Fox Lake, March 30, 1898; Minnesota, Heron Lake, March 16, 1894, Sherburn, March, 23, 1917, Redwing, March 26, 1884, Minneapolis, March 28, 1907, Wilder, March 30, 1917, and Waseca, April 3, 1892; Kansas, Emporia March 17, 1885, Manhattan, March 19, 1897, Topeka, March 25, 1921, Richmond, March 28, 1886, Wichita, March 30, 1917, Onaga, March 31, 1903, and Lawrence, April 2, 1906; Nebraska, Pullman, March 10, 1916, Valentine, March 14, 1893, Nebraska City, March 18, 1909, Whitman, March 21, 1920, Lincoln, March 23, 1900, Falls City, March 24, 1890, and South Bend, March 27, 1899; South Dakota, Sioux Falls, March 27, 1910, Grand View, March 31, 1889, Forest-burg, April 3, 1904, and Huron, April 8, 1887; North Dakota, Bath-gate, April 20, 1891, Larimore, April 20, 1890, Chase Lake, April 22, 1913, Stump Lake, April 26, 1912, and Fargo, April 29, 1914; Manitoba Alexander, April 3, 1895, Reaburn, April 17, 1895, Dalton, April 18, 1889, Portage la Prairie, April 21, 1908, Ossowo, April 22, 1891, Mar-garet, April 27, 1912, and Aweme, April 30, 1901; Saskatchewan, South Qu'Appelle, April 14, 1913, Indian Head, April 18, 1915, Dins-more, April 27, 1909, and Osler, May 1, 1893; New Mexico, Delaware Creek, March 24, 1856; Wyoming, Yellowstone Park, April 11, 1915, and Cheyenne, April 12, 1888; Idaho, Minidoka Bird Reservation, March 22, 1915, and Rathdrum, April 25, 1903; Montana, Neeley, March 1, 1917, Bonner's Ferry, April 15, 1916, and Rouan, April 22, 1917; and Alberta, Flagstaff, April 14, 1915, Carvel, April 27, 1914, Banff, April 29, 1913, and Fort Vermilion, May 8, 1911.

Fall migration.—Late dates of fall departure are: Montana, Terry, October 4, 1903, and Teton County, November 9, 1912; Idaho, Saw Tooth Lake, October 2, 1890, and Meridian, October 24, 1914; Wyom-ing, Yellowstone Park, October 11, 1915; New Mexico, Jornada, Oc-tober 6, 1905, and Chloride, November 28, 1915; Saskatchewan, South Qu'Appelle, November 30, 1913; Manitoba, Aweme, October 20, 1910, Killarney, October 27, 1913, and Margaret, November 2, 1912; North Dakota, Harrisburg, October 18, 1901, Antler, October 23, 1908, and Grafton, November 24, 1914; South Dakota, Wall Lake, October 23, 1908, Sioux Falls, November 28, 1915, and Forestburg, November 30, 1905; Nebraska, Badger, November 10, 1900, and Lincoln, November

18, 1900; Kansas, Onaga, October 26, 1899, and Lawrence, November 6, 1905; Minnesota, Elk River, October 1, 1915, Hutchinson, October 31, 1914, Jackson, November 3, 1902, Minneapolis, November 6, 1906, Lanesboro, November 10, 1892, La Crescent, November 12, 1896, and Heron Lake, November 15, 1914; Wisconsin, Shiocton, November 13, 1882, Milwaukee, November 15, 1914, Elk Horn, December 2, 1919, and Madison, December 12, 1915; Iowa, Gilbert Station, October 22, 1892, Marshalltown, November 1, 1913, Sigourney, November 10, 1920, Emmetsburg, November 18, 1915, and Keokuk, November 18, 1902; Ontario, Todmorden, October 10. 1891, Toronto, October 14, 1898, Point Pelee, October 15, 1906, Ottawa, October 27, 1916, and Kingston, October 30, 1905; Michigan, Manchester, October 17, 1894, Manistee, October 20, 1904, Sault Ste. Marie, October 24, 1922, Ann Arbor, October 30, 1915, Hillsdale, November 3, 1894, Detroit, November 6, 1919, and Vicksburg, December 5, 1909; Ohio, Lakeside, November 5, 1920, Bowling Green, November 11, 1916, Scio, November 14, 1922, Youngstown, November 22, 1913, Oberlin, November 26, 1906, Canton, December 3, 1911, and Sandusky, December 15, 1910; Indiana, Indianapolis, October 16, 1915, Bicknell. October 27, 1914, New Harmony, October 27, 1902, and Lake Maxinkuckee, October 30, 1906; northern Illinois, La Grange, October 21, 1916, Lake Forrest, November 6, 1906, and Illinois River, November 14, 1912; Quebec, Montreal, October 24, 1892; Maine, Pittsfield, October 8, 1895, Portland, October 9, 1905, Saccarappa, October 18, 1890, and Westbrook, October 24, 1904; New Hampshire, Durham, October 10, 1897; Vermont, Rutland, October 10, 1916; Massachusetts, Lynn, October 23, 1912, Newtonville, November 3, 1911, Jamaica Plain, November 30, 1900, and Boston, December 30, 1909; Rhode Island, Newport, November 14, 1871, and Point Judith, November 30, 1900; Connecticut, East Hartford, October 2, 1888, Meriden, October 25, 1915, and Portland, November 14, 1892; New York, Consook Island, November 4, 1881, Orient Point, November 8, 1907, Great South Bay, November 17, 1905, Crugers Island, November 19, 1921, Brooklyn, November 22, 1914, and Branchport, November 23, 1906; New Jersey, Bernardsville, October 25, 1910, Camden, October 29, 1915, Morristown, November 10, 1885, and Pennsville, November 25, 1914; and Pennsylvania, Bridesburg, October 17, 1913, Berwyn, November 1, and Beaver, November 2, 1899, State College, November 5, 1916, Armingo, November 11, 1912, Lake Sheriden, November 21, 1911, and Erie, December 6, 1900.

Casual records.—The coot has been reported as rare at Anticosti Island and it has occurred once at Nain, Labrador, while there also is a record from St. Johns, Nova Scotia, and one from Otter Brook, Sable Bay, Quebec, March 12, 1914. Two have been reported from Greenland, both in 1854, one from Godthaab and the other from Jacobs Haven, near Disco; and Willett reports a specimen taken near Sitka,

Alaska, in September, 1908, stating that two or three others have been taken in that same region in the fall. He also reports three seen at St. Lazaria Island, Alaska, on September 9, 1913.

Egg dates.—California: 58 records, April 11, to August 2; 29 records, May 19 to June 19. Central Canadian Provinces: 20 records, May 16 to June 20; 10 records, June 1 to 7. Minnesota and the Dakotas: 16 records, May 10 to July 6; 8 records, May 27 to June 4. Colorado· 6 records, April 27 to July 2.

REFERENCES TO BIBLIOGRAPHY

REFERENCES TO FIELD MAPPY

REFERENCES TO BIBLIOGRAPHY

ABBOTT, CLINTON GILBERT.
    1907—Summer Bird Life of the Newark, New Jersey, Marshes. The Auk,
        vol. 24, pp. 1–11.
ADAMS, ERNEST.
    1900—Notes of the California Clapper Rail. The Condor, vol. 2, pp. 31, 32.
ALLEN, ARTHUR AUGUSTUS.
    1915—The Behavior of the Least Bittern. Bird-Lore, vol. 17, pp. 425–430.
ALLEN, JOEL ASAPH.
    1900—The Little Black Rail. The Auk, vol. 17, pp. 1–8.
AMES, JAMES HENRY.
    1902—Solution of the "Ornithological Mystery." The Auk, vol. 19, pp.
        94, 95.
ANDERSON, RUDOLPH MARTIN.
    1894—Nesting of the Whooping Crane. The Oologist, vol. 11, pp. 263, 264.
    1907—The Birds of Iowa. Proceedings of the Davenport Academy of
        Sciences, vol. 11, pp. 125–417.
AUDUBON, JOHN JAMES.
    1840—The Birds of America. 1840–1844.
BAILEY, FLORENCE MERRIAM.
    1910—Wild Life of an Alkaline Lake. The Auk, vol. 27, pp. 418–427.
BAILEY, HARRY BALCH.
    1881—Forest and Stream Bird Notes.
BAILEY, SAMUEL WALDO.
    1915—The Plum Island Night Herons. The Auk, vol. 32, pp. 424–441.
BAIRD, SPENCER FULLERTON; BREWER, THOMAS MAYO; and RIDGWAY, ROBERT.
    1884—The Water Birds of North America.
BALES, BLENN R.
    1911—Some Notes from Pickaway County, Ohio. The Wilson Bulletin,
        vol. 23, pp. 43–48.
BANGS, OUTRAM.
    1899—A New Rail from Southern California. Proceedings of the new Eng-
        land Zoological Club, vol. 1, pp. 45, 46.
BARKER, SAMUEL H.
    1901—Does the Green Heron Fish in Deep Water? Bird-Lore, vol. 3, p.
        141.
BARROWS, WALTER BRADFORD.
    1913—Concealing Action of the Bittern (*Botaurus lentiginosus*). The Auk,
        vol. 30, p. 187.
BARTLETT, A. D.
    1866—Notes on the Breeding of several Species of Birds in the Society's
        Gardens during the year 1865. Proceedings of the Royal Society
        of London, pp. 76–79.

BAYNARD, OSCAR E.
    1912—Food of Herons and Ibises.   The Wilson Bulletin, no. 81, vol. 24,
        pp. 167–169.
    1913—Home Life of the Glossy Ibis (*Plegadis autumnalis*, Linn.).   The Wil-
        son Bulletin, vol. 25, pp. 103–117.
BEEBE, C. WILLIAM.
    1909—An Ornithological Reconnaissance of Northeastern Venezuela.   Zoo-
        logica, vol. 1, nos. 2 and 3.
BEEBE, WILLIAM.
    1918—Jungle Peace.
BEEBE, C. WILLIAM, and BEEBE, MARY BLAIR.
    1910—Our Search for a Wilderness.
BENNERS, GEORGE B.
    1887—A Collecting Trip in Texas.   Ornithologist and Oologist, vol. 12, pp.
        49–52, 65–69, and 81–84.
BEYER, GEORGE EUGENE; ALLISON, ANDREW; KOPMAN, HENRY HAZLITT.
    1908—List of the Birds of Louisiana.   The Auk, vol. 25, pp. 173–180 and
        439–448.
BISHOP, LOUIS BENNETT.
    1904—The Eggs and Breeding Habits of Some Comparatively Little Known
        North American Birds.   Abstract of the Proceedings of the Lin-
        naean Society of New York, nos. 15 and 16, pp. 48-61.
BODKIN, A. E. and MATTLEY, C. T.
    1921—Shooting Notes.   Timehri.   The Journal of the Royal Agricultural
        and Commercial Society of British Guiana, vol. 7 (new series) pp.
        115–125.
BONHOTE, JOHN LEWIS JAMES.
    1903—Field Notes on some Bahama Birds.   Avicultural Magazine, vol. 8,
        p. 278; vol. 9, pp. 19, 54 and 87.
    1907—Birds of Britain.
BOWDISH, BEECHER SCOVILLE.
    1891—Notes on the Virginia Rail.   The Ornithologist and Botanist, vol. 1,
        pp. 73–74.
    1902—Birds of Porto Rico.   The Auk, vol. 19, pp. 356–366.
BOWLES, JOHN HOOPER.
    1893—A Peculiarity in the Nesting Habits of the Virginia Rail.   Ornithol-
        ogist and Oologist, vol. 18, pp. 115, 116.
    1909—The Birds of Washington.
BREHM, A. E.
    1871—Zur Fortpflanzungsgeschichte des Purpurhuhns.   Journal für Orni-
        thologie, vol. 19, pp. 34–39.
BRETHERTON, WILFRED A.
    1891—The Great Blue Heron.   Ornithologist and Oologist, vol. 16, pp.
        90–91.
BREWSTER, WILLIAM.
    1881—With the Birds on a Florida River.   Bulletin of the Nuttall Ornitho-
        logical Club, vol. 6, pp. 38–44.
    1883—The Scarlet Ibis in Florida.   Bulletin of the Nuttall Ornithological
        Club, vol. 8, pp. 185–186.
    1886—Breeding of the White-faced Glossy Ibis in Florida.   The Auk, vol.
        3, pp. 481–482.
    1888—Description of Supposed New Birds from Lower California, Sonora,
        and Chihuahua, Mexico, and the Bahamas.   The Auk, vol. 5, pp.
        82–95.

BREWSTER, WILLIAM—Continued.

1891—A Study of Florida Gallinules, with some notes on a Nest found at Cambridge, Massachusetts. The Auk, vol. 8, pp. 1–7.

1901—An Ornithological Mystery. The Auk, vol. 18, pp. 321–328.

1902—Voices of a New England Marsh. Bird-Lore, vol. 4, pp. 43–56.

1902a—Birds of the Cape Region of Lower California. Bulletin of the Museum of Comparative Zoology at Harvard College. vol. 41, No. 1.

1906—The Birds of the Cambridge Region of Massachusetts. Memoirs of the Nuttall Ornithological Club, No. 4.

1907—Notes on the Black Rail of California. The Auk, vol. 24, pp. 205–210.

1911—Concerning the Nuptial Plumes worn by certain Bitterns and the Manner in which they are Displayed. The Auk, vol. 28, pp. 90–100.

BREWSTER, WILLIAM; and CHAPMAN, FRANK MICHLER.

1891—Notes on the Birds of the Lower Suwanee River. The Auk, vol. 8, pp. 125–138.

BROOKS, WINTHROP SPRAGUE.

1923—An Interesting Adaptation. The Auk, vol. 40, pp. 121–122.

BROWN, C. BARRINGTON.

1876—Canoe and Camp Life in British Guiana.

BRYANT, HAROLD CHILD.

1919—Evidence as to the Food of the Wood Ibis. The Condor, vol. 21, pp. 236 and 237.

BRYANT, HENRY.

1861—[On some birds observed in East Florida.] Proceedings of the Boston Society of Natural History, vol. 7, pp. 5–21.

BRYANT, WALTER E.

1893—Notes on the Food of Birds. Zoe, vol. 4, pp. 54–58.

BULL, CHARLES LIVINGSTON.

1911—Under the Roof of the Jungle.

BURMEISTER, HERMANN.

1856—Systematische Uebersicht der Thiere Brasiliens, vol. 2, p. 425.

BURNS, FRANK L.

1915—Comparative Periods of Deposition and Incubation of Some North American Birds. The Wilson Bulletin, vol. 27, pp. 275–286.

BURTCH, VERDI.

1917—Nesting of the Florida Gallinule. The Auk, vol. 34, pp. 319–321.

BUTLER, AMOS WILLIAM.

1897—The Birds of Indiana. Department of Geology and Natural Resources. Twenty-second Annual Report.

CAHN, ALVIN R.

1915—Notes on a Captive Virginia Rail. The Auk, vol. 32, pp. 91–95.

1923—Louisiana Herons and Reddish Egrets at Home. Natural History, vol. 23, pp. 471–479.

CAMERON, EWEN SOMERLED.

1906—Nesting of the Great Blue Heron in Montana. The Auk, vol. 23, pp. 252–262.

1907—The Birds of Custer and Dawson Counties, Montana. The Auk, vol. 24, pp. 241–270.

CARRIGER, HENRY WARD; and PEMBERTON, JOHN ROY.

1908—Some Notes on the Great Blue Heron. The Condor, vol. 10, pp. 78–81.

CHAPMAN, FRANK MICHLER.

> 1892—Notes on Birds and Mammals Observed near Trinidad, Cuba, with Remarks on the Origin of West Indian Bird Life. Bulletin of the American Museum of Natural History, vol. 4. pp. 279–330.
>
> 1900—Bird Studies with a Camera.
>
> 1902—Flamingoes' Nests. Bird-Lore, vol. 4, pp. 177–181.
>
> 1904—Young Flamingos. Bird-Lore, vol. 6. pp. 193–198.
>
> 1905—A Contribution to the Life History of the American Flamingo (*Phoenicopterus ruber*) with Remarks upon Specimens. Bulletin of the American Museum of Natural History, vol. 21, pp. 53–77.
>
> 1908—Camps and Cruises of an Ornithologist.
>
> 1908a—The Home-Life of the American Egret. Bird-Lore, vol. 10, pp. 59–68.
>
> 1914—The Roseate Spoonbill. Bird-Lore, vol. 16 pp. 214–217.

CLARK, JOHN NATHANIEL.

> 1884—Nesting of the Little Black Rail in Connecticut. The Auk, vol. 1, pp. 393, 394.
>
> 1897—The Little Black Rail. The Nidologist, vol. 4, pp. 86–88.

COBB, STANLEY.

> 1906—A Little Black Rail in Massachusetts. Bird-Lore, vol. 8, pp. 136, 137.

COHEN, DONALD A.

> 1895—The California Clapper Rail. The Oologist, vol. 12, pp. 171–173.

COOKE, WELLS WOODBRIDGE.

> 1897—The Birds of Colorado. The State Agricultural College, Bulleti 37.
>
> 1897a—The Scarlet Ibis in Colorado. The Auk, vol. 34, p. 316.
>
> 1914—Distribution and Migration of North American Rails and their Allies. Bulletin of the U. S. Department of Agriculture, No. 128.

CORDIER, ALBERT HAWES.

> 1923—Birds, their Photographs and Home Life.

COUES, ELLIOTT.

> 1865—Ornithology of a Prairie-Journey, and Notes on the Birds of Arizona The Ibis, 1865, pp. 157–165.
>
> 1872—Key to North American Birds.
>
> 1874—Birds of the North-West.

COURT, EDWARD J.

> 1908—Treganza Blue Heron. The Auk, vol. 25, pp. 291–296.

DAWSON, CHARLES B.

> 1917—Some Colony Birds, Part 3. The Journal of The Royal Agricultural and Commercial Society of British Guiana, vol. 4 (ser. 3), pp. 38–57.

DAWSON, WILLIAM LEON.

> 1903—The Birds of Ohio.
>
> 1909—The Birds of Washington.
>
> 1915—The Breeding of the Snowy Egret in California. The Condor, vol. 17, pp. 97–98.
>
> 1922—A New Breeding Record for California. The Journal of the Museum of Comparative Oology, vol. 2, pp. 31, 32.
>
> 1923—The Birds of California.

DICKEY, DONALD R.

> 1923—Description of a New Clapper Rail from the Colorado River Valley. The Auk, vol. 40, pp. 90–94.

DICKEY, DONALD R. and VAN ROSSEM, ADRIAN J.
  1924—A New Race of the Least Bittern from the Pacific Coast. Bulletin of the Southern California Academy of Sciences, vol. 23, pp. 11 and 12.

DRESSER, HENRY EELES.
  1866—Notes on the Birds of Southern Texas. The Ibis, 1866, pp. 23–46.

EDWARDS, WILLIAM H.
  1847—A Voyage up the River Amazon, including a Residence at Para.

ELIOT, WILLARD.
  1892—The Wood Ibis. The Oologist, vol. 9 pp. 143–144.

EMERSON, WILLIAM OTTO.
  1885—California Clapper Rail. Ornithologist and Oologist, vol. 10, pp. 142, 143.

ERICHSEN, WALTER JEFFERSON.
  1921—Notes on the Habits of the Breeding Water Birds of Chatham County, Georgia. The Wilson Bulletin, vol. 33, pp. 16–28 and 69–82.

EVANS, WILLIAM.
  1891—On the Periods occupied by Birds in the Incubation of their Eggs. The Ibis, 1891, pp. 52–93.

FAXON, WALTER.
  1896—John Abbot's Drawings of the Birds of Georgia. The Auk, vol. 13, pp. 204–215.

FIGGINS, JESSE DADE.
  1925—Twice-told Tales. Proceedings of the Colorado Museum of Natural History, vol. 5, pp. 23–31.

FINLEY, WILLIAM LOVELL.
  1906—Herons at Home. The Condor, vol. 8, pp. 35–40.

FISHER, ALBERT KENRICK.
  1893—The Death Valley Expedition. North America Fauna, No. 7.

FORBUSH, EDWARD HOWE.
  1912—A History of the Game Birds, Wild Fowl and Shore Birds of Massachusetts and Adjacent States.
  1914—The Sora Rail. Bird-Lore, vol. 16, pp. 303–306.

GABRIELSON, IRA N.
  1914—Ten Day's Bird Study in a Nebraska Swamp. The Wilson Bulletin, No. 87, vol. 26, pp. 51–68.

GIBBS, MORRIS.
  1899—The Sora. The Oologist, vol. 16, pp. 151–153.

GIFFORD, EWARD WINSLOW.
  1913—The Birds of the Galapagos Islands. Proceedings of the California Academy of Sciences, Ser. 4, vol. 2, p. 1.

GILLETT, DANA C.
  1896—Two Interesting Birds of Tonawanda Swamp. The Oologist, vol. 13 pp. 29–30 and 50–52.

GIRAUD, JACOB POST.
  1844—The Birds of Long Island.

GOSS, NATHANIEL STICKNEY.
  1891—History of the Birds of Kansas.

GOSSE, PHILIP HENRY.
  1847—The Birds of Jamaica.

GRAYSON, ANDREW JACKSON.
  1871—Natural History of the Tres Marias and Socorro. Proceedings of the Boston Society of Natural History, June 7, 1871.

GRINNELL, JOSEPH.
  1900—Birds of the Kotzebue Sound Region.   Pacific Coast Avifauna, No. 1.
  1908—The Biota of the San Bernardino Mountains.   University of Califor-
      nia Publications in Zoology, vol. 5, pp. 1–170.
  1914—An Account of the Mammals and Birds of the Lower Colorado Val-
      ley.   University of California Publications in Zoology, vol. 12, pp.
      51–294.
GRINNEL, JOSEPH; BRYANT, HAROLD CHILD; and STORER, TRACY IRWIN.
  1918—The Game Birds of California.
GRISCOM, LUDLOW.
  1915—The Little Black Rail on Long Island, N. Y.   The Auk, vol. 32, pp.
      227, 228.
GROSS, ALFRED O.
  1923—The Black-crowned Night Heron (Nycticorax nycticorax naevius) of
      Sandy Neck.   The Auk, vol. 40, pp. 1–30 and 191–214.
HAGERUP, ANDREAS THOMSEN.
  1891—The Birds of Greenland.
HAGMANN, GOTTFRIED.
  1906—Ornithologisches von der Insel Mexiana, Amazonenstrom.   Ornithol.
      Monatsberichte, 1906, pp. 107–111.
  1907—Die Vogelwelt der Insel Mexiana, Amazonenstrom, Zoologisches
      Jahrbuch, vol. 26, pt. 1, Reprint. pp. 11–62.
HARLOW, RICHARD C.
  1913—Nesting of the Black Rail (Creciscus jamaicensis) in New Jersey.   The
      Auk, vol. 30, p. 269.
HATCH, PHILO LUOIS.
  1892—Notes on the Birds of Minnesota.
HENNINGER, WALTHER FRIEDRICH.
  1910—Notes on some Ohio Birds.   The Auk, vol. 37, pp. 66–68.
HENSHAW, FREDERICK WILLIAM.
  1918—Some pugnacious Coots.   The Condor, vol. 20, p. 92.
HOWE, REGINALD HEBER, Jr.
  1902—Notes on various Florida Birds.   Contributions to North American
      Ornithology, vol. 1, pp. 25–32.
HOWELL, ALFRED BRAZIER.
  1917—Birds of the Islands off the Coast of Southern California.   Pacific
      Coast Avifauna, No. 12.
HOWELL, ARTHUR HOLMES.
  1911—Birds of Arkansas.   U. S. Dept. of Agriculture Biological Survey
      Bull. No. 38.
HOYT, R. D.
  1905—Nesting of Ward's Heron.   The Warbler, vol. 1, pp. 114–115.
HUDSON, WILLIAM HENRY.
  1888—Argentine Ornithology.
  1902—British Birds.
HUEY, LAURENCE M.
  1915—Random Notes from San Diego.   The Condor, vol. 17, pp. 59–60.
  1916—The Farallon Rails of San Diego County.   The Condor, vol. 18, pp.
      58–62.
HUNTINGTON, DWIGHT W.
  1903—Our Feathered Game.
HUXLEY, JULIAN S.
  1924—Some Points in the Breeding Behaviour of the Common Heron.   Brit-
      ish Birds, vol. 18, pp. 155–163.

INGERSOLL, ALBERT M.
    1909—The Only Known Breeding Ground of *Creciscus coturniculus*. The
        Condor, vol. 11, pp. 123–127.
INGRAHAM, DAVID POWERS.
    1894—Do Wading Birds Swim? The Nidiologist, vol. 2, p. 25.
JACKSON, THOMAS HOOPES.
    1887—The Limpkin and its Nest and Eggs. Ornithologist and Oologist,
        vol. 12, pp. 159–160.
JOB, HERBERT KEIGHTLEY.
    1905—Wild Wings.
KAPPLER, AUGUST.
    1854—Zes Jaren in Suriname.
    1887—Surinam, sein Land, seine Natur, Bevolkerung und seine Kultur-
        Verhaltnisse.
KNIGHT, ORA WILLIS.
    1908—The Birds of Maine.
LAING, HAMILTON M.
    1915—Garoo, Chief Scout of the Prairie. Outing, 1915, pp. 699–710.
LANGILLE, JAMES HIBBERT.
    1884—Our Birds and Their Haunts.
LEOTAUD, A.
    1866—Oiseaux de l'ile de la Trinidad (Antilles).
LLOYD, C. A.
    1895—Stray Notes from Pirara. Timehri. The Journal of the Royal Agri-
        cultural Society of British Guiana, vol. 9 (new series) pp. 220–232.
    1897—Nesting of Some Guiana Birds. Timehri. The Journal of the Royal
        Agricultural and Commercial Society of British Guiana, vol. 9 (new
        series) pp. 1–10.
LORENZ, TH.
    1871—Die Lasurmeise (Cyanistes cyanus). Journal für Ornithologie, vol.
        19, pp. 124–130.
LOWE, WILLOUGHBY P.
    1894—The Scarlet Ibis (Guara rubra) in Colorado. The Auk, vol. 11 p.
        224.
MACFARLANE, RODERICK ROSS.
    1908—List of Birds and Eggs Observed and Collected in the North-West
        Territories of Canada, between 1880 and 1894. Through the Mac-
        kenzie Basin, by Charles Mair.
MACKAY, GEORGE HENRY.
    1893—Behavior of a Sandhill Crane. The Auk, vol. 10, p. 300.
MALTBY, FRED.
    1915—Nesting of the Yellow Rail in North Dakota. The Oologist, vol. 32,
        pp. 122–124.
MAYNARD, CHARLES JOHNSON.
    1888—Notes on the Breeding Habits of the American Flamingo, etc. The
        Oologist, vol. 5 pp. 108–110.
    1896—The Birds of Eastern North America.
MCATEE, WALDO LEE.
    1911—Winter Ranges of Geese on the Gulf Coast; Notable Bird Records for
        the same Region. The Auk, vol. 28, pp. 272–274.
MCILHENNY, EDWARD AVERY.
    1912—How I made a Bird City. Reprinted from Country Life in America.

McKechnie, Frederick B.

1906—A Late Spring Record for the Yellow Rail (*Porzana noveboracensis*) in Massachusetts, with Remarks on the "Ornithological Mystery." The Auk, vol. 23, pp. 457–458.

Mearns, Edgar Alexander.

1895—Description of a New Heron (Ardea virescens anthonyi) from the Arid Region of the Interior of North America. The Auk, vol. 12, pp. 257–259.

Merrill, James Cushing.

1879—Notes on the Ornithology of Southern Texas, Being a List of Birds observed in the vicinity of Fort Brown, Texas, from February, 1876, to June, 1878. Proceedings of the United States National Museum, vol. 1, pp. 118–173.

Miller, Richard F.

1910—Notes on the Florida Gallinule (*Gallinula galeata*) in Philadelphia County, Pa. The Auk, vol. 27, pp. 181–184.

Morris, Francis Orpen.

1903—A History of British Birds. Fifth Edition.

Morris, Robert O.

1905—The Gadwall and Yellow Rail near Springfield, Mass. The Auk, vol. 22, pp. 207–208.

Murchison, A. C.

1895—Nesting of the King Rail. The Nidiologist, vol. 2. pp. 141, 142.

Nelson, Edward William.

1877—Birds of North-Eastern Illinois. Bulletin of the Essex Institute, vol. 8, pp. 90–155.

1883—The Birds of Bering Sea and the Arctic Ocean. Cruise of the Revenue-Steamer Corwin in Alaska and the N. W. Arctic Ocean in 1881.

1887—Report upon Natural History Collections made in Alaska.

Northrup, Edwin F.

1885—A visit to a Heronry. Ornithologist and Oologist, vol. 10, pp. 11–13.

Nuttall, Thomas.

1834—A Manual of the Ornithology of the United States and Canada: Water Birds.

Oberholser, Harry Church.

1912—A Revision of the Subspecies of the Green Heron (*Butorides virescens* Linnaeus). Proceedings of the United States National Museum, vol. 42, pp. 529–577.

1912a—A Revision of the Forms of the Great Blue Heron (*Ardea herodias* Linnaeus). Proceedings of the United States National Museum, vol. 43, pp. 531–559.

Osgood, Wilfred Hudson.

1904—A Biological Reconnaissance of the Base of the Alaska Peninsula. North American Fauna, No. 24.

Palmer, William.

1909—Instinctive Stillness in Birds. The Auk, vol. 26, pp. 23–36.

Patterson, Arthur H.

1905—Nature in Eastern Norfolk.

Peabody, Putnam Burton.

1922—Haunts and Breeding Habits of the Yellow Rail. The Journal of the Museum of Comparative Oology, vol. 2, pp. 33–44.

PEARSON, THOMAS GILBERT.
  1899—Notes on Some of the Birds of Eastern North Carolina. The Auk,
      vol. 16, pp. 246–250.
  1912—The White Egrets. Bird-Lore, vol. 14, pp. 62–69.
  1922.—Herons of the United States. Bird-Lore, vol. 24, pp. 306–314.
PEARSON, THOMAS GILBERT; BRIMLEY, CLEMENT SAMUEL, and BRIMLEY, HERBERT
    HUTCHINSON.
  1919—Birds of North Carolina.
      North Carolina Geological and Economic Survey, vol. 4.
PELZELN, AUGUST VON.
  1871—Zur Ornithologie Brasiliens.
PEMBERTON, JOHN RAY.
  1922—The Reddish Egret of Cameron County, Texas. The Condor, vol.
      24, pp. 3–12.
PENARD, FREDERIK PAUL; and PENARD, ARTHUR PHILIP.
  1908—De Vogels van Guyana (Suriname, Cayenne en Demerara). vol. 1.
PENNANT, THOMAS.
  1776—British Zoology, vol. 2.
PERICLES, EUGENE.
  1895—Nesting of the Great Blue Heron. The Oologist, vol. 12, pp. 179–181.
PETERS, JAMES LEE.
  1925—Notes on the Taxonomy of Ardea canadensis Linne. The Auk, vol.
      42, pp. 120–122.
PHELPS, FRANK M.
  The Resident Bird Life of the Big Cypress Swamp Region. The Wilson
      Bulletin, No. 87, vol. 26, pp. 86–101.
" PICKET "
  1883—Forest & Stream, December 20, 1883, p. 407.
PRESTON, JUNIUS WALLACE.
  1893—Some Prairie Birds. Ornithologist and Oologist, vol. 18, pp. 81, 82·
PRILL, ALBERT G.
  1922—Nesting of the Sandhill Crane, Warner Valley, Oregon. The Wilson
      Bulletin, vol. 34, pp. 169–171.
QUILLIN, ROY W. and HOLLEMAN, RIDLEY.
  1918—The Breeding Birds of Bexar County, Texas. The Condor, vol. 20,
      pp. 37–44.
RACEY, KENNETH.
  1921—Notes on the Northwest Coast Heron in Stanley Park, Vancouver,
      B. C. The Canadian Field-Naturalist, vol. 25, pp. 118, 119.
RAMSAY, R. G. WARDLAW.
  1923—Guide to the Birds of Europe and North Africa.
RAY, MILTON SMITH.
  1902—Rambles about my Old Home. The Osprey, n. s., vol. 1, pp. 23–26.
REID, SAVILLE G.
  1884—The Birds of Bermuda. Part IV in Contributions to the Natural
      History of the Bermudas. Bulletin U. S. National Museum, No. 25
RHOADS, SAMUEL N.
  1892—The Birds of Southwestern Texas and Southern Arizona observed
      during May, June, and July, 1891. Proceedings of the Academy
      of Natural Sciences of Philadelphia, Jan. 26, 1892.
RICH, WALTER HERBERT.
  1907—Feathered Game of the Northeast.

RIDGWAY, ROBERT.

1880—On the Supposed Identity of *Ardea occidentalis*, Aud., and *A. würd-emanni*, Baird. Bulletin of the Nuttall Ornithological Club, vol. 5, pp. 122, 123.

1882—On an Apparently New Heron from Florida. Bulletin of the Nuttall Ornithological Club, vol. 7, pp. 1–6.

1890—Observations on the Farallon Rail (*Porzana jamaicensis coturniculus* Baird). Proceedings of the United States National Museum, vol. 13, pp. 309–311.

ROBERTS, THOMAS SADLER.

1879—Notes on some Minnesota Birds. Bulletin of the Nuttall Ornithological Club, vol. 4, pp. 152, 155.

ROCKWELL, ROBERT BLANCHARD.

1910—Some Colorado Night Heron Notes. The Condor, vol. 12, pp. 113, 121.

1912—Notes on the Wading Birds of the Barr Lake Region, Colorado. The Condor, vol. 14, pp. 117, 131.

SANFORD, LEONARD CUTLER; BISHOP, LOUIS BENNETT; and VANDYKE, THEODORE STRONG.

1903—The Waterfowl Family.

SAUNDERS, HOWARD.

1889—An Illustrated Manual of British Birds.

SAUNDERS, WILLIAM E.

1918—An Episode with the Virginia Rail. The Ottawa Naturalist, vol. 32, p. 77.

SCHLEGEL, H.

1863—Muséum d'Histoire Naturelle des Pays-Bas. Revue méthodique et critique des collections deposées dans cet etablissement, vol. 5.

SCHMIDT, MAX.

1880—On the Duration of Life of the Animals in the Zoological Garden at Frankfort-on-the-Main. Proceedings of the Zoological Society of London, pp. 299–319.

SCHOMBURGK, RICHARD.

1848—Reisen in Britisch-Guiana, vol. 3, Versuch einer Fauna und Flora von Britisch-Guiana.

SCHOMBURGK, ROBERT H.

1840—Mr. Schomburgk's recent Expedition in Guiana. Annals of Natural History, vol. 4, pp. 346–348 and 399–400.

1841—Twelve Views in the Interior of Guiana.

SCOTT, WILLIAM EARL DODGE.

1881—On birds observed in Sumpter, Levy, and Hillsboro Counties, Florida. Bulletin of the Nuttall Ornithological Club, vol. 6, pp. 14–21.

1887—The Present Condition of Some of the Bird Rookeries of the Gulf Coast of Florida. The Auk, vol. 4, pp. 135–144; 213–222; 273–284.

1888—Supplementary Notes from the Gulf Coast of Florida, with a Description of a New Species of Marsh Wren. The Auk, vol. 5, pp. 183–188.

1889—A Summary of Observations on the Birds of the Gulf Coast of Florida. The Auk, vol. 6, pp. 13–18.

1890—An Account of Flamingoes (*Phoenicopterus ruber*) observed in the Vicinity of Cape Sable, Florida. The Auk, vol. 7, pp. 221–226.

SEEBOHM, HENRY.

1884—History of British Birds.

SELBY, PRIDEAUX JOHN.
  1833—Illustrations of British Ornithology.
SELL, R. A.
  1917—Some Notes on the Effects upon the Bird Life of the Corpus Christi
    Storm of August 18, 1916. The Condor, vol. 19, pp. 43–46.
  1918—The Scarlet Ibis in Texas. The Condor, vol. 20, pp. 78–82.
SENNETT, GEORGE BURRITT.
  1878—Notes on the Ornithology of the Lower Rio Grande of Texas. Bul-
    letin of the United States Geological and Geographical Survey,
    vol. 4, pp. 1–66.
SHAW, JOHN.
  1635—Speculum mundi.
SIM, ROBERT J.
  1911—Notes on Captive Paludicolae. The Wilson Bulletin, vol. 23. pp.
    75–78.
SIMMONS, GEORGE FINLAY.
  1914—Notes on the Louisiana Clapper Rail (*Rallus crepitans saturatus*) in
    Texas. The Auk, vol. 31, pp. 363–384.
  1915—With *Rallus* in the Texas Marsh. The Condor, vol. 17, pp. 3–8.
  1915a—On the Nesting of Certain Birds in Texas. The Auk, vol. 32, pp.
    317–331.
SMITH, J. B.
  1894—"High Jinks" of the Great Blue Heron. The Nidiologist, vol. 2,
    pp. 10 and 11.
STEPHENS, FRANK.
  1909—Notes on the California Black Rail. The Condor, vol. 11, pp. 47–49.
STODDARD, HERBERT L.
  1916—The Black Rail (*Creciscus jamaicensis*) at Chicago, Ill. The Auk,
    vol, 33, pp. 433–434.
SUTTON, GEORGE MIKSCH.
  1924—A Visit to a Wood Ibis Colony. Bird-Lore, vol. 26, pp. 391–395.
TAVERNER, PERCY ALGERNON.
  1922—An Aquatic Habit of the Great Blue Heron. The Canadian Field-
    Naturalist, vol. 36, pp. 59, 60.
TAYLOR, EDWARD K.
  1897—Ardea herodias Nests on the Ground. The Nidiologist, vol. 4, pp.
    100, 101.
THAYER, JOHN ELIOT.
  1909—Two letters from W. W. Brown, Jr. The Condor, vol. 11, p. 142.
THAYER, JOHN ELIOT; and BANGS, OUTRAM.
  1909—Description of a New Subspecies of the Snowy Heron. Proceedings
    of the New England Zoological Club, vol. 4, pp. 39–41.
  1912—A New Race of Great Blue Heron from Espiritu Santo Island, Lower
    California. Proceedings of the New England Zoological Club, vol.
    4, pp. 83, 84.
" THOMPSON, ERNEST EVAN " =SETON, ERNEST THOMPSON.
  1890—The Birds of Manitoba. Proceedings of the United States National
    Museum, vol. 13, pp. 457–643.
TORREY, BRADFORD.
  1889—The "Booming" of the Bittern. The Auk, vol. 6, pp. 1–8.
TOWNSEND, CHARLES WENDELL.
  1905—The Birds of Essex County, Massachusetts. Memoirs of the Nuttall
    Ornithological Club, No. 3.

TOWNSEND, CHARLES WENDELL—Continued.
  1920—Supplement to the Birds of Essex County, Massachusetts. Memoirs
        of the Nuttall Ornithological Club, No. 5.
TREGANZA, ANTWONET, EDWARD and ALBERT OWEN.
  1914—A Forty-five Year History of the Snowy Heron in Utah. The Con-
        dor, vol. 16, pp. 245–250.
TYLER, JOHN G.
  1913—Some Birds of the Fresno District, California. Pacific Coast Avifauna,
        No. 9.
VAN HEURN, W. C.
  1912—Enkele Maanden Ornithologiseeren in Suriname, 29 Mei–22 October
        1911. Club van Nederlandsche Vogelkundigen, Tweede Jaarver-
        slag. Reprint, p. 17.
VISHER, STEPHEN SARGENT.
  1910—Notes on the Sandhill Crane. The Wilson Bulletin, vol. 22, pp. 115–
        117.
WARREN, EDWARD R.
  1904—A Sandhill Crane's Nest. The Condor, vol. 6, pp. 39, 40.
WAYNE, ARTHUR TREZEVANT.
  1905—Breeding of the Little Black Rail, (*Porzana jamaicensis*), in South
        Carolina. The Warbler, vol. 1, pp. 33–35.
  1905a—Notes on Certain Birds Taken or Seen near Charleston, South Car-
        olina. The Auk, vol. 22, pp. 395–400.
  1906—A Contribution to the Ornithology of South Carolina, chiefly the
        Coast Region. The Auk, vol. 23, pp. 56–68.
  1910—Birds of South Carolina. Contributions from the Charleston
        Museum, No. 1.
WAYNE, ARTHUR TREZEVANT.
  1922—Discovery of Breeding Grounds of the White Ibis in South Carolina.
        Bulletin of the Charleston Museum, vol. 17, pp. 27–30.
WEBER, JAY ANTHONY.
  1909—The Virginia and Sora Rails Nesting in New York City. The Auk
        vol. 26, pp. 19–22.
WELLS, JOHN GRANT.
  1886—A Catalogue of the Birds of Grenada, West Indies, with Observations
        thereon. Proceedings of the United States National Museum, vol
        9, pp. 609–633.
  1902—Birds of the Island of Carriacou. The Auk, vol. 19, p. 239.
WETMORE, ALEXANDER.
  1916—Birds of Porto Rico. U. S. Dept. of Agriculture, Bulletin No. 326.
  1916a—The Speed of Flight in certain Birds. The Condor, vol. 18, pp.
        112–113
  1920—Observations on the Habits of Birds at Lake Burford, New Mexico.
        The Auk. vol. 37, pp. 221–247 and 393–412.
WHEELOCK, IRENE G.
  1906—Nesting Habits of the Green Heron. The Auk, vol. 23, pp. 432–436
WILLETT, GEORGE.
  1906—The Southern California Clapper Rail Breeding on Fresh Water. The
        Condor, vol. 8, p. 151.
  1919—Bird Notes from Southeastern Oregon and Northeastern California.
        The Condor, vol. 21, pp. 194–207.
WILLETT, GEORGE; and JAY, ANTONIN.
  1911—May Notes from San Jacinto Lake. The Condor, vol. 13, pp. 156–160.

WILLIAMS, JOHN.
    1918—Some Florida Herons.   The Wilson Bulletin, vol. 30, pp. 48–55.
WILSON, ALEXANDER.
    1832—American Ornithology.
WITHERBY, HARRY FORBES, and OTHERS.
    1920—A Practical Handbook of British Birds.
WRIGHT, ALBERT HAZEN; and HARPER, FRANCIS.
    1913—A Biological Reconnaissance of Okefinokee Swamp: The Birds.   The
        Auk, vol. 30, pp. 477–505.
WÜRDEMANN, GUSTAVUS.
    1861—Letter relative to the obtaining of Specimens of Flamingos and other
        Birds from South Florida.   Annual Report of the Smithsonian Insti-
        tution for 1860, pp. 426–430.
YARRELL, WILLIAM.
    1871—History of British Birds.   Fourth Edition.   1871–1885.   Revised and
        enlarged by Alfred Newton and Howard Saunders.

INDEX

INDEX

	Page
Abbott, Clinton G.—	
on Florida gallinule	348
on least bittern	85
Adams, Ernest, on California clapper rail	269, 270
Ajaia ajaja	13
ajaja, Ajaia	13
alba, Guara	23
Allen, Arthur A., on least bittern	89, 90
American bittern	72
American coot	358
American egret	133
American flamingo	1
americana, Fulica	358
americana, Mycteria	57
americanus, Megalornis	219
Ames, J. H., on yellow rail	322
Anderson, R. M., on whooping crane	220, 221
Anthony green heron	195
anthonyi, Butorides virescens	195
Aramus vociferus vociferus	254
Ardea cinerea cinerea	131
herodias fannini	114
herodias	101
hyperonca	127
sanctilucae	130
treganzai	123
wardi	118
occidentalis	93
wuerdemanni	97
atra, Fulica	356
Audubon, J. J.—	
on American egret	134, 141, 142
on black-crowned night heron	207, 209
on clapper rail	277, 280, 281, 282
on Florida gallinule	351
on great blue heron	101, 109, 111
on great white heron	99, 100
on green heron	186
on king rail	260, 262, 263
on least bittern	88
on limpkin	255, 257, 258
on little blue heron	181
on Louisiana heron	174
on purple gallinule	341, 343
on reddish egret	158, 162
on roseate spoonbill	17, 19, 20, 21
on scarlet ibis	34
on snowy egret	147, 151, 152
on sora rail	304, 308
on Virginia rail	293
on Ward heron	122
on white ibis	24, 25, 28, 30, 32
on whooping crane	226, 228
on wood ibis	61, 62, 64
on yellow-crowned night heron	214, 216, 217
on yellow rail	317, 322

	Page
Bailey, Florence Merriam, on American coot.	365
Baird, Brewer, and Ridgway—	
on purple gallinule	343
on sora rail	311
Bales, B. R., on least bittern	85, 87
Barker, Samuel H., on green heron	191
Barrows, Walter B., on American bittern	79
Bartlett, A. D., on scarlet ibis	44
Bassett, Bartlett E., on great blue heron	109
Baynard, Oscar E.—	
on American egret	140
on black-crowned night heron	208
on glossy ibis	46, 48, 49, 50
on little blue heron	182
on Louisiana heron	174
on snowy egret	151
on white ibis	31
Beebe, William, on scarlet ibis	35, 39, 41, 42, 44
Belding rail	266
beldingi, Rallus	266
Benners, G. B., on roseate spoonbill	19
Bingham, Hiram, on jabiru	71
Bishop, Louis B.—	
on Florida clapper rail	287, 288
on Wayne clapper rail	290, 291
bittern American	72
bittern, Cory least	88
bittern, least	84
black-crowned night heron	197
black rail	326
blue heron, great	101
blue heron, little	177
Bodkin, G. E., and C. T. Matthey, on scarlet ibis	43
Bonhote, J. L.—	
on American flamingo	10
on corn crake	357
on spotted crake	302
Botaurus lentiginosus	72
Bowdish, B. S.—	
on green heron	190
on Virginia rail	294
on yellow-crowned night heron	213, 217
Bowles, J. Hooper—	
on northwest coast heron	114, 116, 117
on Virginia rail	295
Bradshaw, Fred, on whooping crane	224, 225, 228
Brandt, Herbert W.—	
on little brown crane	233, 234, 235
on purple gallinule	341
Brehm, A. E., on scarlet ibis	42
Bretherton, Wilfred A., on great blue heron	110
Brewster egret	156
Brewster, William—	
on American bittern	73, 81
on Belding rail	266

Page

Brewster, William—Continued.
on Farallon rail............................ 333
on Florida gallinule................. 346, 347, 353
on Frazar green heron.................... 194
on glossy ibis............................ 46
on green heron........................... 190
on "kicker"........................... 326, 331
on least bittern.......................... 90
on limpkin............................... 258
on scarlet ibis........................... 34
on sora rail............................. 309
Brewster and Chapman, on Florida clapper
rail..................................... 287
brewsteri, Egretta candidissima............. 156
Brooks, Allan, on northwest coast heron. 114, 116, 117
Brooks, W. Sprague, on green heron.......... 191
Brown, C. Barrington, on jabiru............. 69
brown crane, little........................ 231
Brown, D. E., on northwest coast heron...... 117
Brown, Wilmot W., jr.—
on Belding rail.......................... 267
on Espiritu Santo heron.................. 130
Bryant, Harold C., on wood ibis............ 63
Bryant, Henry—
on limpkin........................... 257, 259
on sandhill crane........................ 245
on wood ibis............................ 64
Bull, Charles L., on scarlet ibis.......... 36, 42
Burmeister, Hermann, on scarlet ibis....... 39
Burtch, Verdi—
on Florida gallinule..................... 350
on Virginia rail......................... 295
Butler, Amos W., on sandhill crane......... 246
Butorides virescens anthonyi.............. 195
frazari.................... 194
virescens.................. 185
cachinnans, Gallinula chloropus............. 346
caerulea, Florida......................... 177
Cahn, Alvin R.—
on reddish egret................ 160, 162, 165
on Virginia rail......................... 296
California clapper rail.................... 267
California heron.......................... 127
Cameron, E. S.—
on great blue heron...................... 107
on little brown crane.................... 238
Camp, R. D., on reddish egret........... 161, 164
canadensis, Megalornis.................... 231
mexicanus, Megalornis......... 250
pratensis, Megalornis........... 253
candidissima brewsteri, Egretta........... 156
candidissima, Egretta............ 146
Egretta candidissima........... 146
carolina, Porzana........................ 303
Carriger, H. W., and J. R. Pemberton on
California heron...................... 128, 129
Casmerodius egretta...................... 133
Chambers, W. Lee, on light-footed rail...... 272
Chapman, Frank M.—
on American egret.............. 137, 138, 141
on American flamingo........ 1, 4, 5, 6, 7, 8, 9, 10
on least bittern......................... 90
on little blue heron................. 179, 183
on roseate spoonbill.................. 13, 17
on Ward heron........................... 121
on white-faced glossy ibis.............. 55

Page

chloropus cachinnans, Gallinula............. 346
cinerea, Ardea cinerea.................... 131
cinerea, Ardea....................... 131
clapper rail............................. 277
clapper rail, California.................. 267
Florida................. 287
Louisiana.............. 283
Wayne................. 290
Yuma................. 275
Clark, John N., on black rail.......... 326, 327
coast heron, northwest.................... 114
Cobb, Stanley, on black rail........... 329, 330
Cohen, Donald A., on California clapper
rail.................................. 269, 271
Conover, H. B., on little brown crane....... 235
Cooke, Wells W.—
on sandhill crane........................ 241
on scarlet ibis.......................... 34
on sora rail............................. 310
on whooping crane....................... 220
coot, American........................... 358
European......................... 356
Cordier, A. H.—
on little blue heron......... 179, 180, 183
on Ward heron........................... 120
corn crake............................... 337
Cory least bittern....................... 88
Coturnicops noveboracensis................ 316
coturniculus, Creciscus.................. 332
Coues, Elliott—
on American bittern...................... 72
on sandhill crane.................... 247, 249
on scarlet ibis.......................... 34
on Treganza heron....................... 123
on whooping crane.................. 219, 227
on wood ibis............................ 63
Court, Edward J., on Treganza heron........ 124
crake, corn............................. 337
crane, Florida sandhill.................. 253
little brown...................... 231
sandhill......................... 241
whooping......................... 219
Creciscus coturniculus................... 332
jamaicensis.................... 326
crepitans, Rallus longirostris............ 277
Crex crex............................... 337
crex, Crex.............................. 337
Crispin, William B.—
on American bittern...................... 76
on great blue heron..................... 104
Dawson, Charles B., on scarlet ibis. 40, 41, 42, 43, 44
Dawson, W. Leon—
on California clapper rail............... 271
on California heron..................... 129
on king rail............................ 263
on light-footed rail.................... 275
on sandhill crane....................... 249
on snowy egret.......................... 150
on sora rail............................ 306
on yellow rail.......................... 319
Dichromanassa rufescens.................. 157
Dickens, Elizabeth, on great blue heron..... 112
Dickey, D. R.—
on Anthony green heron.................. 196
on Yuma clapper rail............. 275, 276, 277

Dresser, H. E.—   Page
  on corn crake_____ 338
  on European coot_____ 356, 357
  on spotted crake_____ 301, 302
Edwards, William H., on scarlet ibis_____ 36, 37, 41
egret, American_____ 133
    Brewster_____ 156
    reddish_____ 157
    snowy_____ 146
Egretta candidissima brewsteri_____ 156
        candidissima_____ 146
egretta, Casmerodius_____ 133
elegans, Rallus_____ 260
Eliot, Willard, on wood ibis_____ 58, 64
Emerson, W. Otto, on California clapper rail_ 269
Erichsen, W. J.—
  on American egret_____ 136
  on great blue heron_____ 113
  on green heron_____ 186
Espiritu Santo heron_____ 130
European coot_____ 356
European heron_____ 131
Evans, William—
  on corn crake_____ 337
  on European coot_____ 356
Evermann, Barton W., on California clapper
  rail_____ 268
exilis exilis, Ixobrychus_____ 84
  hesperis, Ixobrychus_____ 84
  Ixobrychus exilis_____ 84
falcinellus, Plegadis_____ 45
fannini, Ardea herodias_____ 114
Farallon rail_____ 332
Faxon, Walter, on scarlet ibis_____ 34
Figgins, J. D., on scarlet ibis_____ 34
Finley, William L.—
  on black-crowned night heron___ 202
  on California heron_____ 127
Fisher, A. K., on little brown crane_____ 237
flamingo, American_____ 1
Florida caerulea_____ 177
    clapper rail_____ 287
    gallinule_____ 346
    sandhill crane_____ 253
Forbush, Edward H., on sora rail_____ 306, 310, 313
Frazar green heron_____ 194
frazari, Butorides virescens_____ 194
Fulica americana_____ 358
  atra_____ 356
Gabrielson, Ira N.—
  on American bittern_____ 76, 77, 79
  on least bittern_____ 87
Gallinula chloropus cachinnans_____ 346
gallinule, Florida_____ 346
  purple_____ 339
Gibbs, Morris, on sora rail_____ 306, 307
Gifford, Edward W.—
  on American flamingo_____ 6, 11
  on yellow-crowned night heron___ 213
Gillett, Dana G., on great blue heron_____ 104
Gilmour, Neil, on whooping crane_____ 222
glossy ibis_____ 45
glossy ibis, white-faced_____ 52
Goss, N. S.—
  on king rail_____ 263
  on whooping crane_____ 226

Gosse, P. H.—   Page
  on black rail_____ 329
  on purple gallinule_____ 344
Grayson, A. J., on yellow-crowned night
  heron_____ 213
great blue heron_____ 101
great white heron_____ 93
green heron_____ 185
green heron, Anthony_____ 195
    Frazar_____ 194
Grinnell, Bryant, and Storer—
  on California clapper rail_____ 267, 268, 269, 270
  on light-footed rail_____ 272
  on little brown crane_____ 237, 239
  on wood ibis_____ 63
Grinnell, Joseph—
  on American coot_____ 361
  on little brown crane___ 233, 234, 235, 237, 238
  on Treganza heron_____ 124, 125
  on white-faced glossy ibis_____ 55
Griscom, Ludlow, on black rail_____ 329
Gross, Alfred O., on black-crowned night
  heron_____ 200, 201, 202, 203, 205, 207, 208, 210
Guara alba_____ 23
Guara rubra_____ 33
guarauna, Plegadis_____ 52
Hagerup, A. T., on spotted crake_____ 301
Hagmann, Gottfried—
  on jabiru_____ 66, 68, 69
  on scarlet ibis_____ 37, 41
Harlow, R. C.—
  on American bittern_____ 76
  on black rail_____ 328
  on great blue heron_____ 104
  on least bittern_____ 86
Hastings, Walter E., on great blue heron___ 105, 106, 109
Hatch, P. L.—
  on American bittern_____ 75
  on Virginia rail_____ 294
Henderson, A. D., on great blue heron_____ 105
Henninger, W. F., on king rail_____ 261
Henshaw, F. W., on American coot_____ 364
herodias, Ardea herodias_____ 101
  fannini, Ardea_____ 114
  herodias, Ardea_____ 101
  hyperonca, Ardea_____ 127
  sanctilucae, Ardea_____ 130
  treganzai, Ardea_____ 123
  wardi, Ardea_____ 118
heron, Anthony green_____ 195
  black-crowned night_____ 197
  California_____ 127
  Espiritu Santo_____ 130
  European_____ 131
  Frazar green_____ 194
  great blue_____ 101
  great white_____ 93
  green_____ 185
  little blue_____ 177
  Louisiana_____ 167
  northwest coast_____ 114
  Treganza_____ 123
  Ward_____ 118
  Würdemann's_____ 97
  yellow-crowned night_____ 213

Page

Hersey, F. Seymour—
  on little brown crane_____ 233, 238
  on Virginia rail_____ 294
hesperis, Ixobrychus exilis_____ 84
Holland, Harold M., on light-footed rail_____ 273
Holt, Ernest G.—
  on great white heron_____ 97, 98
  on Ward heron_____ 98
  on Würdemann heron _____ 98
Howe, Reginald Heber, Jr., on American flamingo_____ 3
Howell, A. B.—
  on California heron_____ 129
  on light-footed rail_____ 275
Howell, Arthur H.—
  on great blue heron_____ 109
  on little blue heron_____ 182
Hoyt, R. D., on Ward heron_____ 118
Hudson, W. H.—
  on European coot_____ 357
  on jabiru_____ 66
Huey, Laurence M.—
  on Anthony green heron_____ 196
  on Farallon rail_____ 334, 335, 336
  on Yuma clapper rail_____ 276
Huntington, Dwight W., on whooping crane_ 227
Huxley, Julian S.—
  on European heron_____ 133
  on Louisiana heron_____ 169, 173, 175
Hydranassa tricolor ruficollis_____ 167
hyperonca, Ardea herodias_____ 127
ibis, glossy_____ 45
  scarlet_____ 33
  white_____ 23
  white-faced glossy_____ 52
  wood_____ 57
Ingersoll, A. M.—
  on Farallon rail_____ 333, 336
  on light-footed rail_____ 273, 274
Ingram, D. P., on American flamingo_____ 11
Ionornis martinicus_____ 339
Ixobrychus exilis exilis_____ 84
  hesperis_____ 84
  neoxenus_____ 88
jabiru_____ 66
Jabiru mycteria_____ 66
Jackson, Thomas H., on limpkin_____ 255
jamaicensis, Creciscus_____ 326
Job, Herbert K., on American egret_____ 142
Kappler, August, on scarlet ibis_____ 36, 41, 43
Kennard, Frederic H., on limpkin_____ 256
king rail_____ 260
Knight, Ora W., on great blue heron_____ 108
Laing, Hamilton M., on sandhill crane___ 247, 248
Langille, J. H.—
  on American coot_____ 364
  on sora rail_____ 310
Law, J. Eugene—
  on California heron_____ 129
  on light-footed rail_____ 274
least bittern_____ 84
least bittern, Cory_____ 88
lentiginosus, Botaurus_____ 72
Léotaud, A., on scarlet ibis_____ 40, 41
levipes, Rallus_____ 272
light-footed rail_____ 272

Page

limpkin_____ 254
little blue heron_____ 177
little brown crane_____ 231
Lloyd, C. A.—
  on jabiru_____ 67, 68
  on scarlet ibis_____ 37
longirostris crepitans, Rallus_____ 277
  saturatus, Rallus_____ 283
  scotti, Rallus_____ 287
  waynei, Rallus_____ 290
Lorenz, Th., on scarlet ibis_____ 44
Louisiana clapper rail_____ 283
Louisiana heron_____ 167
Lowe, Willoughby P., on scarlet ibis_____ 34
MacFarlane, R. R., on little brown crane ___ 234
Mackay, George H., on sandhill crane_____ 246
Maltby, Fred, on yellow rail_____ 319
martinicus, Ionornis_____ 339
Mattingly, A. H. E., on snowy egret_____ 153
May, John B., on great blue heron_____ 110
Maynard, C. J.—
  on American coot_____ 365, 366
  on American egret_____ 140
  on American flamingo_____ 3, 9
  on reddish egret_____ 164
  on sora rail_____ 309
  on Ward heron_____ 121, 122
  on Wayne clapper rail_____ 291
  on yellow-crowned night heron_____ 215, 216
McIlhenny, Edward A., on snowy egret___ 150, 154
McKechnie, F. B., on yellow rail_____ 317, 322
McMullen, T. E., on black rail_____ 329, 330, 331
Mearns, Edgar A., on Anthony green heron __ 195
Megalornis americanus_____ 219
  canadensis_____ 231
  mexicanus_____ 250
  pratensis_____ 253
  mexicanus_____ 241
Merrill, J. C., on white-faced glossy ibis_____ 53
mexicanus, Megalornis_____ 241
  canadensis_____ 250
Mitchell, Catherine A., on great blue heron _ 102
Moore, N. B.—
  on Florida clapper rail_____ 289
  on sandhill crane_____ 245, 246, 249
Morris, Francis O., on corn crake_____ 337
Morris, Robert O., on yellow rail_____ 323
Munro, J. A., on northwest coast heron_____ 116
Murchison, A. C., on king rail_____ 261, 263
Mycteria americana_____ 57
mycteria, Jabiru_____ 66
naevius, Nycticorax nycticorax_____ 197
Nelson, E. W.—
  on black rail_____ 326
  on little brown crane_____ 232, 233, 235, 237, 238
  on whooping crane_____ 220
neoxenus, Ixobrychus_____ 88
Nicholson, Donald J., on black rail_____ 328
night heron, black-crowned_____ 197
night heron, yellow-crowned_____ 213
Northrup, Edwin F., on great blue heron ___ 104
northwest coast heron_____ 114
noveboracensis, Coturnicops_____ 316
Nuttall, Thomas—
  on scarlet ibis_____ 34
  on whooping crane_____ 226, 227, 228

	Page
Nyctanassa violacea	213
nycticorax naevius, Nycticorax	197
Nycticorax nycticorax naevius	197
obsoletus, Rallus	267
occidentalis, Ardea	93
Osgood, Wilfred H., on little brown crane	238
Palmer, William, on Louisiana heron	175
Patterson, A. H., on European heron	132
Peabody, P. B., on yellow rail	317, 318, 320, 321, 322, 323
Pearson, T. Gilbert—	
on American egret	137, 143
on limpkin	254
on little blue heron	177, 179
on reddish egret	165
on snowy egret	152
Pelzeln, August von, on scarlet ibis	44
Pemberton, J. R.—	
on jabiru	67, 70, 71
on reddish egret	161
Penard, F. P., and A. P., on scarlet ibis	37, 38, 39, 40, 41, 42, 43
Penard, Thomas Edward, on scarlet ibis	33
Pennock, C. J.—	
on black rail	331
On Florida clapper rail	288, 289
on Florida gallinule	346
on limpkin	255, 259
on little blue heron	178, 179
on white ibis	24
Pericles, Eugene, on great blue heron	104
Peters, James L., on sandhill crane	241
Phelps, F. M.—	
on sandhill crane	244
on wood ibis	58
Phoenicopterus ruber	1
"Picket," on whooping crane	226, 227
Plegadis falcinellus	45
Plegadis guarauna	52
Pope, E. F., on Louisiana clapper rail	285
Porzana carolina	303
porzana	301
porzana, Porzana	301
pratensis, Megalornis canadensis	253
Preston, J. W., on whooping crane	221
Prill, A. G., on sandhill crane	244
purple gallinule	339
Quillin and Holleman, on purple gallinule	341
Racey, Kenneth, on northwest coast heron	115
rail, Belding	266
black	326
California clapper	267
clapper	277
Florida clapper	287
king	260
light-footed	272
Louisiana clapper	283
sora	303
Virginia	292
Wayne clapper	290
yellow	316
Yuma clapper	275
Rallus beldingi	266
elegans	260
levipes	272
longirostris crepitans	277

	Page
Rallus, longirostris saturatus	283
scotti	287
waynei	290
obsoletus	267
virginianus	292
yumanensis	275
Ramsay, R. G. W., on spotted crake	302
Rathbun, S. F., on sandhill crane	244
reddish egret	157
Reid, Saville G., on American bittern	82
Rhoads, Samuel N., on roseate spoonbill	20
Rich, Walter H., on yellow rail	323
Ridgway, Robert—	
on Farallon rail	332
on Würdemann's heron	97
Roberts, Thomas S., on Florida gallinule	349
Rockwell, Robert B.—	
on American coot	360
on black-crowned night heron	201
roseate spoonbill	13
ruber, Phoenicopterus	1
rubra, Guara	33
rufescens, Dichromanassa	157
ruficollis, Hydranassa tricolor	167
sanctilucae, Ardea herodias	130
sandhill crane	241
sandhill crane, Florida	253
Sanford, L. C., on sora rail	312
Santo heron, Espiritu	130
saturatus, Rallus longirostris	283
Saunders, W. E.—	
on European coot	356, 357
on Virginia rail	298
scarlet ibis	33
Schlegel, H., on scarlet ibis	39
Schmidt, Max, on scarlet ibis	44
Schomburgk, Richard—	
on jabiru	68
on scarlet ibis	37, 41
Schomburgk, Robert H., on jabiru	67, 70
Scott, W. E. D.—	
on American flamingo	2, 9
on Florida clapper rail	287, 289
on reddish egret	157, 164, 166
on roseate spoonbill	13
scotti, Rallus longirostris	287
Seebohm, Henry, on European coot	357, 358
Selby, P. J., on European coot	357
Sell, R. A., on scarlet ibis	35
Sennett, George B.—	
on American egret	138
on snowy egret	149
Seton, Ernest Thompson—	
on sandhill crane	242, 249
on whooping crane	220, 227, 229
Sharples, R. P., on great blue heron	103, 112
Shaw, John, on European heron	132
Sherman, Althea R., on sora rail	306
Sim, Robert J., on sora rail	309
Simmons, George Finlay—	
on least bittern	86
on Louisiana clapper rail	283, 284, 285, 286
Skinner, M. P., on great blue heron	110
Smith, J. B., on California heron	127
snowy egret	146
sora rail	303

	Page
spoonbill, roseate	13
spotted crake	301
Sprunt, Alexander, jr.—	
on Florida gallinule	349
on purple gallinule	341
Stephens, Frank, on Farallon rail	333, 335, 336
Stoddard, H. L., on black rail	330
Stuart, George H., 3d, on black rail	328
Sutton, George M., on wood ibis	60
Taverner, P. A., on great blue heron	110
Taylor, Edward K., on California heron	128
Thayer and Bangs—	
on Brewster egret	156
on Espiritu Santo heron	130
Thayer, John E., on Belding rail	267
Torrey, Bradford, on American bittern	80
Townsend, Charles W.—	
on American bittern	77, 82
on American coot	364
on corn crake	337
on European coot	356
on European heron	131
on great blue heron	111
on green heron	185
on spotted crake	301
on Virginia rail	292, 297
Treganza, A. E. and A. O., on snowy egret	149
Treganza, A. O.—	
on Treganza heron	124
on white-faced glossy ibis	54
Treganza heron	123
treganzai, Ardea herodias	123
tricolor ruficollis, Hydranassa	167
Tyler, John G.—	
on American coot	360, 363
on Anthony green heron	196
on California heron	126
Van Heurn, W. C., on scarlet ibis	36, 39, 41, 42
Van Rossem, A. J.—	
on Anthony green heron	196
on light-footed rail	274
violacea, Nyctanassa	213
virescens anthonyi, Butorides	195
Butorides virescens	185
frazari, Butorides	194
virescens, Butorides	185
Virginia rail	292
virginianus, Rallus	292
Visher, Stephen S., on sandhill crane	242
vociferus, Aramus vociferus	254
vociferus, Aramus	254
Ward heron	118
wardi, Ardea herodias	118
Warren, Edward R., on sandhill crane	244
Wayne, Arthur T.—	
on black rail	330
on king rail	260, 261, 264

	Page
Wayne, Arthur T.—Continued.	
on purple gallinule	340, 343
on Wayne clapper rail	292
on white ibis	27, 31
on yellow-crowned night heron	215, 217
on yellow rail	324
Wayne clapper rail	290
waynei, Rallus longirostris	290
Weber, J. A.—	
on sora rail	303
on Virginia rail	293, 295, 304
Wells, J. G.—	
on purple gallinule	343
on yellow-crowned night heron	215
Wetmore, Alexander—	
on American coot	359, 360, 363
on American egret	140
on black-crowned night heron	208
on California heron	130
on Florida gallinule	352
on little blue heron	182
on snowy egret	151
on Treganza heron	125, 126
Wheelock, Irene G., on green heron	186, 187, 188
white-faced glossy ibis	52
white heron, great	93
white ibis	23
whooping crane	219
Willett, George—	
on American egret	137
on light-footed rail	273
Willett, George, and Antonin Jay, on white-faced glossy ibis	53
Williams, John, on Louisiana heron	171
Williams, Moses, jr., on American coot	365
Wilson, Alexander—	
on clapper rail	282
on great blue heron	103, 109
on scarlet ibis	34
on snowy egret	148, 151
Witherby's Handbook—	
on corn crake	337
on European coot	356
on spotted crake	301
wood ibis	57
Wright and Harper, on sandhill crane	246
wuerdemanni, Ardea	97
Würdemann, Gustavus, on American flamingo	2
Würdemann's heron	97
Yarrell, William—	
on corn crake	338
on spotted crake	302
yellow-crowned night heron	213
yellow rail	316
Yuma clapper rail	275
yumanensis, Rallus	275

PLATES

PLATE 1. AMERICAN BITTERN. American bittern on its nest with
4 small young, photo purchased from S.S.S. Stansell.

PLATE 2. AMERICAN FLAMINGO. *Upper:* American flamingo colony alarmed. *Lower:* American flamingo colony at ease. Photos by Dr. Frank M. Chapman, in the Bahama Islands, June, 1904; presented by him and by courtesy of D. Appleton & Co.

PLATE 3. AMERICAN FLAMINGO. *Left:* American flamingo, feeding small young. *Right:* Large young flamingos, feeding. Note the adult attitude. Photos by Dr. Frank M. Chapman in the Bahama Islands, June, 1904; presented by him and by courtesy of D. Appleton & Co.

PLATE 4. AMERICAN FLAMINGO. *Upper:* American flamingos in flight. *Lower:* Young American flamingos resting. Note the folded legs. Photos by Dr. Frank M. Chapman; presented by him and by courtesy of D. Appleton & Co.

PLATE 5. ROSEATE SPOONBILL. *Upper:* Nest and eggs of roseate spoonbill, Cuthbert Lake, Florida, May 1, 1903, referred to on page 15. *Lower:* Another nest and eggs in the same locality, March 30, 1908, referred to on page 15. Photos by the author.

PLATE 6. ROSEATE SPOONBILL. *Upper:* Young roseate spoonbills in their nest, Cuthbert Lake, Florida, May 1, 1903, photo by
the author, referred to on page 15. *Lower:* Older young of the same
species, Alligator Lake, Cape Sable, Florida, May, 1903; presented
by Herbert K. Job.

PLATE 7. WHITE IBIS. Rookery of white ibises at Orange Lake, Florida, presented by Oscar E. Baynard.

PLATE 8. WHITE IBIS. *Upper:* White ibises on a favorite perch in a big rookery in Victoria County, Texas, May 30, 1923; photo by the author, referred to on page 24. *Lower:* Nest of eggs of white ibis, Orange Lake, Florida; presented by Oscar E. Baynard.

PLATE 9. WHITE IBIS. Nests of white ibises, Cuthbert Lake, Florida, May 1, 1903. Photos by the author; referred to on page 25.

PLATE 10. WHITE IBIS. *Upper.* Young white ibises about five days old; presented by Oscar E. Baynard. *Lower:* Young white ibis nearly ready to leave the nest, Alligator Lake, Cape Sable, Florida, May, 1903; presented by Herbert K. Job.

PLATE 11. GLOSSY IBIS. *Upper:* Glossy ibis building its nest.
Lower: Nest and eggs of glossy ibis. Photos taken at Orange Lake,
Florida, in 1912, by Oscar E. Baynard and presented by him; referred
to on page 47.

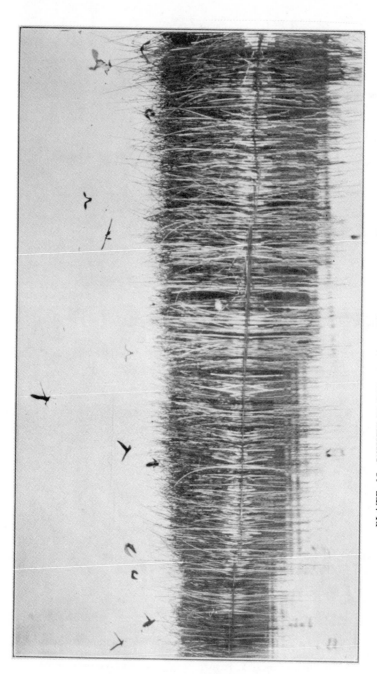

PLATE 12. WHITE-FACED GLOSSY IBIS. Nesting site of white-faced glossy ibis, Malheur Lake, Oregon, presented by William L. Finley and H. T. Bohlman.

PLATE 13. WHITE-FACED GLOSSY IBIS. *Upper:* Young white-faced glossy ibises, in their nest. *Lower:* Nest and eggs of white-faced glossy ibis. Photos by George Willett and Antonin Jay, taken at San Jacinto Lake, Riverside County, California, May 28, 1911, presented by them, referred to on page 53.

PLATE 14. WHITE-FACED GLOSSY IBIS. White-faced glossy ibis
on its nest, Malheur Lake, Oregon, presented by William L. Finley
and H. T. Bohlman.

PLATE 15. WOOD IBIS. *Upper:* Wood ibises on their breeding grounds, Polk County, Florida, March 8, 1925, taken by the author, referred to on page 59. *Lower:* Another photograph, same locality and date, presented by Clarence F. Stone.

PLATE 16. WOOD IBIS. *Upper:* Nests and young of wood ibis, Polk County, Florida, May 31, 1925, presented by Oscar E. Baynard. *Lower:* Nests and eggs of wood ibis, Polk County, Florida, March 8, 1925, Photo by the author, referred to on page 59.

PLATE 17. WOOD IBIS. *Upper:* Nesting tree of wood ibis, Okaloa-choochee Slough, Hendry County, Florida, March 23, 1914, presented by Frederic H. Kennard, referred to on page 59. *Lower:* Young wood ibises in the rookery at Alligator Lake, Cape Sable, Florida, January 29, 1924, presented by Ernest G. Holt.

PLATE 18. JABIRU. Home of the Jabiru, near Barinas, Venezuela, presented by Hon. Hiram Bingham.

PLATE 19. JABIRU. A jabiru family at home, near Barinas, Venezuela, presented by Hon. Hiram Bingham.

PLATE 20. JABIRU. Nest of jabiru about 60 feet up in an immense dead tree, near Corumba, Matto Grosso, Brazil, October 30, 1912, presented by J. R. Pemberton.

PLATE 21. AMERICAN BITTERN. Nest and eggs of American bittern, Duck Lake, Oakland County, Michigan, May 27, 1923, presented by Walter E. Hastings.

PLATE 22. AMERICAN BITTERN. Nests, eggs and young of American bittern, Colorado, presented by the Colorado Museum of Natural History.

PLATE 23. AMERICAN BITTERN. *Left:* Nest and eggs of American bittern, Branchport, New York, May 21, 1912. *Right:* American bittern on its nest, in hiding pose, Branchport, New York, May 18, 1912. Photos presented by Verdi Burtch.

PLATE 24. LEAST BITTERN. *Upper:* Nesting site of least bittern, Merritt's Island, Florida, April 26, 1902. *Lower:* Nest and eggs of least bittern in the above locality. Photos by the author, referred to on page 85.

PLATE 25. LEAST BITTERN. Nest and eggs of least bittern, near Omaha, Nebraska, June 22, 1901, presented by Frank H. Shoemaker.

PLATE 26. LEAST BITTERN. *Left:* Least bittern on her nest, in a button bush, Camden, New Jersey, May 29, 1916. *Right:* Young least bitterns, four days old, in another nest, June 6, 1916. Photos presented by Julian K. Potter.

PLATE 27. LEAST BITTERN. *Left:* Female least bittern, in broken reed posture on her nest, Ithaca, New York, June 3, 1914, presented by Dr. Arthur A. Allen. *Right:* Young least bittern, twenty days old, Oakland County, Michigan, July 11, 1922, presented by Walter E. Hastings.

PLATE 28. GREAT WHITE HERON. *Upper:* Nesting site of great white heron, Oyster Key, Bay of Florida, April 29, 1903. *Lower:* Nest, eggs and young of great white heron in above locality. Photos by the author, referred to on page 95.

PLATE 29. GREAT WHITE HERON. *Upper:* Two nearly full grown young of great white heron in their nest, Oyster Key, Bay of Florida, April 29, 1903. *Lower:* Another nest with half grown young of great white heron in above locality. Photos by the author, referred to on page 95.

PLATE 30. GREAT BLUE HERON. Part of a colony of 300 nests of great blue heron, Livingstone County, Michigan, May 1, 1921, presented by Walter E. Hastings.

PLATE 31. GREAT BLUE HERON. *Upper:* Nests of great blue heron, Yellowstone River, Montana, June 29, 1905, probably *treganzai*, presented by E. S. Cameron. *Lower:* Nest and eggs of great blue heron, Skull Creek, Saskatchewan, June 5, 1905, photo by the author, referred to on page 105.

PLATE 32. GREAT BLUE HERON. *Left:* Young great blue heron, about half grown, presented by the Colorado Museum of Natural History. *Right:* Young great blue heron, nine weeks old, Yellowstone River, Montana, presented by E. S. Cameron. Both probably *treganzai.*

PLATE 33. GREAT BLUE HERON. Great blue herons and their nests, Livingstone County, Michigan, April 30, 1923, presented by Walter E. Hastings.

PLATE 34. *Left:* NORTHWEST COAST HERON. Colony of northwest coast herons, Stanley Park, Vancouver, British Columbia, June 6, 1922, presented by J. A. Munro, courtesy of Canadian National Parks Branch, referred to on page 115. *Right:* TREGANZA HERON. Nest of double-crested cormorant in foreground and nest of Treganza heron in background, Bird Island, Great Salt Lake, Utah, presented by A. O. Treganza, referred to on page 124.

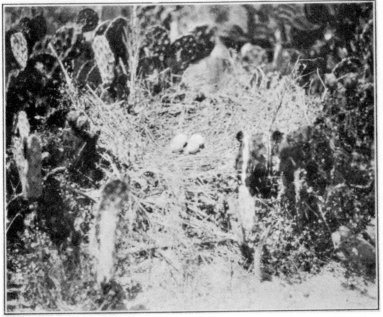

PLATE 35. WARD HERON. *Upper:* Ward herons on their nests, Bird Key, Boca Ceiga Bay, Florida, March 11 and 17, 1925, referred to on page 235. *Lower:* Nest of Ward heron in prickly pear cactus, Bird Island, Laguna Madre, Texas, presented by George Finlay Simmons, referred to on page 120.

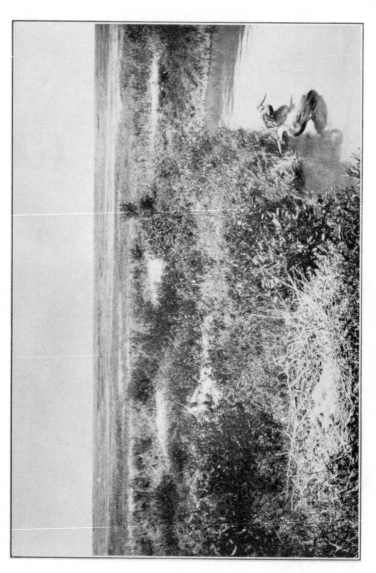

PLATE 36. CALIFORNIA HERON. Nesting site of California herons, on the ground in a salt marsh, Redwood City, California, April 7, 1907, presented by J. R. Pemberton, referred to on page 128.

PLATE 37. CALIFORNIA HERON. Colony of California herons, 41 nests, and black-crowned night herons, 28 nests, in a large syca-more tree, San Francisco Bay region, California, presented by William L. Finley and H. T. Bohlman, referred to on page 127.

PLATE 38. AMERICAN EGRET. *Upper:* American egret on its nest, Bird Key, Boca Ciega Bay, Florida, March 11, 1905, referred to on page 135. *Lower:* Nest and eggs of American egret, Cuthbert Lake, Florida, May 1, 1903, referred to on page 134. Photos by the author.

PLATE 39. AMERICAN EGRET. American egret poses, photos by
Howard T. Middleton, presented by the Eastman Kodak Co.

PLATE 40. AMERICAN EGRET. *Upper:* American egret regurgita-
ting food for its young. Note the lump in its throat; young six
weeks old. *Lower:* American egret incubating. Photos by Oscar E.
Baynard at Orange Lake, Florida, presented by him.

PLATE 41. SNOWY EGRET. *Upper:* Nesting site of snowy egrets, nests in small trees and bushes. *Lower:* Nest and eggs of snowy egret, in a prickly pear cactus. Photos taken by the author on an island in Galveston Bay, Texas, May 5, 1923, referred to on page 148.

PLATE 42. SNOWY EGRET. *Upper:* Young snowy egrets, near Rose-
land, Florida, 1920, presented by Dr. A. H. Cordier. *Lower:* Snowy
egrets in the rookery at Orange Lake, Florida, presented by Oscar
E. Baynard.

PLATE 43. SNOWY EGRET. Nest and eggs of snowy egret, near Los Banos, California, June 4, 1914, presented by W. Leon Dawson.

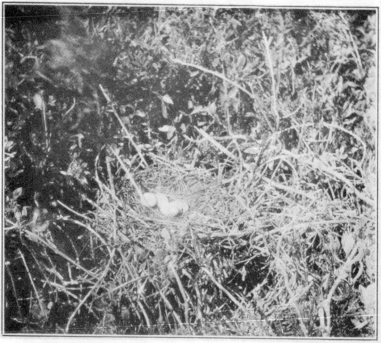

PLATE 44. REDDISH EGRET. *Upper:* Colony of reddish egrets, Green Island, Texas, 1923, presented by Dr. A. H. Cordier, referred to on page 160. *Lower:* Nest and eggs of reddish egret, Chain of Islands, San Antonio Bay, Texas, May 16, 1923, photo by the author, referred to on page 159.

PLATE 45. REDDISH EGRET. Reddish egret incubating, Green Island, Texas, presented by Alvin R. Cahn.

PLATE 46. REDDISH EGRET. Two poses of reddish egret, Green Island, Texas, presented by Alvin R. Cahn.

PLATE 47. LOUISIANA HERON. Nests of Louisiana heron, St. Johns River, Florida, April 18, 1902. Photos by the author, referred to on page 170.

PLATE 48. LOUISIANA HERON. *Upper:* Various herons and egrets in flight, Chain of Islands, San Antonio Bay, Texas, May 16, 1923, referred to on page 171. *Lower:* Louisiana heron standing on its nest in a bunch of canes. Galveston Bay, Texas, May 5, 1923, referred to on page 171. Photos by the author.

PLATE 49. LOUISIANA HERON. *Left:* Unfledged young Louisiana heron, Green Island, Texas, presented by Dr. A. H. Cordier. *Right:* Young Louisiana heron, fully grown and in juvenal plumage, Breton Island Reservation, Louisiana, June 24, 1910, photo by the author.

PLATE 50. LOUISIANA HERON. *Upper:* Louisiana heron turning
its eggs, Avery Island, Louisiana, presented by Prof. Julian S. Huxley
and George F. Simmons. *Lower:* Louisiana heron, shielding its young
from the rain, Orange Lake, Florida, presented by Oscar E. Baynard.

PLATE 51. LITTLE BLUE HERON. *Upper:* Colony of little blue herons, South Carolina, May 8, 1907, presented by Dr. Frank M. Chapman, courtesy of D. Appleton & Co. *Lower:* Nest of eggs of little blue heron, St. Johns River, Florida, April 20, 1902, photo by the author, referred to on page 178.

PLATE 52. LITTLE BLUE HERON. *Upper:* Nests of little blue heron, near Mount Pleasant, South Carolina, May 20, 1915. *Lower:* Nest with small young of little blue heron, in above locality. Photos by the author, referred to on page 178.

PLATE 53. LITTLE BLUE HERON. *Left:* Little blue heron about to feed its young. *Right:* Little blue heron incubating. Photographs by Dr. Arthur A. Allen, Kissimmee Prairie, Florida, April 22 and 23, 1924, presented by him.

PLATE 54. GREEN HERON. Nests and eggs of green heron, Westport, Massachusetts, May 30, 1907, photos by the author, referred to on page 187.

PLATE 55. GREEN HERON. *Upper:* Green heron on its nest, Avery
Island, Louisiana, presented by Prof. Julian S. Huxley and George
F. Simmons. *Lower:* Green heron approaching its nest, Ithaca,
New York, June 15, 1914, presented by Dr. Arthur A. Allen.

PLATE 56. GREEN HERON. *Upper:* Young green heron, 15 days old. *Lower:* Same bird, 19 days old. Photos taken June 23 and 27, 1913, and presented by Charles A. Gianini.

PLATE 57. ANTHONY GREEN HERON. *Upper:* Nest and eggs of Anthony green heron, Fairbank, Arizona, presented by Francis C. Willard. *Lower:* Nest and nine eggs of Anthony green heron, San Diego County, California, May 30, 1915, presented by Donald R. Dickey, referred to on page 196.

PLATE 58. BLACK-CROWNED NIGHT HERON. *Upper:* Distant view of the rookery of black-crowned night herons at Barnstable, Massachusetts, presented by Dr. Alfred O. Gross, referred to on page 198. *Lower:* Some nests in the above rookery, July 3, 1918, photo by the author.

PLATE 59. BLACK-CROWNED NIGHT HERON. *Upper:* Nest and eggs of black-crowned night heron, Clear Lake Reservation, California, May 27, 1923, presented by J. Elliot Patterson. *Lower:* Nest and eggs of same species, in a pitch pine tree, Barnstable, Massachusetts, May 30, 1919, photo by the author, referred to on page 199.

PLATE 60. BLACK-CROWNED NIGHT HERON. Black-crowned night heron, standing on its nest, in the tules, Malheur Lake, Oregon, presented by William L. Finley and H. T. Bohlman.

PLATE 61. BLACK-CROWNED NIGHT HERON. *Upper:* Young black-crowned night herons, about a week old, near Barr, Colorado, May 31, 1907. *Lower:* Same brood, about three weeks old, June 15, 1907. Photos presented by Robert B. Rockwell; referred to on page 201.

PLATE 62. BLACK-CROWNED NIGHT HERON. *Upper:* Young black-crowned night herons climbing in tree tops, Barnstable, Massachusetts, July 12, 1913. *Lower:* Climbing antics of another young bird, same locality and date. Photos by the author, referred to on page 204.

PLATE 63. YELLOW-CROWNED NIGHT HERON. *Upper:* Nest and eggs of yellow-crowned night heron, Bird Key, Boca Ceiga Bay, Florida, April 14, 1925, referred to on page 214. *Lower:* Another nest of the same species, St. Johns River, Florida, April 21, 1902, referred to on page 214. Photos by the author.

PLATE 64. YELLOW-CROWNED NIGHT HERON. Two views of a yellow-crowned night heron on its nest, Puzzle Lake, Florida, April 28, 1924, presented by Dr. Arthur A. Allen.

PLATE 65. WHOOPING CRANE. *Upper:* Nesting site of whooping crane. The clear water around the nest shows where the rushes have been pulled up to build it. *Lower:* Young whooping crane, just hatched. Photos by Fred Bradshaw in Saskatchewan, May 28 and 29, 1922, presented by him, referred to on page 222.

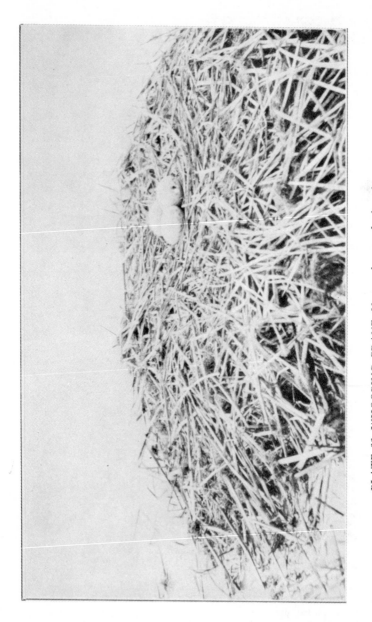

PLATE 66. WHOOPING CRANE. Nest and eggs of whooping crane, Saskatchewan, May 28, 1922, presented by Fred Bradshaw, referred to on page 222.

PLATE 67. LITTLE BROWN CRANE. *Upper:* Nest and eggs of little brown crane, Hooper Bay, Alaska, June 12, 1924. *Lower:* Young little brown cranes, Hooper Bay, Alaska, June 21, 1924; standing bird about two days old and the other half a day old. Photos presented by Herbert W. Brandt.

PLATE 68. SANDHILL CRANE. *Upper:* Flock of sandhill cranes, presented by Hamilton W. Laing. *Lower:* Pair of sandhill cranes, with a newly hatched young in the nest, Kissimmee Prairie, Florida, March 13, 1924, presented by Dr. Arthur A. Allen.

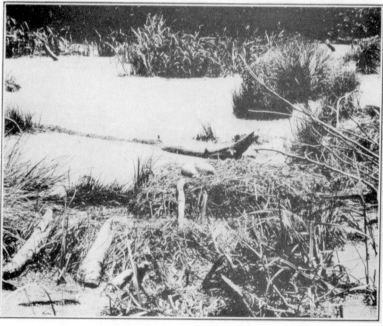

PLATE 69. SANDHILL CRANE. *Upper:* Nest and eggs of sandhill crane, near Bassenger, Florida, March 23, 1924, presented by Ernest G. Holt. *Lower:* Nest and eggs of sandhill crane, Gunnison County, Colorado, June 5, 1903, presented by Edward R. Warren, referred to on page 244.

PLATE 70. SANDHILL CRANE. *Upper:* Nest and eggs of sandhill crane, in open situation among "pond cypress." *Lower:* Another nest in thick growth of pickerel weed. Photos by the author, near Bassenger, Florida, March 21, 1925, referred to on page 243.

PLATE 71. SANDHILL CRANE. *Upper:* Young sandhill crane, just hatched, Kissimmee Prairie, Florida, March 13, 1924. Photos presented by Dr. Arthur A. Allen. *Lower:* Young sandhill crane, about a month old, upper St. Johns River, Florida, April 17, 1924.

PLATE 72. LIMPKIN. *Upper:* Nesting place of limpkin. *Lower:* Nest and large set of eggs of limpkin. Photos presented by Oscar E. Baynard.

PLATE 73. LIMPKIN. Two views of a limpkin on its nest, Upper St. Johns River, Florida, April 18, 1924, presented by Dr. Arthur A. Allen.

PLATE 74. KING RAIL. *Upper:* Nest of King rail, as originally
found, Plant City, Florida, March 30, 1925. *Lower:* Same nest uncovered. Photos by the author, referred to on page 260.

PLATE 75. CALIFORNIA CLAPPER RAIL. Nest and eggs of California clapper rail, near Redmond City, California, April 15, 1911, presented by W. Leon Dawson.

PLATE 76. LIGHT-FOOTED RAIL. *Upper:* Nest and eggs of light-footed rail. *Lower:* Tidal marsh habitat in which above nest was found, Orange County, California, May 14, 1917. Photos presented by Harold M. Holland, referred to on page 273.

PLATE 77. LIGHT-FOOTED RAIL. *Upper:* Light-footed rail, brooding young, San Diego, California, May 13, 1914. *Lower:* Light-footed rail arranging eggs, same locality, May 19, 1914. Photos presented by Donald R. Dickey.

PLATE 78. CLAPPER RAIL. *Upper:* Nesting site of clapper rail. *Lower:* Nest of clapper rail, showing the incline leading to it. Photos by the author, Cobb Island, Virginia, June 25, 1907, referred to on page 278.

PLATE 79. *Upper:* LOUISIANA CLAPPER RAIL. Nest and eggs of Louisiana clapper rail, near Houston, Texas, presented by George Finlay Simmons. *Lower:* FLORIDA CLAPPER RAIL. Nest and eggs of Florida clapper rail, near Safety Harbor, Florida, presented by Oscar E. Baynard.

PLATE 80. WAYNE CLAPPER RAIL. *Left:* Wayne clapper rail on its nest. *Right:* Nest and eggs of same. Photos by B. Rhett Chamberlain, near Charleston, South Carolina, June 10, 1915, presented by him.

PLATE 81. VIRGINIA RAIL. Nest and eggs of Virginia rail, Barr Lake, Colorado, presented by the Colorado Museum of Natural History.

PLATE 82. VIRGINIA RAIL. Two views of Virginia rails at their nest, presented by Jenness Richardson.

PLATE 83. VIRGINIA RAIL. *Left:* Nest with eggs and young of Virginia rail, Branchport, New York, June 12, 1913, presented by Verdi Burtch. *Right:* Young Virginia rail, just hatched, Ithaca, New York, June 15, 1910, presented by Dr. Arthur A. Allen.

PLATE 84. SORA RAIL. *Upper:* Nest and eggs of sora rail, Martha's Vineyard, Massachusetts, May 27, 1900, photo by the author, referred to on page 304. *Lower:* Nest and eggs of sora rail, Harford County, Maryland, May 25, 1899, presented by William H. Fisher.

PLATE 85. SORA RAIL. *Upper:* Female sora rail, incubating, Ithaca, New York, July 26, 1913, presented by Dr. Arthur A. Allen. *Lower:* High-water nest of sora rail, Branchport, New York, May 28, 1914, presented by Verdi Burtch.

PLATE 86. YELLOW RAIL. *Upper:* Nesting site of yellow rail, "the big coulee," Benson County, North Dakota, referred to on page 317. *Lower:* The 1912 nest, as found in above locality. Photos presented by Rev. P. B. Peabody.

PLATE 87. YELLOW RAIL. *Upper:* Fairly open type of nest of yellow rail, rare. *Lower:* The 1912 nest, exposed. Photos by Rev. P. B. Peabody, Benson County, North Dakota, presented by him.

PLATE 88. BLACK RAIL. *Upper:* Nest and eggs of black rail, near
Beach Haven, New Jersey, July 4, 1919. *Lower:* Nesting site in above
locality. Photos presented by J. Fletcher Street, referred to on page
328.

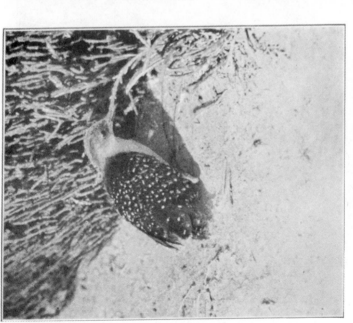

PLATE 89. FARALLON RAIL. *Left:* Farallon rail in San Diego Salt Marsh, San Diego, California, presented by Laurence M. Huey. *Right:* Nest and eggs of Farallon rail in above locality, presented by Donald R. Dickey.

PLATE 90. PURPLE GALLINULE. *Upper:* Nest and eggs of purple gallinule, in a clump of wild parsnip, Lake Apopka, Florida, April 26, 1925, photo by the author, referred to on page 340. *Lower:* Another nest in a clump of *Nymphaea*, presented by Oscar E. Baynard.

PLATE 91. PURPLE GALLINULE. *Left:* Nest and eggs of purple gallinule, South Edisto River rice fields, Charleston County, South Carolina, May 22, 1924, presented by B. Rhett Chamberlain and Alexander Sprunt, jr. *Right:* Nest and eggs of purple gallinule in a clump of cat-tail flags, Pasco County, Florida, April 25, 1925, photo by the author, referred to on page 340.

PLATE 92. PURPLE GALLINULE. Two views of a purple gallinule on its nest, Kissimmee Marsh, Florida, May 7, 1924, presented by Dr. Arthur A. Allen.

PLATE 93. FLORIDA GALLINULE. *Upper:* Nest and eggs of Florida gallinule, among thick flags, Branchport, New York, May 31, 1915, presented by Clarence F. Stone. *Lower:* Nest and eggs of Florida gallinule, among open flags, Gainesville, Florida, May 2, 1924, presented by Ernest G. Holt.

PLATE 94. FLORIDA GALLINULE. *Upper:* Nest and eggs of Florida gallinule, among *Nymphaea* and *Hydrocotyle,* Florida, presented by Oscar E. Baynard. *Lower:* Florida gallinule approaching nest, Cayuga Lake, New York, June 25, 1914, presented by Dr. Arthur A. Allen.

PLATE 95. FLORIDA GALLINULE. *Upper:* Florida gallinule in-
cubating, Branchport, New York, July 5, 1916. *Lower:* Young
Florida gallinule, 5 hours old, Branchport, New York, June 28, 1910.
Photos presented by Verdi Burtch.

PLATE 96. AMERICAN COOT. *Upper:* Distant view of nest of American coot, Steele County, North Dakota, June 8, 1901. *Lower:* Nearer view of same nest with 15 eggs. Photos by the author, referred to on page 360.

PLATE 97. AMERICAN COOT. Nest and eggs of American coot, Barr Lake, Colorado, presented by the Colorado Museum of Natural History.

PLATE 98. AMERICAN COOT. *Upper:* Flock of American coots, with a few teal, Louisiana, December, 1915. *Lower:* Young American coots, a few days old, Manitoba, 1913. Photos presented by Herbert K. Job.

A CATALOGUE OF SELECTED DOVER BOOKS
IN ALL FIELDS OF INTEREST

A CATALOGUE OF SELECTED DOVER BOOKS
IN ALL FIELDS OF INTEREST

THE NOTEBOOKS OF LEONARDO DA VINCI, edited by J.P. Richter. Extracts from manuscripts reveal great genius; on painting, sculpture, anatomy, sciences, geography, etc. Both Italian and English. 186 ms. pages reproduced, plus 500 additional drawings, including studies for Last Supper, Sforza monument, etc. 860pp. 7⅞ x 10¾.   USO 22572-0, 22573-9 Pa., Two vol. set $12.00

ART NOUVEAU DESIGNS IN COLOR, Alphonse Mucha, Maurice Verneuil, Georges Auriol. Full-color reproduction of Combinaisons ornamentales (c. 1900) by Art Nouveau masters. Floral, animal, geometric, interlacings, swashes — borders, frames, spots — all incredibly beautiful. 60 plates, hundreds of designs. 9⅜ x 8¹/₁₆ .   22885-1 Pa. $4.00

GRAPHIC WORKS OF ODILON REDON. All great fantastic lithographs, etchings, engravings, drawings, 209 in all. Monsters, Huysmans, still life work, etc. Introduction by Alfred Werner. 209pp. 9⅛ x 12¼.   21996-8 Pa. $5.00

EXOTIC FLORAL PATTERNS IN COLOR, E.-A. Seguy. Incredibly beautiful full-color pochoir work by great French designer of 20's. Complete Bouquets et frondaisons, Suggestions pour étoffes. Richness must be seen to be believed. 40 plates containing 120 patterns. 80pp. 9⅜ x 12¼.   23041-4 Pa. $6.00

SELECTED ETCHINGS OF JAMES A. McN. WHISTLER, James A. McN. Whistler. 149 outstanding etchings by the great American artist, including selections from the Thames set and two Venice sets, the complete French set, and many individual prints. Introduction and explanatory note on each print by Maria Naylor. 157pp. 9⅜ x 12¼.   23194-1 Pa. $5.00

VISUAL ILLUSIONS: THEIR CAUSES, CHARACTERISTICS, AND APPLICATIONS, Matthew Luckiesh. Thorough description, discussion; shape and size, color, motion; natural illusion. Uses in art and industry. 100 illustrations. 252pp.
                                                    21530-X Pa. $2.50

TEN BOOKS ON ARCHITECTURE, Vitruvius. The most important book ever written on architecture. Early Roman aesthetics, technology, classical orders, site selection, all other aspects. Stands behind everything since. Morgan translation. 331pp.
                                                    20645-9 Pa. $3.50

THE CODEX NUTTALL. A PICTURE MANUSCRIPT FROM ANCIENT MEXICO, as first edited by Zelia Nuttall. Only inexpensive edition, in full color, of a pre-Columbian Mexican (Mixtec) book. 88 color plates show kings, gods, heroes, temples, sacrifices. New explanatory, historical introduction by Arthur G. Miller. 96pp. 11⅜ x 8½.   23168-2 Pa. $7.50

CREATIVE LITHOGRAPHY AND HOW TO DO IT, Grant Arnold. Lithography as art form: working directly on stone, transfer of drawings, lithotint, mezzotint, color printing; also metal plates. Detailed, thorough. 27 illustrations. 214pp.

21208-4 Pa. $3.00

DESIGN MOTIFS OF ANCIENT MEXICO, Jorge Enciso. Vigorous, powerful ceramic stamp impressions — Maya, Aztec, Toltec, Olmec. Serpents, gods, priests, dancers, etc. 153pp. 6⅛ x 9¼. 20084-1 Pa. $2.50

AMERICAN INDIAN DESIGN AND DECORATION, Leroy Appleton. Full text, plus more than 700 precise drawings of Inca, Maya, Aztec, Pueblo, Plains, NW Coast basketry, sculpture, painting, pottery, sand paintings, metal, etc. 4 plates in color. 279pp. 8⅜ x 11¼. 22704-9 Pa. $4.50

CHINESE LATTICE DESIGNS, Daniel S. Dye. Incredibly beautiful geometric designs: circles, voluted, simple dissections, etc. Inexhaustible source of ideas, motifs. 1239 illustrations. 469pp. 6⅛ x 9¼. 23096-1 Pa. $5.00

JAPANESE DESIGN MOTIFS, Matsuya Co. Mon, or heraldic designs. Over 4000 typical, beautiful designs: birds, animals, flowers, swords, fans, geometric; all beautifully stylized. 213pp. 11⅜ x 8¼. 22874-6 Pa. $4.95

PERSPECTIVE, Jan Vredeman de Vries. 73 perspective plates from 1604 edition; buildings, townscapes, stairways, fantastic scenes. Remarkable for beauty, surrealistic atmosphere; real eye-catchers. Introduction by Adolf Placzek. 74pp. 11⅜ x 8¼. 20186-4 Pa. $2.75

EARLY AMERICAN DESIGN MOTIFS, Suzanne E. Chapman. 497 motifs, designs, from painting on wood, ceramics, appliqué, glassware, samplers, metal work, etc. Florals, landscapes, birds and animals, geometrics, letters, etc. Inexhaustible. Enlarged edition. 138pp. 8⅜ x 11¼. 22985-8 Pa. $3.50
23084-8 Clothbd. $7.95

VICTORIAN STENCILS FOR DESIGN AND DECORATION, edited by E.V. Gillon, Jr. 113 wonderful ornate Victorian pieces from German sources; florals, geometrics; borders, corner pieces; bird motifs, etc. 64pp. 9⅜ x 12¼. 21995-X Pa. $2.50

ART NOUVEAU: AN ANTHOLOGY OF DESIGN AND ILLUSTRATION FROM THE STUDIO, edited by E.V. Gillon, Jr. Graphic arts: book jackets, posters, engravings, illustrations, decorations; Crane, Beardsley, Bradley and many others. Inexhaustible. 92pp. 8⅛ x 11. 22388-4 Pa. $2.50

ORIGINAL ART DECO DESIGNS, William Rowe. First-rate, highly imaginative modern Art Deco frames, borders, compositions, alphabets, florals, insectals, Wurlitzer-types, etc. Much finest modern Art Deco. 80 plates, 8 in color. 8⅜ x 11¼. 22567-4 Pa. $3.00

HANDBOOK OF DESIGNS AND DEVICES, Clarence P. Hornung. Over 1800 basic geometric designs based on circle, triangle, square, scroll, cross, etc. Largest such collection in existence. 261pp. 20125-2 Pa. $2.50

150 MASTERPIECES OF DRAWING, edited by Anthony Toney. 150 plates, early 15th century to end of 18th century; Rembrandt, Michelangelo, Dürer, Fragonard, Watteau, Wouwerman, many others. 150pp. 8⅜ x 11¼. 21032-4 Pa. $3.50

THE GOLDEN AGE OF THE POSTER, Hayward and Blanche Cirker. 70 extraordinary posters in full colors, from Maîtres de l'Affiche, Mucha, Lautrec, Bradley, Cheret, Beardsley, many others. 9⅜ x 12¼. 22753-7 Pa. $4.95
21718-3 Clothbd. $7.95

SIMPLICISSIMUS, selection, translations and text by Stanley Appelbaum. 180 satirical drawings, 16 in full color, from the famous German weekly magazine in the years 1896 to 1926. 24 artists included: Grosz, Kley, Pascin, Kubin, Kollwitz, plus Heine, Thöny, Bruno Paul, others. 172pp. 8½ x 12¼. 23098-8 Pa. $5.00
23099-6 Clothbd. $10.00

THE EARLY WORK OF AUBREY BEARDSLEY, Aubrey Beardsley. 157 plates, 2 in color: Manon Lescaut, Madame Bovary, Morte d'Arthur, Salome, other. Introduction by H. Marillier. 175pp. 8½ x 11. 21816-3 Pa. $3.50

THE LATER WORK OF AUBREY BEARDSLEY, Aubrey Beardsley. Exotic masterpieces of full maturity: Venus and Tannhäuser, Lysistrata, Rape of the Lock, Volpone, Savoy material, etc. 174 plates, 2 in color. 176pp. 8½ x 11. 21817-1 Pa. $3.75

DRAWINGS OF WILLIAM BLAKE, William Blake. 92 plates from Book of Job, Divine Comedy, Paradise Lost, visionary heads, mythological figures, Laocoön, etc. Selection, introduction, commentary by Sir Geoffrey Keynes. 178pp. 8½ x 11. 22303-5 Pa. $3.50

LONDON: A PILGRIMAGE, Gustave Doré, Blanchard Jerrold. Squalor, riches, misery, beauty of mid-Victorian metropolis; 55 wonderful plates, 125 other illustrations, full social, cultural text by Jerrold. 191pp. of text. 8⅛ x 11. 22306-X Pa. $5.00

THE COMPLETE WOODCUTS OF ALBRECHT DÜRER, edited by Dr. W. Kurth. 346 in all: Old Testament, St. Jerome, Passion, Life of Virgin, Apocalypse, many others. Introduction by Campbell Dodgson. 285pp. 8½ x 12¼. 21097-9 Pa. $6.00

THE DISASTERS OF WAR, Francisco Goya. 83 etchings record horrors of Napoleonic wars in Spain and war in general. Reprint of 1st edition, plus 3 additional plates. Introduction by Philip Hofer. 97pp. 9⅜ x 8¼. 21872-4 Pa. $2.50

ENGRAVINGS OF HOGARTH, William Hogarth. 101 of Hogarth's greatest works: Rake's Progress, Harlot's Progress, Illustrations for Hudibras, Midnight Modern Conversation, Before and After, Beer Street and Gin Lane, many more. Full commentary. 256pp. 11 x 14. 22479-1 Pa. $6.00
23023-6 Clothbd. $13.50

PRIMITIVE ART, Franz Boas. Great anthropologist on ceramics, textiles, wood, stone, metal, etc.; patterns, technology, symbols, styles. All areas, but fullest on Northwest Coast Indians. 350 illustrations. 378pp. 20025-6 Pa. $3.50

CONSTRUCTION OF AMERICAN FURNITURE TREASURES, Lester Margon. 344 detail drawings, complete text on constructing exact reproductions of 38 early American masterpieces: Hepplewhite sideboard, Duncan Phyfe drop-leaf table, mantel clock, gate-leg dining table, Pa. German cupboard, more. 38 plates. 54 photographs. 168pp. 8⅜ x 11¼. 23056-2 Pa. $4.00

JEWELRY MAKING AND DESIGN, Augustus F. Rose, Antonio Cirino. Professional secrets revealed in thorough, practical guide: tools, materials, processes; rings, brooches, chains, cast pieces, enamelling, setting stones, etc. Do not confuse with skimpy introductions: beginner can use, professional can learn from it. Over 200 illustrations. 306pp. 21750-7 Pa. $3.00

METALWORK AND ENAMELLING, Herbert Maryon. Generally coneeded best all-around book. Countless trade secrets: materials, tools, soldering, filigree, setting, inlay, niello, repoussé, casting, polishing, etc. For beginner or expert. Author was foremost British expert. 330 illustrations. 335pp. 22702-2 Pa. $3.50

WEAVING WITH FOOT-POWER LOOMS, Edward F. Worst. Setting up a loom, beginning to weave, constructing equipment, using dyes, more, plus over 285 drafts of traditional patterns including Colonial and Swedish weaves. More than 200 other figures. For beginning and advanced. 275pp. 8¾ x 6⅜. 23064-3 Pa. $4.00

WEAVING A NAVAJO BLANKET, Gladys A. Reichard. Foremost anthropologist studied under Navajo women, reveals every step in process from wool, dyeing, spinning, setting up loom, designing, weaving. Much history, symbolism. With this book you could make one yourself. 97 illustrations. 222pp. 22992-0 Pa. $3.00

NATURAL DYES AND HOME DYEING, Rita J. Adrosko. Use natural ingredients: bark, flowers, leaves, lichens, insects etc. Over 135 specific recipes from historical sources for cotton, wool, other fabrics. Genuine premodern handicrafts. 12 illustrations. 160pp. 22688-3 Pa. $2.00

THE HAND DECORATION OF FABRICS, Francis J. Kafka. Outstanding, profusely illustrated guide to stenciling, batik, block printing, tie dyeing, freehand painting, silk screen printing, and novelty decoration. 356 illustrations. 198pp. 6 x 9. 21401-X Pa. $3.00

THOMAS NAST: CARTOONS AND ILLUSTRATIONS, with text by Thomas Nast St. Hill. Father of American political cartooning. Cartoons that destroyed Tweed Ring; inflation, free love, church and state; original Republican elephant and Democratic donkey; Santa Claus; more. 117 illustrations. 146pp. 9 x 12.
22983-1 Pa. $4.00
23067-8 Clothbd. $8.50

FREDERIC REMINGTON: 173 DRAWINGS AND ILLUSTRATIONS. Most famous of the Western artists, most responsible for our myths about the American West in its untamed days. Complete reprinting of Drawings of Frederic Remington (1897), plus other selections. 4 additional drawings in color on covers. 140pp. 9 x 12.
20714-5 Pa. $3.95

EARLY NEW ENGLAND GRAVESTONE RUBBINGS, Edmund V. Gillon, Jr. 43 photographs, 226 rubbings show heavily symbolic, macabre, sometimes humorous primitive American art. Up to early 19th century. 207pp. 8⅜ x 11¼.
21380-3 Pa. $4.00

L.J.M. DAGUERRE: THE HISTORY OF THE DIORAMA AND THE DAGUERREOTYPE, Helmut and Alison Gernsheim. Definitive account. Early history, life and work of Daguerre; discovery of daguerreotype process; diffusion abroad; other early photography. 124 illustrations. 226pp. 6⅙ x 9¼.
22290-X Pa. $4.00

PHOTOGRAPHY AND THE AMERICAN SCENE, Robert Taft. The basic book on American photography as art, recording form, 1839-1889. Development, influence on society, great photographers, types (portraits, war, frontier, etc.), whatever else needed. Inexhaustible. Illustrated with 322 early photos, daguerreotypes, tintypes, stereo slides, etc. 546pp. 6⅛ x 9¼.
21201-7 Pa. $5.00

PHOTOGRAPHIC SKETCHBOOK OF THE CIVIL WAR, Alexander Gardner. Reproduction of 1866 volume with 100 on-the-field photographs: Manassas, Lincoln on battlefield, slave pens, etc. Introduction by E.F. Bleiler. 224pp. 10¾ x 9.
22731-6 Pa. $4.50

THE MOVIES: A PICTURE QUIZ BOOK, Stanley Appelbaum & Hayward Cirker. Match stars with their movies, name actors and actresses, test your movie skill with 241 stills from 236 great movies, 1902-1959. Indexes of performers and films. 128pp. 8⅜ x 9¼.
20222-4 Pa. $2.50

THE TALKIES, Richard Griffith. Anthology of features, articles from Photoplay, 1928-1940, reproduced complete. Stars, famous movies, technical features, fabulous ads, etc.; Garbo, Chaplin, King Kong, Lubitsch, etc. 4 color plates, scores of illustrations. 327pp. 8⅜ x 11¼.
22762-6 Pa. $5.95

THE MOVIE MUSICAL FROM VITAPHONE TO "42ND STREET," edited by Miles Kreuger. Relive the rise of the movie musical as reported in the pages of Photoplay magazine (1926-1933): every movie review, cast list, ad, and record review; every significant feature article, production still, biography, forecast, and gossip story. Profusely illustrated. 367pp. 8⅜ x 11¼.
23154-2 Pa. $6.95

JOHANN SEBASTIAN BACH, Philipp Spitta. Great classic of biography, musical commentary, with hundreds of pieces analyzed. Also good for Bach's contemporaries. 450 musical examples. Total of 1799pp.
EUK 22278-0, 22279-9 Clothbd., Two vol. set $25.00

BEETHOVEN AND HIS NINE SYMPHONIES, Sir George Grove. Thorough history, analysis, commentary on symphonies and some related pieces. For either beginner or advanced student. 436 musical passages. 407pp.
20334-4 Pa. $4.00

MOZART AND HIS PIANO CONCERTOS, Cuthbert Girdlestone. The only full-length study. Detailed analyses of all 21 concertos, sources; 417 musical examples. 509pp.
21271-8 Pa. $4.50

THE FITZWILLIAM VIRGINAL BOOK, edited by J. Fuller Maitland, W.B. Squire. Famous early 17th century collection of keyboard music, 300 works by Morley, Byrd, Bull, Gibbons, etc. Modern notation. Total of 938pp. 8⅜ x 11.
ECE 21068-5, 21069-3 Pa., Two vol. set $12.00

COMPLETE STRING QUARTETS, Wolfgang A. Mozart. Breitkopf and Härtel edition. All 23 string quartets plus alternate slow movement to K156. Study score. 277pp. 9⅜ x 12¼.
22372-8 Pa. $6.00

COMPLETE SONG CYCLES, Franz Schubert. Complete piano, vocal music of Die Schöne Müllerin, Die Winterreise, Schwanengesang. Also Drinker English singing translations. Breitkopf and Härtel edition. 217pp. 9⅜ x 12¼.
22649-2 Pa. $4.00

THE COMPLETE PRELUDES AND ETUDES FOR PIANOFORTE SOLO, Alexander Scriabin. All the preludes and etudes including many perfectly spun miniatures. Edited by K.N. Igumnov and Y.I. Mil'shteyn. 250pp. 9 x 12.
22919-X Pa. $5.00

TRISTAN UND ISOLDE, Richard Wagner. Full orchestral score with complete instrumentation. Do not confuse with piano reduction. Commentary by Felix Mottl, great Wagnerian conductor and scholar. Study score. 655pp. 8⅛ x 11.
22915-7 Pa. $10.00

FAVORITE SONGS OF THE NINETIES, ed. Robert Fremont. Full reproduction, including covers, of 88 favorites: Ta-Ra-Ra-Boom-De-Aye, The Band Played On, Bird in a Gilded Cage, Under the Bamboo Tree, After the Ball, etc. 401pp. 9 x 12.
EBE 21536-9 Pa. $6.95

SOUSA'S GREAT MARCHES IN PIANO TRANSCRIPTION: ORIGINAL SHEET MUSIC OF 23 WORKS, John Philip Sousa. Selected by Lester S. Levy. Playing edition includes: The Stars and Stripes Forever, The Thunderer, The Gladiator, King Cotton, Washington Post, much more. 24 illustrations. 111pp. 9 x 12.
USO 23132-1 Pa. $3.50

CLASSIC PIANO RAGS, selected with an introduction by Rudi Blesh. Best ragtime music (1897-1922) by Scott Joplin, James Scott, Joseph F. Lamb, Tom Turpin, 9 others. Printed from best original sheet music, plus covers. 364pp. 9 x 12.
EBE 20469-3 Pa. $6.95

ANALYSIS OF CHINESE CHARACTERS, C.D. Wilder, J.H. Ingram. 1000 most important characters analyzed according to primitives, phonetics, historical development. Traditional method offers mnemonic aid to beginner, intermediate student of Chinese, Japanese. 365pp.
23045-7 Pa. $4.00

MODERN CHINESE: A BASIC COURSE, Faculty of Peking University. Self study, classroom course in modern Mandarin. Records contain phonetics, vocabulary, sentences, lessons. 249 page book contains all recorded text, translations, grammar, vocabulary, exercises. Best course on market. 3 12" 33⅓ monaural records, book, album.
98832-5 Set $12.50

THE BEST DR. THORNDYKE DETECTIVE STORIES, R. Austin Freeman. The Case of Oscar Brodski, The Moabite Cipher, and 5 other favorites featuring the great scientific detective, plus his long-believed-lost first adventure — 31 New Inn — reprinted here for the first time. Edited by E.F. Bleiler. USO 20388-3 Pa. $3.00

BEST "THINKING MACHINE" DETECTIVE STORIES, Jacques Futrelle. The Problem of Cell 13 and 11 other stories about Prof. Augustus S.F.X. Van Dusen, including two "lost" stories. First reprinting of several. Edited by E.F. Bleiler. 241pp.
20537-1 Pa. $3.00

UNCLE SILAS, J. Sheridan LeFanu. Victorian Gothic mystery novel, considered by many best of period, even better than Collins or Dickens. Wonderful psychological terror. Introduction by Frederick Shroyer. 436pp. 21715-9 Pa. $4.00

BEST DR. POGGIOLI DETECTIVE STORIES, T.S. Stribling. 15 best stories from EQMM and The Saint offer new adventures in Mexico, Florida, Tennessee hills as Poggioli unravels mysteries and combats Count Jalacki. 217pp. 23227-1 Pa. $3.00

EIGHT DIME NOVELS, selected with an introduction by E.F. Bleiler. Adventures of Old King Brady, Frank James, Nick Carter, Deadwood Dick, Buffalo Bill, The Steam Man, Frank Merriwell, and Horatio Alger — 1877 to 1905. Important, entertaining popular literature in facsimile reprint, with original covers. 190pp. 9 x 12. 22975-0 Pa. $3.50

ALICE'S ADVENTURES UNDER GROUND, Lewis Carroll. Facsimile of ms. Carroll gave Alice Liddell in 1864. Different in many ways from final Alice. Handlettered, illustrated by Carroll. Introduction by Martin Gardner. 128pp. 21482-6 Pa. $1.50

ALICE IN WONDERLAND COLORING BOOK, Lewis Carroll. Pictures by John Tenniel. Large-size versions of the famous illustrations of Alice, Cheshire Cat, Mad Hatter and all the others, waiting for your crayons. Abridged text. 36 illustrations. 64pp. 8¼ x 11. 22853-3 Pa. $1.50

AVENTURES D'ALICE AU PAYS DES MERVEILLES, Lewis Carroll. Bué's translation of "Alice" into French, supervised by Carroll himself. Novel way to learn language. (No English text.) 42 Tenniel illustrations. 196pp. 22836-3 Pa. $2.00

MYTHS AND FOLK TALES OF IRELAND, Jeremiah Curtin. 11 stories that are Irish versions of European fairy tales and 9 stories from the Fenian cycle — 20 tales of legend and magic that comprise an essential work in the history of folklore. 256pp. 22430-9 Pa. $3.00

EAST O' THE SUN AND WEST O' THE MOON, George W. Dasent. Only full edition of favorite, wonderful Norwegian fairytales — Why the Sea is Salt, Boots and the Troll, etc. — with 77 illustrations by Kittelsen & Werenskiöld. 418pp.
22521-6 Pa. $3.50

PERRAULT'S FAIRY TALES, Charles Perrault and Gustave Doré. Original versions of Cinderella, Sleeping Beauty, Little Red Riding Hood, etc. in best translation, with 34 wonderful illustrations by Gustave Doré. 117pp. 8⅛ x 11. 22311-6 Pa. $2.50

MOTHER GOOSE'S MELODIES. Facsimile of fabulously rare Munroe and Francis "copyright 1833" Boston edition. Familiar and unusual rhymes, wonderful old woodcut illustrations. Edited by E.F. Bleiler. 128pp. 4½ x 6⅜. 22577-1 Pa. $1.00

MOTHER GOOSE IN HIEROGLYPHICS. Favorite nursery rhymes presented in rebus form for children. Fascinating 1849 edition reproduced in toto, with key. Introduction by E.F. Bleiler. About 400 woodcuts. 64pp. 6⅞ x 5¼. 20745-5 Pa. $1.00

PETER PIPER'S PRACTICAL PRINCIPLES OF PLAIN & PERFECT PRONUNCIATION. Alliterative jingles and tongue-twisters. Reproduction in full of 1830 first American edition. 25 spirited woodcuts. 32pp. 4½ x 6⅜. 22560-7 Pa. $1.00

MARMADUKE MULTIPLY'S MERRY METHOD OF MAKING MINOR MATHEMATICIANS. Fellow to Peter Piper, it teaches multiplication table by catchy rhymes and woodcuts. 1841 Munroe & Francis edition. Edited by E.F. Bleiler. 103pp. 4⅝ x 6.
22773-1 Pa. $1.25
20171-6 Clothbd. $3.00

THE NIGHT BEFORE CHRISTMAS, Clement Moore. Full text, and woodcuts from original 1848 book. Also critical, historical material. 19 illustrations. 40pp. 4⅝ x 6. 22797-9 Pa. $1.00

THE KING OF THE GOLDEN RIVER, John Ruskin. Victorian children's classic of three brothers, their attempts to reach the Golden River, what becomes of them. Facsimile of original 1889 edition. 22 illustrations. 56pp. 4⅝ x 6⅜.
20066-3 Pa. $1.25

DREAMS OF THE RAREBIT FIEND, Winsor McCay. Pioneer cartoon strip, unexcelled for beauty, imagination, in 60 full sequences. Incredible technical virtuosity, wonderful visual wit. Historical introduction. 62pp. 8⅜ x 11¼. 21347-1 Pa. $2.00

THE KATZENJAMMER KIDS, Rudolf Dirks. In full color, 14 strips from 1906-7; full of imagination, characteristic humor. Classic of great historical importance. Introduction by August Derleth. 32pp. 9¼ x 12¼. 23005-8 Pa. $2.00

LITTLE ORPHAN ANNIE AND LITTLE ORPHAN ANNIE IN COSMIC CITY, Harold Gray. Two great sequences from the early strips: our curly-haired heroine defends the Warbucks' financial empire and, then, takes on meanie Phineas P. Pinchpenny. Leapin' lizards! 178pp. 6⅛ x 8⅜. 23107-0 Pa. $2.00

WHEN A FELLER NEEDS A FRIEND, Clare Briggs. 122 cartoons by one of the greatest newspaper cartoonists of the early 20th century — about growing up, making a living, family life, daily frustrations and occasional triumphs. 121pp. 8½ x 9½.
23148-8 Pa. $2.50

THE BEST OF GLUYAS WILLIAMS. 100 drawings by one of America's finest cartoonists: The Day a Cake of Ivory Soap Sank at Proctor & Gamble's, At the Life Insurance Agents' Banquet, and many other gems from the 20's and 30's. 118pp. 8⅜ x 11¼. 22737-5 Pa. $2.50

THE MAGIC MOVING PICTURE BOOK, Bliss, Sands & Co. The pictures in this book move! Volcanoes erupt, a house burns, a serpentine dancer wiggles her way through a number. By using a specially ruled acetate screen provided, you can obtain these and 15 other startling effects. Originally "The Motograph Moving Picture Book." 32pp. 8¼ x 11. 23224-7 Pa. $1.75

STRING FIGURES AND HOW TO MAKE THEM, Caroline F. Jayne. Fullest, clearest instructions on string figures from around world: Eskimo, Navajo, Lapp, Europe, more. Cats cradle, moving spear, lightning, stars. Introduction by A.C. Haddon. 950 illustrations. 407pp. 20152-X Pa. $3.00

PAPER FOLDING FOR BEGINNERS, William D. Murray and Francis J. Rigney. Clearest book on market for making origami sail boats, roosters, frogs that move legs, cups, bonbon boxes. 40 projects. More than 275 illustrations. Photographs. 94pp. 20713-7 Pa. $1.25

INDIAN SIGN LANGUAGE, William Tomkins. Over 525 signs developed by Sioux, Blackfoot, Cheyenne, Arapahoe and other tribes. Written instructions and diagrams: how to make words, construct sentences. Also 290 pictographs of Sioux and Ojibway tribes. 111pp. 6⅛ x 9¼. 22029-X Pa. $1.50

BOOMERANGS: HOW TO MAKE AND THROW THEM, Bernard S. Mason. Easy to make and throw, dozens of designs: cross-stick, pinwheel, boomabird, tumblestick, Australian curved stick boomerang. Complete throwing instructions. All safe. 99pp. 23028-7 Pa. $1.50

25 KITES THAT FLY, Leslie Hunt. Full, easy to follow instructions for kites made from inexpensive materials. Many novelties. Reeling, raising, designing your own. 70 illustrations. 110pp. 22550-X Pa. $1.25

TRICKS AND GAMES ON THE POOL TABLE, Fred Herrmann. 79 tricks and games, some solitaires, some for 2 or more players, some competitive; mystifying shots and throws, unusual carom, tricks involving cork, coins, a hat, more. 77 figures. 95pp. 21814-7 Pa. $1.25

WOODCRAFT AND CAMPING, Bernard S. Mason. How to make a quick emergency shelter, select woods that will burn immediately, make do with limited supplies, etc. Also making many things out of wood, rawhide, bark, at camp. Formerly titled Woodcraft. 295 illustrations. 580pp. 21951-8 Pa. $4.00

AN INTRODUCTION TO CHESS MOVES AND TACTICS SIMPLY EXPLAINED, Leonard Barden. Informal intermediate introduction: reasons for moves, tactics, openings, traps, positional play, endgame. Isolates patterns. 102pp. USO 21210-6 Pa. $1.35

LASKER'S MANUAL OF CHESS, Dr. Emanuel Lasker. Great world champion offers very thorough coverage of all aspects of chess. Combinations, position play, openings, endgame, aesthetics of chess, philosophy of struggle, much more. Filled with analyzed games. 390pp. 20640-8 Pa. $3.50

How to Solve Chess Problems, Kenneth S. Howard. Practical suggestions on problem solving for very beginners. 58 two-move problems, 46 3-movers, 8 4-movers for practice, plus hints. 171pp. 20748-X Pa. $2.00

A Guide to Fairy Chess, Anthony Dickins. 3-D chess, 4-D chess, chess on a cylindrical board, reflecting pieces that bounce off edges, cooperative chess, retrograde chess, maximummers, much more. Most based on work of great Dawson. Full handbook, 100 problems. 66pp. 7⅞ x 10¾. 22687-5 Pa. $2.00

Win at Backgammon, Millard Hopper. Best opening moves, running game, blocking game, back game, tables of odds, etc. Hopper makes the game clear enough for anyone to play, and win. 43 diagrams. 111pp. 22894-0 Pa. $1.50

Bidding a Bridge Hand, Terence Reese. Master player "thinks out loud" the binding of 75 hands that defy point count systems. Organized by bidding problem—no-fit situations, overbidding, underbidding, cueing your defense, etc. 254pp. EBE 22830-4 Pa. $2.50

The Precision Bidding System in Bridge, C.C. Wei, edited by Alan Truscott. Inventor of precision bidding presents average hands and hands from actual play, including games from 1969 Bermuda Bowl where system emerged. 114 exercises. 116pp. 21171-1 Pa. $1.75

Learn Magic, Henry Hay. 20 simple, easy-to-follow lessons on magic for the new magician: illusions, card tricks, silks, sleights of hand, coin manipulations, escapes, and more —all with a minimum amount of equipment. Final chapter explains the great stage illusions. 92 illustrations. 285pp. 21238-6 Pa. $2.95

The New Magician's Manual, Walter B. Gibson. Step-by-step instructions and clear illustrations guide the novice in mastering 36 tricks; much equipment supplied on 16 pages of cut-out materials. 36 additional tricks. 64 illustrations. 159pp. 6⅝ x 10. 23113-5 Pa. $3.00

Professional Magic for Amateurs, Walter B. Gibson. 50 easy, effective tricks used by professionals —cards, string, tumblers, handkerchiefs, mental magic, etc. 63 illustrations. 223pp. 23012-0 Pa. $2.50

Card Manipulations, Jean Hugard. Very rich collection of manipulations; has taught thousands of fine magicians tricks that are really workable, eye-catching. Easily followed, serious work. Over 200 illustrations. 163pp. 20539-8 Pa. $2.00

Abbott's Encyclopedia of Rope Tricks for Magicians, Stewart James. Complete reference book for amateur and professional magicians containing more than 150 tricks involving knots, penetrations, cut and restored rope, etc. 510 illustrations. Reprint of 3rd edition. 400pp. 23206-9 Pa. $3.50

The Secrets of Houdini, J.C. Cannell. Classic study of Houdini's incredible magic, exposing closely-kept professional secrets and revealing, in general terms, the whole art of stage magic. 67 illustrations. 279pp. 22913-0 Pa. $2.50

DRIED FLOWERS, Sarah Whitlock and Martha Rankin. Concise, clear, practical guide to dehydration, glycerinizing, pressing plant material, and more. Covers use of silica gel. 12 drawings. Originally titled "New Techniques with Dried Flowers." 32pp. 21802-3 Pa. $1.00

ABC OF POULTRY RAISING, J.H. Florea. Poultry expert, editor tells how to raise chickens on home or small business basis. Breeds, feeding, housing, laying, etc. Very concrete, practical. 50 illustrations. 256pp. 23201-8 Pa. $3.00

HOW INDIANS USE WILD PLANTS FOR FOOD, MEDICINE & CRAFTS, Frances Densmore. Smithsonian, Bureau of American Ethnology report presents wealth of material on nearly 200 plants used by Chippewas of Minnesota and Wisconsin. 33 plates plus 122pp. of text. 6⅛ x 9¼. 23019-8 Pa. $2.50

THE HERBAL OR GENERAL HISTORY OF PLANTS, John Gerard. The 1633 edition revised and enlarged by Thomas Johnson. Containing almost 2850 plant descriptions and 2705 superb illustrations, Gerard's Herbal is a monumental work, the book all modern English herbals are derived from, and the one herbal every serious enthusiast should have in its entirety. Original editions are worth perhaps $750. 1678pp. 8½ x 12¼. 23147-X Clothbd. $50.00

A MODERN HERBAL, Margaret Grieve. Much the fullest, most exact, most useful compilation of herbal material. Gigantic alphabetical encyclopedia, from aconite to zedoary, gives botanical information, medical properties, folklore, economic uses, and much else. Indispensable to serious reader. 161 illustrations. 888pp. 6½ x 9¼. USO 22798-7, 22799-5 Pa., Two vol. set $10.00

HOW TO KNOW THE FERNS, Frances T. Parsons. Delightful classic. Identification, fern lore, for Eastern and Central U.S.A. Has introduced thousands to interesting life form. 99 illustrations. 215pp. 20740-4 Pa. $2.50

THE MUSHROOM HANDBOOK, Louis C.C. Krieger. Still the best popular handbook. Full descriptions of 259 species, extremely thorough text, habitats, luminescence, poisons, folklore, etc. 32 color plates; 126 other illustrations. 560pp. 21861-9 Pa. $4.50

HOW TO KNOW THE WILD FRUITS, Maude G. Peterson. Classic guide covers nearly 200 trees, shrubs, smaller plants of the U.S. arranged by color of fruit and then by family. Full text provides names, descriptions, edibility, uses. 80 illustrations. 400pp. 22943-2 Pa. $3.00

COMMON WEEDS OF THE UNITED STATES, U.S. Department of Agriculture. Covers 220 important weeds with illustration, maps, botanical information, plant lore for each. Over 225 illustrations. 463pp. 6⅛ x 9¼. 20504-5 Pa. $4.50

HOW TO KNOW THE WILD FLOWERS, Mrs. William S. Dana. Still best popular book for East and Central USA. Over 500 plants easily identified, with plant lore; arranged according to color and flowering time. 174 plates. 459pp. 20332-8 Pa. $3.50

MANUAL OF THE TREES OF NORTH AMERICA, Charles S. Sargent. The basic survey of every native tree and tree-like shrub, 717 species in all. Extremely full descriptions, information on habitat, growth, locales, economics, etc. Necessary to every serious tree lover. Over 100 finding keys. 783 illustrations. Total of 986pp.
20277-1, 20278-X Pa., Two vol. set $8.00

BIRDS OF THE NEW YORK AREA, John Bull. Indispensable guide to more than 400 species within a hundred-mile radius of Manhattan. Information on range, status, breeding, migration, distribution trends, etc. Foreword by Roger Tory Peterson. 17 drawings; maps. 540pp.　　　　23222-0 Pa. $6.00

THE SEA-BEACH AT EBB-TIDE, Augusta Foote Arnold. Identify hundreds of marine plants and animals: algae, seaweeds, squids, crabs, corals, etc. Descriptions cover food, life cycle, size, shape, habitat. Over 600 drawings. 490pp.
21949-6 Pa. $4.00

THE MOTH BOOK, William J. Holland. Identify more than 2,000 moths of North America. General information, precise species descriptions. 623 illustrations plus 48 color plates show almost all species, full size. 1968 edition. Still the basic book. Total of 551pp. 6½ x 9¼.　　　　21948-8 Pa. $6.00

AN INTRODUCTION TO THE REPTILES AND AMPHIBIANS OF THE UNITED STATES, Percy A. Morris. All lizards, crocodiles, turtles, snakes, toads, frogs; life history, identification, habits, suitability as pets, etc. Non-technical, but sound and broad. 130 photos. 253pp.　　　　22982-3 Pa. $3.00

OLD NEW YORK IN EARLY PHOTOGRAPHS, edited by Mary Black. Your only chance to see New York City as it was 1853-1906, through 196 wonderful photographs from N.Y. Historical Society. Great Blizzard, Lincoln's funeral procession, great buildings. 228pp. 9 x 12.　　　　22907-6 Pa. $6.00

THE AMERICAN REVOLUTION, A PICTURE SOURCEBOOK, John Grafton. Wonderful Bicentennial picture source, with 411 illustrations (contemporary and 19th century) showing battles, personalities, maps, events, flags, posters, soldier's life, ships, etc. all captioned and explained. A wonderful browsing book, supplement to other historical reading. 160pp. 9 x 12.　　　　23226-3 Pa. $4.00

PERSONAL NARRATIVE OF A PILGRIMAGE TO AL-MADINAH AND MECCAH, Richard Burton. Great travel classic by remarkably colorful personality. Burton, disguised as a Moroccan, visited sacred shrines of Islam, narrowly escaping death. Wonderful observations of Islamic life, customs, personalities. 47 illustrations. Total of 959pp.　　　　21217-3, 21218-1 Pa., Two vol. set $7.00

INCIDENTS OF TRAVEL IN CENTRAL AMERICA, CHIAPAS, AND YUCATAN, John L. Stephens. Almost single-handed discovery of Maya culture; exploration of ruined cities, monuments, temples; customs of Indians. 115 drawings. 892pp.
22404-X, 22405-8 Pa., Two vol. set $8.00

HOUDINI ON MAGIC, Harold Houdini. Edited by Walter Gibson, Morris N. Young. How he escaped; exposés of fake spiritualists; instructions for eye-catching tricks; other fascinating material by and about greatest magician. 155 illustrations. 280pp. 20384-0 Pa. $2.50

HANDBOOK OF THE NUTRITIONAL CONTENTS OF FOOD, U.S. Dept. of Agriculture. Largest, most detailed source of food nutrition information ever prepared. Two mammoth tables: one measuring nutrients in 100 grams of edible portion; the other, in edible portion of 1 pound as purchased. Originally titled Composition of Foods. 190pp. 9 x 12. 21342-0 Pa. $4.00

COMPLETE GUIDE TO HOME CANNING, PRESERVING AND FREEZING, U.S. Dept. of Agriculture. Seven basic manuals with full instructions for jams and jellies; pickles and relishes; canning fruits, vegetables, meat; freezing anything. Really good recipes, exact instructions for optimal results. Save a fortune in food. 156 illustrations. 214pp. 6⅛ x 9¼. 22911-4 Pa. $2.50

THE BREAD TRAY, Louis P. De Gouy. Nearly every bread the cook could buy or make: bread sticks of Italy, fruit breads of Greece, glazed rolls of Vienna, everything from corn pone to croissants. Over 500 recipes altogether. including buns, rolls, muffins, scones, and more. 463pp. 23000-7 Pa. $3.50

CREATIVE HAMBURGER COOKERY, Louis P. De Gouy. 182 unusual recipes for casseroles, meat loaves and hamburgers that turn inexpensive ground meat into memorable main dishes: Arizona chili burgers, burger tamale pie, burger stew, burger corn loaf, burger wine loaf, and more. 120pp. 23001-5 Pa. $1.75

LONG ISLAND SEAFOOD COOKBOOK, J. George Frederick and Jean Joyce. Probably the best American seafood cookbook. Hundreds of recipes. 40 gourmet sauces, 123 recipes using oysters alone! All varieties of fish and seafood amply represented. 324pp. 22677-8 Pa. $3.00

THE EPICUREAN: A COMPLETE TREATISE OF ANALYTICAL AND PRACTICAL STUDIES IN THE CULINARY ART, Charles Ranhofer. Great modern classic. 3,500 recipes from master chef of Delmonico's, turn-of-the-century America's best restaurant. Also explained, many techniques known only to professional chefs. 775 illustrations. 1183pp. 6⅝ x 10. 22680-8 Clothbd. $17.50

THE AMERICAN WINE COOK BOOK, Ted Hatch. Over 700 recipes: old favorites livened up with wine plus many more: Czech fish soup, quince soup, sauce Perigueux, shrimp shortcake, filets Stroganoff, cordon bleu goulash, jambonneau, wine fruit cake, more. 314pp. 22796-0 Pa. $2.50

DELICIOUS VEGETARIAN COOKING, Ivan Baker. Close to 500 delicious and varied recipes: soups, main course dishes (pea, bean, lentil, cheese, vegetable, pasta, and egg dishes), savories, stews, whole-wheat breads and cakes, more. 168pp. USO 22834-7 Pa. $1.75

COOKIES FROM MANY LANDS, Josephine Perry. Crullers, oatmeal cookies, chaux au chocolate, English tea cakes, mandel kuchen, Sacher torte, Danish puff pastry, Swedish cookies — a mouth-watering collection of 223 recipes. 157pp.

22832-0 Pa. $2.00

ROSE RECIPES, Eleanour S. Rohde. How to make sauces, jellies, tarts, salads, pot-pourris, sweet bags, pomanders, perfumes from garden roses; all exact recipes. Century old favorites. 95pp.

22957-2 Pa. $1.25

"OSCAR" OF THE WALDORF'S COOKBOOK, Oscar Tschirky. Famous American chef reveals 3455 recipes that made Waldorf great; cream of French, German, American cooking, in all categories. Full instructions, easy home use. 1896 edition. 907pp. 6⅝ x 9⅜.

20790-0 Clothbd. $15.00

JAMS AND JELLIES, May Byron. Over 500 old-time recipes for delicious jams, jellies, marmalades, preserves, and many other items. Probably the largest jam and jelly book in print. Originally titled May Byron's Jam Book. 276pp.

USO 23130-5 Pa. $3.00

MUSHROOM RECIPES, André L. Simon. 110 recipes for everyday and special cooking. Champignons a la grecque, sole bonne femme, chicken liver croustades, more; 9 basic sauces, 13 ways of cooking mushrooms. 54pp.

USO 20913-X Pa. $1.25

FAVORITE SWEDISH RECIPES, edited by Sam Widenfelt. Prepared in Sweden, offers wonderful, clearly explained Swedish dishes: appetizers, meats, pastry and cookies, other categories. Suitable for American kitchen. 90 photos. 157pp.

23156-9 Pa. $2.00

THE BUCKEYE COOKBOOK, Buckeye Publishing Company. Over 1,000 easy-to-follow, traditional recipes from the American Midwest: bread (100 recipes alone), meat, game, jam, candy, cake, ice cream, and many other categories of cooking. 64 illustrations. From 1883 enlarged edition. 416pp.

23218-2 Pa. $4.00

TWENTY-TWO AUTHENTIC BANQUETS FROM INDIA, Robert H. Christie. Complete, easy-to-do recipes for almost 200 authentic Indian dishes assembled in 22 banquets. Arranged by region. Selected from Banquets of the Nations. 192pp.

23200-X Pa. $2.50

Prices subject to change without notice.
Available at your book dealer or write for free catalogue to Dept. GI, Dover Publications, Inc., 180 Varick St., N.Y., N.Y. 10014. Dover publishes more than 150 books each year on science, elementary and advanced mathematics, biology, music, art, literary history, social sciences and other areas.